THE ECONOMIC
APPROACH TO
PUBLIC POLICY

THE ECONOMIC APPROACH TO PUBLIC POLICY

Selected Readings

EDITED BY

RYAN C. AMACHER
ROBERT D. TOLLISON
THOMAS D. WILLETT

Cornell University Press

ITHACA AND LONDON

HC
105.7
. E27

138916

Copyright © 1976 by Cornell University

All rights reserved. Except for brief quotations in a review, this
book, or parts thereof, must not be reproduced in any form without
permission in writing from the publisher. For information address
Cornell University Press, 124 Roberts Place, Ithaca, New York 14850.

First published 1976 by Cornell University Press.
Published in the United Kingdom by Cornell University Press Ltd.,
2–4 Brook Street, London W1Y 1AA.

International Standard Book Number (cloth) 0–8014–0914–4
International Standard Book Number (paperback) 0–8014–9860–0
Library of Congress Catalog Card Number 75–38425
Printed in the United States of America by Vail-Ballou Press, Inc.
*Librarians: Library of Congress cataloging information
appears on the last page of the book.*

Contents

Preface

This book is the result of the editors' years of experience in teaching courses concerned with the application of the economic approach to questions of social policy. The concept of the collection evolved from an outline prepared for a course on U.S. economic policy, originally offered to undergraduates at Harvard University, and later given at the Fletcher School of Law and Diplomacy. The outline was subsequently revised for a course on the same subject at Cornell's Graduate School of Business and Public Administration. More recent refinements were made in preparing policy-oriented courses for both graduates and undergraduates at the University of Oklahoma, Texas A. & M. University, and Arizona State University. Most of the selections will be of interest to students who have had or are taking an introductory level course in economics. It is our goal to present material on that level that can be useful in a complementary sense to students of political science and public policy. The book also aims to challenge the student by exploring some topics in considerable depth.

We have chosen outstanding contributions, most of which are not otherwise easily available to students. We do not claim, of course, to have exhausted the literature on any of the topics, and the references in each paper are important as a source of further information. In some areas, however, no good summaries existed, and we have filled these gaps with three papers written especially for this volume. These are "The Economic Approach to Social Policy Questions: Some Methodological Perspectives," "A Menu of Distributional Considerations," and "Risk Avoidance and Political Advertising: Neglected Issues in the Literature on Budget Size in a Democracy." All three contain extensive bibliographies. The name index at the end of the volume can also be useful as a guide to the literature.

We are grateful to Roger Sherman and Edward Tower, who commented on earlier outlines of the volume, and we are, of course, indebted to the authors and publishers who allowed us to reprint their papers. Specific acknowledgments appear at the beginning of each selection. Our thanks also go to the staff of Cornell University Press for their help in preparing the manuscript.

RYAN C. AMACHER
ROBERT D. TOLLISON
THOMAS D. WILLETT

List of Contributors

Ryan C. Amacher, Associate Professor of Economics, Arizona State University

James M. Buchanan, University Professor and General Director, Center for Study of Public Choice, Virginia Polytechnic Institute and State University

Christopher K. Clague, Associate Professor of Economics, University of Maryland

Anthony C. Fisher, Associate Professor of Economics, University of Maryland

Kenneth V. Greene, Associate Professor of Economics, State University of New York at Binghamton

Robert L. Heilbroner, Norman Thomas Professor of Economics, New School for Social Research

Roland N. McKean, Commonwealth Professor of Economics, University of Virginia

Charles E. McLure, Jr., Allyn R. and Gladys M. Cline Professor of Economics, Rice University

James C. Miller III, Assistant Director, Wage and Price Council

Dennis C. Mueller, Research Associate, International Institute of Management, Berlin

William A. Niskanen, Professor of Economics, Graduate School of Public Policy, University of California, Berkeley

Arthur M. Okun, Senior Fellow, The Brookings Institution

Mancur Olson, Professor of Economics, University of Maryland

Peter Passell, Assistant Professor of Economics, Columbia University

Mark V. Pauly, Associate Professor of Economics, Northwestern University

Marc Roberts, Professor of Political Economy and Health Policy, Harvard School of Public Health

Leonard Ross, California State Utility Commission

Theodore W. Schultz, Professor Emeritus of Economics, University of Chicago

Charles L. Schultze, Senior Fellow, The Brookings Institution

Martin Shubik, Professor of Economics of Management, Yale University

George P. Shultz, Professor of Management and Public Policy, Stanford University

Robert M. Solow, Institute Professor of Economics, Massachusetts Institute of Technology

George J. Stigler, Walgreen Professor of American Institutions, University of Chicago

Lester C. Thurow, Professor of Economics and Management, Massachusetts Institute of Technology

James Tobin, Sterling Professor of Economics, Yale University

Robert D. Tollison, Professor of Economics, Texas A. & M. University

Gordon Tullock, University Professor of Economics, Center for Study of Public Choice, Virginia Polytechnic Institute and State University

Henry C. Wallich, Member, Board of Governors, Federal Reserve System

Thomas D. Willett, Director of Research and Senior Adviser on International Economic Affairs, U.S. Treasury

THE ECONOMIC
APPROACH TO
PUBLIC POLICY

Introduction

The economic approach to questions of public policy has become an important area of study in most economic curricula, and it is increasingly being incorporated into programs in political science, public policy, and public administration. The thirty-six papers in this volume are intended to be useful in all these areas. Taken together, they demonstrate, through argument and application, the relevance of economics as a guide for social policy. Indeed, they show that the economic approach provides a way of arriving at a fundamentally "correct" view of policy problems.

A good deal of criticism has been leveled at the *relevance* or *usefulness* of "conventional" economics for the discussion of public policy problems. This tendency to reject traditional theory comes particularly from economists of the New Left, whose point of view has been rather extensively aired in several recent readers that present a "radical" approach to social policy issues. While we find this approach useful in raising relevant questions, it has, in our view, produced few, if any, relevant answers. Thus, one of our important objectives in this book is to consider these criticisms. A closely related aim, that stems in large part from our interest and training in applied microeconomics, is to offer an opposing view that stresses the insight that traditional economic theory, broadened as it has been in the last two decades by contributions to the economic theory of public and private behavior, can bring to the analysis of questions of social policy. In this sense the volume has a point of view, of which the reader should be aware.

The volume is divided into five sections. Each begins with a short discussion of the contents of the papers it includes and an assessment of their contributions to the main theme. Part I presents a characterization of the economic approach to social questions. It examines the approach's overall usefulness and its limitations, and considers, from various vantage points, the question of its relevance. Areas of agreement and disagreement among economists are explored. The general view is that while the economic approach may embody implicit value judgments and ideological biases, it is still quite useful in discussing public policy issues; one simply has to be careful to avoid these pitfalls. This section thus serves to warn the reader that he should approach the rest of the volume bearing in mind the possibility that ideology and value judgments may enter scientific discussions of policy.

Part II demonstrates how the economic approach can be applied in a wide range of specific areas of public policy. The papers offer methodological approaches to solving a number of problems of concern to policy makers. Among the areas considered are crime, higher education, the environment, revenue sharing, and public goods.

Part III focuses on the usefulness of economics as a guide to social action in considering questions of equity, justice, and income distribution. These papers illustrate the kinds of insight that conventional economic principles can bring to bear on such issues.

In Part IV economists examine areas traditionally reserved for political scientists. The papers introduce the reader to public choice models and their use in deriving implications of certain assumptions about voter-consumer information, rules of decision, bureaucratic behavior, and so on. These selections consider a substantial number of problems caused by the manner in which we currently make democratic decisions, and indicate some possible directions in which solutions might be sought.

The concluding section, Part V, examines the role of the economist as governmental adviser—a dual role, in which he is both political appointee and representative of the economics profession in the eyes of the public. Among the issues discussed are the effectiveness of various institutional set-ups, the kinds of advice economic advisers can and should give to democratic decision-makers, and the degree to which they are and ought to be independent. Certain conflicts and problems that can arise concerning the behavior of economic advisers are considered, along with a variety of institutional reforms that might reduce these difficulties.

Part I: Perspectives on the Usefulness of Economics as a Guide for Social Policy

The papers in this section discuss the different ways in which the economic approach can play a significant role in the analysis of social policy problems. They have been chosen to offer a range of perspectives on the usefulness of economists in the policy process. The first paper, written by the editors, outlines the main elements of the economic approach. The authors then examine and answer the principal criticisms that have been made against it, considering such issues as the general relevance of economics, the role of assumptions in the economic approach, and the self-interest axiom used by economists. The paper is also concerned with progress in the use of the economic approach, with whether the approach frustrates political consensus, and with whether a conservative bias is inherent in it.

In the second paper Arthur Okun (a former chairman of the Council of Economic Advisers) goes into the characteristics of the economic approach to social policy questions in considerable detail. He also considers the position of the economist versus the special interest and the trade-off between equity and efficiency in economic analysis. Finally, he assays the scope and basis of professional consensus and professional controversy on matters of economic policy.

The third and fourth papers present opposing points of view. In the third, Robert Heilbroner raises the question of the relevance of economics. He discusses problems that he views as inherent in the nature of economic theory. One of his main charges is that economists have ignored many relevant subjects and tend to deal only with quantifiable elements of social activity. Heilbroner essentially argues that there are aspects of the social system that economics cannot illuminate. The fourth selection is Robert Solow's commentary on Heilbroner's paper, which usefully questions the validity of defining the relevance of economics with respect to something else. Solow also discusses the issue of whether economists are conservative by nature, the impossibility of a value-free social science, and problems in doing interdisciplinary research. Ultimately, he considers the general usefulness of economics as an aid in analyzing social problems.

The fifth paper considers the interesting convergence of points of view among economists of the far left and the far right. Mancur Olson and Christopher Clague examine points of agreement and disagreement between groups like the Union of Radical Political Economy and the "Virginia School" (a body of thought largely associated with the name of James Buchanan). These ideologically opposite schools share agreement, the authors show, on many theoretical and policy issues.

Charles Schultze (former Director of the Budget Bureau under President Johnson) argues in the sixth paper that the truth is not that economics is irrelevant, but rather that the tools of economics have not been put to enough use in dealing with social problems. His main point is that neither the radical, who would have men strive for different goals, nor the pragmatist, who wishes to apply the economic approach to social institutions in order to harness self-interest, is irrelevant. Both have important roles to play in solving social problems.

1. The Economic Approach to Social Policy Questions: Some Methodological Perspectives

RYAN C. AMACHER, ROBERT D. TOLLISON, and THOMAS D. WILLETT

In this paper we offer a brief overview of some of the main elements of the economic approach and the major criticisms that have been made of it. An important aspect of the discussion is the question of possible biases inherent in the economic perspective.

We are, of course, offering our own views and in some cases those of other scholars about the nature of the economic approach and the role of the policy economist. The discussion should not be interpreted as outlining an exclusive set of requirements that one must meet in order to be qualified to offer views on economic matters. As will become apparent, our judgment is that the economic approach is very useful and that many criticisms of it can be used in further developing the basic case of economics and the ways in which it can be applied.

I. Elements of the Economic Approach to Social Policy Questions

A first major element of the economic approach is the tendency of economists to look for mechanisms that harness self-interested behavior by individuals. This concern dates from the early classical economists, and its beginnings are usually associated with the work of Adam Smith (*The Wealth of Nations*). This view of individual motivation typically leads economists to give policy advice that emphasizes the manipulation of incentives rather than individual values. We shall investigate this characteristic of the economic approach in greater detail in the next section and the reader will find it illustrated in the readings in Part II of the volume.

A second and related characteristic is that it is usual in economic analysis to take the individual consumer or firm as the unit whose utility is to be maximized, and to build up analysis from the individual unit. (During this century macroeconomics has been a notable exception to this generalization. Recently, however, there has been a strong trend toward a more thorough development of the foundation of macroeconomic theory in terms of the maximizing behavior of individuals.) The basic assumption that underlies this procedure is that individual consumers and producers are the best judges of their own welfare. In looking at public policy questions, this approach leads to the theory of public choice, an approach illustrated by the readings in Part IV. Because of this individualistic starting point for analysis, when the economist looks at collective problems, he tends to look at mechanisms for making decisions, e.g., rules of aggregation or voting rules, and not at outcomes per se. In other words the economist does not tend to see the public interest as distinct from individual preferences and does not spend a great deal of time debating the nature of the public interest, i.e., what outcomes should be as distinct from how they are generated.[1] For him, mechanisms are independent of outcomes. This does not mean, of course, that many economists do not become strong advocates of particular policy positions.

A third major hallmark of the economic approach is that economists tend to be trained to distinguish between positive and normative elements of analysis. A good example of this aspect of the economic viewpoint can be found in discussions of the Phillips curve. The Phillips curve is an economic relation that describes the trade-off between unemployment and inflation. It is typically the case for an economy that these two variables are inversely related, i.e., higher unemployment rates are the price of

1. See Steiner (1970).

lower inflation rates.[2] In this case it is important to know initially what the technical rate of substitution between inflation and unemployment is. In other words the trade-off curve must be plotted. This is the positive element in this analysis. Second, one must choose a particular inflation-unemployment trade-off. This, of course, is the normative element. Indeed, as Sen has pointed out, positive analysis can help one make better value judgments. In Sen's terminology, particular rates of inflation and unemployment are intermediate objectives and not final goals. For example, one can study the costs of inflation without changing one's own values, but knowing how inflation impacts on the poor in a positive sense would aid one in voting on the preferred trade-off. Thus, the development of information in positive analysis could change one's normative evaluation of the trade-offs.[3]

A related issue is whether economics is value-free. In a broad sense it is not, for clearly our values determine to some extent the type of research that we choose to do, what questions we view as important. Economists are, of course, human beings, and as such must be alert to the possibility that personal values may creep into their analysis. The point is to be on guard to distinguish between positive and normative elements in analysis rather than taking the view that technical analysis, as such, is value-loaded, and hence useless. Even recognition that we may never succeed in fully distinguishing between positive and normative elements is not to our minds a reason to abandon the attempt at positive analysis and conclude that because all analysis includes value judgments, any opinion on technical issues is as good as the next. Rather, in an imperfect world, we should strive to approach the ideal of full distinction between positive and normative elements as closely as possible and be on guard for biases that exist in analysis. The view that all analysis is value-loaded leads one to ignore a broad body of useful knowledge. In a reasonably open advocacy process, the competition of ideas should aid in bringing biases and value judgments to the surface.

A fourth major aspect is that economists seek to clarify issues rather than muddle them.[4] The "muddling-through" approach discussed by Charles Schultze in Reading 34 is a good example of a case where a positive description of the policy-making process takes on the attributes of a normative model. Consensus, absence of controversy, and political stability are regarded by some political scientists as the objectives of the political process; in this view there is virtue in blurring issues and mingling

2. For a discussion of the Phillips curve relationship, see Samuelson (1973), and for a discussion of the policy issues relating to the Phillips curve, see Samuelson and Solow (1971).

3. See Sen (1970).   4. We discuss this issue in detail in section III.

ends and means. Economists on the other hand tend to take informed individual choice as their norm, and therefore tend to spend a great deal of effort in clarifying options and in making the opportunity cost of a given choice as clear as possible. This characteristic sometimes creates controversy. A purely political approach might seek to find a consensus without ever asking serious questions about the efficiency of a project, and the economist's tendency to draw attention to the cost of various choices often makes him appear as an agitator, frustrating the attainment of political consensus. Agitation of traditional political thinking can be quite healthy, however, and in a sense it is the role of the economist to be a social accountant, protecting economic efficiency from those who would violate its dictates in search of broad agreement. Because of this tendency to look at opportunity costs, the economist is more likely to recognize the opportunities for substitution among options that exist. He is more likely to be critical of an all-or-nothing approach to public policy; he will probably not, for example, be impressed by claims that a project has to be undertaken at a certain given size to be successful unless clear evidence of economies of scale or indivisibilities in the project are convincingly presented. For the same reasons, an economist would be likely to suggest a great deal of experimenting on a small scale with new public policies.

A closely related point is that economists employ a marginal approach. They are inclined to examine the merits of a small contraction or expansion in a public program, and they look carefully at the change in *marginal* costs and benefits from policy options. In government economists try to use this approach even where "margin" must be broadly interpreted not only as a change in the level of a given project, but also in terms of broad choices among project options. This contrasts with the incrementalism employed by political scientists of the "muddling-through" school of thought.

This section has introduced and highlighted some aspects of the economic approach. We now turn to a consideration of some of the charges that have been made against the economic viewpoint.

II. Criticisms of the Economic Approach: A Rejoinder

Perhaps the most widely voiced criticism of the economic approach is that it is irrelevant and unrealistic. In this section we will examine the charges that traditional economic analysis is irrelevant to today's problems, and that economics is not very useful since it is based on unrealistic assumptions, especially about human motivation. In the same vein, it has been argued that economics is founded on an "immoral" view of man, and we will consider the economist's view of man in this context.

The Relevance of Economics in General

One need only browse through the technical economic journals to find apparent support for the contention that some branches of economics are irrelevant for all (or most) social problems.[5] Indeed, it may be that the increased technical sophistication that has manifested itself in the economic literature in the last few decades has prompted the less technically inclined to level the charge of irrelevance. However, even if one concludes that this literature is of little use in the policy process, it is fallacious to say that all, or even most, branches of economics are irrelevant for social problems.[6] Indeed, the highly technical literature is not always irrelevant for public policy. Although a great deal of it is devoted to mathematical proofs of particular points in economic theory, its interest is not limited to that. Simply because an argument is presented in mathematical terms does not mean it cannot speak to policy problems. For example, a good many arguments in the pure theory of international trade are mathematical in nature and also relevant to aspects of trade policy.[7] For that matter, verbal presentation of economics by no means insures policy relevance, though it is important that the analysis be presented so that nontechnical policy makers find it useful. The distinction between mathematical and nonmathematical economics, then, is not terribly pertinent. What is important is that the economist use good tools and that he address his analysis in a communicative way to relevant policy questions.[8]

Furthermore, many subdisciplines of economics have long histories of research applicable to policy problems. To mention only a few, Industrial Organization, Agricultural Economics, International Economics, and, of

5. For example, see the *Journal of Economic Theory,* the *Review of Economic Studies,* and *Econometrica,* which are largely devoted to mathematical treatments of economic and statistical theory.

6. In fact, there is a substantial body of literature addressed to relevant social questions. Many of the major economics journals such as the *Journal of Political Economy* and the *American Economic Review* devote considerable space to papers dealing with specific policy issues. In addition, there is a growing number of journals devoted almost exclusively to discussions of policy questions. See, for example, *Public Policy, Public Choice, Policy Analysis,* and *The Public Interest.*

7. A good example of this point can be found in Bhagwati (1965), where he develops the analytical differences in tariffs and quotas and concludes that under certain conditions a tariff is to be preferred to a quota where the domestic industry is monopolized. This model is applied to analyze the oil industry in Amacher, Tollison, and Willett (1973).

8. An example of an extremely esoteric, mathematical article that has powerful policy conclusions is the recent paper by Fischer and Cooper (1973). In it they show that long lags do not impair the effectiveness of active stabilization policy, but instead require that stabilization policy be more vigorously used. Variability in these lags, however, does affect stabilization policy and requires that this instrument be applied with caution.

course, Macroeconomics, are areas where such research has long been done. Many of the papers in Part II of this volume are excellent examples of applications of Microeconomics. Indeed, a review of the history of economic thought would reveal that in many cases interest in policy problems has led to important developments in economic theory. This is especially true in the case of International Economics.[9] Thus, though there is a heightened interest in public policy research in the profession today, it is by no means a new thing for economists to be interested in policy. Actually, whether economics is relevant is an empty question; relevant for what is a more correct phrasing.

Our argument to this point, then, is that a great deal of economics, properly applied—including mathematical economics—is relevant to a wide range of social policy questions. While all branches of economics are irrelevant for *some* social questions, relevance depends largely on what questions are being examined. For example, economics can say little about how to resolve family conflicts (although even there it might be of some use). It may be quite useful, on the other hand, in looking for resolutions of social conflicts on a more aggregative scale.

Role of Assumptions in the Economic Approach

The charge of lack of realism is often levied at the assumptions economists use in their analysis.[10] The question here is basic to the role of assumptions in any theory, whether related to economic behavior or to purely physical behavior. Milton Friedman has persuasively argued that the usefulness of a theory should not be judged by the realism of its assumptions.[11] The importance of assumptions in theory is that they allow the model specified to be logically consistent and that they allow the theorist to abstract from the maze of reality and to focus on some fundamental aspect of a social process. Clearly, what matters is the realism of the theory, and this depends on how well it predicts behavior vis-à-vis alternative theories.

Of course, a theory should not be judged *only* by its predictive power.

9. Perhaps the best example of a policy debate that inspired the development of economic theory was the debate in the first half of the nineteenth century over the British Corn Laws. The classical economists were involved, and the idea that emerged led to great developments in the theory of economic rent, international trade, and income distribution. As a result of the debate, the tariff on corn was repealed in 1846. For a discussion of the major classical economists and their positions on the issues, see Gide and Rist (1948).

10. See Ilchman and Uphoff (1969). They argue that economists "too frequently proceed from unrealistic or unacceptable assumptions" (p. 29).

11. " 'Complete realism' is clearly unattainable, and the question whether a theory is realistic 'enough' can be settled only by seeing whether it yields predictions that are good enough for the purpose in hand or that are better than predictions from alternative theories." Friedman (1966), p. 41.

Economic theory has many uses besides prediction. For example, it is a useful way to think about a problem and also a useful teaching device. One cannot always perform a test of a theory, and in this case relevance of assumptions can be an important consideration in thinking about a problem. Where testing of theory is not possible, the art of a good policy analyst lies in "psyching out" the appropriate level of simplification for the problem at hand so that he may concentrate on its fundamental aspects, in effect, discovering how simple a model can be used without serious distortion of the major aspects of the problem.

The ability to perform this function well is a hallmark of a good policy economist. The art comes in the wise choice of simplifying assumptions which depend on the degree of accuracy one needs in the analysis, i.e., how complicated do you need to be? Of course, there may be disagreements over what the fundamental aspects of any problem are. Such disagreements are basically a sign of a healthy science and aid in getting a better feel for the fundamentals. The art of being a good applied economist is related to the advance of the science generally in that some of the most important work comes in "psyching out" the irrelevant and relevant aspects of a theoretical problem. Over time, disagreements over the fundamental aspects of a problem tend to be reduced as economic science advances and an informed consensus emerges. Typically, it is at this stage that positive tests can start to be performed. The hallmark of a good applied economist is his ability to use the economic approach as a thinking device about purely scientific as well as related policy problems.

The Self-Interest Axiom

One important facet of the charges of irrelevance and lack of realism made against economic analysis and assumptions is the question whether man is basically self-interested, whether maximizing behavior accurately describes the real world. Economics, it is claimed, is based on an outdated psychological model of man. This criticism again stems from a mistaken and narrow view of the economic approach. Economists recognize that humans are motivated by complex forces. However, these complex forces are not important in the examination of all questions, and it is often possible to obtain predictive results based on very simple assumptions about human motivation. It is not that the economist views the world in a simple-minded fashion, but rather that it is not necessary for him, in order to make predictive statements, to become involved in a quagmire of behavioral questions about human motivation which are outside the realm of his professional competence. This does not mean that the economist does not know that individual behavior is or can be vastly different from what his assumptions presume, or that he is denigrating the importance and origins of different types of individual behavior. It only means that in considering *some* problems he finds the effects of these differences not significant enough to warrant special attention.

Economists take maximizing behavior as a guideline, but they do not limit their consideration of maximizing behavior to economic variables alone; they also tend to look at broader trade-offs among political and other variables. The economist does not view the concept of self-interest narrowly. Individual choice is simply characterized as utility-maximizing behavior. Many human motivations, including those of love, altruism, and power, result in behavior that can be regarded as utility-maximizing.[12] This is not to imply that economists think that man cannot change or that his preferences cannot be influenced by noneconomic forces. If we turn the economist's self-interest assumption on its head, it is possible to envisage a world of selfless people. But the critic who argues this view should try to develop consistent and predictive models of this form of behavior, and this has not been done. As Solow argues (in Reading 4), in the absence of alternative models we have no choice but to apply the utility-maximizing, self-interest model.

The carping critic does play an important role in pointing out the limitations of analysis. Indeed, alternative kinds of models—an economy of love, if you will—might be quite relevant to describing some forms of human behavior, i.e., family disputes. But it should be stressed that there is competition, even in a world of saints, concerning different views of the general welfare. Consider the differences among competing religions as an example. Indeed, as Buchanan has recently argued, it is in part the reluctance of other social science disciplines to undertake rigorous positive examination of such behavior patterns that has led to the extension of economics into so many areas that were heretofore the realm of the other social sciences.[13]

In general it should be stressed that political economists, from their perspective that men behave in a self-interested way, recognize the importance of institutions, such as markets, that minimize the need for "good action" to solve social problems. In other words, they seek to design institutions that channel self-interest into socially desirable pat-

12. For example, see the analysis of the economics of marriage offered by Becker (1973, 1974).
13. See Buchanan (1972) for a more complete discussion of these points. It should also be mentioned that the fact that there is altruism in the world does not negate the self-interest model and call for a whole new economic theory. Recently David Johnson has demonstrated that standard economic theory is useful when both participants in an exchange have altruistic motivation. See Johnson (1970).

terns, rather than basing social policy on appeals to the love of mankind or attempts to build character.[14]

Thus in considering a particular problem the economist first looks to the market for solutions. If he concludes the market is operating inadequately, he will probably propose a subsidy or tax on the grounds that the use of individual incentives is the most efficient type of intervention in markets characterized by self-interested actors. A real-life example of this can be seen in the recent clamor about the energy crisis. Where the political goal is to reduce fuel consumption, an economist will probably recommend an increase in the price of fuel, rather than suggest a campaign for voluntary energy conservation. There may be circumstances when administrative appeals to good will and voluntary action are quite appropriate, and there are clearly cases where such appeals influence behavior. But to the typical economist, if a substantial reduction in consumption is required, an increase in price is viewed as necessary.

The charge that economic theory is "cold" is largely a result of the fact that economists try to think in a calculating way about things that often have a highly emotional element. This leads those who are critical of the economic approach to the caricature of economic man. Kenneth Boulding in his presidential address to the American Economic Association argued that this attack, which comes from both the left and the right, arises from the economist's neglect of the heroic. While economic man may be a clod to some, Boulding said, heroic man is a fool, and he wondered how economic institutions had survived so long, given the fact that economic man is so unpopular.[15] Somewhere in between the clod and the fool is the human. The important point is that economic theory does not depend on purely economic man to be valid.[16]

Many of the criticisms leveled at economics from other disciplines stem from the tendency of economists to be primarily interested in considerations of economic efficiency. This is a natural result of their training, which teaches them to apply the concept of economic efficiency in a rigorous manner to the problems they choose to investigate. It is incor-

14. The text is really a bad paraphrase of Sir Dennis Robertson's "There exists in every human breast an inevitable state of tension between the aggressive and acquisitive instincts and the instincts of benevolence and self-sacrifice. It is for the preacher, lay or clerical, to inculcate the ultimate duty of subordinating the former to the latter. It is the humbler, and often the invidious, role of the economist to help so far as he can, in reducing the preacher's task to manageable dimensions. It is his function to emit a warning bark if he sees a course of action being pursued which will increase unnecessarily the inevitable tension between self-interest and public duty; and to wag his tail in approval of courses of action which will tend to keep the tension low and tolerable." Robertson (1956), p. 148.

15. Boulding (1969). "No one in his senses would want his daughter to marry an economic man" (p. 10).

16. See Buchanan and Tullock (1962), chapter 2.

rect, however, to say that the economist is not interested in equity. On the contrary, much work in economics is devoted to the concept of equity and its application to different economic problems.[17] (Many of these questions are reviewed in Reading 16.)

Relevance and Progress in the Economic Approach

The general charge that economics is irrelevant is an empty question. In fact there are two basic charges of irrelevancy.[18] One is simply that the economic approach is the wrong kind of approach. This, of course, depends on the question being addressed.

The other charge, that much of abstract economic theory has no applicability, is more related to the issue of the degree of relevance of the economic approach and also to the question of how the economic approach becomes more relevant over time. First, the economic approach becomes more relevant as it investigates real-world problems. One way that it can do this is to broaden its utility-maximization axiom to look at noneconomic factors, e.g., power, love, and so forth, and to look at motives broader than those purely economic in nature. Here we agree with Solow that the best interdisciplinary research is done when individuals from different disciplines look at the same problem from their different perspectives—or better, when one discipline's detailed investigation of a problem leads to a recognition of the need to draw upon other disciplines for a fuller understanding—and not when a group of distinguished theorists from different disciplines is convened to think in an interdisciplinary way. All too often attempts at interdisciplinary thinking end up as exercises in translating terminology from one discipline to another.

A second way in which economics becomes more relevant over time is by broadening the scope of investigation of economic factors. Indeed, while the methodology of modern economics has remained basically the same, there have been significant advances in the conventional models. These models have been expanded to incorporate such factors as the economics of uncertainty, the cost of acquiring information, and the cost of time, to name only a few.[19]

17. See Musgrave (1959), and Musgrave and Musgrave (1974) for some examples of such considerations, and for the application of equity considerations to a specific policy issue, see Amacher, Miller, Pauly, Tollison, and Willett (1973).

18. See Solow (1970).

19. For a review of some of this literature on risk and uncertainty, see Sherman (1974), chapters 7 and 8. For an example of the literature on the cost of acquiring information, see Alchian and Demsetz (1972), and for examples of the literature on the value of time, see Becker (1965), and Sherman and Willett (1972). For useful surveys of modern developments that have enhanced the relevance of economic theory, see H. G. Johnson (1967), chapters 8 and 9.

Economics thus progresses a step at a time by broadening its basic maximizing framework to consider non-economic variables and by broadening its consideration of economic behavior. Of course, these developments may be important in the analysis of some problems and not others. The paper reprinted below as Reading 13 is an example of an analysis that starts from a theoretical proposition and gradually moves into practical considerations. In that paper we extend the original and important theoretical contribution of Ronald Coase, who showed in a quite simple model that in the absence of transaction costs and income effects, the assignment of property rights to one party or another in a given situation does not effect economic efficiency. One obtains the same allocative result regardless of who gets the initial property rights.[20] Coase's paper showed that under very restrictive conditions property right assignment did not matter except on distributional grounds. We push beyond Coase to a specific example where factors such as information and transaction costs make the assignment of property rights an important issue with respect to economic efficiency. This in no way diminishes the importance of Coase's original paper; rather it is an example of how science progresses over time and becomes more relevant. In effect Coase led the way to later, more applied work.[21]

III. Does the Economic Approach Frustrate Political Consensus?

In the early 1960s the role of the economist in government was identified with concepts of cost-benefit analysis and a budgetary process called the planning, programming, and budgeting system (PPB). Cost-benefit analysis is, of course, just applied economics, applied in this case in evaluating public investments, and it has a rather long history in both the United States and Europe.[22] PPB is a budgetary process that emphasizes an economic approach in allocating funds to public programs.[23] Although it has many aspects, the most important for purposes of discussion here is its stress on the statement of program objectives and their attainment at the least cost—in contrast to traditional budgetary procedures,

20. Coase (1960).

21. Another useful example of this process of the broadening of economic theory over time is the broadening of consideration of firm motivation from pure profit maximization to the more general case of utility-maximization. The later theories are especially relevant to bureaucratic firms where the interests of the firm's subcomponents may diverge and profit motivation is not the only objective. This approach can be quite useful in some cases. For a review of some of this literature, see Alchian (1965) and the references cited there.

22. See, for example, McKean (1958), and Ekelund and Herbert (1973). The point here is simply that economic theory is relevant to a large variety of market and nonmarket problems, i.e., it is not simply relevant to private markets or to capitalistic economic systems.

23. See McKean (1958).

which emphasized the purchase of inputs with little or no reference to what was being produced. It is, therefore, in the nature of both cost-benefit analysis and PPB to seek to specify clearly what a program is to accomplish and how it will do it.

It was just this stress on being specific about objectives in government that led some prominent political scientists to criticize PPB and the associated use of cost-benefit analysis.[24] These critics argued that PPB is incompatible with the realities of politics because its stress on efficiency criteria ignores the problems of achieving a political consensus. What the argument comes to is that PPB attempts to separate means from ends, which may be an impossible procedure in a democratic polity. For example, the economist may view defense appropriations as expenditures to guarantee security, while the politician may view them as pork-barrel, i.e., expenditures that benefit the home district. Thus, PPB cannot work if it is conceived of as maximizing a *known* social welfare function subject to some given constraints, because it does not fit political reality.[25] This view assumes that decisions are made on the basis of political advocacy and incrementalism (small, gradual increases in existing programs), in a decentralized pluralistic society.

This argument against the economic approach is, at least in its extreme form, a conservative view. Implicit in it is the assumption that the present political and budgetary processes are optimal, both in the sense of producing desirable results in the present and in the sense of allowing for change and the representation of new ideas and groups over time. The view of decision-making that it represents is a positive description that has taken on normative connotations. The main danger, of course, in taking this model of public decision-making as normative is that the relevant interest groups in the society may not be represented. For example, are consumers represented? [26] Since we have learned from the existing literature on public choice that they are not likely to be, we are led to reject the view that existing patterns of political organization maximize social welfare.[27]

In a less extreme model of this view it is clear that economists sometimes ignore political constraints, because they are not specialized in making such trade-offs. This does not mean, however, that the role of the economist in the policy process should be diminished. Rather, as

24. See Lindblom (1959, 1961) and Wildavsky (1966).

25. Schultze (1968) presents a review of these arguments.

26. We should note in passing that the Council of Economic Advisers has basically served as the advocate of consumers' welfare in deliberations on economic policy. For more discussions of this point, see Readings 35 and 36 in this volume.

27. Schultze (1968), part of which appears as Reading 34, below, offers an effective rebuttal to the more extreme statement of this view, so we will not dwell on it further here.

Schultze has put it, the PPB system has introduced a new set of participants into that process whom he refers to as the "partisan efficiency advocates." [28] Certainly, economists have the same rights as other citizens
when it comes to participating in policy debates and being employed by
government. In this setting their views will dominate only if they prove
successful.

A related criticism of cost-benefit analysis and of the role of economists in government generally is that the analyst may impose his personal
political preferences on his analysis. In other words, cost-benefit analysis
may simply become another form of advocacy for a particular policy.
This is clearly a danger endemic to the application of economic analysis
to public policy problems both in and out of government. Outside of government, in the context of academic debate and publications, one basically relies on competition in the market for ideas to reveal biases. Although there is no way to test conclusively whether this market works
well, it is our feeling as professional economists that it does.[29]

The problem of bias in analysis within government, is likewise lessened by competition among analysts within the federal bureaus and at
later stages by scrutiny from congressional and private economists. Here
it is useful to have some redundance in analysis among bureaus for the
same reason that it is useful to have different people look at the same
problem, i.e., no monopoly of views. Another way to control bias in
such analysis is to separate the functional responsibilities for program
proposal and the like, which belong to operating agencies, from the
evaluation responsibilities for these programs. This is done to some extent in the present budgetary process, where the Office of Management
and the Budget performs the evaluation function. In terms of broader economic policy, one may even wish to establish an independent agency for
evaluation purposes. Gordon Tullock has proposed (see Reading 35 of
this volume) such a role for the Council of Economic Advisers. We have
argued elsewhere (Reading 36), however, that the role of such separate
advisory bodies should be only to supplement, not to replace, the professional economists within the policy formation process.

IV. Is There a Conservative Bias in Economics?

George Stigler has argued that the study of economics tends to make
one politically conservative.[30] Stigler defines a conservative as one who
prefers to see most activity conducted by private enterprise and believes
that competition checks abuses of private power and leads to efficiency
and progress. He argues that the radical reformers (e.g., Henry George,

28. Schultze (1968), p. 101.   29. See Coase (1974).   30. Stigler (1959).

Karl Marx, and Thorstein Veblen) among economists were typically latecomers to economics and brought their philosophy to its study primarily only to pick up its jargon. The scientific training that an economist receives, Stigler believes, tends to make him politically conservative, because the student economist is drilled in the ways that the price system solves social problems. He stresses that it is the area of empirical validation of economic models that produces this (relatively) conservative philosophy. His argument, he points out, is a general one, and exceptions are found within the economics profession.[31] In this section we will elaborate and extend that argument.

As Stigler stresses, the common bond which unites economists and tends to make them politically conservative is their tendency to look for market solution to social problems.[32] They start with society as given and proceed with the analysis from there. This does not mean that the economist necessarily likes the world as he finds it, a charge sometimes made by those unfamiliar with the economic approach. Stigler's definition of *conservative* is expressed in terms of preference for market solutions. Some economists, notably Milton Friedman, would prefer to be labeled classical libertarians. The danger of labeling individuals who prefer market outcomes as conservative is best grasped by considering the reform movements in the Soviet Union, where those preferring markets are the liberal reformers.

There are actually three separate questions in the analysis of social problems: 1. How does the system work? 2. How would one like it to work? 3. How will changes affect the system? This is related to the distinction between positive and normative economics, which we discussed earlier. Most economists are conservative in the sense that economic analysis is typically limited to the first and third questions. There is, however, a considerable amount of literature on the second type of question, and all three types of economic analysis are important. Analysis of the first and third type yields information on "if A, then B" types of social problems. Analysis of the second type develops the properties, either for the economic system as a whole (i.e., general equilibrium analysis) or for isolated policies, of an optimal solution.

There is a criterion that economists have been willing to offer for answering the third type of question and evaluating policy changes. This

31. "In general there is no position, to repeat, which cannot be reached by a competent use of respectable economic theory. The reasons that this does not happen more often than it does is that there is a general consensus among economists that some relationships are stronger than others and some magnitudes are larger than others." Stigler (1959), p. 529.

32. Even Heilbroner, who would be regarded by most as politically liberal, has characterized economics as primarily a study of societies that solve economic problems by the market process. See Heilbroner (1962).

is the criterion of Pareto optimality. The Pareto rule states that any action that benefits some person(s) and harms none can be judged an improvement in social welfare. This rule does embody value judgments, although they are very weak ones. Basically, it implies that individuals are the best judges of their personal well-being and that there should be no objection to actions that enable individuals to increase their welfare without harming anyone. The normal process of exchange guarantees that most Pareto optimal moves are consumated, so this is not usually the type of policy problem faced by decision-makers. A possible role for the economist-policy adviser within the context of the Pareto rule might be that of searching for potential Pareto optimal moves that are not being consumated because of institutional constraints.[33] Finally, it is important to note the distinction between the view that one should make Pareto optimal moves and that one should *only* make Pareto optimal moves. Few economists would quarrel with the former. Many would dispute the latter.[34]

A related point is that economists are conservative in that they take the preferences and actions of men as given, at least in the short run. Indeed, economists have been relatively little interested in what the preferences of individuals are; rather, they take preferences as given and from there predict outcomes and optimal social arrangements. Economists, then, study the "science of choices" as opposed to the "science of preferences." They look only at half, perhaps even the less interesting half, of the problem. Gordon Tullock has gone so far as to suggest a reorientation of teaching and research in the social sciences along these two lines, "the science of choices" and "the science of preferences." [35] This view recognizes that the economic approach is not a universal answer to social problems, but also urges that in the face of human behavior as we find it today, economic models are relevant to a wide variety of problems in the social sciences, including some that are not strictly economic in nature, e.g., political behavior, criminology, and military behavior.

Perhaps a more important distinction in considering whether economists are conservative centers on still another definition of conservatism. It can be argued, as Stigler did, that orthodox economists who have studied the market system are conservative *in the large* because of their predi-

33. For a discussion of this role for economists, see Buchanan (1959). Baumol has argued that the Pareto rule is impractical because it requires unanimity. Furthermore he argues that one-man veto implies one-man rule. Wagner, however, notes that one-man veto does not imply one-man rule because one-man veto means only that one individual can *stop* something from happening and not that one man can *institute* action. See Baumol (1965), pp. 43–44, and Wagner (1973), pp. 36–37.

34. This distinction is discussed in greater detail in Reading 16.

35. Tullock (1972).

lection for democratic capitalism and against radical revolutionary changes in the whole economic and political system. On this point we are in agreement with Stigler. It would, however, be a mistake to classify all economists as conservative *in the small,* that is, in regard to particular programs and policies. Indeed, many orthodox market economists take what can be viewed as radical positions on specific political programs. For example, Milton Friedman is probably best described as conservative in the large in that he does not favor an overthrow of the existing economic and political system. He has, however, supported quite radical specific proposals for reform within the system. For example, he has long advocated flexible exchange rates (now in force), a negative income tax, an all-volunteer army, and the abolition of most regulatory controls of industry by government, all of which represent sharp departures from the existing programs and procedures of democratic capitalism. One could make this same point about many other economists, including Professor Stigler.[36]

Of course, within the discipline of economics there exists a traditional conservative-liberal split in terms of current domestic politics. Politically conservative and politically liberal economists hold much in common, however. Disagreement comes in areas where economic analysis has not settled basic questions of theory or empirical validation, and it is these disagreements among economists that seem to capture the public interest,[37] not their strong agreement on basic issues. One must be careful, then, not to get an exaggerated impression of the degree of disagreement among economists because of the appearance of vigorous debate in some areas.

To digress briefly, an important corollary aspect of the question of conservative bias in professional economics concerns the process by which economic research is disseminated. Here, in a special sense, economics, like most scientific disciplines, is conservative. Scientists tend, as a group, to cling to established paradigms until they are discredited, and the process of advancing a new paradigm, or idea, naturally involves communication with other scientists.[38] The structure of the communication process (e.g., the editorial procedures of the discipline's professional journals) has a profound effect on whether new ideas find a receptive scientific audience. A good example of this problem has recently been pointed out by Robert Ardrey.[39] He documents a case in the

36. See, for example, Friedman (1962).   37. See Friedman (1968).
38. See Kuhn (1964).

39. Ardrey (1961). He argues that in the 1950s no regular scientific journal would publish "The Predatory Transition from Ape to Man," by Raymond Dart. Ardrey considers this a revolutionary research paper that eventually had a large impact in its field (p. 29).

natural sciences where the pace of scientific development was probably retarded by the closed and extremely conservative nature of the scholarly journals in the field.

The process of screening and disseminating research is, therefore, a very important variable in the progress of a discipline, and screening devices can create bias in the dissemination of economic research. While we do not think this is a serious problem in the economics profession, it is well to be on guard against it.

In sum, Stigler presents a convincing case for the political and intellectual conservatism of economists, although one must take care to specify the perspective from which the label *conservative* is attached. Economists are conservative in that they prefer to solve social problems through the market system and in that they take the system as essentially given in the short run. Many are not conservative in the sense of being unwilling to see radical changes in specific policies within the present system in the short run and in more fundamental aspects of the system over the longer run, especially as more knowledge accumulates about what is economically and politically desirable.

V. Conclusion

It is obvious that there are plenty of potential biases in the approach of economists to social policy questions. The best way to guarantee that biases will be exposed is to have an open and representative discussion of policy. The main argument of this paper, however, is that despite its potential biases we should not discard the economic approach. Rather we should use it wisely, attempting to guard against biases, and always distinguishing between the positive and normative elements of any analytical work.

References

Alchian, Armen A. "The Basis of Some Recent Advances in the Theory of the Management of the Firm." *Journal of Industrial Economics*, November 1965.
——, and H. Demsetz. "Production, Information Costs, and Economics Organization." *American Economic Review,* December 1972.
Amacher, Ryan, James Miller, Mark Pauly, Robert Tollison, and Thomas Willett. *The Economics of the Military Draft.* Morrison, N.J.: General Learning Press, 1973.
——, Robert Tollison, and Thomas Willett. "Import Quotas on Foreign Oil: Comment." *American Economic Review,* December 1973.
Ardrey, Robert. *African Genesis.* New York: Atheneum, 1961.
Barzel, Y. "The Market for a Semipublic Good: The Case of the *American Economic Review*." *American Economic Review,* September 1971.

Baumol, William J. *Welfare Economics and Theory of State*. London: G. Bell, 1965 (2d ed.).

Becker, Gary. "A Theory of the Allocation of Time." *Economic Journal*, September 1965.

——. "A Theory of Marriage: Part I." *Journal of Political Economy*, July/August 1973.

——. "A Theory of Marriage: Part II." *Journal of Political Economy*, March/April 1974.

Berg, S. "Increasing the Efficiency of the Economics Journal Market." *Journal of Economic Literature*, September 1971.

Bhagwati, J. "On the Equivalence of Tariffs and Quotas." In R. E. Baldwin et al., eds., *Trade, Growth, and the Balance of Payments: Essays in Honor of Gottfried Haberler*. Chicago: Rand McNally, 1965.

Boulding, Kenneth. "Economics as a Moral Science." *American Economic Review*, March 1969.

Buchanan, James M. "Positive Economics, Welfare Economics, and Political Economy." *Journals of Law and Economics*, October 1959.

——. *The Demand and Supply of Public Goods.* Chicago: Rand McNally, 1968.

——. "Toward an Analysis of Closed Behavioral Systems." In James Buchanan and Robert Tollison, eds., *Theory of Public Choice*. Ann Arbor: University of Michigan Press, 1972 [Reading 21, below].

——, and Gordon Tullock. *The Calculus of Consent*. Ann Arbor: University of Michigan Press, 1962.

Coase, Ronald. "The Problem of Social Cost." *Journal of Law and Economics*, October 1960.

——. "The Market for Goods and the Market for Ideas." *American Economic Review*, May 1974.

Ekelund, R., and R. Herbert. "Public Economics at the Ecole des Ponts et Chaussées, 1830–1850." *Journal of Public Economics*, July 1973.

Etzioni, A. "The Need for Quality Filters in Information Systems." *Science*, January 15, 1971.

Fischer, Stanley, and J. Phillip Cooper. "Stabilization Policy and Lags." *Journal of Political Economy*, July/August 1973.

Friedman, Milton. *Capitalism and Freedom*. Chicago: University of Chicago Press, 1962.

——. *Essays in Positive Economics*. Chicago: University of Chicago Press, 1966.

——. "Why Economists Disagree." In Milton Friedman, *Dollars and Deficits*. Englewood Cliffs, N.J.: Prentice Hall, 1968.

Furubotn, Eirik, and Svetozar Pejovich. "Property Rights and Economic Theory: A Survey of the Literature." *Journal of Economic Literature*, December 1972.

Garvey, W. D., Nan Lin, and Carnot E. Nelson. "Communications in the Physical and Social Sciences." *Science*, December 11, 1970.

Gide, Charles, and Charles Rist. *A History of Economic Doctrines*. Boston: D. C. Heath, 1948.

Heilbroner, Robert L. *The Making of Economic Society*. Englewood Cliffs, N.J.: Prentice Hall, 1962.

Ilchman, Warren F., and Norman Thomas Uphoff. *The Political Economy of Change*. Berkeley: University of California Press, 1969.

Johnson, David, "Some Fundamental Economics of the Charity Market." In
    Thomas Ireland and David Johnson, eds., *Economics of Charity*. Blacksburg,
    Va.: Public Choice Society, 1970.
Johnson, H. G. *Money, Trade, and Economic Growth*. Cambridge: Harvard Uni-
    versity Press, 1967.
Kuhn, T. *The Structure of Scientific Revolutions*. Chicago: University of Chicago
    Press, 1964.
Lindblom, Charles E. "The Science of Muddling Through." *Public Administra-
    tion Review*, Spring 1959.
——. "Decision-Making in Taxation and Expenditures." In National Bureau of
    Economic Research, *Public Finances: Needs, Sources, Utilization*. Princeton:
    Princeton University Press for NBER, 1961.
McKean, R. N. *Efficiency in Government through Systems Analysis*. New York:
    John Wiley, 1958.
Mohring, H. "A Remission from Baumol's Disease: Ways to Publish More Ar-
    ticles: Comment." *Southern Economic Journal*, July 1970.
Musgrave, Richard. *The Theory of Public Finance*. New York: McGraw-Hill,
    1959.
——, and Peggy Musgrave. *Public Finance in Theory and Practice*. New York:
    McGraw Hill, 1974.
Niskanen, William A. *Bureaucracy and Representative Government*. Chicago:
    Aldine, 1971.
Okun, Arthur. "Fiscal-Monetary Activism: Some Analytical Issues." *Brookings
    Papers on Economic Activity*, No. 1, 1972.
Robertson, Dennis H. *Economic Commentaries*. London: Staples Press, 1956.
Samuelson, Paul. *Economics*. New York: McGraw-Hill, 1973.
——, and Robert M. Solow. "Analytical Aspects of Anti-Inflation Policy." In
    M. G. Mueller, ed., *Readings in Macroeconomics*. New York: Holt, Rinehart,
    and Winston, 1971.
Schultze, Charles L. *The Politics and Economics of Public Spending*. Washing-
    ton: The Brookings Institution, 1968.
Sen, Amartya K. *Collective Choice and Social Welfare*. San Francisco: Holden-
    Day, 1970.
Sherman, Roger. *The Economics of Industry*. Boston: Little, Brown, 1974.
——, and Thomas Willett. "The Standardized Work-Week and the Allocation of
    Time." *Kyklos* 25 (1), 1972.
Steinberg, J. L. "European Astronomers Decide to Consolidate Their Journals."
    Science, April 30, 1971.
Steiner, Peter O. "The Public Sector and the Public Interest." In R. H. Haveman
    and J. Margolis, eds., *Public Expenditures and Policy Analysis*. Chicago:
    Markham, 1970.
Stigler, George. "The Politics of Political Economists." *Quarterly Journal of
    Economics*, November 1959.
——. *Essays in the History of Economics*. Chicago: University of Chicago Press,
    1964.
Tollison, R., and T. D. Willett. "A Defense of the CEA as an Instrument for
    Giving Economic Policy Advice: A Comment on Tullock." *Journal of Money,
    Credit, and Banking*, February 1975. [Reading 36, below].

Tullock, Gordon. "Public Decisions as Public Goods." *Journal of Political Economy,* July–August 1971.
——. "Economic Imperialism." In Buchanan and Tollison, eds., *Theory of Public Choice.* Ann Arbor: University of Michigan Press, 1972.
Vandermuelen, A. "A Remission from Baumol's Disease: Ways to Publish More Articles." *Southern Economic Journal,* October 1968.
——. "Manuscripts in the Maelstrom: A Theory of the Editorial Process." *Public Choice,* Fall 1972.
Wagner, Richard E. *The Public Economy.* Chicago: Markham, 1973.
Wildavsky, Aaron. "The Political Economy of Efficiency: Cost-Benefit Analysis, Systems Analysis, and Program Budgeting." *Public Administration Review,* December 1966.

2. Consensus and Controversy in Political Economy

ARTHUR M. OKUN

During the Kennedy and Johnson years, there was a major influx of economists into policy-level positions in the administration. Unlike most of their predecessors, the four Directors of the Bureau of the Budget and the two Under Secretaries of the Treasury for Monetary Affairs who served during the eight years were professional economists. Four new Governors of the Federal Reserve System—a majority of the Board— were chosen from the economics profession. The Pentagon civilian management was also invaded by economists. The Council of Economic Advisers (CEA) thus had much more company than in the past from their professional fraternity brothers.

Under the Nixon administration, it became clear that the phenomenon is bipartisan. The Bureau of the Budget remained the bailiwick of economists; the top management of Treasury became even more "economist," and the Pentagon continued to involve economists at high levels. A distinguished member of the profession was appointed to the newly created White House position of Counselor to the President; an outstanding academic labor economist was named Secretary of Labor. These presidential appointments are a ringing endorsement of the contribution that economists make in the policy process.

The changing of the guard in the executive branch underlines the

Reprinted from Arthur M. Okun, *The Political Economy of Prosperity* (New York: Norton, 1970), pp. 1–23, by permission of the Brookings Institution. Copyright © 1970 by the Brookings Institution, Washington, D.C.

agreements and the disagreements within the profession on public policy. Economists of contrasting political views agree among themselves on many issues. In particular, on a number of issues, a bipartisan majority of the profession would unite on the opposite side from a bipartisan majority of the Congress. However, areas of disagreement within the profession remain important and these are generally linked to differences in social philosophy as well as differences in technical judgments about the workings of our economy. This chapter is devoted to a discussion of the scope and bases of professional consensus and of professional controversy on matters of economic policy.

The economist's influence is best known in the area of policy to influence overall business conditions. The tasks of promoting prosperity and avoiding recession, curbing inflation and achieving price stability—which are the main focus of the subsequent chapters—have long been recognized generally as the territory of the economist. However skeptical the public may be about the ability of economists to solve these problems, it does not know any group that is more reliable. The economist may not be believed or trusted, but he will not be ignored. When called upon to make a major tax decision, every elected federal official—from the President to a freshman member of the House of Representatives—knows that he is traveling on economic terrain and does not need to be reminded to seek the views of economists. He will surely also want to hear opinions from others—especially from the leaders of business and labor. But even these views will be influenced by the economists who advise the leaders of the private economy.

The influence of the economist on policy, however, is not limited to clearly defined *economic* programs and problems. The political decision maker faces thousands of problems which are primarily social or national security or international or racial issues. Yet almost every problem and proposed solution has an economic side, involving material benefits and costs and affecting the use of manpower and capital. One of the major responsibilities of economists in central positions—like the Bureau of the Budget or the Council of Economic Advisers—is to ensure that the economic aspects of such decisions will not be ignored. In many cases, they can demonstrate that alternative programs, equally capable of fulfilling a national security or social objective, deserve widely different grades for economic consequences.

To take one example of relevance in recent years, proposals to reduce pollution surely do not come to the President as *economic* policy. Yet pollution policy has been an area of intensive staff work by economists. This interest was reflected in the 1966 Annual Report of the Council in a small section headed "Rubbish, Garbage, and Junk Automobiles." [1] (Some readers have long felt that the Council's Reports were full of rubbish, garbage, and junk, but this was the first time that the CEA agreed.) More generally, as Charles Schultze has recently discussed in detail, the planning, programming, and budgeting system adopted by the federal government for all agencies in 1965 is developing into a comprehensive and concerted effort to apply the economic yardstick to the many choices in the federal budget. [2]

The Economist's Approach

Obviously economists are individuals with diverse talents and aptitudes: Some are good speech writers; some are imaginative creators of programs and projects; others are excellent salesmen of ideas; a few even turn out by luck to be good administrators. Nevertheless, economists tend to share some common ways of thinking, resulting largely from the training program that our universities give to young people who subsequently are called economists. The program is designed to give the student a particular way of viewing problems and particular skills in solving them; to some extent, it succeeds.

Whatever the problem set before the economist, his technique in solving it reflects his training. The analytical approach to choice is the hallmark of the profession. It is the essence of the discipline to focus on, and especially to quantify, the dimensions of choice—the costs, the benefits, and the alternative ways to achieve a given result. Most of what we know professionally about the process of analyzing choices is surprisingly simple and yet astonishingly useful; apparently the simple truths are not always learned in the school of hard knocks or the temple of common sense.

First, the economist looks for the opportunities sacrificed in selecting any alternative; he is professionally qualified to apply thoroughly and unrelentingly the propositions that you can't get something for nothing and that you can't have your cake and eat it too. Whether some specific federal action is a good thing can be decided only in terms of what the nation has to forgo in order to make the endeavor possible. Every proposal aims to further some worthy objective. A meaningful evaluation requires a careful analysis of what other objectives it may impede either directly, or indirectly by using up resources that could go elsewhere.

1. *Economic Report of the President together with the Annual Report of the Council of Economic Advisers, January 1966*, p. 123.
2. Charles L. Schultze, *The Politics and Economics of Public Spending* (Brookings Institution, 1968).

Second, the economist recognizes that the closest one ever comes to getting something for nothing is by increasing efficiency and productivity. Where that is possible, more can be obtained in one area without sacrificing and taking less in others. The potential for improvement in productivity and efficiency is the great reconciler in economic policies.

Third, the economist takes a marginalist or incremental approach by asking how much *extra* is obtained by doing something *extra*. "What difference does it make?" is the key question. By keeping his eye on this ball, the economist can ensure against post hoc, propter hoc reasoning. The empirical verification and quantification of marginal effects of policy actions are exceedingly challenging. They are the core of the research about economic behavior that is most relevant to policy.

The wise economist knows, however, that merely finding a marginal-this to be compared with a marginal-that is not sufficient for an evaluation. A rigidly incrementalist approach can lose sight of major opportunities. Locating the least soggy spot in a swamp is not optimizing if high ground is accessible outside the swamp. The fruitful applications of global "systems analysis" demonstrate that economists need not succumb to marginalist myopia. Moreover, the economist is trained to recognize the time dimension of the effects that he appraises. Short-run and long-run consequences of programs differ, and the analyst looks beyond immediate results to subsequent repercussions and ramifications.

Fourth, the economist recognizes the diverse uses of resources and the opportunities for substitution among them. These principles often lead to a preference for seemingly roundabout or indirect solutions. The employment problems of textile workers in New England cities may be solved by the development of an electronics industry. A tax cut can create jobs for the poor even though they benefit little directly from lower tax bills.

Because money is fungible—capable of being divided and shifted around—the direct approach that strikes the politician's fancy may not work. It often *seems* most effective to support an earmarked purpose by such direct means as a grant to a locality for education, a tax incentive to a businessman for manpower training, or a gift of food to a less developed country. But it may be virtually impossible to assure that such measures really hit their target. The recipient can respond by spending less of his own funds on the stated objective and more elsewhere, thus turning the aid into a general purpose grant. Hence roundabout routes may be more effective, even if they appear paradoxical to the layman. The man in the street knows that the penicillin designed to cure his sore throat is not injected into his throat; but he does not have similar experience with the flow of economic medicine through the body politic.

Fifth, the economist trained in the Anglo-Saxon tradition has a predisposition to believe that the best way to serve the interest of a rational, well-informed adult is to let him make his own choices insofar as they do not conflict with the welfare of others.

Finally, the economist sees the competitive market and its pricing mechanism as a particularly efficient way of giving expression to individual choices and of reconciling private and public interests.

It is remarkable how many of the campaigns, crusades, and battles of economists in public service are predicated in one way or another on these simple propositions. They are the foundation for a considerable area of agreement within the profession. It is news when economists disagree, but the broad range of agreement among professionals of differing political philosophies often goes unnoticed. In particular, there is widespread professional agreement about things the government should *not* do, what Charles Hitch once called the profession's "non-agenda of government." [3]

An economist interested in public policy is likely to be a free trader. He can demonstrate analytically that, under a broad set of conditions, barriers to the international exchange of goods and services induce a net reduction in worldwide efficiency. He will, of course, recognize exceptions to this rule as well as other cases where, even though the world economy loses, our own nation may come out ahead. But, when he umpires; any protectionist proposal comes up to bat with at least one strike against it.

In domestic areas as well, the economist is likely to be skeptical of proposals that would stifle the price mechanism, whether by setting ceilings or floors on prices or by restraining competitive behavior. Whatever the ideological stripe of an administration or congressional body, its economists are likely to be among those least enthusiastic about agricultural programs based on contrived scarcity, ceilings on interest rates, rapid advances in the minimum wage, floors on rates in transportation industries, resale price maintenance (so-called fair trade agreements), and other controls and constraints on prices or wages. Free choice and competition expressed through purchasing and selling decisions of individual competitors often have a remarkable property of yielding social results that cannot be improved on by public action. At the same time, the market has many defects and shortcomings that require public action. In dealing with these defects, the economist is happiest when he can recommend a public policy that works to perfect the market rather than to overrule or finesse it.

3. Charles J. Hitch, "The Uses of Economics," in Pendleton Herring, Philip E. Mosely, Charles J. Hitch, and others. *Research for Public Policy* (Brookings Institution, 1961), p. 96.

The Economist versus the Special Interest

If economists who vote Democratic and economists who vote Republican are united on many issues in their field of professional expertise, then why are their agreements not always reflected in the law of the land? One answer emerges from a simple review of the programs on which I have suggested that present statutes and professional consensus are at variance. Whatever the economics profession may think about agricultural price supports, high barriers against oil imports, or minimum rates in transportation, some groups in our nation have an obvious stake in these measures. Many of the interest groups in our society want a shield against the market, and some have the political influence and power to get one. Generally these are likely to be producers' groups, and the economist is often cast in the role of the consumer's champion.

In some cases, the producer's interest coincides with, or is consistent with, the public interest. The producer's claim to special treatment may reflect a legitimate gripe or bring to light an imperfection in the workings of the system. Our pluralistic political process relies upon individuals and groups to present their views and press their cases. Ungreased wheels are expected to squeak for themselves.

Yet the producer's interest diverges from the public interest in many areas; such cases have been recognized and amply documented in the literature of economics from Adam Smith to Henry Simons.[4] And the literature of my profession, as well as that of political science, records the potency of special interests. Still it comes as a surprise and disappointment to the novice in Washington to learn just how much such groups influence the legislative process.

The strong and concerted wishes of the few tend to get disproportional weight relative to the weak and diffused interests of the many. The key is not primarily wealth or class; small businessmen and farmers are as powerful in this respect as the mighty giants of the petroleum industry. It takes a well-organized, unified minority willing to put on the line its political support, its votes, and its efforts on the basis of a single group of issues. Thus dairy import quotas involve bread as well as butter to a couple of hundred thousand dairy farmers; they mean at most a few cents a day to a couple of hundred million other Americans. The dairy farmers will know and remember how their congressmen vote on this issue; the

4. Adam Smith, *An Inquiry into the Nature and Causes of the Wealth of Nations* (London: 3rd ed., Methuen, 1922), Vol. 1, esp. Chap. 10, "Of Wages and Profit in the Different Employments of Labour and Stock"; Henry C. Simons, *Economic Policy for a Free Society* (University of Chicago Press, 1948), esp. Chap. 2, "A Positive Program for Laissez Faire: Some Proposals for a Liberal Economic Policy."

housewife will almost certainly either ignore or forget it, and her husband surely will. Political realities impel a congressman to tax the majority of his constituency lightly in order to benefit a small interest group heavily.

Economists in government spend much time and energy rebutting the claims of special interest groups. They have to shoot down repeatedly the lengthy briefs prepared by the economists in the employ of such groups, who eagerly invoke the support and defense of economic arguments to claim that their interest really does coincide with the public interest. The economist in the public service always faces the threat that bad economics will drive out good. And he has to run fast just to avoid losing ground.

In fact, we have run at least fast enough to hold our own in the sixties. Special interest groups have not made new and greater inroads in the law. We can even point to a few areas of progress. American trade policy became freer under Presidents Kennedy and Johnson. President Johnson viewed liberal trade as a fundamental principle and was willing to fight for it. Once, for example, when presented privately with a proposal that was billed as "only a little protectionist," he squashed it with the retort that it reminded him of the girl who was only a little bit pregnant. Also, in the Johnson years, the consumer was provided with a network of safeguards against deceitful and harmful practices, lack of information, and misinformation that impair his free choice in the market.

Finally, the balance of political power was improved by interest groups formed in areas of new government initiative. Organized political expression by the poor and lobbying by educators and even by operators of nursing homes followed the initiation of government programs; these offset some of the power of more traditional special interests. Although the new lobbies could prove troublesome in the future, their interests were generally in tune with national priorities during the sixties.

There have, however, been many instances of frustration and defeat. President Kennedy's program for deregulation of transportation was stillborn in 1962. The response to the 1963 Kennedy initiative for tax reform was most discouraging. After years of internal work to devise a maritime program that might have some chance of enactment, President Johnson's proposals did not gain an inch in the legislative process. Congress failed regularly to act on presidential proposals for more reliance on user charges for federal facilities. On one occasion President Johnson authorized Gardner Ackley and me to get the reaction of some congressional leaders to the Council's argument in favor of repeal of fair trade laws. The first thing that caught my eye in one office was a plaque recording the appreciation of a retailers' trade association for the achievements of that congressman. We did not get an enthusiastic reception.

Given the strength and the bitterness of the opposition, a presidential crusade against shields and subsidies seemed most unpromising. Particularly in the early 1960s, far greater gains were to be made by fighting to enlarge the size of the national economic pie than by pressing proposals to increase equity and efficiency in sharing the pie. Improved overall performance of the national economy could be legitimately sold as good for everybody, and thus fitted into the Johnsonian consensus approach. Where redistribution was at issue, it seemed most important to focus on political power by enhancing the strength of the weak and the disadvantaged at the ballot box and in community decision making. Thus for understandable—though regrettable—reasons, the shields and subsidies continue on the statute books into the seventies.

Efficiency and Equity

The cases where the professional verdict is overruled by the minority can be readily documented and lamented. But there are also many cases in which the economist's answer conflicts with the views of the majority. Often the divergence arises out of public misunderstanding, which then requires mass education in elementary economics. This was particularly important in regard to the tax proposals of 1963 and 1967.

In other cases, however, the economist's judgments about efficiency are rejected because they do not accord with the public's concept of equity. The structure of welfare economics rests on what economists call the "Pareto condition": A measure improves social efficiency if its benefits *exceed* what is required to compensate fully everyone whose welfare is impaired. In fact, the people harmed normally are not compensated and this is a basis for legitimate concern. A democratic capitalism must perform a perpetual juggling act to keep the balance between equity and efficiency. In a society with egalitarian principles, substantial inequality in income and wealth is tolerated only as a concession to efficiency. The inequality arises through the carrots and sticks of a market system. Sometimes the carrots are awarded to the wise, the energetic, and the ingenious; such results square with society's sense of fair play. Even the working of the stick may be supported when it falls on the foolish and the lazy.

In many instances, however, rewards and penalties are not neatly equated with personal merit. Any economics textbook describes some results which are generated by a blind lottery rather than a wise jury. If consumer demand shifts from hats to shoes, then shoe producers are rewarded with greater profits and hat producers are penalized with lower incomes. This redistribution has the socially desirable consequence of encouraging investment and employment in the production of shoes and of discouraging expansion in the hat industry. But the public cannot applaud when some able and honest businessmen fail and some efficient and energetic workers become unemployed. Nor does the nation cheer when some citizens just happen to have the pot of gold land in their laps.

The market generates a distribution of income which is a by-product of its solution of the problems of allocation and production. The solutions to these problems have certain demonstrably ideal properties, but the resulting income distribution has no inherent logic.

It is quite understandable that the distribution result is sometimes deplored by the majority. Some economists who have advised less developed countries report widespread opposition to the allocation of food by market-clearing prices. Cumbersome and inefficient rationing systems are actually preferred. In the view of the public, it is bad enough that food is scarce; it would be unconscionable for food to be expensive too. Support for rent ceilings in this country is analogous: People want to prevent rich landlords from gouging poor tenants. But rent controls destroy incentives to maintain or rehabilitate property, and are thus an assured way to preserve slums. (When I read that some Harvard students were actively campaigning for rent ceilings in Cambridge and Boston, I wondered how many of that group were economics majors.)

The public is usually hostile to the proposal frequently made by economists for charging premium rates on subways, buses, or bridges at peak hours.[5] Here justice seems to be violated because the peak-hour traveler gets the worst service—most crowding, slowest ride, and so forth. If he had any options or a high enough income, he would not be one of the sardines. How can he decently be charged an *extra* fee compared with those who travel in leisurely luxury during slack hours?

These attitudes are not entirely unreasonable and they cannot be dismissed. The economist is challenged to find solutions which preserve efficiency and still meet public standards of equity. He is also challenged to educate the public on the importance of the efficiency criteria he applies. The economist's job is to enlighten democratic decisions—not to attempt to impose technocratic decisions in the policy process.

With a little ingenuity, economists frequently can devise solutions that reconcile efficiency with the democratic notion of equity. This is particularly true in meeting the burdens of transition which so often concern the nation. When workers or firms are displaced by technological advance, aids to relocation and retraining deserve more stress. Adjustment assistance offers a particularly promising approach to ameliorate the impact of

5. See, for example, William S. Vickrey, "Pricing in Urban and Suburban Transport," in American Economic Association, *Papers and Proceedings of the Seventy-fifth Annual Meeting, 1962* (*American Economic Review*, Vol. 53, May 1963), pp. 452–65.

shifts in international trade. When businessmen and workers are severely injured by changing patterns of imports, they can be given temporary aid in shifting to other productive efforts. This means of cushioning the blow need not detract from the efficiency of the national economy and can be far less costly to the nation than the perpetuation of barriers to broader trade with other countries.

The Negative Income Tax

Taxation is a key to linking equity and efficiency. The progressive income tax—despite all the current defects and limitations of our tax laws—is our most important and most efficient means of modifying the upper end of the income distribution. There is a growing—although far from complete—professional consensus [6] in favor of extending the same principle to the low end of the income scale through a negative income tax, which would establish a guaranteed income floor and would provide for a sliding scale of payments diminishing with rises in a family's earnings. The best way for the poor to raise their incomes is, of course, through improved opportunities for gainful employment. More and better jobs for the poor have indeed been the main escape route out of poverty during the sixties. But because of this very progress, relatively more of the poor are now in groups that, because of age, disability, or family situation, are least likely to achieve satisfactory opportunities for work. For these groups, cash benefits are the main hope for raising living standards. While there is a rationale for specific programs of in-kind benefits in the form of food, rent, or medicine, most economists regard the malnutrition, inadequate housing, and poor health of the poor primarily as symptoms of their inadequate income rather than as separate problems to be attacked by different routes. An economist on the CEA staff once offered a typical professional reaction when, after reviewing a host of in-kind proposals, he expressed the hope that money might soon be invented in our society.

Of course, cash benefits are offered to those among the poor who are classified as eligible for welfare. But the eligibility standards reflect an effort to distinguish between the "deserving" and "undeserving" poor—a distinction that defies justification on either philosophical or economic grounds. In practice, the efforts to retain penalties on the "undeserving" adult poor often condemn their children to a life of poverty. As a supple-

6. See, for example, Milton Friedman, *Capitalism and Freedom* (University of Chicago Press, 1962), esp. pp. 190–95; Christopher Green, *Negative Taxes and the Poverty Problem* (Brookings Institution, 1967); Robert Theobald (ed.), *The Guaranteed Income: Next Step in Economic Evolution?* (Doubleday, 1966); James Tobin, Joseph A. Pechman, and Peter M. Mieszkowski, "Is a Negative Income Tax Practical?" *Yale Law Journal,* Vol. 77 (November 1967), pp. 1–27 (Brookings Reprint 142).

ment to other necessary and desirable efforts, a program of guaranteed income could greatly increase the logic and efficiency of public aid to the poor. To be sure, steps would be required to assure that work incentives are maintained. The poor will not work for no added income any more than the rich. But we deal quite effectively with this problem at the upper end of the income scale. Just as the present income tax does not seriously impede incentives to earn high incomes, the negative income tax need not interfere significantly with incentives to augment low incomes.

The negative income tax looks like a "right answer" to a difficult question. Yet public opinion polls record the overwhelming opposition of the American public to any system of guaranteed income that does not depend directly on work efforts. In June 1968, for example, the Gallup Poll found that more than 80 percent of those expressing an opinion favored a plan that provided for an above-poverty income through guaranteed employment opportunity, but more than 60 percent opposed the income floor without a work requirement.[7] These expressions of public opinion suggest that it would be very difficult to enact a full-dress negative income tax under present circumstances. Moreover, they warn us that, even if the negative income tax could be enacted, it might become an instrument of social divisiveness. It might generate a wave of resentment by the middle class and a strong feeling of being demeaned on the part of the recipients. Before economists can conclude that we have the "right answer" in this area, we have to understand and educate the American public. For one thing, it is doubtful that the public realizes how many of the poor are unable to work, by any reasonable standard.

The family assistance program proposed by President Nixon in the summer of 1969 is a major step toward the negative income tax for families with children.[8] It may well be as large a step as our society will accept at this time. The plan effectively eliminates the categories of eligibility for public assistance and hence terminates the pointless distinction between the deserving and undeserving poor. One vestige of this distinction, however, remains in the form of a requirement that recipients of this assistance be prepared to accept "suitable jobs." Given the modest level of the federal payment—$1,600 a year for a family of four—and the 50 percent net retention of earned income, I strongly doubt that the work requirement is seriously needed. Moreover, it would be enforceable only through a revival of strict categorical definitions in a new guise, which

7. *New York Times,* June 16, 1968.
8. Immediately after President Nixon set forth his welfare proposals in August 1969, the Gallup Poll found overwhelming public support for them. See "The President's Address to the Nation on Domestic Programs," *Weekly Compilation of Presidential Documents,* Vol. 5 (Aug. 11, 1969), pp. 1103–12; and *New York Times,* Aug. 31, 1969.

might nullify the progress offered by this program. I would expect good sense to triumph in limiting enforcement to the rare flagrant cases of freeloading. Apparently, some statutory antilaziness requirement is a political imperative for the program. In the days of temperance laws it was sometimes said that the most viable social compromise required that the "drys" get their laws while the "wets" get their liquor. Perhaps, at this juncture in society, the reactionaries must get their work provision when the poor get their aid.

International Exchange Rates

In another important area—international exchange rates—the profession has a "right answer" which is only gradually winning acceptance among bankers, businessmen, and statesmen.

Research economists and academic experts today agree broadly, although not unanimously, that a greater degree of flexibility in exchange rates would be a desirable innovation.[9] Under the present system of pegged exchange rates, changes in relative currency values are difficult to accomplish, so that nations get locked into valuations which are inconsistent with their domestic stabilization objectives. To reconcile the irreconcilable, they often turn to measures which raise barriers to the international flow of goods and capital. Moreover, as a set of administered prices, the pegged exchange system does not provide the flexibility and the opportunities for gradual adjustment and for economizing that would exist under market-determined exchange rates. If marks are scarce relative to francs, the whole philosophy of a market mechanism argues that the relative prices of the two currencies ought to adjust accordingly. But this prescription, broadly accepted by professional economic experts, is still acceptable to only a minority of international traders and investors and dealers in world exchange markets.

Most practitioners in the world economy see flexibility of exchange rates as an additional source of risk and uncertainty.[10] The exponent of greater flexibility can point out that, under the system of pegged rates, the

9. See, for example, Milton Friedman, "First Lecture," in Milton Friedman and Robert V. Roosa, *The Balance of Payments: Free Versus Fixed Exchange Rates* (Washington: American Enterprise Institute for Public Policy Research, 1967), pp. 1–24; George N. Halm, *Toward Limited Exchange-Rate Flexibility* (Princeton University, Department of Economics, International Finance Section, 1969); James E. Meade, "The Case for Variable Exchange Rates," in Warren L. Smith and Ronald L. Teigen (eds.), *Readings in Money, National Income and Stabilization Policy* (Richard D. Irwin, 1965), pp. 505–17. For an opposing expert view, see Charles P. Kindleberger, "The Case for Fixed Exchange Rates, 1969" (paper presented at the Bald Peak Monetary Conference, sponsored by the Federal Reserve Bank of Boston, Melvin Village, N.H., Oct. 9, 1969).

10. See "O'Brien Rejects Floating Rates," *London Financial Times*, Sept. 17, 1969.

relative exchange rate between francs and marks has been highly uncertain at times, and that the major revaluations which occur infrequently can be far more disruptive than gradual adjustments over time. He can also argue that the initiation of greater flexibility in exchange rates would promote the development of better markets offering insurance and hedging opportunities to those who need protection against future changes in exchange rates. He can finally point to commercial, financial, and political uncertainties that simply swamp the exchange rate uncertainty in their impact on world commercial and financial transactions.

Still the doubts and reservations of the skeptics persist. In particular, they can document a generation of unparalleled success in the liberalization and growth of world trade and world capital movements. They can stress the risk of disrupting a system that has been a consistent winner: Why throw in a pat hand? The repeated signs of crisis so evident in the last few years argue for timely preventive action to modify the existing system while it is still a winner. Along with most of my professional colleagues, I believe we must travel the road toward greater flexibility. But more flexible rates will become a correct and feasible answer only when they are better understood by the world financial community. If introduced today, flexible rates might have disruptive results in the short run. Because traders and investors might be frightened away from some international activities, the new system might impose unacceptable transition costs and indeed conceivably might not survive its initiation period.

To make a more flexible system economically reliable as well as politically feasible, intensive education is necessary. In order to convince those affected that legitimate interests can and will be protected, economists must learn to understand the precise character of the concerns and anxieties that international businessmen and bankers feel about greater flexibility. Education has to proceed in both directions. The exchange trader can help to teach the economist how greater flexibility can be tailored to the needs of the currency markets. The economist's basic objective of greater flexibility can be achieved by a number of alternative techniques and the practitioners have much to contribute in drawing up the specific blueprint.

The educational process is developing in encouraging ways. Some outstanding international economists who are exponents of greater flexibility have been discussing the issues with international bankers and traders in meetings of the new Conference on Proposals for Greater Flexibility of Exchange Rates.[11] This is proving to be a flexible exchange of views.

11. The Conference was organized by Robert V. Roosa, Fritz Machlup, and George N. Halm. The first meeting was held Jan. 29–31, 1969, at Oyster Bay, N.Y.; subsequent meetings have been at Burgenstock, Switzerland, June 23–29, 1969, and at the Brookings Institution, Oct. 1, 1969.

What Consensus?

Our ability as economists to influence public policy in the areas of professional agreement is impaired by the difficulty of establishing the existence of consensus. In fact, nobody really knows how to define or measure a consensus, and I could be challenged on a number of areas where I have claimed that the profession is generally agreed.

The economics profession is richly endowed with thousands of qualified experts and, on almost any particular issue, at least a few hundred are likely to differ honestly with the rest of their colleagues. The view of a small minority will get considerable attention in the press just because of its novelty. And when the Congress is looking for the testimony of experts, it makes every effort to select a balanced panel so that both sides can be heard. The staff of one congressional committee had a particularly difficult assignment when, in 1968, it was forced to beat the bushes to find some "respectable" expert who would testify *against* Special Drawing Rights—the widely supported plan for augmenting international liquidity with fiat money.

The existence of a professional consensus in favor of a tax increase in the fall of 1967 was reflected in a petition to the Congress bearing the signatures of 260 economists. Yet it was possible for Senator William Proxmire to state accurately that that list represented less than 2½ percent of the membership of the American Economic Association. In June 1969, a group of sixteen well-known economists covering the political spectrum made a similar plea for extension of the tax surcharge, relying on the prestige of the signatories rather than the count of noses.[12]

Some nations have formed duly constituted nonpartisan or bipartisan groups which can command respect as a kind of Supreme Court of economic advice. Examples are the Economic Council of Canada and the German Council of Experts.[13] But for reasons which I believe compelling, the U.S. Council of Economic Advisers functions in a much more controversial and partisan atmosphere, and makes no claim or attempt to act as a Supreme Court of economic views.

Professional Controversy

The overriding objection to proposals that would focus the activities of the political economist on areas of consensus is precisely that they would

12. *Congressional Record,* Vol. 113, Pt. 19, 90 Cong. 1 sess. (1967), pp. 25063–65; *New York Times,* June 11, 1969.

13. For an interesting comparison of the German institution to the CEA, see Henry C. Wallich. "The American Council of Economic Advisers and the German Sachverstaendigenrat: A Study in the Economics of Advice," *Quarterly Journal of Economics,* Vol. 82 (August 1968), pp. 349–79 [Reading 33, below].

remove him from the areas of controversy. They would limit him to the role of a pure technician. As technicians, economists are not pure; and we are more than technicians. Our philosophical and ideological positions are part of our professional views and our potential contribution.

One has to search hard for professional controversies—even on "purely" theoretical or empirical issues—that are independent of differing ideologies. The best example I can offer is the disagreement among students of business investment regarding the relative importance of internal cash flow, the cost of external capital, and the growth of final demand as determining factors. Even here, the accelerator school, which regards the growth of final demand as the key determinant of investment, seems to have no adherents who are politically conservative.

Most of the key policy controversies among economists reflect different philosophies about the government's role in the society and the economy, and about the relative priority attached to various objectives that we all value to some degree. There is no logical necessity for economists who place a particularly heavy weight on the goal of price stability also to favor a minimum size and scope of the federal budget, or to emphasize the importance of balance-of-payments equilibrium. Yet empircally this association exists. If you knew the views of an unidentified economist on half a dozen controversial issues, you could make a good estimate of his positions on six other issues.

In the areas of fiscal and monetary policy, economists sometimes disagree about the general ability of government to promote better economic performance by discretionary policy decisions. Those who advocate that monetary policy be guided by specific rules have a consistent ideological position reflecting their distrust of judgment and decision making in the bureaucratic process. Apart from this particular debate, the key to varying fiscal-monetary prescriptions lies in differing assessments of the relative social importance of price stability and of high employment. To be sure, the experts differ with one another at times on their forecasts of private demand and on their choice of stabilization instruments. Such differences in technical judgments can lead to occasional disagreements among people with the same philosophical orientation. Thus in some instances Walter Heller and Paul Samuelson disagree on the right prescription; and at times Arthur Burns and Henry Wallich disagree. And, on many occasions, all four agree.

But the ideological differences dominate the disagreements. There are "high-pressure" and "low-pressure" economists, to use Henry Wallich's apt term.[14] History probably does not record a day when Paul Samuelson was advocating restraint while Henry Wallich urged stimulus. When there

14. Henry C. Wallich, "Conservative Economic Policy," *Yale Review,* Vol. 46 (Autumn 1956), p. 68.

are risks to be taken, Samuelson will accept a somewhat greater danger of inflation and Wallich will take somewhat more risk of unemployment. Price stability and high levels of employment are prized by both men, but not with the same relative intensity.

James Tobin has stated the high-pressure creed eloquently:

> . . . The whole purpose of the economy is production of goods or services for consumption now or in the future. I think the burden of proof should always be on those who would produce less rather than more, on those who would leave idle men or machines or land that could be used. It is amazing how many reasons can be found to justify such waste: fears of inflation, balance-of-payments deficits, unbalanced budgets, excessive national debt, loss of confidence in the dollar. . . . Perhaps price stability, fixed exchange rates, balanced budgets, and the like can be justified as means to achieving and sustaining high employment, production, and consumption. Too often the means are accorded precedence over the end. . . .[15]

In the microeconomic area, sharp controversies arise among economists regarding the capability of political action to improve imperfect results of the market's decisions. The areas of consensus described above reflect a general commitment of economists to the impersonal and efficient solutions of the market mechanism in cases where competition prevails, where buyers and sellers are well informed, and where there are no externalities—that is, where benefits and costs are limited to consumers and producers of a given product. In such a world, the scope of microeconomic policy would be limited to modifying income distribution. But these assumptions are not a good description of the real world, and not a perfect description of any specific situation.

Any economist who wants the government to "do something about it" whenever the market falls short of perfection will prescribe an unlimited scope for government intervention. As George Stigler put it in a widely circulated comment, this prescription is like the verdict of the judge in a singing contest who was ready to award the prize to the second singer merely on the basis of having heard the first. The real question is whether any modification that could be introduced by government action would improve the situation.

On the other hand, conditions in the market sometimes fail to bear even a family resemblance to those of the model. Some situations virtually cry out for public intervention. For example, it is cold comfort that, without food and drug regulation, any customer who is fatally poisoned by a medication will never buy that product again. Political solutions can be workable and can improve matters on many occasions when

15. James Tobin, *National Economic Policy: Essays* (Yale University Press, 1966), pp. vii–viii.

the market solution is strongly tainted. And political action can bring the income distribution generated by the market closer into line with our egalitarian principles.

The microeconomic policies and programs of government aim to narrow the wide gap between the ideal world of the competitive model and the complex world we actually inhabit. Obviously, in many areas, the consumer does not receive adequate information to make intelligent choices without government safeguards and intervention. In some areas, economies of scale are so important that effective competition is impossible or woefully inefficient; hence the real choice is between regulated and unregulated monopoly. In such cases as pollution and neighborhood renewal, benefits and costs are not confined to the individual producer and the particular consumer; hence the decisions made by the parties directly involved in a transaction will neglect the interests of many others who have an important stake in the outcome.

Many goods—like national defense and lighthouses—simply cannot be provided by the market, and the government must shoulder the responsibility. Thus public policy aims to ensure competition whenever possible, to improvise substitutes for competition where it cannot work, to improve the flow of information, to supply services which are valued by the public collectively but which would not be adequately supplied in response to private market choice, and to reflect the social costs (and benefits) of production that are not borne (or captured) by the producer.

Health care is one of the many areas where we can see these principles at work. Contagious diseases introduce externalities, giving us all a stake in the health care of our neighbors and pointing toward public programs to ensure vaccination and to prevent epidemics. The generally accepted social principle that the market should not legislate matters of life and death obliges public policy to ensure at least a minimum level of medical care to all. Since the consumer faces enormous informational problems in the choice of highly complex professional medical services, the government has responsibility to set standards for practitioners and to regulate the sale of potentially harmful medicines. Since the supply of medical workers depends on the scale and mix of educational efforts, which cannot be regarded as rapidly responsive to the signals of the market, government action may be needed to shorten the time lags.

The economist has a role to play in shaping programs in such areas. Applying the tools of planning, programming, and budgeting, he can help to appraise the problems of choice in order to fulfill aims at least cost. He can work to achieve objectives with minimum impairment of individual choice. He can underline the opportunities that are sacrificed by adopting medical programs; indeed, it is surprising how often he has to point out that, although medical care is a good thing, it does not follow that everyone ought to have unlimited amounts of it at government expense. Surely there would be a professional consensus of economists against any public program that would give every American as many free pairs of eyeglasses as he would like. But there would not be widespread professional agreement on most of the relevant issues in health policy.

In other policy areas, however, professional agreement is greater because technical elements loom larger and ideological considerations play a smaller role. In the case of water resources, for example, the profession has accepted criteria for measuring costs and benefits, which, in the nature of things, are amenable to quantification. Egalitarian considerations seem far less significant here than in the field of health; and the scope of the public sector is less at issue since water is clearly a public good. In every case, the judgments of economists about policy reflect a blend of technical analysis and social philosophy.

3. On the Limited "Relevance" of Economics

ROBERT L. HEILBRONER

Relevance is a word that makes professors of economics wince these days. There was a time when I could initiate a class into the mysteries of diminishing marginal utility, explaining why the man in the Sahara Desert would not be willing to pay as much for the third pint of water as for the second, confident that when the hands went up it would be because someone was convinced that he ought to pay more, because his *total* utility was greater after three pints than after two. Today when the hands go up, I know what's coming: "That's clear enough, but I don't see how it's relevant."

Is it relevant? Have the refined figments of economics anything to do with ghetto life or the behavior of corporations or the military industrial complex? It is easy to sympathize with the student who chokes on marginal utility while the world seethes outside the classroom. Yet, I do not think that this first attack on the relevance of economics counts for much. For, as his instructor quickly explains, these rarified concepts are essential if economics is to penetrate to the fundamental elements of the social universe. They are as necessary to economics as the abstractions of

Reprinted by permission of the author and publisher from *The Public Interest*, No. 21 (Fall 1970), pp. 80–93. Copyright © by National Affairs Inc., 1970.

time and space are for physics. Indeed, if it could not conceive of an abstraction like marginal utility, economics could not claim to be a social *science*.

Moreover, as the instructor delights in pointing out, some of these remote conceptions contain unexpectedly sharp cutting edges. The rationale for progressive taxation, for example, uses the argument that successive dollars of income, like successive pints of water in the Sahara, yield ever smaller increments of enjoyment to their recipients. Pure competition, another hopelessly "unrealistic" concept that is a favorite target of freshman scorn, turns up, of all places, as the starting point for Marx's analysis of the dynamics of the capitalist process. Indeed, by the time a zealous instructor is through, the danger is that the shoe will be on the other foot, and the class will have been persuaded that "irrelevance" is nothing but the ill-considered objections of those who have not yet mastered the subject.

Yet, it must be clear from the title of this essay that I am not among those who are so persuaded. For behind the question that our student puts, is a deeper issue to which the standard reassurances do not always address themselves. It is that economics exists for a purpose, and is meaningful and useful only insofar as it serves that purpose. The purpose is to enable us better to comprehend the structure and tendencies of the economic order—that is, the institutions and activities that affect the production and distribution of wealth. Insofar as economics gives us this understanding, no matter how abstract or far-fetched it may seem, it is undeniably relevant. But insofar as it fails to do so, no matter how elegant or scientific it may appear, it is not.

I do not think an instructor would take issue with this criterion of relevance. Rather, he would argue that economics meets it very well. Does not the enormous demand for economists, he would ask, imply that the discipline has something to offer for which hardheaded businessmen are willing to pay? Does not the recent creation of a Nobel Prize in economics testify that it is an activity of high public importance? Is not the flattery of imitation paid by other social sciences to the techniques of economics similar testimony from the world of scholarship? What further proof of relevance would one want?

The answer I wish to give is not to denigrate what economics has done. It is to stress what it has failed to do. Obviously, economics throws a good deal of light on the workings of the economic process. But the light is curiously uneven. Some parts of the social machinery are brilliantly lit. Other parts are left shadowy or totally dark. And this uneven lighting, I would maintain, is not merely due to the fact that, like all sciences, economics is more highly advanced in some areas than in others. It is the consequence of the kind of illumination that conventional economic theory sheds. In other words, I believe there are aspects of the economic system that economics, as it now exists, *cannot* light up, no matter how brightly its lamps may burn. For someone who wants to inspect those parts of the machinery, economics today is as useless as a searchlight fixed in the wrong direction.

The Irrelevance of Economists

We shall turn shortly to the problems inherent in the nature of economic theory itself. But first we must take up a touchy subject that cannot be sidestepped. For one reason that part of the social machinery is shrouded in darkness cannot be attributed to the failings of the discipline itself. It lies rather in the fact that economists themselves are at fault for having failed to turn their torches on important issues and problems of our economic order.

Let me give a few instances of this disregard of certain economic problems. One area of nearly Stygian blackness is to be found in the growth of American economic power abroad. Between 1950 and 1969, American overseas investment increased from $12 billion to over $65 billion, giving rise to the familiar charge that American imperialism has become a dominant force in international economic (and perhaps political) affairs. Astonishingly, however, a student of international events who depended for his knowledge of current trends on the professional journals would have remained totally unaware of this portentous development. The statistics of foreign investment were, of course, reported. But I am unaware of an analysis of the politicoeconomic consequences of this economic penetration in the professional literature. Our knowledge of the extent, nature, or effects of American hegemony in foreign investment has been gained almost entirely from the work of Marxian economists or from that of journalists such as Servan-Schreiber.

Another striking evasion is to be found in the professional examination of that central abstraction, the firm. There is a vast literature on the firm, but studying it would leave one curiously uninformed about many aspects of its real-life counterpart, the corporation. Reading professional journals one would not know that corporations affect national policy; that they are centers of powerful propagandistic efforts; that they practice fraud, chicane, and misrepresentation; that they dominate the social and political life of many smaller communities in which they are located, etc. Economists would no doubt offer a number of reasons why these aspects of "the firm" were left unexamined, principal among them being that these were not "economic" questions. But the fact remains that they *were* left unexplored. So far as conventional economics was concerned, these issues simply did not exist.

This roster of ignored subjects could be easily expanded. I do not know of any treatment in the professional literature of the size and distribution of the benefits of the war economy by socio-economic groupings; of any interest in the question of the means by which private wealth and income are preserved from one generation to the next; of any analysis of the benefits accruing from "public" goods by income strata. Even poverty and ecological damage, now fairly common subjects for professional examination, were not issues originally unearthed by economists, although both problems would seem to lie directly beneath their gaze.

This is not to say that nothing has been written on these matters. Here and there an economist has looked in these directions, at aspects of the social machinery that were formerly obscured. Yet I do not think that many will dispute my contention that these are not the kinds of questions that crowd the pages of the economics journals, or that the attitude of most economists has been to avoid rather than to seek out perspectives of this kind.

I would feel somewhat more uneasy in my contention that economists were markedly one-sided in their outlook were not my belief bolstered by the support of an impeccable observer, George Stigler, one of the most respected economists of the conservative Chicago school. In a well-known essay, "The Politics of Political Economists," Stigler has written that "the professional study of economics makes one politically conservative." The reason for this is "the effect of the scientific training the economist receives. . . . It becomes impossible for the trained economist to believe that a small group of selfish capitalists dictates the main outlines of the allocation of resources. . . . He cannot unblushingly repeat slogans such as 'production for use rather than for profit.' He cannot believe that a change in the *form* of social organization will eliminate basic economic problems." [1]

Professor Stigler's point is clear: if economists tend to be conservative, this is because it is the more *intelligent* thing to be. Without conceding that point (for I am by no means convinced by Stigler's examples of the things that economists cannot believe), I would like to raise another, less elegant, explanation for the phenomenon. It is that economists are conservative because they tend to be located in the upper echelons of the pyramid of incomes. The demand for economists has now raised their salaries until (as of 1967) the median pay of an associate professor was $14,000

1. *Quarterly Journal of Economics,* Nov. 1959, reprinted in *Essays in the History of Economics* (Chicago, 1965) pp. 52, 59, 60.

that of a full professor $18,000, and of a "superior" full professor $21,000. This scale of salaries, quite aside from the royalties, consultation fees, foundation grants, etc. which are the common complement of professional pay, suffices to place associate professors in the top 15 per cent of all taxpayers; full professors in the top 5 per cent; and "superior" full professors in the top 2 per cent.

In his article Stigler raises venality as a possible cause for the conservatism of the profession, and dismisses it with the comment that "current rates of pay for good economists are much below what I would assume to be the going rate for a soul." But venality is not the issue at stake. When we seek to explain the prevailing political outlook of other groups in society, it is first and foremost to their place in the socioeconomic spectrum that we look. Thus, if economists are conservative, one *prima facie* reason would seem to be that they simply share the conserving attitudes we find in the top echelons of all societies.

To this one should no doubt add that special contemplative approach of the scholar which in itself tends to militate against "radicalism." But the first consideration remains to be faced: economists fare very well in this social order; why should they search for problems that might ruffle that serene temper on which conservatism always rests? The answer, to come out with it flatfootedly, is that they do not, with the result that the picture of the economic order that conventional economics gives us is not one which might emerge if every portion of the mechanism were illumined as brightly as every other portion, but a partial and selective view from which much that is unpleasant or disturbing has been, no doubt unconsciously, passed over.

Let me now pass to more elevating matters. For there is a second and more interesting reason for the unreliable illumination that economics affords. It is (to continue our metaphor) that the light of economics only seems to work when the machinery of the social system is turning over smoothly, whereas any failure in the social mechanism short-circuits the beam that economics throws.

This will take us into a quick tour of the electrical arrangements. As anyone knows who has ever looked into an economics journal, economics is now a very complicated subject, virtually inaccessible to someone without a fairly thorough grounding in mathematics and statistics. Yet what is really significant about the discipline communicates itself immediately to the most casual browser. It is that economics bases itself on the methods of "real" sciences. In the severity of its language, its omnipresent formulae, the recurrent use of the word "model," there is clear advertisement that the paradigm of elucidation that economics follows is patterned as closely as possible on that of the physical sciences. In particular, economic methods stress rigor of procedure and proof, and a studied absence of value judgments—an approach that finds its ultimate expression in the depiction of the economic process as a series of interconnected mathematical equations.

Now what is astounding about economics—or more accurately, about society—is that this mathematical paradigm actually finds its application to social reality. That is, economics can indeed construct algebraic (or geometrical) analogues of social situations that explicate social action with the irresistible force of a logical demonstration, an achievement before which other social sciences pale with envy.

Because this point is very important, let me explain it in more detail. Economics derives its extraordinary explicative power from two sources. First, unlike its sister social sciences, it carefully limits its concerns to the *quantifiable* aspects of the social process. It is not with the sweat on the laborer's brow or the pleasures on the consumer's palate that economics deals, but only with the units of output the laborer produces or the wages he earns, or with the amounts the consumer expends or the income he enjoys. Thus, economics claims for itself a portion of the social universe that is peculiarly amenable to mathematical representation—a claim that immensely facilitates its treatment of the universe in a "scientific" way.[2]

Second, economics achieves its scientific capability because it discovers two kinds of social behavior at the heart of the economic process, both of which lend themselves with surprising ease to replication through mathematical equations.

The first of these behavior patterns is given its clearest expression in the crossed "curves" familiar to every freshman as the Supply and Demand diagram in chapter one of his textbook. As the freshman quickly learns, the curves describe the fact that buyers and sellers, interacting on a marketplace, will spontaneously discover that there is one "equilibrium" price that clears the market—a price at which the quantities offered for sale will exactly equal those that are sought by the other side.

Entranced by the beautiful simplicity of this truly remarkable diagram, our freshman may not reflect on the still more remarkable property of the social mechanism on which it rests. It is that one and the same economic stimulus—for example, a rise in prices—will result in *opposing* behavior reactions. As prices rise, buyers will reduce the quantities they are willing and able to take from the market, while sellers will increase the quantities they seek to unload on it. From the interaction of these opposite behavioral patterns there then emerges the astonishing possibility of

2. And what about marginal utility? Economics has experienced no end of trouble with utility precisely because enjoyment is not cardinally quantifiable. But it gets around the problem by *ranking* one enjoyment as greater than, equal to, or less than another.

describing a social process by means of two different equations, and the even more astonishing possibility of predicting the outcome of this social process by solving these two algebraic expressions.

A second, although related, characteristic of society offers the economist a second basis for translating social action into mathematical formulae. It is that much economic activity, especially that involving production, can be described as "maximizing subject to constraint." By this the economist means that the profit-seeking firm or individual does not have the capability of increasing its revenues without limit simply by adding more and more inputs. Sooner or later, the hard facts of scarcity, technological barriers or organizational inertias place boundaries in the way of unlimited profit-seeking, usually in the form of ever more steeply rising costs.

So much is no more than common sense. But now follows the achievement of economic science. By calculating the "shape" of the constraints imposed by technology, scarcity, or whatever, the economist finds that he can reproduce in a set of equations the outcome of the interaction between the force of profit-maximizing and the constraints of the physical and institutional world, just as a physicist can give mathematical representation to the forces and resistances of the physical universe. Hence, at least in theory, the economist can *predict* the behavior of the profit-maximizing firm in a model that once against displays the extraordinary property of describing social behavior in mathematical terms.[3]

Thus in the eyes of the theoretical economist, the unusual attribute of economics—its claim to relevance, if you will—lies in its ability to portray important aspects of the social universe in terms of the same kind of determinate models that we use to depict certain processes of the natural universe. What is more, there is no doubt but that this fantastic claim is partly true. There *are* relationships of an opposing-behavior or force-constraint kind that hold with sufficient regularity to enable us to use economics with considerable accuracy as a means of explaining or predicting many economic events. As I have said, the practical usefulness of economics is without question, and much of it derives from this "scientific" base.

Economics and the Real World

There is, however, a problem. It lies in the fact that the premises of opposing-behavior and force-constraint on which so much of the scien-

3. Let me add that these two characteristics of opposing-behavior and force-constraint are not the only bases for scientific economics. Economics also relies on statistical relationships that express "typical" behavior patterns, such as the propensity of individuals to save or spend at different levels of income. Nevertheless, the two relationships discussed above are central to most economic theory.

tific model rests are *behavioral assumptions*, and these assumptions, while valid enough of the time to give the scientific model its usefulness, are not valid all of the time. Behavior, in a word, contains an element of indeterminacy that plays hob both with real social processes and with the accuracy of their representation in mathematical models. For when behavior departs from the pattern on which economic theory is built, the illumination—the relevance—of that theory suddenly disappears.

But how indeterminate is behavior? Clearly, it is not so capricious that Macy's cannot count with considerable assurance on a positive response from buyers when it lowers its prices. In "ordinary" circumstances the behavior of buyers and sellers and producers is sufficiently like that on which economic theory builds its edifice so that economics enables us to make predictions and analyses of considerable accuracy. But conditions, alas, are not always ordinary. Indeed, in precisely those times when we most want the assurance of theoretic reliability—when, for example, times are unsettled, or the economy seems poised at the edge of a boom or bust, or when expectations are particularly labile (such as is the case right now)—the dependability of the behavioral premises rapidly deteriorates.

As it does, the determinacy of the scientific model of society deteriorates as well. In the supply-demand situation, for example, the presumption, as we have mentioned, is that buyers will respond to higher prices by curtailing their activities, while sellers do just the opposite. But once an uncertainty of outlook is introduced into the picture, this assumption disappears. Now buyers may respond to a rise in price by rushing into the market before (they think) prices go higher; and sellers may respond by curtailing their offerings, in the hope of selling them more profitably tomorrow. In that case it is impossible to tell where the "equilibrium" price and quantity will settle, because we do not even know, from moment to moment, where the "curves" themselves are located or in which way they incline. That is why the marvellously sophisticated computer models of the economy, which perform well as long as things fundamentally conform to the behavioral patterns of normality, lose their predictive power totally when a sharp change in the winds of opinion brings about a change in economic habits. It explains also why the government which can build elaborate models of the economy for normal periods, detailing with considerable accuracy the effects of small changes in monetary or fiscal policy, cannot tell in advance how a major change will be "interpreted" by the public.

Although it is less dramatic, a second weakness in the economic depiction of reality further undermines the scientific pretensions of the economic model. This is the assumption that we can actually describe the economic forces that bump up against constraints. When the beginning

student first works with this problem, he finds most interesting the determination of exactly where along its frontiers of possibility a firm will
choose to locate itself. But the more bemusing question is a much simpler
one: will the firm in fact be operating on its "frontiers," or will it be content to get along with something less than the "maximum" profit that the
model assumes as its goal. And the problem is not merely one of deciding
on the degree of fineness of economic accuracy in prediction. For if firms
do not maximize, we have no way of knowing what economic path they
will follow, and the whole scientific reproduction of that part of the social
universe collapses forthwith.

The question then comes down to an empirical one: do firms (or individuals) actually maximize their profits (or utilities) or whatever? What is
embarrassing is that we cannot tell whether they do or not. In part, given
the complexities of technology and the inertias of organization, this is the
result of the fact that it is difficult to determine at any moment what
"maximum" performance for a firm should be. More important, maximization becomes an indeterminate guide because it is impossible to
translate into a prescription for behavior over time. Given the innumerable factors that may affect its sales, a firm may rationally seek to maximize its profits over "the long run" by increasing or decreasing its investment, by pushing product A or product B, by risking an antitrust suit
by aggressive actions or by guarding against one by passive behavior.

The problem is thus that profit-maximizing is a rule of conduct that it is
impossible to specify or detect in the real world. Hence it is virtually impossible either to predict future behavior or to evaluate existing behavior
in the terms of its congruence with an objective standard.[4] The analogy is
that of a physicist who was unable to state whether an object dropped
from a tower was actually falling at the rate predicted by the law of gravity. In such circumstances, the law could no longer serve as a basis for
predicting events in the universe. In similar fashion, our inability to state
whether or not corporations (or individuals) are in fact operating on their
maximizing frontiers vastly reduces the relevance of the scientific model
by which we seek to elucidate the workings of the economic universe.

Economics and Social Change

What we have seen so far is that economics lacks relevance insofar as
its practitioners are loath to apply it to "radical" critiques of the system,
and to the extent that the real world defies the regularities of behavior on

4. The exception is for firms competing under conditions of pure competition. Here there
is an unambiguous rule of profit-maximizing that governs their immediate behavior. But
such firms are themselves the exception in the world of imperfect competition that we find
in actuality.

which the economic model of reality is based. But there is, as well, a
third problem to be faced. It is that economics, by its very insistence on
dealing only with the quantifiable elements of social activity, thereby distorts and misrepresents the activities it seeks to explain. Economics deals
with the economic order as if it were only a mechanism for the generation
and allocation of goods and services. But the fact is that the economic
order is also and inextricably a mechanism for the generation of power
and privilege, life-style and motive. Hence, in wrenching something
called "the economy" from the larger "society," economics performs an
operation that is intrinsically self-defeating. For the economic variables
cannot be excised from the larger social system in which they are embed-
ded and treated as a microcosm of that system without seriously distorting
the relation of the model to the reality.

For example, economic analysis is frequently employed to explore the
"growth paths" over which the economy—and of course the surrounding
society—might travel. But the trouble with the analysis of these growth
paths is that they do not take into consideration the social changes or the
political frictions that growth will generate. The models assume that everything "noneconomic" will go on as it is, so that the only important
changes will be the quantifiable relationships of capital and output and
savings, etc. Yet it is apparent that even a single generation of growth at
the rate of the past will bring average household incomes into the "full
professor" range of $18,000 (in terms of today's purchasing power).
Such an upward shift in the socioeconomic center of gravity is virtually
certain to affect patterns of incentive and activity, particularly among the
lower income groups, and might severely change the distribution of
power among the various groups competing for shares of the national income. Yet, before these potential developments, economics is silent, *although these repercussions are likely profoundly to affect the validity of
the growth projections themselves.*

There is, of course, a reason for this restricted scope of economic analysis. It is that neither economists nor anyone else are in a position to state
with any degree of certainty what the social and political effects of economic change will be. The economist is not heedless as to the wider
implications of the economic model he manipulates. It is rather that he
feels that he cannot say anything "scientific" about them, within the
rules and conventions of the paradigm in which he works.

Here is where the "scientific" model of economics thus meets its ultimate limit. For in its unwillingness to indulge in sociopolitical "guesswork," out of fear of transgressing the limits of proper scientific procedure, economics is placed in a position in which its findings *must* be
partial and incomplete and very possibly erroneous. For every economic

act, from the simplest response to a change in prices to the most complex decisions of an entrepreneur, is also a social act. Every action taken by the actors in a social system is freighted with innumerable significances, which we clumsily categorize under the rubrics of "economics" and "sociology" and "politics," etc. Here is the problem of abstraction that we encountered as the initial stumbling block in the approach to economics, come home with a vengeance at a much deeper level of significance. No one denies that abstraction is an essential precondition for a social science if it is to reduce the complexity of the real world to manageable proportions. But we can now see that the sharper and clearer the abstract model we create, the less "interdisciplinary" that model must be—*and insofar as the reality of the social process is unitary and indivisible, the less reliable as a guide to the social mechanism it must also be.*

Must economics resign itself to the "irrelevance" of an avowedly inadequate grasp of society? Or should economists abandon the scientific paradigm that has given such distinction to their efforts?

There are, so far as I can see, two ways out of the impasse. The first is to seek to widen the existing model of society by deliberately setting out to add as many social and political linkages as possible to the economic armature. The problem is how to go about this ambitious tak. We stand today before the ramifications of social action much as did Linnaeus before the disorganized array of living forms, and we seek, as he did, a principle for introducing order into seeming chaos. Because we do not have that organizing principle, there is little we can do at the moment except to search for one, and that will necessarily impose a considerable burden on economic thought. For the search requires that we bring into sharp focus the hitherto overlooked noneconomic aspects of the familiar economic variables. The economist, in building his models, will have to learn to think in units much richer—but correspondingly much less easily manageable—than heretofore. His one-dimensional "consumers" must now simultaneously assert their existence as voters, members of social groups, role-actors under various forms of stress, etc.; his "firms" must figure as *loci* of political activity and of industrial discipline as well as of production. The state, technological change, economic growth—in short, all the variables that are now disposed of as letters in the equations by which the processes of economic society are described—will have to "mean" something quite different from what they do now.

It is enough merely to suggest such an enlargement of the model to recognize its difficulties. For we are asking for an extension of the orderly patterns of the scientific paradigm to cover a much wider expanse of life than we have hitherto been able to encompass within the bounds of equations. Indeed, it may be that we are asking for an extension of the paradigm beyond the limits to which it can properly be applied. Undoubtedly there are *some* linkages in the social process that patient investigation will enable us to incorporate into a richer model of society, but it seems very probable that many others will remain elusive, or indeterminate (as we have seen economic behavior itself to be under certain circumstances), or simply too complex. In the end, the very ideal of a scientific model capable of representing social change may be beyond hope of attainment.

In that case where can economics go? There is one direction, I would suggest, that would enable it to retain the marvellous architecture of the scientific model, while shedding the restrictions that rob that model of so much relevance. *This would be the conversion of economics into an instrument of social science whose purpose and justification was not so much the elucidation of the way society actually behaves, as the formulation of the ways in which it should behave.* To put it differently, it would change the purpose of economics away from the discovery of the consequences of presumably known behavioral tendencies to the specification of the necessary behavioral patterns to enable society to reach a postulated goal.

This reorientation of economics, which has been called "instrumental" by its originator, Adolph Lowe,[5] would retain the "rigorous" aspect of the scientific method, but would subordinate its "value-free" aspect to an explicit recognition of the subservience of economic techniques to political and social ends. In the instrumental use of economics, the initial task—into which the economist would enter only as a member of the polity, quite without any special claims to expertise or superior wisdom—would be the articulation of desired social destinations or goals. These might be quantitative or qualitative, reformist or revolutionary, and they would be justifiable only by whatever standards of morality prevailed in society at that time. (To the horrified exclamations over such a meddling in human affairs, the instrumentalist answer is that the passive stance of economists today in fact constitutes an affirmative vote for whatever goals are inherent in the given socioeconomic mechanism at the moment.) The first task of an instrumental economics would thus be to raise the problem of social destination to its proper level as the most important decision that must be made by any society.

Once a social destination has been posited (if only as the premises of an economist's model), it then becomes possible to apply the "scientific" procedures of economic analysis, supplemented to whatever extent we can with sociological and political linkages. For the task of the econ-

5. Adolph Lowe, *On Economic Knowledge* (N.Y.: Harper & Row, 1970), as well as *Economic Means and Social Ends,* R. Heilbroner, ed. (N.Y.: Prentice Hall, 1969).

omist—who is now properly on the way to becoming a true social scientist—is to describe the various ways in which a social system that finds itself a point A may begin to move to point B. This description must include not only the necessary technical steps, such as the amassing or reallocation of capital or other resources, but also the sufficient behavioral steps, including the political and social as well as economic actions that will be compatible with the final target. And in turn these behavioral conditions will cause the social scientist to ask what institutional settings, what political directives, etc., may be needed as a still deeper-lying prerequisite for the desired social change.

It is enough merely to specify the width and depth of the necessary instrumental analysis to indicate that such a redirection of economics would be very nearly as challenging as the extension of the scientific model we previously discussed. The difference, however, is that a failure to specify all the various interactions of the social process does not vitiate the instrumental model, as it does the conventional "predictive" model. It simply means that various policies may have to be tried on a pragmatic basis to see how well they succeed in bringing about the desired result. Instrumentalism thus does not require a set of universal laws of behavior, but only a commitment to the conscious subordination of behavior to the requirements of deliberately selected social goals. It is, in Walter Lippmann's apt phrase of many years past, the choice of mastery over drift, with all the dangers and difficulties that any such assumption of control must bring.[6] The justification, if in fact one is needed, is that the social universe, unlike the natural universe, is not a mere collection of objects doomed to obey the laws of nature, but an assembly of human beings who include among their attributes the possibility of affecting the relationships that make up the system of which they are a part. Economics can thus find its ultimate relevance by becoming the instrument through which men can, within the limits of their knowledge and wisdom, use the procedures of science to gain those ends they hold in high value.

6. It may be, of course, that the social goals include freedom of behavior—i.e., the decision not to intervene into the decision-making process. In that case, it may be impossible to achieve other goals that would require the influencing of behavior. In such a case, instrumentalism serves the purpose of making clear what opportunity costs must be borne in opting for behavioral freedom.

4. Science and Ideology in Economics

ROBERT M. SOLOW

These notes are intended only incidentally as a commentary on Robert Heilbroner's article. I take up some of the same questions and give independent answers, sometimes similar to his, sometimes different. The questions confront any teaching economist these days who talks to his students and reads the handwriting on the wall.

Relevance to What?

Utility theory is a prize example of a certain kind of economic theory. It sets out to be an abstract theory of rational choice, free of deep psychology, free of social institutions, applicable equally under capitalism and socialism. Naturally, it turns Freudians purple and sociologists green. Heilbroner's student wants to know if the theory of diminishing marginal utility is relevant. In Perry Mason stories, the judge is supposed to rule on the relevance of some line of questioning *to* something very particular, namely the case being tried. What does the student have in mind? Is diminishing marginal utility relevant to "ghetto life or the behavior of corporations or the military-industrial complex"? I have a short answer to that question: Not very. If the student is interested only in ghetto life, the behavior of corporations and the military-industrial complex, then he can probably survive without knowing much about diminishing marginal utility (though it might actually help with the behavior of some corporations). I have never promised that every bit of economics he learns will be relevant to those three things.

If, on the other hand, Professor Heilbroner's student is interested in the proper scale of fares on public transportation and congestion charges on urban roads, in the hope of making cities more livable, or if he is interested in changing the income-tax schedule so that it will distribute incomes more equally without turning off valuable effort from talented people, or if he wants to think about the way riskiness affects a man's choices of securities for his portfolio (or a government's choices of flood-control projects), then he might do well to master the idea of diminishing marginal utility. I couldn't care less either way, though naturally, I ex-

Reprinted by permission of the author and publisher from *The Public Interest*, No. 21 (Fall 1970), pp. 94–107. Copyright © by National Affairs Inc., 1970.

pect every student of economics to learn about the foundations of the subject, even if bits of what he learns are irrelevant to his special interests.
Do medical students complain that they have to learn about livers when
they are specially interested in ear-nose-throat?

There is, however, a different point to be made here. Since the 1930's
and until recently (perhaps even now), much of the intellectual energy of
the profession has gone into macroeconomics, the analysis of the main
global totals that describe the functioning of the economy as a whole: the
national product, the unemployment rate, the price level, interest rates,
etc. That was certainly relevant to the understanding and elimination of
mass unemployment, which was probably the main domestic social problem of the 1930's. In fact, even unemployment of the magnitude of 7½
per cent of the labor force, as recently as the summer of 1958, was
nothing to sneeze at. I don't think economists need apologize for having
worked hard on macroeconomics into the 1960's. Even now, the combination of 5 per cent unemployment and rising prices poses a mean difficulty for policy. I, personally, think the current inflation has been in-
flated as a social problem, but if fear of it leads to policies which drive
unemployment up to 5 or 6 per cent (and 10 or 12 per cent in the ghetto),
then perhaps macroeconomics still has a bit of relevance.

Many students—and others—are not turned on by macroeconomics
because their feelings about social priorities have changed and are changing. The macroeconomic problems now seem (and no doubt are) less
urgent than the problems of war, poverty, racial discrimination, urban
decay, traffic congestion, and the power of the large corporation. That's
where the relevance is now. Economics tends to respond to shifts of
opinion like this, but not overnight. It takes time for middle-aged men to
change their research interests and their teaching, and it may take even
longer for them to drum up any interesting and useful things to say. The
theoretical analysis may be difficult, and statistical data are rarely available about something that has just now reared up in public consciousness.

After the war, for instance, the economic development of Asia, Africa,
and Latin America became an interesting and important problem, became
suddenly relevant, that is, for the obvious reasons. There were very few
answers to begin with. In time, there came into being a corps of talented
and specialized people whose main interest is the study of, and promotion
of, economic development. It is a difficult matter, in which economic
forces and other forces interact closely; the data are often scarce and
unreliable; analogies to what goes on in developed economies may break
down; powerful interests pull in different ways. Twenty years later, I'm
not sure there are many answers yet, but not for want of looking.

There is already a shift of activity underway in the direction of work on the sort of problems that now seem most urgent. On some of the easier ones, like traffic congestion, there is already a certain amount of knowledge. Others will take more time and more work. (And, by the way, the best allocation of scarce research resources among competing ends is a good exercise in the theory of diminishing marginal utility.)

Are Economists Conservative?

Professor Heilbroner thinks that economists stay away from certain subjects because they are dangerous. To study them is almost automatically to be critical of the System, or at least of the System's pretensions. Because economists are generally conservative, in the sense that they are not disposed to entertain any radical critique of the foundations of the System, naturally they shy away from exposing the seamy side of things. According to George Stigler, economists are generally conservative because the scientific study of economics makes them so. According to Professor Heilbroner, the more likely explanation is that economists tend to take care of the System because the System takes care of them, by paying professors' salaries well into the upper reaches of the income distribution.

I have my doubts about that last bit of reasoning. It seals off discussion. If I disagree on an issue, the implication is that I am a paid lackey of the System. If I protest that I, like Professor Heilbroner, am above that, I am doubly suspect. It is like what happens if I say that Freudian theory is obvious nonsense: I am told that I only say that because of my relation with my mother. I protest that my mother had nothing to do with it. "See!" says my Freudian friend and walks away a sure winner. (Even in the days when I was a close student of Marxism I used to wonder about a similar question: if social theory is part of the ideological superstructure, hence not to be taken at face value, why is not Marxism also part of the superstructure—and in that case why should we take at face value the Marxist notion that social theory is part of the ideological superstructure?) Moreover, I rather suspect that many more radicals are to be found among those, and among the children of those, with incomes near $21,000 than among those with incomes nearer the median. Still, Heilbroner does well to be suspicious.

But I really want to comment on Stigler's proposition, which Heilbroner accepts. I am interested in it because I have been exposed to the scientific study of economics and do not regard myself as politically conservative; and also because it seems to me that economics has quite a strong radical potential too, especially along equalitarian lines.

Are economists really conservative? As it happens, there is now some evidence on that. Recently the Carnegie Foundation collected questionnaire responses from a large sample of academic people. Respondents were asked, among other things, how they would characterize themselves politically among the possibilities of Left, Liberal, Middle of the Road, Moderately Conservative, and Strongly Conservative. Of the economists, 61.7 per cent classified themselves as Left or Liberal, as compared with 47 per cent of the whole sample. The economists were more conservative than the sociologists (80.5 per cent Left or Liberal), political scientists (71.8 per cent), psychologists (69.1), anthropologists (69.4), historians (68.7) and teachers of English (65.8). They were less conservative than mathematicians (47.3), chemists (44.8), physicists (54.4), biologists (44.9), foreign-language teachers (56.0), medical school people (40.6), teachers of education (44.7) and of engineering (28.9).

One might be led to the conclusion that the study of economics makes one more conservative than does the study of sociology or political science, but makes one more radical than does the study of biology or mathematics or chemistry. I suspect that's not a good conclusion either. My guess is that it will be found, for example, that there is a fair correlation of place in the political spectrum with age, and that economists are on the average a bit older than sociologists and perhaps political scientists. (I have no idea about the natural scientists.) There may be other such factors at work. And it may well be that the causal arrow runs from political disposition to choice of field as much as the other way. In any case, it seems to be untrue that economists are particularly conservative, or that the study of economics makes them so.

It may be the case that some radicals unimproved by the study of economics tend to accept certain soft-hearted shibboleths that will not stand up under cold analysis. It may equally be the case that certain conservatives laboring under the same handicap tend to accept certain hard-hearted shibboleths that fare no better: such as that the free market always leads to better results than would come from intervention, or that public enterprise is inherently wasteful, or that steeply progressive taxation is unjust and inefficient, or that the AFL-CIO runs the country.

But then why do economists shy away from those dangerous questions? I think there are different reasons for different questions. Most economists would regard the political and community behavior of corporations as outside their field of competence. Maybe they're too modest. A study of "the size and distribution of the benefits of the war economy by socioeconomic grouping" scares me more by its impossible difficulty than by its possible subversiveness. I doubt that the data are available to do such a study with the rigor and precision the profession now demands. And beyond that, who is to know what Congress would otherwise have done with the resources that it actually voted to the military? (By the way, for an example of what can be done, see "Fiscal Policy and the Poor: The Case of Vietnam," by Charles E. Metcalf, in the Winter 1970 issue of the Kennedy School journal *Public Policy*.) There actually have been attempts to analyze the "benefits accruing from 'public goods' by income strata"; it is indeed a fairly standard exercise, though the results are partly conjectural because simplified rule of thumb is all that is available for working out the incidence of some public expenditures. In the case of United States investment abroad, I don't feel competent to guess at the true state of affairs. I do not mean to suggest that economists are not as much afflicted with blandness as others, or that some may prefer, consciously or unconsciously, to avoid touchy subjects. I do wonder why those touchy questions one is accused of avoiding are so often vague and unanswerable questions.

Value-free Social Science?

It is sometimes said that academic economics and other social science are necessarily ideological, that their alleged "objectivity" is at best naive and more likely fraudulent. The claim to scientific objectivity is a swindle; it permits ideology to masquerade as science.

No doubt some research is slanted; the results are decided before the data are in, or the data are carefully selected to prove a point. One hopes that professional criticism will catch this sort of thing but, inevitably, some of it escapes exposure. Where powerful interests are at stake, some research will be consciously or unconsciously perverted, and the critical mechanism will be diverted or dulled. But that is not what we are talking about now. Something subtler and deeper is supposed to be the case. Social scientists, like everyone else, have class interests, ideological commitments, and values of all kinds. But all social science research, unlike research on the strength of materials or the structure of the hemoglobin molecule, lies very close to the content of those ideologies, interests, and values. Whether the social scientist wills it or knows it, perhaps even if he fights it, his choice of research problem, the questions he asks, the questions he doesn't ask, his analytical framework, the very words he uses, are all likely to be, in some measure, a reflection of his interests, ideologies and values.

It is important to keep these different kinds of biases distinct. Some are more important than others; and, without care, the existence of one kind may be mistakenly thought to imply something about another kind. It is undeniable, for example, that many of the economist's terms, however technically and naturally they are defined, have definite overtones of value. "Equilibrium" is an obvious case in point; "market imperfection" is another. These are, I must stress, technical terms: their definitions are not value-loaded. On the other hand, it may be, as they say, no accident that "equilibrium" sounds good and "market imperfections" are obviously far from perfect. This sort of bias is not really very important. It is also correctible, but rather little follows from that. Suppose "equilibrium" were replaced by a more neutral phrase like "state of rest" or, if that is too evocative, by the mathematical term "singular point." Does anyone think that bourgeois society would totter? Besides, if the concept itself is naturally value-loaded, then I fear that after a few decades people would come to regard a "singular point" as a big deal. But evidently much more than this is at stake.

Here is Gunnar Myrdal, for instance: ". . . no social science or particular branch of social research can ever be 'neutral' or simply 'factual,' indeed not 'objective' in the traditional meaning of these terms. Research is always and by logical necessity based on moral and political valuations, and the researcher should be obliged to account for them explicitly." [1] Myrdal does not mean only that no amount of "objective" collection and analysis of data, no amount of "scientific" theorizing could ever eventuate in a policy recommendation without some reference to a scale of values. That is true, but would hardly be news. It is the orthodox view of the theory of economic policy. But Myrdal speaks of "false claims of being able to ascertain relevant and significant facts . . . without explicit value premises." On the other hand, he is curiously inexplicit about the precise way in which open or concealed valuations manage to shape and color even the simplest factual and analytic research projects. It is a little hard to see how ideology sneaks into an attempt to discover how purchases of frozen orange juice respond to changes in price (even a socialist planning board might want to know that), or—to take something more specifically capitalist—how the plant and equipment spending of corporations is related to their sales and profits, interest rates, stock prices, taxes, and other things. Perhaps the idea is that the demand for orange juice would behave differently in a society with a radically different distribution of income, and certainly the investment study is tied to the institutions of private property. But neither does it seem in principle very ideological to study the working of a capitalist economy, if that is the kind of economy we have.

Sometimes Myrdal says things that seem to contradict his major line. He says at one point: "The relative importance of nature and nurture is a question of facts, and beliefs can be proved to be true or false by research." I don't see how this is consistent with the impossibility of objective social science. Indeed, a statement like the following is capable of

1. *Objectivity in Social Research* (NY: Pantheon, 1969), p. 74.

more than one interpretation. "When these valuations have been brought out into the open, anyone who finds a particular piece of research to have been founded on what he considers wrong valuations can challenge it on that ground. He is also invited to remake the study and remodel its findings by substituting another, different, set of value premises for the one utilized." The difficulty here is to know what it means to "remodel" the findings of research. If it means that the same research results will lead to different practical conclusions with different value premises, we are back to what everyone knows. If it means that somehow the research results will be different, then it is not clear how or why.

The whole discussion of value-free social science suffers from being conducted in qualitative instead of quantitative terms. Many people seem to have rushed from the claim that no social science can be perfectly value-free to the conclusion that therefore anything goes. It is as if we were to discover that it is impossible to render an operating-room perfectly sterile and conclude that therefore one might as well do surgery in a sewer. There is probably more ideology in social science than mandarins like to admit. Crass propaganda is easy to spot, but a subtle failure to imagine that institutions, and therefore behavior, could be other than they are may easily pass unnoticed. It may even be that perfectly value-free social science is impossible, though I regard that claim as unproven about the kind of work that has genuine claims to be science. But suppose it is so. The proper response, I should think, would be to seek ways to make social science as nearly value-free as it is possible to be (and, of course, to be honest about the residue). The natural device for squeezing as much unacknowledged ideology as possible out of the subject is open professional criticism. Obviously, then, one must protect and encourage radical critics. I think that outsiders underrate the powerful discipline in favor of intellectual honesty that comes from the fact that there is a big professional payoff to anyone who conclusively shoots down a mandarin's ideas.

Interdisciplinary Economics?

When you leave your car with an auto mechanic, it doesn't bother you that he will regard it just as an internal combustion engine on wheels. You don't feel it necessary to remind him that it is also a status symbol, an object of taxation, and a possible place to make love. Why, then, is it bound to be wrong for economists to regard the economic system just as a mechanism for allocating resources and distributing income, despite the fact that it also plays a role in the determination of status, power, and privilege? Why should economics be "interdisciplinary?" The answer is, presumably, because otherwise it will make mistakes; the neglect of all but the narrowly economic interactions will lead to false conclusions that could be avoided. The trouble is that the injunction to be interdisciplinary is usually delivered in general, not in particular; it is presented as self-evident, not as a conclusion from the failure of certain narrow undertakings and the success of certain broad ones.

I imagine that biochemistry and biophysics got started not because someone thought that biology should be interdisciplinary as a matter of principle, but because concrete research problems arose on the borderline of the biological and the chemical or physical. I will in a moment mention some problems that lie on the borderline between economics and the other social sciences. I think that the only way the interdisciplinary approach will ever make it will be for someone to make a killing on these or similar problems. But first there is a red herring to be cleared out of the way. The charge that economics limits itself by choice to the "quantifiable" is mistaken. There are plenty of qualitative distinctions that play a central role in economic analysis: employed-unemployed-out of the labor force, owner-renter, export commodity-import commodity, agriculture-industry. Sometimes, when people say that economics limits itself to the "quantifiable" they really mean to the precisely definable. When they want economics to be broader and more interdisciplinary, they seem to mean that they want it to give up its standards of rigor, precision, and reliance on systematic observation interpreted by theory, and to go over instead to some looser kind of discourse in which propositions are not supposed to be tested or testable, and it is never clear what kind of observation would definitely mark a hypothesis as false. One should resist any tendency for bad social science to drive out good. Mind you, economists talk a better game than they play. The fact that one can't experiment but only analyze history's single run of data means that an ingenious and determined man can keep a played-out theory alive for years. Nevertheless, it is a sound instinct to want to look at "the numbers," because they define, in a sense, what you're talking about. But any precisely defined measurement or observation would do as well.

There really are some problems outstanding that seem to call for an interdisciplinary approach. For example, five years ago the National Commission on Technology, Automation and Economic Progress tried to survey existing knowledge on job satisfaction and dissatisfaction under modern industrial conditions. There was pitifully little. With all the talk about alienation, dehumanization, and the loss of satisfaction from work, you would think that many researchers would be trying to find out the facts, by asking questions and by devising more direct measurements, by trying to figure out what aspects of particular routines are most destructive of satisfaction, and what loss of production would result from changing the routines. But apparently not so, unless the last five years have seen more such work than the period before.

Here is another example. Every discussion among economists of the relatively slow growth of the British economy compared with the Continental economies ends up in a blaze of amateur sociology. The difference is the bloody-mindedness of the English worker, the slowness of English management to adopt new products or new processes or new ideas, the elaborately amateur character of English business practice, the excessive variety of English goods corresponding to a finely stratified society, or the style of English education and the attitudes it imprints on graduates, or the difference is all of these in unspecified proportions. This may be a complicated way to admit ignorance. More likely it suggests that the identifiable purely economic factors do not account for the full difference between the growth of productivity in Britain and in, say, Germany or Sweden. It is a fair, if very complicated, problem in social science to measure the other social forces that operate on the level of output per man and the growth of output per man, and perhaps to estimate the extent to which each of them is responsible for the British lag.

Finally, more in the spirit of the game, let me mention a much more vague sort of problem. It will, I fear, be more attractive to some, primarily because it is less capable of an answer. Never mind, here it is. One has the impression that wages and prices in the United States are rising a bit faster than they "ought to." More precisely, statistical analysis of the past gives us certain relations connecting the rate of wage inflation, say, to other things in the economy; given the current state of those other things, the rate of wage and price inflation may now be a little higher than the historical relation would predict.

By itself that would be nothing remarkable. Econometric relations have been known to break down before. Sometimes they never recover; sometimes the data creep back into consistency with the old relation and one must then try to decide whether the interlude has something systematic to teach or was simply the result of what is grandly called a random shock. What is interesting is that much the same thing seems to be happening simultaneously in other countries as well. The British are threatened with a wage explosion though unemployment is unusually high. The same seems to be true in Germany, with quite a different labor-market tradition. I am told, casually to be sure, that the same thing is happening in Sweden and France and probably elsewhere; they are all "off the curve" in the same direction. Why? Is it to do with rising standards of living, or with the attitudes of younger workers, or is it just a random shock?

Heilbroner is rather pessimistic about the prospects of a broadened interdisciplinary economics. So am I. If there is any hope for it at all it will come from solving well-defined, maybe even "quantifiable" problems, not from methodological precept.

Obviously, economists do recommend policies. These recommendations must rest on some ethical judgments or values. What are they? Sometimes they are rather "low-order" or specific value judgments with which no one would quarrel unless he were especially quarrelsome: unemployment is a bad thing; or inflation is a bad thing; it is better that people should have adequate food and housing than that they should not. Sometimes there is room for argument, or at least there is argument: if I say that unemployment is a worse thing than inflation (quoting some numbers, of course), someone may disagree. But at a deeper level, the theory of economic policy is supposed to rest on a "weak"—that is, widely acceptable—fundamental value premise: a change in economic arrangements is a good thing if it makes everyone better off, or at least no one worse off (counting the possibility that there are initially gainers and losers, but the gainers compensate the losers, so that in the end everyone gains). There are obvious technical problems with this criterion: for example, does "everyone" include foreigners and unborn generations? But they need not concern us here.

To get anywhere, there must be room in economic theory for tougher value judgments that weight the welfare of one person or group against the welfare of another. But the basic principle that makes market mechanisms attractive to economists is the one I have just stated.

What does it mean for someone to be "better off"? Many criteria are possible: you could say that a man is better off if he makes a bigger contribution to the health of the State or the glory of God. In economic theory, however, it has usually meant that he is better off *in his own estimation*. If you want to know whether A prefers working over a hot stove or in a nice cool sewer, you ask him; or better still, you offer him a choice between the two jobs and see which he chooses. Similarly for bundles of consumer goods. This criterion is clearly a certified product of nineteenth-century liberal individualism, and in that sense economics is permeated with individualism.

This individualist orientation and the accompanying doctrine of "consumer sovereignty" are under attack these days, usually for the wrong reasons. It is said that ordinary people can not be entrusted with the judgment of their own welfare, not even with the choice of the things they buy. This is because they are ignorant of "true" satisfaction, or because they are manipulated by advertising, or because their tastes, such as they are, have been formed by a wicked society to preserve itself. We are all, or most of us, in the position of the Indian brave who has been hooked on cheap fire water by the greedy fur trader; in what sense is he better off because he willingly trades muskrat for rotgut?

No one can deny that advertisers advertise, and must have some effects (though one could argue about how much) on the preferences of consumers. It is certain that our preferences are far more social than biological or individual in origin. What should we conclude from these propositions? From the first, perhaps that advertising ought to be limited by taxation or regulated as to truth. From the second, what? Not, I hope, that individuals' judgments about their own welfare should not be respected, whatever their origin. One need only ask what could be put in their place—presumably the judgments of an elite. The attack on consumer sovereignty performs the same function as the doctrine of "repressive tolerance." If people do not want what I see so clearly they should want, it can only be that they don't know what they "really" want.

Now there are critical things that need be said about individualist welfare economics, but they are rather different things, well known inside the profession but not always understood outside it. For example, as I mentioned earlier, the individualist criterion is not complete. There are many questions on which it does not speak at all, and it *must* be supplemented by sharper value judgments that each society must make in its own characteristic way. For example, the strict individualist criterion does not imply that it would have been a good thing for the English government to have relieved starvation in Ireland during the potato famine. It was, however, a fallacy for the English to believe, as some of them did, that the criterion did imply that it would have been a bad thing. It is simply a separate decision. The individualist criterion does not say that the rich should be taxed to help the poor, nor that they shouldn't. It does say that if you decide to do so, it is in general better to give the poor money than to give them what you think they ought to consume. It takes a bit more than diminishing marginal utility to imply that you should in fact redistribute income toward the poor, but it sure helps, as Professor Heilbroner remarked.

This is not a trivial matter. I said that the choices must be made, and default is merely a way of making them. The radical critique is right that merely to mumble something about not interfering with the market is to favor the current holders of wealth and power.

Another problem arises not so much with the individualist welfare criterion itself as with its implementation through the market. The market mechanism works best when it deals with "private goods" which have to be divided up among individuals or families and consumed by them separately. When "consumption externalities" are important, when one person's consumption decisions have a strong effect on the satisfactions of others, or where different people consume the *same* "public good," like clean air or weather forecasts, the market need not work so well, and other, more directly political, decision methods may take its place. The trouble is that each producer and consumer compares the market price with benefits to himself; other benefits and costs are not taken into any-one's account. This is also a serious matter. As standards of living rise, population density increases, and technological interactions grow more pervasive, it may be that a greater and greater part of economic life will have to come under these rules of the game, which may turn out to be quite different from the rules of the private-property game.

But notice that neither of these problems I have sketched involves superseding the individual as the best judge of his own satisfactions.

Is Science Necessary?

The modern critics of economics and the other social sciences rarely seem to do any research themselves. One has the impression that they don't believe in it, that the real object of their dislike is the idea of science itself, especially, but perhaps not only, social science. A sympathetic description of their point of view might be: if the ethos of objective science has led us to where we are, things can hardly be worse if we give it up. A more impatient version might be: what good is research to some-one who already knows? The critics, whether from the New Left or else-where, do not criticize on the basis of some new discovery of their own, but on the basis that there is nothing worth discovering—or rather that anything that is discovered is likely to interfere with their own prescriptions for the good society. My own opinion is that the good society is going to need all the help it can get, in fact more than most. A society that wants to be humane, even at the cost of efficiency, should be looking for clever, unhurtful, practical knowledge.

Even Professor Heilbroner, who is a reasonable man, speaks of the "scientific" paradigm, in quotes, as if there is some other way to find out about the world. There is no other way. Economics can be better or worse science, but it has no other choice. Breadth is not the issue either. What Thomas S. Kuhn remarked about natural science holds for social science too: ". . . though the scientist's concern with nature may be global in its extent, the problems on which he works must be problems of detail." I do not fully understand Heilbroner's "instrumental" road to relevance, but so far as I do understand it, it seems likely to make more, not fewer, demands on "positive" economics. It is hard enough to understand the working of the institutions we have; to understand the working of hypothetical institutions may sound easier, but only because our mistakes would be less likely to be found out.

My argument about science is not a defense of what is sometimes called "scientism." The possibility of scientific economics (whether pure or merely as nearly pure as one can make it) does not entail the impossibility or the degradation of intellectual dissent and thoroughgoing criticism of the justice and quality of social and economic institutions. It seems reasonable, however, that whatever results can be established (after the most abrasive criticism) by economic science ought to set certain ground rules for philosophical and ideological discussion of economic institutions. The two kinds of activity ought to be distinguished, if not necessarily separated, simply because the reasons for believing one kind of statement are different from the reasons for believing the other. The main trouble with the attack on "scientism" of someone like J. P. Nettl[2] is that it fails to come to terms with genuine, limited, reasonably "objective" social science. The free-floating intellectual's social imagination is not completely free to float.

It makes no sense to squabble over which is the "higher" and which is the "lower" form of intellectual effort. But there is sense in a determined effort to see both that issues of value-conflict do not get smothered in smooth pseudo-science and that questions susceptible of a scientific answer not get submerged in a flood of ideology impervious to analysis and evidence.

5. Dissent in Economics: The Convergence of Extremes *

MANCUR OLSON and CHRISTOPHER K. CLAGUE

I.

Who are the discontented economists? In some ways and on some days almost all economists are discontented. Every economist who advances the field—and there have been a fair number of advances in recent

2. J. P. Nettl, "Ideas, Intellectuals, and Structures of Dissent," *On Intellectuals,* edited by Philip Rieff (N.Y.: Doubleday, 1969).

Reprinted from *Social Research,* 38 (Winter 1971), pp. 751–776, by permission of the publisher and authors.

* The authors thank the National Science Foundation and Resources for the Future for bearing some of the expenses involved in preparing this article.

years [1]—must have been dissatisfied with some aspect of the existing state of economic knowledge. Great as the prestige of economics is in comparison with the other social sciences, most economists would readily concede that there are many inadequate models, dubious assumptions, and areas of ignorance in the discipline. But it is not these ubiquitous and partial discontents that concern us here: It is rather those that involve impassioned objections to the direction in which the mainstream of economic thought is flowing.

This fundamental dissent appears to have been growing in recent years. Small but apparently increasing numbers of economists are demanding what some of them call a "paradigm change" in the sense of Kuhn—a change of conception that would do to orthodox economics what Copernicus did to Ptolemaic astronomy or Einstein did to Newtonian physics. In contrast to some of the long-standing dissenters, such as the "institutionalist" economists, the growing groups of dissenters are ardently opposed to the prevailing social system, public policy, and political leadership. They believe that much current thought in economics is merely a rationalization for the existing social organization or public policy, or even an apology for the sins of the establishment.

II.

The most conspicuous dissenters in economics today are the "radical economists." They are an outgrowth of the "new left," or more precisely proponents of the new left who happen to be economists. Some of those who are casually categorized with the new left are simply orthodox Marxists, and some of those who are called radical economists are in reality classical economists of the Marxian persuasion. But the sense of growth and novelty, at least in the United States and probably also in some parts of continental Europe,[2] comes from what is actually new in the new left and from what is truly radical in radical economics, and this new left or radical development is what interests us here. It is evident in the outbreak of appeals for a new paradigm in economics, in the spread of conferences with clear (if not self-conscious) new left or radical labels, and in the rapt attention given to the Union for Radical Political Econo-

1. An incomplete list: the concept of human capital; the incorporation of risk into models of economic behavior, particularly the management of financial assets; new theories incorporating the role of technology in comparative advantage and direct foreign investment; new theories of corporate behavior based on assumptions alternative to profit maximization; the application of economic concepts to political behavior.

2. In a leading British center for the study of economics, Cambridge University, where one of the authors of this paper (Olson) visited during part of the time when this paper was being written, some of the younger economists who claimed to be at the far left had a clean-shaven, conventional style and a fidelity to Marx reminiscent of the old left.

mists that was founded in September, 1968. Though very few established economists take radical economics seriously, many graduate students in economics (and some of the most talented) are fascinated by it.

The other main group of discontented economists is not so conspicuously discontented, partly because of differences of age and style. Indeed, the economists in this group—or rather collection of subgroups—should not by some standards be classified as dissenters at all, especially in view of the respectability and even eminence that some of them enjoy. Yet in a meaningful sense they are profoundly discontented about the direction in which modern society has been moving and with the economic thinking that has facilitated this movement. They are the economists who object so regularly to the passing of *laissez faire,* to "Keynesian" and post-Keynesian fiscal policies, to the threat to individual liberties they see in the welfare state, and to the economic analyses and prescriptions that have encouraged a generation or more of "creeping socialism."

The typical (or rather prototypical) economists of this sort are those who speak of themselves as the "Virginia School" and have been greatly influenced by the work of James Buchanan. Though Buchanan is himself one of the most respected men in the economics profession, he and most of his followers seem deeply disturbed by the direction of much economic thinking today. Buchanan and many of his disciples point out that, when most economists today find externalities, monopoly, or other problems that can lead markets to fail to operate in an optimal way, they typically advocate government intervention. This, Buchanan and those of his persuasion emphasize, involves a *non sequitur.* It does not follow from the fact that a market fails to bring optimality that government intervention will improve matters. This point has been stated most pungently by George Stigler, who though not in the Virginia School is related to it. Stigler has said that economists who, upon finding market failure, advocate government intervention without further inquiry, are like the Roman Emperor who is supposed to have judged a music contest with two contestants, and who, having heard only the first, gave the prize to the second.

This sensitivity to the shortcomings of government has helped lead James Buchanan, Roland McKean, Gordon Tullock, and other members of the Virginia School to develop deductive or economic models of political or governmental behavior, most of which imply that democratic governments with the usual constitutions or decision rules will tend to work very badly indeed. Buchanan and Tullock, in their influential book on *The Calculus of Consent,*[3] have emphasized the shortcomings of majority

3. Ann Arbor: University of Michigan Press, 1962.

rule and the advantages of constitutions requiring something close to unanimous consent [4] before governments can take action. Only the requirement of unanimity can insure that governments won't use a citizen's resources in a different way than the citizen would have wished, and any Pareto-superior policies (those that increase efficiency) should (as Kurt Wicksell pointed out long ago) be able to command essentially unanimous support anyway, since distribution of the gains must exist that would leave everyone better off (or some better off and none worse off). At the same time local governments are to have a greater share of whatever governmental activity remains. To say that this sort of work reflects and encourages skepticism about government does not, of course, deny its scientific worth. The contributions of the Virginia School can readily be integrated with, and have already contributed to, the work that other economists with a variety of different political perspectives have been doing on public or nonmarket decisions.

The Virginia School descends from Frank Knight and other forebears of the Chicago School, which has the same enthusiasm for *laissez faire* libertarianism, the same susceptibility to politicians like Goldwater, and the same dislike of Keynesian economics and the welfare state. Though it seems odd to treat so eminent an economist as discontented, an examination of Milton Friedman's views on practical policy, particularly as they are expressed in his book on *Capitalism and Freedom*, [5] shows that he is in a profound sense a dissenter. He treats all government actions, and particularly those of central governments, as above all an actual or potential threat to individual freedom. He would like to return the schools to private enterprise (with compulsory attendance and financial vouchers), cut out most public support for higher education, eliminate compulsory saving through social security, replace most social and welfare services by a (very modest) negative income tax, see labor unions lose most of their power, rely on a nondiscretionary monetary policy, and repeal all laws prohibiting racial discrimination by individuals. Anyone with these views is apt to be profoundly disturbed (even, perhaps alienated) by the direction in which the United States and most other societies are moving.

III.

If it is accepted that the growth and vitality of dissent in American economics has come from the radical economists on the one side and the

4. Even the most advantageous proposals cannot be expected to pass when complete unanimity is required for action. Any individual could insist that he would give his indispensable favorable vote only if he got most of the total gain from adoption of the proposal. Since this would be a rational strategy for others as well, unanimity could not be expected, at least not without altogether excessive bargaining costs.

5. University of Chicago Press, 1967.

Chicago-Virginia Schools on the other, the next question is: What are the discontents? There are a great many, but four are particularly significant: First there is the complaint to which we have already referred, that mainstream economics is often a rationalization for the prevailing public policies, political leadership, and the social system; second, the complaint that orthodox economics fails to take political or social factors into account; third, that economics today is preoccupied with technical elegance and detail to the neglect of policy relevance; fourth, that traditional economics neglects the forces that form and change preferences.

Some of these discontents, and the policy recommendations that are related to them, bring us to a point which some readers will probably find unconvincing, and which a few may find repugnant. This is the point that, far to the left as the radicals are, and far to the right as the Chicago-Virginia groups are, and harsh as their comments about one another can sometimes be, there is an underlying unity in the discontents, and to a degree even in the policy objectives, of these two sides. To use an unoriginal simile, the two sides resemble each other in much the way a negative resembles a print. But this unity is *not* the often noticed authoritarianism [6] that makes many Marxist-Communist type old leftists and many fascistic or dictatorial rightists so similar. It is a far different kind of unity—one which can tell us something constructive about one of the most profound problems confronting modern societies.

This unity is evident in some of the discontents mentioned above. With respect to the first discontent, we have already pointed out that both sides often regard mainstream economics as the servant of the "liberal establishment." The radical economists could hardly be more explicit about this.[7] The Chicago-Virginia group does not make the same complaint in such a striking way, but some of its members have said almost the same

6. The intolerance of opposing points of view that is sometimes observed in new left audiences, and the desire for drastic measures to deal with crime and student disorder of some old right economists, have understandably invited the speculation in some quarters that there are authoritarian tendencies in even some of the most liberal, if not anarchistic circles. Even if one were to assume (which we do not) that these allegations were true, that still would not be relevant here. We are concerned with the (admittedly sometimes inchoate) ideas and policy objectives that dissenting economists have put forth, rather than with anyone's psychology, and the ideas and policy objectives under consideration are the opposite of authoritarian.

7. Michael Zweig, "A New Left Critique of Economics," pp. 25–31 in: (David Mermelstein, ed.), *Economics: Mainstream Readings and Radical Critiques* (New York: Random House, 1970); Paul Sweezy, "Toward a Critique of Economics," *Monthly Review,* January 1970; (reprinted in URPE, Spring 1970) pp. 1–8, James Weaver, "Toward a Radical Political Economics," *The American Economist,* XIV (Spring 1970), pp. 57–61.

Back in 1959, in a much less discontented period, George Stigler approvingly noted the tendency of economics to conservatize its students and practitioners. See "The Politics of Political Economists," *Quarterly Journal of Economics,* LXXIII (November 1959), pp. 522–532.

thing. Buchanan, for example, has argued that many "mainstream economists conceive themselves to be members of an 'establishment elite' who
somehow have a divine right to advise whatever government may exist
toward doing the things that this elite knows is really 'good' for society at
large," and that the policies they prefer are pinkish if not worse.[8]

The second complaint is that mainstream economics neglects or is
naive about government and politics. Though several mainstream economists have worked on models of public choice, it is certainly true that
most mainstream economists have no explicit model of government and
politics. The typical economist, while naturally mindful of the desirability
of free markets when they are feasible and competitive, may also often
implicitly assume that public officials will normally be reasonable and
well intentioned. He often also has the faith that the government, despite
acknowledged faults, can recognize problems and devise and implement
solutions that will serve the public reasonably well. This faith underlies
the claim that his research has relevance for policy.

The radical economists regularly deplore the fact that most economists
abstract from (or deal implicitly and naively with) government and politics. They believe that an economic theory that abstracts from the relationship between the economy and political or social developments cannot be relevant to the great questions of our time. Like Marx, they
believe that governments reign in the interests of the ruling class. As they
see it, those policies that appear to favor the oppressed classes were in
fact passed to preserve the existing system. They are openly cynical about
those who have authority, not only in the United States but in other countries (including the Soviet Union) as well.

Interestingly enough, the effort to incorporate political and governmental behavior explicitly into economic theory is the principal distinguishing feature of the Virginia School. Buchanan's and Tullock's Center
for the Study of Public Choice at the Virginia Polytechnic Institute has
proclaimed, in the brochure that describes its program for potential graduate students, that the central shortcoming in most economics today is the
failure to incorporate government and politics into the framework of eco-

---

8. From a letter in which Buchanan kindly commented on a draft of this article, a
revelant passage is as follows:
". . . let me try to clarify my own position a bit. What I have said, and repeatedly, is
that most mainstream economists act *as if* they are advising the despot, or a despot.
That is to say, as Wicksell noted, they put themselves always in the idealized position
of advising a despot, whose own ideas, as it turns out, are their own. This is different
from saying that they serve the men who actually hold power, which is the radical
position. It is even more true, however, that the idealized despot whom the mainstream
people serve is 'pink' or even a deeper shade than any who might actually be in power.
. . . The difference between this and the radical way of putting this is to say that the
mainstream economists are hardly 'democrats' at all, whereas maybe, at base, both my
position and the radical position could be treated as this."

nomic theory. As we have already pointed out, the economists in the Virginia School have already succeeded in developing a number of relatively rigorous models of political and governmental behavior. In these models there is no trace of the tacit assumption of many mainstream economists that government will normally be guided by some conception of the public interest: The Virginia School consistently and explicitly assumes that voters and public officials alike are normally rational and self-interested.

Though the members of the Chicago branch have not usually developed abstract models of political behavior, some of them have emphasized the need for such models. And they almost surely share the assumption that political behavior is normally self-interested and the pessimistic predictions about how governments will work in practice. Certainly Milton Friedman has made many policy recommendations, such as his advocacy of a *non-discretionary* monetary policy (a predetermined annual increase in the money supply that cannot ordinarily be changed by monetary or political authorities) that is difficult to understand solely in terms of his monetary theory or his confidence in the robustness of the model of perfect competition.

The third complaint is that economics is preoccupied with technical intricacies that have little relevance to the urgent problems of our time.[9] Economists on the far left are fond of saying that elaborate mathematical models are being developed to answer questions that are utterly trivial. Some of the radical economists who make this complaint are themselves adept at technical economics and, strangely, even continue to practice it part of the time. Again, this complaint comes from the right wing as well. The aforementioned announcement from Buchanan's and Tullock's center at the Virginia Polytechnic Institute explicitly states (and even italicizes) the argument that the Virginia School's analysis is more "relevant" than other varieties of economics. Though his substantial theoretical contributions make it clear that Buchanan has a considerable aptitude for technical reasoning, he argues that too many economists are concerned with esoteric technical questions that are about as practical as the medieval disputes about how many angels could dance on the head of a pin, but that things are beginning to change—what he calls the "Samuelsonian" period will soon be coming to end. The same point seems to hold true, though perhaps less clearly, for the Chicago School. Technically gifted as Friedman and many other members of the Chicago School are, their work reveals much less fascination with technical detail than, say, that of Yale or MIT economists.

To be sure, much of the complaint about preoccupation with narrow

9. Sweezy, *op. cit.* (January 1970); Weaver, *op. cit.* (Spring 1970).

technical matters—perhaps most of it—does not come from the political extremes. The institutionalists, among others, have been reiterating this complaint for a long while. And a substantial and perhaps increasing proportion of the mainstream economists with considerable technical skill are also concerned about an excessive interest in technical intricacy.[10]

Yet there probably is a genuine causal connection between the degree and intensity of political commitments of economists and their success in treating the technical tools of economics as a means rather than an end. The economists with political passions as intense as those at the poles of the political spectrum want to tell us something about the real world as they see it, and accordingly tend to use elaborate technical arguments only when they are needed to make the point. An unusual political perspective, moreover, can help an economist to look at an old problem from a new angle. As the innovations of the Chicago and Virginia Schools remind us, many advances in economics have come from men with ardent, and often extreme, political views. If we claim in economics that necessity is the mother of invention, we should also own up to the fact that ideological passion is often the father.

The fourth complaint—against the neoclassical assumption that peoples' tastes are fixed, or at least determined exogenously (outside the system neoclassicists study)—shows that the argument offered in this paper can easily be pushed too far. The assumption that tastes can be taken as given lies at the core of the mainstream economics, for its abandonment calls into question not only the efficiency of the competitive market, but also many of the tools economists use to study efficiency. Radical economists often attack this assumption, not only because they are aware that this is the Achilles heel of neoclassical economics, but probably also because they are particularly interested in the factors that influence individual preferences or "consciousness." Many radicals dislike the preferences that most people in the modern world now have; they feel that capitalist society makes people competitive, selfish, materialistic, submissive, and insufficiently spontaneous.[11] In the United States today (and most of them would say, probably in the Soviet Union as well) most work is boring and dehumanizing, but instead of changing the nature of work, which is perfectly possible, society trains children, particularly through the schools, to submit to an alienating environment. Some radicals believe that appropriate changes in socialization could bring about substantial

10. Wassily Leontief's presidential address at the 1970 meetings of the American Economic Association, published in the *American Economic Review* (March 1971).

11. Although they criticize capitalism for inducing these traits, the radicals are not enamored of the Soviet Union and would probably say that Soviet society suffers from these same defects.

changes in human nature, and perhaps even create a "new man," who would not have to be offered material incentives.

At the same time, we should not forget that radical economists and others in the counterculture implicitly or explicitly assume that individual wants, even given the indoctrination by the present system, have some stability and legitimacy, as when they emphasize that everyone should be allowed to do "his own thing" and encourage individual spontaneity. We must also remember that radical economists have not been altogether alone, even when they have been questioning the assumption that tastes are exogenously determined: This has been a primal point in J. K. Galbraith's recent writings, and it has also been a source of uneasiness for many mainstream economists.[12]

On the other side, the Chicago-Virginia Schools have been particularly defiant in saying individual tastes are beyond their purview. In their view, neither the economist nor anyone else should presume to judge the propriety of other individuals' tastes. Nor are they very interested in why tastes are what they are. They have moreover been particularly skeptical about the possibility of changing human nature and vigorously opposed to any government efforts to try.

IV.

The similarity of new left and classical liberal economists shows up not only in complaints but in policy preferences as well. Fundamentally, both the new left and classical liberal economists want societies in which the individual has what the new left calls his right to do "his own thing," and what economists of the right call "individual liberty." the "liberation" that both sides believe in is not mainly the right to vote, form organizations, or speak against the government, which rights already exist in the countries where most of the dissenting literature is written, but rather the almost unlimited right for each *individual* to *do* what he pleases, whatever the majority through democratically elected government or private social pressure might have ordained. It is the rights of the minority, even the minority of one, against the majority, that they cherish. The concern about what the classical liberals call "economic freedom" and "individual liberty" goes back, of course, to the nineteenth-century liberals and utilitarians, among whom John Stuart Mill is perhaps prototypical; it is what has always distinguished them from Burkean or Hegelian conservatives. The concern about what the new left calls

---

12. Mainstream economists tend to regard the assumption that tastes are exogenous either as a workable approximation of reality, or else hold to it because they don't see any superior alternative. If this assumption is abandoned, the discipline's standards of precision and verifiability would be drastically lowered.

unresponsive bureaucracy and the right to choose a new life style is what mainly distinguishes it from the old left with its familiar fondness for nationalization, central planning, and the Soviet example.

No doubt, at least partly because they have been working on it far longer, the classical liberals have come much closer to working out a positive policy. But there are the germs of positive proposals on the new left side as well, and beneath the vastly different rhetoric one can see that they have much in common with those of the classical liberals on the right. This should not be surprising, given the uneasiness about the majority and the establishment on both sides.

The old right advocacy of *laissez faire* (or something close to it) obviously rests to a considerable degree on the argument that it protects the rights of individuals, especially those in minorities. If decisions about the mix of outputs to be produced and the allocation of resources are made by a centralized government, however democratic it might be, all of those individuals who preferred a different output mix and distribution of resources have to put up with whatever was chosen by majority rule. If there is the usual dispersion of preferences, most of the people in the society would not have preferred precisely what was chosen, and those with extreme preferences have to put up with something far different from what they wanted. In a market free of externalities or public goods, by contrast, each individual can use his resources in whatever way he prefers and consume any mix of goods he can afford. Thus the free market provides a range of freedom of action that will be especially important to those with unusual preferences, which a society without markets [13] could not provide, however complete its adherence to the usual democratic procedures. It is mainly for this reason that classical liberal economists oppose compulsory social security contributions and national health schemes, which must take away the individual's freedom to decide how much to spend on retirement or medical care.

The Chicago School has not been logically quite complete or theoretically altogether explicit in its advocacy of the classical liberal philosophy, for it has not offered a theoretical justification for the decentralized and constitutionally confined type of government it prefers. But the Virginia School has been admirably complete and explicit here. It has conceded to mainstream economists that, where public goods (roughly, goods such that nonpurchasers cannot, as in the case of pollution abatement and defense, be kept from consuming them) involving large numbers of people are concerned, government provision is necessary. But it has also

---

13. It would not necessarily require private enterprise, in the sense of privately owned firms, to allow this freedom of action; publicly owned or worker controlled firms that competed in free markets, could, at least in principle, provide the same result.

gone on, as we know, to argue that the needed collective goods could be provided efficiently, and with an enormously reduced risk of violating individual freedom to spend, by constitutional rules requiring something close to unanimity for action. It has also argued theoretically that with a decentralized or localized governmental system the infringements on individual liberty will be much less than with centralized government. This is not only because each individual can in principle have a larger say in a small government than a large one, but also because (as the late Charles Tiebout best explained) individuals can often migrate to the jurisdictions that come closest to providing the mix of expenditure and level of taxes that they prefer. The Virginia School has gone on to offer detailed models that illuminate these and other aspects of the classical liberal philosophy of government.

The new left directs most of its enmity at the "power structure" or "establishment" rather than at markets (except insofar as markets are thought to lead to a concentration of wealth and hence of political power). The main policy proposals that have come from the new left concern "decentralization" and "democratic participation," and these proposals could hardly be directed against the market. This suggests not only a gradual abandonment of the old left antipathy to markets, but also a skepticism about bureaucracy, government, and majority rule quite like that of the Chicago and Virginia Schools.

There is a striking illustration of the common denominator in new left and classical liberal policy preferences in Angus Black's *Radical's Guide to Political Economy*.[14] This remarkable book has the new left rhetoric and complaints about the whiskey drinking critics of the drug culture that might be expected in a *Radical's Guide*. The welfare system, it says, is run by "highly paid busybodies who make sure the money is being spent in a manner that will please middle class holier-than-thous"; it is worried about "government Fascists imposing their uptight, puritanical values on the rest of society." But the policy recommendations are exactly (yes, exactly) those that Friedman has made familiar in his more (indeed, far more) sedate style. They are Friedmanite even down to the anti-Keynesian monetarism ("the government causes inflation by making available too many pieces of paper with slaveowning national heroes on them"). The key to the book may well be Black's attitude to the government:

. . . great exploitation and monopoly power exist in this so called "great land of ours." What may not be so obvious, though, is that our representative government has been and continues to be a partner to all of this. . . .

14. Angus Black, *A Radical's Guide to Political Economy* (New York: Holt, Rinehart and Winston, 1970), pp. 2, 85, 86.

We have a representative government. It represents the rich oil man, the rich cattle raiser, the rich wheat grower, the rich steel producer, the rich doctor, the rich dentist, and the rich lawyer. If you ever got anything good out of your government you can be sure that some rich sonofabitch got even more by letting you get yours. . . .

My plea is clear . . . less government today, even less tomorrow.[15]

Black's book by itself by no means proves our point. One swallow doesn't make a summer. His pro-market views are not typical of radical economists. His claim to be radical would be denied by many. His book, taken all by itself, might signify nothing more than that writings of the Chicago persuasion are often assigned in courses, and that they make sense to a student with a radical style and value judgments. There is also a need for evidence that some such ideas have attracted widespread attention on the left, and that they are not simply a result of persuasion by the Chicago or Virginia Schools.

Fortunately, there is a good deal of evidence of just that sort. Consider, for example, the following passages from Charles Reich's *The Greening of America,* which is probably the best selling new left book ever written, and which was written by a lawyer who obviously has not borrowed his ideas from the Chicago or Virginia Schools:

Poverty, distorted priorities, and law making by private power . . . are not the accidents of a free economy, they are intentionally and rigidly built into the laws of our society by those with powerful influence. . . .

What the New Deal did was to create . . . to carry out its reforms, a new public state, matching in size and power the private corporate state. . . . The dominating concept was that all private activity, individual or corporate, was subject to restriction, licensing, or regulation "in the public interest."

What the theory neglected was the possibility that the two kinds of power might join. And this is what did happen . . . to form the inhuman structure in which we now live—The American Corporate State.

It is not the misuse of power that is an evil; the very *existence* of power is an evil. . . .

The foundation of Consciousness III is liberation . . . Consciousness III starts with self. In contrast to Consciousness II, which accepts society, the public interests, and institutions as the primary reality, III declares that the individual self is the only true reality. . . .

Activist political radicals . . . fail to recognize that bureaucratic socialism or communism presents many of the same evils as America, and that in America capitalism is now only a subordinate aspect of the larger evil of the uncontrolled technological state.

Marcuse . . . recognized that excess repression was the central fact of our so-

15. These quotations are from different parts of the book, but are perfectly representative.

ciety, and that it led inevitably to the state which must seek to dominate both those who live within it and those beyond its borders. . . .

The plan, the program, the grand strategy is this: resist the state, when you must; avoid it, when you can.[16]

Nor is the new left anti-authority, the-less-government-the-better attitude peculiar to the United States. Though it is relatively rare in some other countries, such as Great Britain, it has certainly been evident on occasion in parts of the Continent. There is something of this attitude in the writings of Rudi Dutschke, the former leader of student protests in West Germany, on "Anti-authoritarianism." [17] And in France, the student revolt that culminated in the nearly successful revolution of May, 1968, certainly did have a new left, anti-authoritarian quality (the Communist Party, of course, opposed the revolutionary effort for a good while). Daniel Cohn-Bendit, a most important figure in that uprising, opposed bureaucracy and authority even to the point of refusing to create a hierarchy of leadership for his own protest movement.[18]

Though the main source of new left skepticism about government and organized authority is the feeling that hierarchies push people around, there is also the belief of radical economists and other new leftists that bureaucracies are inefficient. Charles Reich has been quite explicit about how ineffective many New Deal and other government reforms proved to be, and on how it is inherently very difficult to design and implement effective government policies to deal with social ills.[19] In emphasizing the ineptness of government and bureaucracy the radical economists again

16. Charles Reich, *The Greening of America* (New York: Random House, 1970). The quoted passages are drawn from many different sections of the book; there is no one place where all of Reich's arguments of the sort cited are drawn together. Some passages in the book that run counter to those cited in the text could also be found, but the strand of thought evident in the quotation is nonetheless a fundamental part of the book.

17. See his essay reproduced in Carl Ogelsby's *New Left Reader* (New York: Grove Press, 1969).

18. See his essay written with Gabriel Cohn-Bendit, also reproduced in Ogelsby's *New Left Reader*. See also Herbert Marcuse, "An Essay on Liberation," and Mermelstein's introductory remarks on "Visions of a Good Society," in Mermelstein, *Mainstream Economics and Radical Critiques*. For an interesting study of Marcuse's thought on this as well as other questions, see Alasdair MacIntyre, *Marcuse* (London: Fontana/Collins, 1970).

19. Witness the following passages from his book: "The first thing we might observe is the phenomenon of tremendous lag in American governmental actions. The reforms of the New Deal were mostly responses to ills that had been diagnosed many decades earlier. . . .

"It is now clear how incredibly difficult it was and is to attempt to apply rational control and social self-protection to the chaotic forces of industrialism. There is the difficulty of diagnosis, the difficulty of getting prompt action once the diagnosis is made, and still greater difficulty of following through, the impossibility of conducting experiments, and the danger that solutions may give rise to problems of their own, perhaps even greater than the

obviously have much in common with the classical liberals; there is, for example, a good deal of similarity between the radical economist David Gordon's analysis in his book on *Problems of Political Economy* [20] and the relatively conservative views in Edward Banfield's well-known book on *The Unheavenly City*. [21] Each argues that the government's manpower training programs, criminal rehabilitation efforts, and social welfare services have accomplished little for the poor and cannot be expected to accomplish much, at least given present institutions.

The radicals' conviction that governments and other hierarchies are the source of the oppression, yet at the same time often unable to solve real problems, may provide a hint about how to interpret (or develop) new left proposals for "decentralization" and "democratic participation." These policy objectives, like most of those from the new left, are (to put it kindly) not yet very specific. It won't be possible to say for sure just what the radicals are after until they set out their objectives more clearly. But it is entirely possible that the radical demands for decentralization and democratic participation can usefully be interpreted as embryonic left-wing versions of the political economy of the Virginia School. In any event, something resembling the Virginia School's conception of an ideal policy is implicit in the values and assumptions of some of the radicals. On this interpretation, the new left plea for decentralization is the belief that each neighborhood or minority should have some of the authority that now is exercised by higher levels of government. Similarly, the demand for democratic participation, when applied as it is to societies that already have democratically elected governments, can be interpreted as an argument that each minority should have the right to veto at least some legislative and administrative actions, even when these actions have been decided upon by constituted bodies or authorities in democracies operating by majority rule.

Even if, as may well be the case, this interpretation of the new left approach to decentralization and democratic participation goes too far, it is nonetheless indisputable that the radical economists are far more cautious about government, hierarchy, and centralized planning than any other group of dissenting economists, except the classical liberals.

---

problems which called them forth. This New Deal was our first great attempt at social control, and . . . in large measure it failed.

"America's political system, supposedly the sector of the state most subject to popular influence, is perhaps the most rigid and least democratic of all. It is far easier to get a change in religious ceremonies than a change in government policy."

20. Lexington, Mass.: D.C. Health, 1971.

21. Banfield is a political scientist, but he is familiar with the work of the Chicago and Virginia Schools, and his book would surely gain assent from most of the members of these two schools.

Though the American Institutionalists and the German Historical School of economics share the radical economists' opposition to both the technical tools and substantive conclusions of mainstream economics, they have been inclined toward increases in planning, institutionalization, and government intervention.[22] The German Historical School was once even fairly favorable to mercantilism.[23] J. K. Galbraith and his followers are another source of criticism of mainstream economics, but Galbraith emphasizes the shortcomings of most existing markets and the inevitability of planning. And the old left, it goes without saying, has always wanted more centralization, nationalization, and planning. Thus, however much the radical uneasiness about centralized or hierarchical arrangements may be qualified, it remains in striking contrast to all of the other dissenting schools in economics, except for those of the libertarian right.

There is an historical precedent for the curious unity of the new left and old right economists. Marx was developing his ideas at about the same time that *laissez faire* liberalism was coming into ascendancy. This was also the period when anarchism was developing. It is surely significant that all three of the great ideologies of the mid-nineteenth century had within them a profound distrust of government. As is well known, Marx believed that the government was always the instrument of the dominant class, so that in capitalist societies it was controlled by the hated bourgeoisie; he opposed all of the governments that existed in his day. And as for his ultimate ideal, it was a stateless as well as a classless society. Obviously the *laissez faire* ideology wanted as close to a stateless society as was feasible. Anarchism fits the generalization as well as any ideology conceivably could. The suspicion of government in all three of these diverse ideologies suggests that, while the new-left/classical-liberal approach is not in keeping with the intellectual trends since the depression of the 1930s, it nonetheless has deep historical roots.

22. See our colleague Allen Gruchy's 1968 presidential address to the Association for Evolutionary Economics published in the *Journal of Economic Issues,* III (March 1969), 3–17.

23. And this was partly because it was regarded as a good method for building the national state. The German Historical School developed the interesting argument that mercantilism was at least partly justified when applied in Western Europe from approximately the fifteenth to the eighteenth centuries, because the national protectionist policies combined with opposition to feudal restrictions on trade, and the promotion of monopolies and regulation by the central government, tended to weaken the parochial authorities that had been dominant in feudal times and strengthen the national state. It may be that this approach had a special appeal in Germany in the nineteenth century because of the fact that a national government was attained there only in the latter part of the century. This would hint that classical liberal and new left ideologies can be expected to prosper only in countries and periods that have for some time had a strong central government.

V.

Can the gripes and ideas of the dissenting economists have any value to those who are not on the political extremes? We believe that they can, not only because there is no necessary connection between the political affiliation of those who express a view and its truthfulness or usefulness, but also because the new left and old right economists have been concerned about problems that are probably becoming more important as time goes on.

The problems that governments need to deal with are primarily those involving collective goods and externalities. Public or collective goods and externalities can for the present be defined as goods (or bads) that will not have a price in a market under conditions of *laissez faire,* because there is no way, at least when the number of firms or individuals is very large, for the market to charge the recipients of the goods or the generators of the bads the (positive or negative) price they would need to be charged to obtain economic efficiency. In the case of pollution, which we mentioned earlier, the market does not charge individuals a price for the pollution they create, nor would it reward a businessman if he were to take it upon himself to provide the good of a cleaner environment. Thus there is a need for coercion and therefore government to compel the generators of the bads to limit the damage they do and to obtain the resources needed to produce the desired goods that the market does not produce.

Though there are some exceptions (like the decline of contagious disease), in general it is probably true that externalities and collective goods may be becoming relatively more important over time in developed societies. As population increases and economic growth proceeds, and as more of the population and activity take place in metropolitan areas, the problems of pollution and congestion may very well increase, at least in the absence of any government action. It may also be the case that education and research are becoming relatively more important over time, and these activities are probably more externality-intensive than average. To the extent that externalities and collective goods are in fact becoming more important, the emasculation of government that many dissenters want becomes more dubious. At the same time, the apparent growth of externalities and the indisputable increase in the share of resources used by governments also means that an increasing proportion of the decisions that affect people's lives are made by governments rather than individuals, and that the public sector problems which the dissenters are concerned about are becoming ever more important.

It is all too easy to assume, as many mainstream economists and others do, that the political process will work out more or less reasonable legislation to deal with these problems, and that the politicians and government officials will work effectively to further some generally acceptable conception of the public interest, rather than for narrower interests. To say the very least, this is only an optimistic assumption: There is no rigorous body of theory that would predict that rational individual behavior in a typical democratic system will lead to an efficient, or even a workable, outcome. And the historical experience is by no means always encouraging. It would seem that the new left conviction that those who already have the private and public power will run things in their own interest, and the Virginia School models of political behavior, deserve a wider examination.

Consider also the private, in the sense of nongovernmental, hierarchies. They too have become bigger and more pervasive. Though there are good studies that suggest that industrial concentration by industry has not been increasing over the course of the century, the absolute size of firms has enormously increased with the growth of markets and of multiproduct and multinational firms. Though the typical steel mill has been owned by a large corporation for a very long while, it is only recently that the local hamburger stand has become part of a huge and at least partly hierarchical enterprise. The growth in the size of universities has already been pointed out, but not that of many other nonprofit organizations, from the hospital in which a child is born to the church which buries him. Though in some contexts economies of scale have been exaggerated, there does seem to have been a striking growth in the size of enterprises and institutions in modern times which must be due mainly to such economies. They could for all we know become even more significant in the future.

The gains from exploiting these economies of scale are important and obvious enough, but there are, as the new left is quick to remind us, problems too. The large hierarchies seem to be deficient both in responsiveness to the individual and in their capacity to generate a sense of community. The individual, whether as employee, customer, client, student, or whatever, often feels in a weak position vis-à-vis the huge bureaucracy, particularly if he is not adept at understanding the ways of bureaucracy. Even if a substantial number of relevant individuals want a change, it may be difficult for the large organization to react quickly. The residents of a ghetto can sometimes elect a black mayor, but the policeman on the beat will change only very slowly, if at all. The impersonality and scale of the modern bureaucracy can also work against the development of a sense of community which is evidently widely desired. In the absence of a sense of common purpose and mutual loyalties, the power of those at the top of a bureaucracy can be bitterly resented, whether it is exercised reasonably or not—that at any event is what *seems* to be happening with increasing frequency these days. Given the ubiquity of large hierarchies and the apparently increasing resentment of their power structures, there is surely a case for more careful research into the substantial area of nonmarket economics and social and political interaction within the large bureaucracy.

There is surely also something to be said for the radical economists' complaint about the assumption that tastes are exogenous. Clearly the corporations and other large organizations of the private sector spend a good deal on advertising and community relations. Clearly governments spend a lot on schools and the comments of their leaders are a principal subject of the media of public communication. A lot of this expenditure of resources is designed to change individual tastes or values, and it would be surprising if it were all without effect.

To be sure, the complaint is sometimes exaggerated; it is certainly not true that consumers buy whatever corporate hierarchies dictate that they buy. There are hundreds if not thousands of companies that can advertise even at a national level; there may be only four companies from which an American can buy a domestically produced car, but there are thousands that have assorted products which he can spend his money on. Each of these companies is in competition with *all* of the others for the consumer's dollar. With this degree of competition among products, each firm has an incentive to adjust to any preexisting predilections, practical requirements, or latent desires that the public has, even if it should be the only firm in its particular industry. Thus consumers must continue to have a striking *independent* influence on the goods the system produces, i.e., a large measure of consumer sovereignty.

Yet the need to take account of changes in tastes, or at least those that have their origins in the working of the system economists analyze, remains. It is said that 7,000 new products were offered in American supermarkets in a single year.[24] In view of the fact that some resources were required to shift from the old to the new, some of these new products may very well have reduced rather than increased human welfare. Some of those who bought some new products may have thought they were getting something better, when in fact they were not, and given continued advertising might even have persisted in the error. The advertising may also have created needless anxieties about personal odors, social adjustments, and the like. Quite apart from gratuitous new products, advertising can remind poorer consumers of what they are missing, and to the extent it does not inform, or even misleads consumers, it involves a waste

24. Alvin Toffler, *Future Shock* (New York: Bantam Books, 1970), p. 71.

of resources. It would be possible to create a government agency that had full power to control advertising and the introduction of new products. But before anyone proposes this, he should first consult the old right economists about how efficient the regulatory agency would be, and the new left economists about who would ultimately control it.

There is probably also a need to give serious attention to the dissenters' complaints about the preoccupation with technical intricacy at the expense of relevance in mainstream economics. There are some forces that may make the degree of technicality in economics often greater than is optimal. In economics and some other fields the market for the output of practitioners is mainly determined by other professionals in the same field. Whereas the carpenter's work is judged by the buyers of houses, the economist is judged by other economists. There are notable exceptions, as when economists work for governments or business firms. But in the main, the economist, and the practitioners of other disciplines whose output may also often be without immediate monetary value, must live by pleasing universities or foundations, and the decisions of these institutions are usually made by professionals in the same field as the person doing the research. This may be on balance the best way to handle things, but it has the important consequence that work is judged in terms of the interest it has for other practitioners of the same craft, rather than in terms of the extent to which it serves some practical purpose. Since craftsmen usually take pride in the tools of their trade, those who judge work in their own field will normally give special weight to the extent to which the tools of the trade have been skilfully used. We can well imagine that, if a carpenter's school were to support all carpenters, more fancy cabinets and fewer livable houses would be constructed. Similarly, economists and many other academic professionals may give relatively more weight to technical proficiency, and less to substantive insight, than those who ultimately gain from an advance of economic understanding would want them to do. This tendency is perhaps reinforced by the fact that intricate technical work may provide a quicker and easier measure of an economist's industry and intelligence than the analysis of a problem to which existing techniques cannot fruitfully be applied. Though the complexity and logical correctness of technical work is relatively easy for skilled professionals to assess, and such work can be richly rewarded even when its substantive value is questionable, efforts to understand and discuss problems that are not now ordinarily amenable to a highly technical treatment, and which partly for that reason have not always been studied by economists, are not so readily assessed nor so regularly rewarded, however urgent the need for attention to these problems may be. Since many of society's most serious problems do not lend themselves to displays of technical virtuosity at the present stage, it is not surprising that they do not attract the attention of economists interested in maximizing their professional reputations and rewards.

These areas of neglect and difficulties in mainstream economics might seem to justify the demands of some radical economists for a new paradigm. In fact, Kuhn's concept of paradigm change is not altogether adequate as a description of intellectual advance in economics, and it certainly does not explain the emergence of radical economics. Kuhn argued that it is the accumulation of anomalies—observations that the received theory does not correctly explain—that leads to a revolutionary change in the theory. But in economics, and presumably in social science generally, much of the impetus for new developments comes from changes in the society and what it wants. The economists' postwar interest in economic development and the current interest in problems of race and poverty clearly had little if anything to do with any anomalies. As for the radical economists themselves, they do not base their case on the argument that mainstream economics fails to answer the questions it sets for itself, but that these questions are either trivial or, at any rate, not the most important ones. There are to be sure anomalies in economics, but they troubled mainstream economists long before the radical economists made the scene.

Some of those who demand a paradigm change in economics also neglect the extent to which theoretical revolutions incorporate or subsume the orthodoxies that preceded them. Science, even at its most primitive, proceeds cumulatively. Newton even in his distant day could say that, if he had seen further than his predecessors, it was "because he stood on the shoulders of giants." So does the economist. The marginal utility revolution took place a century ago, but even then it did not throw out Ricardo's theories of rent and comparative advantage, or many of the insights of Adam Smith, but rather led to their incorporation into the main body of neoclassical theory. Nor did the Keynesian revolution suggest that the quantity of money never had any influence on the price level; it rather subsumed the quantity theory of money in a model which added, among other things, the demand for money as an asset.

We would accordingly conjecture that if there is a paradigm change in economics, as there could be at any time, it will add a great deal more than it throws away. Surely no complete or ideal theory could do without some of the concepts economists use today. Yet we must be uneasy about the many aspects of reality that interact with variables that the economist studies, but which he often leaves out of account. As the dissenting economists have reminded us, we economists (or someone else) must take better account of the government and the other hierarchies that increasingly influence our lives, and grapple with the forces that change tastes. Someone must, in short, take account of the politics in large organizations and the sociology behind changing values. Perhaps, if there is a paradigm change in economics, it will be in the form of a unified approach to social science.

6. Is Economics Obsolete? No, Underemployed

CHARLES L. SCHULTZE

The current disenchantment, particularly among the young, with the optimistic, problem-solving approach to social issues that characterized the 1960s not surprisingly has rubbed off on economics. As a number of other articles in this symposium demonstrate, many members of the economics profession now question the relevance and meaning of the fundamental assumptions underlying the economics that is currently taught and practiced. Some of the critics have been saying these things for several years but have only lately found someone to listen. A few are recent converts from orthodoxy. And among the younger members of the profession, these critical views are becoming fairly widespread.

There is merit in some of the criticism, but little in the general notion that economics has grown obsolete or irrelevant. The indictment against it should read not that economics is irrelevant but that its very relevant tools have been too sparingly applied to the kinds of problems now confronting us. In some instances, economics is a victim of its own highly relevant successes.

One of the major counts in the indictment is that Keynesian economics is incapable of handling the central policy issue of the era: how to make full employment compatible with reasonable price stability. Yet, in the twenty-five years since the Second World War, a period during which Keynesian fiscal policy emerged from advanced theory courses to become the conventional wisdom of Presidents, unemployment in no year averaged more than 7 per cent compared with the 1930s, during which unemployment never fell below 14 per cent. The major depressions and massive financial panics that sporadically afflicted industrial economies

Reprinted from the *Saturday Review*. Copyright 1972 by Saturday Review Co. First appeared in *Saturday Review* January 22, 1972. Used with permission.

for the century-and-a-half before 1940 are no longer even a dim threat. And aside from the brief aftermath of World War II, the inflations that quite rightly gave Americans cause for worry have not exceeded 5 or 6 per cent per year at their worst, a far cry from the persistent rates of 10 and 20 per cent per year with which some nations of the world have been living for decades.

Modern economics can and has successfully prescribed the means of preventing large-scale unemployment without bringing on major inflation. It can devise, and has devised, ways of preventing major inflation without precipitating serious depressions. Although the prescriptions of economists are not solely responsible for the sharply improved postwar performance of the Western economies, they surely played a major role. What we now label a failure of theory and policy has been a roaring success by pre-Keynesian standards.

The puzzle economics has not yet solved, and which critics quite properly point to, is the worrisome, but far from catastrophic, inflation that appears when overall demand and supply come into balance during periods of high, but not excessive, prosperity. Yet this failure may stem not so much from shortcomings of the basic theoretical apparatus as from the difficulty of making precise measurements. Economics has little difficulty in prescribing counterbalances to large swings in prices and employment. But in recent years we have been dealing with variations in the employment rate between 3.5 and 6 per cent and with differences of 2 to 3 per cent in the rate of inflation. And within these ranges the analysis of how wages and prices interact and the prescribing of policy require more precise and complex measurements than we have yet devised. Still, a good carpenter can make a perfectly satisfactory joint with instruments that would be useless for calibrating the tolerances in an Apollo guidance mechanism. Which is by no means to say that the carpenter should throw away his tools as being irrelevant to modern society.

A better understanding of the inflation that accompanies high (even though not excessively high) employment may not ultimately rest on some radical new breakthrough in economic theory. Rather it may well result from gradual improvement in our knowledge about labor markets, about the role of people's expectations during inflation, and about how the market power of unions and business is translated into specific wage and price decisions. Policy instruments to deal with the problem may correspondingly be found in improvements in manpower training programs and antitrust policy, and in the gradual development of wage-price standards sufficiently flexible to avoid smothering the economy in regulation, yet tough enough to influence a key decision when it counts.

Whatever the outcome, any successful prescription for jointly achieving full employment and price stability will undoubtedly contain a large dose of what I may loosely call Keynesian economics—extended, modified, and supplemented, but not abandoned.

Another major indictment against contemporary economics runs approximately like this: Because economics ignores the substantial economic power now concentrated in large firms and unions, and because on a larger scale it accepts the fundamental status quo of current power relationships in society and ignores the relationship between the distribution of power and the distribution of income, it either has no policy prescriptions for pressing social problems or offers ameliorative remedies that only scratch the surface.

To some extent, the charge that modern economics has produced little in the way of remedies for the current siege of social problems is valid, but paradoxically this is so for reasons precisely opposite to those advanced by economics' critics. Economics may be faulted, not because it possesses a theoretical apparatus of no relevance to current social problems, but because in many cases it has failed to apply, or only recently begun to apply, an apparatus that is particularly well suited to dealing with a large segment of those problems.

Much of economics deals with the problem of how a decentralized decision-making system can be made to provide proper incentives so that individual decision-makers, apparently pursuing their own ends, nevertheless tend to act in a way consistent with the public good—the "invisible hand" of Adam Smith. Since time immemorial it has been too often assumed that the apparatus of analysis which dealt with this problem applied only to the private market and that the public sector of the economy must operate by a completely different set of rules. Yet, a little reflection will demonstrate that many of the major social problems with which government is now seized require solutions under which the decisions of thousands of communities and millions of individuals are somehow channeled toward nationally desired objectives.

Cleaning up environmental pollution, changing the delivery structure of an ineffective and inequitable medical-care system, providing compensatory educational programs, and offering training and labor market opportunities to the previously disadvantaged depend for their success or failure on day-to-day decisions made by particular communities, business firms, and individuals throughout the nation. No program that merely seeks to transfer these hundreds of thousands, indeed millions, of decisions to a few officials in Washington can hope to be effective. Nor, conversely, can any program that simply shovels federal revenues to state and local governments, and then hopes for the best. Somehow institutional frameworks and incentives that guide a multitude of particular decisions toward national ends have to be developed.

And here, traditional economics and its incentive-oriented apparatus suggest a number of approaches. The major problems of environmental pollution, for instance, stem from the fact that air and water are given free to all comers, and like any good that is given away these commodities will be overused; with no incentives to conserve them, neither individuals nor business firms will lend their talents toward developing and using new conservation technology. But old-fashioned economic analysis suggests that placing a stiff charge on the dumping of pollutants into the air or water will marvelously stimulate the discovery of production methods that reduce pollution, just as the rising cost of labor has promoted a steady growth in techniques to increase output per man-hour, at a rate that roughly doubles the efficiency of labor every twenty-five years. Economics also brings into question whether it makes any more sense to rely solely on detailed regulation and court decision for minimizing pollution than it would to use these devices for minimizing other industrial costs.

As for health care, conventional economics indicates that the nation can hardly hope to have an efficient use of scarce medical resources when the current health care system provides a powerful set of incentives to waste and misdirect those resources: insurance plans that cover hospitalization but not office visits, thereby encouraging excessive use of hospitals; private and governmental insurance that reimburses hospitals on a cost-plus basis, penalizing the efficient and rewarding the inefficient; financial rewards keyed to dramatic intervention (the cardiac surgeon) but quite niggardly for the practice of preventive medicine; etc.

In the area of public education, economic analysis points to the difficulty of getting superior performances from a monopoly with a captive market (the public school system of the inner city) and can help design means of introducing incentives for improvement and innovations. It also emphasizes the impossibility of designing and enforcing urban land-use plans in an economic environment where many aspects of the tax laws and land laws provide large positive incentives for urban sprawl. It provides insights into the problem of urban congestion by showing how most auto users are not now required to pay the real social costs that their ride imposes on other citizens and how this fact provides incentives for socially excessive use of crowded highways.

As these examples indicate, many of our social problems arise because the current system of markets, laws, and customs provides positive incentives for individuals, business firms, and local communities to engage in what can objectively be called antisocial conduct. Correspondingly, substantial improvement in these areas is most unlikely to come from governmental programs that rely principally on traditional, centralized decision-making, but must rest in part on a restructuring of incentives and institutions—a task for which economics, far from being obsolete, has been too little used.

In terms of social problems, economic analysis also has a relevant role to play as a bearer of unpleasant truths—that in some areas of social policy the nation is seeking to pursue conflicting goals. It is literally impossible, for example, to design a welfare program that simultaneously meets four often-sought goals: providing a generous minimum income to the poor; preserving incentives for productive work by avoiding a rapid reduction in welfare benefits as recipients begin to earn outside money; instituting welfare reform in a way that does not reduce the income of any beneficiaries under the current system; and preventing such large budgetary costs that those not far above the poverty line have to be taxed heavily to support those just below it. No program can do all of these things simultaneously.

In the same vein, a public service job program must seek a compromise between two conflicting objectives: to provide wages and working conditions sufficiently attractive to appeal to the unemployed and the low-paid casual worker and to avoid drawing workers away from productive jobs elsewhere. A national medical program cannot at one and the same time guarantee virtually all the medical care private citizens can demand regardless of income, provide a financial mechanism and a set of incentives that hold down escalation of costs and avoid comprehensive detailed regulation of medical care by Washington bureaucrats.

Pointing out relevant truths of this sort, however, appears to be one of the factors underlying the charges of irrelevancy leveled against economics. Such observations about conflicting objectives imply the need for compromise. But to those for whom compromise is inherently evil, and for whom most problems fundamentally trace back to the greed of the power structure, calling attention to the technical difficulties that would face even a liberated world seems to be irrelevant at best and obstructionist at worst.

A similar reaction, perhaps, will greet the assertion that there are many social issues in which economics should not be expected to play a central role. Economists can seek to ferret out the economic consequences of racial discrimination and help in devising means to expand opportunities for racial minorities. But the eradication of discrimination itself will necessarily depend heavily on a combination of legal steps, education, and political leadership. Economists can trace many of the causes of financial crisis now afflicting large central cities. But the job of rationalizing the archaic jumble of local government in metropolitan areas, thereby providing a viable economic base for large cities, is a task beyond what should be expected of economists. While many of our social ills have major economic consequences, there are some that will yield only to political solutions.

One area in which the economics profession has a decidedly mixed record is the field of income distribution. The problem is not so much a deficiency in economic theory as it relates to income distribution but rather a tendency on the part of the profession to exhibit an excessive concern for efficiency as compared with equity in dealing with situations where the two are in conflict.

An economic system can be very efficient in providing private and public goods to meet the demands generated by a very lopsided income distribution—fine mansions, good public protection, and rapid mass transit for affluent suburbanites while the poor live in hovels, are victimized by crime, and spend inordinate amounts of time getting to work. The formal structure of economics recognizes that its rules for an efficient allocation of resources are blind with respect to the distribution of income; that efficiency considerations alone cannot justify policies which have significant effects on that distribution; and, conversely, that policies which redistribute income in a direction society thinks more just may be warranted even when those policies reduce efficiency. Most economists working in the field of taxation have paid close attention to matters of distribution, and the large majority have raised their voices in favor of strengthening the redistributive features of the tax system. On the other hand, in many areas of public policy, economists as a body have had a bias toward letting efficiency considerations rule.

Higher efficiency, however, is often secured at the expense of particular groups of workers and individual communities. It is not so much that the remedies for these problems need be sought in protectionism, subsidies to dying industries, or rigid featherbedding work rules. Rather, an affluent society might well be expected to provide better income guarantees to workers than ours now does, particularly to older workers, whose skills have been rendered obsolete by economic change and growth. Economists have generally been much more active in pointing to the efficiency gains of unimpeded economic change than in devising means of minimizing its impact on particular workers and communities. In a similar vein, it is only recently that economists and statisticians have begun to look deeply into the often perverse income distribution consequences of many public programs—farm subsidies, low tuition at state universities, urban highway building, irrigation and flood control projects, and the like.

Paying more attention to the problems of income distribution, however, would not rescue conventional economics from attack. To the Western economist, income distribution problems can be approached through such pragmatic measures as reforming the tax system, restructuring welfare programs, and providing more equal educational opportunities. But to radical critics, these are Band-Aid measures. The basic cause of maldistribution of income, they say, is the maldistribution of power that inevitably accompanies a market-oriented free enterprise system. Any pragmatic measures will eventually be perverted by the holders of economic power to their own ends. Only the demise of the market system itself will make it possible to provide a just distribution of the fruits of man's productive activity.

Here indeed is a fundamental difference in approach. An evaluation of the merits of the case would go far beyond the scope of this article, and, in any event, logical argument seldom makes converts in this controversy. I cannot resist pointing out, however, that in any complex society, whatever its original structure, there is a tendency for power, influence, and wealth to become concentrated in relatively few hands, and this is particularly true whenever societies seek to provide incentives for abundant production. Eternal vigilance is the price of an egalitarian distribution of income. Even in the "post-revolutionary state," the old pragmatic measures of progressive taxation, transfer payments such as welfare benefits, and equal educational opportunities would still be important tools for securing a just distribution of income.

There remain two major areas in which even the most sympathetic view of modern economics would have to concede that charges against the state of the art do strike home. One involves the behavior of producers, the other, that of consumers.

The panoply of tools with which economics seeks to explain how resources are allocated in the private market relies quite heavily on the premise of profit-maximizing firms, each responding to but not controlling the market in which it operates and making decisions subject to reasonably good knowledge about the future consequences of those decisions. For purposes of analyzing the long-run effects of economic policy actions, this "model" of the world is quite serviceable. In the long run, firms do seek to maximize profits; they cannot control basic changes in their economic environment; and there is sufficient feedback from their decisions to provide reasonably accurate information. But in the short run, the behavior of firms with respect to modest changes in prices, wages, and investment policy is much less predictable. They can insulate their own markets against moderate threats; their search for long-run profits is roughly consistent with a number of alternative short-term strategies; and before the feedback from their decisions reaches them, they are faced with great uncertainty.

The inability of economic theory to predict the short-run behavior of firms might not be so important except for the problem of inflation. The long-run allocation of resources, and the shift in price relationships that brings it about, probably does proceed much in the manner explained by economic theory. But it may take place around a generally rising price trend. And unlike market shares, inflation is generally irreversible. A series of short-term decisions on the part of many firms and unions can lead to continuing inflation. The weakness of current economics in predicting the short-run behavior of modern firms and unions thus turns into a serious deficiency in terms of the ability of economists to explain today's inflation *cum* unemployment.

The second charge hits home in the sensitive area of consumer preference theory. Traditional economics takes consumer tastes and preferences as given. It neither looks behind them nor seeks to weigh their relative merits. This approach has two consequences. First, the economist has little to say about the social implications of advertising practices that create and destroy preferences, nor about the social waste represented by the resources devoted to the satisfaction of manipulated tastes. Nor does he have anything to contribute to the deeper problem of the way in which basic preferences themselves respond to economic development, except to note that "yes, this does indeed happen, and the sociologists better get to work."

Second, and perhaps more important, the economist, by taking individual preferences as given and absolute, sharply limits the field of his analysis when it comes to many matters of public policy. The tools of economics are designed to show how resources can best be deployed to meet society's wants. By its assumption that the relevant social wants are based on the existing preferences of individuals, and that those preferences cannot be questioned, economics has erected a barrier against the use of its analysis in some of the most important matters of public policy. The economist can give advice on the efficiency of the policy instruments chosen to meet an objective. But when it comes to choosing among different objectives, the economist qua economist must be silent. Personal tax cuts that increase society's consumption of beer and whitewall tires hold equal status with increased public expenditures for education. Choice between the two is a "value judgment," which he must eschew.

One promising line of research has been suggested as a means of breaking this impasse. Individual tastes and preferences are themselves hierarchical. Many of our wants are means to a higher set of goals. The demand for the services of physicians and hospitals is itself a means of attaining a higher end, the maintenance of health. The demand for automobiles is (in part, at least) a demand for transportation. To the extent that preferences are considered means to an end, rather than ends themselves, they can be judged in terms of their efficiency—how well does the satisfaction of a particular "lower-order" preference contribute to the attainment of the "higher-order" goal. At least some preferences can be looked at critically and not accepted unquestionably. Once the question of efficiency is introduced, economics is back on familiar ground. It is peculiarly suited to analyze matters of efficiency.

No one has pursued this line of approach at any great length. Whether it will pay off, in terms of providing a more solid footing for economic theory than the shifting sands of "absolute preferences," cannot be foretold. Barring some progress in this area, economics must stand guilty on part of one count of the indictment against it.

Reflection on the nature of radical criticism of economics leads to one further comment. Economics is fundamentally a discipline that deals with man as he is. At its best, economics seeks to harness man's very human motivations to the public interest. Much of the New Left is interested in changing man, elevating his motives, reducing his greed, and intensifying his love for his fellow man. Economics is a social science, but love is a religion. They are both relevant, but they are not on the same plane of discourse. The economist, for example, generally thinks it naïve to hope that pollution will somehow be conquered by bringing public pressure on corporations to exercise "social responsibility." But he does advocate changes in the structure of incentives and the network of contract laws to create a situation in which it becomes a corporation's own self-interest to act "responsibly."

To the young radical, such technical solutions, which accept and play upon man's drive for material advancement, seem shabby and mean. The evangelism of love and understanding mingle curiously with an intolerant hate for institutions built on the search for money and wealth. But they mingle no more curiously than in the Epistles of St. Paul. There is need for both the pragmatist who would harness in the public service man's drive for worldly goods and the idealist who would lift man's drive to more lofty goals. Neither is irrelevant.

Part II: Application of Economic Thinking to Some Particular Social Problems

This section is broken into four subsections that illustrate the application of economic analysis to broad issues of social policy. The purpose is not to suggest that economics provides all the answers to these questions, for they are clearly interdisciplinary. Rather, the aim is to illustrate that economics can offer important insights into a much broader range of questions than those usually associated with economic behavior.

Subsection A is concerned with crime and punishment. The first paper, by Gordon Tullock, using the examples of motor vehicle code violations and tax evasion, demonstrates that the economic approach can be used in a computational way to define optimal laws. Tullock stresses that one needs empirical information in order to make computations in such matters. Still, the economic approach provides a thought process through which it is possible to analyze public policy toward crime. In the second paper Lester Thurow outlines the decisions concerning equity that society must make before it calls upon the efficiency experts to make law enforcement more effective. Public investment analysis, he forcefully demonstrates, cannot be conducted independently of normative questions concerning the goals of public activities—e.g., where should squad cars patrol?

In subsection B we turn to the application of the economic approach to higher education. In the first paper Theodore Schultz develops an argument, based on his considerable contributions to human capital theory, that stresses the idea of higher education as a form of investment. Schultz emphasizes that the central economic concept in planning higher education should be rate of return on investment. He goes on to discuss within this analytical framework such issues as the major functions of higher education, the real cost of human capital formation, and, importantly, the effects of education on the distribution of income. In the second paper Robert Tollison and Thomas Willett examine proposals for full-cost pricing of educational outputs and the greater use of markets to organize higher education. They also discuss the role of public aid to education under a full-cost pricing scheme.

Subsection C consists of three papers concerned with environmental problems. The first is a book review by Peter Passell, Marc Roberts, and Leonard Ross. They examine three recent "doomsday" volumes and point out some typical fallacies that can be avoided by applying the economic approach to environmental and natural resource problems—most notably the fallacy that the world cannot adjust to scarcity. In the second paper Anthony Fisher examines the relationship between population and environmental quality. He argues that economic theory supported by empirical evidence suggests that the deterioration of the environment is not primarily a population problem, but rather comes about because of pervasive price distortions. The third paper is a reprint of an article by the editors that uses the economic approach to examine ways of protecting endangered predators. Although the particular problem is a limited one, the analysis is relevant for a wide variety of policy questions related to the environment. In addition the paper presents an application of the Coase theorem, considers liability assignment in environmental policy, and discusses the development of fiscal mechanisms to yield information on desirable levels of externality control.

The fourth subsection is concerned with revenue sharing and the drawing of political boundary lines. In the first paper Gordon Tullock examines the trade-offs that have to be made to determine the optimal size of government. He looks at trade-offs involved in internalizing externalities, economies of scale in the production of governmental output, and decision-making costs. It is his conclusion that while a highly centralized government may be the most orderly, one would be mistaken in thinking it the most efficient. In the second paper Charles McLure questions the view that revenue sharing is the essence of rational fiscal federalism. Basing his argument on a well-known normative model of fiscal federalism, he contends that the so-called state-local financial crisis is caused primarily by a failure to adopt more suitable fiscal arrangements. McLure also considers the structure of federal grants programs.

A. CRIME AND PUNISHMENT

7. An Economic Approach to Crime *

GORDON TULLOCK

Among the various approaches to the study of crime, the economic perspective has been one of the least developed and utilized.[1] The purposes of this article are to demonstrate the utility of the economic perspective and to present some simple computational tools in two areas of the law which the reader is likely to have fairly extensive personal experience—motor vehicle code violations and tax evasion. In the case of the former, we are not only fully experienced, but we also have a very good and clear idea in our own minds of the consequences of the violation. While our knowledge and experience in regard to tax evasion are rather less than those concerning violations of the traffic code, most of us have at least contemplated padding our expenses on the income tax form, and we find very little difficulty in understanding why other people actually do it fairly regularly.

In addition to reader knowledge based on experience, there is a further advantage to discussing motor vehicle offenses and tax evasion. The customary element in such laws is extremely small. Most of our laws on crime came down from great antiquity and hence contain all sorts of quaint nooks and corners. The motor vehicle law is almost entirely a creation of the 20th century and is periodically changed quite drastically. Similarly, the income tax code is largely a recent development, and in this case is being continuously changed by both legislative enactment and the actions of various administrative bodies. Thus, we do not have to deal with the weight of immemorial tradition when we turn to these problems.

Reprinted from *Social Science Quarterly,* 50 (June 1969), pp. 59–71, by permission of the publisher and author.

* This article is part of a larger project in which efforts are made to apply economic reasoning to many aspects of law including more serious crimes than are discussed herein.

1. The approach is new only in terms of the 20th century. Bentham, Mill and a number of other 19th-century scholars took a rather similar approach to crime. Unfortunately, the modern apparatus of welfare economics or cost-benefit analysis was not available to the 19th-century scholars and hence they were not able to make as strong a case for their position as can now be made. For a recent example of much the same approach see Gary Becker, "Crime and Punishment: An Economic Approach," *Journal of Political Economy,* 74 (March–April, 1968), pp. 169–217.

Illegal Parking

To begin, let us consider the most common and simplest of all violations of the law, illegal parking. This is a new problem. In the days of yore, there were not enough idle vehicles to require special parking laws; when, however, common men began to buy automobiles, the number of vehicles was such that simply permitting people to park where they wished along the side of the street led to very serious congestion. The number of spaces was limited, and rationing on a first come, first served basis seems to have been felt to be unsatisfactory.[2] In any event, the proper governmental bodies decided that there should be a "fairer" distribution of parking space, and it was decided that individuals should vacate spaces at some specified time, frequently an hour, after they occupied them.

The question then arose as to how to assure compliance. The method chosen was to fine noncompliance. The police were instructed to "ticket" cars which parked beyond the time limit, and the owners of the ticketed cars were then fined a small sum, say ten dollars. Thus, the individual could choose between removing his car within the prescribed period or leaving it and running some chance of being forced to pay ten dollars. Obviously, the size of the fine and the likelihood that any given car owner would be caught would largely determine how much overparking was done. The individual would, in effect, be confronted with a "price list" to overpark, and would normally do so only if the inconvenience of moving his car was greater than the properly discounted cost of the fine.[3]

Not all overparking is the result of a deliberate decision, however. Clearly a good deal of it comes from absentmindedness, and part is the result of factors not very thoroughly under control of the car owner. Nevertheless, we do not in general feel that the fine should be remitted. The absence of a criminal intent, or indeed of any intent at all, is not regarded as an excuse. When I was working in the Department of State in Washington, I served under a man who got several parking tickets a week. I think that I knew him well enough to be sure that all of these violations occurred without any conscious intent on his part. He would get involved in some project and forget that he was supposed to move his car. The

2. We are now discussing the early development of parking regulations. The relatively recent invention of the parking meter has changed the situation drastically and will be discussed later.

3. I am indebted to Professor Alexandre Kafka for the "price list" analogy. He insists, following his own professor, that the entire criminal code is simply a price list of various acts.

District of Columbia was levying what amounted to a tax on him for being absentminded.

As far as I could tell, the police force of Washington, D.C., was not particularly annoyed with my superior. Apparently, they thought the revenue derived paid for the inconvenience of issuing tickets and occasionally towing his car away. Suppose, however, they had wanted to make him stop violating the parking laws. It seems highly probably that a drastic increase in the fines would have been sufficient. Absentmindedness about ten dollars does not necessarily imply absentmindedness about 100 or even 1,000 dollars. With higher fines he would have felt more pressure to train himself to remember, to avoid parking on the public streets as much as possible, and to arrange for his secretary to remind him. Thus, the fact that he was not engaging in any calculations at all when he committed these "crimes" does not indicate that he would not respond to higher penalties by ceasing to commit them.

So far, however, we have simply assumed that the objective is to enforce a particular law against parking. The question of whether this law is sensible, or how much effort should be put into enforcing it, has not been discussed. In order to deal with this problem, let us turn to a more modern technology and discuss a metered parking area. In such areas the government in essence is simply renting out space to people who want to use it. It may not be using a market-clearing price because it may have some objectives other than simply providing the service at a profit, but this does not seriously alter the problem. For simplicity, let us assume that it is charging market-clearing prices. It would then attempt to maximize total revenue, including the revenue from fines and the revenue from the coins inserted in the parking meters minus the cost of the enforcement system. We need not here produce an equation or attempt to solve this problem, but clearly it is a perfectly ordinary problem in operations research, and there is no reason why we should anticipate any great difficulty with it.

Other Motor Vehicle Laws

However, parking is clearly a very minor problem; in fact, it was chosen for discussion simply because it is so easy. In essence, there is very little here except calculation of exactly the same sort that is undertaken every day by businessmen. For a slightly more complicated problem, let us consider another traffic offense—speeding. Presumably, the number of deaths from auto accidents, the extent of personal injuries and the material damage are all functions of the speed at which cars travel.[4]

4. Recently this relationship has been somewhat obscured by the publication of Ralph Nader's *Unsafe at any Speed*. It is undoubtedly true that cars can be designed to reduce

By enforcing a legal maximum on such speed, we can reduce all of them. On the other hand, a legal maximum speed will surely inconvenience at least some people, and may inconvenience a great many. The strictly material cost of lowering speeds is easily approximated by computing the additional time spent in traveling and multiplying this by the hourly earning power of an average member of the population. This is, of course, only an approximation, leaving out of account such factors as the pleasure some people get out of speed and the diversion of economic activity which would result from the slowing of traffic. Nevertheless, we could use this approximation [5] and the costs of deaths, injuries and material damage from auto accidents to work out the optimal speed limit, which would be simply the limit which minimized total costs in all of these categories. The computation would be made in "social" terms because the data would be collected for the whole population. Individuals, however, could regard these figures as actuarial approximations for their personal optima.

To the best of my knowledge, no one has ever performed these calculations in a reasonably direct and precise way. Presumably the reason for the omission is an unwillingness to consciously and openly put a value on deaths and injuries which can then be compared with the strictly material costs of delay. When I point out to people that the death toll from highway accidents could be reduced by simply lowering the speed limit (and improving enforcement), they normally show great reluctance to give any consideration to the subject. They sometimes try to convince themselves that the reduction would not have the predicted effect, but more commonly they simply shift quickly to another subject. They are unwilling, for reasons of convenience, to approve a substantial lowering of the speed limit, but they do not like to consciously balance their convenience against deaths. Nevertheless, this is the real reasoning behind the speed limits. We count the costs of being forced to drive slowly and the costs of accidents, and choose the speed limit which gives us the best outcome. Since we are unwilling to do this consciously, we probably do a bad job of computing. If we were willing to look at the matter in the open, consciously to put a value on human life, we could no doubt get better results.

As an example of this reluctance to think about the valuation we are

---

fatalities in accidents and, for that matter, that highways can be designed to reduce accidents. Recent discoveries of methods of reducing skidding by improved highway surfaces probably indicate that there is more potential in highway improvement than in car redesign. Nevertheless, for a given car and highway, speed kills.

5. For those who object to approximation, more elaborate research, taking into account much more of the costs of slowing down traffic, could be undertaken.

willing to put upon deaths and injury in terms of our own convenience, a colleague of mine undertook a study of the methods used by the Virginia Highway Commission in deciding how to improve the roads. He found that they were under orders to consider speed, beauty, and safety in presenting projects for future work. The beauty was taken care of by simply earmarking a fixed part of the appropriations for roadside parks, etc. For speed they engaged in elaborate research on highway use and had statistical techniques for predicting the net savings in time from various possible changes. It was the possibility of improving these techniques which led them to invite my colleague to make his study. For safety, on the other hand, they had no system at all.

It was clear that they did take safety into account in designing roads, and spent quite a bit of money on various methods of reducing the likelihood of accidents. They did not, however, have any formula or rule for deciding either how much should be spent on safety or in what specific projects it should be invested. They must have had some trade-off rule which they applied. This rule, however, remained buried in their subconscious even though they used fairly elaborate and advanced techniques for other problems. This is particularly remarkable when it is remembered that, given any exchange value, the computations of the amount to be spent on safety would be fairly easy.

If, for example, it is decided that we will count one fatal accident as "worth" $500,000 in inconvenience to drivers (measured in increased travel time), then, with statistics on accidents and volume of traffic, it would be possible to work out how much should be spent on safety and how much on speed. Since the Highway Commission did not spend all of its money on safety, some such "price" for accidents must have taken some part of its reasoning, but rather sophisiticated engineers were unwilling to admit, probably even to themselves, that this was so. Perhaps more surprising, my colleague fully approved of their attitude. Basically a "scientific" type, with a great interest in statistical decision theory, he felt that here was one place where careful reasoning was undesirable. He did not want to consider ratios between deaths and convenience himself, did not want the people who designed the highways on which he drove to consciously consider them, and did not want to discuss the subject with me.

But even if we do not like to critically examine our decision process, clearly the decision as to the speed limit is made by balancing the inconveniences of a low limit against the deaths and injuries to be expected from a high one. The fact that we are not willing to engage in conscious thought on the problem is doubly unfortunate, because it is difficult enough so that it is unlikely that we can reach optimal decisions by any but the most careful and scientific procedures. The problem is stochastic on both sides since driving at a given speed does not certainly cause an accident; it only creates a probability of an accident. Similarly, our convenience is not always best served by exceeding the speed limit, so we have only a stochastic probability of being inconvenienced. There will also be some problems of gathering data which we do not now have (mainly because we have not thought clearly about the problem) and making reasonable estimates of certain parameters. In order to solve the problem we need a table of probabilities rather like Table 1. Obviously, with this table, and one more thing, a conversion factor for deaths and delay, we could readily calculate the speed limit which would minimize the "cost" of using the road.[6]

Table 1. Effects of speed limits

Speed limit (mph)	Deaths per 100,000,000 miles	Costs of delay
10	1	$50,000,000,000.00
20	2	35,000,000,000.00
30	4	22,500,000,000.00
40	8	15,500,000,000.00
50	16	5,000,000,000.00
60	32	2,000,000,000.00
70	64	500,000,000.00

Equally obviously, no direct calculation of this sort is now undertaken, but our speed limits are set by a sort of weighing of accident prevention against inconvenience. The only difference between our present methods and the ones I have outlined is that we are frightened of having to admit that we use a conversion ratio in which lives are counted as worth only some finite amount of inconvenience, and we refuse to make the computations at a conscious level and hence are denied the use of modern statistical methods.

Having set a speed limit, we now turn to its enforcement. If, for example, the limit is 50 MPH, then it does not follow the people who drive over that speed will automatically have accidents. Nor does it follow that driving at 51 MPH is very much more likely to lead to an accident than driving at 50 MPH. The use of a simple limit law is dictated by the problems of enforcement rather than the nature of the control problem it-

6. Note that I am ignoring all consequences of accidents except deaths and that it is assumed that the speed limit is the only variable. These are, of course, simplifying assumptions introduced in order to make my table simple and the explanation easy. If any attempt were made to explicitly utilize the methods I suggest, much more complex data would be needed. The figures are, of course, assumed for illustrative purposes only.

self. If we had some way of simply charging people for the use of the streets, with the amount per mile varying with the speed,[7] this would permit a better adjustment than a simple speed limit. In practice, the police and courts do do something rather like this by charging much higher fines for people who greatly exceed the speed limit. Let us, however, confine ourselves to the simple case where we have a single speed limit, with no higher fines for exceeding it by a sizable amount.

Our method of enforcing this law is in some ways most peculiar. In the first place, if a citizen sees someone violating this law and reports it, the police will refuse to do anything about it. With one specific exception, which we will footnote in a moment, you cannot be penalized for speeding unless a police officer sees you do it. Think what burglars would give for a similar police practice in their field of endeavor.

A second peculiarity is that the penalty assessed is unconnected with the attitude of mind of the person who violates the speed limit.[8] Driving at 70 MPH may get you a fine of 100 dollars or a ten-year sentence, depending upon the occurrence of events over which you have no control. Suppose, for example, two drivers each take a curve in the highway at 70. The first finds a police car on the other side, gets a ticket and pays a fine. The second encounters a tractor driving down his side of the road and a column of cars on the other side. In the resulting crash, the tractor driver is killed, and the outcome may be a ten-year sentence for the driver of the car.[9] We can assume both men exceeded the speed limit, for the same motives, but the second had bad luck. Normally we like to have penalties depend upon what the defendant did, not on external circumstances beyond his control. (The only other situation in which this kind of thing is done involves the rule which makes a death caused while committing a felony murder regardless of the intent.)

The peculiarity of this procedure is emphasized when it is remembered that the man who risks being sent up for ten years for killing someone in an accident almost certainly had no intent to do so. He was driving at high speed in order to get somehwere in a hurry, an act which normally leads to a moderate fine when detected. The heavy sentence comes not from the wickedness of his act, but from the fact that he drew an unlucky

7. Needless to say, the cost of driving 50 MPH in a built-up area would be higher than in the open countryside.

8. There is a partial and imperfect exception to this for certain special cases. The man who speeds to get his wife to the hospital before the birth of their child is perhaps the one who gets the most newspaper attention.

9. Note that the rule that a traffic offense is prosecuted only if seen by a police officer is not followed in the event of a serious accident. A third driver may be imagined who took the curve at the same speed and met neither the police nor the tractor. He would, of course, go off scot-free even if his offense were reported to the police.

number in a lottery. The case is even clearer in those not terribly rare cases where the accident arises not from conscious violation of the law but from incompetence or emotional stress (losing one's head). In ordinary driving we frequently encounter situations where a small error in judgment can cause deaths. A man who has no intent to drive carelessly may simply be a bad judge of distance and try to pass a truck where there is insufficient room. An excitable person may "freeze" when some emergency arises, with the result that there is an accident which could easily have been prevented. Both of these cases might well lead to prison terms in spite of the complete lack of "criminal intent" on the part of the defendant. "If a driver, in fact, adopts a manner of driving which the jury thinks dangerous to other road users . . . then on the issue of guilt, it matters not whether he was deliberately reckless, careless, momentarily inattentive, or doing his incompetent best." [10]

As anybody who has studied game theory knows, a mixed strategy may pay off better than a pure strategy. It may be, therefore, that the combination of three different treatments is better than a simpler rule providing a single and fairly heavy penalty for speeding, regardless of whether you hit anyone or happen to encounter a policeman while engaged in the criminal act. But, although we must admit this possibility, it seems more likely that a single penalty based on the intent of the individual would work better in preventing speeding. The probable reason for the rather peculiar set of rules I have outlined is simply the functioning of the court system. If someone who disliked me alleged that he had seen me speeding and I denied it, the court would have to decide who was lying without much to go on except the expressions on our faces. Since "dishonesty can lie honesty out of countenance any day of the week if there is anything to be gained by it," this is clearly an uncertain guide. Thus, under our current court system, permitting people to initiate prosecutions for speeding by stating that they had seen someone doing so would almost certainly mean that innumerable spite cases would be brought before the courts, and that the courts would make many, many mistakes in dealing with them.

Similarly, the use of two sets of penalties for speeding, depending on factors not under the defendant's control, is probably the result of judicial performance. Charging a very heavy fine or relatively brief imprisonment for every speeding conviction would very likely be resisted by judges who do not really think speeding is very serious unless it kills somebody. That this is the restriction cannot strictly be proven but at least some evidence can be provided for it. In Virginia, as in many states, multiple con-

10. Hill v. Baxter, 1 *QB* (1958), p. 277.

victions for traffic offenses can result in removal of the driving license. The state has encountered real difficulty in getting its judges to carry out this provision. Under the conditions of modern life the deprivation of a driver's license is a real hardship, and judges apparently do not like to impose it for a speeding offense simply because the offender has been convicted twice before. Similarly, if a license is suspended, the courts are unlikely to inflict a very heavy penalty on the man who drives anyhow, provided he avoids killing someone.[11]

It is probable that problems of judicial efficiency account for another peculiarity of the motor traffic code; i.e., it is almost impossible for an individual to defend himself against the accusation. Normally the police officer's testimony is accepted regardless of other evidence. Further, in general, the penalty exacted for the average minor violation of the code is small if the defendant pleads guilty, but high if he does not. Parking offenses, for example, may very commonly be settled for one or two dollars on a guilty plea, but cost ten to twenty if you choose to plead not guilty. This amounts to paying the defendant to plead guilty. As almost anyone who has had any experience with a traffic court is aware, most of the people who get tickets are indeed guilty, but those who are not guilty normally plead guilty anyway because of this system of enforcement.

Obviously we could apply the same line of reasoning to deal with all other parts of the traffic code. The problem is essentially a technological one. By the use of some type of exchange value and evidence obtained from statistical and other sources, we could compute a complete traffic code which would optimize some objective function. In practice we do not do this because of our reluctance to specify an exchange value for life. Nevertheless, we get much the same result, albeit with less accuracy and precision, by our present methods.

Tax Evasion

Turning now to the income tax law, we must begin by noting that apparently almost anybody can get special treatment. The present laws and regulations are a solid mass of special rules for special groups of people. There are innumerable cases where some particularly wealthy man or large corporation has succeeded in obtaining special tax treatment. Nevertheless, we can consider how the existing tax code should be enforced.

11. Possibly, given the difficulties of enforcement, a restriction of the license rather than a removal might be wise. Restricting the license of a multiple offender to a limited area, including his home, a couple of shopping centers and his place of employment, together with a low speed limit, say 30 MPH, might appeal to judges who would be unwilling to remove the license totally. Judges might also be more inclined to give heavy sentences to people who violate such restrictions than to people who continue to drive to work in spite of the lack of a license.

Unfortunately, even the enforcement is full of loopholes. In the first place, there are a great many people (special classes that readily come to mind are doctors, waitresses, and farmers) who have special facilities for evading the income tax. It is also widely believed that certain groups (the farmers in particular) have been able to make use of their political power to see to it that the Internal Revenue Service does not pay as much attention to detecting evasion by them as by other groups. Nevertheless, we can assume that the tax code contains within it both a set of special privileges for individuals and instructions for evasion which apply only to certain classes, and hence that the true tax law is residual after we have knocked all these holes in what was originally a rather simple piece of legislation.

There are further difficulties. The individual presumably is interested in the taxes being collected from other people because he wants the government services which will be purchased by them. He would prefer to be left free of tax himself, but this is unfortunately not possible. He, in a sense, trades the tax on his own income for the benefit which he obtains from the purchase of government services by the entire community. It is by no means clear that for everyone the present amount of government services is optimal. If I felt that the total amount of government services being purchased today was excessive (i.e., that lower tax rates and lower levels of service were desirable), presumably I would feel relatively happy about systematic evasion of a tax law on the part of everyone. On the other hand, if I felt that the present level of government services was too low and the taxes should be higher, I might conceivably feel that "overenforcement" is desirable.

Even if I am happy with the present level of government expenditures, it is by no means obvious that I should be terribly much in favor of efficient enforcement of the revenue code. I might favor a revenue code which sets rates relatively high and an enforcement procedure which permits a great deal of evasion to lower rates and better enforcement procedures which brought in the same revenue. Surely I would prefer the former if I had some reason to believe that I would be particularly able to evade the taxes. But even if I assume that everyone will have about the same ability to evade, I might still prefer the higher rates and higher level of evasion. Nevertheless, it seems to me that most people would prefer the lowest possible level of tax for a given net return. I have been unable to prove that this is optimal,[12] but it does seem to me to be reasonable that this would be the appropriate social goal. In any event, that is the assumption upon which our further calculations are built. It would be rela-

12. I sincerely hope that some of my readers may be able to repair this admission.

tively easy to adjust these calculations to any other assumption on this particular matter.

Table 2. Definitions of symbols

C_P	= Private cost of enforcement (includes cost of incorrect tax penalties)
C_R	= Cost of revenue protection service
I	= Income
I'	= Some part of income
L_C	= Likelihood of compliance
L_D	= Likelihood of detection of evasion
N	= Social return on tax (excess burden not subtracted)
P	= Penal rate for detected noncompliance
R	= Tax rate
T_R	= Tax revenue (net of direct enforcement costs)

Under these circumstances and on these assumptions, the return in taxation to the government from various levels of enforcement can be seen by Equation 1, which is fairly lengthy but really simple. (See Table 2 for definitions of symbols.)

(1) $$T_R = L_C \cdot R \cdot I + (1 - L_C) \cdot I' \cdot L_D \cdot P - C_R$$

The first term on the right of the equal sign is the likelihood that individuals will fully comply with tax laws, multiplied by the tax rate and income. Note that this is deliberately somewhat ambiguous. It can be taken as any individual's tax payments or the payments for the economy as a whole, depending on which definition we choose for income. We add to this the probability that an individual will attempt to evade payment of taxes on all or part of his income, times the probability of detection of his evasion, times the penalty he will be compelled to pay on the evasion. This gives us the total return which the community will receive. There is, of course, the cost of maintaining the inspection and revenue collection system, which is subtracted from this output in the final term C_R.

Ignoring, for the moment, the taxpayer's propensity toward accepting risks, the condition for a favorable decision to attempt *to evade* the tax legally payable on some particular portion of his income is

(2) $$L_D \cdot P \cdot I' < R \cdot I'$$

That is to say, if the likelihood of detection times the penalty he must pay on detection is less than the rate that he would legally pay, he would appropriately attempt to evade. It will be noted that both in this inequality and in the previous equation there is an implicit assumption that the individual will be able to pay a fine if he is found to have evaded the tax law. The reason that the individual is normally able to pay a fine is simply that in general those who get into income tax difficulties are well off.

Nevertheless, although this is a very good approximation, it is not entirely accurate. The income tax authorities do sometimes attempt to put people in prison for tax evasion. In general, the Internal Revenue Service has a dual system. If you make a "tax saving" which is relatively easy for them to detect, they will normally adjust your return and charge you a relatively modest interest payment. If, on the other hand, you do something which is quite hard to detect, which normally means a directly dishonest statement, they assess a much heavier penalty. From their standpoint no doubt this is sensible as a way of minimizing enforcement costs.

There is another peculiarity of the income tax policing process. Usually the policeman himself (i.e., the Internal Revenue man) simply assesses a deficiency on the face of the form if he does not suspect what is technically called evasion. This is usually the complete legal proceeding. In small cases the individual normally pays, although he may complain to the person making the assessemnt. It is highly probable that in this matter, as in other small claims litigation, there is a great deal of inaccuracy on both sides. Since these are small matters, the use of a cheap but relatively inaccurate procedure is optimal. For major matters, however, very elaborate legal proceedings may be undertaken. These proceed at first through the administrative channels of the Internal Revenue Service and turn to the regular courts only if all administrative methods are exhausted. Here one would anticipate a great deal more care and far fewer errors, and there is no doubt that this is the case.

Returning, however, to our basic equations, it will be noted that the likelihood of quiet compliance (i.e., the likelihood of the income-tax payer's making no effort to evade) is a function of the likelihood of detection of evasion as shown in Equation 3:

(3) $\qquad L_C = g(L_D)$

The likelihood of detection of evasion in turn is a function of two things, as shown in Equation 4:

(4) $\qquad L_D = h_1(C_R) + h_2(C_P)$

One of these, of course, is simply the amount of resources that we put into the revenue service. The second, however, is the resources that we force the private taxpayer to put into keeping records and filing returns and doing other things which make it easier to enforce the tax revenue code. Thus, Equation 1 was incomplete. Equation 5 shows the net social benefit or loss from the tax, including the factor C:

(5) $\qquad N = L_C \cdot R \cdot I + (1 - L_C) \cdot I' \cdot L_D \cdot P - C_R - C_P$

It will be noted that I have, for these computations, ignored problems of excess burden.

The term C_P is interesting and very comprehensive. It not only includes the troubles involved in filling out the income tax forms, which we all know may be considerable, but also the necessity of keeping our accounts in such form that the Internal Revenue Service may survey them. It includes the possibility that we will be audited even if we have not violated the law. It does not include any penalty which we might incur if we have violated the law, because that is included under P. It includes a number of other things which are somewhat less obvious, however. It includes the inconvenience we might suffer occasionally when the Internal Revenue Service is investigating a potential violation of the internal revenue code by someone other than ourselves; we might, for some reason, have some evidence which the Internal Revenue Service wants and be compelled to furnish it. It also includes the possibility that the Internal Revenue Service will wrongly suspect us and will then assess an incorrect fine upon us. Lastly, of course, it includes legal expenses involved in all of the above. Thus, it is by no means a small figure.

Still, the problem is relatively easy. We should simply, maximize N.[13] Examination of this equation indicates some superficially not terribly probable consequences. We could, for example, be in favor of increasing enforcement even though we know it is likely to raise our own payments. It will be noted that there is nowhere in the equation the assumption that we will obey the law and others will not. If we really believe that the government money is being spent for something worthwhile, then we make a net gain of some nature from increasing N. It is true that the N in our equation represents this net gain very crudely, since it takes a total figure rather than a marginal figure, but we need not worry about this.

As noted above, we might feel it desirable to include some kind of risk aversion factor. If the penalty for evasion of the tax code is quite large, let us say 25 times the tax that is evaded, and if we feel that there is a fair probability of the Internal Revenue Service going wrong in assessing such penalties, then our term C_P could be large. This might still maximize the value of N, but if we are risk avoiders, we might prefer a lower value of N in order to avoid the risk of being assessed such a very large penalty.

But these are refinements. Basically we could calculate an optimum tax enforcement policy from a set of equations such as those here. I think that

13. J. Randolph Norsworthy has studied present-day Internal Revenue procedures on the assumption that they behave somewhat in accord with the instruction of maximizing T_R. His methods are quite different from ours, but his doctoral dissertation is well worth studying: Tax Evasion, University of Virginia, 1965.

if the reader considers his own reactions he will realize that his own attitude towards the income tax authorities is based upon something like this form of reasoning. He does, of course, hope that the income tax authorities will give him special treatment and does his best to obtain it. But insofar as this special treatment has already been taken into account, his behavior would be appropriately described by Equation 2. His behavior with respect to general social policy in this period would then be described more or less by a desire to maximize N in Equation 5. There may be some people who have strong moral feelings about their own payments under the income tax, but I have never run into them. Most of my friends will talk about the desirability of the income tax, but I also find them discussing in detail what they can get away with. In fact, I suspect that moral considerations are less important in tax enforcement than any other single part of the law.

Summary

In this article we have discussed two areas of the law with which the reader is likely to have fairly great personal experience. We have demonstrated in both cases that very simple computational tools defining an "optimum law." Application of these computational tools would, it is true, require the development of certain empirical information we do not now have, but they are nevertheless suitable guides to further work. Further, our computational tools in this respect are simply formalizations of the thought processes now used by most people in dealing with these matters.

8. Equity versus Efficiency in Law Enforcement

LESTER C. THUROW

Coincident demands for "law and order" and efficiency in government expenditures are leading to the use of systems analysis or cost-benefit analysis in law enforcement activities. The RAND Corporation is working to increase the efficiency of the New York City Police Department; the Institute for Defense Analysis is doing research for the Justice Department. Different enforcement techniques, crimes, regions, pieces of equip-

Reprinted without appendix from *Public Policy*, Summer 1970, pp. 451–462, by permission of the publisher and author.

ment, and social groups are examined to determine where the greatest reduction in crime can take place for the least cost.

Large gains in efficiency are possible in law enforcement. In a recent application of cost-benefit techniques to the problem of enforcing the minimum wage, overtime, and equal pay laws, the U.S. Department of Labor's enforcement budget could have been reallocated to increase the benfits from law enforcement twelvefold.[1] Alternatively, the current level of benefits could have been achieved while cutting the enforcement budget almost 90 percent.

Efficiency and equity are both among the goals of law enforcement, but efficiency cannot be defined without specifying the definition of equity or justice. Depending on the definition of equity, different law enforcement practices will be inefficient or efficient. Conversely, the specification of efficient law enforcement practices implies some particular definition of equity. For example, assume that efficiency is defined as the maximal reduction in the incidence of crime for a given law enforcement budget.

Such a definition implies that the purpose of law enforcement is the prevention of crime and not the capture of criminals. Resources would only be devoted to capturing criminals if it were found that capturing criminals deters future crimes. In addition, such a definition of efficiency implies that all crimes are equally serious, or it requires some explicit weighting of the importance of different types of crime. To meet the postulated goal of efficiency, efficiency experts would look for those criminals whose preferences are easily altered, those criminals who find criminal activities marginally attractive, and those crimes easiest to prevent. These are the points where the greatest reductions in crime can occur for a given expenditure of resources, and they are the points where existing resources would be used. Pursuit of such a goal of efficiency would leave different groups or individuals with very different probabilities of being victimized. Different types of criminals would face different probabilities of being caught. Some laws would be more strictly enforced than others. Some areas would have more police protection than others.

As this example indicates, a very particular definition of equity (or inequity) emerges from our definition of efficiency, but corresponding problems flow from definitions of equity. Assume that equity is defined in such a way that police resources must be used to equalize the probabilities of being victimized, the probabilities of being caught, the severity with which each law is enforced, and the police protection for each area.

1. Lester C. Thurow and Carl Rappaport, "Law Enforcement and Cost-Benefit Analysis," *Public Finance* (Spring 1969).

This definition may constitute an inconsistent set of goals (equalizing the probability of being victimized may require more police protection in one area than in another), but it also implies an increase in the incidence of crime for a given law enforcement budget. Police resources are to be used in areas where crime prevention is difficult or impossible. The result is fewer resources for areas where crime prevention is easy, and a higher total incidence of crime. Thus, the definition of equity cannot be chosen without realizing that it has an impact on either the incidence of crime in society or on the size of the law enforcement budgets necessary to achieve some specified incidence of crime.

Before efficiency experts can allocate an enforcement budget, society must determine the equity constraints within which it wishes to be efficient. The purpose of this article is to outline the decisions about equity which society must make before it calls in the efficiency experts.

Equity Goals: The Victim

Does society want the police to investigate every complaint? Typically complaints do not occur in those areas where the greatest possible reductions in crime per dollar of expenditure occur. Broader social goals, such as the desire to make everyone feel important, may call for the investigation of every complaint, but minimizing the incidence of crime argues for the reverse. At current budget levels many law enforcement agencies are complaint agencies. Most of their time is required to investigate every complaint. To be efficient they must stop investigating all complaints. What they should do depends on the value society assigns to making people feel important *vis-a-vis* reducing crime.

Before law enforcement activities can be efficiently organized, society must decide how it wants criminal losses to be distributed. Does society have some responsibility to see that losses are either equally or randomly distributed? In the first case each person must suffer equal losses from criminal activities. In the second case each person faces the same expected loss, although the actual losses will differ. Some individuals are simply the unlucky victims of crime. Or perhaps society wants criminal losses to be either progressively or regressively distributed. Should criminal losses rise as a proportion of income as income increases, or should criminal losses fall as a proportion of income as income increases? Should the rich or the poor suffer the burden of criminal losses? Should black and white losses be equal?

If losses must be distributed in some specified manner, this aim constitutes a severe constraint on the deployment of police resources. It substantially raises the costs of reducing crime to some specified incidence.

Enforcement budgets must be allocated to areas where enforcement is costly.

In determining its standards of equity, society must decide how much it should act to offset individual decisions. The problem is especially acute with crime. Individuals do not decide to be the victims of crime as they decide to be mountain climbers. Someone else decides to make them victims, but individuals can act in ways which will result in different probabilities of being victimized. Should police resources be used to protect a person who does not lock his car?

The incidence of crime is uneven under present enforcement procedures, but this fact does not justify plans designed to yield uneven enforcement. If one of the items in the social contract between individuals and society is the prevention of criminal activites, society probably has a responsibility to distribute equitably the incidence of crime. Efficiency must be achieved within this equity constraint and not at the expense of it.

One solution is to make compensatory payments to the victims of crime. The consequences are to be equalized, although the expected losses are not. Compensation is paid to the victim since compensation is the efficient method of making the consequences equal, not because society is responsible for crime. The costs of crime prevention rise, but not as much as if preventative measures must ensure equal losses for each individual. Compensation is cheaper than enforcement procedures, since the costs of deterring many types of crime exceed the costs of allowing those crimes to occur. Compensation allows the police to relax ex-ante equity constraints on their method of operations, but preserves ex-post equity. If large gains in efficiency are to be realized, compensation becomes a necessity. Without it, the resulting inequities are probably intolerable. They might be no larger than the present inequities, but they would be consciously planned inequities rather than historical inequities.

Economic losses can be handled by compensation, but human life and human injuries present more complicated problems. In many cases, especially in the case of death, the victim cannot be compensated. As a result, society may require that law enforcement activities for crimes against persons must be organized to provide equal protection. If such is the case, law enforcement resources must be shifted from protecting those groups who now have a low probability of being victimized by criminal attacks to protecting those groups who now have a high probability of being victimized. If it is more expensive to protect the latter group than the former group, as is probably the case, society is faced with the dilemma of either allocating more resources to crime prevention or allowing the total number of criminal attacks to rise. For a given law enforcement budget, equalizing the probability of being injured may increase the average probability of being injured.

Compromises are possible. Some level of minimal protection can be provided with efficient allocation above the minimal level. But where should this line of minimal protection be drawn? To answer the question, society must decide how it wants criminal losses to be distributed.

Equity Goals: The Criminal

The pursuit of efficiency raises problems of equity among criminals themselves. Does society have any responsibility to equalize the probability of being captured and punished? What if it proves to be easy to catch and punish criminals of a particular race, income class, living in a particular area, or committing certain crimes? Should law enforcement activities be concentrated on that area, race, income class, or crime? The minimal incidence of crime dictates concentration. Equity may not.

By committing a crime, does an individual stand outside of society and not merit equal treatment? Traditionally, equal treatment has been limited to legal procedures after capture. Does it or should it be extended to the probability of being captured? Does justice mean equalizing the probabilities of being convicted after being captured, or does it mean equalizing the probabilities of being convicted after committing a crime? In the former case the probabilities of being captured can be unequal; in the latter case they must be equal.

Equity also becomes important in society's use of punishments to deter crime. Two different crimes may be equivalent in terms of their social costs. Strong punishments may be an effective deterrent for one crime and not the other. Should punishments for the deterable crime be higher than those for the nondeterable crime? If punishments differ, two individuals in equal positions are being treated unequally. If punishments are not strengthened for the deterable crime, law enforcement will be less efficient. Should an individual be more harshly punished because he happens to commit a crime where other individuals will be affected by his punishment? Should the individual be held accountable for the indirect (demonstration) costs of his action as well as the direct costs? Similar problems arise if punishments have different effects on different areas, income classes, and races.

In all of these decisions, society's definition of horizontal equity, equal treatment of equals, becomes important. Are two men in equal or unequal positions if they commit crimes that have the same direct consequences, but crimes which differ in terms of their indirect or demonstration effects? Without a social decision on the concrete definition of horizontal equity, it is impossible to determine what law enforcement techniques are proper or improper.

Similar problems arise with respect to vertical equity, the fair treatment of individuals who commit crimes with different direct social consequences. Punishment should fit the crime, but does the crime include only the direct effects of the crime, or does it include the indirect demonstration effects of the crime? If there is a demonstration effect, one crime causes others to commit crimes. Should the first criminal be punished because other people will follow his example?

Punishments raise another problem of equity. The death penalty might be an effective deterrent to minor crimes, but it would hardly be equitable to the individual. Society must not only decide upon its standards of horizontal and vertical equity among criminals, but it must also decide upon the degree of progression in criminal penalties. How should the severity of the penalty rise as the severity of the crime rises?

Punishment as deterrent may also clash with punishment as rehabilitation. Rehabilitation may require progressive prisons with halfway houses and released time. Progressive prisons may be less effective deterrents to crime. What if progressive prisons succeed in rehabilitation, but increase the incidence of crime by reducing the deterrent effects on others? Is the function of prisons to rehabilitate criminals or to deter crime? The two goals may conflict. How is the conflict to be decided?

Equity for victims and equity for criminals may also conflict. Reducing the incidence of crime in ghetto areas to levels commensurate with suburban areas may make the probability of capturing a black criminal higher than that for a white criminal. How do we weight the two types of equity? How should society balance its equity goals when they are in conflict?

Conclusions

The conflict between equity and the minimal incidence of crime is real. Real resources are required to equalize the probability of being robbed in the ghetto and in suburbia. For a given law enforcement budget, equalizing the probability of being robbed or being caught will increase the probability of being robbed. To achieve the lowest average probability of being robbed, equity must be ignored.

The actual costs of achieving equity will depend on further empirical information. Because empirical data on law enforcement are lacking, very little work has been done on determining what activities deter crime and what activities do not. Perhaps the conflict between efficiency and equity will not be severe. More probably it will be acute. Cost-benefit analysis looks for differences in the deterability of crime. Resources are concentrated where they have the largest effects. The problem of equity does not arise if there are no differences in the deterability of crime, but the efficiency problem does not arise either. Resources are equally efficient in all areas. They do not need to be redistributed. Existing evidence and common sense would indicate that there are differences in the deterability of crime. There are gains in efficiency to be made. There are problems of equity to be considered.

Several points should be emphasized. (1) All evidence would suggest that large gains are possible in law enforcement efficiency. (2) Before systematic analysis can be applied to obtain these gains, society must determine its canons of equity with respect to both criminals and victims. Techniques are ultimately efficient only if they meet society's standards of equity. (3) Current law enforcement techniques ignore both equity and efficiency. The incidence of crime and the probability of being captured are not equally distributed. The strict pursuit of efficiency probably would not result in a more inequitable distribution of the costs of crime, but it would result in a different distribution. Consciously planned inequities would be substituted for historically sanctioned inequities.

Theoretically, the legislatures which make the laws and provide law enforcement budgets should resolve the difficult conflicts between equity and efficiency. They should decide how the costs of criminal activities should be allocated among victims. They should decide how punishments should be allocated among criminals. Unfortunately, there seems little likelihood that legislatures are going either to address or to solve these problems. Therefore the executive branch of government, the courts, and the legal profession are going to have to face the conflict between equity and efficiency.

I realize that standards of equity cannot be set by efficiency experts, but I would like to make several suggestions. Congress has given us a hint as to how the losses from criminal activities might be distributed across income classes. Currently the federal individual income tax rate for persons with taxable incomes from $0 to $500 is 14 percent, while the marginal tax rate on persons with incomes from $22,000 to $26,000 is 55 percent. According to the tax laws, a loss of 14 cents for the person with an income of $0 to $500 is supposed to cause the same reduction in welfare as a loss of 55 cents for the person with an income of $22,000 to $26,000. Criminal losses could be regarded as a social tax like any other tax. Consequently, for every $1 suffered in criminal losses by the man with an income of $0 to $500, the man with an income of $22,000 to $26,000 should suffer criminal losses of $3.93 [($1/.14) (.55)] if their welfare losses are to be equal. Either the ex-ante distribution of crime prevention measures or ex-post compensation could be used to achieve this result.

When criminal losses involve human life, there is no alternative but to allow equality to dominate. No compensation can be paid to the victim. Consequently, ex-ante crime prevention measures must be distributed to equalize the probability of being killed.

There are two directions in which society might move when it considers the problems of equity among criminals. (1) Society might decide that individuals stand outside of our society when they commit criminal acts. Consequently, it is not interested in treating criminals equitably, but is only interested in protecting potential victims. Some criminals will be punished harshly, some will be punished lightly, and some will not be punished. These decisions will simply be made on the basis of how they affect the probability that an individual will be victimized. Police departments and other law enforcement agencies will be told to worry about protecting victims and protecting the innocent, but not to worry about treating criminals equitably. (2) Society might decide that criminals stand inside society and require the same equitable treatment that is afforded victims. Consequently, law enforcement agencies must make an attempt to equalize probabilities of being caught and punished across crimes, groups, and regions.

Our current legal system is halfway between these extremes. It is interested in equalizing the probability of being punished given that the criminal has been caught, but it is not interested in equalizing the probability of being caught. There does not seem to be any logical basis for this distinction. To have one type of equality without the other is to have a façade of equity, but a reality of inequity. Recent Supreme Court rulings protecting the defendant could be completely implemented and our legal system might still favor the white crook over the black crook. They may have very different probabilities of being caught.

Difficult choices between equity and efficiency are inherent in law enforcement. The police are currently making these choices implicitly. The pursuit of efficiency means that the choices must be made explicitly. Perhaps this is the real benefit of systems analysis or cost-benefit analysis. Using it requires someone to set out explicitly a set of equity constraints. Techniques for achieving efficiency are not in any inherent conflict with equity. They are a means of forcing us to achieve both equity and efficiency. From my perspective of having served as an efficiency expert for law enforcement agencies, I would argue that the current interest in police efficiency without a discussion of equity is misplaced, since society has not made enough equity decisions even to begin to be efficient.

B. HIGHER EDUCATION AND THE DISSEMINATION OF INFORMATION

9. Resources for Higher Education: An Economist's View *

THEODORE W. SCHULTZ

It would be convenient, in good grace, and not too difficult to make a strong case for more funds for higher education. Such a case could be made convincing by simply projecting the recent high rate of increase in higher education, with student enrolment and the cost per student continuing to rise, by proclaiming that soon virtually every high school graduate will require some higher education. This would set the stage for universal higher education with the implication that it should become more nearly free to students and would stress the necessity of supporting more quantity and more quality everywhere. Thus, it would seem that there are reasons aplenty for more federal funds, preferably without public control, and for a public package that would finance everybody.

But I would serve you badly by making such a case. The problems here that await solution cannot be treated in so convenient a manner. Even the preliminary task of identifying the problems that matter is a major undertaking. I am attracted to Professor Shackle's (1966) distinction between poetry as a search for beauty and policy as a search for solutions to problems. Our search is for solutions to the problem of financing higher education. Raising money falls on the President, whereas the task of finding beauty is left to students. While bards with beards protest, poets command a low price. University administrators who are successful financiers are scarce and dear.

Although poetry is an art, not all of financing is problem solving; for it seems to be true that it has many of the earmarks of an art, subject to

Reprinted from the *Journal of Political Economy*, May/June, 1968, pp. 327–347, by permission of The University of Chicago Press and the author. Copyright 1968 by The University of Chicago.

* This paper was prepared for a trustees' conference, American Council of Education, Dallas, January 26, 1968. C. E. Bishop, Mary Jean Bowman, Milton Friedman, Zvi Griliches, A. C. Harberger, Lewis C. Solomon, and Finis Welch commented critically on my first draft, and I am indebted to them. I have also profited from a number of comments made by those who attended and participated in the Dallas meeting.

convention and tradition, as is the art of the poet in his use of words. It could be said that reason, theory, and analysis are quite impotent in challenging any of the following propositions: it is better to maintain an old college than to move it to a superior location; it is better to add new university functions than to eliminate those that have become obsolete; it is better to accommodate classes that have become virtually empty than to reallocate faculty to gain efficiency; it is better simply to project past upward trends than to explain them with the view of altering their course for the better; and it is better to obtain additional outside funds than to raise tuitions.

Turning to economic analysis, my plan is to begin with a comment on some of its limitations; then to present a set of propositions and their implications for higher education; and last, to sketch the search for solutions to financing higher education.

I. From Preferences to an Agenda of Economic Problems

Consider first the cultural values that determine the preferences of parents, students, and society for higher education. How they may be changed for the better is beyond the economic calculus; such a reform must rest on cultural and political considerations rather than on economic choices among economic opportunities. Economists start with preferences and build on them, treating them as given. Economists have developed powerful analytical techniques, and they are skilful in using them in specifying and identifying the "revealed preferences" of people. With regard to the technical properties of resources, there are some that are "fixed." They consist of particular "original" resources and their attributes—for example, the physical dimensions and space of the United States and the inherited abilities of students and teachers. Other technical properties are not altogether fixed but nevertheless cannot be altered much in any short period of time—for example, the absolute magnitude of the endowment of human and material capital, including the state of knowledge. At best, this endowment can be enlarged somewhat but it would be in the small, and to this extent economics would have something to say on the worthwhileness of such small changes.

When you ask economists for their agenda of problems pertaining to education, you are asking for additional trouble. Propositions about education that have long been treated as self-evident and settled are placed in doubt. The grand monolithic social value of higher education is seen as many little values, each of which is up against a schedule of marginal costs. There is no free instruction. Thus, one must ask: Is the additional cost worth the additional satisfactions and earnings? Is it worth as much as the value from an equal expenditure in some other private or public activity? If the federal government were prepared to appropriate an additional billion dollars, would society gain as much from allocating it to higher education as it would from using it for the conservation of natural resources, reducing water and air pollution, providing more medical care, slum clearance, or for the reduction of poverty? Would an additional billion dollars reduce the job discrimination against educated Negroes, the rate of economic obsolescence of acquired education, or the inefficiency with which resources are allocated within higher education? Would it improve the career choices of students? Would it reduce the social and economic inequities which presently characterize the personal distribution of resources going into higher education? These are some of the troublesome problems on the economists' agenda.

II. From Propositions to Implications

While altruism is not at the heart of the relationship between education and economics, both gain from an exchange of products. To broaden the exchange, economists are offering some new propositions which should prove useful in planning and in financing education. Of these, there are seven which I shall offer for your consideration. Let me indicate what they are about. Organized education produces an array of different forms of human capital of varying durability. Higher education is engaged in three major types of production activities which entail discovering talent, instruction, and research. But it is not renowned for its gains in the productivity of teachers and students. Educational planning overlooks most of the real costs of higher education because of its omission of the earnings foregone by students. Long-term projections of the demand for higher education are conjectures that undervalue flexibility and overvalue formulas. The advantages of thinking in terms of the rates of return to investment in education and the requirement of efficiency prices in allocating investment resources in accordance with the standard set by the relative rates of return on alternative investment opportunities are strong and clear. There is, however, much confusion with regard to the welfare consequences of higher education, including the consequences of the way in which it is financed and the resulting personal distribution of costs and benefits. I now turn to the meaning of these propositions.

1. Education Is a Form of Human Capital

It is *human* because it becomes a part of man, and it is *capital* because it is a source of future satisfactions, or of future earnings, or both of these. Thus far, however, the concept of human capital has contributed more to economic thinking than it has to the solution of problems in education. In economics, it has become a seminal concept entering into many parts of economic analysis. In international trade, it points to the solution of the Leontief paradox, showing why capital-rich countries nevertheless export goods which are labor intensive; for we discover that labor entering into these goods requires much human capital. The differences among countries in their capital endowments, when both physical and human capital are taken into account and under the assumption of factor-price equalization, go a long way toward explaining the differences in income per worker among them.[1] When considering the international movement of human capital and the growing international markets for particular high skills, the so-called brain drain is straightaway a form of maximizing economic behavior. In internal migration also, human capital is a critical explanatory factor. In solving the long-standing puzzle of the *residual,* where the rate of increase in output exceeds the rate of increase in inputs, it has contributed much. As a part of an all-inclusive concept of capital, advances in specification and measurement of the services of capital explain most of the observable economic growth (Jorgenson and Griliches, 1967). Furthermore, it sets the stage for a generalized theory of capital accumulation in which investment resources are allocated in accordance with the priorities set by the relative rates of return on all material and human investment opportunities (Schultz, 1967*a*).

There are the following particular implications of this proposition for planning and financing higher education: (1) The human capital that is formed by higher education is far from homogeneous. Parts of it are for consumption and parts are for production. Moreover, both the consumer and producer components are of many different types. To lump them in allocating resources to higher education is bad economics. (2) The value of each type of human capital depends on the value of the services it renders and not on its original costs; mistakes in the composition and size of the stock of each type, once made, are sunk investments. (3) The formation of most of these types of capital requires a long horizon because the capabilities that the student acquires are part of him during the rest of his life. (4) The value of the benefits of higher education accruing to students privately consists of future earnings and of future non-pecuniary satisfactions. Although it is difficult to measure the latter, they are nevertheless real and important. (5) Although human capital as such cannot be bought and sold, it is comparatively easy to estimate the value of the producer services of this capital because they are priced in terms of wages and salaries in the labor market. (6) Human capital, like reproducible ma-

---

1. Here I am indebted to Professor Anne O. Krueger, University of Minnesota, for her paper (1967).

terial capital, is subject to obsolescence. The traditional tax treatment of depreciation is outmoded inasmuch as it excludes human capital. Although earnings foregone do not enter into taxable income, none of the direct private costs is treated as capital formation. The upper limit of the life of this capital is the remaining lifespan of individuals after they have completed their formal education. An increase in longevity may decrease the rate of depreciation; earlier retirements may work in the opposite direction. More important is the obsolescence from changes in demand for high skills, changes which are a consequence of the characteristics of our type of economic growth. It should be possible to provide instruction that would be less subject to this type of obsolescence than it is presently. Educational plannings should search for ways and means of improving higher education in this respect by substituting long-life for short-life instructional components so that it can ride better the changing demands for high skills. Continuing education after graduation is a form of maintenance. (7) Capital formation by education sets the stage for thinking of education as an investment.

2. The Three Major Functions of Higher Education are Discovering Talent, Instruction, and Research

Each of these activities requires analysis to determine how efficiently it is organized and whether too few or too many resources are allocated to it. But it must be admitted in all honesty that hard facts and valid inferences pertaining to these issues are about as scarce as they are in the pork-barrel realm of rivers and harbors. What is an efficient organization of each of these three activities in higher education, thinking in terms of scale of organization, specialization, location of colleges and universities, and, importantly, the *complementarity between the discovery of talent, instruction, and research?*

Taking the system of higher education as it is, with regard to instruction, economists have made substantial progress in specifying and identifying the economic value of higher education, as it increases the value productivity of human agents as workers. Less, although some progress, has been made in getting at the economic value of university research. The much neglected activity is that of discovering talent. It, too, can be approached by treating it as a process which provides students with opportunities to discover whether they have the particular capabilities that are required for the type and level of education at which they are working.

The value of the research function has received a lot of puffing but little analysis. It has prestige, but what about performance? With regard to organized agricultural research, where it is a part of land-grant universities, there are some studies with some hard facts. The payoff on this type of research has been very high.[2] But there are no economic studies to my knowledge of other types of organized university research. Is it organized efficiently in terms of combinations of scientific talent, scale of organization, complementarity with Ph.D. research and with other research centers, and division of labor between basic and applied research? Is it for profit or on public account? Despite the importance of these questions and the wide array of experience from which we can learn, scientists are woefully unscientific in the impressionistic answers they give to this question.[3]

The economic value of instruction is appropriately considered under the section on the rate of return.

There are many signs that indicate that one of the strongest features of U.S. higher education is in discovering talent. Although we are far ahead of western Europe in this activity, the payoff to additional resources used for this purpose is still in all probability very high. If so, three implications are worthy of note: (1) relatively more resources should be committed to this activity; (2) resources should be allocated specifically to support it; and (3) the organization and budgets of higher education should be planned to perform this activity efficiently.

3. There Are Few or No Gains in the Measured Productivity of Labor Entering into Higher Education

It follows that if the price of this labor rises and if its productivity remains constant (other things unchanged), the price of the services it renders must rise; that is, the cost of higher education per student must rise. The crude facts, as we observe them, are consistent with this proposition. But these facts do not measure changes in the quality of the educational product which has been rising markedly in many fields. The advance in knowledge is probably the main reason; and here we have a strong clue to the complementarity between instruction and research.

Nor do we know the possibilities of economizing on the labor entering into education by substituting other educational inputs for this labor or by reorganizing the educational process and therby obtaining gains in the productivity of teachers and students in terms of the time they spend teaching and learning. These possibilities are undoubtedly of substantial importance, but it is doubtful that they will be found predominantly in

2. See Schultz (1967*b*).   3. For a thoughtful exception, see Brooks (1967).

new learning machines, television instruction, or in the computerization of educational activities; instead, they are mainly to be had by many small innovative reorganizations of the instructional interplay between teachers and students that will reduce the time spent by each in achieving a given educational product.

The reasons why it is so difficult to make these gains are fairly obvious. The product of teaching and learning is highly labor intensive, like that of barbers. At best, it would appear that there is little room for non-labor inputs. Nor are cheaper inputs the solution, that is, substituting low quality, less costly teachers and students for high quality persons. Although the difficulties here may seem insurmountable, it should be remembered that in classical economics, manufacturing carried the promise of decreasing cost whereas the outlook for agriculture was increasing cost per unit of product. But economic development in Western countries has more than offset the drag of diminishing returns to land in farming, and the gains in labor productivity in agriculture have been exceeding those in manufacturing. Not so long ago, the conventional view was that the retail sector could not gain appreciably from labor-saving developments, but it has in fact made much progress on this score. The present conventional view that the educational sector is destined to continue as it is in the amount of time required of students and teachers may also prove wrong.

The major real problems awaiting solution in higher education in economizing on the time of students and teachers are in large part a consequence of the traditional decision-making process in colleges and universities, the ambiguity which conceals the value of the product that is added, and the lack of strong incentives to innovate. On theoretical grounds there is room for more progress. Decision-making theory is not empty as a guide in improving the traditional process. A theory of the allocation of time (Becker, 1965b), is now at hand for determining how efficiently the time of students is allocated. Requiring college students to spend twenty hours a week in class, as is required of many students, may be anything but efficient. The implication is that we might find fifteen, or ten, or even fewer hours more efficient. But we really will not know what could be achieved by such innovations until we have undertaken carefully planned experiments to discover what the results would be. The specifications of the value added to the capabilities of students by the educational process are being clarified, for example, in the search for a better mix of instructional components which would have a longer life than the present mix.

4. Earnings Foregone by Students Are Well Over Half of the Real Costs of the Human Capital Formation

In 1959–60, U.S. "direct" expenditures for higher education minus auxiliary enterprises and capital outlay plus implicit interest and depreciation of physical property came to about $4,350 million, but the earnings foregone by college and university students exceeded this figure. Yet we omit these earnings foregone in our planning and financing approach to higher education. We keep them concealed by not entering them in our college and university plans or in our national income and capital formation accounts. The omission of these earnings foregone by students seriously distorts our view of the economics of higher education. Let me turn to the major implications of this omission of earnings foregone: (1) higher education (leaving university research aside) is more than twice as costly as is revealed in our budgets; (2) it is simply impossible to plan efficiently when over half of the real costs are treated as "free" resources; (3) there is no incentive to economize on the time of students in educationing planning under existing circumstances; (4) educational planners receive no signals that the value of the time of students is rising relative to material inputs; (5) the rate of return to investment in higher education is grossly overestimated when earnings foregone are omitted; (6) so-called free education is far from free to students and their parents, which in turn implies that many families with low incomes cannot afford to forego the earnings of their children; and (7) savings, investment, and capital formation are all substantially understated in terms of national accounting.[4]

5. Long-Term Projections of the Demand for Higher Education Are Beset with All Manner of Uncertainty

These projections are conjectures that can be very misleading. As a consequence, flexibility is undervalued and formulas are overvalued in educational planning. Economic logic tells us that in coping with uncertainty it is necessary to remain sufficiently flexible so that one can act efficiently when new and better information becomes available. But such flexibility is not costless; thus, the prospective additional gains from flexibility must be reckoned against the additional costs. Furthermore, to the extent that these projections can be made more reliable, the need for and cost of acquiring flexibility can be reduced.

The now available projections of the demands for higher education can

4. See the excellent treatment of these issues by Simon Kuznets (1965), pp. 228–34.

be substantially improved. What we have are numbers which are not a reliable source of information. The concept of demand for education
requires clarification; as it is presently used, it is beset with ambiguity.
So-called need is not demand, because the concept of demand implies
prices and quantities. But the relevant prices, whether they are shadow
prices or actual prices, are not specified in the numbers which are being
projected. The demand behavior of students for places in colleges and
universities is a useful approach. Another approach is to determine the
demands for the particular capabilities that come from the teaching and
learning in higher education—demands that are derived from the production activity of the economy. But it is unfortunately true that there is as
yet no satisfactory theory which connects ex post rates of increase in the
demands for the satisfactions and earnings that accrue to college and university students with future rates of increase in these demands. Projections, of course, abound, but they are in principle as naïve as exponential
population projections. You can take your choice, and if you happen to
be correct, it will not be because of reason but because of luck.
Manpower studies do not provide the answer, nor are the sophisticated
programming models as yet providing an answer.

The rise in income per family undoubtedly increases the demand for
the consumer satisfactions from higher education; the income elasticity of
the demand for this consumer component is probably such that it is a superior good with a fairly high elasticity. But the demand for the producer
component is very hard to determine because it is derived from the production activity of the economy and because the sources of change in
these derived demands over time are still far from clear. Furthermore, the
observable responses of students to the array of different prices that
students pay for higher education are confounded by all manner of pricing
policies and changes in these policies over time.

The lessons to be drawn from all of this are as follows: (1) The game
of numbers as it is now played produces unreliable projections of the
demand for higher education. (2) Some improvements can be achieved by
clarifying and analyzing the economic demands in terms of the factors
that determine changes in these demands. (3) But this approach is also
severely limited because as yet there is no economic theory for determining the changes in the demands for higher education that are derived from
our type of economic growth. (4) At best, any long-term projections of
the demands for higher education are subject to many unknowns and to
much uncertainty. (5) To be prepared to cope with these, it is the better
part of wisdom to pay the price of developing flexibility in the institutional structure of higher education and also within colleges and universities so that they will be capable of adapting their activities to new infor-

mation, with regard to demands, as it becomes available. (6) Fixed formulas, like the parity formula in agriculture, lead to inflexibility, and, over time, to serious distortions, and they should therefore be avoided in planning and financing higher education.

6. Seeing That Education Is an Investment in Human Capital, the Central Economic Concept in Planning and Financing It Should Be the Rate of Return to Investment [5]

The advantages of this concept are that it has a firm foundation in economic theory, that it is applicable to both private and public allocative decisions, that in practical economic affairs it is widely used and understood, and that it leads to efficient allocations when all investments are made in accordance with the priorities set by the relative rates of return on alternative investment opportunities. Although it is difficult to use this concept as an allocative guide in view of the way in which education is organized, it is the economist's key in solving the problem of allocating resources; the solution is in equalizing the rates by always allocating investment resources in favor of the highest rate of return.

The practical difficulties in using this concept in education are predominantly consequences of a type of organization which is not designed to provide most of the necessary information and which lacks strong incentives to use the available information. Consider the cost of college and university instruction: earnings foregone by students, which are well over half of the real cost, are concealed; the depreciation and the rate of interest on the investment in buildings used for classrooms, laboratories, offices, and libraries are also as a rule concealed; the cost of university research and of discovering talent is rarely identified and separated from the cost of instruction. It is also true that the price that the student pays for educational services is only remotely related to the real cost of producing them, and therefore private choices by students, however efficient they are privately, are not necessarily efficient socially. Nor can the allocation of public funds to higher education be made socially efficient under circumstances where information on cost is so inadequate. Consider also the returns that accrue to students and society from these educational services: the organization of higher education provides little or no economic information on returns, pecuniary and non-pecuniary, to guide students in making their career choices—not even the starting salaries of college graduates; foundation and public subsidies are accepted and awarded to students to get them to enter particular fields without regard to the depressing effects of the increase in supply that is thereby induced

5. For a more extended treatment of this approach, see Schultz (1967a).

upon the lifetime earnings of those who are and will be in these fields; there is inadequate information on the effects upon returns of differences in innate ability of students, in their motivations, and of the differences in the effectiveness of college teaching; although these returns are subject to uncertainty, it is not a unique, distinguishing mark, because other investments are also subject to uncertainty. In general, colleges and universities and public bodies that provide funds are poorly organized to provide the necessary information on cost and returns or to use whatever information is available.

Meanwhile, economists, who have taken a hand in estimating the returns to education, have made substantial progress.[6] These estimates and those pertaining to cost have reached the stage where they are becoming useful allocative guides. But so far, the returns from the non-pecuniary satisfactions that accrue to students have not been reckoned. Nor are the estimates of social returns in good repair.

Turning back to the rate of return as the central concept, the alternative investment opportunities are of course numerous, not only between human and material capital but within each of these two sets. Is there evidence that private educational choices are privately efficient; that is, do private rates of return on education tend (1) to be equal among educational options and (2) to be comparable to private rates of return on other private investments? The evidence implies inefficiencies. To illustrate, consider the available estimates on alternatives within education: In terms of equalizing the rates of return, elementary and secondary schooling appear to have priority. All of the estimates with which I am familiar show the highest private rates of return to elementary schooling. (A word of caution—estimates of foregone earnings are probably somewhat too high for college students in light of new evidence which shows an increasing proportion of college students employed part time while attending college; and, for students in their last two or three years of elementary school, there probably are some earnings foregone which have not been reckoned in the estimates of private rates of return.) We need to remind ourselves that there are still some children who are not completing the elementary grades; and what is more important is the underinvestment in the quality of elementary schooling, especially in many rural areas.[7] While the private rate of return on the investment resources entering into high school education is not as high as that on elementary schooling, it nevertheless appears to be about twice as high as that indicated for private investment in completing college. In Table 1, the private rates of return

6. See especially Becker (1964a) and Hanoch (1965).
7. See Schultz (1964), pp. 12–34, and Welch (1966).

to white males after personal taxes, in 1958, are 28 per cent for high school graduates and 14.8 per cent for college graduates. Thus, in allocating resources within education with a view to equalizing the rates of return, the implication is that elementary and secondary schooling appears to be subject to underinvestment relative to higher education. Nevertheless, comparing columns (2) and (4) in Table 1, the private rates of return to white male college graduates after personal taxes, without any allowance for the private satisfactions that accrue to students, are on a par with the private implicit rates of return to material capital *before personal taxes* on the income from this capital.

Table 1. Estimates of private rates of return, United States

Year	High school graduates: white males after personal taxes (%) * (1)	College graduates: white males after personal taxes (%) * (2)	Corporate manufacturing firms after profit taxes but before personal taxes (%) † (3)	U.S. private domestic economy: implicit rate of return after profit taxes but before personal taxes (%) ‡ (4)
1939	16	14.5		...
1949	20	13.+	7.0	12.6
1956	25	12.4	(for	14.4 (1955–56)
1958	28	14.8	period	12.3 (1957–58)
1959	Slightly higher than in 1958		1947–57)	9.7
1961	Slightly higher than in 1958			11.2 (1960–61)
1963–65	...	...		13.3

* From Becker (1964*a*), p. 128.
† Also from Becker (1964*a*), in which he draws on a study by G. J. Stigler (see p. 115 and n. 2).
‡ From Jorgenson and Griliches (1967), p. 268.

7. Education Changes the Distribution of Personal Income

The general extension of education and the additional earnings from these forms of human capital have probably been a major factor during recent decades in changing the distribution of personal income. Not only has the supply of educational opportunities increased markedly over time, but the inequality in the differences in the supply of these opportunities has been reduced, without doubt, in elementary and secondary schooling. The differences in the innate capacity of individuals to benefit from investment in education probably remains unchanged for the population as a whole, but the distribution of this capacity of those attending college changes over time as the proportion of individuals of particular age classes attending college increases. A recent study by Becker, to which I shall refer again shortly, treats human capital as the key to a theory of the distribution of personal income.

Higher education is certainly *not neutral* in its personal income distribution effects; some individuals and families undoubtedly gain future income streams partly at the expense of others. Whether it is, in general, regressive or progressive depends on the distribution of the personal costs and personal benefits of higher education. There are many opinions but few hard facts on this issue.[8]

In clarifying public policy choices, it is necessary to distinguish between the objective of economic efficiency and that of reducing the inequality in the distribution of personal income. There are circumstances when a particular policy will advance the economy toward both objectives; for example, when there is excessive unemployment, a fiscal-monetary policy that reduces such unemployment would normally contribute to both objectives. Similarly, when there is an underinvestment in elementary schooling (that is, a high rate of return to additional investment in such schooling) a policy to invest more in universal elementary schooling of high quality contributes both to economic efficiency and to reducing the inequality in personal income. But under other circumstances, the attainment of one of these objectives is in part at the expense of the other. At this point, the rating of social values underlying such policy choices enters.

I assume that it is not necessary to belabor the fact that economic efficiency rates high among the social values of our society.[9] This assumption is implicit in my formulation of the six propositions already considered; the principal implications derived from them all pertain to economic efficiency. But how high a social value does our society place on reducing the inequality in personal income? The rating of this social value is not so clear as that which is socially assigned to economic efficiency. Nevertheless, there are strong indications that it also is an important social value. I shall proceed on the assumption that there is a social preference for less inequality in the distribution of personal income than that which prevails presently. Moreover, I shall assume that this social preference is such that society is prepared, should it be necessary, to forego some economic efficiency to bring about somewhat less inequality in the distribution of personal income. Proceeding on this assumption, it becomes relevant and important to determine what the income distribution effects of higher education are, and how they can be altered for the better at the least cost in terms of allocative efficiency.

Although higher education is in all probability far from neutral in its

8. For a general approach to the many factors entering here, see Bowman and Anderson (1966), pp. 177–214.
9. See Macfie (1943).

effects on the distribution of personal income, it is surprising how little is actually known about these effects. It could be that the financing of higher education is in general quite regressive. It is plausible that it is regressive because it adds to the value of the human capital of those who attend college relative to those who do not go to college, because it increases the lifetime earnings of college graduates in part at the expense of others, and closely related, because higher education provides educational services predominately for students from middle and upper income families and a part of the cost of these educational services is paid for by taxes on poor families. It appears to be true that a much smaller proportion of the undergraduate students in publicly financed institutions receive financial aid for reasons of their having inadequate income than do undergraduate students in private colleges and universities. In either case, the financing is such that substantial amounts of valuable assets are being transferred by society to a particular intellectually elite set of individuals.

In retrospect, given the type of growth that has characterized our economy and the remarkable increase in the stock of education per worker in the labor force, the gains in elementary and secondary schooling and in higher education taken as a whole have been instrumental, it seems to me, in reducing the inequality in the distribution of personal income. The hypothesis which I proposed some time back (Schultz, 1962) with regard to this issue continues to be consistent with the evidence thus far available. In terms of the income effects of additional education per worker, this hypothesis is: The rise in the investment in education relative to that invested in non-human capital increases total earnings relative to total property income, and property income is distributed much less equally than the earnings of persons from labor. Therefore, investment in schooling reduces the inequality in the distribution of personal income. The hypothesis proposed here is that these patterns of investment are an important part of the explanation of the observed reductions in the inequality of distribution of personal income.

Becker and Chiswick have been analyzing the effects of schooling on the distribution of personal income. For adult white males and for the states within the United States, they report that "about one-third of the differences in inequality between states is directly explained by schooling, one-third directly by the residual, and the remaining one-third by both together through the positive correlation between them (Becker and Chiswick, 1966).

In a more recent report, Chiswick gives the following results from his analysis of North-South differences: "The education component . . . can 'explain' half of the North-South differences in income inequality. The proportion is slightly lower for white males and slightly higher for all males" (Chiswick, 1967, p. 35).

But neither the hypothesis which I have advanced nor the evidence on the income effects of schooling from Becker and Chiswick implies that the income effects of higher education per se are progressive rather than regressive. It is indeed regrettable that studies to determine what these income effects are have not been undertaken.

In developing an analytical approach bringing economic theory to bear on the effects of human capital on the distribution of personal income, the recent pioneering work of Becker (1967) is full of promise. His distinction between the "egalitarian" and "elite" views is helpful in clarifying the problem. He identifies the egalitarian view with supply conditions; the objective is to reduce the inequality in the differences in the supply of educational opportunities. The elite view, on the other hand, turns on the demand conditions; the actual investment and earning differences are primarily a consequence of differences in the capacity of individuals to benefit from investment in education and from other forms of human capital. What Becker's analytical approach will show when it is applied to higher education is still in the realm of unfinished business.

III. Searching for Solutions

My list of problems that await solution is indicated by the implications that have been derived from the preceding propositions. Although it is a long list, it consists of two major parts in terms of economic logic. The first part pertains to resources for higher education allocated in accordance with the test of economic efficiency; the second part pertains to allocations that reduce the inequality in the distribution of personal income. Rest assured, I shall not present a national budget for higher education all properly allocated. I shall try, however, to clarify some of the organizational changes that would strengthen the tendency toward a more efficient allocation of resources in the area of higher education.

The purpose of the organizational changes on which I shall concentrate is to improve the possibilities of making optimum allocative decisions pertaining to higher education. The substantive changes relate to economic incentives and information. The decisions that are dependent on these incentives and the state of information consist of economic decisions by students, college and university administrators, and public (social) bodies. The ideal from an economist's point of view is a form of organization that would assure the necessary incentives coupled with optimum information in allocating investment resources to higher education in accordance with the relative rates of return on alternative investment opportunities, an organization in which the rate of return is functionally the price at the intercept of the supply of education services and the demand for them.

But, in making these organizational changes, it will be important not to lose sight of the advantages of the existing organization of higher education that are consistent with this ideal. Among them are: (1) in terms of career choices, higher education in the United States offers students many options; (2) in discovering talent, it has in all probability no equal; (3) the process of admitting many students who do not graduate is not necessarily wasteful, especially when they can readily enter the labor force; (4) there is substantial economic complementarity between discovering talent and instruction and between research and instruction, despite the common view to the contrary; (5) although it is obvious that colleges and universities tend to serve an elite, measured in terms of intellectual capacity to benefit, they provide places for a much larger proportion of college-age youth than is traditionally served, for example, in western Europe; (6) no college or university has a monopoly of the supply of these educational services, and, on the contrary, there are many more institutions than would be necessary to assure competition if it were strictly a business sector; (7) as suppliers of these services, colleges and universities show some tendency to adjust to changes in demand, although this tendency could be substantially strengthened; (8) last, and very important, there is much more economic competition within higher education and between it and other sectors of the economy than meets the eye. Colleges and universities purchase virtually all of their instructional inputs in competitive markets. Most of the budget is for faculty, and the job market for their services in this country is actively competitive among colleges and universities and between them and government. Business, too, bids for many of these skills. The range in salaries is subject to some constraints, partly corrected by adjustments in work arrangements. The earnings foregone by students are also determined in a competitive job market. Surely it would be shortsighted to overlook or impair these advantages in our quest to improve the possibilities of making optimum allocative decisions.

How, then, can we strengthen the tendency toward a more efficient allocation of resources? The required changes in organization to achieve this objective are fundamentally of two parts, namely, better economic incentives and better information for those who make the allocative decisions.

But who should make these allocative decisions? Who is best qualified? There are those who contend that students and their families are best qualified. To support this contention, they appeal to consumer sovereignty and to private self-interest for privately efficient investment in education. Others contend that there are external economies or social benefits that accrue not to the student but to others in society and that these decisions can best be made by public or other social bodies. Those who know and administer the affairs of our colleges and universities see the importance of academic entrepreneurship in managing this complex set of activities, and it can be argued that they are best qualified.

How much truth is there in each of these contentions? Is it all with one and none in the others?

1. On Behalf of Student Sovereignty

The key to student sovereignty is the private self-interest of students, which provides the necessary economic rationale. Student self-interest is also sufficient to bring about an efficient allocation of investment resources to education under the following conditions: (1) competition in producing educational services along with efficient prices of these services, (2) students acquiring optimal information, (3) an efficient capital market serving students, and (4) no social benefits (losses) from higher education.

A clear view of the gains to be had from hitching higher education to the private self-interest of students is blurred by arguments about the underlying conditions. But surely competitive pricing of educational services is in the realm of possibilities. Student loans from public and private sources can be devised to supply the necessary capital. How to reckon the social benefits (losses) of higher education is much more difficult. But if student sovereignty has an Achilles' heel, it is in the domain of information, a long-standing controversial issue as unsettled today as it was when classical economists divided on this issue.[10]

In enlarging the scope and improving the performance of student sovereignty in allocating resources to higher education, the gaps in information and the distortions in incentives really matter. On earnings foregone, students are well informed, but on their capabilities as students they are in doubt. With regard to the benefits that will accrue to them, the state of information is far from optimum. But much worse still is the lack of information on the differences in the quality of the educational services of different colleges and universities. Nowhere are students confronted by prices for these services that are equal to the real cost of producing them, and therefore the prices to which they respond are not efficient prices. As a consequence, no matter how efficient students are privately in their decisions, from the point of view of the economy as a whole, the allocation of resources to higher education will not be efficient.

10. See E. G. West (1964).

2. On Reckoning Social Benefits (Losses)

When this box is opened, we are in trouble. There is so little agreement on what this box contains. It is hard to distinguish between fact and fiction because the task of specifying and measuring these benefits has been grossly neglected. No wonder that claims and counterclaims are the order of the day. Most of us have a vested interest in higher education which is hard on objectivity. We are prone to lay claim to most of the advances in knowledge from which social benefits are undoubtedly large. University research and instruction are as a rule joint products; at the Ph.D. level, graduate instruction and research are highly complementary. Are there identifiable social benefits from instruction that do not accrue to the college student from his private investment in education? It is plausible that having neighbors who are educated gives a family with such neighbors some positive satisfactions. It is also plausible that having co-workers who are educated is a source of additional satisfactions. It has been argued that parts of our public administration, namely, individuals coping with our "income tax forms," give rise to an administrative social benefit. But it is also plausible that the private benefits of education accruing to college students leave some other persons worse off. It is argued that some elementary school teachers *favor* the children from homes with (college) educated parents and that this favoritism leaves other children worse off. It is also alleged that in buying and selling homes some educated families act to exclude uneducated families from acquiring property (homes) in their particular neighborhoods.

But it is all too convenient to engage in double counting. Education, no doubt, increases the mobility of a labor force, but the benefits in moving to take advantage of better job opportunities are predominately, if not wholly, private benefits. Educated labor has access to more of the relevant economic information than uneducated labor; but here, too, the benefits from this advantage presumably accrue to the persons who have the education. The cultural component embodied in higher education is the source of another benefit which invites double counting. There is also a tendency to claim that higher education makes for better citizens and for a better political democracy. It could be, but our belief with respect to these benefits is a matter of faith. It is not obvious that the political self-interest of college graduates results either in more responsible citizenship or in a more perfect government than the self-interest, say, of high school graduates.

To the extent that there are benefits that accrue to persons other than to the student acquiring the education, there could be underinvestment in higher education, regardless of how efficient students are privately in their investment in education. But there is an important set here that does not qualify, namely, those benefits accruing to the student that make the private investment at least as good an investment in terms of the rate of return as that on alternative investment opportunities. Under these circumstances, presumably, privately efficient investment by students would suffice to bring forth the required education and assure whatever benefits might accrue to others, as was true in the case of Henry Ford and his very profitable Model T.

Suppose, however, that there are some potential college students who would not benefit enough privately to warrant the investment privately and that there were some social benefits which were sufficient when added to the benefits accruing to the student privately to raise the (social) rate of return sufficiently to make it a good investment, by the standard set by the priorities of the relative rates of return on alternative investment opportunities—then, under these circumstances, some underinvestment in higher education at the margin would be implied.

It follows, of course, that if there were no such social benefits, this bit of economic logic would be wholly empty. Thus, we are back to a question of fact—namely, are there in fact any such benefits that can be identified and that are subject to measurement?

3. On Academic Entrepreneurship

In terms of managerial decisions, the complexity of the modern university places an extraordinary burden on its administrators. But by what economic test are their decisions to be judged? The market test is severely circumscribed by the constraints placed on student sovereignty. Endowment income, private gifts, and public funds confound any economic test of an efficient allocation of resources. Innovation should be rewarded, but where are the incentives to innovate? Surely under the dynamic conditions that now characterize higher education, academic entrepreneurship should be given a vastly better opportunity than is presently possible to allocate resources efficiently.

These observations with respect to student sovereignty, social benefits, and academic entrepreneurship would appear to lend support to the following organizational changes in higher education.

With Respect to the Private-Decision Domain of Students

In providing economic incentives that would be allocatively efficient, the ideal price to students for the educational services they acquire should be neither more nor less than the real cost of producing these services. But much of the argument on the differences between private and public tuitions is beside the point. Equalization of tuitions would merely replace one type of price distortion by another type because of the marked differences in the quality and real cost of the educational services that colleges and universities supply.

This important organizational change implies, however, several complements: (1) that there be developed a capital market that would provide funds to students so they could invest in themselves, which would call for large increases in funds for public loans to students in view of the limitations of the private capital market, (2) that a program of private and public subsidies would be required to finance those, and only those, qualified students who for welfare or social-efficiency reasons should attend college but who privately would not enrol, even if there were student loans, and (3) that although the improvement in information that is implicit in the change in pricing set forth above would be very substantial, much more would have to be spent in moving to an optimum in producing and distributing the other types of information already referred to.

On the Social Benefits of Higher Education

In producing these education services, the required organizational changes pertaining to incentives and information are not easy to determine. Consider the problem that arises in planning and financing these components so that public and social bodies would become efficient in allocating investment resources for these purposes: what are the pertinent educational activities that render social benefits? University research is in substantial part one of them. So is a part of the activity pertaining to the discovery of talent. Let me elaborate briefly on why this may be true. My conception of the cost and returns pertaining to the *discovery of talent* could qualify here. There are many colleges that admit at least two freshmen for every one who will survive to graduation. If these colleges charged full costs, I would assume that this ratio of entering freshmen to graduating seniors would decline sharply—and suppose then that for every ten freshmen, nine could graduate. Presently, the half of entering freshmen who discover that they lack the capabilities and motivation to complete college drop out and enter the labor market, benefiting sufficiently from the year or more they spent in college to have made their private investment in that amount of college work a good investment privately, although when the subsidy entering into their instruction is taken into account, it was in itself a poor investment. But suppose now that out of the entering freshmen who would not have sought admission at full costs there were a substantial number of students (say, a tenth of the seniors who complete college) who did not know they had the necessary capabilities. These discovered students could (should) pay full cost; but they would not have become college educated had it not been for the extra cost of the discovery process. It would be a matter for public policy to decide whether this extra cost was worthwhile. A part of instruction may also belong here; but the instruction that accrues wholly to the benefit of students is excluded. It must be admitted that it is exceedingly difficult to specify the particular types of information and the nature of the incentives that would prove strong and clear in attaining these purposes. Here we have one of the major unsolved problems in planning and financing higher education.

College and University Administrators

Academic entrepreneurship can be made much less frustrating and at the same time much more efficient once the private decision-making domain of students is made subject to the constraints of a pricing policy, complemented by adequate student loans and by subsidies to attain the particular welfare and social-efficiency purposes set forth above. But more than this would be required in terms of information and incentives. The value of the time of students would have to enter; it is, however, easy to measure, using earnings foregone. The value of faculty time is also readily available information, in view of the open market competition for their services; but the internal organization of colleges and universities is anything but efficient in allocating their services within the institution. The most important informational component that is lacking is the *value added* by the instruction, by research, and by the activity which I have called "discovering talent." But if we put our minds to it, I am sure we could do a good deal in determining the amount of value added by each of the different activities and proceed from there to internal organizational changes that would provide incentives to take advantage of such information in our academic entrepreneurial and management endeavors.

References

Becker, Gary S. "Human Capital and the Personal Distribution of Income: An Analytical Approach" (W. S. Woytinsky Lecture No. 1). Ann Arbor: Univ. Mich., 1967.

——. *Human Capital*. New York: Columbia Univ. Press, 1964. (a)

——. "A Theory of the Allocation of Time," *Econ. J.*, LXXV (September, 1965), 493–517. (b)

Becker, Gary S., and Chiswick, Barry R. "Education and the Distribution of Income," *A.E.R.*, LVI (May, 1966), 368.

Bowman, Mary Jean, and Anderson, C. Arnold. "Distributional Effects of Educational Problems," in *Income Distribution Analysis*. Raleigh: N.C. State Univ., 1966.

Brooks, Harvey. "Can Science Be Planned?" in *Problems of Science Policy: Seminar at Jouy-en-Josas on Science*. Paris: Organization Econ. Cooperation and Development, 1967.

Chiswick, Barry R. "Human Capital and the Distribution of Personal Income by Regions." Ph.D. dissertation, Columbia Univ., New York, 1967.

Hanoch, Giora. "Personal Earnings and Investment in Schooling." Ph.D. dissertation, Univ. Chicago, 1965.

Jorgenson, D. W., and Griliches, Z. "The Explanation of Productivity Change," *Rev. Econ. Studies*, XXXIV (July, 1967), 249–83.

Krueger, Anne O. "Factor Endowments and Per Capita Income Differences among Countries." Unpublished MS, Dept. Econ., Univ. Minn., 1967.

Kuznets, Simon. *Modern Economic Growth*. New Haven, Conn.: Yale Univ. Press, 1965.

Macfie, A. L. *Economic Efficiency and Social Welfare*. London: Oxford Univ. Press, 1943.

Schultz, Theodore W. "Reflections on Investment in Man," *J.P.E.*, LXX (Part II, Suppl.; October, 1962), p. 2.

——. "Underinvestment in the Quality of Schooling: The Rural Farm Areas," in *Increasing Understanding of Public Problems and Policies*. Chicago: Farm Found., 1964.

——. "The Rate of Return in Allocating Investment Resources to Education," *J. Human Resources*, II (Summer, 1967), 293–309. (*a*)

——. "World Agriculture in Relation to Population, Science, Economic Disequilibrium and Income Inequality: Reflections and Unsettled Questions," Part II. Unpublished paper presented at International Association of Agricultural Economists, Sydney, Australia, August, 1967. (*b*)

Shackle, G. L. S. "Policy, Poetry and Success," *Econ. J.*, Vol. LXXVI (December, 1966).

Welch, Finis. "The Determinants of the Return to Schooling in Rural Farm Areas, 1959." Ph.D. dissertation, Univ. Chicago, 1966.

West, E. G. "Private versus Public Education," *J.P.E.*, LXXII (October, 1964), 465–75.

10. The University and the Price System

ROBERT D. TOLLISON and THOMAS D. WILLETT

There is little disagreement that the higher education industry in the United States is facing a financial crisis of considerable proportion. Virtually no institution is immune. Even heavily endowed Harvard University ran its first deficit ($-$ \$760,000) since World War II during 1969–70. While most universities have survived by cutting expenditures, many smaller institutions have been forced to close. For example, the State of

Reprinted from the *Journal of Economics and Business*, 25 (Spring–Summer 1973), pp. 191–197, by permission of the publisher.

North Dakota recently offered for sale the Ellendale Branch of the University of North Dakota. The institutions that remain open are necessarily searching for ways to resolve their financial difficulties. Examples of less drastic solutions are abundant. Hiram Scott College recently dismissed almost one-third of its faculty members in an attempt to keep the school open. Columbia University recently announced that its graduate program in linguistics would be phased out. Several schools (e.g., NYU) have made major cuts in their athletic programs.

The current financial crisis does not mean that the existence of higher education in America is in serious danger, or even that it will be radically reduced in size relative to other sectors of the economy. A crisis literally means a turning point after which things will not be the same again. With respect to the size of higher education, it is the rapid expansion of past years that will no longer be the same. The current economic conditions of the industry, rapidly increasing costs, and a slackening in the rate of growth of demand are of necessity forcing both the universities and the public to reexamine the traditional methods of financing higher education in the United States. The outcome of such reexamination may well lead to a restructuring of pricing and financing policies which will be of much greater importance for the quality and efficiency of higher education in the United States than is the decline or cessation of the growth of the size of the industry. While all of the possible alternatives cannot be discussed, several aspects of the proposals made by a number of economists will be considered for full-cost pricing of the outputs to higher education and the greater use of markets to organize activities in higher education.[1]

The Logic of Full-Cost Pricing

The basic rationale for full-cost pricing of higher education (combined with government provision of ample loan funds to students who do not have access to competitive loan terms in the private market) is that in

---

1. A variety of statements of this argument are found in Alchian [1; 2], Alchian and Allen [3; 4], Buchanan and Devletoglou [5], Friedman [11], and Mishan [15]. An excellent discussion of the differential pricing of the various outputs of colleges and universities and the relationships of such a pricing system to subsidies for basic research in educational institutions appears in Kaysen [14]. Also of interest in this area is [19]. Finally, see the papers in the special issue of the *Journal of Political Economy: Investment in Education: The Equity-Efficiency Quandary* (May-June 1972).

We should also clarify here that tuition and fees are not the only costs associated with undergraduate education. Foregone earnings and related costs may account for more than half of the total costs of private undergraduate education. Since the demand for undergraduate education is a derived demand (i.e., it is valued as a factor of production and not in and of itself), the level of the nontuition costs will affect the derived demand for educational outputs.

most areas of higher education the private rate of return to student investors appears to be sufficiently high to provide adequate incentives for
socially optimal levels of demand for education, if student investors have
access to loan funds on reasonable terms.[2] The major public commitment
to financing undergraduate higher education would be the provision of a
stock of loan funds to supplement the financing available from the private
market.[3] Initial loans would be repaid over time out of the higher earnings of graduates, and, hence, be available for relending to a later generation of students.

As it is frequently presented, the logic of the full-cost pricing argument
is not fully developed. Full-cost pricing of university education is typically conceived as an average cost fee to be charged to all students at a
given school.[4] Tuition would be higher under this scheme than it is currently, but it would remain, as under the present practice, a standard fee
faced by all undergraduate students. (Traditionally distinctions are made
only between graduate and undergraduate fees.)

This pricing procedure ignores relative cost and demand differences for
activities within the university. A course in high-energy physics, for example, is relatively more costly to offer per student than a classics course
under current pedagogical practices in these fields. Likewise, a lecture
course for 500 students is less expensive than 20 courses for 25 students
each. Substantial cost differences between courses and departments may
result from the types of facilities required (laboratories and equipment,
for instance), the number of students in the class, and salaries of instruc-
tors (or costs of tapes). There are also differences in demand for courses,
reflecting primarily differing student tastes among courses and also differing student incomes (e.g., wealthier students may demand more polo
courses), and the price of any close substitutable or complementary
courses offered in the university. Under these conditions a standard, full-
cost tuition price would in effect charge the classics student for part of the

2. The evidence that there are significant external benefits to justify public support of undergraduate education in general is not strong. See Hansen [12].
3. This discussion is primarily about the undergraduate output of the higher education industry at this point. It is suspected that graduate professional education would be subject to
the same general analysis. However, graduate education and the basic research output of the
industry may call for public support in some form in the full-cost pricing university since
relevant external benefits may exist from these activities if they are left entirely to private
action. The financing of some other outputs of the university is discussed in the next section.
4. Two exceptions are Daniere [7] and Cartter [6]. Cartter discusses the inefficiencies of
having only a single price for the whole educational purchase but does not go on to advocate
greater use of the price system. Further discussion of the use of differential prices in universities appears in [22].

cost of the education of the physicist. In effect, a standard, full-cost fee would redistribute welfare from students in low-cost disciplines to students in high-cost disciplines and from students with a heavy mix of lectures to students with a heavy mix of seminars. To be consistent, the full-cost pricing argument should imply that the university employ a differential pricing system for each different activity within the university. Otherwise, students in the relatively costly areas of university education still do not pay their way, and the pricing mechanism does not serve its functions of allocation and calling forth production to the degree possible within the university. It would appear that charging a single, standard fee for quite varied educational packages is neither efficient nor equitable. The equity aspect of cost-based pricing is discussed later.

Marginal cost pricing should invoke significant changes in the way undergraduate teaching services are supplied. For example, the use of lectures as the primary method for dispensing knowledge in the university originated during a period in which the production of books was by hand. Hence, there was a strong case for lectures, even where they merely fulfilled the often quoted function of directly transferring information from the lecturer's notes to the students' tablets without passing through the students' minds. In the modern university this pattern of teaching has not changed radically even though underlying costs of books versus lectures has obviously changed tremendously and new alternatives have been made available by advancing technology. Perhaps one of the reasons for this unchanged pattern of teaching is the absence of differential prices for undergraduate offerings. The introduction of cost-based pricing would spur universities to seek more efficient approaches to teaching, especially of large undergraduate courses.

As noted above, the concern here is about applying the logic of full-cost pricing to the supply of undergraduate education. Such pricing policies need not be limited to the undergraduate classroom. Other areas that immediately come to mind are athletics and computer services [20]. At Cornell University ice hockey is a very popular sport. The team usually wins the Ivy title and less often, but fairly frequently, wins the NCAA title. Tickets are in high demand, and evidences of a shortage in the market for ice hockey tickets are abundant. How does Cornell price hockey tickets? One would think this could be a potentially lucrative source of income for the university to shore up its operating deficit. Unfortunately, the story does not run this way. Each fall the tickets are allocated to those students, faculty, and townspeople who are able to stand in line for the longest periods of time (for faculty and townspeople overnight, for the students over several days and nights). Simple economic analysis would suggest higher prices to ration the fixed number of tickets, but this response has not been forthcoming from the university.[5]

It would be administratively infeasible for each activity or class within the university to be priced according to relative cost. There is a trade-off between the gains from proper pricing and the administrative and nuisance costs of keeping track of and collecting varying fees. There seems little doubt that an optimum compromise would display more extensive usage of differential pricing in our colleges and universities than is common today. The appropriate extent of differential pricing would no doubt have to be determined by trial and error, but advocates of full-cost tuition should recognize that some differential pricing is required if students are to pay for the full cost of their respective educational investments.[6]

The introduction of full-cost pricing in higher education might help to increase the degree of competitiveness among universities. Many cartel-type arrangements (e.g., standardization of entrance requirements), which serve to inhibit competition among schools, exist under the present financing system of higher education where student-consumers do not bear the full costs and have less incentive to shop around for the most efficiently supplied educational consumption bundle that they desire and can afford.[7] The introduction of full-cost pricing to higher education, especially in terms of the greater use of marginal-cost pricing, would increase competition in the university sector as student-consumers were provided with additional information about their planned consumption choices.[8] Static gains of greater efficiency in the allocation of existing resources in higher education and dynamic gains such as greater innovation and entry into (and exit from) the industry would be forthcoming.

5. From the point of view of utility-maximizing university administrators, underpricing popular athletic events may be rational even though it conflicts with general economic efficiency. We will not speculate here on the motives that may lead to this result. The interested reader is referred to A. A. Alchain and W. R. Allen's treatment of the allocation of Rose Bowl tickets in [3].

6. A theoretical point that needs to be cleared up is the link between university total revenue and marginal cost pricing procedure. In other words, would an administratively optimal set of differential prices yield enough revenue to the university to cover its costs? The answer is most likely yes because over the relevant range of outputs produced in the various university activities there are probably roughly constant returns to scale so that by charging long-run marginal costs (i.e., incremental capital costs) revenue would cover costs.

7. See Buchanan and Devletoglou [5] for discussions of this point. These authors in general do not feel that the present university system exhibits a great deal of competitiveness, except perhaps for faculty members. This is a tricky position, however. For example, the cartel arrangements that exist between universities are probably regional or state wide in character (e.g., the Ivy League), and there thus would probably be significant price and service competition among the various regional cartels. For a contrasting view on the competitiveness of the higher education industry, see [9].

8. See Stigler [21] for the argument that better informed consumers make cartel-like arrangements more costly to maintain.

(For example, physics courses at smaller schools may turn out to be less expensive than those offered at larger schools, and students would have the more general option of cheap versus expensive physics courses.) In effect, greater information about prices for educational services should aid in promoting a responsive and efficient university system.

Competition among full-cost pricing universities would also ease the problems caused by the higher subsidies in the price of public institutions. As one would expect from simple economic behavior, the present system is characterized by overcrowding and pressures for expansion in subsidized public institutions and by less than optimal use of capacity and pressures to reduce programs in most privately supported institutions, especially small private schools. Full-cost pricing, with whatever public aid is deemed desirable for undergraduate education flowing to students and not to institutions, would help to correct this problem by putting equivalent quality units of educational supply on an equal footing in the marketplace.

The Role of Public Aid under Full-Cost Financing

The application of the logic of full-cost financing to the university does not mean that all university activities have to "stand on their own bottom in the market place." To the extent that faculty activities such as research or student (graduate and undergraduate) consumption of certain educational programs generate positive and marginally relevant externalities for society at large, public aid can generally be justified to support these activities. For any given level of aid for such purposes there remains the question of how the aid should be given—to individuals or institutions?

In the case of the research and graduate teaching functions of the university, which might broadly be characterized as the discovery and preservation of knowledge and culture, the case for aid to institutions seems greater than the case for aid to undergraduate student education. In this instance one is partially giving a subsidy to create an environment in which research can take place. The ideal arrangement here is probably a combination of institutional overhead grants at moderate levels and individual grant applications for large projects. Further, given the uncertainties associated with public investments in research, there may be additional advantages to some decentralization of grant-giving for individual research projects. Institutional grants or large unrestricted grants to individual researchers would be a way to accomplish such decentralization.

Public authorities would have to make judgments on whether research grants, especially to individuals, were marginal or inframarginal. In other words, do the grants promote additional (or better quality) work by a researcher in an area in which the public authority is interested, or do they simply subsidize the researcher for work that he or she would have done anyway? This is a judgmental question for public authorities, but clearly one of which they should be aware. Other trade-offs would exist for assessing public investments in university research (e.g., number of researchers versus quality of their work), but in general it would appear that a mixed system of institutional and individual aid aimed at maximizing the relevant social gains from research is optimal.

In the case where the training and education of students generates positive and marginally relevant externalities, we would suggest that the issue of institutional versus individual aid be resolved in favor of aid to individual students and not in deviations from full-cost pricing by universities. Such a policy would maximize student (i.e., consumer) choice in the selection of schools, and minimum quality constraints could be maintained in this procedure by limiting the grants to use at certified schools only.

There may be a case for giving institutional aid for the education of undergraduate students per se on a strictly transitional basis. For example, one may wish to keep in operation schools that otherwise might be forced to close down (perhaps for a short time) during the transition from one type of financing system to another. Likewise, it might be worthwhile to encourage diversity by subsidizing entry by schools offering a differentiated product.[9] Such institutional financial support should definitely be for a limited duration only and should probably be heavily weighted toward loans rather than grants.

With the possible exception of some minimum quality constraints, the choice of school for any publicly supported student should be left in the hands of the student-consumer. This right would put such students on equal footing with those students paying full costs, and in general student sovereignty can promote an efficient allocation of students among schools with respect to the type of educational consumption desired. As noted previously, this allocation should make universities more competitive and

9. It may be desirable to subsidize graduate students, who will naturally be integrated into the research function of the university, via institutional grants to universities, or for that matter, to groups of universities.

Another important issue which is not considered here is what should be the mix of local, state, and federal finance for the support of higher education and what types of aid (research versus student) should be paid by each governmental level. These are complicated questions on which the existing economic theory of fiscal federalism offers the somewhat limited guidance of the form "those who receive the benefits should pay." A voting system is proposed to resolve problems of how to articulate local, regional, and federal stakes in public goods such as higher education produces when benefits spill over a number of jurisdictions in Mueller, Tollison, and Willett [16].

call forth a variety of educational institutions in response to consumer demand.[10]

It should be mentioned that the corollary issue is how much student sovereignty to allow within a given university. Two of the major problems that one faces in choosing a mix of student and professor sovereignty are the student's competency to tell whether he is getting a good education and the present merger of teaching and evaluation.[11] In general, given the nature of the educational product, full consumer sovereignty within universities would not be desirable; neither is full professor sovereignty desirable. Groping around somewhere in between is probably the best that can be expected with perhaps a variety of mixes of faculty and student control in different schools. For example, a fraction, but not all, of teachers' salaries might be paid directly by students.[12] Thus a system of full consumer sovereignty in the choice among universities is suggested with only limited consumer sovereignty in choices within any given university as an attractive approach to the protection of both the student and the integrity of higher education.

Even if one felt that students were fully competent to judge the educational services they were purchasing, full student payment directly to teachers (the fullest embodiment of consumer sovereignty) would not be desirable under our present institution because of the merger of the two functions of teaching and evaluation or certification in the role of the American professor. Buying an education is quite a different thing from buying a grade or a favorable recommendation. While the available evidence is far from clear cut, fear has already been expressed in many quarters that as mild an institutional change as the regular publication of student evaluations of courses has caused slippage in the degree of objectivity with which grades are assigned. Any such tendency could be much more strongly pronounced where the professor was directly dependent on

10. There is no presumption here that the average quality of higher education would deteriorate under such a system. Indeed, it may even improve, especially with respect to variables such as the amount of (quality-adjusted) value-added per student. This could happen where students demand those educational experiences which maximize (ex ante) their expected lifetime income. Hence, the amount of time it takes to obtain certain degrees may fall or rise as market conditions dictate. In this process, current academic standards would change, but in terms of the way differential pricing would merge the higher education sector with the rest of the economy, there is no presumption that these changes would reflect lower quality educational outputs. After all, higher education as an industry derives its rationale for existence from the way it fits into the general economic process.

11. An interesting possible example of the latter is discussed in a recent article in *Science* where evidence was reported that there was a significant correlation between student grades and the rankings given by students to professors.

12. A colleague (Seymour Smidt) has suggested that a way to accomplish this would be by earmarking a part of tuition payments for this purpose.

student purchasers for the majority of his income. It would be possible to separate more formally the functions of teaching and evaluation by making greater use of standardized tests or external examinations, as is done in Great Britain and in India. There are both advantages and disadvantages to such a separation, and it does not seem clear to us at this point whether such a separation would be desirable or not.

Possible Objections to Full-Cost Pricing

In trying to anticipate objections to differential pricing of higher education resources, the question of income distribution comes foremost to mind.[13] Is the poor student not priced out of the small seminar, the "hard" sciences, and other high marginal cost activities in the university? Indeed, does not the full-cost pricing procedure discriminate against the poor student no matter how universities choose to set full-cost fees? And would not this be compounded if, as some have suggested, a disproportionate number of poor students prefer to go into the hard sciences?

In considering these questions, it is important to clarify what is meant by the term "poor students." Almost all students are poor in the sense that their current income is low, but generally when such arguments are made, the term is used to refer to students where families are of low income. It can be argued that the most important definition of "poor" for educational purposes should be in terms of expected lifetime earnings, and today almost no student who obtains admission to a college or university is poor in this sense [13, pp. S288–89]. The real problem is whether students can borrow on reasonable terms against their expected earnings. Government policies to assure the availability of such borrowing opportunities in the face of imperfections in private capital markets are an essential part of any rational approach to the allocation of resources in higher education. This is true under present university pricing practices and would be even more important under full-cost pricing. Government provision for borrowing opportunities is especially needed to finance education because in the private market the right of individuals to sell stock in themselves based on their expected future earnings is constitutionally prohibited. Even when individuals do have access to competitive market terms, they have the choice only of fixed obligation borrowing. Despite the high average rates of return on investments in higher education, there is also considerable dispersion in these rates, and for the individual student undertaking a fixed obligation of the size necessary to finance his college education (much less graduate school), the investment may carry substantial personal risk. Thus, the proposals for government

13. General discussions of equity in the provision of higher education are found in Schultz [19; Reading 9, above], Hansen [12], and Johnson [13].

programs which would in effect give individuals the opportunity to equity finance their education by incurring the obligation of an income tax surcharge rather than a fixed obligation are particularly attractive.[14]

But suppose in full awareness of this analysis and in the presence of appropriate programs for higher educational finance there are still perceived to be marginal externalities for the general taxpaying public from undergraduate educational consumption and investment of students from low-income or minority group backgrounds (or for students who concentrate in fields such as the hard sciences that have been given national priority). Would this not then require deviations from the principle of full-cost pricing of undergraduate education? The answer is that it depends. In the case of minority students, for instance, the perceived externality is associated with the individual being educated. In such circumstances, as noted above, the appropriate policy is a direct subsidy to the student for educational expenses, not deviation from full-cost pricing by the university.[15]

On the other hand, in the case of wanting to induce additional students into a particular field such as physics, the perceived externality is associated with the educational activity, and the appropriate policy is a subsidy to the activity. This policy will lead to deviations from costs of prices charged students for the educational activity. The policy does not contradict the principle of full-cost pricing, since the case for the subsidy is that society consumes some the benefits (i.e., the student and society share in the consumption of the benefits of education), and they together through direct government subsidy plus student fees pay the full cost of the joint product. The minority student who went into physics would, in effect, receive a double subsidy.[16]

Actually, with a given total supply of educational resources within the

14. See, for example, Nerlove [17] and the references cited there.

15. The present system of subsidizing (through the general tax system) the consumption of higher education through less than full-cost tuition (for example, students' fees covered 21 percent of the 1965–66 current fund revenues of colleges and universities) results in a substantial income transfer from lower to higher income groups, a practice not in keeping with normal principles of fiscal equity. See Hansen [12, pp. S264–65] and the references cited there. Less than full-cost tuition and fees means also that rationing of admissions takes place according to nonprice criteria. See Nerlove [17, p. S180].

From the perspective of public officials or individual schools, grant aid designed to attract certain types of students should be marginal and not inframarginal. In other words, grant aid should affect allocative decisions by students and not simply increase the rents earned, for example, by very bright minority students. In practice it would not be possible to estimate each student's reservation price, but in principle this is what one should attempt to do.

16. For completeness a third category of externalities should be mentioned which is not associated directly with the individual nor exclusively with his course of study, but rather the particular use made of the education after graduation. The special fellowship programs for future teachers illustrates the existence of this type of perceived externality. Here again,

university, allocation decisions could equally well be based on shadow prices and student coupons. Where important externalities were felt to be present (for example, in the case of low-income minority students), extra coupons could be given. Likewise, performance by students could be encouraged by the award of additional coupons. Whether voting by dollars or points, students' decisions would give a better evaluation of their demands for different classes with respect to their costs and provide better signals for the allocation of resources in higher education.

When the relative costs of courses are reflected in different prices, will a majority of the students still complain about large lecture sections taught by graduate students (rather than smaller seminars taught by the best known figures on campus)? This question is hard to answer, but experiments with marginal cost-pricing systems should provide useful information. Certainly, it is not stranger that at the same price students would prefer the latter than that, given the choice of the same price for steak and hamburger, they would choose steak.

In general, then, the income distribution objection is really a special case of the university producing a special type of public output, and the general principle should apply that subsidies should be given to the appropriate activities where deemed desirable. Indeed, one may wish to extend traditional thinking about the types of subsidies that are desirable; for example, to consider systematically offering lower costs for the first and perhaps second year of higher education. The SUNY system currently does this. Such a subsidy would be consistent with the implementation of marginal cost pricing since presumably first and second year courses will be less costly per student because of standardized curricula and large classes.

Another objection to differential pricing in the university has been raised by Eckstein; namely, that the capitalization problem faced by the student investing in higher education is likely to be biased [8]. The benefits of the investment in college education (higher expected earnings) are much less well-defined and certain than are the immediately obvious costs of the investment (borrowing, drawing down family savings, and the like). The distant benefits of the educational investment are capitalized imperfectly while the costs are accurately capitalized. Thus, high marginal cost activities in the university (e.g., the hard sciences) would not be undertaken in correct amounts by investing students. Indeed, the same argument could be levied against the full-cost argument regardless of its incarnation.

Without questioning the validity of this argument, it could be argued

---

would not government activity aimed primarily at improving the attractiveness of teaching positions be more appropriate than such special fellowships?

that differential pricing under a viable full-cost financing scheme might well have a healthy demonstration effect by causing student educational investors to investigate the potential benefits of alternative educational investments.[17] This effect would largely take the form of information gathering about potential benefits and could have an important impact in rationalizing the allocation of labor resources in the college and post-college trained segment of the labor force. Casual empiricism suggests that good advising about career choices is one of the areas in which the higher education industry today generally performs poorly. While the full extent of the current glut of new doctorates in English and history could not have been predicted without foreknowledge of the current financial squeeze, the supply side effects of recent PhD production with respect to the normal growth of demand was very apparent to many experts long before oversupply became generally recognized. Greater attention to career prospects cannot assure the absence of expectations which are frustrated, but we believe that the incidence of such disappointments could be substantially reduced. The incidental benefits of better career planning which might be generated by differential pricing could prove to be quite substantial.

Conclusion

It is recognized that there are a number of practical difficulties in implementing a system of differential pricing and the accompanying organization of markets in higher education, and a substantial amount of work remains to be done to design an operational system of pricing and public aid for individual universities which would approximate optimality. But the scope for improving the production and use of resources in higher education through the implementation of such policies should be substantial. It is felt that the expected benefits are amply sufficient to justify the costs of experimenting with the implementation of such policies. It is unclear to what extent the application of differential pricing and markets would prove to be most efficient. (For instance, should each course carry its own price, or should there be only several classes of courses for pricing purposes?) We are so far from an efficient solution at present that the appropriate direction for movement seems clear. A modest step in this direction was recently taken by the State Higher Education System in New York to charge different tuition rates for beginning and advanced undergraduate study in recognition of the substantial difference in their average costs.

17. See Freeman [10] for the argument and evidence that student educational investment decisions do respond to market incentives.

References

1. A. A. Alchian, "The Economic and Social Impact of Free Tuition," *The New Individualist Review*, 8:42–58 (Winter 1968).
2. ——, *Pricing and Society*, London, The Institute of Economic Affairs, 1967.
3. —— and W. R. Allen, *University Economics*, 2d ed., Belmont, Cal., Wadsworth Press, 1967.
4. ——, "What Price Free Tuition?" *Michigan Quarterly Review*, 7:269–72 (October 1968).
5. M. Buchanan and Nicos Devletoglou, *Academia in Anarchy*, New York, Basic Books, 1970.
6. A. M. Cartter, "The Economics of Higher Education," *Contemporary Economic Issues*, ed. Neil Chamberlain, Homewood, Ill., Richard D. Irwin, Inc., 1969.
7. Andre Daniere, *Higher Education in the American Economy*, New York, Random House, 1964.
8. Otto Eckstein, "The Problem of Higher College Tuition," *Review of Economics and Statistics*, Supplement: 71 (August 1960).
9. Stephen Enke, book review of *The Economics of Harvard* by Seymour E. Harris, *Journal of Economic Literature*, 9:467–68 (June 1971).
10. R. B. Freeman, *The Market for College-Trained Manpower: A Study in the Economics of Career Choice*, Cambridge, Mass., Harvard University Press, 1971.
11. Milton Friedman, "The Role of Government in Education," *Economics and Public Interest*, ed. R. Solo, New Brunswick, N.J., Rutgers University Press, 1955.
12. W. L. Hansen, "Equity and the Finance of Higher Education," *Journal of Political Economy*, 80:S260–73 (May–June 1972, Part 2).
13. H. G. Johnson, "The Alternatives Before Us," *Journal of Political Economy*, 80:S280–89 (May–June 1972, Part 2).
14. Carl Kaysen, "Some General Observations on the Pricing of Higher Education," *Review of Economics and Statistics*, Supplement: 55–60 (August 1960).
15. E. J. Mishan, "Some Heretical Thoughts on University Reform," *Encounter*, 32:3–15 (March 1969).
16. D. C. Mueller, R. D. Tollison, and T. D. Willett, *Public Choice in a Constitutional Democracy* (in preparation).
17. Marc Nerlove, "On Tuition and the Costs of Higher Education: Prolegomena to a Conceptual Framework," *Journal of Political Economy*, 80:S280–89 (May–June 1972, Part 2).
18. T. W. Schultz, "Optimal Investment in College Instruction: Equity and Efficiency," *Journal of Political Economy*, 80:S2–30 (May–June 1972, Part 2).
19. ——, "Resources for Higher Education: An Economists' View," *Journal of Political Economy*, 76:327–47 (May–June 1968).
20. Seymour Smidt, "Flexible Pricing of Computer Services," *Management Science*, 14:B-581–B-600 (June 1968).
21. G. J. Stigler, "A Theory of Oligopoly," *Journal of Political Economy*, 72:44–61 (February 1964).

22. R. D. Tollison and T. D. Willett, "A Proposal for Marginal Cost Financing of Higher Education," *Public Finance* 27:375–80 (No. 3, 1972).

C. THE ENVIRONMENT

11. Economists on the Doomsday Models: A Review of *The Limits to Growth*, by Donella H. Meadows et al, and *World Dynamics* and *Urban Dynamics*, by Jay W. Forrester

PETER PASSELL, MARC ROBERTS, and LEONARD ROSS

"If this doesn't blow everybody's mind who can read without moving his lips," writes "Up the Organization"-man Robert C. Townsend, "then the earth is kaput." Anthony Lewis of The New York Times deems it "likely to be one of the most important documents of our age" and learns from it "the complete irrelevance of most of today's political concerns" to the world's long-run travail. The authors' press agents describe the book as a "rediscovery of the laws of nature" through the medium of the computer.

The book is "The Limits to Growth," and its message is simple: Either civilization or growth must end, and soon. Continued population and industrial growth will exhaust the world's minerals and bathe the biosphere in fatal levels of pollution. As the authors summarize, "if the present growth trends . . . continue unchanged, the limits of growth on this planet will be reached sometime within the next hundred years."

"The Limits to Growth" is a product of an interdisciplinary M.I.T. team led by Dennis Meadows. It is financed and publicized as part of the "Project on the Predicament of Mankind," an activity of the Club of Rome. The Club of Rome is a four-year-old international organization of 75 technocrats and businessmen self-described as an "invisible college" dedicated to probing "the complex of problems troubling men of all nations," including poverty, degradation of the environment, alienation of youth, rejection of traditional values, and monetary disruptions. These

Reprinted from *The New York Times Book Review*, April 2, 1972, by permission of the authors.

"seemingly divergent" problems are, says the Club, in reality part of a single "world problematique," which can now be analyzed with the help of computers. Using techniques developed by M.I.T. systems-engineer Jay Forrester, the Meadows team claims to have limned the underlying fallacy of industrial expansion.

"The Limits to Growth," in our view, is an empty and misleading work. Its imposing apparatus of computer technology and systems jargon conceals a kind of intellectual Rube Goldberg device—one which takes arbitrary assumptions, shakes them up and comes out with arbitrary conclusions that have the ring of science. "Limits" pretends to a degree of certainty so exaggerated as to obscure the few modest (and unoriginal) insights that it genuinely contains. Less than pseudoscience and little more than polemical fiction, "The Limits to Growth" is best summarized not as a rediscovery of the laws of nature but as a rediscovery of the oldest maxim of computer science: Garbage In, Garbage Out.

"Limits" approaches the problem of predicting the future straightforwardly enough, employing the time honored technique of mathematical simulation. Simulation has proved invaluable as a device for testing engineering designs at little cost and no risk to lives. For instance, instead of simply building a prototype aircraft and seeing if it flies, the airplane's characteristics are condensed to a series of computer equations which simulate the airplane in flight. The Apollo moon rocket made thousands of trips in an I.B.M. 360 before it was even built. Economists also use simulation, though their successes have been modest. Simulation models have a rather spotty record in using current data to predict national income, unemployment and inflation even a year or two in advance.

But "Limits" is cast from a more heroic mold than any engineering or economic study to date. The Meadows team focuses its attention on the whole world and extends its time horizon to centuries. Factors the researchers believe influence population and income are boiled down to a few dozen equations. The crucial variables—population, industrial output, raw materials reserves, food production and pollution—all interact in ways that are at least superficially reasonable: Population growth is limited by food output, health services and pollution; industrial growth and agricultural growth are limited by resource availability and pollution. "Limits" is thus able to create a hypothetical future based on knowledge of the past.

As a first approximation of the future, the authors assume that the world is utterly incapable of adjusting to problems of scarcity. Technology stagnates and pollution is ignored, even as it chokes millions to death. A shortage of raw materials prevents industry and agriculture from keeping up with population growth. World reserves of vital materials (silver, tungsten, mercury, etc.) are exhausted within 40 years. Around 2020 the pinch becomes tight enough to cause a fall in per capita income. A few decades later, malnutrition and lagging health services abruptly reverse the climbing population trend. By the year 2100 the resource base has shrunk so badly that the world economy is unable to sustain even 19th-century living standards.

Scientists should have few objections to this grim scenario, even though it is based on what the Meadows team admits are crude assumptions. The scenario does plausibly illustrate the need for continued scientific progress to sustain current levels of prosperity. The quality of life in the future surely depends on the progress of technology and, to a lesser extent, on our willingness to limit population growth. But that should come as no surprise to a world that is already enormously dependent on modern techniques: If the telephone company were restricted to turn-of-the-century technology 20 million operators would be needed to handle today's volume of calls. Or, as British editor Norman Macrae has observed, an extrapolation of the trends of the 1880's would show today's cities buried under horse manure.

By the same measure, the simulation provides some small insight into the probable hazards of continued indifference to pollution and population growth. Current industrial and agricultural practices dump vast quantities of debris into the biosphere which would ultimately leave the air unfit for humans and water unfit for fish. Unchecked, the world's population is likely to double by the year 2000, with most of the burden on less developed countries. The future would be grim indeed if Con Ed were indefinitely allowed to ignore what comes out of its stacks or if Colombia permitted 20 million people to jam the barrios of Bogota. Had the "Limits" team concluded on this note, they would have had an acceptable point—but one quite independent of their elaborate computer simulation. It doesn't take a $10-million machine to figure out that only science—and the will to use it intelligently—could keep us ahead of population growth.

The authors, however, have much more in mind. They are out to show that pollution and malnutrition cannot be attacked directly, but only by stopping economic growth. They argue that any reasonable modification of their equations to account for new technology, pollution and population control might postpone collapse but would not avoid it. Under the most sanguine conditions imaginable, they say, growth must end within 100 years. Even if technology doubled known resources and crop yields, pollution were cut by three-fourths, and birth control eliminated all unwanted pregnancies, growth would turn out to be self-limiting. In no more than a century, the collective weight of food shortages, raw material depletion and pollution would reverse expansion. Hence the only way to avoid collapse and its attendant miseries is to halt growth now. "Limits" preaches that we must learn to make do with what we already have.

It is no coincidence that all the simulations based on the Meadows world model invariably end in collapse. As in any simulation, the results depend on the information initially fed to the computer. And the "Limits" team fixes the wheel; no matter how many times you play there is only one possible outcome. Critical to their model is the notion that growth produces stresses (pollution, resource demands, food requirements) which multiply geometrically. Like compound interest on a savings account, these stresses accumulate at a pace that constantly accelerates: Every child born is not only another mouth to feed but another potential parent. Every new factory not only drains away exhaustible resources but increases our capacity to build more factories. Geometric (or as mathematicians prefer to call it, exponential) growth must eventually produce spectacular results. If the Indians who sold Manhattan 300 years ago for $24 could have left their money untouched in a bank paying 7 per cent (a number chosen no more arbitrarily than many in "Limits") they would have more than $25-billion today.

While the team's world model hypothesizes exponential growth for industrial and agricultural needs, it places arbitrary, non-exponential, limits on the technical progress that might accommodate these needs. New methods of locating and mining ores, or recycling used materials, are assigned the ability to do no more than double reserve capacity; agricultural research can do no more than double land yields; pollution can cut emissions from each source by no more than three-fourths. Hence the end is inevitable. Economic demands must outstrip economic capacities simply because of the assumption of exponential growth in the former.

It is also disconcerting to note that one earlier variant of the world model, which does manage to avoid collapse, is not even discussed in "Limits." In "World Dynamics," the Forrester book which sets forth the basic simulation, one scenario has crowding reduce the population growth rate to zero before pollution, food shortages and depletion overtake the planet. But the "Limits" researchers jigger the assumptions just enough to eliminate this noncatastrophic possibility. In the "Limits" version pollution is less controllable and crowding actually increases birth rates. The world economy overshoots its sustainable limits and, obligingly, collapses. Where even Forrester's model provides hope, the "Limits" team prudently fudges the result.

"The Limits to Growth" is not the first research effort to explore the dangers of exponential growth. Nor, once again, was it necessary to use fancy computer techniques to justify what so obviously follows from the assumptions. The Rev. Thomas Malthus made a similar point two centuries ago without benefit of computer printouts or blinking lights. Malthus argued that people tend to multiply exponentially, while the food supply at best increases at a constant rate. He expected that starvation and war would periodically redress the balance.

Still, "The Limits to Growth" might be excused in spite of its lack of originality and scent of technical chicanery if those dismal assumptions behind the calculations were accurate. It is true that exponential growth cannot go on forever if technology does not keep up—and if that is the case we might save ourselves much misery by stopping before we reach the limits. But there is no particular criterion beyond myopia on which to base that speculation. Malthus was wrong; food capacity has kept up with population. While no one knows for certain, technical progress shows no sign of slowing down. The best econometric estimates suggest that it is indeed growing exponentially. The Forrester-Meadows team could have performed a service by citing hard evidence to discredit these estimates, if they have any. Instead they simply assume a bleak future for technology, announce that their own estimates are generous, and conclude that under any hypothesis about scientific progress growth must end. Heads you lose; tails you lose.

Natural resource reserves and needs in the model are calculated on the most conservative assumptions about the ability of the world economy to adjust to shortages. This is largely due to the absence of prices as a variable in the "Limits" projection of how resources will be used. In the real world, rising prices act as an economic signal to conserve scarce resources, providing incentives to use cheaper materials in their place, stimulating research efforts on new ways to save on resource inputs, and making renewed exploration attempts more profitable.

In fact, natural resource prices have remained low, giving little evidence of coming shortages. And the reasons are not hard to find. Technical change has dramatically reduced exploration and extraction costs, while simultaneously permitting the substitution of plentiful materials for scarce ones—plastics for metal, synthetic fibers for natural, etc. Moreover specialists usually agree that cheap energy is the critical long-run constraint on output of raw materials. Given enough energy, minerals might be reclaimed from under the sea, or from seawater itself. A virtually infinite source of energy, the controlled nuclear fusion of hydrogen, will probably be tapped within 50 years.

"Limits" also assumes that abatement practices will at best reduce pollution by three-quarters. Yet that goal could be accomplished using techniques that exist today and ignores the promise of innovations still under development. Relatively pollution-free autos are within reach if we have the political will to insist; electric power could be generated with minimal pollution if we are willing to pay a reasonable price.

Forrester's attempt to predict the future of the world via computer simulation has precedent in his own earlier attempt to predict the future of the cities. The approach of his "Urban Dynamics" is substantially the same as "World Dynamics." Rather simply motivated equations are created as proxies for the forces that mold the economic structure of urban areas. Simulation then allows the analyst to extrapolate the past and present into the future.

The urban model seeks to explain the sickness of American cities and test the efficacy of various remedies. Forrester's urban system stylizes the economy of the city as a concentration of business enterprises populated by the people who seek to work in them. His city is economically viable only if its tax base of successful businesses and employed workers is large relative to the demands placed on the city by the unemployed or endemically poor. High tax rates drive business away and further erode the revenue base by discouraging middle and upper income taxpayers from living in the central city.

Just as "World Dynamics" provided a rationale for an end to growth, "Urban Dynamics" provides a computerized justification for benign neglect. Expenditures on low-income housing and antipoverty programs turn out to be counter-productive. They lure more poor people and thereby aggravate the problem of holding on to prosperous taxpayers. Even if the funds for renewal come from outside sources, says Forrester, the cities are left with an increased burden on local services and few new taxpayers. By the logic of the model, the cities can be saved if outside aid is used only to demolish existing housing without replacement. Plots vacated by the poor provide building sites for new industries. Federal aid devoted to lowering tax rates would have much the same effect; businesses and wage earners are attracted by more favorable conditions.

As in the world model, the urban model critically depends on the assumptions upon which it is based. Forrester derives the assumptions straight from his own intuition and in the process generates some results worthy of Lewis Carroll. By his assumption, any policy that attracts business to the city brings with it a flood of poor people looking for jobs. Since Forrester's hypothetical businessman or employed worker is loath to pay taxes, the only way to prevent his flight to the suburbs is to deny poor people a place to live in the city. The healthy city, "Urban Dynamics" style, depends for its continuing prosperity on a massive shortage of low-income housing.

Forrester also avoids some troublesome questions that arise from the restricted purview of his model. One urban area may be able to attract a tax base by damn-the-poor policies, but what if all communities follow that prescription? Most Americans already live in or around cities. Where will the would-be rich urbanites come from and where will the impoverished go? Nothing in the "Urban Dynamics" formula would raise the total level of resources available for community welfare or eliminate the fact that shuffling the poor around won't solve the problem of poverty for the nation as a whole. It seems a pity to attempt the rehabilitation of central cities by the same methods that the suburbs used to destroy them.

If the world and urban model researchers were more modest in the reforms they recommend, and if they were dealing with a less credulous press, one might excuse their efforts. But "Urban Dynamics" has found many sympathetic readers, and "The Limits to Growth" appears on its way to even greater influence. Zero-growth ideology is being generalized from population—where it makes a good deal of sense—to production, where it makes almost no sense at all. A society prepared to throw out the baby should at least clean up the bathwater. Stopping growth is a sane way to curb pollution only if society doesn't have the nerve to do the job directly. But a world too timid to require smokestack precipitators would hardly jump at the chance to shut down factories. Conversely, if we ever did have the willpower to halt growth, we could use that resolve affirmatively to enhance the quality of life. The President who could convince Congress to forbid new capital investment could find money for comfortable mass transit and could put teeth into antipollution laws.

Fifteen years ago, nuclear incineration was the fashionable apocalypse. The doomsday clock on the cover of The Bulletin of Atomic Scientists marched inexorably toward midnight. Today the vision is mass death from insecticide poisoning, climatic changes, or some other form of retribution from an angry biosphere. None of these fears is chimerical. Ecologists are surely right in shaking us from our unconcern about the side-effects of growth. A fair volume of propaganda is tolerable—indeed necessary—to counter years of smug neglect.

But there is a real danger involved in exploiting modern society's intimations of disaster. Ecologists studying pest control have taught us that the remedy is often worse than the affliction. This principle has an intellectual analogue. To insist that pollution control is pointless without a halt to growth is not simply wrong; it is noxious. Instead of inspiring a zero-growth policy, it is more likely to rationalize even further stalling over the few basic steps needed to curb pollution. Con Ed can fume away, secure in the knowledge that the fault is not theirs but all mankind's.

The planet certainly has its problems—and maybe even a "problematique" or two. But public-relations stunts which imply a false inevitability of doom do not speed the day of salvation. Crying wolf is too important a function to be left to invisible colleges.

12. Population and Environmental Quality

ANTHONY C. FISHER

A number of recent studies have emphasized a connection between environmental quality and population size and growth.[1] Indeed, deteriorating environmental quality, as measured by such indices as increasing air and water pollution and increasing congestion in various kinds of public facilities, is seen by some as primarily a population problem. Thus Mayer argues: "Our housing problem; our traffic problem; the insufficiency of the number of our hospitals, of community recreation facilities; our pollution problem, are all facets of our population problem." [2] This conclusion seems plausible; more people in a given area presumably results in more crowding of facilities and a greater generation of wastes, discharged into environmental media as residuals in the production and consumption processes. It would follow, moreover, that a remedy lies in somehow stabilizing population, and indeed at a level much below today's.

I shall argue, on the contrary, that economic theory, supported by some evidence, suggests that this is not the case, i.e., that deteriorating quality is not *primarily* a population problem.[3] More specifically, the following propositions may be advanced: (1) the rate of population growth may be expected to persist, perhaps to decline still further, and to spread to currently less developed areas; (2) there is, nonetheless, a real and quite probably increasing problem of quality deterioration; and (3) the deterioration arises, most fundamentally, from a pervasive price distortion, and the remedy lies in policies to correct the distortion which are largely unrelated to population control.

Reprinted from *Public Policy,* Winter 1971, pp. 19–35, by permission of the publisher and author.

1. See, for example, P. Ehrlich, *The Population Bomb* (New York: Ballantine, 1968).

2. J. Mayer, "Toward a Non-Malthusian Population Policy," *Columbia Forum* (Summer 1969), 12.

3. A similar argument is made in B. Wattenberg, "Overpopulation as a Crisis Issue: The Nonsense Explosion," *New Republic* (April 4, 1970).

Before proceeding with the demonstration of these propositions, let me define the problem more precisely. The old Malthusian questions of population versus food (or even other traditional limiting resources, such as minerals) is not at issue. It is recognized that in large areas of the world, even in some local areas of the U.S., starvation and malnutrition constitute grave threats to human health and survival. Whether this situation is improving or not is a matter of some controversy. It is my impression that, very recently (within, say, the last few years), students of the problem have become increasingly optimistic. The so-called "green revolution" in food production, involving development and wide application of new types of fertilizers, along with other, much more exotic innovations, offers the prospect of removing, perhaps for centuries, food as a limiting factor to population growth.[4] More generally, to quote Krutilla, "Those who take an optimistic view would hold that the modern industrial economy is winning its independence from the traditional natural resources sector to a remarkable degree."[5] And these developments refer only to gross production of food, or more generally, energy. If, as discussed below, the rate of population growth continues to decline, and the decline continues to spread, the picture becomes still brighter. In any case, the main concern here is with environmental quality in an affluent society, and its relation to population size and growth, and not with the old Malthusian question, which is admittedly still relevant in some areas, and perhaps ultimately relevant in all.

Also not at issue is the relation of migration to environmental problems, except insofar as it affects fertility. Clearly the high concentrations of population resulting in part from large unplanned migration from rural to urban areas have something to do with congestion and pollution problems in these areas. This is not a problem of global or aggregate population growth, but rather of the distribution of population.[6]

I. Trends in Population Growth

Let us consider the first proposition: The rate of population growth has been declining, and may continue to decline. The facts of past decline are given in Table 1 for the U.S. (figures for other developed areas would show the same broad trends).

It can be seen that both birth rates and death rates have been declining

4. Mayer, *op. cit.*, 10–12.
5. J. V. Krutilla, "Conservation Reconsidered," *American Economic Review*, LVII (September 1967), 778.
6. This point is made in detail by Wattenberg, *op. cit.*, 19, who notes that in the last eight years one out of three counties in the United States actually lost population, and three out of five had a net outmigration.

Table 1. Birth and death rates in the U.S. for the selected years, 1820–1968

Year	Birth rate	Death rate	Natural growth rate
1820	55.2	?	3+(?)
1840	51.8	?	3 (?)
1860	44.3	18.7 *	2.56
1880	39.8	19.8 *	2.00
1900	32.3	17.2	1.51
1920	27.7	13.0	1.47
1940	19.4	10.8	.86
1960	23.7	9.6	1.41
1968	17.4	9.6	.78

Sources: 1820–1950, *Historical Statistics of the United States, Colonial Times to 1957* (Washington, D.C., 1960), pp. 23, 27; 1957–1960, *Natality Statistics Analysis, United States 1963* (Washington, D.C., 1966), p. 2 and *Mortality Trends in the United States, 1954–1963* (Washington, D.C., 1966), p. 3; 1968, *Monthly Vital Statistics Report, Annual Summary for the United States, 1968* (Washington, D.C., 1968), p. 1.

* Death rates for 1860 and 1880 are for Massachusetts only. Massachusetts death rates in the twentieth century have averaged about a point higher than U.S. rates, so that U.S. rates in 1860 and 1880 were probably about a point below those listed.

throughout this century and, as far as the figures can take us, through most of the nineteenth century as well, with the larger absolute decline in birth rates resulting in a fall in the rate of population growth (neglecting net migration) from probably more than 3 percent per year in 1820 through about 2.5 percent per year in 1860 to less than .8 percent per year in 1968. Before examining the reasons for this long decline and attempting to predict the course of future population growth, let us take a closer look at the figures. The low (below trend) birth rate for 1940 may be explained by a slow emergence from the depression, adding a cyclical component to the secular. During World War II birth rates were up a bit, and just after the war they jumped abruptly (stock adjustment?) to a level above the trend, reaching a peak in 1947. There were small fluctuations in the late 1940s and early and middle 1950s, with a peak in 1957. Since 1957, birth rates have been steadily declining in the U.S. through a variety of lesser cyclical fluctuations, resuming apparently the long downtrend. While a more detailed breakdown of vital statistics could facilitate a very short-run prediction of future birth rates, I believe an application of economic theory can carry us further.[7]

Recall that for Malthus, the dynamics of population growth worked exclusively through changes in mortality. A temporary increase in income, due perhaps to a better-than-average harvest one year, would lead to a reduction in infant and other mortality and thence to an increase in population. The increase could only be temporary, however, as diminishing returns to (agricultural) production drove (per capita) income down, even-

7. Wattenberg, *op. cit.,* notes declining fertility rates over the last decade, but does not attempt to analyze the causes.

tually to below the subsistence level, where the "positive" checks of famine, pestilence, and war could be relied upon to increase infant and other mortality, reducing population until (per capita) income climbed back to the subsistence level. A permanent increase in population could come only through a permanent increase in income, due perhaps to technological progress. The increase in income would, however, in the absence of fertility control, eventually just support a larger population at the subsistence level.

Malthus did see how technological progress could, for a time, outdistance population growth and raise per capita incomes, but obviously he could not and did not foresee how it could continue to do so indefinitely. Also, he gave scant attention to the possibility of progress in fertility control, more or less dismissing it as "vice," an "unnatural" means of population control. Yet we have seen that falling birth rates have been associated with development in the U.S. and elsewhere. How has this come about, and is it likely to continue?

Cipolla, in his fascinating survey of the economic history of world population, observes that there has been associated with industrialization first a drop in the death rate, and then, after some lag, a drop in the birth rate.[8] He does not, however, inquire into the mechanism of the falling birth rate, and this we must do in order to make predictions about future movements. What we need, then, is a theory of population in which the control works through fertility. Such a theory has been formulated by Becker[9] and elaborated by Mincer,[10] and it can provide an explanation of a number of observations, in particular of the secularly falling birth rate.

In Becker's model, utility-maximizing households determine the number of children they want subject to relative price, income, and technological constraints. Thus as family income rises (if children are not an "inferior good"), the number of children desired increases. On the other hand, as the relative "price" or cost of having and raising children rises, the number of children desired decreases. Also, since the technological constraint is essentially knowledge of contraception, technological progress clearly results in fewer children.

Falling birth rates may then be explained, at least in part, by the domi-

8. C. M. Cipolla, *The Economic History of World Population* (Baltimore: Penguin, 1962), pp. 82–91.

9. G. S. Becker, "Economic Aspects of Fertility," in Universities-National Bureau Committee for Economic Research, *Demographic and Economic Change in Developed Countries* (New York: National Bureau of Economic Research, 1958).

10. J. Mincer, "Market Prices, Opportunity Costs, and Income Effects," in Carl F. Christ *et al.*, *Measurement in Economics* (Stanford, Calif.: Stanford University Press, 1963).

nance of combined technical and relative price effects over an income effect. What has all of this to do with industrialization? Obviously, industrialization has brought rising incomes and, other things equal, they would be expected to lead to higher birth rates. Industrialization has also fostered the development and spread of contraceptive knowledge which, other things equal, would lead to lower birth rates. More subtly, industrialization and associated urbanization have increased the cost of having and raising children, and this fact, along with the growth in contraceptive knowledge, can explain the falling birth rate. Let us examine some of the reasons for the relative price effect.

It is fairly clear that the value of a child's services in the household, which is one (negative) component of price, typically falls with urbanization. In a rural or farm household a boy can be employed in planting and harvesting and general maintenance, and a girl can help in the processing and preparation of food crops, making clothing, and so on. The banning of child labor, and compulsory education laws, make it difficult to convert value-in-kind in the rural sector to money returns in the urban industrial sector. There seems in addition to have been a shift in preferences for what Becker calls ''higher quality'' children, children with, for example, increasingly greater amounts invested in their education beyond the legal minimum in formal schooling. For given expenditure, higher quality means lower quantity.

An important positive component of the cost of a child is, as Mincer demonstrates, the mother's opportunity cost. This cost may be roughly approximated by her foregone earnings. Growing opportunities for women in the urban market economy can be expected to lead a woman to the joint decision to participate in the labor force, and to defer or limit numbers of children. It is not that families have refrained from having children because the wife is working; rather, a shift in relative prices, with home work becoming relatively more ''expensive'' in terms of foregone market income, has resulted in movement out of the home (child-bearing and child-rearing) and into the market. Thus, as birth rates have fallen (see Table 1), the labor force participation rate of married women has risen from 5 percent in 1890 to 40 percent today.

Related to this movement may be the deferral of marriage and especially family formation (with the reduction in child-bearing years leading, perhaps, to a reduction in numbers of children) by young men and women investing in the increasingly greater amounts of education demanded by the modern industrial, or postindustrial, economy.

Further aspects of the relative price effect of economic development on birth rates might be distinguished, but the main tendency seems clear. Broadly, it is for lower birth rates in response to shifting opportunities.

Before assessing the implications of price, income, and technological changes on future fertility patterns (and, given apparently stable mortality, on population growth) in the developed areas, we might make an additional related observation on the situation in the currently less developed areas. There may be a sort of feedback relationship between mortality and fertility, in the sense that current birth rates are a function of (in addition to the price, income, and technological variables considered above) expected death rates. That is to say, as Schultz points out, "The established regime of childhood mortality may influence parents in planning their lifetime reproductive behavior to compensate for what they expect to be the incidence of death among their offspring." [11] Some evidence in support of this hypothesis is cited from a study by Fredericksen of birth and death rates in Ceylon, Mauritius, and British Guiana.[12] If true, it provides a further explanation of falling birth rates in earlier years (during the period of falling death rates) in the developed areas, and a further prediction of falling birth rates in future years in the less developed areas.

As to future birth rates and population growth in the U.S. and other developed areas, one is made wary of prediction by the poor past performance of the demographers.[13] Their predictions are essentially extrapolations of trends, modified somewhat by changing age, race, and other distributions of the population but neglecting consideration of underlying economic determinants. Might we not, employing the tools of economic theory, do better? Of course, some guesswork is still involved. My guess, then, is that the economic development that has characterized the past century will (for some decades, at least) continue, that it will continue to be associated with changes in technology and in relative opportunities, and that these changes will continue to be associated systematically with slowly falling, or at the very least not rapidly rising, birth rates.[14]

Moreover, to the extent that some current social movements are suc-

11. T. P. Schultz, "An Economic Model of Family Planning and Fertility," *Journal of Political Economy,* LXXVII (March/April 1969), 160.

12. H. Fredericksen, "Determinants and Consequences of Mortality and Fertility Trends," in *Public Health Reports,* vol. LXXXI (Washington, D.C.: U.S. Public Health Service, 1966).

13. The U.S. Census Bureau has in fact just recently announced major downward revisions in its population projections for the next 30 years, based apparently on the falling birth rates of the last few years (*Washington Post,* August 13, 1970). The high projections had been based on the relatively high birth rates of the late 1950s and early 1960s.

14. A caution here is suggested by a purely demographic consideration. The large numbers of births in the early and middle 1950s mean that large numbers of women will be entering the child-bearing ages in the early and middle 1970s. This may result in some deviation from the long trend, perhaps even in increasing birth rates for a few years.

cessful, the tendency for birth rates to fall may be strengthened. I am referring to (1) the movement to limit population by changing preferences and relative opportunities, and (2) the movement to "liberate" women. The population movement involves attempts to persuade prospective parents to have fewer children, increasing public and private activity to disseminate knowledge of contraception, and even a proposal (by Senator Packwood) to in effect change the tax incentive structure for the production of children by instituting a declining scale of income tax exemptions for children. Similarly, the focus of "women's liberation" on providing more challenging and remunerative opportunities for women may be expected to lead additional women out of the home and into the market—although the widespread institution of "free" child care centers, another objective of the movement, could work in the opposite direction by reducing child care costs.

Even should population in the U.S. continue for some decades to grow at a rate of about 1 percent per year—the current rate *including* immigration—clearly this, *in itself,* would have little effect on the quality of the environment—nor would cessation of growth, *in itself,* be likely to result in any improvement in quality. To understand this point, let us consider briefly some trends in the indices of environmental quality—pollution and congestion—and then attempt an alternative explanation of these phenomena.

II. Evidence on Deterioration of the Quality of the Environment

Although congestion is a recognized fact of life in most urban areas, some particularly striking figures reflect the growing congestion of natural or wild areas. Thus over a period of just twelve years, from 1947 to 1959, man-days of use in wilderness areas of the U.S. national forests increased from 306,800 to 1,399,000 [15]—an increase of 356 percent, as compared to an increase of just over 20 percent in population over this period. Current density and rates of increase are even greater for the national parks.[16]

With respect to air quality, although considerable evidence has been accumulated over the last few years on levels of pollution and, to a much lesser extent, on the effects of various pollutants, not too much is known about trends. This is, as Freeman observes, because "random factors

15. University of California Wildland Research Center, *Wilderness and Recreation: A Report on Resources, Values and Problems* (Outdoor Recreation Resources Review Commission Study Report No. 3; Washington, D.C.: Government Printing Office, 1962), pp. 226–229.

16. Mayer, *op. cit.,* 12.

[such as weather] tend to obscure trends over the relatively short periods of time covered by most available time series on air quality.'' [17] Obviously, pollution has increased over time in the U.S., if we go back far enough. On the other hand, no trend emerges from an array of figures on major pollutant concentrations in seven major cities in the U.S. over the period 1962–1966. [18] Further, there is even some evidence for a downtrend in the average level of particulates, the most visible of pollutants, in 64 cities over the period 1957–1963. [19] In Los Angeles, smog was not perceived as a problem during the early years of rapid population growth. It came rather suddenly in the early 1940s, associated perhaps with World War II industrialization. And in spite of continued rapid population growth over the last several years, the smog problem has not worsened; indeed, it may have improved slightly. In Pittsburgh, definite improvement over a period of about twenty years has been detected, with no corresponding decrease in population. These (and other) apparently perverse relationships are, as we shall see, to be explained by pollution control policies not related to population.

It should be obvious, even from these somewhat sketchy figures and examples, that there is currently no simple relationship between population and environmental quality in the U.S. By some measures, quality is deteriorating much more rapidly than population is increasing. By others, quality seems to be holding the line, if at costly and dangerously low levels, as population is increasing. There are, however, some qualifications.

The first is that, again, it must be emphasized that we are concerned with aggregate population growth, and not with the (mal) distribution of population stemming from large migrations to urban areas unprepared to handle the resulting congestion.

The second is that, obviously, quality deterioration did not become significant until some lower bound or threshold concentration of population, or perhaps more importantly, economic activity, was reached. But it does not follow, as we shall see, that the only solution, or even the best solution, is now somehow drastically to reduce population and economic activity.

The third is that beyond some upper bound, continued population growth, even at a rate of less than 1 percent per year, is impossible. This has to do with the extreme deterioration of quality associated with an approach to "standing-room-only." But often-expressed inferences of

17. A. M. Freeman, "The Quality of the Natural Environment" (background paper prepared for the Panel on Social Indicators, Department of Health, Education and Welfare, 1968), p. 30.

18. *Ibid.,* pp. 27, 28.   19. *Ibid.,* p. 30.

imminent disaster from compound population growth are quite unwarranted.[20] This is because with compound growth most of the increase in absolute numbers comes toward the end of a given period, when the (constant) rate of increase is applied to an increasingly larger base. Thus if the population of the U.S. is now 200 million and grows constantly at a rate of 1 percent per year, in 100 years it will have reached a level of approximately 540 million, in another hundred years approximately 1,458 million, and in another hundred years approximately 3,937 million. In the first hundred years the increase is 340 million, in the second it is 918 million, and in the third 2,479 million. The latter figure would, by the way, give the U.S. (including Alaska) a population density of a little over 1,000 per square mile, or about double the current density in India—uncomfortable, although still some distance from "standing-room only." I am certainly not advocating, or even predicting, this sort of sustained growth. It seems probable that unless birth rates in the U.S. decline still further within the next hundred years or so, new versions of the old Malthusian checks can be expected to reassert themselves—certainly at some point well before "standing-room-only" can be realized. On the other hand, several more decades of growth at present rates of less than 1 per cent or even slightly higher seem feasible, if not optimal.

A much more relevant problem is: What, if not increasing population, is the source of the pervasive and quite probably growing deterioration of environmental quality? And what policies are likely to be helpful in improving quality? It is with these questions that the remainder of this article is concerned.

III. Prices and Quality

The phenomena of pollution and congestion cited earlier as examples of environmental decay are often characterized by economists as "external costs," or "externalities." [21] In altering or expanding its operations an economic unit (individual, firm, or even public agency or municipality) may be imposing costs on others, in addition to its costs of operation. Thus a factory discharging quantities of smoke may be increasing costs for nearby farmers, if the smoke has deleterious effects on the growth or health of the farmers' crops or livestock. Similarly, a logging or pulp-making operation polluting a stream may increase the costs of obtaining drinking water or water recreation facilities for downstream users. With respect to congestion, the problem arises because additional users of a fa-

20. See, for example, Ehrlich, *op cit.*, for perhaps the most prominent expression of this position.
21. For a rigorous definition and discussion of the concept of externality, see J. Buchanan and W. Stubblebine, "Externality," *Economica,* XXIX (November 1962).

cility may, beyond some level of use, impose costs on other users. To take perhaps the most commonly cited example, additional motorists on a highway will increase the travel time, and perhaps also the fuel and maintenance costs, of other motorists.

These examples could be multiplied, but the underlying principle would be the same. It is that external costs in the forms of pollution and congestion are imposed as a consequence of failure to price (or otherwise effectively ration) scarce environmental resources. Thus air, water, and even open land have traditionally been "free goods" for the disposal of gaseous, liquid, and solid wastes. Also traditionally "free" or otherwise unrestricted has been access to (for example) crowded highways and national parks. But as Ayres and Kneese point out in a stimulating study of the relationship of some economic processes to environmental quality, air and water (and, I would add, open land) are, in reality, "common property resources of great and increasing value presenting society with important and difficult allocation problems which exchange in private markets cannot resolve." [22] As Kneese shows in a related article in this issue ["Strategies for Environmental Management," *Public Policy*, Winter 1971], the problems do not arise at low levels of use, given the capacity of the common property resources to absorb and assimilate wastes. The problems would also not arise if these resources were in private ownership and claims could be exchanged in competitive markets. But these conditions do not hold in a real economy, nor can they be expected to. Thus if a firm (or a householder, or a municipality) had to pay a price for the right to discharge wastes, it may be expected that it would either treat the wastes, seek a new location, or adopt an alternative cheaper production process perhaps involving some recycling; or, failing any of these, simply cut back on production and the associated generation of wastes. Similarly, as a number of writers have shown,[23] the levying of a toll or charge on the use of a public highway or other facility will tend to reduce the level of use, providing potential users with an incentive to seek alternative modes of transport or other substitutes for the tolled facility.

This view of the environmental quality problem carries with it an implicit solution. It is that, in principle, optimal levels (conceivably zero) of various types of pollution and congestion could be achieved by "internalizing externalities," i.e., by pricing relevant environmental resources—and at a rate equal to the (marginal) social cost of their use. In

22. R. U. Ayres and A. V. Kneese, "Production, Consumption, and Externalities," *American Economic Review*, LIX (June 1969), 283.

23. See, for example, M. Marchand, "A Note on Optimal Tolls in an Imperfect Environment," *Econometrica*, XXXVI (July-October 1968).

such an amended pricing system, costs formerly external would be absorbed by those responsible, presumably leading them to modify or curtail activities giving rise to such costs. This is further spelled out by Kneese with special reference to water quality.

The policy of internalizing externalities through a modified incentive structure is widely recognized by economists as likely to be helpful in improving the allocation of resources,[24] and in fact it is embodied in a number of current legislative proposals, from President Nixon's (1970) State of the Union message and a follow-up on environmental quality, to legislation introduced by Senators Nelson and Proxmire and others.[25]

It must be recognized that measurement of losses from air or water pollution or from various types of congestion presents some formidable problems. Further, some aspects of environmental management necessarily involve public investment (e.g., in research and development of sewage facilities, mass transit systems, and so forth). What, then, are the best policy hopes for improving environmental quality?

Obviously, internalizing known externalities where feasible will be optimal. But in the absence of perfect knowledge and perfect pricing mech-

24. See, for example, K. Boulding, "The Economics of the Coming Spaceship Earth," in Henry Jarrett (ed.), *Environmental Quality in a Growing Economy* (Baltimore: Johns Hopkins Press, 1966). Boulding notes (p. 13) that "many of the immediate problems of pollution . . . arise because of the failure of the price system, and many of them could be solved by corrective taxation. If people had to pay the losses due to the nuisance they create, a good deal more resources would go into the prevention of nuisances." It must, however, be noted that some rather subtle issues concerning the feasibility and optimality of corrective taxation have been raised in the literature. A detailed discussion of these issues is beyond the scope of the present article, but the interested reader might consult, among others, R. H. Coase, "The Problem of Social Cost," *Journal of Law and Economics*, III (October 1960); O. A. Davis and A. Whinston, "On Externalities, Information and the Government-Assisted Invisible Hand," *Economica*, XXXIII (August 1966); F. T. Dolbear, "On the Theory of Optimum Externality," *American Economic Review*, LVII (March 1967); J. M. Buchanan, "External Diseconomies, Corrective Taxes, and Market Structure," *American Economic Review*, LIX (March 1969). Very briefly, I would assert that none of these critiques seriously weakens the case for corrective taxation and public investment to internalize the widely diffused external effects typically associated with pollution and congestion phenomena.

25. In the State of the Union message, the President says that ". . . the price of goods should be made to include the costs of producing and disposing of them without damage to the environment." In a message to Congress released February 10, 1970, he specifically proposes that "failure to meet established water quality standards . . . be made subject to court-imposed fines of up to $10,000 per day." Along these lines, Senator Proxmire, joined by nine other senators from both parties, has introduced a bill to impose a system of effluent charges, with the revenue collected going into regional water quality management. Senator Nelson has introduced a bill to require manufacturers to pay a fee for selling their goods in containers that cannot be either recycled or easily degraded, also with revenue going to state and local agencies for construction of solid waste facilities.

anisms we need not accept the status quo. Other means of control, having more or less relation to the optimal, have been suggested. Let us examine them briefly.[26]

It has been widely suggested that an effective way to control pollution is simply to set maximum physical emission or discharge levels, with significant penalties attached to their violation. This policy is, however, just a special case of the graded schedule of charges or penalties envisioned in the optimal pricing system. It is essentially a sort of "all-or-nothing" tax on externalities, with a heavy penalty for exceeding allowable limits and no penalty at all for not reaching the limits. In cases where accurate measurement of costs associated with a range of pollution or congestion levels is not technically or economically feasible, it may well be a good policy. Still better, presumably, would be a graded system of charges bearing some relation to costs.

As noted above, a program of public investment in research and development of alternative, less socially costly methods of production and associated treatment of waste materials may be worthwhile. Also, provision of such facilities as highways and large recreation areas has traditionally fallen within the public sector. The case for public investment also rests on the presence of externalities—here, benefits from an investment which cannot be appropriated by private investors. And subsidies to private research and development in, for example, new methods of recycling residuals or otherwise altering a production or consumption process to reduce residuals discharged in harmful form can be viewed as elements of socially optimal pricing to internalize externalities—in this case, putting a *negative* price on *improvement* of environmental quality.

Related to these measures would be subsidies for the treatment of wastes from a given process. Such subsidies are likely to be inefficient, however, for a number of reasons given by Kneese in his criticism of current policies for water pollution control. For these reasons, a tax on pollution giving the polluter an incentive to seek the least (social) cost process (which could turn out to be treatment of wastes from an existing process), or public investment in some form of abatement if the polluter is a public agency, are to be preferred.

A major theme that emerges from many discussions of policies to improve environmental quality, or at least to prevent its further deterioration, is that a fundamental re-ordering of preferences must be accomplished, involving an acceptance of reduction in rates of growth of personal income, and even in levels of personal income, in exchange for

26. For a clear, detailed discussion of the superior features of the proposed marginal social cost pricing scheme, see L. E. Ruff, "The Economic Common Sense of Pollution," *The Public Interest,* No. 19 (Spring 1970).

benefits from enhanced quality of the common property resources (air, water, open space, and so forth).[27] While it is quite true that cutting back the level of economic activity would (given the existing structure of relative prices and associated choice of technologies) reduce the pollution and congestion loads placed on the environment, the implicit assumption of fixed prices is misleading. It is hoped that enough has been said to suggest that changing the structure of prices and associated technologies can accomplish the objective in less costly fashion. Some reduction in growth or level of income as traditionally measured, e.g., by GNP, is a price that must be paid for better quality, but the reduction will be minimized by the discriminating pricing policy. Further, it is not clear how an undiscriminating slowdown, much less reversal, of economic activity could be brought about without inducing widespread hardship. For example, perhaps the most important source of reduction in poverty in the last decade (if not before) has been aggregate economic growth.[28] It seems far preferable, then, to channel growth out of harmful paths rather than to stop it completely.

We come, finally, to population policy. In attempting to better environmental quality through reducing population we face much the same problems as in attempting to better quality through reducing aggregate economic activity. For given per capita incomes and relative prices, reducing population may indeed be expected to reduce the loads on environmental resources. But even with population somehow permanently reduced, expanding economic activity will, if otherwise unregulated, increase the loads to undesirable levels. Moreover, it is hard to see how the necessary very substantial reduction could be brought about. Short of disaster, no one is predicting that population can be or will be reduced below current levels, only that its rate of growth can be or will be reduced, perhaps to zero in the near future. Unless, then, we want to return (as we probably cannot) to perhaps pre-industrial levels of population and economic activ-

27. See, for example, a number of the contributions to G. de Bell (ed.), *The Environmental Handbook* (New York: Ballantine, 1970). This alternative is also discussed by L. Mayer, in an article, "U.S. Population Growth: Would Slower Be Better?" *Fortune* (June 1970). A stimulating statement of the case against a policy of encouraging rapid economic growth is found in E. J. Mishan, *The Costs of Economic Growth* (New York: Praeger, 1967). As I understand him, however, Mishan is not so much opposed to increasing personal incomes as he is to some of the undesirable side effects, the external "costs of growth" of the sort we have been discussing. His own policy recommendation is to internalize these external costs through corrective taxation and the price system (pp. 53–57), exactly as proposed above.

28. Even Anderson, who takes a fairly pessimistic view of future reduction in poverty from this source, indicates that it has been important in the past: W. H. L. Anderson, "Trickling Down: The Relationship between Economic Growth and the Extent of Poverty among American Families," *Quarterly Journal of Economics*, LXXVIII (November 1964).

ity with their (for the most part) uncongested environmental common property resources, there is no alternative to dealing directly with our environmental problems.

Thus the reason that population and economic activity have increased over the last several years in Los Angeles without further deterioration of air quality is simply that controls on emissions have been imposed. Conversely, were population stabilized and controls lifted, I would confidently predict rapid further deterioration. And does Mayer,[29] for example, really believe that the flow of 26 billion bottles he cites as discarded annually over the American landscape would, in the absence of incentives for consumers to save and return them, or for producers to supply degradable containers, somehow evaporate, or even be diminished, were population growth somehow reduced immediately from .8 percent per year to zero—or even below—as he advocates?

Again, using our example of growing congestion in outdoor recreation areas: Could not a system of user charges, ideally related to external costs of use, be instituted to reduce congestion (and damage to the areas)? Something like this is already done for some types of use, such as hunting. Very substantial license fees or day-use fees or both limit numbers of hunters and thus, along with individual bag limits, protect the game for sustained hunting and other uses (e.g., research). It is an extension of policies of essentially this sort that is likely to be most effective in protecting the wider environment.

IV. Conclusions

I have tried to demonstrate, and then to relate, several propositions on population and environmental quality. The propositions are (1) that the rate of population growth in the U.S. and other developed economies has been declining, and is likely to continue to decline; (2) that this fact is not very relevant for problems of environmental quality in these areas, which will continue to worsen even in the presence of zero population growth or absolutely reduced population; (3) that the more fundamental source of most quality problems is a distortion of the structure of relative prices, caused in turn by the pervasive presence of technological externalities in production and consumption; and (4) that the most effective policies for improving quality involve essentially correcting the distortion—internalizing externalities in a very broad sense.

Finally, I should like to make it clear that none of the above is intended as opposition to population control, especially in poorer areas. Rather, it is intended to suggest that it is misleading to assert that population control can, *in itself,* be expected to do much for environmental quality.

29. Mayer, *op. cit.,* 13.

13. The Economics of Fatal Mistakes: Fiscal Mechanisms for Preserving Endangered Predators *

RYAN C. AMACHER, ROBERT D. TOLLISON, and THOMAS D. WILLETT

The recent mass killings of eagles in Wyoming have prompted considerable discussion of ways both to control and to preserve endangered predators.[1] On the one hand, ranchers and farmers are concerned about losses of valuable livestock, and on the other, conservationists are worried about the eventual extinction of predators such as the bald eagle. What can economists say about efficient social arrangements to handle this type of problem, where the private activities of ranchers and conservationists may not reveal all of the costs and benefits of controlling and preserving these birds?

The current federal law protecting eagles stipulates a fine of $500 or six months in prison (or both) for the killing or possession of bald or golden eagles. Permits can be obtained to kill golden eagles that are destroying property, but in the face of growing demand to protect these birds, none have been issued since 1969.

There is evidence that ranchers are willing to pay a bounty on eagles to protect their livestock. A recent estimate of $25 per eagle paid by one Wyoming rancher was presented to the Environmental Subcommittee of the Senate Appropriations Committee.[2] This evidence indicates that the law, which places a value of $500 per eagle plus a possible prison sentence on the killing of eagles, does not prevent the systematic hunting of these birds. The monetary equivalent of the probability of a $500 fine and

Abridged and reprinted from *Public Policy,* Summer 1972, pp. 411–441, by permission of the publisher.

* The authors are grateful to Dennis C. Mueller and Marc J. Roberts for helpful comments on an earlier draft of the paper. Any remaining errors are our responsibility.

1. See, for example, the discussion in *Predator Control and Related Problems* (Hearings before the Subcommittee on Agriculture, Environmental, and Consumer Protection, Committee on Appropriations, U.S. Senate; Washington: Government Printing Office, 1971).

2. James O. Vogan, pilot of a predator-hunting helicopter, testified that he had "personal knowledge of the shooting of over 500 eagles on one ranch in Wyoming. These eagles were shot from aircraft and include both golden and bald eagles." In later testimony he produced his notebook which showed "there had been at that date 377 eagles killed, at $25 per head, which comes to $8,425." *Ibid.,* pp. 153, 192.

six months in prison being applied plus the cost of killing an eagle is not sufficient to eliminate the expected return from killing eagles of about $25 per eagle. Why not? The main reason is that the law is costly to enforce because of the technical difficulty of discovering violations of the law. For example, the span of geography within which violations can occur is large enough to make detection of violations difficult and costly. In this case the probability of the $500 fine being applied is so low as to make the expected cost (i.e., the probability of being apprehended times the fine) much less than the $25 bounty. In fact, under these conditions it might be argued that the fine would have to be raised to a very high level to be an effective deterrent, to approximate in terms of the amount the rancher can expect to pay on a statistical basis the value to the society and all its members of losing an additional eagle (the marginal social cost).[3]

Even if this were sufficient to raise the expected cost of killing eagles to a level high enough to discourage most hunting, serious questions about the equity aspects of such a policy can be raised. The prosecution of a violation where only a small percentage of violators are caught and prosecuted would result in an *ex post,* or after-the-fact, penalty to the few violators who happen to be caught that would not fit well into some doctrines of "fairness." [4] The widespread public reaction against "making a scapegoat" of Lt. Calley is an example of this type of consideration.[5] Further, and importantly, almost all of the costs of preserving eagles under the fine-and-imprisonment approach are placed on ranchers, since the "cost" of preservation in this case is the ranchers' stock losses. Such

3. This is analogous to the case of ineffective $25 littering fines where the probability of being arrested is so low that the fine has no deterrent effect. In other words, the potential offender may calculate the value of the stated fine for littering times the probability that he will be caught and decide that the gains from littering exceed these expected costs. It should be noted, however, that in general risk-averse decision-makers would value the fine negatively more highly than its expected value. For the analytical background and some discussions relating to the economic approach to illegal activity, see G. Becker, "Crime and Punishment: An Economic Approach," *Journal of Political Economy,* LXXVI (March–April 1968), 169–215; M. Pauly and T. Willett, "Two Concepts of Equity and Their Implications for Public Policy," *Social Science Quarterly,* LIII (June 1972), 8–19 [Reading 19, below]; and G. Tullock, "An Economic Approach to Crime," *ibid.,* L (June 1969), 59–71 [Reading 7, above].

4. See Pauly and Willett, *op. cit.,* for a discussion of *ex ante* and *ex post* equity.

5. It also appears that the government's response to these eagle killings will be to amend the present law by substantially increasing the fine and imprisonment term for killing bald or golden eagles without a permit. The House of Representatives passed a bill in February 1972, proposing to raise the fine to $5,000 and/or one year in jail ($10,000 and two years for subsequent violations) and confiscation of any killing equipment (including helicopters). The Senate has yet to act on this bill. [The Senate subsequently passed the House version of the bill.] Although this approach may lead to some decrease in eagle killing, high enforcement costs will probably still make increased fines and punishments within the range of political feasibility an ineffective method of protecting these predators.

a distribution of costs does not correspond closely to either of the two contending canons of tax equity, the benefit and the ability-to-pay criteria. In fact, the two major equity criteria for taxation would imply that either conservationists (the benefit criterion) or rich people (the ability-to-pay criterion) bear the costs of eagle protection.[6]

In light of these considerations, what changes could be made in the existing procedures for protecting the eagles? More generally, how is correct information obtained on the demand for a good such as the preservation of eagles which has both public and private aspects? When faced with a case where private behavior may not reveal *all* the costs and benefits associated with a given activity, of which the eagle problem is an example, and economist's standard reaction is to see whether a different assignment of property rights can solve the problem.

Coase has shown that in the absence of transaction costs and in the presence of a small number of affected parties, an optimal allocation of resources would be forthcoming even without liability assignment for damages.[7] He pointed to the reciprocal nature of social cost relationships

6. The criteria for tax equity associated with the benefit and ability-to-pay criteria are discussed in most, if not all, public finance textbooks. An excellent discussion of these principles and their doctrinal origin is contained in R. A. Musgrave, *The Theory of Public Finance* (New York: McGraw-Hill, 1959), chaps. 4 and 5. Essentially, the benefit principle implies that publicly produced goods and services be priced in terms of an individual consumer-voter's *willingness* to pay for a (marginal) unit of output, where willingness to pay is indicated by the individual's (presumably) revealed marginal preferences for that output. The ability-to-pay principle, on the other hand, uses income or wealth as a proxy for the capacity of individuals to be taxed for public goods and services.

7. For Coase's original article, see his "The Problem of Social Cost," *Journal of Law and Economics,* III (October 1960), 1–44. A good basic presentation of Coase's argument, and of current externality and public goods theory in general for those unfamiliar with this literature, is contained in Robert Bish, *The Public Economy of Metropolitan Areas* (Chicago: Markham, 1971), especially chap. 2. For further discussions of transaction costs and liability rules, see G. Calabresi, "Transaction Costs, Resource Allocation and Liability Rules: A Comment," *Journal of Law and Economics,* XI (April 1968), 67–73; H. Demsetz, "Some Aspects of Property Rights," *ibid.,* IX (October 1966), 61–70, and "The Exchange and Enforcement of Property Rights," *ibid.,* VII (October 1964), 11–26; and A. Lerner, "The 1971 Report of the President's Council of Economic Advisers: Priorities and Efficiency," *American Economic Review,* LXI (September 1971), 527–530. For recent discussions of liability assignment in pollution control, see R. Zerbe, "Theoretical Efficiency in Pollution Control," *Western Economic Journal,* VIII (December 1970), 364–376, and "Theoretical Efficiency in Pollution Control: Reply," *ibid.,* IX (September 1971), 314–317; D. Shoup, "Theoretical Efficiency in Pollution Control: Comment," *ibid.,* 310–313; and H. Demsetz, "Theoretical Efficiency in Pollution Control: Comment on Comments," *ibid.,* 444–446. For recent discussions by economists of the relation of population to environmental quality and policy strategies for environmental management in general and for water pollution control in particular, see A. C. Fisher, "Population and Environment Quality" [Reading 12, above], A. V. Kneese, "Strategies for Environmental Management," A. M. Freeman, III, and R. H. Haveman, "Water Pollution Control River Basin Authorities, and Economic Incentives: Some Current Policy Issues," and M. J. Roberts,

and argued that bargaining between affected parties will internalize social costs under these conditions. In other words, bargaining is perfect under these conditions. Where bargaining is imperfect in the presence of transaction costs (and ignoring distributive justice), Coase frames the issue in terms of what is the least resource cost manner in which to correct for a social cost.

In the context of imperfect bargaining among the parties in a social cost relationship, the real point of considering changes in the assignment of property rights is to change the relevant transaction costs. For instance, in the case of air pollution, an assignment of property rights over the atmosphere to the public and assignment of liability for violating these rights to polluting firms and individuals (e.g., a pollution tax) may represent a feasible approach to this social cost problem.[8] In effect this approach lowers transaction costs relative to the case where firms have the right to pollute and large members of affected parties face high transaction costs in any attempts to organize and bargain over the level of pollution. A pollution tax may enable more efficient bargaining to take place between the affected parties via, for example, the level of pollution tax set through administrative or political processes.

The problem of devising a scheme to protect the eagle is parallel to some extent to that of the pollution example. That is, for the eagle problem, transaction costs and other costs of internalizing the relevant externalities (i.e., those social costs and benefits that are worth the cost of internalizing them) are significant and warrant the investigation of alternative liability assignment schemes. The costs relevant in the eagle problem, characterized as transaction costs, can be more specifically outlined. The high costs of enforcing the existing system of fines, already men-

---

"Organizing Water Pollution Control: The Scope and Structure of River Basin Authorities," all in *Public Policy*, XIX (Winter 1971), 19–142 consecutively. It should also be noted that externality theory is presently in a state of flux with some of its paradigms in question. Without going into considerable detail in interpreting these developments here, the best that can be done is to cite some of the contributions to these intellectual developments. See especially C. J. Goetz and J. M. Buchanan, "External Diseconomies in Competitive Supply," *American Economic Review*, LXI (December 1971), 883–890, especially n. 13, p. 888; H. Shibata, "Pareto-Optimality, Trade and the Pigovian Tax," *Economica*, XXXIX (May 1972), 190–202; J. M. Buchanan and W. C. Stubblebine, "Pareto-Optimality and Gains-from-Trade: A Comment," *ibid.*, 203–204; W. J. Baumol, "On Taxation and the Control of Externalities," *American Economic Review*, LXII (June 1972), 307–322, and J. M. Buchanan, "The Institutional Structure of Externality" (unpublished manuscript, January 1971). Finally, for a recent survey article in this area see E. J. Mishan, "The Postwar Literature on Externalities: An Interpretative Essay," *Journal of Economic Literature*, IX (March 1971), 1–28.

8. See, for example, the discussion in U.S. Council of Economic Advisers, *The Economic Report of the President* (Washington: Government Printing Office, 1971), Chapter IV.

tioned, are one example. In addition there are the possible costs involved with obtaining an incorrect revelation of demand for eagle protection under various liability assignments. These costs will be expressed in terms of protecting "too many" or "too few" eagles, owing to the fact that under some liability assignments information forthcoming about how many eagles to preserve may be biased. There are also those costs due to any redistribution of welfare and efficiency costs introduced by a liability scheme using public financing, where some individuals do not care about the preservation of eagles over the relevant range of public financing or some individuals care about their preservation at different levels of intensity but face identical tax charges for this service. It is the trade-offs among the various costs that differentiate the alternative liability assignment schemes for protecting eagles.

The eagle is taken as an example for discussion, but the principles involved are applicable to situations involving other endangered predators, such as the mountain lion and the timber wolf. Indeed, the analysis may be helpful in illuminating the public policy trade-offs of similar types of activity which embody all or some of the characteristics (which will be made clear as the analysis is developed) of the eagle problem.

I. Private Liability Assignment for Eagles

At present eagles are construed to be in the public domain and are held responsible for the damage they cause. Therefore, given the technical difficulties of identifying which eagle kills what sheep and of policing the consequent general killing of eagles by ranchers, some eagles pay for the cost of these damages with their lives. However, the eagles cannot bargain with ranchers for their own protection. In fact no very good market exists to equate costs and benefits in this case. The "fine plus jail" possibility might be seen as a "price," but in addition to the administrative difficulties noted above, the price-setting mechanism involved is quite unresponsive to local supply-demand considerations.

Suppose the property rights for eagles were transferred to conservative groups and their supporters, and these groups were made legally liable for the damage caused by eagles. If conservation groups accepted this liability, it might be possible to approach a "correct" population of eagles through bargaining between the "owners" of eagles and those harmed by the preying of eagles. Optimality here would be defined in terms of how many eagles conservationists would be willing to "own" (i.e., protect), given the predator damage accounted for by eagles.[9] In addition, under

9. See Section III for the discussion of the optimality conditions for any publicness components of the demand for eagle preservation and the application of the appropriate tax or subsidy to the use of land near where eagles live to obtain proper resource allocation to

this reform the cost of preserving eagles would be distributed in greater accordance with the benefit principle of taxation (see footnote 6) in the sense that those who value the preservation of eagles would probably bear the majority of the costs of such a program. Note that this argument ignores the problem of getting all who care about eagles to enroll in the relevant conservation organizations. If beneficiaries conclude that others will pay, so that they need not contribute (i.e., they will be "free-riders"), too few eagles will be demanded.

Supposing, as some conservation groups argue, that ranchers now overstate eagle damage, a correctly operating eagle market would result in a much larger eagle population.[10] If, on the other hand, the ranchers are correct in assessing eagle damage as high, the correct eagle population might be quite small. In any event, assigning liability would help to permit a determination of the optimal eagle population through bargaining between conservationists and ranchers.[11] Note, however, that in the proposed market where conservationists had to pay for the eagle damage, the ranchers would still have an incentive to exaggerate damage. The point is that one would have a party with an interest in accurate data, and an impartial scheme on the insurance adjuster model might arise. Conservationists are now demanding an unchecked eagle population because they bear minimal (if any) costs in supporting the preservation of eagles; ranchers demand a very small eagle population because they bear, or at least think they bear, most of the costs of a large eagle population.

Only if ranchers are fully compensated for what they view as eagle damage, including all costs incurred in making and documenting claims, will they have no incentive to kill eagles.[12] Since documentation will be

---

ranching on which to base a determination of the proper number of eagles to preserve. Also, in this preliminary discussion of liability assignment it is assumed that all ranchers are fully compensated by owners for losses due to eagles. Thus, by definition the existing eagle population becomes the optimal one to preserve. The case where the existing population is too large or too small is treated later in the paper.

10. For a discussion of research summarized by the National Audubon Society and designed to refute reportedly exaggerated Department of Agriculture estimates of stock losses due to predators, namely eagles, see C. B. Pfeiffner, "Eagle Shooters Are Mostly Misguided," *Washington Post,* September 24, 1971, p. D9. Some of this summarized research appears to have applied convincing techniques (e.g., the chemical analysis of eagle droppings from a number of nests) to demonstrate that government estimates were somewhat too high. These results, however, have little impact on the analysis here, since what is behaviorally relevant is what farmers and ranchers actually *believe* their losses due to eagles are.

11. Since a substantial number of eagles are killed by poison, it may be necessary to compensate ranchers for losses due to predators other than eagles in order to protect eagles. This increased cost of eagle protection would probably stimulate conservation groups to search for species-specific methods of controlling predators.

12. Those individuals who kill eagles purely for "sport" could be dealt with through

costly, it must either be part of the compensation or done free by public officials. Otherwise, it might be cheaper to kill eagles than to put in a claim for damage. It is difficult to say *a priori* whether or not such documentation costs would in general be less than the analogous enforcement costs of the present fine system.

However, one must also be careful not to overcompensate for losses. If the compensation exceeds the cost of the damage, it would become profitable to be victimized. Ranchers would have an incentive not to take "normal" precautions to protect their livestock. Taken to an extreme where damage was very profitable, a rancher might continually "raise" new eagles, which in turn would only be destroyed by conservationists. The ranchers would be seeking to avoid such payments. Taking into account the relative risks and costs of setting the wrong level of compensation, it would probably be best to err in this regard a little on the high side if the existing stock of eagles is quite low from an ecological point of view, or the probability of the survival of the species. The effects of overcompensation (too many eagles) would be more easily reversible than those of undercompensation (too few).

This issue is just one example of the often-ignored need to consider whether natural processes can be easily reversed when devising public policy. Such asymmetries are pervasive in conservation problems (e.g., cutting redwoods, damming the Colorado River, and so forth) and have not received the attention they deserve from economic analysts. By removing the economic incentive for killing eagles, such a scheme could be quite effective in preserving eagles. Two closely related questions remain, however. First, is the eagle worth the costs of saving it, and if so, how many should be preserved? The second question is how should the preservation of the eagles (i.e., the payment of compensation for damages caused by eagles) be financed? The relationship between the two questions is that alternative financing mechanisms may yield more or less information about the socially "correct" level of demand for eagles.

The consideration of these problems involves a more detailed analysis of the economics of the proposal to assign ownership rights for eagles to conservationists. The general reader may not wish to work through this analysis and may wish to proceed instead to the conclusion in Section V. However, most readers would probably find it useful to at least skim the intervening sections.

---

other legal methods, perhaps through astronomical fines. Once the rancher is fully compensated he would no longer sponsor eagle killing and may be equally incensed by the "sport" hunters, thereby making protection costs lower.

II. Will Purely Private Finance Preserve Enough Eagles?

The scheme advanced above does have its difficulties. As noted, under purely private financing of compensation there is the problem of avoiding strategic behavior by members or potential members of conservation groups. Members might place false, low valuations on their desired eagle populations in the hope of "free-riding" on the contributions of others. Thus, an individual contributor might rationalize that if he does not contribute or contributes very little, while other contributors kick in their full share, he can enjoy the common output (eagle preservation) at little or no personal cost. In essence he cannot be excluded, since the costs of exclusion are prohibitive once the common output has been provided by the (presumed) contributions of others. However, when all contributors behave in this way simultaneously, a much less than appropriate level of compensation would be forthcoming from purely voluntary contributions. Indeed, under some conditions the common output may not be supplied at all. Needless to say, the motivation of conservationists is not being questioned in making such an argument. Presumably these individuals desire to preserve the eagle, but the structure of choice under purely voluntary compensation biases the outcome against expressing the "correct level" of demand for such a good. Indeed, the situation described is one where purely self-interested economic man dominates, but not completely. The existence of Kantians (especially rich ones) and others who behave with respect to their conceptions of what is good for all would cause some voluntary contributions to be forthcoming.[13]

The preservation of eagles can be viewed as a public good with a high

13. The concept of free-riding behavior has been employed in the development and discussions of public goods theory. It is generally considered that such behavior is more likely to occur and to be severe when large rather than small groups are involved. This is due primarily to the higher transaction costs in larger groups where there are no predefined rules to internalize such behavior. Though probably not as prohibitive as in large groups, transaction costs in small groups in the absence of predefined rules are still important and take the form of the administrative problems of eliciting options, nonrelevation of preferences, and the cost of bargaining when small numbers are involved. It is argued that free-riding behavior can be detected *and* deterred at relatively lower costs in small groups. This is a tricky question, however, since some small groups supplying a public good may be able easily to detect free-riding but not be able to deter it (at least strongly). A possible example of this is behavior by participants in the international monetary system where detection of free-riding is reasonably easy, but ability to apply sanctions under the present institutional structure of the system is weak. For discussion of this example, see L. H. Officer and T. D. Willett, "The Interaction of Adjustment and Gold Conversion Policies in a Reserve Currency System," *Western Economic Journal,* VIII (March 1970), 47–60. For an analytical discussion of free-rider behavior in public goods theory and a bibliography of the relevant literature, see J. M. Buchanan, *The Demand and Supply of Public Goods* (Chicago: Rand McNally, 1968), chap. V.

skewed demand ranging from that of the conservationists who value highly the (marginal) eagles preserved (Amacher and Tollison) to others in the collectivity who may place a zero (or perhaps negative) value on the preservation of the marginal eagles (Willett).[14] For this type of good, public financing through the general tax system will redistribute welfare, since individuals who do not value eagle preservation would be charged for this service *and* those who place positive, but different, marginal evaluations on eagle preservation may be charged the same tax-price. For example, following an equity criterion of benefit taxation where individual users of a public good are taxed in proportion to their evaluations of the (marginal) amount of the good or service consumed, financing eagle preservation through the federal income tax would involve such a redistribution of welfare.[15] Furthermore, there may be an efficiency loss associated with purely public financing of eagle preservation, since the level of demand for eagles may be different than in a completely optimal scheme where tax prices closely approximate the distribution of demand. In other words, the point is that the level of preservation is presumably set by what people would be willing to pay in a good financing scheme, and not simply by what they do pay under financing mechanisms.[16] In any scheme to pay for losses due to eagles, the trade-offs between the free-riding and public-finance types of nonoptimality need to be consid-

14. Defining eagle preservation as a public good is done in the sense that it enters more than one person's utility function, and thus all externalities can be treated as public goods. It is not necessary in this view that everyone value the public good the same or, indeed, that everyone receive the same physical service flows from the good. For further elaboration of this point see P. A. Samuelson, "Pure Theory of Public Expenditure and Taxation," in J. Margolis (ed.), *Public Economics* (Amsterdam: North-Holland, 1969), and J. M. Buchanan, *ibid.*, chap. 4. Also, one should see a recent exchange on the links between public goods and external effects in the *Journal of Political Economy*. See E. J. Mishan, "The Relationship Between Joint Products, Collective Goods, and External Effects," *Journal of Political Economy*, LXXVII (May–June 1969), 329–348; J. Boyd, "Joint Products, Collective Goods, and External Effects: Comment," *ibid.*, LXXIX (September–October 1971); 1138–1140; D. Bradford, "Joint Products, Collective Goods and External Effects: Comment," *ibid.*, 1119–1128; E. James, "Joint Products, Collective Goods, and External Effects: Comment," *ibid.*, 1129–1135; N. Singer, "Joint Products, Collective Goods, and External Effects: Comment," *ibid.*, 1136–1137; and E. J. Mishan, "Joint Products, Collective Goods, and External Effects: Reply," *ibid.*, 1141–1150.

15. It should be noted that this is not an unusual situation for taxpayers, as similar transfers of welfare probably occur with respect to a significant number of public outputs. Thus, while the analysis of the eagle problem can be viewed as a proposal to extend the application of the benefit criterion in public finance, the main issue at stake is simply that the existing fine and imprisonment system does not deter the killing of eagles, and the application of the benefit criterion along with the other elements of the proposal presented in this paper may adequately protect the eagle.

16. For the analytical discussion of how prearranged tax shares (e.g., in a constitutional setting) may affect the amount and mix of public goods demanded by voter-taxpayers, see J. M. Buchanan, *The Demand and Supply of Public Goods, op. cit.*, chaps. 7 and 8.

ered, and a range of schemes can be discussed in terms of this trade-off.

To get around the limits of purely voluntary contributions, one could require through law that conservation groups compensate ranchers. Free-riding behavior might well be somewhat less of a problem under this scheme as long as there were individuals who received benefits from belonging to conservation groups (i.e., these would be individuals who would not drop out of conservation clubs as the price of membership rose due to liability for eagle damage). This scheme would, in effect, increase the price of belonging to a conservation club. Membership in conservation clubs would decrease as a result. The magnitude of the decline would depend upon how sensitive the demand for membership in such groups was to price (i.e., the demand elasticity) and on the amount of the increase. Unfortunately, there is no estimate of the strength of either element, but it can be conjectured that it would be enough to make the scheme unworkable, since as each person left, the price to remaining members would rise.

However, if enforcement costs were low, the proper liability assignment might be on the rancher (i.e., the ranchers had to pay for killing as they do today). In this case farmers might attempt to insure against losses due to eagles. Since enforcement costs are high, however, such a scheme, like the current fine procedure, would probably not work. Ranchers would probably not buy insurance, which would be more expensive the higher the costs of documenting losses, and instead just kill eagles and hope to avoid having to pay up.

A possible method of attempting to estimate the private, or purely voluntary, demand for eagles would be for, say, the Interior Department to auction off permits to own eagles, rather than assign specific liability to conservation groups.[17] A market exchange process would then result to

17. See U.S. Council of Economic Advisers, *Economic Report of the President, op. cit.,* for the discussion of such a proposal to deal with environmental pollution. Also, see Lerner, *op. cit.,* and J. Stein, "The 1971 Report of the President's Council of Economic Advisers: Micro-Economic Aspects of Public Policy," *American Economic Review,* LXI (September 1971), 531–537, for further discussions of the Council's proposals in this area. Stein's analysis is criticized in S. Peltzman and T. N. Tideman, "Local Versus National Pollution Control" (Harvard Institute of Economic Research, Discussion Paper Number 216, November 1971). Acutally, both Stein and Peltzman and Tideman miss several important trade-offs in the issue of local versus national pollution control. Space does not permit a consideration of these trade-offs here as they are not directly relevant to the eagle problem. The interested reader may see R. Sherman and T. D. Willett, "Regional Development Externalities and Tax-Subsidy Combinations," *National Tax Journal,* XXII (June 1969), 291–293, and R. D. Tollison and T. D. Willett, "Intergovernmental Spillovers and the Theory of Clubs and Alliances" (mimeographed; Cornell University, 1972). Also, see the discussion in C. McLure, Jr., "Revenue Sharing: Alternative to Rational Fiscal Federalism?" *Public Policy,* XIX (Summer 1971), 457–478 [Reading 15, below] on the possible appropriateness of a federal minimum pollution charge with localities allowed within this constraint to pur-

reveal price and quantity data for the preservation of eagles as conservationists and ranchers traded and held these permits over time. Such a method essentially forces private action in this case. However, to the extent that the ownership of a permit (i.e., the preservation of eagles) generates benefits not captured by the owner, free-riding behavior may appear, and the price and quantity data generated by such an auction system would not be fully accurate.

Furthermore, there is still the problem of enforcement costs under this scheme. Shifting to private liability for eagles would not avoid these costs, and either government or private action would have to insure that the eagles that were owned via the permit scheme were not illegally killed. In terms of the incentive to cheat under this scheme the rancher or sportsman, for example, would have no economic incentive to bid more for a permit than the expected value of the cost of being caught and prosecuted for killing an eagle without a permit.[18] Surreptitiously killing eagles may simply be less costly under some circumstances. In general, however, if compensation for eagle damages and documentation costs is promptly forthcoming from the "owners" of eagles, the enforcement costs with respect to ranchers should fall under the permit scheme. If the compensation scheme is costly or complex for ranchers, they may make expected value computations on, for example, the probability of winning a damage suit times the value of their losses that will lead them to kill eagles in any event.[19]

Thus, although the permit-auction system is an attractive way to get data on the demand for eagle preservation, it does not avoid free-riding behavior. It suggests also the possibility of providing less protection than schemes where the compensation procedures are not left entirely to private action through the courts.

It is useful to consider a hypothetical permit market for eagles to clarify the various issues posed in the eagle problem. If a permit is issued for every eagle, the relevant supply curve *in a given period* is a vertical line above the existing population of eagles. The market price per eagle in this time period for a given eagle population would thus be demand-determined at the point where the demand curve for holding eagle permits in-

---

chase their preferred levels of environmental quality. Discussion of the appropriate level of government to deal with the preservation of eagles is in Section IV below.

18. Actually, a risk-averting rancher would be willing to pay somewhat more to avoid the risky situation of killing eagles without a permit.

19. It is possible that if the rancher views the right to buy a permit to kill an eagle as more reasonable than the present fine and jail rules, he might lose more utility from violating the rules of the more reasonable system. Thus, he might have less tendency to break the reasonable rule, even where obtaining compensation was costly, and enforcement costs could fall under these circumstances as a consequence.

tersects the vertical supply curve of eagles. Figure 1 illustrates such a hypothetical market for eagles.

On the vertical axis is measured the price per unit for eagles, and on the horizontal axis is measured quantities of eagles per time period. In any given short-run time period, the length of which would be determined mainly by the biological process of reproduction among eagles (or the ease with which eagles could be hunted and killed), there is a given number of eagles such as depicted by the supply curve, S (or point Q'_E, along the horizontal axis). The permit-auction system involves issuing a permit for each eagle and then selling these permits at auction to all interested buyers. A market price for eagles, P'_E, is thereby established where aggregate demand (drawn linear for convenience) intersects aggregate supply at A.

When viewed as a hypothetical market, the various analytical issues posed by assigning liability for eagles can be delineated. One set of problems, discussed extensively above, is to avoid free-riding behavior, which in terms of Figure 1 means that the demand curve for eagles may be biased downward. A closely related question is whether resource allocation with respect to ranching in areas where eagles prey is efficient. Since the social costs in the eagle problem are caused by the proximity of

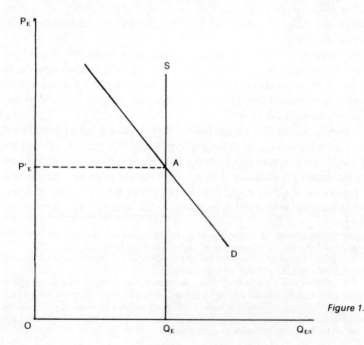

Figure 1.

eagles and livestock, the relationship between the two is reciprocal, as stressed in the previous discussion of Coase's paper, and in resource cost terms one has to determine whether it is cheaper to move eagles away from the sheep, or vice versa. In the presence of transaction costs, this issue involves placing the appropriate unit tax or subsidy on ranching in these areas.

The problems of obtaining an estimate of the demand for eagles and efficient resource allocation on land where eagles prey interact in the sense, for example, that placing the appropriate unit tax or subsidy on ranching activity in areas where eagles live may move one along the aggregate curve for eagles. This will happen because placing the appropriate unit tax or subsidy will shift the long-run supply curve of eagles, which is a function of the marginal damages imposed by various populations of eagles and is positively sloped with respect to price as depicted in Figure 2 below, and thereby invoke a movement along the aggregate demand curve for eagles. These two problems interact to determine *how many* eagles to preserve, and they are considered in detail in the next section.

A second and closely related problem area, which is treated in detail in Section IV, is how to adjust the number of permits issued over time if the correct market demand curve gives a market price (for the moment ignoring the possibility of government holding permits) for eagle damages that is either too high or too low to maintain the existing stock of eagles.

It should be stressed that a pure auction system where one can buy the rights to kill *or* maintain birds is probably not much of an improvement over the present fine-and-imprisonment scheme. The problem of enforcement costs would still be present under such a scheme, and if, for example, conservationists bid up the market price for eagles to a high enough level, ranchers may make expected value calculations which will lead them to kill eagles illegally. Thus the mere act of establishing private liability for eagles does not necessarily lead to a good system for preserving these birds. In fact, to lower enforcement costs, the ranchers' incentive to kill eagles has to be reduced by paying compensation.

This is a primary difference in the policy problems of the eagle and the environment. In the latter case the establishment of a market for certain environmental rights may be enough to obtain an efficient solution to the problem. In the case of eagles compensation must be paid to ranchers to get around the problem of enforcement costs. The problem with compensation schemes, however, is to offset potential free-riding behavior in purely private action by introducing public finance in some form.[20] A possible scheme involving public finance is presented in the next section.

20. A related problem in the permit system, which complicates obtaining a good estimate of conservationist demand, is that each person or group buying a permit has to guess how

III. The Role of Public Financing: A Levering Scheme of Financing Eagle Preservation

The preceding argument suggests that a form of compensation through the public sector is required to offset the problem of free-riding and enforcement costs with the purely voluntary schemes. The rationale for this is that by requiring individuals to pay prearranged tax shares, all individuals are presumably aware that contributions for public outputs will be forthcoming generally. One thus has to pay for public outputs, and the incentive to free-ride is sharply reduced. Individuals should now reveal their preferences (to an approximation) for public outputs through political processes, since they are now in the inverse behavioral position from that of the free-rider; namely, they have to pay for public goods regardless of whether they want them or not. Thus, revelation of preferences may become a dominant strategy for individual voters-taxpayers.[21] However, while public finance options may sharply reduce the incentives for free-riding, they involve possible inequities and efficiency costs in the financing of such a public good as eagle preservation.

At an extreme of full public financing would be the paying of all compensations financed through the general income tax system. The advantage of paying for eagle damages in this manner is that everyone is constrained to contribute, and the free-rider incentive is reduced. In addition, since there would be an opportunity cost to conservationists in terms of other foregone public outputs under this scheme, conservationists and other protectors of eagles would have a greater incentive to make the appropriate calculations concerning the number of eagles to be preserved.[22]

---

many will end up in the hands of would-be killers of eagles. This problem can be addressed by introducing supplementary public finance, for example, to buy and hold eagle permits (discussed in the next section) and by careful management of the long-run supply of eagles by public authorities in the face of varying levels of forthcoming compensation for eagle damages (discussed in Section IV).

21. It should be noted that the above discussion ignores the problem that under pure public finance there may be incentives to *overstate* one's preferences, since taxes for particular outputs are not adjusted to varying demands. One may overstate his preferences in this case since any given individual bears only a small percentage of costs in each case.

22. An example of a public finance scheme involving essentially no opportunity cost to those wishing to protect eagles would be to allow registered conservationists to earmark part of their tax bill to compensate for predator losses. This alternative is not an attractive financing system in this case because it places a zero opportunity cost in terms of foregone public outputs on the conservationists. In other words, the earmarking of taxes for predator protection would only infinitesimally offset the amount of welfare, defense, and other public outputs that these individuals consume. In practice this procedure would turn out to be little different from the present situation, in which the conservation groups demand unchecked eagle populations. Earmarking would also create problems in matching earmarked funds with total losses due to eagles and other predators. For example, should the earmarked

One might find that under financing through the general tax system the result hinges on the sensitivity of the political process to conservationist pressure groups. Still, this method represents an alternative way to get an approximation of the demand for eagles that avoids free-riding problems, given the total losses imposed by eagles.

However, the demand for the preservation of eagles as a public good, although shared to some extent by large numbers of citizens, is probably greatest for conservationists, and may even be geographically concentrated in areas where eagles live.[23] The full public financing scheme may thus not appropriately reflect the degree of skewness in the public demand associated with preserving eagles and would introduce an inequity on the benefit criterion to the extent that citizens who place a zero value on eagle preservation are charged for such a service and citizens who place a positive, but different, valuation on the marginal eagle preserved are charged the same tax-price. In essence, welfare with respect to the preservation of the eagle would be redistributed among taxpayers in some manner according to the relation between the distribution of demand for eagle preservation and individual shares in pure public finance. For example, why should Willett, who does not value the preservation of (marginal) eagles at all, be charged by the government for such a service? And with respect to Amacher and Tollison, who do wish to see eagles preserved, but Tollison loves (marginal) eagles twice as much as Amacher, why should they face the same tax-price (assuming they earn equivalent taxable incomes) for this service? These questions suggest that on an equity criterion of benefit taxation a financial scheme is needed that places a differentially higher burden on the conservationist. Indeed, if conservationists also tend to be rich, then the ability-to-pay criteria for

proportion be fixed or variable? If earmarking oversubscribes losses due to eagles, should rebates be made to other public programs or to subsidizing eagle production? These problems combine to exclude earmarking as an attractive alternative in handling compensation for predator damages. This does not mean that earmarking incremental taxes is not a valuable fiscal device in some uses. For a theoretical comparison of the properties of public outcomes under financing through general funds and earmarking, see J. M. Buchanan, "Economics of Earmarked Taxes," *Journal of Political Economy,* LXXI (October 1963), 457–462; and G. Goetz, "Earmarked Taxes and Majority Rule Budgetary Process," *American Economic Review,* LVIII (March 1968), 128–136.

23. The reasoning here would be the "out of sight, out of mind" sort of argument which J. M. Buchanan ("What Kind of Redistribution Do We Want?" *Economica,* XXXV [May 1968], 185–190) raised with respect to the externality generated by the poor. Thus, those who do not see the eagles may experience no gain or loss from their existence or nonexistence. Although this is probably not the case with the public good associated with eagles, should these conditions hold, the financing of the preservation of eagles could be appropriately undertaken by the various governments in the geographic areas where eagles live. See McLure, *op. cit.,* for further analytical discussion of the appropriate level of government to finance various types of public outputs.

taxation would also imply higher taxes on conservationists for this service.

There may be an efficiency cost to pure public finance as well. Such a cost would take the form of obtaining a different level of demand from pure public finance as opposed to that obtained under a more optimal financing scheme. For example, the level of pure public finance may be constrained by those taxpayers with low marginal evaluations for eagle preservation in the sense that these individuals may carry majority weight in the legislative process which would set a level of finance for eagle damages. A more flexible financing scheme may thus garner more revenue for compensating damages and thereby preserve more eagles.

The general problem posed by eagles, then, is to preserve the advantages of public finance in avoiding free-riding behavior while avoiding as far as possible the inequity and efficiency costs involved in pure public finance. A possible method to approximate the correct public-private mix of compensation would be to allow conservationists to lever their voluntary contributions through the fiscal system by having the government approximate the "publicness" element in the demand for eagle preservation with a matching contribution of some magnitude. Such a scheme could be envisaged as ranging from a zero matching contribution by government (pure private action by conservationists) to full or greater matching (in the extreme, full public financing with perhaps a subsidy for eagle production) and thereby encompass the full range of public-private interactions. The degree of matching would obviously depend on the amount of public goods demand estimated for eagles. By allowing conservationists to lever their contributions, some of the free-riding incentives might be internalized, since conservationists would now have the knowledge that in some form related to their contributions others were constrained to contribute to the financing of the program. Thus, the incentive to free-ride is reduced, although probably not completely eliminated. In an ideal sense, where such factors as transaction and information costs are negligible, the levering scheme allows government to trade off between the problems caused by free-riding and public finance precisely. Starting from the position of no matching by government, one would trade off the nonoptimality of the estimated impact of free-riding behavior against the nonoptimalities of assuming an increasing degree of financing the public good through the fiscal system. In addition, the application of such a system for preserving eagles seems justified on equity grounds.

It should be noted that under feasible conditions it may be difficult to estimate the above trade-offs. The scheme would probably involve some leverage for conservationists, although there would be room in such a program for voluntary incentives to function. The trade-offs in this model could not be made with extreme precision in practice. However, the model does allow trade-offs to be made between public and private action, in comparison with the present fine-and-imprisonment system which essentially places trade-off coefficients of 1 and 0 (i.e., all-or-none) on public and private action to protect eagles, with ranchers bearing the brunt of the costs of eagle preservation.[24]

The levering system as presented here is distinct from the auction-permit system. It would be operated separately with some agency collecting forthcoming public and private funds and paying off documented damage claims or using the funds to preserve eagles in the most efficient way. As pointed out earlier, compensation must be paid in the case of eagles to avoid enforcement cost problems, and the levering scheme accomplishes the compensation requirement.

However, the levering scheme also embodies the problem of demand estimation for the public component of forthcoming compensation. In this regard one may be interested in the possible use of the permit system to obtain estimates of the aggregate demand for eagles. For example, government may wish to propose various matching ratios in response to private purchases of permits (e.g., government purchases one-half a permit for each private permit bought). In an ideal sense the "market price" established for eagles should be the same in the levering scheme of compensation with the optimal public-private mix of finance and in the auction-permit system with government matching of private purchases. Operationally, the latter approach could be viewed as a way to derive estimates of the optimal public-private mix of finance to pay compensation in the pure levering scheme.

The levering scheme with ownership rights for eagles can thus aid in the determination of the correct number of eagles to preserve by obtaining an estimate of the demand for this service which is (to an approximation) unbiased and adheres more closely to the benefit principle of taxation. There remains, however, the second problem, in determining the optimal eagle stock, of being sure that resource allocation to ranching on the land where eagles prey is efficient. For example, if the differential advantages of raising sheep in eagle areas are low, conservationists or government may find that using forthcoming private and public contributions to buy the land near where eagles prey to establish sanctuaries or bribing land-

24. The trade-off procedure could be extended to other public-private relationships. Matching grant devices are frequently employed in intergovernmental relationships between the national and state and local governments, but have not (to our knowledge) been used by governments in dealing with private groups or individuals.

owners to restrict the use of their land is desirable, if this is less costly than paying for the livestock damage by eagles under current land use (or perhaps that some mix of these methods is optimal). Since the relevant negative externality is caused by the proximity of livestock and eagles (i.e., is reciprocal), one should in general consider the costs of moving eagles away from the sheep as well as the costs of moving sheep away from the eagles. (It appears, however, that in the present case the latter procedure is not a least-cost alternative.) Where transactions costs are zero and the possibility of threats to "blackmail" compensation is absent, then on efficiency grounds all that is needed for these allocative effects to be properly internalized is that property rights be clearly established, irrespective of to which party or parties they are given. Ranchers and conservationists would then bargain out an efficient solution.[25]

Where transactions costs or threats of blackmail are high, however, the most efficient action may be to implement a unit tax and/or subsidy (for not using the land to raise livestock) scheme on ranching activity in the areas where eagles live. The appropriate unit tax or subsidy (or combination) would depend on the real opportunity cost caused by the optimum number of eagles and would probably vary with the nearness of the land to the eagles. The optimum number of eagles is probably the existing population of these birds, and this point is discussed below. The efficient unit tax or subsidy must still, however, be placed on ranching, since without, for example, such a subsidy ranchers would have incentives to overutilize the land near to the eagles with respect to purposes, such as lamb-raising, which would increase the negative externality caused by the "correct" stock of eagles.

Thus, an appropriate unit tax or subsidy must be applied, as the number of eagles to preserve and resource allocation to ranching in the area are interdependent (see the discussion below). Faced with an appropriate unit subsidy for abstaining (at the margin) from raising lambs, ranchers would make socially optimum decisions on land use, since they would be confronted with the correct opportunity cost for the raising of livestock on land near where eagles live. An efficient unit tax on ranching could confront ranchers with the same opportunity costs and elicit a similar resource allocation. In the face of such policy instruments, it may become more efficient for ranchers to switch to livestock on which eagles

---

25. As the reader will recall, these are the type of questions of efficiency in resource allocation raised by Coase in his classic article on social cost (*op. cit.*). See G. A. Mumey, "The 'Coase Theorem': A Re-examination," *Quarterly Journal of Economics,* LXXXV (November 1971), 718–723, for a discussion of threats to blackmail compensation. Income effects are also neglected. On this point see E. J. Mishan, *op. cit.,* and R. Sherman and T. Willett, "Regional Development Externalities and Tax-Subsidy Combinations," *op cit.*

do not prey or to move the raising of lambs to areas where eagles do not prey.[26]

Ideally, once the efficient unit tax or subsidy is established, the optimal eagle population will change. To see this effect in terms of the hypothetical market for eagles, the concept of a longer-run supply curve for eagles must be introduced. Such a curve would have the normal positive slope (with respect to price) associated with supply curves and would be a function of the (marginal) damages imposed by various potential populations of eagles. In effect this curve represents the long-run marginal cost or damage schedule for eagles and is defined over periods long enough to adjust the supply of eagles upward or downward (see footnote 33 below). A long-run supply curve for eagles is depicted by LRS (drawn linear for convenience) in Figure 2.

The effect of placing the efficient unit tax or subsidy on ranching activity is to shift the long-run supply function from LRS to LRS' in Figure 2. In essence, the long-run marginal cost curve for protecting eagles is low-

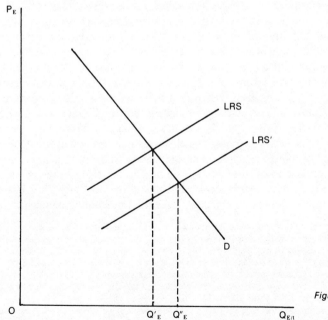

Figure 2.

26. See Coase, *op cit.*, and R. Turvey, "On Divergences Between Social Cost and Private Cost," *Economica*, XXX (August 1963), 309–313, for discussions of determining efficient alternatives in production. Turvey's paper is an excellent short summary of many of the analytical points contained in this section.

ered due to the fact that ranchers no longer have incentives to overutilize the land near to where eagles live in such a way as to increase the externality imposed on them by any given stock of eagles. The optimal long-run eagle population would thus change from Q'_E to Q''_E in Figure 2. The extent of any shift in the long-run supply curve and therefore in the optimal eagle population would be determined by conditions in the ranching industry. (Qualitatively, for example, one could say that where producers earn large differential rents in the area, the extent of the shift will be less, and vice versa.)

As is clear in Figure 2, the shift in long-run supply moves one along the aggregate demand curve for eagles, lowering price and increasing quantity demanded. Forthcoming compensation to protect eagles may increase, decrease, or remain the same, depending on whether demand is elastic, inelastic, or unit elastic over the relevant range. In general, one would want to compute the cost of the unit tax or subsidy for different levels of demand for eagles, and vice versa, and set the eagle population and the tax or subsidy at the intersection of two such schedules. Such a process would establish equilibrium values for these variables.[27]

Actually, in this case, since the fine and imprisonment system is not effective and liability for losses due to eagles presently rests with the ranchers, land usage near where eagles live probably already reflects livestock losses due to eagles. An approximation to the proper unit tax or subsidy can thus be taken from the damage caused by the existing eagle population, if existing land uses reflect these damages. The efficient tax or subsidy must still be placed on ranchers, however, since under a (assumed) bias-free private-public financing scheme, full compensation would probably be forthcoming for all losses due to the current stock of eagles, and without the appropriate unit tax or subsidy ranchers would have an incentive to overutilize the land near to the eagles, thereby causing damages by the existing stock of eagles to be too "high."[28] Under these conditions, however, one could take the forthcoming compensation

27. For a clear statement of the theoretical issues involved with reciprocal externalities and for references to the literature on this problem, see Wallace E. Oates, *Fiscal Federalism* (New York: Harcourt Brace Jovanovich, 1972), chap. 3, especially Appendix A. Also, for the discussion of reciprocal externalities which are termed "non-separable" and for which there may be no efficient solution (in game-theoretic terms, the absence of dominance), see O. Davis and A. Whinston, "Externalities, Welfare and the Theory of Games," *Journal of Political Economy,* LXX (June 1962), 241–262.

28. The reason that the efficient unit tax or subsidy must be placed on ranchers even though existing land values may reflect the preying of eagles is analogous to Coase's (*op. cit.*) example of crop damage caused by sparks from a railway. With liability on the railroad company for crop damage, farmers would not have the proper incentives for crop-raising near the railroad right-of-way without the appropriate tax or subsidy.

for the existing stock of eagles as fairly indicative of the appropriate number to support.

There may also be discontinuities in the reaction functions of the two parties in this case, so that the originally determined optimal eagle population is still the optimal one after the efficient tax or subsidy is put on. If the existing number of birds turned out to be smaller or larger than the forthcoming compensation would support, then adjustments in the stock of eagles and subsequently adjustments in the optimal unit tax or subsidy on ranchers could be undertaken. Given, however, the consideration of possible discontinuities in reaction functions and the fact that land values near to the eagles probably already reflect losses due to eagles, the problems of reaching the correct stock of eagles via the levering scheme and correct resource allocation by ranchers via the appropriate unit tax or subsidy are probably not too serious, and in terms of efficient public policy the difficulty of approaching the economist's optimal solution may not be great in this case.

In an ideal sense, then, the dynamics of reaching the desired eagle population is a function of adjustments in both the relevant demand and supply curves. As noted at several points above, however, the implicit dynamic involved in determining the number of eagles to preserve and the correct resource allocation to ranching discussed in this section assumes that enough funds will be forthcoming to preserve the existing stock of these birds. Assuming that in a given period the above adjustments have been made, there remains, however, the related problem of how to adjust the stock of eagles over time if forthcoming compensation is not sufficient (or more than sufficient) to support the existing population of eagles. This problem will be treated in the next section.

The problem in giving private liability for eagles to determine the correct level of demand (the optimal private-public mix of finance) is illustrative of an important problem in operationalizing public goods theory. The normative model used by economists in discussing public goods is essentially the Samuelsonian pure public good model where the satisfaction of the (total) condition, where *vertically* summed marginal evaluations for this good are equal to its marginal cost, is stressed. The marginal conditions (if desirable to be satisfied at all as guides to how much of the public good to produce) imply differential benefit taxes. However, the marginal evaluations on which such taxes would be based are essentially subjective phenomenon, not observable by external observers, and are subject to bias in the sense of free-riding behavior by individuals as discussed above. One is thus left with the important operational problem of how to obtain unbiased revelations of individuals' marginal evaluations for public goods.[29] Note that there is also the more general problem of whether current authorities have the incentives to supply correct amounts of public goods, even though they may have reliable demand estimates, a problem which cannot be considered in detail in this paper.[30]

IV. Adjustments in the Stock of Eagles

For the moment let it be assumed that a procedure can be devised and followed so that the aggregate demand for eagles can be accurately estimated.[31] Assume some plan which either issues permits or else operates

29. P. A. Samuelson is credited with presenting the modern general equilibrium statement of public goods theory in two basic papers. See his "The Pure Theory of Public Expenditure," *Review of Economics and Statistics*, XXXVI (November 1954), 387–389, and "Diagramatic Exposition of a Theory of Public Expenditure," *ibid.*, XXXVII (November 1955), 350–356. An excellent bibliography on public goods theory current through 1968 appears at the end of the chapters in J. M. Buchanan, *The Demand and Supply of Public Goods, op. cit.* The concept of subjective cost which, as noted, is important in the case of public goods, is stressed in J. M. Buchanan, *Cost and Choice* (Chicago: Markham, 1970). The reason that the text states that the marginal conditions in the public good case may not have to be met can be clarified. In the pure public good case there is a dilemma. Welfare maximization implies that where the marginal cost of adding another consumer to a public good *already produced* is zero, then marginal units of the good should be priced equal to zero. Since pure public goods, by definition, exhibit the property of being available equally to all at zero marginal cost to any voter-consumer, then static welfare maximization implies zero marginal cost to any voter-consumer, then static welfare maximization implies zero prices for voter-consumers in this case. However, if such a policy is followed, no information about demand for the good or about the desirability of any given level of present or future production of the good is obtained. Pricing the public good via differential benefit taxes would provide this information to a degree. Hence, there is a dilemma between pricing and not pricing in the case of pure public goods, which presumably would be resolved in favor of information and pricing under most circumstances. This problem is discussed in considerably greater detail in the literature cited above.

30. See Mueller, Tollison, and Willett, "Solving the Intensity Problem in Representative Democracy" (mimeographed; Cornell University, 1972) [Reading 30, below], for a normative model of public choice which contains a good demand estimation procedure (point voting) and in which politicians have incentives to behave responsively to the underlying preferences of their constituents for public goods. For other references to the literature on models of public choice, see the references cited in *ibid.*

31. There is very little literature addressed to this form of the problem of estimating demand for public goods. Recent additions include a paper by Y. Barzel, "The Market for a Semipublic Good: The Case of the *American Economic Review*," *American Economic Review*, LXI (September 1971), 665–674, in which he claims to have estimated the demand for a semipublic good (*The American Economic Review*), when in fact he only estimates the private elements of demand in this case (a point which he does not bring out clearly in his paper); and a piece by Bohm, "An Approach to the Problem of Estimating Demand for Public Goods," *Swedish Journal of Economics* (March 1971), 55–66, in which he discusses a possible survey research method to obtain unbiased responses about the demand for pure public goods. To take an example from Bohm's discussion, by making the means and distribution of payments for public goods highly uncertain, strategic free-riding behavior may

to compensate ranchers for losses due to eagles (or perhaps to reallocate their production). Whatever scheme is used, one might find "too many" eagles, so that the market price of permits or the level of compensation would not be high enough to maintain the existing population of eagles.

The compensation scheme may be difficult to adjust in these circumstances. A peculiarity of compensation in the eagle question is that there would probably be a sharp discontinuity in the schedule relating eagle deaths to levels of compensation around the level of full compensation. In other words, suppose that under a good financing system funds were forthcoming to an extent of 70 percent of the total cost of damage by the current stock of eagles. Such partial compensation would probably only deter some killing of eagles, and there would seem to be little correspondence between the percent "parity" of compensation and the resulting level of private killing of eagles. One would not easily alter quantity killed by making small adjustments in this parity level. There are thus strong advantages to keeping compensation at full market value of damages so as to eliminate the private incentives to kill eagles.

If not enough (or too much) in funds were available for preserving the current stock of eagles, it might be better policy to keep compensation at 100 percent, but lower (increase) the quantity of damage by *systematically* reducing (enlarging) the stock of eagles. This could be done by varying the number of permits issued and allowing game wardens or hunters to kill off the excess eagles. The supply of eagles could thereby

---

be avoided if the individual more or less responds with a "What the hell, why not tell the truth?" attitude. Or better yet, individuals may follow their enlightened (Kantian) self-interest under such circumstances. Also, such an estimation procedure does not have to be costly, since stratified random sampling can be used to determine demand in large polities. The methodological difference between Bohm's approach that tries to make the financing procedure unknown to decision-makers and the traditional approach initiated by Wicksell that stresses making the means of financing each expenditure perfectly clear with self-financing taxes should also be noted. For Wicksell's classic article, see K. Wicksell, *Finanztheoretische Untersuchungen* (Jena: 1896), a major portion of which is translated in "A New Principle of Just Taxation," in R. A. Musgrave and A. T. Peacock (eds.), *Classics in the Theory of Public Finance* (London: Macmillan, 1958), pp. 72–118. Other literature on the problem of estimating demand for public goods includes E. A. Thompson, "A Pareto Optimal Group Decision Process," *Papers on Non-Market Decision Making*, I (1966); M. L. Eysenback, "Note on a Pareto-Optimal Decision Process," *Public Choice*, V (Fall 1968), 105–107; E. A. Thompson, "A Pareto Optimal Group Decision Process: A Reply," *ibid.*, 109–112; M. I. Kamien and N. L. Swartz, "Revelation of Preference for a Public Good with Imperfect Exclusion," *ibid.*, IX (Fall 1970), 10–30, and "Exclusion Costs and the Provision of Public Goods," *ibid.*, XII (Spring 1972), 43–56; E. M. Clarke, "Multipart Pricing of Public Goods," *ibid.*, XI (Fall 1971), 17–34; T. N. Tideman, "The Efficient Provision of Public Goods," in Selma Mushkin (ed.), *Public Prices for Public Products* (Washington, D.C.: The Urban Institute, 1972); and D. C. Mueller, R. D. Tollison, and T. D. Willett, *op. cit.*

be adjusted to a level that the forthcoming compensation would support.[32] In essence, one manages this system of eagle preservation on the supply side by killing off or subsidizing the production of eagles, as the case may be.[33]

Under a permit scheme the population could be controlled more directly, since, by asking unused permits to be turned in, public officials would know the number killed in any year. Since varying the stock of permits will vary (positively) the number exercised, adjustment to equilibrium could be achieved. In either scheme accurate eagle census and reproduction data would be required. Note that in equilibrium some eagles might well be killed, if in the absence of hunting the population would tend to grow above desired levels.

In practice, however, it should be stressed that the public-private financing scheme may not be exactly optimal or unbiased, and care would have to be taken in judging an existing population of eagles as "too large."[34] Indeed, since the mix of public and private contributions might

32. Alternatively, if the demand for the preservation of eagles were geographically concentrated, forthcoming compensation might be enough to pay off all losses in that area, with losses in other areas going uncovered. Increases or decreases in the funds for compensation would then be reflected in expansions or contractions of the area over which eagles were protected and full compensation for damages was guaranteed.

33. Another manner in which to view the process of adjusting the stock of eagles discussed in this section is to consider the problem in terms of the long-run supply curve for eagles introduced in Figure 2. As noted above, to introduce long-run supply the horizontal axis in Figure 2 was redefined with respect to the longer period of time required to adjust the population of eagles. (It is defined in Figure 1 as the time period that the current population of eagles exists, e.g., the period of time between breedings.) Such a curve would be a function of the marginal costs or damages imposed by the various potential populations of eagles. Connecting the points on such a long-run schedule where low marginal damages (i.e., a low market price for eagles in a given period) implies a low quantity of eagles supplied, and vice versa, one would obtain a positively sloped and more elastic supply curve for eagles over this longer period of time. Actually, the authorities who run this type of program would largely determine the degree of elasticity in eagle supply over the long run, as they are the ones responsible for adjusting eagle supply based on forthcoming compensation to protect the largely fixed present supply of birds (as depicted in Figure 1). The sense in which the concept of long-run supply could be useful for these authorities is that it may be useful to forecast future possible adjustments in the eagle population, perhaps based on present trends in forthcoming compensation. Thus, the authorities may be interested in estimating the elasticity of the long-run supply for eagles and the presumed direction of movement along this curve as part of an effort to plan future possible adjustments in the number of eagles. This is a reasonably important problem in this case, since to obtain any significant degree of elasticity in the supply of eagles, especially with respect to increases in their numbers, may require a long period of time. Also, the downward adjustment in the long-run quantity supplied of eagles, while quite elastic in the sense that game wardens could simply kill off birds, is a tricky problem in terms of externality theory and is discussed below.

34. An example of a possible bias in the public-private financing scheme is that the demand of future generations for the existence of eagles may not be counted. Indeed, how

depend on the number of eagles over which demand is distributed, the public contribution would probably become larger if eagles became more scarce.

The relation of the number of eagles to the degree of public financing also raises a problem endemic to an externality such as eagle losses where reversibility is either impossible (the species becomes extinct) or becomes very costly (in the absence of large-scale capacity to hatch eagles in a laboratory setting, the expense of careful protection of a small number of eagles over the long time span required to increase the eagle population). In terms of the initial establishment of such a program, it might be efficacious to be sure of full compensation and to be wary of reducing the existing stock of eagles on the presumption that this stock is too large, since in the short run and without perfect demand information, it may be less costly to err on the side of having "too many" rather than "too few" eagles.[35]

V. Summary and Conclusions

Eagles are at present construed to be in the public domain (i.e., unowned) and are "protected" by a fine and imprisonment penalty, which places the costs of preserving eagles primarily on ranchers. The difficulty of policing the fine system makes it unlikely that politically feasible fines will deter the killing of eagles, and the assignment of the costs of eagle preservation to ranchers in this system appears unjustified on equity grounds. Assignment of liability for damage done by eagles to private individuals or groups who desire to protect the eagle would aid in determining the appropriate number of eagles to preserve, and in achieving a more equitable distribution of the costs of maintaining these birds. The mere assignment of private liability, for example by selling rights to eagles,

---

and whether there is a need to estimate such a demand is a controversial issue. See, for example, the discussion of this point in Mishan, *op. cit.* The problem of a "too small" eagle population has been tossed about loosely in the analysis. Such a condition implies that the production of eagles should be subsidized, if this is possible to conceive. The functional equivalents of this activity might consist in spending the additional funds to protect eagles from accidental death and the like, or for subsidies for research to raise eagles in captivity or in a laboratory setting, or even to public production, as with fisheries. The latter prospects for raising and perhaps producing eagles in captivity are not so farfetched as they might seem. See, for example, the report on "Three Golden Eagles, the Product of Artificial Breeding, Hatched," *New York Times,* May 21, 1972.

35. Lerner (*op cit.*) discusses the problem of water pollution when, depending on the recovery characteristics of the stream or lake, reversibility may not be very costly. Thus, the appropriate public policy may be to start off at a suboptimal level of pollution control and "work up" to optimality. In the case of the eagle, this does not seem feasible, since upward reversibility in the stock of eagles is hard to accomplish given present technology. Also, Lerner has an interesting discussion of whether to set price or quantity in his pollution control example, which involves estimating the demand for a public good under uncertainty.

will not overcome the enforcement cost problems of the present fine and imprisonment system. Ranchers may still make expected value calculations which will lead them to kill eagles illegally. Compensation must be paid to ranchers to protect eagles effectively. The issue becomes, how should compensation be financed? The problem with purely private financing of compensation is that free-riding behavior may cause contributions to be suboptimal. Purely public finance also involves inequities and efficiency costs. A levering scheme involving a mix of public and private finance is thus proposed that would permit a matching public contribution as an offset to free-riding problems and allow for private contributions to obtain a more equitable distribution for the costs of preserving eagles and a better estimate of the demand for eagles. The trade-offs in the public and private components of the levering scheme involve attempting to offset one set of problems against the other. This scheme, with the fiscal system making up the difference between the amount of private compensation forthcoming and the full level of damages, eliminates the ranchers' incentive to continue killing eagles (documentation would also be part of the compensation). If compensation were prompt and equitable, there should be no incentive for ranchers to kill eagles. Adjustment in resource allocation to ranching on the land near where eagles live would also have to be undertaken under this scheme, through the appropriate tax or subsidy on livestock-raising in the area; otherwise, ranchers might overutilize the land near the eagles for purposes which would cause the damages imposed on them by the eagles to be "too large." If desirable, changes in the stock of eagles could be undertaken, based on the relation between damage done by the present supply of these birds and the amount of compensation forthcoming from a good public-private mix of finance over a time period long enough to be sure that the direction and extent of the change desired in the eagle population was fairly clear to the relevant authorities. It is probably a good guess that the existing eagle population would be either optimal or too small in terms of potential demand under a good mix of public and private finance.[36]

36. An analysis of the available statistical data on sheep and lamb losses allows us to make some *very rough* estimates of the amount of compensation required. In Wyoming eagles were reported to have killed 8,200 lambs (no sheep) valued at $165,700 during 1969. These losses represented 6.8 per cent of Wyoming's 1969 sheep and lamb losses from all predators ($2,454,900). A 16-state area (containing 76 percent of the total sheep and lamb population) survey by the Department of Interior estimated by extrapolation of average figures, 1970 sheep and lamb losses from all predators (within the 16-state area) to be valued at $16,955,820. If the Wyoming eagle loss rate is applied to this total loss, an upper bound should be set on the losses due to eagle killings. (It should be an upper bound because the Wyoming eagle population is not representative of the 16-state area.) Such a calculation places eagle damage to sheep and lamb herds (within the 16-state area) at approximately $1.2 million. See R. Reynolds and O. Gustad, "Analysis of Statistical Data on Sheep

Public policy toward predators developed historically as an administrative response to demands for predator *control* by ranchers and farmers. Today, however, the existence of various species of predators is threatened, and other segments of society are demanding public policies to *preserve* these species. Unfortunately, eagles and other endangered species cannot protect themselves from modern man.[37] The fine and imprisonment system which has been developed for their protection threatens to become a *de facto* system for the extinction of these species because the politically feasible forms of this system do not sufficiently deter the continuing killing of these animals. The recent mass killings of eagles in Wyoming are an excellent, although disturbing, reminder of this point. If government officials, conservationists, and others who care about protecting endangered predators are sincere in their desires to formulate public policy to preserve these species, then the approach proposed in this paper is an administratively feasible way to accomplish this goal, and it merits their careful scrutiny.

D. REVENUE SHARING AND THE DRAWING OF POLITICAL BOUNDARY LINES

14. Federalism: Problems of Scale

GORDON TULLOCK

The modern explanation of Democratic government is based firmly on the theory of economic externalities. Individual choices in a situation in which externalities are important may lead to highly inefficient resource use. Government is one way, and frequently the most convenient way, to deal with this problem. This approach also gives an idea of the optimal size of the government or governments. It may be said that the governmental unit chosen to deal with any given activity should be large enough to "internalize" all of the externalities which that activity generates. It would appear that most students do not really aim at totally internalizing

Losses Caused by Predation in Four Western States During 1966–1969" (mimeographed; Bureau of Sport Fisheries and Wildlife, U.S. Department of Interior, May 1971). The dollar magnitudes involved in the proposed system of eagle control and preservation in this paper are thus not startlingly high.

37. Actually, before the development of firearms, helicopters, and DDT, eagles were not too badly off in this regard.

Reprinted from *Public Choice*, Spring 1969, pp. 19–29, by permission of the publisher and author.

all external effects of the given action, but merely internalizing most of them, say 90 per cent. The reason that I am confident that this is so is that they almost never discuss local border effects. Any geographically delimited governmental unit must have a border, and if its function is to deal with an externality producing activity, then its actions just inside the border will normally produce an externality just outside the boundary. Thus total internalization would normally require boundaries which ran along some very impressive natural barrier. Such a minor matter as street-cleaning might require a continental or even world-wide governmental unit to totally internalize its effects.

If we assume, however, that it is not (for some reason) desirable to internalize all externalities, only most of them, then the existence of externalities even when handled in this very crude way, does give a guide for governmental size. National defense would require larger units to internalize 90 per cent of the externalities than would garbage removal. The exact percentage of externalities which are to be internalized, however, is not normally discussed. A policy of internalizing 99 per cent of the externalities would produce much larger governmental units than would a policy of internalizing 80 per cent. We will later see that this is not an insoluble problem.

A second factor traditionally considered in discussion of the size of governmental units is the optimal scale of production for the governmental service. Economies of scale, of course, can be regarded as externalities, but let us discuss them either as a special kind of externality or as a separate phenomenon. There is, in fact, a good deal of literature dealing with local government which simply seeks the most efficient operating unit in terms of scale economies. If costs of providing governmental services do vary as the size of the operating unit is changed, this should somehow be taken into account in designing an optimal system of governmental units. Assuming that the governmental unit is to provide its own facilities, then there would be arguments for choosing the governmental unit in such a way as to give the most efficient production unit. This might or might not be the same size as would be chosen on straight externality grounds. The two considerations, however, can be easily combined. In Figure 1, I have put the cost of choice of some governmental unit on the vertical axis, and the absolute size on the other. The external cost (EC) line shows the cost inflicted by the continued existence of noninternalized externalities, and it slopes down to the right throughout its range. If we arbitrarily aim at an internalization of 90 per cent of the externalities, then the optimal governmental size would be A. If, on the other hand, we were only interested in efficiency in producing the governmental service, then we would choose a governmental unit which

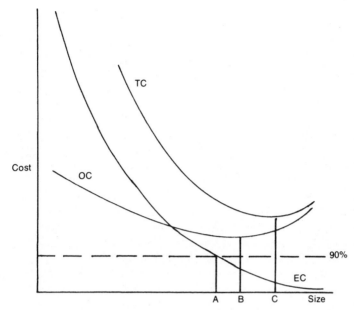

Figure 1.

minimized the operating cost (OC), and this would be at B. Geometrically summing these two cost lines (TC) gives us C as the optimal size of the governmental unit. Note that the optimum size in terms of economies of scale. This is a simple consequence of the fact that the external cost line is continuously downsloped to the right while the "scale" cost comes down and then goes up.

But although I have drawn a correct conclusion from assumptions which a short time ago had been accepted as the modern tradition, the work of our host, Dr. Ostrom, has fairly conclusively demonstrated that there is a hidden, and untrue, assumption in the reasoning. [Tullock is referring to Vincent Ostrom, host at a conference in June 1967 at the University of Indiana. A paper by Ostrom precedes this paper in *Public Choice*.] The economies of scale are relevant to the choice if a governmental unit itself must produce the particular governmental service. If it can purchase it from a specialized producer, then the economies of scale cease to have relevance to the decision as to the size of the governmental unit. I need not repeat here the work of Dr. Ostrom, but I take it that we can agree that only conservatism and organizational rigidities prevent widespread purchase of services by governmental units of any size from organizations large enough to obtain the full benefit of any economies of scale which may exist. Thus the "optimal size" of the government as a producer of services can be dropped from the rest of this paper even though it has played a notable role in the recent literature about local governments.

But this leaves us only with the externality criteria, which provides no maximum size for the governmental unit at all. I have introduced an ad hoc assumption that we only try to internalize something like 95 per cent of the externalities from each activity, but this is clearly arbitrary. Not only is it arbitrary, but I have been unable to find [1] any previous example of its use. My only excuse for introducing it is that externality arguments are used in a way which implies that something like this is at the back of the mind of their authors. Clearly, however, it is an inadequate criterion. If there is not a counterbalancing factor, the more of the externality that is internalized the better. That there are other factors, I presume we all agree. Clearly continental or even world governmental agencies for street cleaning or fire protection are not desirable.

There are, in fact, factors which lead to the optimal size of the governmental unit normally being smaller than is necessary to internalize *all* externalities. The first of these is simply that the smaller the governmental unit the more influence any one of its citizens may expect to exert, consequently, the smaller the unit, the closer it will come to fitting the preference patterns of its citizens. This is true of all forms of government, although it is easier to analyze the matter formally when we consider democratic governments.

That the average level of adjustment of government to its citizens desires must increase as the size of the government is reduced, can be very readily proved by a technique invented by Pennock.[2] Suppose some governmental unit makes its decisions by majority rule. A majority of its citizens prefer policy A to $\overline{A}$. The government therefore carries out policy A which pleases the majority and displeases the minority. Suppose the area is now divided into two units, and each of these units votes on the issue. There may be a majority for A in both of the new, smaller units, and there certainly will be such a majority in at least one of them. If both new units have majorities for A, then A will be applied in both areas and there is no change in satisfaction. If, however, one of the new units has a majority for $\overline{A}$, then the total number of people in the society who are getting their wish in the matter must go up.[3] Although Pennock devel-

1. In an admittedly rather cursory survey of the literature.
2. "Federal and Unitary Government-Disharmony and Frustration," *Behavioural Science,* IV (April, 1959), 147–57.
3. A numerical example may be helpful. Suppose the original unit had a voting population of 10,000, of whom 6,000 favored A and 4,000 favored $\overline{A}$. It is broken into two units

oped this argument for simple majority voting, it may readily be extended to any voting rule.

This principle is perfectly general, and clearly indicates that the individual will suffer less cost from governmental activities of which he disapproves the smaller the government. This cost would probably take the form shown on Figure 2.

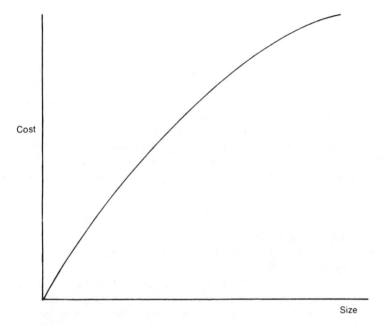

Figure 2.

Surely this cost is a strong offset to gains which can be made by expansion of the governmental unit. We could add this line on to those of Figure 1 to get an improved optimum size, but there are other costs of governmental expansion.

Suppose you normally eat in restaurants and that there are a considerable number of competitive restaurants to choose among. For the first stage of our model assume that all of these restaurants have a la carte menus. The customer thus chooses each item separately. Let us now assume that all of the restaurants, perhaps as the result of an unwise law, shift to a system under which they list a number of complete meals on

of 5,000 voters, and in one of these we find a majority, say 3,000 to 2,000, for Ā. The other small unit would have 4,000 for A and 1,000 for Ā. Before the division 6,000 voters got what they wanted, under the new arrangement 7,000 do.

their menus, and you must choose from among these without any substitution being permitted. Let us carry this procedure further and assume that the restaurants begin requiring their customers to purchase meals for a full day as a bloc. The restaurants publish daily menus in which you can choose among a dozen or so full menus for the day. Menu A, for example, would consist of toast and coffee for breakfast, vegetable soup and cottage cheese salad for lunch, and roast beef, spinach and carrots for dinner, one cup of coffee being served with each meal. Menu B, on the other hand, might be less obviously aimed at people who intend to reduce, and so on through menus C . . . N. The individual is still exercising freedom of choice in a competitive market, but I think it would be agreed that his satisfaction would have declined. We can extend the example by assuming fixed weekly menus among which choice is to be made, monthly, or even yearly menus.

The declining degree of satisfaction as the unit of choice is raised comes from two interrelated factors. In the first place it is harder to provide as wide a total range of choice if the unit of choice is large. Consider the breakfast menus of a typical restaurant, for example. If they offered nothing but fixed breakfasts, and simply presented all of the possible combinations which could be made from their present menu, they would have a book instead of a page or two. Further, the customer obviously would not wade through the innumerable combinations in search of his optimum. He would look at the first page or so and make his choice from this restricted set of choices.

The second problem is related to communication theory. When you choose an item to buy, among other things, you give the restaurant owner information about your tastes which will permit him to adjust his offerings so as to please you and get a competitive advantage over the other restaurants. By restricting the number of choices you can make, the information content of the total "communication" between you and the restaurant manager is reduced. As a consequence it is less likely that the choices with which you will be presented in subsequent periods will be as desirable as they would be if the solution process were more highly segmented. People who have unusual combinations of tastes would be particularly disadvantaged by the procedure of grouping decisions into large bundles.

The relevance of all of this to the scale of government may not be obvious, but the selection of a governmental unit involves a decision on the size of the bundles of alternatives which will be chosen among in future elections. The situation is depicted in Figure 3.

On the vertical axis the scope of the governmental unit is shown. This

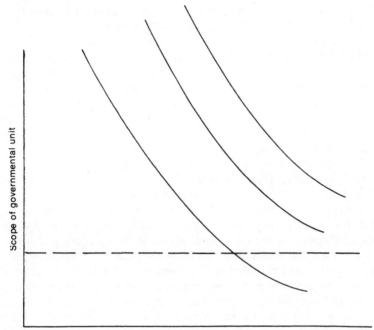

Figure 3.

Size of governmental unit or number of citizens

means, quite simply, the number of activities that it carries out with re-spect to any citizen or group of citizens. On the horizontal axis is shown the number of citizens for which it performs these activities. The total number of activities, thus, increases as you move up and to the right. Since the governmental unit will be elected to deal with all of the activi-ties covered, the farther to the right and up on the figure, the higher the cost imposed by the necessity of making choices in large bundles. If the scope of governmental activities is held constant and the size of it is increased, as along the dotted line, then the cost of the increase would be shown by a cross-section of Figure 3 which would look like Figure 2.

There is a final cost associated with enlarging government units which is extremely popular these days; this is the cost of bureaucracy. The New Left and other groups which we may loosely call "Libertarian" are deeply distressed at the amount of bureaucracy in our society. It is cer-tainly true that the longer the chain of officials that runs between the voter making the choice and the actual provision of the product, the more noise is introduced into the process by the individual bureaucrats who have their own preference functions and by the problems of information transmission.[4] This cost, like the others, steadily increases as the size of bureaucracy grows; in fact it might well increase at the increasing rate—i.e. it might be an exponential function of the size of the government unit. Here again, this function could be represented by a figure like 3. Figure 3 could also represent the sum of all of the costs we have been discussing.

Note that the figure says nothing at all about the total size of "government," taking that term to mean the sum of all governmental organizations. Many American cities and states have numerous different elected officials dealing with different governmental functions. If people actually made independent choices instead of voting a party ticket, then the scope of each governmental agency chosen by the voter might be quite small while the total scope of "government" was very large.

Now, having three costs which vary with the governmental unit dealing with any particular activity, we might simply add them and find the minimum total cost point and choose that as the optimum size for the governmental unit dealing with that particular problem. It should be noted that if you have a large number of government activities being carried on by different governmental units, presumably there will be externalities generated by the individual government activities which affect the others. As a simple example, the fire department in many ways makes traffic control difficult. These externalities, external effects of one government agency on another, would themselves be dealt with by other government agencies which would have the specific purpose of providing through taxes and subsidies for internalizing these externalities in the actual operating units.

The end product of our reasoning, if we stop now, would be a genuinely Rube Goldberg arrangement in which the individual citizen would be a member of a vast collection of governmental units, each of these governmental units being to some respect of a different geographical coverage than the others and each one dealing with a separate activity. The reason for this would be simply that each type of government activity has slightly different externality from the others and as a consequence each one repuries a different size. Some of these governmental agencies would be engaged in providing services for the citizen and others would be engaged in internalizing the externalities generated by the individual agencies on each other.

It is, I presume, reasonably clear that this system would not be an optimum government organization. With each individual a member of 5,000

4. See Oliver E. Williamson, "Hierarchical Control and Optimum Firm Size," *Journal of Political Economy* (April 1967), 123–38.

or perhaps 50,000 different governmental units it would be quite impossible for him to engage in the most rudimentary supervision of his servants. It is, indeed, unlikely that the average citizen would even know the names of the people who are running for office in many of these "governments." If we contemplate an actual voter attempting to deal with this multitude of governmental units, it is fairly certain that he would not even bother to participate in the elections which controlled very many of them. The bulk of them would be, from this standpoint, quite uncontrolled. It is clear that this pattern would be very, very far from optimum.

In actual economic life we also deal with situations in which the individual cannot hope to make rational decisions for himself. I do not make even the slightest effort to decide the detailed specifications of the automobile that I buy; I leave that to other people and choose among the alternative packages of characteristics that are presented to me. In some cases I hire the services of a specialized consultant, a doctor for example, who will give me advice on what type of unit I should consume. Clearly the same method would be suitable when purchasing government services.

So far we have not specified how individuals choose the government service which is performed. It might, for example, be arranged so that each of our multitudinous governmental units submits all its detailed administrative decisions to a public plebiscite. Clearly, this is not what we normally observe and we would be surprised if it would be optimum. What we normally do is simply appoint an agent to deal with government activities. Here again, the resemblance to the private economy is considerable. The difference is largely that we appoint our agents in a different manner—through elections instead of through contract. If then, we assume that the government agencies which we have set up to deal with these specific problems will be controlled by some kind of a special agent or board of agents and the voter selects these agents or boards of agents, let us say at the end of the year, we have greatly simplified the task the voter has in making decisions about these services. Similarly the private economy greatly simplifies *its* purchasing decisions by grouping the characteristics of automobiles and letting individuals choose among baskets of such characteristics. But though this greatly simplifies matters we still find ourselves with some five to ten thousand decisions for the voter to make. Clearly the grouping of the process should be carried further. We must appoint agents to deal not with the individual government activities but with whole clusters of such activities.

How, then, would we determine the optimum site of such clusters? There is a fairly simple analytical answer to this question; unfortunately actually applying it may be extremely difficult. On Figure 4 the horizontal axis represents the degree of dispersion of governmental activities. It is assumed that as you move to the right the government is first halved and then each of the halves cut in half and etc. Somehow this process is assumed to be continuous in order to give us smooth curves. Curve C represents the cost inflicted on the voter through poor control as the scale of government organizations are shifted. At the left where he faces a single choice, let us say once a year a package of policies covering all government policies in the whole of the country, his costs are quite high. As the government is broken into smaller fragments his costs go downward. After a while, however, it begins to be difficult for him to make individual choices for each of the fragments and at this point his cost begins to go up again. Eventually in the Rube Goldberg model of a few paragraphs back they might well be much higher in this highly differentiated government than they are in a monolithic government.

Line E is the cost that will be imposed through grouping governmental units in nonoptimum ways, the optimum way being defined in the way we have done before. We assume that, as you move from left to right, not only is the government split into smaller and smaller pieces, but that all of the splitting of the government is done in such a way as to be the

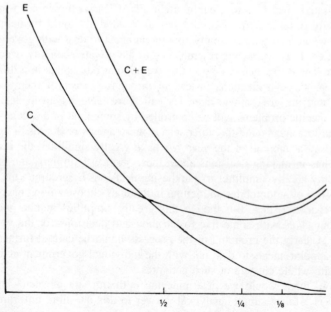

Figure 4.

"most efficient" arrangement for that particular degree of differentiation in government.[5]

This curve falls monotonically from the left to the right and eventually reaches a point of zero when the differentiation of the government functions has exhausted the full possibilities of the economies by this method—that is when every government function is at its most efficient size. The total costs then of having any particular degree of division of governmental functions can be shown by summing costs C and E as on the diagram. The low point on this curve would be the optimum degree of differentiation of the government. It will always lie to the right of the low point on the C curve simply because E is monotonically decreasing. It might not lie very much to the right.

The division of the functions of the government, if it is to be efficient, will take a good deal of care. You can't just randomly allocate several functions to one bureau; there are efficiency considerations here too. In general we need not concern ourselves with the details of these efficiency considerations here but one point should be made. It is not necessarily true that all functions in a given geographic area should be run by the same unit. One can well imagine, let us say, the voters of the state of Indiana, instead of voting for the state of Indiana government and a city government, voting for two governments for the Indiana area, each of which dealt with a different aspect of affairs.

We have now what appears to be a theoretical structure for deciding the degree to which the government should be federalized. A society actually applying our solution would require a good deal of empirical research which has not yet been done. If I may be permitted to offer a guess, I would imagine that it would end up with each individual being a member of somewhere between five and eight separate government units. These government units would not necessarily bear any particular resemblance to our present governments. It is, for example, quite possible theoretically that we would have two "national" governments, one of which, let us say, dealt with national defense and the other with all other activities which required nationwide organization.

We should, of course, make every effort to make the voting itself an efficient choice process. As to one example, we could use what used to be called the Soviet system. Voters can elect small governments which themselves elect the next higher unit(s) of government. A scheme in which small government units create larger government units is far more efficient than one in which large government units subdivide their control.

5. In practice of course, splitting the government evenly into two parts or evenly into four parts or evenly into eight parts would be unlikely to be the efficient arrangement. You might find 65 per cent in one group and 35 per cent in another.

The city of Chicago, for example, would be better off controlling its own destiny and participating in electing a government of Illinois than if the government of Illinois had two subdivisions, one of which dealt with the city of Chicago and one of which dealt with the rest of the state, the reason being simply that the downstate voters would have less influence on the city of Chicago under the former system.

Another rather simple method of improving efficiency of the voting process is to arrange that people defeated in the election process, but who nevertheless do reasonably well, are given an opportunity to act as sort of public auditors over the behavior of the people who win. As is rather well known, I am a proponent of proportional representation. If we have proportional representation, and if, let us say, five members were elected to duty on a governing board, whatever that board is, making the sixth highest ranking candidate auditor and giving him full access to all records would provide an excellent control without much burden on the voters. Today we have auditors but we usually elect them separately, thus requiring an additional vote and complicating the election process.

In sum, many students seem to think that a highly centralized government is the most efficient government. It would be more accurate to say that centralized government is the most orderly government. If we want the voters' wishes to be served by the government, then a system under which the voters are able to communicate those wishes to the government through the voting process in a more detailed and particular way is more efficient. We cannot carry this detailed voting, however, to its logical extreme because the information costs put on the voter are too great. Still it is probable that we could rearrange things in the United States so that the voter had to know less in order to cast an intelligent vote than he now does—i.e. we could get rid of the long ballot. At the same time we could give the voter considerably more control over his future and his fortunes. The most efficient government is not the most orderly looking government but the government that comes closest to carrying out the wishes of its masters.

15. Revenue Sharing: Alternative to Rational Fiscal Federalism? *

CHARLES E. McLURE, Jr.

I. Introduction

By the end of the 1960s, the fiscal plight of state and local governments in the United States had reached what some observers considered crisis proportions. Strongly felt needs for expenditures were growing more rapidly than revenues from existing taxes. Yet governing bodies considering new or higher taxes seemed to fear being impaled on one of the horns of a serious dilemma: Imposing or increasing progressive personal income taxes or taxes on businesses, especially corporations, might stifle economic development in the state or locality; but raising generally regressive property and sales taxes seemed to run directly counter to the new-born war on poverty. Either choice was likely to be politically unpopular. Thus President Nixon's proposal to share federal income tax revenues with state and local governments received overwhelming endorsement from the mayors and governors of America. Increases in state and local expenditure requirements would be met in part with revenues from the progressive federal income taxes, which tend, under normal conditions (unlike most state and local taxes) to grow at a faster pace than the expenditures they finance. Through revenue sharing the fiscal crisis would be averted, but without raising either regressive state and local taxes or taxes that might drive economic activity from a state or locality. This plan, it appeared, would assure the fiscal viability of American federalism.

This article questions the implication that revenue sharing is the *essence* of rational fiscal federalism. It argues that revenue sharing is needed, if at all, primarily as an alternative, or at best a supplement, to a

Reprinted from *Public Policy*, Summer 1971, pp. 457–478, by permission of the publisher and author.

* A more detailed exposition of the theme of this paper, including more extensive references to the literature, was presented at a symposium on Political Aspects of Intergovernmental Resource Allocation at the University of Maryland on May 12, 1970 under the title "Economic Aspects of Alternative Methods of Intergovernmental Financing." The author is grateful to Malcolm Gillis, Dennis Mueller, Robert Tollison, Thomas Willett, Robert Floyd, Ralph Burns, and Gerald Stone for their comments on an earlier draft of the present paper. Although he accepts sole responsibility for the ideas expressed, he recognizes that they are almost certainly not entirely his own.

more rational way of financing federalism, and that the state-local financial crisis is in large part the result of failure to adopt more suitable fiscal arrangements. This argument is based upon a well-known normative model of fiscal federalism elaborated in section III. The implications of that model for federal and for state and local finance are explored in greater detail in sections IV and V. The structure of federal grants, including revenue sharing, is considered in section VI, and concluding remarks are offered in the final section. But before examining these points it will be worth while to digress briefly to ask why we might expect the fraction of the GNP devoted to government activities to grow over time.

II. Fiscal Mismatch and Revenue Sharing

Some people seem shocked by the growth in the proportion of national output devoted to providing government services. To many it seems unnatural that the public sector should grow more rapidly than the rest of the economy. The view that something is amiss finds its most vocal expression in resistance to tax increases, or "taxpayer revolts."

Yet explanations for the relative growth of the public sector are not hard to find. The demand for public services might well rise faster than income, even if the relative costs of public and private goods were constant. This is especially true because urbanization, population growth, and increased density create enormous demands for public services such as police and fire protection, streets and highways, public utilities and waste disposal, and education.

But relative costs do not remain constant. Because the public sector is extremely labor-intensive, it experiences little productivity gain, and costs rise faster than those in the private sector, where there are substantial increases in output per unit of labor. If the demand for public services is fairly insensitive to this shift in relative costs, any income-induced tendency for the relative growth of the public sector is compounded.[1] Thus it may be unsettling that a continually rising portion of national output is devoted to the activities of governments, but it is not unnatural, and it need not be shocking.

In practical terms this increase in the public share of national output is likely to be most troublesome at the state and local level. Due to its large

1. See William J. Baumol, "Macroeconomics of Unbalanced Growth: The Anatomy of Urban Crisis," *American Economic Review* (June 1967), 415–426. For an empirical analysis of this thesis, see D. F. Bradford, R. A. Malt, and W. E. Oates, "The Rising Cost of Local Public Services: Some Evidence and Reflections," *National Tax Journal* (June 1969), 185–202. Isolating the demand and supply influences does, of course, involve a horrendous identification problem.

defense component, the federal budget may not rise much faster than national output over the long run. Moreover, the revenues from federal income taxes grow faster than GNP. Thus there is a tendency for federal receipts from stable tax rates to grow faster than expenditure needs. While this "fiscal dividend" may create a contractionary tendency in the economy in the absence of repeated federal tax cuts or expenditure increases, it can hardly be termed a fiscal crisis.[2]

On the other hand, the revenue requirements of states and localities grow faster than national output—both because demands for services are highly responsive to growth in income and because of seemingly inflexible demands in the face of rising unit costs. Moreover, revenues from the taxes traditionally used by these governments grow more slowly than national output. As a result, revenue needs outstrip tax receipts unless tax rates are continually raised. From the perspective of the states and localities, "fiscal mismatch" does indeed wear the face of fiscal crisis.

One of the solutions offered is, of course, for the federal government to share its tax revenues with the states and localities. Such a scheme would obviate the need for cutting federal taxes while raising state and local taxes and transferring to the federal level functions best performed at a lower level. Moreover, the progressive federal income taxes would be used to finance state and local activities, avoiding the need either to expand the use of regressive state and local taxes or to risk driving industry from a state or locality using more progressive levies. Finally, the fiscal strength—and therefore the viability—of decentralized federalism would be preserved.[3]

III. The Musgrave-Tiebout Layer-Cake Model

In his monumental treatise on *The Theory of Public Finance*, Musgrave argued that policymaking is improved if government activities in the realms of resource allocation, income distribution, and stabilization of the economy are thought of as the functions of three distinct "branches" of government, each branch acting on the assumption that both of the others are doing their jobs. The allocation branch would provide public goods,

2. For an analysis of the fiscal dividend through 1976 projected in the U.S. Budget for Fiscal 1972, see Charles L. Schultze, Edward R. Fried, Alice M. Rivlin, and Nancy H. Teeters, *Setting National Priorities: The 1972 Budget* (Washington, D.C.: The Brookings Institution, 1971), pp. 319–333.

3. Most of the early literature on revenue sharing has been brought together in the three-volume collection by the U.S. Congress, Joint Economic Committee, *Revenue Sharing and Its Alternatives: What Future for Fiscal Federalism?* (Washington, D.C.: Government Printing Office, 1967). The present paper was originally written as a commentary on general revenue sharing, that is, before the 1972 budget proposed special revenue sharing. It is noted in section VI below that the distinction between general and special revenue sharing is probably more apparent than real.

subsidize activities that might otherwise be carried on at suboptimal levels because of external economies, and penalize activities creating external diseconomies. The distribution branch would engage only in tax-transfer operations designed to bring the distribution of income resulting in the marketplace more nearly into line with society's views of equity. Finally, the stabilization branch would adjust the over-all level of taxation to assure the maintenance of full employment and price stability.

Building on the work of Tiebout, Musgrave and others have argued that the distribution and stabilization functions should be discharged primarily by the central government, largely for practical reasons. State and local governments cannot be expected to contribute significantly to efforts to stabilize the economy, because their ability to borrow is severely restricted and they lack the tools of monetary policy. Equally important, the "leakages" from one state or locality into imports from the rest of the nation would so greatly reduce the multiplier that no one state or local government could be very successful in stabilizing even its share of the national economy. Thus it is not realistic to expect stabilization policy to be implemented except by the federal government.

Despite efforts and appearances to the contrary, state and local governments may also be unable to engage in effective policies of income redistribution. Attempts at progressive taxation (via personal or corporation income taxes or both) may tend to repel industry and geographically mobile high-income individuals and stunt economic development to such a degree that it is actually relatively immobile lower income individuals who bear the real burden of the nominally progressive taxes. If this is true, it would seem best not even to attempt significant redistribution at the state and local levels.[4] Moreover, there are important, though debatable, philo-

4. Musgrave's tripartite view of the public sector received its most familiar treatment in the first two chapters of Richard A. Musgrave, *The Theory of Public Finance* (New York: McGraw-Hill, 1959). That numerous studies have shown that the allocation and distribution functions are not logically separable does not mean that the three-branch view is not a useful construct for clarifying thinking on policy issues. Musgrave's early contribution to the development of the layer-cake model, which appears on pages 131–132 and 179–183 of his treatise, built upon Charles M. Tiebout, "A Pure Theory of Local Expenditures," *Journal of Political Economy* (October 1956), 416–424, and in turn influenced Tiebout's "An Economic Theory of Fiscal Decentralization," in *Public Finances: Needs, Sources, and Utilization* (Princeton, N.J.: Princeton University Press for the National Bureau of Economic Research, 1961), pp. 79–122. Other contributions to the development of the economist's layer-cake model of fiscal federalism, as well as evidence that existing institutions bear a closer resemblance to "marble cake" are cited in Dick Netzer, *State-Local Finance and Intergovernmental Fiscal Relations* (Washington, D.C.: The Brookings Institution, 1969) esp. pp. 10–14.

The difficulties any state or local government would encounter in pursuing an independent stabilization policy are described in Wallace E. Oates, "The Theory of Public Finance in a Federal System," *Canadian Journal of Economics* (February 1968), 37–54. Oates also

sophical reasons for preferring that the federal government be the final arbiter of income distribution. These are not discussed here.

On the other hand, state and local governments suffer no similar disadvantage when it comes to the activities of the allocation branch. So long as the benefits of public services bear a reasonably close relation to the taxes paid to finance them, there may be relatively little reason to fear tax-induced migration of businesses or persons. In fact, Tiebout has argued that if households are sufficiently mobile with regard to residential location, differences in the market baskets of public services available in different communities allow consumers to optimize their consumption of these services that within each community must be consumed in equal amounts by all. Similarly, so long as adequate income redistribution is being implemented at the federal level, there is little reason to object to whatever pattern of taxation at the state and local level reflects benefits received from public services. Even regressive state and local taxes would be acceptable if offset by a sufficiently progressive tax structure at the federal level.

Thus we have a "layer-cake" normative model of the public household. In it the federal government would assume responsibility for stabilizing the economy, redistributing income according to social consensus, and providing public services that are nationwide in scope. The state and local governments, on the other hand, would provide public services that are geographically more limited, financing them primarily with benefit taxes. The division of functions and tax bases among the various levels of subnational government would depend on the geographic extent of benefits, economies of scale in production and administration, decision-making costs, the mobility of taxpayers and recipients of benefits of public services, and the advantages of vote trading in expressing intensity of feeling.[5]

---

elaborates the layer-cake model with regard to the distribution and allocation branches, reaching the conclusions that "Like the Stabilization Branch, the Distribution Branch is in general seriously constrained in its operations at sub-central levels of government. . . . [M]obility would largely defeat the purpose of the program" (p. 45) and "The economic case for federalism is found in the Allocation Branch" (p. 50). Assertions such as those by Oates and the ones in the text about the net effects of nominally progressive state and local taxes are based largely on theoretical analysis. Given their crucial role in the formulation of a theory of fiscal federalism, they deserve severe empirical scrutiny.

5. For a survey of attempts to measure some of these, see Werner Z. Hirsch, "The Supply of Urban Public Services," in Harvey S. Perloff and Lowdon Wingo, Jr. (eds.), *Issues in Urban Economics* (Baltimore: Johns Hopkins Press for Resources for the Future, 1968), pp. 477–526. The long-neglected point on the advantages of combining functions in one government in order to facilitate vote trading is made in an unpublished paper by Dennis C. Mueller.

IV. Implications for Federal Tax Policy

Benefits of public services provided by state and local governments (excluding transfers) are generally distributed in a pattern that is "pro-poor"; that is, the value of public services represents a greater fraction of the incomes of the poor than of the wealthy.[6] Thus benefit taxation would probably be regressive taxation, and reliance upon it by state and local governments could equitably be increased only if the distribution function were indeed being discharged effectively by the federal government. As it is, the progressivity of the federal tax system is in many cases more apparent than real. For this reason thorough-going reform of the federal income tax, including initiation of systematic low income relief, is the *sine qua non* of rationalizing fiscal federalism in line with the layer-cake model.

What kind of federal tax reform is required by the layer-cake model? This is a question that only social consensus can answer. But it would probably include the traditionally espoused closing of loopholes—more recently given the euphemism "tax preferences"—the exclusion of interest on state and local bonds, the preferred treatment of long-term capital gains, the excess of percentage over cost depletion, and so on. These blatant violations of a comprehensive definition of income for tax purposes serve as a rallying point for those who oppose any increases in potentially regressive benefit-related state and local taxes, as well as creating substantial horizontal inequities and reducing the over-all progressivity of the federal income taxes.[7] Beside being justified on its own merits, such tax reform might help to break the political log-jam preventing adequate financing of state and local governments.

In addition, the redistribution activities of the federal "layer" would need to include low income relief. To increase the taxes most appropriate to the financing of state and local governments without providing such relief would be to impose an onerous burden on those families at the bot-

6. Such a pattern is reported in Irwin W. Gillespie, "Effects of Public Expenditures on the Distribution of Income," in Richard A. Musgrave (ed.), *Essays in Fiscal Federalism* (Washington, D.C.: The Brookings Institution, 1965), pp. 122–186; and in George A. Bishop, *Tax Burdens and Benefits of Government Expenditures by Income Class, 1961 and 1965* (New York: Tax Foundation, 1967).

7. A recent exchange over the feasibility of employing the Haig-Simons definition of income for tax purposes long favored by economists is contained in Boris I. Bittker, Charles O. Galvin, R. A. Musgrave, and Joseph A. Pechman, *A Comprehensive Income Tax Base?* (Branford, Conn.: Federal Tax Press, 1968). For a lucid discussion of the distributional implications of existing tax "preferences," see Joseph A. Pechman, *Federal Tax Policy* (Rev. Ed.; Washington, D.C.: The Brookings Institution, 1971), chap. 4. It should be noted that limiting tax preferences would have been far preferable to the alternative minimum tax on preference items adopted in the 1969 tax law.

tom of the income scale—and one which no amount of federal tax reform or even conventional tax relief would offset: to reduce the income taxes of those not paying income taxes is to provide no relief at all!

Low income relief could be provided in a number of ways, although most economists would probably prefer that it be done through a negative income tax. Under such a scheme low income families would receive transfers based on the amount by which their incomes fell short of a socially chosen break-even point, just as now taxes are levied on the excess of income over the break-even point.[8] A negative income tax would assist low income families precisely because they are poor, rather than because they belong to groups with many poor families. This latter approach, which is typical of many existing programs, frequently results in assistance to high income families and exclusion of poor ones. Ideally the negative income tax would replace all these inferior approaches to the alleviation of poverty.

V. Implications for State and Local Finance

Adoption of the layer-cake model of financing federalism, including the federal tax reform suggested above, would have a number of important fiscal implications for state and local governments. Most fundamentally, it would relieve these governments of the need to employ progressive taxes and eschew regressive ones. If adequate progressivity were assured by the federal revenue system, state and local governments would not be placed in the (for them) awkward position of trying to effect income redistribution. They could concentrate on providing the services most appropriate to them, financing them largely with benefit taxes. Even

---

8. Although the idea is implicit in Musgrave's distribution branch, perhaps the most famous discussion of the negative income tax is that in Milton Friedman, *Capitalism and Freedom* (Chicago: University of Chicago Press, 1962), chap. 12. Problems of implementation are discussed in James Tobin, Joseph A. Pechman, and Peter M. Mieszkowski, "Is A Negative Income Tax Practical?" *Yale Law Journal* (November 1967), 1–27. The conceptual relationship between negative income taxation and the conventional income tax is discussed in the present author's "Negative Income Taxation and the Ability to Pay," *Rivista di Diritto Finanziario e Scienza della Finanze* (Spring 1973). President Nixon's Family Assistance Plan has many of the attributes of a negative income tax, although a quite incomplete one. A scheme for combining large transfers to those unable to work with low marginal tax rates on those able to work is described in Richard Zeckhauser and Peter Schuck, "An Alternative to the Nixon Income Maintenance Plan," *Public Interest* (Spring 1970), 120–130.

Considerable analysis has recently been devoted to the proposition that society may be concerned about the consumption of *particular* goods and services by the poor as well as levels of income-in-general. It may also be that redistribution through provision of public services to the poor is favored over general redistribution because it is felt to involve fewer disincentive effects. Whether this feeling is correct depends on whether public services are complementary to private consumption or are substitutes for it.

if such taxes tended to be regressive, it would be of secondary importance, so long as adequate progressivity were provided by the federal tax
system. In this regard one is reminded of Galbraith's call in *The Affluent
Society* for liberals to cease their insistence that every increase in government programs be financed by progressive taxes, since the net result is
likely to be underprovision of public services of especial importance to
low income groups. If the federal tax system provided adequate progressivity and low income relief, Galbraith's point would be even stronger.

More specifically, adoption of the layer-cake model would necessitate
the transfer of some traditionally state and local activities to the federal
level, increased state and local use of benefit taxes and charges based on
environmental degradation, and reduced reliance on local property taxes
and state corporation income taxes. These implications and the residual
role to be played by state and local sales and income taxes are discussed
in the remainder of this section. Intergovernmental transfers are examined
in the next section.

Transfer of functions. One potential way to relieve the fiscal stress on
state and local governments would be to transfer some of their activities
to the federal government. Under the scheme described here, welfare activities at *all* levels of government would be largely superseded by a federal negative income tax. Besides rationalizing the welfare system and
providing considerable direct relief for state and local budgets, adequate
redistribution at the federal level would allow states and localities to raise
additional revenue from potentially regressive benefit-related taxes, as
noted below. Moreover, it is suggested below that the federal government
should carry more of the burden of financing education. But outside these
fields the prospects for directly reducing the fiscal mismatch by transferring functions do not seem particularly bright. The economic case for fiscal federalism is based on the limited geographic extent of benefits and
the costs of decision-making, and is bolstered by the political case for the
separation of powers in a democracy. Besides the inherent political
dangers of centralization, transfer to the federal government of activities
better carried on at the state or local level could result in both greater
costs of public services and decisions less responsive to the desires of citizens. Thus there appears to be little reason to hope for fiscal salvation of
state and local governments from this approach, which in many respects
rests on the denial of the very basis of fiscal federalism.[9]

Fiscal environmental controls. In an earlier, pre-industrial age the capacity of air and water to absorb man's wastes so greatly exceeded his
production of wastes that it may have been sensible for it to be free. But

9. This is not to argue, however, that either the existing political boundaries or the
division of responsibilities among governments is optimal; see Netzer, *op. cit.*, pp. 14–26.

waste production has grown to the point where in many places it has virtually overwhelmed the essentially static assimilative capacity of air and water. This has occurred in large part because allowing free use of air and water for waste disposal is no longer sensible social policy. Faced with the alternatives of dumping wastes into a stream or lake at no cost or installing expensive equipment to treat them, any firm concerned with earning profits is likely to choose the former, even if the decision results in a more than offsetting increase in costs to society. Because the once abundant assimilative capacity of the environment has become scarce, but still carries a zero price, it is overburdened, and pollution results.

The economists' solution is, of course, to raise the price of using air and water for waste disposal. This could be accomplished by imposing taxes on the discharge of wastes, with the charge being varied to take account of the damage caused. The hypothetical firm's choice would then be between cleaning up its discharge and paying the "effluent charge." If the system of effluent charges were appropriate, enough firms would choose the former course to bring the amount of "pollution" to socially acceptable levels.[10]

There are many good reasons for making effluent charges the heavy artillery in the war against pollution, although this is not the place to discuss them in detail. Most fundamentally, such taxes would have an advantage shared by few others. Ordinarily we worry about a given tax's becoming too high because taxes distort choices: Income taxes discourage work effort, and excise taxes discriminate between products. But the effluent tax *"distorts" our choices away from pollution*. More important in the present context, effluent charges are a potentially important source of public revenue. It is anomalous indeed that at a time of severe financial crisis at the state and local level, the scarce common property resources of air and water should continue to be free for anyone to use as a

10. References to "socially optimal levels of pollution" may seem repulsive, if not a contradiction in terms. But it is economically nonsensical as well as unrealistic to expect man's activities to have *no* impact on the environment. The key is, of course, to devote resources to achieving a better environment up to the point that at the margin the costs are equal to the benefit—where costs and benefits are as inclusively defined as is appropriate.

Probably the most vocal spokesman for the economists' solution, which goes back at least as far as A. C. Pigou, has been Allen V. Kneese, whose works, including (with B. T. Bower) *Managing Water Quality: Economics, Technology, Institutions* (Baltimore: Johns Hopkins Press, 1968), are among the most authoritative in the field. For a concise critique of existing practices in the area of water quality management and the case for effluent charges, see Kneese, "Strategies for Environmental Management," *Public Policy* (Winter 1971), 37–52. Purists will note that allocative efficiency ideally requires payments to those suffering the remaining pollution as well as charges on the polluters. Given the practical difficulties in implementing such a payment scheme and the need for action, the present author would be willing to risk the inefficiencies involved in employing only the tax half of the tax-subsidy scheme.

receptacle for wastes. A tax on pollution, besides improving the environment, would raise some badly needed revenue.

A potentially important, but seldom noticed, disadvantage of effluent charges (or any other scheme that would cause social costs of pollution to be reflected in market prices) is that they would be paid disproportionately by the poor, since they would raise prices of widely consumed goods. In the absence of low income relief their regressive incidence may effectively rule out the widespread use of effluent charges. But if low income allowances are set with due regard to the higher costs of environmentally cleaner production, there need be no conflict between equity and ecology.

There remains the question of whether taxes levied on pollution by only some states and localities would not drive away economic activity. This can be answered on several levels. First, there is almost certainly some threshold of pollution at which an industry would become *personna non grata* in a community. We have learned to live without abattoirs and tanneries in our central business districts, and as pollution worsens (and our awareness of it increases) we may be willing to do without other polluting activities in our midst.

Second, pollution may be almost as likely as high taxes to drive out economic activity. A state may be able to attract manufacturers by offering lax legal treatment of pollution. But in the process it may create quite literally a climate that is unattractive—or actually repulsive—to the increasingly vital segment of the economy that is footloose and locationally dependent on the residential choices of its owners, executives, or professional personnel.[11] Whether the state's laxity would result in a net gain in locational advantage (ignoring for the sake of argument the increased pollution residents would have inflicted upon them) is problematical at best. And the mood of America does not seem to be to ignore pollution.

Finally, the federal government could establish a basic pollution charge to be applied uniformly throughout the nation, with credit allowed for similar state or local levies. This would forestall in large part any tendency toward a "pollution competition" analogous to—but potentially more ominous than—the "tax competition" that has figured so heavily in the fiscal crisis of the state and local governments. Those states that so desired could go beyond the basic uniform national charge with relatively little fear of loss of industry, and all states would gain substantial revenue.

Increased benefit taxation. It has been argued above that to the extent

11. In this respect, see Jean Gottman, "The Rising Demand for Urban Amenities," in Sam Bass Warner (ed.), *Planning for a Nation of Cities* (Cambridge, Mass.: M.I.T. Press, 1966), pp. 163–177.

possible state and local governments should employ taxes, charges, and user fees that act as prices for services provided. As an example—but an important one—students (or their parents) could be charged fees to cover much of the costs of education, the fees being determined on the basis of the expected marginal private benefits from schooling. Financing from general funds would be limited to the expected marginal (external) social value of education.[12]

Such a system of fees, supplemented by subsidies from general revenues, would do much to rationalize the provision of public services, and not only in education. Most obviously, it would reduce the burden on general financing, which in the case of education means the property tax. This would lessen the local fiscal crisis. Moreover, people would be more likely to get what they want in the way of public services, and nothing else, if charges were more closely related to benefits. As a corollary, though raising state and local taxes will never be painless (nor should it be), resistance to increased taxes would probably be lessened if the link between benefits and services were more direct. Again, the fiscal crisis might be alleviated.

Further fiscal relief for state and local governments is suggested by an examination of the geographic extent of the spill-overs and external benefits of education. In an earlier period of relatively immobile labor, local financing of the public or external aspects of education may have made sense. But with the advent of more nearly national labor markets, local financing of education has resulted in substantial spill-overs of benefits between jurisdictions. This, plus the inherently national scope of many of the external benefits of education, suggests that more of this service should be financed nationally, rather than locally.[13]

As noted above, benefit taxation and effluent charges would in general be regressive, and relatively greater reliance on them would be acceptable only in the context of tax reform and low income relief. But it might

12. This approach is an application of the ideas in Richard A. Musgrave, "Provision for Social Goods," in J. Margolis and H. Guitton (eds.), *Public Economics* (New York: St. Martin's Press, 1969), pp. 124–144. Although it need not be, this scheme could be employed to stimulate competition among public schools or even between public and private schools via a tuition voucher scheme of the type Friedman has proposed, *op. cit.*, pp. 85–107.

13. See, for example, Burton A. Weisbrod, *External Benefits of Public Education: An Economic Analysis* (Princeton, N.J.: Princeton University Industrial Relations Section, 1964). It seems that education results in geographic spill-overs of benefits largely because a service that produces essentially private human capital is publicly financed. Private financing of this private capital formation would largely eliminate the spill-overs Weisbrod considers. Of course, private capital markets would need to be vastly improved. Federal subsidies would then be necessary primarily to compensate for the nationally experienced external aspects of education.

reasonably be asked why we should bother to implement low income relief (and tax reform) and then employ regressive taxes, rather than simply providing public services free of charge and financing them with progressive taxes.

The answer goes to the heart of Musgrave's tripartite view of budgetary policy. According to that view, poor people should be assisted *because they are poor,* and not because they consume education, or any other public service. Conversely, if resource allocation is to be optimal, people of all income levels should as nearly as possible *pay for what they consume,* including public services. In the context of fiscal federalism, we have argued, the redistribution function is best handled at the federal level and many allocation functions at the state or local level.

Property taxation. The property tax is doubtlessly not the worst tax ever conceived by man. But there is little good that can be said about it, except that it yields enormous revenues, that local governments can administer it, and that "old taxes are good taxes." Certainly it cannot be justified, except in the grossest way, under either the benefit or ability-to-pay principles of taxation. Even for property taxes on residences used to finance education, the link between benefits and tax liabilities is quite tenuous; for nonresidential property and for other services it is virtually nonexistent. Thus the tax, especially the part on improvements, distorts economic decisions and stymies the redevelopment of America's central cities. So far as ability to pay is concerned, the tax makes no allowance for debt, and applies to corporations as well as to natural persons. Ability-to-pay taxation would require a tax on the *net* wealth of *individuals,* if anything. Thus reduced reliance on the property tax should receive priority if and when the present fiscal squeeze on local governments abates. As noted above, increased federal financing of education would tend in this direction.

Yet there is considerable truth to the adage that old taxes are good taxes. Because existing property taxes may have been capitalized in lower property values, eliminating them would result in unwarranted capital gains to present owners of property, beside costing substantial revenue. Thus perhaps they should be lowered gradually by not applying them at existing rates to new improvements, rather than by lowering all rates.

Another lesson from the archies of fiscal theory is that taxes on land (site values) involve no economic distortion. Thus while local governments should reduce taxes on improvements and personal property— which do distort economic decisions—they could increase their taxation of land values. Of course, raising tax rates on land would inflict capital losses, and is therefore open to questions as a matter of equity. But relatively little can be said against taxing increments to land values, especially since many of these are the results of social action and the sheer pressure of population, rather than the actions of private entrepreneurs.[14]

State corporation income taxes. As a federal levy, the corporation income tax makes sense only because it yields substantial revenue and prevents retained earnings from going untaxed. It cannot be justified under either benefit or ability-to-pay principles of taxation.[15] On balance the tax adds to the progressivity of the tax system if it is not shifted, but it results in substantial horizontal inequities. Low income families may pay high (corporation) taxes on the share of corporation profits attributable to them, while high income individuals can use the capital gains loopholes to pay no more than the corporate tax rate on their share of profits. And if the corporation tax is shifted, it is an incredibly complex and capricious means of collecting a sales or payroll tax. Under either shifting assumption the tax distorts a multitude of economic decisions. These distortions involve corporate versus noncorporate forms of business organization, differences in amenability of various industries to noncorporate organization, the choice between debt and equity finance in the corporate sector, and the capital-labor mix in both sectors, not to mention those induced by special provisions in the tax law itself.

As a state levy, the corporation tax is even worse. It contains all the faults of the federal tax. But in addition, a tax on profits is uniquely unsuited for use by states that constitute only a small and very open part of a national economy. Most obviously, each state is reluctant to use the tax for fear of driving out economic activity. But a more fundamental problem exists. By their very nature, the profits of an interstate corporation, being the residual of revenues over costs, cannot be divided uniquely and scientifically among the various states. In practice they are allocated among the states on the basis of arbitrary formulas. But economic theory suggests that the state corporation profits tax should be reflected in higher

14. For further discussion of this point, see Dick Netzer, *The Economics of the Property Tax* (Washington, D.C.: The Brookings Institution, 1966), pp. 197–213. Of course, existing owners may have bought in anticipation of future gains, and ideally they too should not bear the capital losses occasioned by such a tax. The tax could be phased in over some time, but at some point a line must be drawn.

15. This point is discussed, for example, in Musgrave, *The Theory of Public Finance, op. cit.,* pp. 173–175. For a contrary view, see Richard Goode, *The Corporation Income Tax* (New York: Wiley, 1951). Of course, by the same token that the corporation income tax prevents retained earnings from going untaxed, it results in the double taxation of dividends. The only perfect solution would be to integrate the personal and corporation income taxes. See Pechman, *Federal Tax Policy, op. cit.,* pp. 140–147.

The empirical literature on the shifting of the corporation income tax is too extensive to review here. All but the most recent contributions are surveyed in Peter Mieszkowski, "Tax Incidence Theory: The Effects of Taxes on the Distribution of Income," *Journal of Economic Literature* (December 1969), 1103–1124.

product prices in a taxing state to the extent that it is allocated on the basis of sales by state of destination and in lower factor returns to the extent that it is based on sales at origin, on property, or on payrolls.[16] This being the case, it would be more efficient for the state to tax retail sales or personal income directly than to use the corporation income tax. The objection that such a policy would lower progressivity over-all is, of course, met by noting (1) that the progressivity added by state corporation income taxes may be largely illusory, and (2) that ideally adequate progressivity would be provided by the federal tax system, in any case.

The residual: broad-base taxes. The shifts in government financial practices proposed above (and others suggested by the layer-cake model) would have far-reaching effects upon expenditures and revenues at all levels of government. Whether on balance they would relieve the fiscal difficulties of states and localities is uncertain, although it seems likely that they would. In any case there may remain a gap between the expenditure needs and the revenues of those governments. Such a gap would most reasonably be filled in one of two ways: through increases in broad-based taxes such as sales or income taxes or through grants from the federal government.

Either general sales taxes or flat-rate personal income taxes would be a reasonable choice to fill the gap, since either consumption or income can be argued to reflect fairly accurately the benefits of public services.[17] With the activities of the distribution branch being handled at the federal level, the choice between the two might rest largely on administrative considerations. State income taxes have the potential administrative advantage of using the pre-existing federal tax base, but only if most of the

16. For the development of this point, see the present author's "The Interstate Exporting of State and Local Taxes: Estimates for 1962," *National Tax Journal* (March 1967), 49–77; and "The Inter-regional Incidence of General Regional Taxes" *Public Finance* (1969), 457–183. This is the reasoning underlying the presumed inability of state and local governments to effect redistributional policies noted in section III. As noted in footnote 4 above, it should be subjected to thorough empirical testing. Furthermore, we are faced here with a largely unresolved problem in the methodology of incidence analysis. The statements in the text may be true for any one state's tax, but the tax may be borne by profits if all states use it. Whether it is more appropriate to consider each state individually or all states together is an unresolved question. The remarks in this section apply *a fortiori* to local taxation of corporations, which fortunately is seldom proposed.

17. Whether sales or income is the better measure of benefits of government services is a complicated question that need not concern us here; for a more complete discussion, see the present author's "Economic Aspects of Alternative Methods of Intergovernmental Financing," *op. cit.* Briefly, the choice hinges upon (1) whether saving should be included in the tax base and (2a) whether the income tax should be levied where income is earned or where the income recipient resides or (2b) whether the sales tax should be collected where production or consumption occurs.

inequities and distortions of the latter are accepted.[18] Using the federal tax base for income taxation at the local level, either directly or through a piggy-back on the state tax, is also feasible.

On the other hand, there is no federal sales tax for the states to piggy-back. But states seem to be quite able to implement retail sales taxes without federal administrative assistance, although with higher rates problems of the taxation of interstate commerce would be compounded.[19] Finally, local sales taxes can be applied piggy-back fashion to state sales taxes.

VI. Intergovernmental Grants

A more radical way to fill the remaining revenue gap at the state and local levels would be grants from the federal government. President Nixon's proposal for revenue sharing is a variant of this approach. It would provide both largely unconditional grants (general revenue sharing) and block grants for broadly defined functional categories (special revenue sharing).

Unconditional grants. Theoretically, unconditional grants have no place in the layer-cake model described above. Thus revenue sharing seems to be needed primarily because present fiscal institutions diverge so widely from the layer-cake model. Yet the difference between financing any residual fiscal gap through broad-based state and local taxes or through unconditional federal grants or general revenue sharing may be

18. This accentuates the case for federal tax reform. Of course, even if they were based on the federal definition of income for tax purposes, state income taxes need not automatically include all the tax preferences in the federal statutes, although in fact they are likely to do so for political reasons. Integration of federal personal and corporate income taxes is especially vital in this context. If the states were to eschew taxing corporate income, as suggested above would be appropriate, a method of taxing retained earnings under state personal income taxes would be essential. The easiest way would be through levying a piggy-back state tax on an integrated federal income tax.

Because it is assumed that income redistribution is handled at the federal level, only flat-rate state income taxes are considered here. Moreover, because income and sales taxes are treated here as an extension of benefit taxation, it is only consistent to argue that no deductions should be allowed for them in computing federal income tax liabilities. On the other hand, state incomes taxes should apply to income net of federal tax just as sales taxes apply to consumption made from after-tax income.

19. Even if the federal government were to adopt a value-added tax, a simple state piggy-back would not be easy to implement. On the other hand, states and localities could fairly easily supplement a federal sales tax imposed at the retail level. This is discussed in greater detail in the author's "TVA and Fiscal Federalism," *National Tax Journal*, forthcoming. For a recent exchange on the pros and cons of a federal tax on value added, see Dan Throop Smith, "Value Added Tax: The Case For," and Stanley S. Surrey, "Value Added Tax: The Case Against," *Harvard Business Review* (November–December 1970), 77–94.

more apparent than real, especially if federal credit were allowed for state and local income taxes. The federal taxes used to finance the grants may be somewhat more progressive and would interfere less with economic decisions than those the states and localities would use. Moreover, there is likely to be some interstate redistribution if the gap is filled by grants. But if for administrative reasons the state and local taxes would be applied piggyback fashion to federal taxes, it may make little difference which approach is employed. The amount of difference depends in large part upon the formula by which the grants are awarded.

Grants with an equalization provision would result in more interstate redistribution than if the states and localities levied their own taxes to fill the gap. But one might ask whether this is desirable. For one thing, equalizing grants may distort economic choices toward location in low-productivity regions because of the federal contribution to public services provided by states and localities there.

More basically, one must question the entire rationale for equalization provisions in grants. Presumably these provisions are intended either to allow all regions to provide certain minimum levels of public services for their citizens or to reduce differences in the interstate distribution of income. But neither of these arguments is convincing, so long as there is an adequate federal program of low income relief. First, it is not clear that citizens of the poor region, given adequate incomes, would not prefer more private goods and services to some externally determined minimum level of public services. Only if failure to meet the minimum standard involves serious social costs to the rest of the nation would there seem to be a case for federal action to assure the minimum. But unconditional grants are an extremely clumsy way of achieving minimum service standards; categorical grants are much more efficient instruments for this purpose, as noted below.

Second, if the program is an approach to income redistribution, it is also extremely clumsy. Equity involves the incomes of *people,* and not the incomes of *regions.* Equalization provisions at their worst could result effectively in transfers from poor people in wealthy states to rich people in poor states.[20] Clearly, equalization provisions in grants are not a good substitute for low income relief. And more to the point, they might not even be sensible in a fiscal system that included low income relief.

Similar observations can be made about formulas that reward tax ef-

20. This problem could be overcome by limiting the geographic areas eligible to receive equalizing grants quite strictly to those with high concentrations of poverty. Carried to the extreme, this means that grants would be made to poor families, as under the negative income tax—although presumably in the form of vouchers usable only for the provision of public services.

fort. For any number of reasons private response will not provide some services in optimal quantities; this is the very basis of the economic case for government. Moreover, where there are important benefit spill-overs between states, the independent actions of the various states may leave public services underprovided. This is the justification for categorical federal grants. But there is nothing that suggests that the quest for optimal provision of public services is likely to be furthered by a federal subsidy to tax effort, *per se*.

Categorical grants. One argument often advanced in favor of general revenue sharing is that it would not distort the preferences of lower-level governments in the way existing categorical grants do; being provided with almost no strings attached, the shared revenues would be available for these governments to spend as they desired, rather than being limited to specific categories.[21] This argument deserves further examination, with the crucial question being the definition of "distortion."

Spill-overs of benefits between governmental jurisdictions provide the *raison d'être* of categorical grants. Because a given government can be expected to take little account of benefits it provides to nonresidents, it is likely to underprovide services characterized by substantial benefit spill-overs. Categorical grants for such services may be provided by a higher level of government in order to induce the subordinate levels to provide more of the service in question. Thus the preferences of the lower-level government are "distorted" in the direction of greater output than would be demanded in the absence of the categorical grant. But ideally this induces a more nearly optimal level of output of these spill-over-prone activities for the nation as a whole. Seen in this way the alleged distortion is largely illusory, the illusion resulting from a misunderstanding of the purpose of categorical grants.

On the other hand, the categories for grants can be specified so narrowly that distortion does in fact occur in a real sense. In this case, gains could be achieved by loosening some of the restrictions on the use of federal funds. Whether in fact existing grant categories are too narrowly

21. A clear example of this argument is contained in the following quotation from the Task Force of the Republican National Committee, "Financing the Future of Federalism: The Case for Revenue Sharing," in U.S. Congress, Joint Economic Committee, *Revenue Sharing and Its Alternatives: What Future for Fiscal Federalism?* vol. II, p. 795:

> Too often, States have programmed activities for which national grants in aid are available, without due regard to whether such programs are as essential as some others for which national grant money is not available but for which there is a greater need within the State. Thus grant programs have frequently had the effect of skewing State plans and budgets toward problem areas which are considered important in Washington, but not necessarily within the State. Moreover, Federal matching-fund requirements have frequently dictated types of approaches to problem areas and have hogtied state budgeting.

defined is impossible to say without detailed analysis, although it seems likely that they are. If so, it would be desirable to consolidate some of the categories. But again, one can go too far in this direction. Removing all, or nearly all, strings on the use of federal grants, as would be done under President Nixon's proposal for special revenue sharing, would largely abrogate the purpose of the grants. Ideally the categories would be so drawn that programs with national ramifications would be subsidized through categorical grants, but substitute means of meeting a given objective would not be proscribed.[22]

VII. Concluding Remarks

The thrust of this article has been that revenue sharing deserves support not so much because of its own merits as because of the irrationality of the present institutions of fiscal federalism. If the layer-cake model were followed more closely, the case for revenue sharing would be much diminished, if not eliminated. State and local governments would undertake the provision of those public services most appropriate to them, using benefit taxes to a greater extent than now, confident that the progressive taxes and low income relief provided by the federal budget would offset the (perhaps otherwise insufferable) burden of these regressive taxes on low income families. There would be little reason for states and localities to levy the kinds of taxes most likely to drive out industry and distort locational decisions, since adequate progressivity would be provided at the federal level.

Rationalization of fiscal federalism along these lines should relieve the fiscal crisis of the state and local governments, but some residual fiscal gap may remain. To fill the gap these governments could supplement benefit-related taxes with broad-based taxes on sales or income. In the latter case the taxes could be applied to the federal tax base, and federal credits could be allowed for them. Alternatively, the federal government could simply share its income tax revenues with the states and localities. This would substantially simplify the tax collection process.

Note, however, that this argument for revenue sharing is substantially different from that usually advanced. It sees revenue sharing not as the essence of rational fiscal federalism, but as one of several means of filling any gap remaining after fiscal federalism has been rationalized along the lines of the layer-cake model. Viewed in the light, revenue sharing as usually proposed can be seen to be only a stop-gap measure offered in lieu of a more sensible set of fiscal institutions. Revenue sharing may be

---

22. This is essentially the conclusion reached regarding special revenue sharing in Schultze, *et al.*, *Setting National Priorities: The 1972 Budget, op. cit.*, pp. 160–161 and 169–171.

a desirable second-best solution to the fiscal woes of federalism. But we should never forget that it is no more than that. Whether revenue sharing becomes the law of the land or does not, attention should not be diverted from federal tax reform and the initiation of a comprehensive program of low income relief, as these are essential to the rationalization of fiscal federalism—besides being highly desirable on their own merits. In this regard, it is instructive to quote a recent statement by Dick Netzer:

Thus, I have come to view federal revenue-sharing as something of an expedient, while we await long-dealyed structural solutions which may never arrive; in my ideal system of fiscal federalism, the federal role in income redistribution would be greatly expanded, the federal income tax perfected, federal functional grants for activities like education increased, and state-local revenue systems greatly changed, in the direction of benefit taxation.[23]

It is worth noting that Netzer classifies himself as "an early and noisy advocate of revenue sharing."

23. Dick Netzer, "Comment on Murray L. Weidenbaum's 'Sharing Federal Revenues with State and Local Governments,' " presented at the annual meetings of the Regional Science Association, November 6, 1970.

Part III: Economists on Equity, Justice, and the Distribution of Income

One of the main charges made against the economic approach to social policy questions is that it ignores, or is not a useful way to discuss, problems of equity, justice, and income distribution. In this section we seek to examine its utility in each of these areas.

The first paper, written by the editors, surveys a wide range of contributions by economists to discussions of the major normative and positive trade-offs involved in public policy concerning income distribution. It examines both general and specific criteria for redistributing income. Mechanisms for redistribution, the impact of public sector decisions, and positive theories of income redistribution are also discussed.

In the second paper James Tobin (a former member of the Council of Economic Advisers) distinguishes between general and specific egalitarianism and discusses several illustrative cases of the latter. The mainstream of the economics tradition, believing that specific interventions introduce inefficiencies, has been correct, he argues, to insist the general taxation (positive and negative) is the best way to moderate inequalities of income and wealth in a competitive market economy. He points out, however, that in some cases it may be necessary to adopt nonmarket distribution of commodities essential to life and citizenship.

In the third paper George Stigler presents and illustrates the "law" of public income distribution put forward by Aaron Director, professor of economics at the University of Chicago Law School. Director's law states that public expenditures are made for the primary benefit of the middle classes, and are financed in considerable part by taxes on the poor and the rich. This paper is an example of positive economic analysis, which seeks to explain the types of government income redistribution which actually occur—as contrasted with normative analysis, which seeks to give guidelines as to how income should be distributed.

The fourth selection is a paper by Mark Pauly and Thomas Willett, which examines the meaning of equity—a concept that runs through most discussion of public policy, but in many cases is not clearly defined. The paper clarifies some aspects of this problem by distinguishing between *ex ante* and *ex post* equity. The authors use the example of the military draft to develop their concepts, but they proceed to show their much wider applicability to issues such as voting rights. They also consider cases where *ex ante* and *ex post* equity converge.

In the final paper in this section, Dennis Mueller, Robert Tollison, and Thomas Willett present a more general model of the theory of justice advanced by the philosopher John Rawls. The model they propose avoids the problem of Rawls' argued formulation in terms of a limited definition of a just decision and yet retains the important idea of justice as fairness and the contractarian approach. This more general theory, they argue, constitutes a bridge between the pure utilitarian theories and the social contract doctrines. The theory's advantages are demonstrated by applying it to a problem discussed by Rawls, intergenerational equity, and comparing the two solutions.

16. A Menu of Distributional Considerations

RYAN C. AMACHER, ROBERT D. TOLLISON, and THOMAS D. WILLETT

In this essay we attempt to identify the major normative and positive questions involved in public policy concerning the distribution of income. We intend it to be a useful guide to the relevant trade-offs involved in typical economic approaches to income distribution, which are illustrated in the papers that follow. The discussion cannot be divided into neat separations, as the various questions about income distribution are intermixed in a complex way.

We begin in section I with an examination of the equity of the distribution of income produced by a free market and consider some of the reasons why this distribution could be viewed as unacceptable. Section II then examines some *general* criteria for the distribution of income, and the separation of income distribution from the market outcome. Section III discusses arguments for specific types of income redistribution. In section IV we examine mechanisms, both voluntary and mandatory, for the redistribution of income. Section V discusses the effect of some aspects of public sector decisions on the distribution of income, and in section VI we turn to a consideration of two positive theories of income redistribution.

I. Does the Market Produce Equitable Outcomes?

Assuming a perfectly competitive market for the factors of production (land, labor, capital, and entrepreneurship) and abstracting from the question of "unearned income," what determines the laissez faire distribution of income, and is it a "just" or "equitable" solution? Economic theory gives us an unambiguous answer to the first question. The second, however, is more complicated and will be the principal topic of this essay.

The return (rent, wages, interest, and profits) to the factors of production and hence the distribution of income, is determined by the supply of and demand for factors of different kinds and qualities. This functional distribution of income is treated in economic theory as a reflection of choices made by individuals in the market place. The demand for factors of production, including labor, is a demand derived from the demand for the good the factors are combined to produce. A factor has no intrinsic market value. Its value is derived (hence "derived demand") from what it produces. The differences in income that do exist are a result of a combination of elements including differences in productivity and in the demand for the final product. In an "adequately" competitive factor market, we would expect that the monetary advantages plus the non-monetary advantages (negative and positive) in various lines of employment would be roughly equal. For example, unpleasant or risky occupations must have a higher monetary wage, *ceteris paribus,* to attract workers. Recognition of this principle is reflected in many of the programs associated with the all-volunteer-army. Likewise, return to capital must be higher in higher risk industries.[1]

This competitive market solution is a reward both to the value of the input and to the value of the output of the productive unit. Given factor inputs of equal physical productivity, the highest reward will go to the factor unit employed in the industry producing products most highly valued on the market. Conversely, labor inputs employed in the same industry will be rewarded with respect to their physical productivity, the more productive factor receiving the more remuneration at the margin. Additionally, the return to the factor will be affected by the physical productivity of the other factor units it is combined with and by the relative

---

1. For a more elaborate treatment of marginal productivity theory, see Friedman (1962) and Becker (1971).

amounts of each factor employed. Thus it is possible that factors of "equal quality" receive different remuneration, depending upon what other factors of production they are combined with. A good example of this point is the return to the management of General Motors versus the return to the management of a "small home-town" plant. The managers of General Motors receive a higher return, for one reason, because they are combined with larger amounts of capital, which raises the value of units of managerial decision-making.

An important aspect of this determination of the distribution of income is that it is associated with efficiency in resource allocation. If other things are equal, factors flow to those employments with the highest remuneration, i.e., those in which their productivity is most highly valued. Such a system has value because it rewards productivity rather than determining factor remuneration by some other ethical, nonmarket standard. Administrative wage systems that tend to be largely egalitarian in ethic, rewarding longevity and the like, tend to promote uneconomic behavior. A good example can be found in the wage practices of most colleges or universities, where the factors are producing an output that is not always directly marketed and remuneration must therefore be administratively determined. With faculty it is sometimes difficult to measure productivity. This produces the curious situation in which administrators often turn to rewarding inputs (e.g., time spent at work) because they find it difficult or unpleasant to monitor and reward outputs. The faculty predictably responds by inputting a very visible amount of "service activities" (committee work, memo writing, etc.) Perhaps an even better example of how such non-market remuneration practices can interfere with efficiency can be found in the staffing and remuneration of some secretarial pools. If the reward to the factor, in this case secretaries, is not for productivity, but rather for observed inputs, one of two effects will follow. If input reward takes place in an area with competing opportunities for secretarial employment, e.g., a university surrounded by industrial-commercial demands for secretarial service, the productive ("good") secretaries will simply be bid away from the university. On the other hand, if the university is a monopsonist (the major employer of secretaries in the area), the "good" secretaries will tend to react like the unproductive ("bad") secretaries, because there is little reward for productivity.

In freely operating markets the return to factors of equal productivity will tend to equality. This is an important cornerstone of positive economics. It enables economists to analyze many problems concerning factor movements and changes in factor shares in the face of changed market conditions. But while the traditional theory of income distribution is a positive theory of income determination in a free market system, it does provide an implicit normative standard of distributive justice.

In a normative evaluation of the market-produced distribution of income, the important question is whether man deserves what he produces. An alternative popular slogan reads, "From each according to his ability, to each according to his need." Of course, this slogan hardly suggests the difficulties that would be encountered in making such an alternative income distribution operational. There would be the obvious problem of defining "needs" and many other less obvious problems concerning incentives, as discussed in our previous examples. However, distributive injustice typically arises from some original distribution of resources, i.e., one person is born healthy and another is born lame. Thus, while we can correct for original injustices (and this paper will discuss various ways to do so), we may wish to reward according to productivity after making such corrections. This is because it is difficult to determine what principle to apply, and reward according to productivity may be a widely accepted principle. In addition, it is associated with the efficient operation of the economic system.

We should stress that we are not attempting to bias the reader against an alternative ethic to marginal productivity theory that might stress "needs." On the contrary, we are now going to examine the basis on which one might object to a market-produced distribution of income. In this discussion the marginal productivity theory of income distribution, which we briefly sketched, will serve as a useful benchmark as we consider some additional *normative* and *positive* questions concerning the distribution of income. As we shall see, many of the normative questions arise because the market is not the only institution affecting the distribution of income in most societies.

Market Imperfections

We have been assuming a perfectly competitive market for the factors of production. The existence of market imperfections presents the first reason why the market-produced income distribution might be viewed as inappropriate. Market imperfections cause a welfare and an income loss to consumers. This can be simply demonstrated. Consider Figure 1. Assume the long-run marginal cost function is the horizontal line LRC. Equilibrium price in pure competition would be Pc and monopolization would result in a price of Pm with output falling by XmXc. The dead-weight loss from monopoly is represented by triangle ABC. This is a dead-weight loss because it is consumer surplus that would have been gained

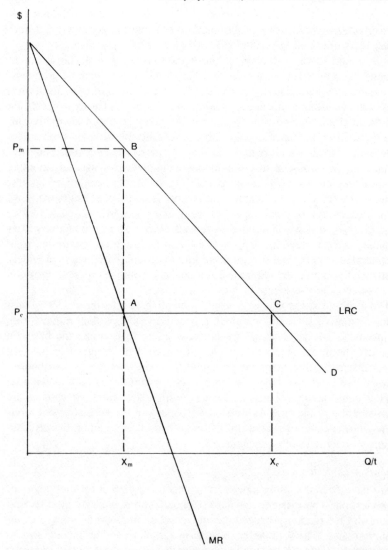

Figure 1.

by consumers but now vanishes into thin air.[2] No one captures this real income. On the other hand, rectangle PcABPm is consumer surplus that

2. In this example we have assumed that the average cost is the same in the industry in pure competition and monopoly. It is likely that average cost would be higher under monop-

is lost to consumers, but is captured by shareholders in the monopoly firm. It might therefore be argued that within the context of the competitive model this income should be redistributed to consumers.[3] Many popular arguments for income redistribution are based on such market imperfection arguments.

An obvious solution to the problem of monopoly imperfection would be to correct for the market imperfection that produced the monopoly profits. For example, instead of taxing "unearned" oil income, one might more easily, and with less distortive effect, attempt to make the industry more competitive. This, of course, would correct for present and future monopoly profits, but not those that occurred in the past. Another indirect and probably inefficient way to adjust for market imperfections is through progressive income taxation. Thus, aside from other arguments for progressive taxation, one might argue that progressiveness adjusts for these unearned income streams where they are positively correlated with income.[4] Of course, one must trade off these sorts of adjustments in the tax system against the disincentive effects on labor supply that are generally associated with a highly progressive income tax.

The Role of Economic Rents

A popular reason for objecting to the market-determined distribution of income is the existence of economic rents in the price system. To an economist, rent is a return in excess of a factor's opportunity cost. For example, when a market wage is set for volunteer soldiers, some soldiers will receive rents (or quasi-rents) in the sense that the *market* wage exceeds their supply prices. Indeed, all but the marginal volunteer soldier will receive rents. In this section we will discuss the role of three separate categories of economic rent: rents that have to be paid but not necessarily received, monopoly rents, and windfall profits.

The problems involved in the first case are best illustrated by the old fallacy in Henry George's single-tax proposal, to tax only income from land. This fallacy involved the failure to distinguish between the fact that the supply of *all* land is completely inelastic with respect to price (rent),

---

oly. This is important because it causes an understatement of the profit rectangle and the welfare loss triangle in empirical work. The waste of resources due to this cost inefficiency represents an additional welfare loss that has been estimated to be larger than the dead-weight-loss triangle taken alone. See Comanor and Leibenstein (1969).

3. For summaries of the empirical attempts to measure the welfare loss due to monopoly, see Scherer (1970), chapter 17, and Sherman (1974), chapter 19. Most empirical studies have assumed that consumers and producers have the same marginal utility of income and have attempted only to measure the dead-weight loss.

4. For some of the other arguments for progressive taxation, see Blum and Klaven (1953).

and the fact that the supply of land to alternative uses is quite elastic. Thus, price serves the function of allocating land to competing uses, even where it is not possible to induce increases in the total supply of land. The land payments must be paid in order for this allocative function to operate, though it is not absolutely necessary that they be received.

We have distinguished two basic cases. In the first the relevant supply function is completely inelastic with respect to price (the supply of all land). In this case rent does not have to be paid, since there is no allocative function to be performed. In the second case, there are rents associated with positively sloped supply functions for any factor of production. Here, rents must be paid in order to obtain the proper allocative result, but they do not necessarily have to be received. Therefore, one may object to the receipt of such rents and propose to tax them away.

Of course, it would be administratively complicated to tax any such rents without distorting the economy. Even in the case where the supply schedule is perfectly inelastic, it is difficult to determine the relevant alternatives to judge exactly what constitutes the rent component (under market price, but above the supply curve). For example, Joe Namath earns rents in the sense that there is a perfectly inelastic supply of his quarterbacking talent. One might argue that all these rents could be taxed away without reducing his supply of quarterbacking services. But what is the relevant size of his rent? Should it be calculated on his next best football alternative, or on his next best non-football alternative? This is a crucial distinction in taxing any rent generated in the price of any factor of production, since a mistake in deciding a factor's supply price and relevant size of rent would lead to allocative distortions.

The other two categories of rents are monopoly rents and windfall profits. Monopoly rents accrue due to a market imperfection such as we discussed earlier in this section. As we noted, perhaps the best way to deal with this type of rent is to correct for monopoly power through antitrust policy. One could, however, propose to tax such monopoly returns as "excess" profits.

As a distinct category of rents, windfall gains are typically a result of unanticipated changes in the price system. Many proposals to tax such windfall profits are presently being heard. Taxation is especially desired when such returns are thought to be "unearned" or related to market imperfections, such as monopoly. The best current example of this attitude is the clamor about windfall profits in the oil industry.

In a more fundamental sense, however, one again encounters the problem described above in determining the amount of the gain that should be properly treated as a windfall. That is, what portion of windfall profits must be paid, but not received? Often what is thought to be a windfall gain is a return to risk bearing and other entrepreneurial activities that are necessary to stimulate future expansion of production. Consider for example, the role of entrepreneurs and speculators in the price system. What annoys some people is that certain individuals earn large amounts of income (and lose large amounts of income) by buying and selling future rights to resources or by being in the right place at the right time. It then appears that the individual receives a windfall or unearned gain if oil is discovered under his land, if the price of the crop he is raising goes up, etc. Those who are offended by this perhaps feel as they do because these returns seem uncorrelated with physical endeavor or some similar effort. However, in an economic sense these returns cannot be viewed as unearned. Rather, they are typically returns to functions like risk bearing, associated with the ability or willingness to attempt to predict the future. It is an important task in the price system where one has stocks of goods, such as agricultural goods, that are periodically produced, to allocate the fixed stock over the period until new production comes on the market. In this situation, entrepreneurs and speculators fill a useful social function by assuming the risks of future price changes, and thereby enabling producers to specialize in production and to plan production on the basis of solid price contracts. Speculators as a group cannot make profits by inducing price fluctuations, unless they possess monopoly power.

So while windfall gains and losses may be of concern in the sense that they do not have to be received, i.e., they are a by-product of unanticipated price changes, one must be careful to avoid confusing windfalls with *bona fide* returns to economic functions. Of course, as with rents in the first category, any proposal to tax windfall profits will be fraught with administrative difficulty if it seeks to avoid creating allocative distortions in the price system.

The Role of Chance

Another reason that the market-determined distribution of income may be unsatisfactory is that substantial elements of chance are associated with it. An individual's future income is subject to a considerable degree of uncertainty. To a great extent this uncertainty may not be avoidable privately, and hence where most people are risk-averters, government programs of an egalitarian nature affecting either income distribution or the distribution of specific commodities may appear.[5] Thus privately uninsurable risk may lead to income redistribution becoming a valid function

5. For a highly original general consideration of the role of chance in explaining income redistribution, see Head (1966). For a treatment of government redistributive programs as social insurance, see Buchanan (1967), and for an example of the implications of this argument for the size of the budget in total, see Greene (1973).

of the state. Government may respond to such risks either by acting *ex ante* (before the fact) to reduce the risk itself or by acting *ex post* (after the fact) through insurance payments. Examples of the former are preventative public programs, such as public health and education programs designed to help prevent illness or accident and programs to regulate product safety. Institutions such as social security, unemployment insurance, progressive income taxation, and stabilization policy are examples of *ex post* governmental policies that respond to some extent to risk-aversion among voters. It should also be noted that to some degree it is possible to trade off among policy instruments to reduce risk. Thus, efficient stabilization policy can be traded off against unemployment insurance, and public health programs against medical insurance.

Summary

We have reviewed marginal productivity theory and discussed some reasons why a market-produced distribution of income might not be generally acceptable. We now turn to a discussion of some general schemes for changing this market-determined distribution.

II. Should Income Distribution be Completely Separated from Market Outcomes?

Economists have been reluctant to make interpersonal comparisons of utility. This has somewhat restricted their analysis of distributional problems. The basic reason for this reluctance is that value judgments are necessary to judge alternative distributions of income, and to an economist value judgments are not scientific data. However, various economists and philosophers have developed general distributional schemes which depend in one way or another on interpersonal comparisons. In this section we examine some examples of these schemes and the value judgments that underlie them.

Distribute Income to Maximize Satisfaction

A good utilitarian would argue that income should be distributed to maximize satisfaction. Of course, this is a difficult criterion to agree upon since there is no scientific way to compare degrees of satisfaction. Operationally, it would be difficult, if not impossible, to obtain reliable measures of satisfaction since each individual would have a clear incentive to lie, and even if reliable measures for individuals could be obtained, economists have long argued that there is simply no way to make interpersonal comparisons of satisfaction. Say, for example, that we wish to tax Sid E. Slicker $100 and redistribute it to John S. Okie. It is impossible for us to know whether the satisfaction Slicker gave up by consuming $100 less champagne is less than the satisfaction Okie received by consuming $100 more Coors beer.

Distribute Income on Computed Egalitarian Lines

Since general schemes like "maximizing satisfaction" are both theoretically and operationally impossible to implement, it might make sense to distribute income on some computed egalitarian basis. Plato was explicit on such a rule. He argued that no one in a society should be more than four times richer than the poorest member.[6] Abba Lerner has asserted ". . . if it is desired to maximize the total satisfaction in a society, the rational procedure is to divide income on an equalitarian basis." [7] Lerner bases his argument on some simple utilitarian assumptions. He assumes that the marginal income-utility schedules for all individuals decline. He allows for differences in levels and slopes of these marginal utility schedules but is unable to determine which individual is attached to which schedule. He therefore concludes that since it is impossible to conclude who has higher and lower income-utility schedules, any move toward greater equality is likely to increase total welfare.[8]

Lerner's argument has been open to various interpretations. Some contradict others, but all view it as authoritative. In a later note, Lerner himself states that there can be no certain gain from redistribution if we are ignorant of the individual's utility function. He does maintain, however, that redistribution would maximize the *probable* total satisfaction.[9]

Once such a normative decision to redistribute is made, the question then becomes one of determining an operational egalitarian basis. Again, economists have done little work in this area because of their unwillingness to make the necessary value judgments. Recently, however, Ray Fair has attempted to present a normative model for the optimal distribution of income. Fair assumes that everyone should be weighted equally in the social welfare function, that all should be given equal opportunity to reach their potential, and freedom to maximize their individual utility function. He then solves this model for alternative sets of assumptions to examine the model's sensitivity to key parameters.[10]

6. See Fair (1971).   7. See Lerner (1944), p. 32.
8. See Lerner (1944), p. 40.
9. In an exchange with Breit and Culbertson (1970) in the *American Economic Review* he amends this statement by inserting the phrase, "the rational procedure, in the absence of the knowledge that would enable us to equalize the marginal utilities, is to maximize the probable total satisfaction, i.e., to divide. . . ." Lerner (1970), p. 442. For an examination of the assumptions Lerner makes, see Breit and Culbertson (1970).
10. See Fair (1971).

Minimum Income

Perhaps one workable approach is for everyone in a jurisdiction to be guaranteed at least some minimum income, by means of a guaranteed annual income or negative income tax. The negative income tax is appealing to economists for a number of reasons. In the first place, it concentrates public funds on the poor rather than attempting to have them trickle down through a large welfare bureaucracy. The same amount of redistribution therefore costs less because it is directed specifically at poverty, eliminating the need for intermediary agencies. Perhaps most importantly, however, the negative income tax does not eliminate work incentives. A negative income tax at a fractional rate gives greater incentive to earn extra income than present welfare programs because the recipient is able to retain a portion of each dollar earned.[11]

In any event, once the idea of a negative income tax or guaranteed annual income is accepted, the question becomes what this minimum should be. Again this has to be a strictly normative decision; economic theory can give us no clue as to what level is the right one. The most workable approach here seems to be that of calculating a typical break-even budget at current prices.

Rawls' Difference Principle: A Specific-Egalitarian Scheme

John Rawls has constructed a social contract theory of moral and political philosophy.[12] He divides collective choice into four stages: (1) social contract, (2) constitution, (3) legislature, and (4) judiciary and administration. In the first stage the decisions on equality and inequality are made. The individuals consider this problem, not knowing what position they will occupy. These mutually disinterested individuals are assumed to know "general facts" about human society, and the result of the "experiment" is that all rational, egotistic individuals adopt the same set of *fair* "rules" as a social contract. Rawls devotes a great deal of effort to demonstrate that two principles will emerge from this original position. The second principle, the difference principle, requires that choices always be made so as to maximize the expected position of the worst-off individual in the society. As Rawls discusses this concept, it is equivalent to the maximin strategy in game theory and assumes an extreme degree of risk aversion. This would mean that we would raise the minimum level of income to the maximum possible, given the constraint that these raises might affect the total level of income. In other words, we trade off ef-

11. For a thorough discussion of the negative income tax, see Friedman (1968).
12. See Rawls (1971).

ficiency for equality until the disincentive effects become too costly to go further. Again the determination of this maximum is a normative decision. It might, as Rawls argues, be possible for unbiased decision-makers to reach unanimity on the maximum.[13]

Summary

It is possible, of course, to combine several of the preceding schemes into one argument for redistribution. For example, it may be decided to trade off the problems of excess burden from taxation and the consequent effects on total income and distribution, in effect, to maximize income equality *ex post,* subject only to the excess burden constraint. This is quite similar to the Lerner argument discussed above in the sense that its ethical basis assumes diminishing marginal utility of income, because it assumes that greater income equality implies that social satisfaction is maximized.

III. Specific Criteria for Income Distribution

We have been discussing general ethical schemes for income redistribution. In this section we will examine some specific criteria for redistribution.

Should Strings be Attached?

A question basic to discussions of income redistribution is what should be redistributed? In other words, should general money grants be given, or should the redistribution be in the form of goods (in kind)? A related question if money is redistributed is whether conditions should be attached to the transfer.

The argument that money should be given instead of certain goods is part of the argument that lump-sum transfers of general purchasing power are the optimal form of transfer. A transfer of money gives more options and maximizes the freedom of the recipient, i.e., places him on the highest indifference curve.[14] This is the traditional welfare analysis of transfers of money and is based solely on the welfare of the recipient.[15]

13. For a criticism and extension of Rawls' arguments, see Mueller, Tollison and Willett (1974b).

14. See Scitovsky (1951).

15. Recently, however, J. D. Rodgers has argued that, from the point of view of the donor, if general welfare is the interdependency in the donor's utility function that causes the redistributive transfer, than the lump sum transfer is optimal. If the interdependency depends upon a specific externality generated by the poor, Pareto optimality involves the transfer of particular commodities. See Hochman and Rodgers (1973) and the reference cited there for an in-depth treatment of the optimal form of income transfer.

Specific Externalities

James Buchanan has argued that, in examining the question of whether strings should be attached, maximizing the freedom of the recipient is not a relevant consideration; one should instead talk about maximizing the freedom of the donor.[16] This implies either money or in-kind transfers, whichever the donor specifies. This argument applies whether we are discussing negative externalities (e.g., the poor) or positive externalities (e.g., what is "best" for students to read).

A transfer is more likely to be granted conditionally when the motivation for it is not concern over the welfare of the recipient, *per se*. This motivation may stem from a distaste for a particularly noxious externality (à la Buchanan) or even from a desire to influence behavior in a certain way. That is, it may stem from a desire to reduce the cost of policing against a certain action, or a fear that unless some redistribution takes place the poor will become unruly (e.g., it will be a "hot summer"). These are distinctly separate motivations, but they produce the same distributional response, and they both imply that it is the freedom of the donor that should be maximized. Where these motivations are important to the donor, it is likely that strings will be attached to the transfer. Probably the best example of such conditional granting of transfers is the requirement that able-bodied males must be willing to accept work if it is offered. In effect, the argument here is that in-kind transfers to reduce specific externalities may be quite rational from the point of view of the donor-voter. This is supported in a positive sense by the observation of the large numbers of such specific transfers in practice.

"Basic Needs"

Many of the transfers that we observe are in-kind transfers of specific commodities, e.g., the surplus commodity food program and Salvation Army soup kitchens. Grants and transfers of this kind may result when those initiating the transfer are concerned with what they consider "basic needs." The transfer is not so much based on the desire to reduce income inequality, but rather is designed to insure that basic needs, such as food and shelter, are provided. James Tobin has called motivation of the latter sort *specific egalitarianism*.[17] Tobin feels that most economists are general egalitarians, to the extent they are egalitarian, because they recognize the inefficiencies introduced by specific interventions. The majority of the

    16. See Buchanan (1968).
    17. See Tobin (1970), and Tobin (1952). Musgrave's (1959) concept of "merit wants" is quite similar to Tobin's discussion of specific egalitarianism. For an example of medical care as a form of specific egalitarianism, see Lindsay (1969).

electorate, however, are specific egalitarians. If this observation is correct, one can expect most public transfers to be transfers in kind, or with strings attached.

Redistribution as Jobs

In opposition to the belief that recipients prefer the money transfer to the in-kind or strings-attached transfer it is sometimes argued that the poor do not want welfare, but rather, meaningful jobs. This is, in essence, a call for in-kind transfers in the form of jobs, sometimes publicly provided. This argument can often be added, in a subtle fashion, to arguments for short-term expansionary monetary and fiscal policy. Generally, however, public works are viewed as inferior to tax cuts as a method to pursue short-run expansionary policy.[18] In the discussions preceding the "economic summit" in October 1974 it was argued that publicly provided jobs were needed to cushion the harshness of contractionary monetary and fiscal policy.

Redistribution to Special Interests

An interesting variety of redistribution is the type where the recipients attempt to conceal from themselves and others that a transfer is being made. This constitutes backdoor welfare, i.e., transfers from the general public to special interest groups via some form of trade restricting legislation. Arguments for such action appear frequently in the international trade literature, but the direct advocacy of tariffs and quotas is by no means the only way special interest groups try to obtain backdoor welfare.[19] A good example of another means used is the mink breeders' association's argument that its members need protection from the cheap mink being imported from Eastern Europe. In effect, the mink breeders are asking for an income transfer from consumers of mink. It is an income transfer because the tariff or quota will allow the price of mink to be higher than it would be in the absence of import restrictions. The transfer is well camouflaged and many of the industry leaders and producing firms would object strenuously to putting their argument for protection in these terms. Nevertheless, the protection represents a transfer to the protected industry.

In fact, it might well be argued that every lobbyist in Washington is really an entrepreneur for backdoor welfare, that the laws they urge produce these transfers and also lead to unproductive entrepreneurial activ-

18. For a discussion of some of these arguments for expansionary fiscal policy see Samuelson (1973), chapter 41, esp. pp. 825–833.

19. For good examples of some of these arguments for tariffs, see Yeager and Tuerck (1966).

ity.[20] Examples here are investment in tax avoidance and the employment of tax lawyers and accountants.

Adjustment Assistance

Still another specific argument for income redistribution concerns individuals whose incomes are affected by changes in governmental policies such as procurement, tariffs, quotas, or by technological change. An example might be individuals who lose jobs when a mill is closed by a new environmental policy because it has been polluting a stream. Or the loss of employment may be caused by the mill's loss of a government contract or its inability to meet foreign competition. The issue here is whether individuals so affected should be compensated or paid adjustment assistance for the loss of employment or the costs of moving to a new job.

On a practical plane, adjustment assistance may be viewed as a useful tool to achieve Pareto-optimal social policy.[21] In this sense adjustment assistance can be used as compensation to make the removal of a trade barrier politically feasible. Whether such compensation should be paid in any given situation depends, of course, on who has the property rights. As in the case of monopoly, removal of a trade barrier can be viewed as benefiting consumers via lower supply prices while harming those factors of production benefiting from the monopoly restriction. In such cases it is generally true that where there are no transaction costs for consumers to organize, consumers can buy out (i.e., compensate) monopolists and still come out ahead.[22] There is a presumption, then, in favor of giving property rights for compensation to the affected factors of production. However, in the absence of public intervention, transaction costs to the large number of affected consumers would be prohibitive. Each consumer benefits by a small amount from the removal of a trade barrier, and no one consumer has a large personal incentive to organize other consumers to pay for the removal of a barrier since it would be largely other consumers who benefited from such activity. It is just uneconomic (i.e., the costs are greater than the personal benefits) for any one consumer to undertake to organize all consumers in such a case. Viewed in this manner, adjustment assistance is a public policy that mediates between those who are harmed and consumers who gain by the removal of a trade barrier in such a way as to reduce transaction costs to consumers (actually taxpayers viewed as consumers).

20. For a treatment of resources "invested" in these types of activities, see Tullock (1967).

21. See Reading 1 in this volume for a discussion of Pareto optimality.

22. Buchanan and Tullock (1968) argue that monopoly benefits tend to be capitalized at the moment of creation and that current owners do not differentially benefit. Bierman and Tollison (1970), on the other hand, argue that under realistic assumptions monopoly rents

As this discussion suggests, establishing property rights to compensation, or adjustment assistance, would be a difficult practical matter. Why, for example, would such assistance be limited to dislocations caused by changes in international competition? How does one differentiate between dislocations brought about by regional resource movements (e.g., north to south) and those resulting from international trade? To displaced workers, there is no difference in the two cases. Or, if adjustment assistance raises the possibility that further government action may be forthcoming that will make movement unnecessary, will management and labor in these industries be encouraged to invest in political action to secure the change in policy they desire, i.e., to make relocation unnecessary? [23]

Or, to take a more extended example of a practical problem in implementing adjustment assistance, consider a common argument that suggests that, where one factor is more mobile than the other, the relatively less mobile factor bears the brunt of adjustment costs. This is true as stated, but it does not necessarily follow that *labor* is always the factor that bears the heavier dislocation costs. Certainly labor is less mobile than financial capital. But where capital takes the form of investment in fixed plants and facilities, it is quite a tricky question to generalize about the relative mobility of capital versus labor. The correct answer would depend on a careful analysis of each particular case. The increased international mobility of capital is thus not clear proof that labor bears the larger proportion of adjustment costs resulting from international competition. While the increased mobility of capital does cut down on labor's ability to win large wage settlements, this is a completely different point from which factor bears the major proportion of the dislocation costs.

Of course, problems of the practical politics of adjustment assistance and the philosophical and theoretical underpinnings of such a policy are difficult to keep completely separate in any discussion. The question of who has property rights in such cases clearly raises both practical and philosophical issues. When we speak of a philosophical explanation of adjustment assistance, however, what we have in mind is a rationale for such a policy as a part of a broader social or constitutional arrangement. One such argument would suggest that individuals may find it advantageous to insure against employment loss or dislocation at a constitutional stage of choice where decision makers must choose social rules under uncertainty. This type of choice might be made for efficiency or equity reasons. In efficiency terms private insurance markets may not

---

are not completely discounted at the moment of their creation due to the uncertainty surrounding future antitrust action against the firm, so that these rents are partially transferred forward in time.

23. See Yeager and Tuerck (1966), and Tullock (1967).

emerge to internalize completely the costs of temporary employment loss and dislocation. In equity terms constitutional decision makers would expect that adjustment costs would fall heavily on low-income workers and may want to institute adjustment assistance as a result. As we noted above, however, it is not always true that low-income workers bear the heaviest portion of adjustment costs. A further difficulty may be encountered here too. Workers may not want to adjust and might prefer to maintain trade barriers and their present jobs rather than receive adjustment assistance.[24]

Redistribution via a Third Party

Redistribution through a third party is best described by use of an example familiar to many: that of overclaiming on insurance claims. Each individual acts like a perfect competitor in the sense that the behavior of the rest of society is treated as exogeneous. The result is that the harmed individual has an incentive to overclaim whenever possible. If successful, such action results in an income transfer from the insuring public toward those making claims.[25] Of course, there are incentives for the insurance companies to police this type of behavior. In addition, if insurance rates were to go up as a result of overclaiming to the point that loss insurance was no longer a "fair bet," people would start to self-insure.

Another type of redistribution through a third party is that which results from crime. Income is redistributed from the victim to the criminal. The overclaiming discussed above and tax evasion are examples of white-collar crimes which redistribute income. Hard core crimes, e.g., muggings and holdups, also represent income transfers toward the criminal. A related question that might be considered in discussing income redistribution concerns public compensation to the victims of such crimes.

Distribution of Political Income [26]

We conclude this section with a discussion of a specific proposal to redistribute a particular type of income, political income. Before we begin, it is important that we distinguish clearly between *ex ante* and *ex post* eq-

24. For an example of some of these arguments, see Yeager and Tuerck (1966), e.g., "Mushroom-growers don't want to be sent to Detroit" (p. 259).

25. In some sense it might be argued that such transfers are "equitable" because there are more costs on the harmed party than those of the loss of property alone. In this sense overclaiming is compensation for psychological costs. There is some empirical evidence to support this argument because, except for an occasional fire, we find few examples of people in the business of "losing" property in order to make claims.

26. This discussion follows closely the arguments in Mueller, Tollison, and Willett (1974a). See the original for references and a complete discussion.

uity.[27] *Ex ante* equity refers to fairness in the sense that risks or opportunities before the fact are equalized, i.e., all runners start at the same mark. *Ex post* equity is fairness in the sense of actual outcomes of social processes involving risk and uncertainty. In most cases, *ex post* equity is probably of greater importance, though not always—not, for instance, in cases where equality of opportunity is the objective, or where it is desirable to introduce a mechanism to achieve *ex ante* equity (or some combination of the two concepts) because *ex post* equity is impossible or too costly to achieve. Most programs to achieve greater equity contain some mixture of the two; for example, mechanisms such as Fair Employment Laws can be viewed as generating greater *ex ante* equity, or equality of opportunity, while a progressive income tax can be viewed as generating greater *ex post* equality, but each also exerts certain effects in the other direction. The two concepts of equity are, however, separable. One might therefore support programs that have as their goal *ex ante* equality of income, but not support *ex post* schemes for equality.

We have seen that there is a connection between political power and income distribution. It is, therefore, important to investigate the distribution of political income. Such investigation has been characterized primarily by discussion of the analogous problem of generating mechanisms to achieve *ex ante* equality of opportunity to participate (e.g., one man, one vote). Perhaps the primary reason that this form of *ex ante* equality has been stressed in the literature and institutions of democracy is that it is considered a basic sort of right, or value judgment, which goes hand in hand with political democracy. Possibly a second important reason is that only minor disincentive effects are associated with guaranteeing this form of political equality.[28]

Given the relative lack of disincentive effects associated with mechanisms for reallocating voting rights, it is interesting that establishing an *ex post* equality of the distribution of political income has never seriously been considered. In markets for private goods, each voter-consumer allocates his income so that the expected marginal utility from each dollar vote on a good is equal. Planned consumption at equilibrium prices is identical to actual consumption. In the absence of mistakes due to lack of sufficient information, this assures equality between expected and actual utility. These conditions are not likely to hold where public goods are allocated via one-man, one-vote majority rule. The utilities a voter ex-

27. For an extended treatment of the two concepts of equity, see Pauly and Willett (1972), and the references cited there.

28. For a discussion of the decision to vote considered by a rational economic calculus, see Tollison and Willett (1973).

pects from each vote may vary widely. And there can exist a large divergence between what he expects (hopes?) to receive in public goods as indicated by his voting decisions and what he actually receives after all votes are cast and counted.

These two characteristics of voting have been typically described as giving rise to problems of "minority rights" or the "tyranny of the majority." It is important to note, however, that these characteristics create *two separate problems*, which require separate remedies.

The problem created by differing intensities of preference among voters can be solved by introducing point voting. To begin with, voters and issues must be grouped into polities such that in any given polity each voter has an "equal stake" (in terms of his potential aggregate utility change) in the *set* of issues to be decided. That is, governmental units are broken up into, say, neighborhood, city, regional, and national jurisdictions, so that the integral of voters' utility distributions over the issue set to be decided by a given polity is approximately equal. Each member of a polity is given an equal number of vote-points to be allocated over the set of issues to be decided by the polity. If the voters honestly allocate the vote-points in proportion to their relative intensities of preference on all issues (i.e., if they do not engage in strategic behavior), the point allocations will reflect each voter's marginal rates of substitution between issues. If the equal-stake criterion is met, the total expected utility of every voter in a polity will be equal, and the outcomes obtained from aggregating the point-vote allocations will maximize the utility gains of the community from voting. The equal-stake criterion produces *ex ante* political equality for each voter over the set of issues, while point voting allows each voter to achieve *ex ante* equality on every single issue by revealing his relative intensities of preferences over the issue set. Together they form a system for achieving *ex ante* political equality for each voter on every issue.

There are two contexts in which one can conceive of equalizing the distribution of political income *ex post*. First, one could adjust each individual's vote stock at the beginning of a voting period, depending upon his success over *all* previous periods. Suppose that in the first round an individual won on issues totaling 90 per cent of his vote-points, while the average voter won only 70 per cent. If the initial stock was 100 votes, the individual would be given 80 votes at the start of period two. If he again won on 90 per cent, he would win on 72 vote-points, and his tax for the next period would be 2 votes. He would thus have 78 votes for period three, and as long as he continued to win on 90 per cent of his vote-point allocations, he would be winning on issues totaling 70 vote-points, the average for the community. If on some round either his tastes or the community's changed so that he won on only half of his allocations, his total successful allocations would fall to 39. In the next round his cumulative overall tax would be $20 + 2 - 31 = -9$, and he would receive 109 votes. If he continued to win on only 50 per cent of his vote-point allocations, his vote holdings would continue to rise until he began receiving 140 vote-points, assuming the average voter was still winning on 70 vote-points.

This procedure is a compromise between the *ex ante* egalitarian condition embodied in the equal-stake criterion, and a full *ex post* equality of political income as described below. The stability of voter preferences, and therefore of voter winning percentages, is relied upon to adjust the vote holdings so that each voter's expected successful vote allocations, based on past outcomes, are the same for the coming round. (If the voters' winning percentages are not stable over time, there is no long-run tyranny of the majority problem, and hence no need to adjust individual vote stocks.) In the above example, the voter would continue to get 70 vote-points, the community's average. No adjustments would ever be made, however, for the 22 "extra" vote-points he won in the first two rounds. He is always "ahead of the game" by that amount. Alternative tax-subsidy schemes could be designed to achieve equal cumulative, *ex post* political income, but these would have the serious disadvantage of requiring a constant potential total utility gain for each voter from period to period. No such restrictive assumption is required under the lagged vote-tax scheme, since its goal is merely to equate each voter's *expected* winning number of vote-points in the coming period. If these expectations are based on each voter's past history of successes, and the stability of these winning percentages are taken into account, individual vote stocks could be adjusted to bring *ex ante* and *ex post* political income into equality over time. The voter who has done badly in the past can only write these losses off, and console himself with the knowledge that he may expect a more equal share of the public-good pie in the future, whatever the size of that pie might be.

Alternatively, one might decide to equalize the realized utility gains over the set of issues a polity decides at any point in time, by a system of taxes and subsidies on voting rights, *and* a sequential, non-binding series of votes on issues. Such a system could achieve *full ex post* equality of political income. Initial votes would be tentative, subject to the vote-income distribution that resulted from voting. As an example, suppose that, after the initial vote, the set of outcomes was such that each voter had on average decisions corresponding to 70 per cent of his vote-point allocations satisfied. If a particular voter won on a set of issues corresponding to 90 per cent of his vote-point allocations after the first round, then his total vote holdings would be reduced for the second round of voting. Thus, vote stocks would be adjusted by taxing abnormally high winners (say a tax of 20 votes on the 90 per cent winners) and subsidizing losers, after which the vote-points would be cast again. Over a series of recontracts with adjusted stocks of vote-points, the gains from winning and losing would be equalized. To avoid excessive recontracting under this scheme, one might be satisfied with bringing everyone to within 5 or 10 points of the average utility gain.

The best examples of such systems in the private sphere can be found in some handicapping systems in sports. The player draft in professional sports, where successful teams are penalized in an effort to make the season more equal *ex ante,* has much the same purpose as the vote tax: to avoid long winning streaks.

Summary

This section considered specific schemes for redistributing private and political income. An important conclusion is that while complete *ex post* equality is not possible or even desirable when we are discussing the distribution of private income, the *ex post* equality of political income is possible and perhaps feasible.

IV. Mandatory versus Voluntary Mechanisms for Redistributing Income

There are many ways that the types of general or specific transfers we have been discussing can be carried out. The manner in which redistribution is accomplished can influence the type and amount of the ultimate transfer. In this section, then, we will examine some of the different mechanisms for redistribution.

Private versus Collective Redistribution

Private redistribution through charity takes place voluntarily. Such transfers can spring from a variety of motivations, all linked to some form of concern on the part of an individual for other individuals in society. The analytical term for such concern is utility interdependence.[29] Interdependence of utility functions exists for any one of a number of reasons, ranging from a desire for social justice to a feeling that the life style of those who are poor is offensive. The important point about such transfers is that they are voluntary and hence may be presumed to be Pareto-optimal in the sense that both parties are made better off. Thus the income equality achieved via private charity can be characterized as a

29. For examples of some of these models, see Hochman and Rodgers (1969), Olsen (1969), and Johnson (1970).

pure public good. Nonetheless, private charity may produce "too little" redistribution. In a large group the individual may feel that he does not have to contribute, since he assumes everyone else will. There is in large groups a tendency to free-ride in this way and in practice to give very little to charity. The reason, as Gordon Tullock has so aptly put it, is that the two drives, to consume and to help the poor, are in conflict. The result is that people generally talk as if they are charitable, but in practice demonstrate that they are not as charitable as they profess to be.[30] Of course, if everyone were to follow this strategy, there would be no private redistribution. Such an argument provides a basis for collectivizing the function of income redistribution. The person who gives to others because he gains personal satisfaction from the act does not present a free-rider problem. However, if the personal gain the giver receives is seeing less poverty in the world, the act of others giving diminishes his need to give, and the free-rider problem can arise.

An important variable in determining the amount of private redistribution is the size of the group in which the distribution takes place.[31] If we are dealing with a relatively small, homogeneous group, the proportion of private redistribution increases. This is observable in such groups as the Mormon Church and certain Amish sects, and is consistent with the view that the externalities associated with poverty are more significant (i.e., observable) the smaller the group size. Thus, one might predict that in a collective context a small country with a relatively homogeneous population, e.g., Sweden, would be likely to practice more redistribution than a large "melting pot" country like the United States.

Tullock has alerted us to the possibility that collectivization of charity might lead to an overinvestment in charitable activity.[32] He suggests that this could come about because individuals, in voting for more collectively supplied charity, face a potential prisoner's dilemma. It is less costly for the individual to vote to tax everyone $100 for charity than it is to donate $100 to charity, because there is only a small probability his vote will be influential. But the aggregation of votes could produce a situation where, in attempting to buy charity at a "discount price," the individual is forced to pay the full price, a purchase he would not have freely made.

We have to this point been discussing the theory that those who are relatively rich use the state as a mechanism for transferring income to the

30. "Indeed, if I ask my students or my faculty colleagues how much they personally give to the poor, it often turns out to be a small amount—in many cases zero. They very commonly explain their attitude by saying that they prefer governmental charitable activity." See Tullock (1971) p. 387.

31. For a discussion of the effects of group size, see Hochman and Rodgers (1973).

32. See Tullock (1971).

poor. There is, however, another theory: that the poor use the state as a means of extracting transfers from the rich.[33] This view is grounded on some empirical evidence: the poor vote, and the amount of redistribution that takes place does seem to be a function of the degree to which they vote.[34]

Legislative versus Constitutional Decisions

A second question regarding redistribution mechanisms relates to whether redistribution should result from legislative or constitutional decisions. A major problem with legislative decisions on redistribution is that the way is opened for a whole range of backdoor, special-interest type of transfers, and the relative political power or impotency of the recipients and donors comes into play. Constitutional strictures with respect to some egalitarian principle can help to insure greater impartiality in the system. Redistribution decided upon at the constitutional level places fundamental constraints on the economic rules of the society, especially on legislative and judicial decision-making, and if one feels that, once the parliamentary stage is reached, the rich will receive more benefits because of their political power, it makes sense to incorporate a greater amount of redistribution at the constitutional stage. The vote-tax discussed above is an example of such a mechanism.

It has been argued that the basic rules of the game affecting the distribution of wealth should be made at a constitutional stage,[35] with only short-run decisions handled at the parliamentary stage. This theory is like that of Rawls, although it is more general in nature.

Musgrave distinguishes in his discussion between allocation and distribution branches of the budgetary process. The distribution branch designs a tax-transfer mechanism to secure the desired distribution, while the allocation branch provides for public goods and finances them by imposing the allocatively appropriate benefit taxes. Although the two branches are interdependent, Musgrave argues that decisions on redistribution and the level of social goods should be made independently.[36]

Samuelson has, however, insisted that it is incorrect to separate the two branches in this way.[37] His argument follows directly from formal public goods theory, where there can be shown to exist a whole sub-infinity of

33. For a representation of this view, see Downs (1957).

34. See Fry and Winters (1970).

35. For a discussion of the constitutional and legislative role in redistribution see Buchanan and Tullock (1969), Mueller (1973), and Mueller, Tollison, and Willett (1974c), and their references.

36. See Musgrave (1959), Musgrave (1969), and Musgrave and Musgrave (1973).

37. This is a very cryptic treatment of Samuelson's position. For the complete argument, see Samuelson (1954, 1969).

Pareto-optimal outcomes, each depending on a different initial distribution of income. Thus, where you end up is not independent of where you start, and Samuelson consequently argues there is no *analytical* case for separation of the branches. He takes the view that, given that preferences are known, nothing is gained by separating the two branches because if one is optimal, the other must also be optimal. Musgrave argues that the distinction provides a bridge to an operational theory of the public sector and that it is analogous to using the private market mechanism for efficient allocation of goods and then making adjustments through a tax transfer process after a subsequent examination of a given distribution.

While Samuelson's argument is theoretically correct, Musgrave's separation of allocation and distribution has much practical appeal. Recent developments in the theory of public choice emphasize a distinction between constitutional and legislative decisionmaking. In this approach the distribution parameters are set at the constitutional stage and allocative decisions are handled as a part of normal legislative business. This procedure is quite similar to Musgrave's separation of allocation and distribution, although there is a formal analytical mechanism to determine the initial distribution of income via some ethical choice process at the constitutional stage.[38]

Summary

This section considered problems associated with the issue of mandatory versus voluntary mechanisms for income redistribution. We now turn to the question of the importance of government decision-making in the distribution of income.

V. Governmental Decisions and Income Distribution

At the outset we argued that the market was not the only institution that determined the distribution of income. We now turn to examine some of the ways in which public policy decisions influence income distribution.

Redistribution via the Bureaucracy

Without doubt, large governmental investment projects affect the distribution of income. The relevant questions thus become whether or not decisions on such projects should take distributional considerations into account and, if so, what equity weighting system should be used in cost-

38. Mueller, Tollison and Willett (1974b) envision an intermediate stage of constitutional choice where society opts for a utilitarian principle of maximizing the average economic well-being of the society. Such a society could approach the difference principle (Rawls' maximin) as its absolute level of income rose. In effect, such an argument implies that security is a luxury good, i.e., the society opts for more of it as its income increases.

benefit programs. Musgrave feels that distributional considerations should not enter such governmental calculations, but should be adjusted separately.[39] At perhaps the other extreme, Weisbrod suggests a weighting system arrived at by assuming that past congressional action reflected the true social welfare function.[40] In his recent book Mishan points out that the basis for cost-benefit analysis is a search for a Pareto improvement and that conventional cost-benefit analysis bears no relation to the notion of maximizing or increasing total utility.[41] Cost-benefit analysis should instead be regarded as an extension of the market system that helps select projects where benefits exceed costs. Mishan points out that once these Pareto-based allocative principles are altered by an equity-based weighting scheme, public investment projects might be agreed to even though the costs exceed the benefits.[42] In addition, equity weighting cannot guard against regressive public expenditure projects because projects can be approved if the rich people that are benefited are numerous and the poor that are damaged are few.

The difficulty in any weighting scheme, apart from Mishan's objections, is the problem of where the economist derives the necessary equity weights. Certainly he should not base them on past congressional or executive action, or on the tax system, as these weights are a function of a political process which has all sorts of biases (e.g., geographical representation, seniority, lobbying). Perhaps the best that is attainable is to have the broad sweep of projects distributionally balanced—rather than to be much concerned with any one project from a distributional viewpoint. This comes back to the Musgrave point that the distributional consideration should be achieved through a separate adjustment, and the Mueller argument that rules concerning equity should be established at the constitutional stage.

Social Rate of Discount

An important question affecting the distribution of income between present and future generations is what approximate rate of discount should apply to public investment projects? There is voluminous literature on this subject and no particular consensus among economists about whether the appropriate rate is above or below the market rate of interest.[43] The distributional issue inherent in the selection of the appropriate rate is that a below-market social rate of discount not only increases the

39. See Musgrave (1969).
40. See Weisbrod (1968). Musgrave comments that if past congressional action is correct, why is cost-benefit analysis needed? See Musgrave (1969), p. 803.
41. See Mishan (1973).   42. See Mishan (1973) p. 23.
43. In particular, see Baumol (1968), and the references cited there.

relative size of government, but also redistributes income toward the future since it encourages longer-lived public investments. Aside, then, from the analytical merits or demerits of such a policy, it involves a perverse redistribution of income from present to future citizens [44]—perverse since, because of the normal workings of compound growth, future citizens will be richer than present citizens.

Non-Renewable Resources

A related argument is that unregulated market activity will lead to too rapid a depletion of non-renewable resources. This is based on a belief that a market system will generally fail to lead to correct investment and production decisions because private decision-makers fail to use socially appropriate discount rates. The argument is that the private rate of interest may exceed the rate at which society as a whole should discount future income, that the market rate of interest exceeds the social rate of time preference. The reasons generally advanced for this assertion are that individuals discount the riskiness of future events and that they do so at too high a rate because some of these risks are individual risks and not risks to society as a whole. As a result market rates of interest are too high. If this argument is correct, non-renewable resources will be exploited too rapidly and exhausted before the socially optimal time. There is not unanimity of view within the economics profession as to whether this argument has substance. Divergent opinions have been expressed, particularly in the literature on growth as an objective of government policy and in the partially related literature on the appropriate discount rate to be used in government decision-making.[45] It must be recognized that the contrary point of view requires government policies to influence rates of investment and exploitation to achieve economic efficiency and does not advocate that resources be singled out for special treatment. In other words, whatever general tax incentives or other measures are deemed desirable should be applied to all firms. There is no economic case for applying special measures to certain industries.

Summary

It should be clear that the question of the effect of individual governmental policies on the distribution of income is a complex issue. In some cases it is almost impossible to determine the effect of single policy, and the complexity is compounded when we examine the effect of all governmental programs. As we stressed earlier, perhaps the best answer is that the broad sweep of projects be distributionally balanced.

44. This argument was originally made by Tullock (1964).
45. See Tobin (1964), Stein (1964), Baumol (1968), Singer (1972), and Solow (1974).

VIII. Positive Theories of Income Redistribution

The preceding discussion has centered on a consideration of some basic motivations that lie behind various arguments for income redistribution, and the conclusion is that redistribution follows from any one of a number of benign and non-benign motives. There have been very few attempts to distill these arguments into a positive theory of income redistribution based on the usual self-interest models employed by economists. Two exceptions here are the positive theories expounded by George Stigler and Gordon Tullock, who consider why people might try to redistribute income to themselves rather than to others.[46]

Stigler, in expounding "Director's Law," theorizes that the government will use its coercive power to extract resources that would not be forthcoming through voluntary agreement in the society. Any group that can gain control of the government machinery can use this power to its own benefit. Stigler argues that the group that controls government is the middle class and hence most public expenditures are made for the benefit of the middle class.

Along similar lines, Tullock argues that only a small portion of the massive amounts of government transfers go to the poor. In the nature of the voting process, he says, resources will be taken from the rich, but it is not entirely clear how they will be distributed. Since the middle income groups will be crucial in obtaining the 51 per cent agreement needed to take resources from other members of society, he expects that money will flow from both ends of the income ladder toward the middle.

Both Tullock and Stigler argue that the state is used primarily for the taking of resources, and political power will be used to advance this end. As a result income redistribution will be in reality a method by which the dominant political group, the middle class, extends its power. Both Tullock and Stigler present examples, such as farm policy, education, etc., where examination of the incidence of the benefits supports this hypothesis. The lesson that should be drawn here is that the real reason for income redistribution and the expressed political motivation are often quite different. Of course, these arguments are closely related to some of those that were treated earlier. In fact, they are forms of special interest redistribution or redistribution via bureaucracy. In the latter case, Tullock's point that in most cases transfers do not reach the poor is particularly telling. It agrees in this respect with recent theories of bureau supply that

46. See Stigler (1970), and Tullock (1971). Of course, Pareto-optimal redistribution is a selfish argument for income transfers. It has perhaps been unfairly identified with altruistic motivations. Also, along the lines of Stigler and Tullock, one should read Buchanan, *The Limits of Liberty* (forthcoming).

emphasize the maximization of bureaucratic income as a goal of bureaus.[47]

IX. Conclusion

We have considered some of the normative and positive arguments concerning income distribution. There are many ways of looking at the question of the distribution of income and obviously many trade-offs to be considered in determining an "optimal" or "acceptable" answer to it. Our approach has been agnostic in that we sought only to sketch the relevant questions and trade-offs. We remain agnostic in conclusion, since the resolution of distributional questions is something on which we cannot pronounce as economists. Rather, we hope that the menu of distributional considerations that we have presented will be helpful to individuals in coming to grips with the basic trade-offs involved in setting distributional policy.

References

Baumol, W. "On the Social Rate of Discount." *American Economic Review,* September 1968.

Becker, Gary. *Economic Theory.* New York: Alfred A. Knopf, 1971.

Bierman, Harold, and Robert Tollison. "Monopoly Rent Capitalization and Antitrust Policy." *Western Economic Journal,* December 1970.

Blum, Walter, and Harry Klaven. *The Uneasy Case for Progressive Taxation.* Chicago: University of Chicago Press, 1953.

Breit, W., and W. P. Culbertson. "Distributional Equality and Aggregate Utility: Comment." *American Economic Review,* June 1970.

Buchanan, James M. "Positive Economics, Welfare Economics, and Political Economy." *Journal of Law and Economics,* October 1959.

――. *Public Finance in the Democratic Process.* Chapel Hill: University of North Carolina Press, 1967.

――. "What Kind of Redistribution Do We Want?" *Economica,* May 1968.

――. *The Limits of Liberty: Between Anarchy and Leviathan.* Chicago: University of Chicago Press, forthcoming.

――. "The Political Economy of the Welfare State." Proceedings of the Capitalism and Freedom Conference in honor of M. Friedman's 60th birthday, forthcoming.

――, and Gordon Tullock. *The Calculus of Consent.* Ann Arbor: University of Michigan Press, 1962.

――, and Gordon Tullock. "The 'Dead' Hand of Monopoly." *Antitrust Law and Economics Review,* Summer 1968.

Comanor, William, and Harvey Leibenstein. "Allocative Efficiency, X-efficiency and the Measurement of Welfare Loss." *Economica,* August 1969.

---

47. See Niskanen (1971).

Downs, A. *An Economic Theory of Democracy*. New York: Harper and Row, 1957.

Fair, Ray C. "The Optimal Distribution of Income." *Quarterly Journal of Economics,* November 1971.

Friedman, Milton. "Choice, Chance, and the Personal Distribution of Income." *The Journal of Political Economy,* August 1953.

——. *Price Theory: A Provisional Text*. Chicago: Aldine, 1962.

——. "The Case for the Negative Income Tax." In Melvin Laird, ed., *Republican Papers*. New York: Praeger, 1968.

Fry, B. R. and R. F. Winters. "The Politics of Redistribution." *American Political Science Review,* June 1970.

Greene, Kenneth. "Attitudes Toward Risk and the Relative Size of the Public Sector." *Public Finance Quarterly,* April 1973 [Reading 29, below].

Head, John G. "On Merit Goods." *Finance Archive,* March 1966.

Hochman, H. M., and J. D. Rodgers. "Pareto Optimal Redistribution." *American Economic Review,* September 1969.

——, and James Rodgers. "Utility Interdependence and Income Transfers through Charity." In Kenneth Boulding, Martin Pfaff, and Anita Pfaff, eds., *Transfers in an Urbanized Economy*. Belmont, Cal.: Wadsworth, 1973.

Johnson, David. "Some Fundamental Economics of the Charity Market." In Thomas Ireland and David Johnson, eds., *Economics of Charity*. Blacksburg: Va.: Public Choice Society, 1970.

Lerner, A. *The Economics of Control*. New York: Macmillan, 1944.

——. "Distributional Equality and Aggregate Utility: Reply." *American Economic Review,* June 1970.

Lindsay, Cotton M. "Medical Care and the Economics of Sharing." *Economica,* November 1969.

Mishan, E. J. "A Survey of Welfare Economics, 1939–1959." *Economic Journal,* 1970.

——. *Economics for Social Decisions*. New York: Praeger, 1973.

Mueller, D. C. "Constitutional Democracy and Social Welfare." *Quarterly Journal of Economics,* February 1973.

——, Robert D. Tollison, and Thomas D. Willett. "On Equalizing the Distribution of Political Income." *Journal of Political Economy,* March/April 1974a.

——, Robert D. Tollison, and Thomas D. Willett. "The Utilitarian Contract: A Generalization of Rawls' Theory of Justice." *Theory and Decision,* 1974b [Reading 20, below].

——, Robert D. Tollison, and Thomas D. Willett. "Solving the Intensity Problem in Representative Democracy." 1974c, Mimeo. [Reading 30, below].

Musgrave, Richard A. *The Theory of Public Finance*. New York: McGraw-Hill, 1959.

——. "Provision for Social Goods." In J. Margolis and H. Guitton, eds., *Public Economics*. New York: St. Martin's Press, 1969.

——. "Cost Benefit Analysis and the Theory of Public Finance." *Journal of Economic Literature,* September 1969.

——. "Pareto Optimal Redistribution: Comment." *American Economic Review,* December 1970.

——, and Peggy B. Musgrave. *Public Finance in Theory and Practice*. New York: McGraw-Hill, 1973.

Niskanen, William. *Bureaucracy and Representative Government*. Chicago: Aldine, 1971.

Olsen, E. O. "A Normative Theory of Transfers." *Public Choice*, Spring 1969.

Pauly, Mark V., and Thomas D. Willett. "Two Concepts of Equity and their Implications for Public Policy." *Social Science Quarterly*, June 1972 [Reading 19, below].

Rawls, John. *A Theory of Justice*. Cambridge: Harvard University Press, 1971.

Samuelson, P. A. "The Pure Theory of Public Expenditure." *Review of Economics and Statistics*, November 1954.

——. "Price Theory of Public Expenditure and Taxation." In J. Margolis and H. Guitton, eds., *Public Economics*. New York: St. Martin's Press, 1969.

——. *Economics*. New York: McGraw-Hill, 1973.

Scherer, F. M. *Industrial Market Structure and Economic Performance*. Chicago: Rand McNally, 1970.

Scitovsky, T. *Welfare and Competition*. Homewood, Ill.: Richard D. Irwin, 1951.

Sherman, Roger. *Economics of Industry*. Boston: Little, Brown, 1974.

Singer, N. *Public Microeconomics*. Boston: Little, Brown, 1972.

Solow, Robert M. "The Economics of Resources or the Resources of Economics." *American Economic Review*, May 1974.

Stein, H. "Comment." *American Economic Review*, May 1964.

Stigler, George J. "Director's Law of Public Income Redistribution." *Journal of Law and Economics*, April 1970 [Reading 18, below].

Tobin, James. "A Survey of the Theory of Rationing." *Econometrica*, October, 1952.

——. "Economic Growth as an Objective of Government Policy." *American Economic Review*, May 1964.

——. "On Limiting the Domain of Inequality." *Journal of Law and Economics*, October 1970 [Reading 17, below].

Tollison, Robert, and Thomas Willett. "Some Simple Economics of Voting and Not Voting." *Public Choice*, Fall 1973 [Reading 27, below].

Tullock, Gordon. "The Social Rate of Discount and the Optimal Rate of Investment." *American Economic Review*, May 1964.

——. "The Welfare Costs of Tariffs, Monopolies, and Theft." *Western Economic Journal*, June 1967.

——. "The Charity of the Uncharitable." *Western Economic Journal*, December 1971.

Weisbrod, Burton. "Income Redistribution Effects and Cost Benefit Analysis." In Samuel Chase, ed., *Problems in Public Expenditures Analysis*. Washington: The Brookings Institution, 1968.

Yeager, Leland, and David Tuerck. *Trade Policy and the Price System*. Scranton, Pa.: International Textbook Company, 1966.

17. On Limiting the Domain of Inequality *

JAMES TOBIN

The most difficult issues of political economy are those where goals of efficiency, freedom of choice, and equality conflict. It is hard enough to propose an intellectually defensible compromise among them, even harder to find a politically viable compromise. These are ancient issues. The agenda of economics and politics have always featured policies whose effects on economic inequality and on efficiency in resource allocation are hopelessly intertwined. But it is only in the last five years that they have regained the center of attention of American economists, with whom stabilization, full employment, and growth took the highest priority for the preceding three decades.

When a distinguished colleague in political science asked me about ten years ago why economists did not talk about the distribution of income any more, I followed my *pro forma* denial of his factual premise by replying that the potential gains to the poor from full employment and growth were much larger, and much less socially and politically divisive, than those from redistribution. One reason that distribution has returned to the forefront of professional and public attention is that great progress was made in the postwar period, and especially in the 1960's, toward solving the problems of full employment and growth.

It is natural that debate should now focus on intrisically harder issues of the composition and distribution of the national product, and it is also natural, though disappointing, to find people with short memories questioning whether full employment and growth ever were problems worth worrying about. There are of course other reasons for the recent shift of emphasis, notably the belated commitment of the society to racial equality and the diffuse concern for social justice that is one feature of the cultural revolution of the young.

American attitudes toward economic inequality are complex. The egalitarian sentiments of contemporary college campuses are not necessarily shared by the not-so-silent majority. Our society, I believe, accepts and

* The Fifth Henry Simons lecture, delivered at the Law School, University of Chicago, April 16, 1970.

Reprinted from the *Journal of Law and Economics*, October 1970, pp. 263–278, by permission of the publisher and author.

approves a large measure of inequality, even of inherited inequality. Americans commonly perceive differences of wealth and income as earned and regard the differential earnings of effort, skill, foresight, and enterprise as deserved. Even the prizes of sheer luck cause very little resentment. People are much more concerned with the legitimacy, legality, and fairness of large gains than with their sheer size.

But willingness to accept inequality in general is, I detect, tempered by a persistent and durable strain of what I shall call *specific egalitarianism*. This is the view that certain specific scarce commodities should be distributed less unequally than the ability to pay for them. Candidates for such sentiments include basic necessities of life, health, and citizenship. Our institutions and policies already modify market distributions in many cases, and the issues raised by specific egalitarianism are central to many proposals now before the country.

The trained instincts of most economists set them against these policies and proposals. To the extent that economists are egalitarians at all, they are general egalitarians. The reason is their belief that specific interventions, whether in the name of equality or not, introduce inefficiencies, and the more specific the intervention the more serious the inefficiency. Henry Simons eloquently articulated these instincts and proposed a clearcut practical resolution of the conflict between efficiency and equality.[1]

Simons' design is a very attractive one, deceptively so. He splits economic policy into two departments, one for equity and one for efficiency. Problems of equity and social justice are resolved at the most general level, in legislation for taxation of income and wealth. As for efficiency, the objective of government policy is to make markets work competitively. The government does not intervene in particular labor or product markets on behalf of distributive justice. Reformers interested in reducing, or increasing, economic inequality are referred to the Ways and Means Committee. They cannot seek these ends by fixing milk prices or minimum wages or oil imports or apartment rents or wheat acreage or subway fares—or, for that matter, by rent subsidies or food stamps. Simons says, "It is urgently necessary for us to quit confusing measures for regulating relative prices and wages with devices for diminishing inequality. One difference between competent economists and charlatans is that, at this point, the former sometimes discipline their sentimentality with a little reflection on the mechanics of an exchange economy."[2]

While concerned laymen who observe people with shabby housing or too little to eat instinctively want to provide them with decent housing and adequate food, economists instinctively want to provide them with

1. Henry Simons, *Economic Policy for a Free Society* (1948).
2. *Id.* at 83.

more cash income. Then they can buy the housing and food if they want to, and if they choose not to, the presumption is that they have a better use for the money. To those who complain about the unequal distribution of shelter or of food, our first response—and Simons'—is that they should look at the distribution of wealth and income. If the social critics approve that distribution, then they should accept its implications, including the unequal distribution of specific commodities. If they don't like it, then they should attack the generalized inequality rather than the specific inequality. Economists, especially some trained at the University of Chicago, think they can prove that, given the distribution of generalized purchasing power, competitive production and distribution of specific commodities will be optimal.

This answer rarely satisfies the intelligent egalitarian layman. He knows, partly because he has learned it from economists, that there are pragmatic limits on the redistributive use of taxation and cash transfers. These instruments are not as neutral in their allocative effects as Simons appeared to believe; they may seriously distort choices between work and leisure, selections of occupations and jobs, allocations of savings among competing investments, etc. We have yet to conjure into reality the economist's dream tax—the lump sum tax that no one can avoid or diminish by altering his own behavior.

Simons knew, no doubt, that progressive taxation was not neutral in its allocative effect, but he was writing in the days of small government and was not contemplating very heavy taxes. Nor does he seem to have contemplated what we now call negative taxes, although such transfers would have been a logical extension of his program.

Serious redistribution by tax and transfer will involve high tax rates, as the following simple calculation illustrates. Suppose the government gives every citizen a certain amount $m (a guaranteed minimum income) and collects by income tax enough to pay these grants and to finance government activities which cost $c per capita. Tax rates must be high enough to collect the fraction $(m + c)/\bar{y}$ of total income, where $\bar{y}$ is average income per capita. If the guarantee level m is a quarter or a third of mean income, and especially if the government is purchasing for substantive use any significant fraction of national output, the necessary tax rates will be so high that incentive and allocational effects cannot be ignored.

The layman therefore wonders why we cannot arrange things so that certain crucial commodities are distributed less unequally than is general income—or, more precisely, less unequally than the market would distribute them given an unequal income distribution. The idea has great social appeal. The social conscience is more offended by severe inequality in nutrition and basic shelter, or in access to medical care or to legal assistance, than by inequality in automobiles, books, clothes, furniture, boats. Can we somehow remove the necessities of life and health from the prizes that serve as incentives for economic activity, and instead let people strive and compete for non-essential luxuries and amenities?

This is essentially what the United States and other countries did in the second World War when the supplies of normal consumption goods were drastically limited by the drafts of resources for the war effort. The public was not taxed enough to accomplish this transfer of resources in the market, in large part because of fear of the disincentive effects of the high tax rates that would have been necessary. Prices and wages were controlled to repress, and postpone, the latent inflation. At the controlled prices there was chronic excess demand for consumption goods, and market distribution of these goods was supplanted by a more egalitarian distribution via official and unofficial rationing. Incentives to work, beyond sheer patriotism, were maintained by the prospect that incomes, though inconvertible into consumption at the time, would become convertible later, after the end of the war.

Specific egalitarianism takes a number of different forms, with a number of different motivations and rationalizations. There are some commodities where strict equality of distribution is deemed a crucially important objective, so important that society cannot permit an individual even voluntarily to transfer his share to someone else. These "commodities" include civil rights and privileges—and their converse, civil obligations—where equality among citizens is basic to the political constitution. The vote is a prime example, the military draft possibly another. The category includes also biological or social necessities which are scarce in aggregate supply, so scarce that if they are unequally distributed, some citizens must be consuming below a tolerable minimum. Examples include essential foods in wartime, and probably medical care here and now. In these cases there is a strong paternalistic element in the state's insistence that the individual may not, even voluntarily, transfer his ration to someone else.

At the other end of the spectrum there are commodities of ample supply, or at least of potentially ample supply, where the egalitarian objective is, so to speak, one-sided, not a strictly equal distribution but an assured universal minimum. Ample aggregate supply means that if everyone received only the tolerable minimum, there would be a surplus. Food and possibly housing are examples in the United States today.

In every case a crucial issue is the elasticity of supply, in the short run and the long run, of the commodity in question. When the scarce commodity is in fixed supply, then arrangements for distributing it equally, or on any other non-market criterion, can be made without worrying about efficiency. This is also the case in which social concern about specific inequality makes the most sense.

In wartime Britain tea was in short and inelastic supply; there was no way by which selling it to the highest bidder could increase the imports; and it made sense to worry specifically about the fairness of the distribution of tea. In peacetime United States there is social concern about inequality of access to medical care: luxury medical care for the rich uses resources that could be saving the lives or life chances of the poor. Specific redistribution makes sense if medical care, like tea in wartime Britain, is in inelastic supply. It makes less sense if additional medical care can be obtained by drawing resources from other uses. To that degree the medical deprivations of the poor can be laid to rich consumers of automobiles, boats, and higher education as fairly as to rich over-consumers of the services of physicians and hospitals.

The state has at its disposal a number of instruments for modifying or supplanting the market distribution of a commodity. By market distribution, I mean the distribution among consumers that would result from the expenditure of their money incomes after taxes and cash transfer payments, in the absence of any interventions to set prices or allocations. The concept is clear for privately produced goods and services. But some "commodities" of interest are produced and dispensed by the state; indeed some are rights or privileges rather than goods and services in the usual sense. In the case of state-controlled commodities, I shall use the term market distribution to refer to the result of auctioning the supply to the highest bidders.

One instrument is to forbid the delivery of the commodity to consumers without the surrender of *ration tickets,* of which the government controls the allocation. Ration tickets may be either *personal* or *transferable*. A second instrument is the *commodity voucher* or *stamp,* of which the government likewise controls the allocation. The consumer can use the voucher or stamp only for a specific commodity or class of commodities. The government redeems in cash the vouchers presented by a supplier. Like ration tickets, vouchers can be either personal or transferable. Finally, although ration tickets are usually necessary but not sufficient to purchase a rationed good, it is possible for ration tickets to serve also as vouchers. I shall find it convenient to use these terms in a figurative sense, that is, to apply them to a number of situations which can be described as if there are ration coupons and vouchers even though such pieces of paper do not or need not literally exist.

I propose now to discuss a number of illustrative cases of specific egalitarianism, actual or proposed.

Wartime Rationing

The rationing of scarce necessities of life in time of war or its after-math is, as noted above, a common example of specific egalitarianism. It is worth further brief discussion, because it illustrates some of the issues and problems that arise in contemporary manifestations of specific egalitarianism.

One common system was specific rationing. Ration tickets for a single commodity, sugar or orange juice or tea or meat or gasoline, were distributed equally or in relation to some criteria of need. They were not transferable, either for money or for other ration coupons. The rationale was a combination of egalitarianism and paternalism. Rich children should not have all the orange juice, and no family should bargain away its children's vitamins even if the parents want to do so. Of course, even though ration tickets themselves are not transferable, it is difficult to prevent informal or black market exchanges and sales of the commodities themselves, except when the commodities are highly perishable or personal.

Once delivery of a commodity is effectively forbidden except in exchange for ration tickets, the government has at least indirect control of the money price. Left to the market, the price will be set so that the available supply will be equal to ration-limited demand. This could be as low as zero if the ration coupons cover no more than the available supply. If the government sets a positive price, then it will induce some consumers to leave coupons unused; the real value of remaining coupons will correspondingly increase. Conversely, if coupon values are set too high then a positive money price will arise in order to squeeze out excess consumers.

If equality is really the aim, if consumption is to be strictly independent of unequal money income, then a positive money price must not be allowed to squeeze anyone out. Indeed, ration tickets must double as vouchers, with the government paying the suppliers by redeeming the ration-vouchers with money.

If the supply is inelastic, as was typically the case in wartime, the terms of redemption are purely a distributive matter, as between the general taxpayers and the suppliers of the scarce commodity. But if the supply is responsive, then the government's payment will be one of the determinants of the future supply.

Another model is the negotiable ration ticket. Ration coupons are equally distributed, and the scarce commodity cannot be purchased without one. But coupons can be transferred. The rich and eager can consume an above average share of the commodity, but only by transferring purchasing power over other goods to the poor and indifferent. Equality of specific consumption is not maintained, but those who wish more than their share must find and compensate someone willing to get along with less. The same effect could be achieved by giving everyone a lump sum dollar grant and levying a tax on the consumption of the commodity, just enough to pay for the grant. The advantage of the ration mechanism is that the market makes what would be a difficult calculation for the tax collector. The equity of the system is that high consumers of the scarce commodity, rather than general taxpayers, are made to subsidize the poor and other low consumers.

The transferable ration system does not give the right signals when supply is elastic. It does not make sense to levy an excise tax on an essential commodity in short supply. The way out is for the government, in effect, to buy the supply at its supply price and to distribute it by ration-vouchers at a lower money price or free.

Voting

There are some rights and privileges, and some duties, which the society desires to distribute precisely equally among its members, or among a subgroup of its members. The distribution is supposed to be wholly independent of income and wealth. Furthermore the distribution is supposed to be independent of individual preferences; society would not approve an individual's voluntary assignment of his share to someone else even if the assignee were of equal or lower income.

Perhaps the clearest example is the vote in a democratic polity. The modern democratic ethic excludes property qualifications, obvious or disguised, for the suffrage. Votes are not transferable; buying or selling them is illegal, and the secret ballot makes such contracts unenforceable. In some countries, indeed, citizens are penalized simply for not voting. Any good second year graduate student in economics could write a short examination paper proving that voluntary transactions in votes would increase the welfare of the sellers as well as the buyers. But the legitimacy of the political process rests on the prohibition of such transactions. A vote market would concentrate political power in the rich, and especially in those who owe their wealth to government privilege.

The instrument used for equal distribution of the vote could be described, in the terms previously introduced, as a non-transferable combined ration ticket and voucher. Obviously an egalitarian distribution can be enforced without any loss of efficiency. The aggregate supply of votes is intrinsically inelastic. Allowing a free market in votes could not augment the power of the electorate as a whole; it would serve only to redistribute it differently.

The Draft

Military service is a duty rather than a right, but the same issues arise with respect to its distribution. In some nations it is regarded as a non-negotiable obligation of citizenship, just as the vote is a non-negotiable right. This conception applies in some countries even in peacetime. But the notion that the obligation should not be distributed among citizens on the basis of income and wealth is of course strongest in wartime, when it becomes a matter of distributing risks of death and injury. The national conscience was scandalized, at the time and in retrospect, by the civil war spectacle of rich fathers' purchasing substitutes for their drafted sons. The power of the purse saved the life of one boy in exchange for the death of another. Subsequent draft laws in this country have excluded this kind of transaction.

Nevertheless many of the criteria of selective service are highly corre-lated with economic status. The correlation is difficult to avoid so long as selections must be made, so long as the number of persons needed in the armed services is smaller than the physically eligible population. That is one reason why the draft today is so much more difficult and socially divisive a problem than it was in the second World War. Although equal-ity of exposure could be achieved in current circumstances by short en-listments, too rapid a turnover would make it impossible for the armed services to accomplish their missions.

In these circumstances a lottery, with no deferments, is the only egali-tarian device available. Forbidding the exchange of a vulnerable draft number for a safe number is conceptually equivalent to prohibiting the sale of votes or of ration tickets—once again a paternalistic insistence on an egalitarian distribution takes precedence over the standard economist's presumption that a voluntary exchange increases the welfare of both par-ties.

A further condition of a strictly egalitarian solution is hardly ever squarely faced. The possibility that poor young men may risk their lives for money can be wholly avoided only by prohibiting volunteering or by setting soldiers' pay well below effective civilian alternatives.

A volunteer army is subject to the same objections on egalitarian grounds as a free market in negotiable military obligations. It is just a more civilized and less obvious way of doing the same thing, that is, allo-cating military service to those eligible young men who place the least monetary value on their safety and on alternative uses of their time. There is one important difference, however. With a volunteer army, the general taxpayer must provide the funds necessary to draw into military service the number of soldiers needed. With a free market in draft obligations, much of this burden is picked up by the draftees who are buying substitutes, or by their families. The general taxpayer bears only the costs of the official soldiers' pay, which in a draft system is of course below the market supply price. Young men who escape the obligation are, in effect, taxed to pay the young men who take it on. It is certainly not obvious that the volunteer army solution, whatever its other merits, is the more equitable of these two arrangements.

As for efficiency on the supply side, it is not clear whether the size of the armed forces should be regarded as a fixed demand for manpower independent of its cost. If so, then there is no problem of resource allocation, only a problem of equitable distribution, and nothing is lost by an egalitarian draft. It may be argued, on the other hand, that voters, the Congress, the President, and the Pentagon would and should attune their foreign policies and military technologies to the costs of military manpower, and that the draft biases their decisions toward using more military personnel than they would if defense budgets reflected the true marginal costs. The volunteer army solution would correct this distortion. In principle it could also be corrected within the framework of the opposite solution, a stochastic draft with volunteering prohibited, but with military pay set at the conjectural supply price of the size army the government wants.

Rights to Bear Children

Contemporary worries about the prospects of overpopulation have led to spreading conviction that society will eventually have to control population growth by rationing births. The Zero Population Growth movement, popular on campuses, wants every mother to be limited to two children. We can imagine that medical technology will some day permit social control of periods of fertility.

I am not interested in discussing here whether worries about overpopulation are justified or whether, even if they are, society should in fact regulate births. What is relevant to my subject is how such regulation would be carried out. Should each and every mother be limited to two children or less? Or should each woman be issued two—or two and a fraction tickets, whatever is consistent with zero population growth—and be allowed to transfer whole or fractional tickets to other women? Or should the government fix an annual quota of births and auction the tickets to the highest bidders?

The first system is the most egalitarian, but excludes many voluntary transfers of "birth rights" that would in principle increase the utility of all parties concerned. The second system allows such transfers, but also opens up the possibility that rights to have children will be concentrated in the rich. At least the poor and others who give up their rights will be well compensated. This is not the case under the third system, the auction, where the rich can still buy up the rights but to the benefit of the general taxpayer rather than of would-be mothers who lose out in the auction.

Education

The American system of elementary and secondary education is one of non-transferable ration vouchers, along with a paternalistically motivated compulsory requirement for minimum consumption. Every child is entitled to free schooling. His "ticket" cannot be transferred to anyone else; there is no direct way in which one parent, by accepting less schooling for his child, can provide more for another. A child may use his "voucher" only in the public schools. If he does not use it, he must buy an approved substitute version of the same commodity. His voucher is no good for that purpose, but neither is he limited by his ration. His parent may purchase for him as much education, beyond the minimum requirement, as he chooses.

In recent years support has been growing for what I shall call an extended voucher system, under which the education voucher is usable in any approved school of the parent's choice, not just in public schools. I note in passing that the advocates of the extended voucher system find it possible to reconcile some paternalism with their libertarian principles. They do not propose to abandon compulsory education and to compensate non-consumers of public education in money.

One of the effects of the present arrangement is to require high income parents who wish their children to have more or better education than the public schools provide to pay not only the extra costs but also part of the expenses of educating the children of the less affluent. In this respect the present system is a measure of specific egalitarianism. The proposed reform would shift the burden now borne by those who opt out of the public system to the society at large in higher taxes, or to the lower-income consumers of public education in lower quality.

Reducing the cost of luxury education would no doubt increase the demand for it, and draw teachers and other resources into it, partly from the public schools, partly but more slowly from the rest of the economy. Whatever its other merits, principally in encouraging greater competition and innovation in the supply of education, the extended voucher proposal would increase the inequality of education. This effect could be largely avoided by restricting the use of the vouchers to those private schools that hold other charges on the parents to zero or within prescribed limits.

Another difficulty with the extended voucher proposal arises from the externalities of the educational process—that is, the contributions to the education of students made by other students. The relationships here are complex and uncertain, and excessive heterogeneity in schools and classrooms may be as unproductive as excessive homogeneity. But the evidence seems to be that some racial, social, and intellectual heterogeneity is productive. A major problem of American education today is that public schools, reflecting and in turn influencing residential patterns, are becoming increasingly homogenous. The proposed extension of the voucher system might well accentuate this trend, by making it cheaper for parents to group their children homogeneously in private schools.

This possibility raises the question of how much selectivity in admission and retention private schools eligible for parentally disposed funds would be allowed to practice. So long as schooling is compulsory, there must be some schools that cannot be selective. Are public schools to become the residual depository for all students that publicly financed private schools cannot or will not cope with? To some degree, this is already true, and private and parochial schools gain reputations for intellectual achievement, discipline, and good behavior, simply by pushing difficult and risky cases back to the public schools. Perhaps beneficiary schools should be required to admit all applicants—or in case of oversubscription to select among them in an unbiased way—and to dismiss or suspend students only by the same rules as apply to the public schools.

Medical Care

There are not many commodities in prosperous peacetime America that are scarce in the sense in which some necessities of life were scarce in wartime, but this could be said of medical care. The available supplies of physicians, hospitals, and other personnel and facilities are still low relative to the needs of the population. Even if the supplies were equally distributed, the medical needs unmet at the margin would evidently be far from trivial. This fact is, of course, the basic reason for social concern about the inequality of access to medical care. If people differed only in the attention they received with respect to cosmetic or orthodontic problems, or the number of psychoanalyses they enjoyed, or the hotel-like amenities provided to new mothers, inequality of medical care would not be a big issue. What is disturbing to many observers is the suspicion that chances of death and disability are unequally distributed, that some people consume for trivial purposes resources that could be crucial to the health of others.

In the case of medical care, equality would mean that the treatment of an individual depends only on his medical condition and symptoms, not on his ability or willingness to pay. Everyone would be compelled to have the same medical insurance policy, and no one could obtain medical care except on the terms prescribed in the common policy. This would be, in principle, a non-transferable ration-voucher system, as defined above in other illustrations. But ration-vouchers for medical care would be complicated contingent claims, and stating their value in services so as to balance demand and supply would be extremely difficult.

If medical care were delivered through a ration-voucher system, the government would in effect be purchasing *all* the services of physicians, hospitals, and other suppliers. The prices paid would have to be set so as to draw new resources into the medical industry. Past experience suggests, however, that the mechanism of supply response to price is slow and imperfect, and there may well be more effective ways to get new doctors, medical schools, hospitals, and clinics than simply to add to the rents of the present practitioners.

The system just sketched is compatible with a great deal of decentralization and free choice, but there is no getting around the fact that it is socialized medicine. It is hard to see how there can be equality of medical care otherwise. Although this prospect may shock many people today, including many at the University of Chicago, it would not have shocked Henry Simons. In 1934 he wrote, in connection with his proposal for a rigorously thorough and progressive income tax, as follows: "On the expenditure side, we may look forward confidently to continued augmenting of the 'free income' of the masses, in the form of commodities and services made available by government, either without charge or with considerable modification of prevailing price controls. There are remarkable opportunities for extending the range of socialized consumption (medical services, recreation, education, music, drama, etc.). . . ." [3]

The system toward which the country is moving is quite different. More and more medical vouchers are being provided, through Medicare, Medicaid, and perhaps in the not too distant future, universal health insurance. But no formal rationing is being imposed. Inequality is reduced as the medical care of the poor is brought up to a minimum standard, but the rich can buy medical care in higher quantity and quality. The addition of voucher demands to the unrestricted private market drives prices up. If the government fixes the money value of its vouchers too low, doctors shift their attention to other patients. If the government tries to regulate all fees, not just those charged voucher patients, the result is informal rationing and queuing, with considerable inefficiency, inequity, and annoyance. There will be no good solution short of the day when resources for medical care are so abundant that a hypochondriac can consume them for

3. *Id.* at 68.

low priority purposes, if that way of spending money suits his taste, without depriving someone else of vital care.

Food Stamps

The society's propensity to give assistance to the poor in kind rather than in cash is most clearly evidenced by the political popularity of food stamps and housing subsidies. These are what I earlier called one-sided egalitarian measures. The intent is to increase the consumption of these necessities of life by the poorly nourished and poorly housed, not to reduce the luxury amounts going to heavy consumers. Indeed these commodities are not, in aggregate, scarce in the sense that medical care is in short supply. Food supplies can easily and quickly be expanded in response to new demand, and present supplies are ample, if equally distributed, for meeting socially accepted standards of nutrition. There is no reason that gourmets and gourmands in particular, rather than high-income people in general, should pay for raising the food consumption of the poor.

Paternalism is presumably the motive for assisting poor people with food vouchers rather than generalized purchasing power. But the actual and proposed systems do not live up to the rationale, which would imply compulsory nutrition in the manner of compulsory education. Given the fungibility of stamps and foods, the plans do not even insure adequate diets for their beneficiaries. And, although based on the premise that adequate income is no guarantee of adequate nutrition, income-conditioned food vouchers do nothing to insure adequate nutrition for those whose incomes make them ineligible. In short, food vouchers are just an inferior currency, and taxpayers' funds would be better spent in general income assistance. It is quite true that society has an obligation to protect children whose parents cannot be trusted to nourish them. But this obligation is independent of the size and source of the parents' income.

Subsidized Housing

Paternalism once again is a major reason for society's willingness to subsidize the housing rather than the incomes of the poor. No doubt the neighborhood effects of poor housing, including the fact that it is a particularly visible manifestation of poverty, help to explain the appeal of subsidized housing. A paternalistic policy of housing vouchers is far more likely to be successful than food vouchers, because housing services are much less transferable and fungible.

Engineering a less unequal distribution of housing services is, however, particularly difficult because the services are generated by a specific housing stock inherited from the past. No doubt the resources invested in the current stock are more than enough to meet minimal standards for the whole population. But the high degree of inequality of density and quality built into the present stock limits the possibilities of equalizing its use in the short run. Likewise, expansion of the supply of housing services can occur only as fast as the stock can be augmented. It would take a long time for the market by itself to adapt the supply of housing to a significantly less unequal distribution of general income and wealth.

Present policies are neither fair nor effective. The income tests for housing subsidies are not very severe compared to the tests imposed for current and proposed cash assistance programs. Housing subsidies would be very expensive if everyone who could meet the income tests actually received them. But the subsidies are available only for an accidentally or arbitrarily selected few. The result is that some low income taxpayers are subsidizing the rents of families with equal or higher incomes. One reason that the spread of subsidized low-rent housing is slow is that, with minor exceptions, subsidies are connected only with designated new construction. Perhaps the concentration on new construction reflects the ambivalence of motivation for the programs, which are designed to make cities look better as well as to help low-income families. If the latter purpose is to be sought with housing vouchers, it would make sense to use them to improve the allocation of existing as well as new structures. A disadvantage of the present approach is that it publicly tags the residents of subsidized projects as recipients of public assistance.

I personally see little convincing justification in the long run for specific egalitarianism in housing. There are numerous reasons for preferring a system in which everyone can and does buy decent housing to his taste in the same market. But it does not follow that the supply of housing can be left to the market as now organized and regulated. There are too many cases of racial discrimination, too many ways in which zoning ordinances, building codes, and land taxes favor low-density housing, too many restrictive practices in the home-building industry, too many government subsidies to affluent home-owners, etc. Poor people ought to be given dollars—or housing vouchers if that is preferred—that they can spend for housing anywhere. But at the same time governments do have an obligation to see that these dollars and vouchers have some value.

In conclusion, I believe that Simons and the mainstream of the economics tradition have been right to insist that general taxation, positive and negative, is the best way to moderate the inequalities of income and wealth generated by a competitive market economy. I have no doubt that a cash negative income tax would be, dollar for dollar, the most effective anti-poverty and pro-equality program that could be adopted at this time.

At the other end of the economic spectrum, the urgency of reform of income and estate taxation was scarcely diminished by the tax legislation of 1969. The interests opposed to egalitarian reform of the tax-and-transfer system are formidable. The cause could use some enthusiastic and intelligent support, and it deserves more energy and attention than most youthful egalitarians in our midst have been giving it. Still more fundamental, and certainly more difficult, are policies to diminish the distribution of income before taxes and transfers. These include removal of those barriers to competition, whether private or governmental in origin, which protect some positions of high wealth and income. They include efforts to diminish inequalities of endowment of human capital and of opportunity to accumulate it.

These approaches to the problem of economic inequality deserve priority, but they do not entitle us to dismiss out of hand every proposal for specific egalitarianism or to acquiesce in a market distribution of every scarce commodity. It does make sense in some cases to adopt non-market egalitarian distributions of commodities essential to life and citizenship. It makes sense when the scarcity of the commodity cannot be overcome by drawing resources from the general economy. Difficult practical cases arise when, as in the cases of medical care and housing, supply is inelastic in the short run but responsive to increased demand in the long run. In some instances, notably education and medical care, a specific egalitarian distribution today may be essential for improving the distribution of human capital and earning capacity tomorrow.

18. Director's Law of Public Income Redistribution

GEORGE J. STIGLER

Almost a decade ago Aaron Director proposed a law of public expenditures: Public expenditures are made for the primary benefit of the middle classes, and financed with taxes which are borne in considerable part by the poor and rich. The law was empirical, and the present essay seeks not only to present and illustrate the law (which its inventor refuses to do) but to offer an explanation for it.

The philosophy of Director's Law is as follows. Government has coercive power, which allows it to engage in acts (above all, the taking of

Reprinted from the *Journal of Law and Economics,* April 1970, pp. 1–10, by permission of the publisher and author.

resources) which could not be performed by voluntary agreement of the members of a society. Any portion of the society which can secure control of the state's machinery will employ the machinery to improve its own position. Under a set of conditions to be discussed below, this dominant group will be the middle income classes.

I. Director's Law Illustrated

A reasonably rigorous demonstration that the state redistributed income in favor of the middle income classes would require vast empirical studies of the distribution of public revenues, non-revenue burdens, and benefits, by income class. We are content here to defend the plausibility of Director's Law.

The distribution of incomes of parents of students in California institutions of higher education is highly skewed toward larger incomes (see Table 1). California is a relatively wealthy state so somewhat lower incomes would be received by parents in other states, but no defensible adjustments of the data would qualify the assertion that the colleges of America are populated by the children of the middle and upper classes. The rough estimates of the distribution of state and local taxation by income classes are persuasive: public provision of higher education redistributes income from the poorer to the higher income classes.

The same redistributive effect, one may conjecture, was achieved in equal degree by the public provision of high school education thirty years ago, and even today the parents of high school *graduates* are primarily in middle and upper income classes. In the nineteenth century the same

Table 1. Distribution of parents of students in California colleges and universities by income, 1964, and related data

Income class	1964 percentage of parents		1964 percentage of all U.S. families	1965 state and local taxes as per cent of income	1961 share of total state and local taxes paid
	State colleges	University of California			
Under $4,000	4	5	26	11	17
$ 4,000–$ 8,000	27	19	38	10	46
$ 8,000–$14,000	48	38	27	9	27
$14,000 and over	21	39	9	8	9

Sources: Parents' income: J. Edward Sanders and Hans C. Palmer, The Financial Barrier to Higher Education In California; A Study Prepared for the California State Scholarship Commission (1965). Family income: U.S. Bureau of the Census, Statistical Abstract of the United States, Table 472, at 324 (1968) [approximate]. Taxes as per cent of income and share of total taxes: Tax Burdens & Benefits of Gov. Expenditures by Income Class, 1961 and 1965, Tables 7, B-9 (Tax Foundation, 1967) [approximate].

analysis would apply to elementary public schools; the *graduates* of elementary schools in 1900 were probably largely from middle income class families.

The main beneficiaries of several other traditional governmental functions appears to be much the same. Fire and police activities, for example, are clearly middle-income oriented to the extent that they protect property, and it would be interesting to investigate the extent to which such activities are provided more liberally in middle than in lower income areas of cities. But the major examples of the use of the state by the middle classes lie elsewhere:

1. *Farm policy*. The basic method of assisting farmers has been to raise prices by restricting output, and the restriction of output has been based upon the use of land. The beneficiaries of the policy have therefore been the farm land owners, not the poorer farm laborers and tenants. The burden of the system has been placed upon the consumers of farm products—a regressive excise tax, in effect—as well as on the public treasury. The redistribution of income has therefore much exceeded direct governmental expenditures.[1]

2. *Minimum wage laws*. The main beneficiaries of minimum wage legislation have been two types of workers. The first is the higher paid Northern worker (in textiles, for example) who received some measure of protection from the Southern, low-wage branch of the industry. The second class of beneficiaries has been the better-paid workers, for whom the lower-paid workers are an important substitute. The income redistribution, which is not part of the public budget, is financed by the workers who are displaced by the minimum wage statute and the consumers who purchase the products of low-wage industries.

3. *Social security*. The social security system taxes most heavily, relative to the benefits they will receive,

    i.   Those who begin work early, as compared with those who continue in school.

    ii.   Those who die early, as compared with those who live longer.

    iii. Those families in which the wife works, relative to those in which she does not.

    iv. Those who were young, as compared to those who were old, when first covered by the law.

1. See John E. Floyd, "The Effects of Farm Price Supports on the Returns to Land and Labor in Agriculture," 73 J. of Pol. Econ. 148 (1965).

All of these effects are in favor of the middle classes. There are other effects which run in favor of lower income classes (for example, benefits are a lower fraction of average wages as wages rise), but it is quite possible that the system on balance redistributes income to the middle classes.[2]

4. *Public housing*. The public housing program has had for its primary purposes the reduction in the density of population and improvement in the quality of structure, with the implicit rise in housing costs offset to some extent by public subsidies. Even when the new housing is made available to those displaced, many of the displaced cannot be rehoused in the area, and of course the more attractive housing attracts the competition of those who are better off. The public housing has therefore at a minimum injured many of the poor, and in good measure benefited the non-poor.[3]

5. *Tax exempt institutions*. One form of subsidy is tax exemption, and if we examine the classes of institutions which were given tax exemption, we find that they were primarily those which served the middle classes. Churches are the largest of the tax exempt institutions, but educational and medical institutions are equally directed to the middle classes.

6. *Welfare expenditures*. Public charitable expenditures in the nineteenth century could be viewed as the transfer to the state of burdens otherwise necessarily borne by the well-to-do. The great modern programs presumably involve net transfers to the poor and are therefore apparently contradictory to Director's Law. We shall return to this category of state expenditures.

There remains that enormously expensive social activity, war. Have the middle classes been the special beneficiaries of war? Possibly some wars, such as the American Revolution, could be viewed as levying a highly progressive tax on the wealthy loyalists. Modern wars, however, are not easily viewed as profitable to any income class (although by devices such as conscription the middle classes reduce the costs to *them*). Simply to put aside a large subject which should not be dismissed simply as pathological, wars will be adduced neither as support nor counter-evidence on Director's Law.

2. This argument implicitly assumes that workers bear the tax; if consumers bear a portion, the conclusion is even more likely.
3. See Martin Anderson, *The Federal Bulldozer: A Critical Analysis of Urban Renewal, 1949–1962* (1964).

II. The Bases for Voter Coalitions

A majority coalition of voters may be formed upon any of a variety of bases: religion, nationality, region, industry, or income, to mention only a few historically important bases. If the coalition of voters is to make effective use of the political machinery of the state to redistribute income, it must find a state activity (expenditure) whose benefits flow to the coalition in greater proportion than the taxes which will finance the activity.

In the nineteenth century there were relatively few available tax bases or functions (expenditure categories) which were closely related to income. The federal governmental revenues (the Civil War period aside) were either custom duties or excises upon liquor and tobacco, and of course the burden of commodity taxes is only loosely related to income. The overwhelming preponderance of state and local governmental revenues came from the general property tax, which again bore only a loose relationship to income. (The tax on land, indeed, would be capitalized and have no necessary relationship to even property incomes at later times.) In the nineteenth century, in summary, only unconcealable assets (real property) and commodities which passed through bottlenecks (a port, or large production processes) and were inelastic with respect to taxes were feasible objects of taxation.[4]

If the state is to be used to redistribute income, the activities it undertakes are also limited. Normally it will not be possible to give any commodity (or sell it at subsidized prices) to a particular class, unless the allotments of the commodities to individuals can be effectively rationed, because the members of this class will simply resell the commodity to other classes. Redistribution is a form of discrimination, and is subject to the usual limitation that the classes discriminated against not be able to deal with the classes who are favored. Services are generally non-transferable, and on reflection it is a remarkable fact that the state has almost never supplied anything but services.[5]

---

4. The elasticity of supply with respect to taxes is determined by both demand and supply elasticities. Let $f(q)$ be the demand price and $h(q)$ the supply price, so before tax $f(q_0) = h(q_0)$. After a unit tax of t, the equilibrium is given by

$$f(q_0 + \Delta q) + t = h(q_0 + \Delta q),$$

and expanding in a Taylor series,

$$\Delta q = \frac{t}{h'(q_0) - f'(q_0)}$$

and the elasticity of output with respect to the tax is

$$\frac{\Delta q}{q} \Big/ \frac{t}{p} = \frac{1}{\frac{1}{\epsilon} - \frac{1}{\eta}}$$

where ϵ is the elasticity of supply and η the elasticity of demand.

5. When a commodity producing industry seeks governmental benefits, it generally

In the nineteenth century there were relatively few services which the state could supply only to favored income groups. The protective functions (the courts and police functions, in particular) and a measure of transportation and educational services were of special value to the upper income classes, but as with taxes the relationship to income was not close.

With both expenditures and taxes largely unrelated to income in the nineteenth century, we are not surprised that relatively little use was made of the state as an instrument of income redistribution. One may conjecture that other bases of classes (regional, urban v. rural) entered largely into the determination of public activities.

Increasingly in the twentieth century income has become a more important basis of political classes. Income taxes and an almost unlimited variety of excise taxes gradually became feasible, that is collectible at tolerable costs. A modern state is by no means unrestricted in its ability to assign tax liabilities to various income classes—in fact even the ability of families to divide income among members is an important restriction. Nevertheless changes in economic organization (for example, employment by large organizations rather than self-employment) and in the recording of economic information have greatly increased the power and flexibility of taxation.

There has been a corresponding enlargement of the eligible expenditure programs. Services have increased generally as a part of modern living— education and health services are examples. Direct transfer payments have also become practicable, although many such payments are still unrelated to income (for example, the subsidies to sugar and farm products).

As income has become a widely usable basis for tax and expenditure programs, we conjecture that both the extent of governmental activities and their income redistribution effects grow.

III. Notes on a Theory

Let us henceforth assume that income is the strategic basis for the formation of voting coalitions. The actual income distribution of a society may be presented as a conventional frequency distribution, which is shown in Figure 1.

In each income interval there is also a given number of possible voters (adults). The number of possible voters increases with income: low income families are often single persons, and high income families will

---

prefers output or entry restriction because the benefits of direct subsidies are likely to be dissipated by competition of firms in the industry. Hence the opposition of farm groups to the Brennan plan: the supply of poor farmers is more elastic than the supply of farm land.

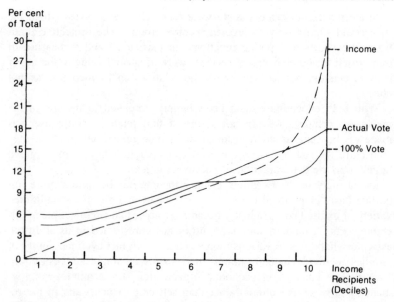

Figure 1.
  Source: U.S. Bureau of the Census, Statistical Abstract of the United States, Income, 1966 in Table 472 at 324 (1968).

also contain more grown children and dependents. If every adult were to vote, we would have a distribution of voters by income of the type (labelled "100 per cent Vote") illustrated in Figure 1.

The actual number of votes cast will differ from the maximum possible votes for two reasons. The first is that the dominant coalition can impose a variety of restrictions upon voters which decreases the voter participation of other income classes. In particular, upper income classes increase their share of votes if they impose literacy requirements, poll taxes, and residence requirements (which affect most the more migratory persons). Registration requirements have recently been shown to have a substantial influence upon the fraction of eligible voters who actually vote.[6] The second reason for differential voting is that individuals outside the majority coalition will receive smaller benefits from voting. The distribution of actual voters will be skewed to the right; it is labelled "Actual Vote" in Figure 1.

When only excises and real property were feasible bases of taxation, the distribution of tax revenues by income class would be relatively

6. See Stanley Kelley, Jr., Richard E. Ayers, & William G. Bowen, "Registration and Voting: Putting Things First," 61 Amer. Pol. Sci. Rev. 359 (1967).

regressive—perhaps similar to the tax revenue curve displayed in Figure
2. The distribution benefits of eligible expenditures (education, justice)
might be that shown in the same figure; other potential public functions
would be excluded because they put a larger tax than benefit upon the
majority coalition of voters. The net redistribution of income by income
class would be obtained by subtracting the tax distribution from the expenditure distribution (assuming budget balancing). There would be as
many possible income redistribution curves as there were possible combinations of tax and expenditure programs.

Each income class would of course prefer that income redistribution
which benefited it the most, and if a single income redistribution met this
requirement of 51 per cent of the voters, it would be chosen. As a rule,
however, different fiscal programs would be preferred by different income classes, and then the program to be chosen must represent a compromise. The program displayed in Figure 2 would be chosen only if the
area under the votes curve to the right of A contained a majority, and if
no alternative program offered more to some majority.

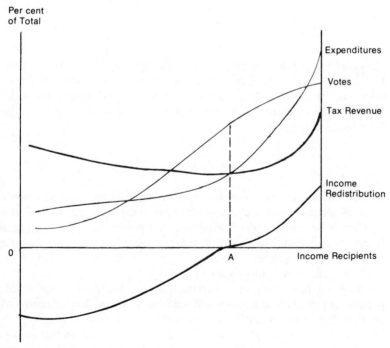

Figure 2.

At the present time both taxes and expenditures can be much more closely assigned to particular income classes. Suppose now that taxes could be made strictly proportional to income, and expenditures consisted of uniform family subsidies. Then the difference between the income curve and a uniform curve ($^1/_{10}$ of subsidies received by each income decile) would represent the gains or losses to an income class from recourse to the political machinery.

Under these restrictive conditions—proportional taxation and uniform subsidies—the gain to any decile income *class* from a K per cent tax would be readily calculated:

1. Let its pre-tax income be (s_iN), where N is national income.
2. The tax upon it would be Ks_iN.
3. The uniform income class subsidy would be one-tenth of the total tax receipts, or $KN/10$.
4. Hence the subsidy to the class would exceed its tax if

$$\frac{KN}{10} > Ks_iN$$

or

$$\frac{1}{10} > s_i.$$

Hence all income deciles with less than one-tenth of income would gain. If they contained a majority of the votes, they would vote for redistribution, and if they had less than a majority, the government would not engage in redistributive activities. Since the gain to an income decile from redistribution is

$$KN\left(\frac{1}{10} - s_i\right) \qquad \cdot \qquad \left(s_i < \frac{1}{10}\right),$$

it rises with the tax rate until $K = 1$. Absolute leveling of income would have self-defeating disincentive effects upon the rich, so that rate of taxation would be imposed which maximized the present value of a perpetual stream of redistributions, taking account of the effects of taxes upon the supply of large incomes. A variant of this scheme is analyzed in the mathematical notes to this paper.

The fiscal machinery of government is not limited to such simple policies as proportional taxation and uniform subsidies. Tax systems may be made regressive in certain regions and progressive in others, not only by income tax rate schedules but by deductions (costs of owned homes) and by excises on suitably chosen commodities. Expenditures, as we have seen, can be concentrated on certain income classes by subsidizing goods and services which primarily these income classes consume.

The increase in the flexibility of taxes and expenditure programs works toward a larger role for government, and toward programs which redistribute income increasingly toward lower income classes. As the amount that can be collected from upper income classes increases, and the amount that can be given directly to the lower income classes increases, the potential rewards from redistribution rise for the lower income classes. In the long run the middle classes may have been beneficiaries of this process because they were in coalition with the rich in the nineteenth century, and are entering into coalition with the poor today.

MATHEMATICAL NOTES

1. Let families be ranked over the interval $(0,1)$ by income. At any point x on the interval,

$v(x)$ is the number of votes of family x

$y(x)$ is the income of family x.

The votes in the successful coalition are given by

$$V_c = \frac{1}{V_t} \int_{x_0}^{x_1} v(x)dx > 1/2, \tag{1}$$

where V_t is the total number of votes.

Let us consider a case in which taxes are levied at a uniform rate t on families *outside the coalition*, and the receipts distributed only to members of the majority coalition. The tax receipts will be

$$T = t \left\{ \int_0^{x_0} y(x)dx + \int_{x_1}^1 y(x)dx \right\}. \tag{2}$$

Suppose we add a small increment of wealthier families to the coalition: they will possess

$v(x_1)(\Delta x)_u$ votes.

Correspondingly we must subtract an equal number of votes from the lower incomes to maintain a minimum majority:

$v(x_0)(\Delta x)_L$ such that

$$v(x_1)(\Delta x)_u = v(x_0)(\Delta x)_L. \tag{3}$$

This reconstitution of the coalition will reduce aggregate taxes (and hence benefits for the members of the coalition) if

$t\{y(x_1)(\Delta x)_u - y(x_0)(\Delta x)_L\} < 0,$

or, using equation 3, if

$$y(x_1)(\Delta x)_u - y(x_0)(\Delta x_u)\frac{v(x_1)}{v(x_0)} < 0$$

or

$$\frac{v(x_0)}{y(x_0)} < \frac{v(x_1)}{y(x_1)}. \tag{4}$$

But $\dfrac{v(x)}{y(x)}$ is a decreasing function of x for all x, so (4) holds for all x. Hence the successful coalition is that for which $x_0 = 0$, and x_1 is given by (1). This conclusion ignores the question of marginal incentives, to which we turn.

2. The system of uniform taxation of the non-members of the coalition founders on the problem of marginal incentive, that is, the families with income above x_1 have after tax incomes of $(1 - t) y(x), x > x_1$, and this may be less than x_1. If one exempted $y(x_1)$, the tax would become $t'[y(x) - y(x_1)]$, where t' is the new rate. The reconstitution of the coalition by adding $(\Delta x)_u$ and deleting $(\Delta x)_L$ must be such that the limits set by disincentives be taken into account.

19. Two Concepts of Equity and Their Implications for Public Policy [1]

MARK V. PAULY and THOMAS D. WILLETT

The concept of "equity" is one which runs through most discussions of public policy, and yet in many contexts there seems to be no very clear idea of just what equity means. Presumably, the term implies that equals should be treated equally, that unequals should be treated unequally, and that the differences in treatment should be "fair." But even when it can be determined who are equals for a particular purpose (which is no mean task) the question remains of what constitutes equal treatment.

A prominent example of this difficulty is the controversy surrounding the military draft. Almost everyone agrees that the system of military manpower procurement should be equitable, but is has not been clear what "equitable" means in this context. No general consensus appears to have developed on which of the major suggested alternatives to the draft—the lottery, Universal Military Training or Service or a voluntary professional army—is the most equitable.[2] The problem in this case is one of determining equitably who will serve in the armed forces when not all are needed. Several years ago we suggested that much of the divergence of views on this question arises from a failure to distinguish between quite separate and distinct concepts of equity, between what we called *ex ante* and *ex post* equity.[3]

Since having first stressed the importance of this distinction we have become aware of its applicability to a much wider range of public policy

Reprinted from *Social Science Quarterly*, 53 (June 1973), pp. 8–19, by permission of the publisher and authors.

1. An earlier version of this paper appeared as "On the Distinction Between *Ex Post* and *Ex Ante* Equity," *Harvard Institute of Economic Research Discussion Paper No. 153*, (Dec., 1970). For helpful comments we are especially indebted to Charles Fried, James C. Miller, Dennis C. Mueller, Roger Sherman, and Robert Tollison. Sole responsibility is of course the authors'.

2. At least one has not yet been indicated in the major public opinion polls. Though as we have made clear in earlier writing, our own position is strongly in support of a volunteer army and while we are naturally pleased at President Nixon's adoption of this goal, the polls indicate substantially less than general support for this policy among the polity. We have of course also moved toward a lottery as an interim policy.

3. Mark V. Pauly and T. D. Willett, "Who 'Should' Bear the Burden of National Defense?" in James C. Miller, ed., *Why the Draft? The Case for a Volunteer Army* (Baltimore: Penguin Books, 1968), pp. 58–68.

questions than just the military draft. The purpose of this paper is to indicate this greater scope of applicability by considering a number of other areas of debate over public policy which we feel the distinction between *ex ante* and *ex post* equity helps to clarify. We shall begin by reviewing this distinction and its application to the military draft.

The Concept of *Ex Ante* and *Ex Post* Equity

We can perhaps best illustrate our distinction between *ex ante* and *ex post* by giving a simple example. Suppose that a group of six people, each member of which has the same wealth, is called upon to make a payment of $60. One way to allocate the burden of payment would be to assign numbers from one to six to each of the persons, and then to roll an unbiased die to determine which individual should pay the entire $60 amount. Another way would be for each person to make a payment of $10. Which is the fairer way to finance the payment? The answer clearly depends upon the concept of equity employed. The first method is "fair" by the standard of what may be called before-the-fact or *ex ante* equity. Each individual has an equal chance of incurring the obligation of payment. That is, *ex ante* equity is attained when risks or opportunities are equalized.[4] The second method of financing is equitable in an *ex post* or after-the-fact sense. Each individual ends up paying an equal share. *Ex post* and *ex ante* equity are not, of course, mutually exclusive (and in the second method of payment described above they coincide), but the presence of one need not in general imply the other.

Which system is preferable? If individuals are risk-averters, that is, if they dislike risky situations, then they would prefer that the choice be made by the second method. Before the die is rolled, each individual has a one-in-six chance of paying $60, or an expected (average) value of $1/6 \times \$60 = \$10$. Under the second method, each individual also pays $10 directly, but he no longer experiences the risk of a chance situation. Other things being equal, if individuals dislike risk they prefer a situation which is equitable *ex post* to one which is equitable *ex ante*.

An Application to the Military Draft

The use of a lottery or random system to select individuals to perform military service has been advocated by many, including the National Ad-

4. This concept of justice is close to that of Harsanyi. See J. C. Harsanyi, "Cardinal Utility in Welfare Economics and in the Theory of Risk-Taking," *Journal of Political Economy,* 61 (Oct., 1953), pp. 434–455; J. C. Harsanyi, "Cardinal Welfare, Individualistic Ethics, and Inter-personal Comparisons of Utility," *Journal of Political Economy,* 63 (Aug., 1955), pp. 309–321; and the discussion of these and related work by Rawls, Vickrey and others in Amartya K. Sen, *Collective Choice and Social Welfare* (San Francisco: Holden-Day Inc., 1970), Chaps. 5 and 9.

visory Committee on Selective Service (the Marshall Commission) and Eli Ginzberg,[5] as the fairest method of selection and recently has been incorporated into U.S. military manpower policy.[6] The lottery is, however, equitable only in an *ex ante* sense. Even if problems of exemption, of variation in the demand for servicemen, and of discrimination on the basis of sex could be overcome, an ideal lottery could only equalize the *risk* of being drafted. Still there would be great difference between those who are unlucky enough to have their numbers come up, and those who are lucky and avoid service altogether. Some men would still be conscripted while others would not be. Consequently it would not be true in an *ex post* or after-the-fact sense that all young men would bear equal shares of the burden of national defense. Some—those whom the lottery selected—would clearly pay much more than others. Hence, there would still remain an *ex post* inequity.

One way of attaining *ex post* equity in a limited sense is of course to require every one to serve. If the army needed, say 25 percent of equitable young men to serve for two years, one could have all eligible young men serve for six months (Universal Military Training). Such an arrangement would, however, be highly inefficient because of increased training costs and brief periods of military usefulness. To overstate the case, we might think of UMT in terms of our previous example as taxing each of the group $360 and then throwing away the extra $300. In such a case we could alternatively invoke Gregory Vlastos' concept that the requirement of equalitarian justice is not "equality as such, but equality at the highest possible level." [7] In such a way one may escape the nonsensical implications of more narrow definitions of equity or equality of treatment such as that as long as the King deliberately cuts off his own right hand, it is equitable for him to require all of his citizens to do likewise. In Vlastos' sense UMT with below market wages would not be equitable because draftees' utility levels would be unnecessarily low.[8]

Another way of producing approximate *ex post* equity under conscription would be to compensate those who do serve at a rate which makes them approximately as well off as they would have been if they had not

5. Eli Ginzberg, "The Case for a Lottery," *The Public Interest,* 5 (Fall, 1966), pp. 83–89.

6. For an interesting discussion see Stephen E. Fienberg, "Randomization and Social Affairs: The 1970 Draft Lottery," *Science,* 171 (Jan. 22, 1971), pp. 255–261.

7. Gregory Vlastos, "Justice and Equality" in Richard B. Brandt, ed., *Social Justice* (Englewood Cliffs, N.J.: Prentice Hall, 1962), p. 62.

8. Where capital markets are imperfect this conclusion holds even when UMT is not technically inefficient, i.e., even when there is a real demand for all available manpower to be used in the military service. See Thomas D. Willett, "Another Cost of Conscription," *Western Economic Journal,* 6 (Dec., 1968), pp. 425–426.

been drafted. That is, each individual in the army would be as well off as would a similar individual in civilian life. Ginzberg suggested that "fringe benefits" be added to the lottery as partial compensation in order "to make the incidence of luck less brutal." In order to eliminate fully the differential effects of risk, however, full compensation would have to be paid and conscription would no longer be necessary. Each one of those selected would, ideally, receive a wage package just large enough to entice him to choose the military service voluntarily as an occupation. If he did not receive this much compensation, then he would choose civilian life, and would not be as well off in the army as he would have been as a civilian. This is the chief characteristic of an all-volunteer army—the absence of inequitable taxation specifically placed on military personnel. In an all-volunteer army, no individual bears an unfair burden because he chooses military service voluntarily (though the tax structure which raises funds for national defense could, of course, still be inequitable in any one of a number of aspects). Insofar as military service itself is concerned, *ex post* equity is achieved. And since everyone has an equal risk of being conscripted—zero— *ex ante* equity is also achieved. Notice that in this context the relevant question is not who serves, but who bears the cost over and above general taxation.

It is doubtful that either those who favor a random draft or those who favor a volunteer army, would approve of the way in which the burden of paying for national defense is distributed by the draft were the distribution of this burden made clear to them.[9] But suppose that both groups did agree that it was fair for many young males to pay substantially high taxes (in the neighborhood of an average of 50 percent of civilian income). Then remaining differences of opinion about whether which of the two methods of military manpower procurement, a draft or the volunteer army, is "fairer" could be traced to the use of those two distinct notions of equity.

Cases Where *Ex Ante* Equity May Be Most Desired

A move from the present system of conscription toward a volunteer army is one which would bring both greater equity (in the senses discussed) and greater efficiency. But in many other cases, attainment of full *ex post* equity might be accompanied by undesirable characteristics. Thus we often settle for or prefer *ex ante* equity, with perhaps a measure of *ex post* equity, to full *ex post* equity. Consider the following examples.

9. On this distribution, see Mark V. Pauly and Thomas D. Willett, "Who Bears the Burden of National Defense?" in Miller, *Why the Draft?* pp. 53–57; James C. Miller and Robert Tollison, "The Implicit Tax on Reluctant Military Recruits," *Social Science Quarterly,* 51 (March, 1971), pp. 924–931; and references cited in these works.

Ex Ante *Equity and Equal Opportunity*. The great amounts of public funds devoted to primary and secondary education are primarily designed not to correct existing inequities in the incomes of parents, but to give all children a more equal chance in securing further income.[10] Equality of opportunity is the goal here, and identical results in later life will not occur for all children, even if they have the same opportunities.

There are numerous examples of other public programs designed to produce, not *ex post,* but *ex ante* equity. Even with widespread availability of public education, not all will earn the same incomes and attain the same social status. Some will be (relatively) losers and others winners, so that *ex post* equity is not likely to be attained by a system whose goal is equal opportunity for all. That the final outcome is unequal does not prove that the system itself is inequitable in an *ex ante* sense, however. If *ex post* equity is also desired, one should not criticize a system designed to achieve only *ex ante* equity for not attaining a different goal.

Ex Post *Equality and Moral Hazard*. The easiest way to attain *ex post* equity is to tax the winners to compensate the losers. Such a goal is reflected in our progressive income tax. Other social welfare programs, such as Aid to Dependent Children, may be looked upon as an attempt to attain some degree of *ex post* equity, to help out the unlucky with the gains of the favored. Indeed, the whole congeries of welfare programs can be looked upon as an attempt to make the incidence of luck less brutal. But full attainment of *ex post* equality through taxation and expenditure policy is prevented by consideration of the effect of such schemes on work incentives.[11] One of the social costs of the attainment of greater *ex post* equity, by, for example, a guaranteed annual income, might be the reduction in effort that would accompany it.

An individual who is a risk-averter might reasonably support such welfare programs, even if he were philosophically opposed to income redistribution.[12] There is always the possibility that anyone might have a streak of bad luck and be pleased to take advantage of programs designed to palliate the effect of that luck. In a sense, welfare programs provide a kind of "income insurance." Individuals pay taxes as premiums, in the expectation that if, by chance, they should experience a significant decrease in income, they would be able to collect from that "insurance."

10. This is, of course, not the only rationale for allocating public funds to education.

11. Many may also question the morality of receiving "unearned income" which conflicts with the just dessert concept of justice. For an interesting discussion of this view see Kenneth Boulding, "Social Justice in Social Dynamics," in Brandt, *Social Justice,* esp. pp. 82–84.

12. See, for instance, William Breit and William Culbertson, "Distributional Equality and Aggregate Utility: Comment," *American Economic Review,* 60 (June, 1970), pp. 435–441, and references cited there.

But the problem of incentives is also analogous to a problem in insurance called "moral hazard."[13] Ideally, an event to be insurable should be completely random. If the individual can alter his behavior in such a way as to make an event more likely to happen (by starting a fire, for instance) then the event may not be completely insurable. Since individual incomes are subject not only to random disturbances arising from events over which they have no control but also depend on the individuals' supply of work effort, incomes may well not be strictly insurable. Hence, on these grounds, one might prefer not to provide complete *ex post* equity.[14]

Other Examples of the Use of *Ex Ante* and *Ex Post* Equity

The distinction between *ex ante* and *ex post* equity also is useful because it suggests that there is often more than one way of defining what is "fair" in a given situation, even when all agree on general principles. The following examples are suggested.

Traffic Violations and Conflicting Views of Fair Legal Treatment. Consider the case of a motorist who passes a stop sign at an intersection at which there is rarely cross traffic. If he simply runs the stop sign and is caught, he will get a ticket and, generally, have to pay a rather small fine. But suppose, while running the stop sign, some other motorist runs into another car. The fact that the other car happened to be there is, from the viewpoint of the second offending motorist, purely a chance event. Yet the legal penalties levied on the motorist who hit the random car will generally be much higher than those levied on the lucky motorist who passed through without incident.

Does this constitute fair legal treatment? From an *ex post* viewpoint, the motorist involved in a collision through negligence clearly has worked much graver harm than the motorist who only disobeys a legal injunction. So we could claim that, in terms of *ex post* equity, the law which punishes the hapless driver is fair, as is the general provision of law in cases of negligence which in general allows damaged parties to sue only those who injured them through negligence, not those whose negligence might have contributed to their injury, but did not.

13. See, for instance, Mark V. Pauly, "The Economics of Moral Hazard," *American Economic Review*, 58 (June, 1968), pp. 531–537.

14. A corollary is that on efficiency grounds there should be greater insurance provided in areas where moral hazard is low than where it is high. Examples where greater amounts of social insurance should probably be allocated on efficiency grounds include compensation of victims of crime (where victims have taken reasonable precautionary measures) and catastrophic coverage programs for medical insurance. On the latter see Martin Feldstein, "A New Approach to National Health Insurance," *The Public Interest*, 23 (Spring, 1971), pp. 93–105; and Mark V. Pauly, "An Analysis of Government Health Insurance Plans for Poor Families," *Public Policy*, 19 (Summer, 1971), pp. 489–522.

But from an *ex ante* viewpoint, it seems clear that both motorists are equally guilty, since both, we may assume, faced the same risk of collision before running the stop sign. Since the risk was the same, one might argue that the penalty should be the same. Tullock has been the most forceful advocate of the point that it is unfair to require an individual to be liable in civil law for negligence-caused damages, since he is not especially guilty, only especially unlucky.[15] If all motorists who sometimes disobey traffic laws are risk-averters, they would favor a system in which fines are raised somewhat in order to provide a pool from which damages could be paid for the random damages party. If all motorists do sometimes disobey laws and are risk-averters we might even go further and suggest that the state compensate those injured by damages from funds raised from some more general tax, such as a gasoline tax. There is clearly a moral hazard problem here, since the likelihood of larger fines if involved in an accident may make motorists more alert when running stop signs, but the quantitative importance of this factor would probably not be great.

Tradeoffs Between Ex Post *and* Ex Ante *Equity: Voting Rights and Law Enforcement.* A second example shows the contrary case in which the *ex post* equity to which we are accustomed can be converted into *ex ante* equity. Consider the way in which elections are conducted. We generally regard it as just or fair to give each citizen a vote. But suppose that instead of having all citizens who wished to do so vote, individual persons were selected at random, and given a ticket which would permit them to vote. For instance, such tickets might be given to a random one percent sample of the population. Then the election would be decided by these voters only. Such a procedure would probably be much cheaper than the current method of voting, and would be likely to reduce vote fraud too. If the sample was truly random, the results would in the large number case, come very close to those of a universal election, and the procedure would save a lot of people the trouble of taking off from work and going to the polls. In cases where the sample method yielded close results, a general balloting could be held.

Here the purpose is not to comment on the desirability of the two schemes, but to assess the kind of equity displayed in each.[16] The usual method of voting is an example of *ex post* equity. Ideally, each person

15. Gordon Tullock, "An Economic Approach to Crime," *Social Science Quarterly,* 50 (June, 1969), pp. 59–71 [Reading 7, above].

16. For such analysis see Dennis C. Mueller, Robert D. Tollison, and Thomas D. Willett, "Representative Democracy Via Random Selection," *Public Choice,* Spring, 1972, pp. 57–68 [Reading 26, below].

would be permitted to vote. The sampling method is the *ex ante* equitable analog of this. It is not *ex post* equitable, since some would vote while others would not. But it is *ex ante* equitable, since before the sampling all face the same chance of being chosen. Because of the lower cost of obtaining *ex ante* equity in this case many individuals may prefer the method which has only *ex ante* equity,[17] while at the same time not wishing to purchase a lower cost method of selection which did not have this attribute (for instance, selection by a group of voters chosen by the government in power).

Another example is the question of the appropriate level of fines or punishment for illegal activity. Consider for instance the problems of speeding or highway littering. Suppose that if it were decided that an appropriate deterrent would be the certainty of a $5 fine for any littering and that such a fine would be just in the sense of approximately commensurate with the nature of the "crime." The cost of assuring that every litterer was detected and apprehended would be very high. However, it has not escaped the notice of public officials, at least in an intuitive sense, that the deterrence equivalent of a sure $5.00 fine may also be achieved by an infinite number of combinations of higher fines and lower probabilities of being apprehended. For instance, if the typical potential litterer was risk neutral, then a 50 percent probability of a $10 fine or a 10 percent chance of a $50 fine or a 1 percent chance of a $500 fine would each have an equal deterrent value.

Holding constant the level of technology of detection and enforcement, the further one moves along the spectrum in the direction of higher fines, but lower risk of punishment, the less will be the direct cost of law enforcement, but the greater will the *ex post* inequity placed on those who happen to be caught. Society clearly faces a tradeoff concerning how much it is willing to pay for a greater degree of *ex post* equity. As long as the procedure for catching violaters is roughly random, a high degree of *ex ante* equity can still be obtained.

This is not to suggest that *ex ante* equity is a full substitute for *ex post* equity, but by explicitly recognizing the concept one is lead to ask further questions about enforcement procedures in situations in which there is a

17. Voting by all qualified citizens would of course provide both *ex ante* and *ex post* equity given that a "just" definition of qualified was used. We should note, however, that in another sense even full exercise of voting rights is still only *ex ante* equitable. This is because even where voting power is equalized different individuals may be more or less successful in converting their votes into the passage of policies. Thus the *ex post* distribution of utility generated by the political process might be quite uneven despite full *ex ante* equality having prevailed in the sense of completely equalitarian distribution of voting rights.

substantial probability of any particular individual violator not being apprehended.[18] For instance, if it were discovered that with respect to a particular situation the enforcement mechanism was systematically biased (when it was originally thought that it was not) then it might be appropriate to consider the desirability of allocating a greater level of resources to law enforcement to either increase the probability of apprehension across all individuals, i.e., reduce the degree of *ex post* inequity, or to correct or reduce the present biases in the enforcement mechanism (greater supervision of patrolmen on the beat?) i.e., reduce *ex ante* inequities, or some combination of the two.

A similar situation holds with respect to legal procedures after someone is arrested. There is evidence of wide variation in the penalties of individuals convicted of similar offenses.[19] Again society is faced with the questions of whether these variations are *ex ante* equitable in the sense of being randomly distributed and even if they are, whether "sufficient" *ex post* equity is obtained or whether more resources should be devoted to standardization of outcomes.

Two other relationships between concepts of equity and costs and efficiency of law enforcement should be mentioned. One is that if different types of individuals are more or less likely to commit crimes (or to have crimes comitted against them) then maximum efficiency in crime prevention would dictate that resources be allocated such that the probabilities of being arrested (or being protected) will differ for different individuals, creating *ex ante* inequities.[20] *Ex post* equity would require that all crime be prevented or that full compensation be paid (and in some cases such as homicide this would not be possible). As Thurow has stressed, there is a tremendous need for public decision makers to face up explicitly to such equity-efficiency tradeoffs.

The second question is that of giving operational meaning to the concept that to render a verdict of guilty juries should feel the defendant to be guilty beyond reasonable doubt. If we are not all knowing, the question is in part that of balancing the risk that an innocent man is found guilty against the risk that a guilty man is allowed to go free. For a given

18. A good example where this is relevant is the case of the recent illegal killings of eagles in the Western United States. See, for instance, Ryan Amacher, R. Tollison, and T. D. Willett, "The Economics of Fatal Mistakes: Fiscal Mechanisms for Preserving Endangered Predators," *Public Policy*, 20 (Summer, 1972), pp. 411–441 [Reading 13, above].

19. See, for instance, H. Zeisel, "Methodological Problems in Studies of Sentencing," *Law and Society Review*, 3 (May, 1969).

20. See Lester C. Thurow, "Equity Versus Efficiency in Law Enforcement," *Public Policy*, 19 (Summer, 1971), pp. 451–462 [Reading 8, above]. In this excellent paper Thurow does distinguish between *ex ante* and *ex post* equity.

level of technology for discovering the truth the two types of risk are uniquely related.[21] Reducing the risk of one type of mistake increases the risk of the other. Even if we can secure perfect *ex ante* equity in the sense that irrelevant characteristics (such as the length of one's hair) do not affect the probabilities of conviction, we must make an equity judgment in balancing off the risks of either type of mistake. Further, even though we can never hope to reach a state in which no mistakes are made (the condition necessary for full *ex post* equity to prevail), the levels of resources devoted to law enforcement and the courts can affect the magnitude of discrepancy between the degree of *ex ante* and *ex post* equity. The choice between the two types of risk must be made in conjunction with the decision of how much to invest in avoiding mistakes. Presumably the lower the level of resources devoted to law enforcement and hence the greater possibility of making a mistake in the courts, the greater would be the degree of benefit of the doubt that we would want to give to defendants because the lower level of resources devoted to law enforcement would imply a lower level of public concern with crime prevention and hence a lower view of the cost of letting a guilty man go free.[22] Again these are tradeoffs which should be faced up to for they are made implicitly when they are not explicitly. It is probably the desire not to face up to the fact that *ex post* inequities (mistakes) do exist that has retarded discussion of *ex ante* equity aspects of the problem.

Cases Where Ex Post *Equity Is Not Possible.* In the previous example of voting we discussed a case in which *ex post* equity, though the most desirable form of equity in these cases, may be only marginally preferred to *ex ante* equity which could be achieved at substantially less cost. In these cases the difference in the "quality" of equity might not be worth the price differential and the less preferred form chosen.

The extreme of this situation would be where one form was preferred but is not physically possible to obtain (i.e., has an infinite price) because of the discrete nature of the situation. An example is the problem of the lifeboat which will hold only a certain number of people which is smaller than the number of current survivors. If 10 is the maximum number of people that the boat will hold without sinking and there are 11 people, the

---

21. The problem is identical to that of balancing Type 1 and Type 2 errors in the theory of statistics.

22. This statement of course assumes that there exists an efficient allocation of resources across all aspects of law enforcement. On the economics of crime and optimal allocation of resources in law enforcement see Gary Becker, "Crime and Punishment: An Economic Approach," *Journal of Political Economy,* 76 (March/April, 1968), pp. 169–217; William M. Landes, "Law and Economics" in *51st Annual Report* (National Bureau of Economic Research, 1971), pp. 2–8; Tullock, "An Economic Approach to Crime," and references cited in these works.

narrowly defined *ex post* equitable solution of assigning 10/11 of a space to everyone will mean that all 11 will die. This clearly violates common sense and Vlastos' more sophisticated concept of equalitarian justice. In this case the best course of action (assuming the 11 are similar or identical in all major respects) is to seek *ex ante* equity by drawing lots or some other similar method. Indeed this principle has been established in the U.S. courts.[23]

Imaginative Approximation of Ex Post *Equity: A Problem from Illinois Politics.* The same type of situation appeared to have occurred in the vagaries of Illinois politics.[24] In setting up the apparatus for the election of "nonpartisan" delegates to a convention to rewrite the Illinois Constitution, the General Assembly provided that the Secretary of State should list candidates for delegates on the ballots in the order in which their applications were received. Since it is believed that voters often mark the first name of a column of names when the candidates are unknown to them, the top place on the ballot was a political plum. A number of candidates therefore camped out in front of the door to the Secretary of State's office the day before applications were due. But the Secretary of State had mail delivered through a back door and chose to recognize (presumably by opening first) the applications of candidates whose names he knew or who had been put up by the major political parties.

A suit followed, and the Federal Court ordered that, rather than the Secretary's method, a random selection process should be used to determine the order in which the names are listed in each district. This was a method which was clearly equitable *ex ante,* since each candidate faces the same probability that his name will be chosen first. But it was still inequitable *ex post,* since only one candidate's name will appear first and those of the others will not. Since only one name can be at the top of the ballot, *ex post* equity could not be produced directly.

However, in this case with some imagination the apparent impossibility of obtaining *ex post* equity could be escaped. Since there are many ballots in each district, *ex post* equity could be approximated by rotating the names of the candidates on ballots, and distributing those ballots in a random fashion. The Chicago Bar Association suggested a similar method, in which the ballot positions would be rotated for each precinct, the precincts presumably being chosen on a random basis. In either case, the

---

23. See the discussion and references in Fienberg, "Randomization and Social Affairs."
24. For an account of the controversy, see "Powell Defies U.S. Court's Con-Con Rule; Won't Have Lottery He Asserts," *Chicago Tribune,* (Aug. 10, 1969), sec. 1, p. 25; and "Edict in Con-Con Upheld; Scott Favors Lottery Order," *Chicago Tribune,* (Aug. 12, 1969), p. 1.

object would be to place each candidate's name on the top of the ballots of equal numbers of randomly selected voters. This should minimize the benefit of first position to any particular candidate.

The Convergence of Ex Post *and* Ex Ante *Equity as Time Periods Lengthen: Speeders and Constitutions.* The large number effect invoked in the preceding example may influence an individual's opinion about what is "fair" treatment, even when they agree on general principles of equity. Let us return to our motorist example, and suppose that patrolling of the intersection is itself a random variable. Police ticket not all law-breakers but motorists they select at random, and they do this often. *Ex ante* this is fair to all lawbreaking motorists who ever use the intersection, since they face the same risk per try of being caught. But *ex post* it would appear to be unfair, since some lawbreakers receive tickets while others do not. The tourist who has used the intersection for the only time in his life may therefore feel that he has been treated unfairly, even if he did pass the stop sign. But the commuter who passes by every day would probably feel less unfairly treated, since his expected fine for any reasonably long period of time can be known in the sense that he could estimate, with a reasonable degree of accuracy, the number of times per year he would be likely to be caught and the amount of the fine.

In other words, the longer the functional time horizon being considered (in the sense of number of trials or plays), the closer total *ex post* equity will tend to coincide with *ex ante* equity. In general then in continuous play games we may need to pay little attention to specific *ex post* outcomes, concentrating instead on the *ex ante* fairness of the game.

Perhaps the longest run type of consideration of this type would be constitutional decisions which determine the rules of the game for an individual's lifetime. If individuals do not have knowledge of where they will come out *ex post* on the income distribution they may be in especially good positions to make determinations of rules for *ex ante* equity in a manner "unbiased" by current positions. Thus we would expect that in a society of individuals all of whom combine self interest and equalitarian instincts we would observe greater consensus over appropriate (i.e., equitable) fiscal structure, the more distant in the future these rules are to take effect and the longer they would be expected to remain in force.[25]

---

25. This latter consideration is important as long as the date of implementation is not so far in the future that individual actors have no idea where they (or their descendants) will come out on the income distribution. On delayed implementation of constitutional changes see, Mueller, Tollison, and Willett, "Representative Democracy"; Dennis C. Mueller, "Constitutional Democracy and Social Welfare," *Quarterly Journal of Economics,* February, 1973; and references cited in these papers.

Summary

We have argued that there is an important distinction between two concepts of equality which we have termed *ex ante* and *ex post* equity respectively. We believe that more general recognition of these two distinct concepts should help to clarify discussion of a number of issues of public policy. We do not feel that one can draw firm conclusions as to the greater appropriateness of one concept or the other. Both are important.

In most cases we feel that the *ex post* aspects of a policy are probably of greater importance than the *ex ante* aspects, but there are important exceptions—for instance, where equality of opportunity is the objective. Further there are many instances in which even though *ex post* equity is the more desirable characteristic, it may be impossible or very expensive to achieve and the substitution of *ex ante* equity or some combination of the two may be desirable.

While situations can exist where policies meet both criteria fully, for instance, in the case of a volunteer army in place of conscription or the Chicago Bar Association's proposal for solving the balloting problem in Illinois, the more general case appears to be where the public must trade off the lower desirability and lower cost of *ex ante* equity against the greater desirability and greater cost of *ex post* equity. Law enforcement is one area in which such tradeoffs are particularly important. Public attention needs to be focused on such tradeoffs for in the absence of rational debate the questions do not disappear; they are decided implicitly rather than explicitly and frequently by *ad hoc* rather than democratic procedures. Our distinction between *ex ante* and *ex post* equity cannot provide unique solutions for these questions, but it can make important contributions to focusing questions and clarifying issues. This is all that we can ask of concepts.

20. The Utilitarian Contract: A Generalization of Rawls' Theory of Justice *

DENNIS C. MUELLER, ROBERT D. TOLLISON, and THOMAS D. WILLETT

In a series of major papers culminating in *A Theory of Justice,* [1] John Rawls constructs an alternative to utilitarianism by developing a social contract theory of moral and political philosophy. Unfortunately, Rawls formulates the two basic principles upon which the theory rests in such a way as to restrict (unduly) the contract theory's applicability (see Section I). In this paper we present a more general discussion of the theory of justice that avoids the problems of Rawls' formulation and yet retains the important idea of justice as fairness and the contractarian approach (Section II). Later it is argued that this more general theory constitutes a bridge between the pure utilitarian theories and the social contract doctrines (Sections V and VI). The theory's advantages are demonstrated by applying it to a problem discussed by Rawls, intergenerational equity, and comparing the two solutions (Section III). Further comparisons are made and inferences drawn in the concluding three sections.

I. A Critique of the Difference Principle

Rawls divides the collective decision process into four stages: (1) social contract, (2) constitution, (3) legislature, and (4) judiciary and administration (pp. 195–201). The social contract is a set of rules covering the fundamental principles upon which social relationships are built: justice, honesty, equality, natural duties, etc. The contract is an abstract embodiment of these principles, and "the procedure of contract theories, then, is a general analytic method for the comparative study of conceptions of justice" (p. 121).

Individuals start from an original position in which they are currently

Reprinted with permission from *Theory and Decision,* IV/3, pp. 345–369.

* Without implicating them, we would like to thank James M. Buchanan and David Lyons for comments on an earlier draft of this paper.

1. John Rawls, *A Theory of Justice,* Harvard University Press, Cambridge, Mass., 1971. Future page references to the book are placed in parentheses. Some of Rawls' basic ideas were set forth earlier in his "Justice as Fairness," *The Philosophical Review* 57 (1958) 164–94.

equal and uncertain of their future positions (see in particular Chapter 3). They are assumed to be able to conduct a *Gedankenexperiment* in which they are ignorant of all characteristics peculiar to themselves (e.g., tastes, economic position, age, generation) and devoid of personal conceptions of the general good or special features of psychology such as aversion to risk or liability to optimism or pessimism.[2] These mutually disinterested individuals are assumed to know "general facts" about human society. The outcome of the experiment is that all rational, egoistic individuals adopt the *same* set of fair principles as a social contract.

The outcome of unanimity in the original position follows because all are convinced by the same arguments and "therefore, we can view the choice in the original position from the standpoint of one person selected at random" (p. 139). In effect there is no problem of obtaining unanimity since individuals are assumed to be devoid of special personal characteristics and in possession of the identical general information about themselves, and there is therefore only one decisionmaker (everyman). There are thus no problems of bargaining or reaching unanimous agreement on the social contract in the original position.[3]

Rawls devotes a great deal of effort to try to demonstrate that the following two principles will emerge from the original position:

First: each person is to have an equal right to the most extensive basic liberty compatible with a similar liberty for others (p. 60).

Second: social and economic inequalities are to be arranged so that they are both (a) to the greatest benefit of the least advantaged and (b) attached to offices and positions open to all under conditions of fair equality of opportunity (p. 83).[4]

2. Rawls later (p. 159) notes that some philosophers have thought that ethical first principles should be independent of all contingent assumptions. He criticizes this view as supposing that persons in the original position know nothing about themselves. However, this seems to be the nature of what he assumes about individuals in the original position.

Rawls later also (p. 160) says that one cannot do without a conception of the good on the basis of which individuals rank alternatives. This seems inconsistent with his discussion of the original position.

3. Rawls charges (p. 141) that utilitarianism "improperly extends the principle of choice for one person to choices facing society." As noted in the text, he does the same thing in his definition of the original position.

At several points Rawls raises the issue of what happens in the original position if not all agree (see in particular pp. 142–50) on conceptions of justice or other matters. One way to handle this problem is simply to rule some possible exchanges out (e.g., those between basic liberties and economic and social benefits). This is really beside the point, given Rawls' definition of the original position. Indeed, Rawls shows no inclination to consider alternative models of constitutional choice where individuals are different and unanimity is hard to obtain and where constraining the constitutional choice set may be quite useful.

In Section V we consider this issue further in the context of a discussion of the various types of original positions or constitutional settings that have been discussed in the literature.

4. These two principles are discussed and redefined at numerous places (e.g., pp. 60–83 and pp. 150–88).

These two principles are regarded as a special conception of justice derived from the general conception of justice embodied in the following principle:

All social values—liberty and opportunity, income and wealth, and the basis of self-respect—are to be distributed equally unless an unequal distribution of any, or all, of these values is to everyone's advantage (p. 62).

Throughout most of the book, Rawls focuses on the special conception of justice in which the two principles are treated separately and serially, i.e., the first principle is given priority over the second, and no one's liberty can be reduced even in turn for an economic gain by every citizen. He justifies this lexicographic ordering of the two principles on the grounds that a condition of moderate scarcity prevails in the society (p. 127). Thus, he assumes a society sufficiently wealthy to *afford* to give liberty priority over economic gain (p. 152). We shall have some comments on the lexicographic ordering of these two principles in Section IV. Our focus in this section, however, is on Rawls' defense of the second principle, the difference principle.

The difference principle requires that choices always be made so as to maximize the expected position of the worst off individual in the society. As Rawls discusses this concept, it is equivalent to the maximin strategy in game theory and assumes an extreme degree of risk aversion, as can be seen from the following example. Suppose an individual can purchase a chance to play a game that pays $200 if a fair coin turns up heads and nothing if it turns up tails. A risk neutral individual will pay $100 to play the game, the expected value of the outcomes. A risk taker would pay more than $100 and a risk averter less. But it would only be the most extreme type of risk averter who would pay nothing at all to play (not even a penny, say). Yet this is precisely the behavior the maximin strategy dictates. To pay anything and lose is always to come out worse than one can by avoiding the game. More generally, a maximin strategist will only pay L dollars for a chance to play a game $(p: W, L)$, where p is the probability of winning W and $(1-p)$ the probability of winning L. His choice will be independent of the values of $W, L,$ and p. A maximin strategist will never risk a loss however small for a gain, however large and however high the probability of winning.

When applied to the social contract or constitution drafting decisions, this principle requires that each individual choose the set of rules that maximizes the welfare levels of all other citizens, and any information, even of a general nature, that might lead him to make probability estimates about his being one of the worst-off citizens.[5]

5. Rawls curiously does not credit Sen with developing the standard critique of the difference principle that it is (an unlikely) special case of expected utility maximization under

Rawls (following Fellner) attempts to justify the maximin strategy at the social contract and (implicitly) constitutional stages on three grounds: (1) The decisionmaker does not know and therefore takes no account of the probabilities of the various outcomes, (2) he considers the gains above the minimum payoff unimportant, and (3) he regards the worst potential outcomes under other decisions as unacceptable (p. 154). The choice of the maximin strategy does not necessarily follow, however, from these three arguments.

Rawls argues that in the original position ". . . the veil of ignorance excludes all but the vaguest knowledge of likelihoods. The parties have no basis for determining the probable nature of society, or their place in it" (p. 155). Individuals may be wary of probability calculations if any other course is open to them. But it is a great leap from wariness about probability calculations to a strategy in which individuals behave as if they were 100 percent certain of the worst outcome.

The mere absence of objective probability estimates is not a sufficient condition for asserting that the maximin strategy is the only rational decision rule. Although uncertainty about the probabilities of success and failure may increase risk aversion, it need not discourage gambling entirely. If our hypothetical gambler were told the coin to be flipped was biased in some unspecified way, he *might* offer less to play the game, but he would not necessarily refuse to play altogether as assumed under maximin.

In his second justification of the difference principle, Rawls restricts its applicability to situations in which the gains to other members of society achieved under other decision rules are inconsequential. This justification of the maximin strategy leaves open the question of what principles govern a just society when the gains to other citizens under different decision rules are not small. And what criterion is used to determine when the gains are small enough to ignore and when they are not? Rawls recognizes this difficulty on p. 157 with the following example:

	States	
Strategies	0	n
	$1/n$	1

uncertainty. See Amartya K. Sen, *Collective Choice and Social Welfare,* Holden-Day, San Francisco, 1970, pp. 135–41. He recognizes clearly, however, that the choice between his principles and some concept of average utility is perhaps the central problem in his theory (p. 150). He recognizes that maximin is not a suitable guide to choices under uncertainty, but goes on to argue that ". . . it is attractive in situations marked by special circumstances" (p. 151). His aim is to show that his definition of the original position embodies these special circumstances where maximim is a rational decision rule.

Given these two sets of payoffs, a maximin strategist always chooses the second. Yet, a high enough n surely makes this behavior implausible. Rawls skirts this counterexample by arguing that "part of the answer is that the difference principle is not intended to apply to such abstract possibilities."

However, the possibilities where n can be large in the original position are not so abstract in nature. For example, as we will discuss in Section III, decisions must be made on intergenerational equity and societal saving rates. This is not an inconsequential decision, and application of Rawls' difference principle carries the implication that society undertakes no net saving or dissaving. Taxation and redistribution decisions would also be made in the original position, and these would not be abstract possibilities where the gains to other citizens under alternative decision rules are small.

As the other part of the answer, he assumes "the possibilities which the objection envisages cannot arise in real cases; the feasible set is so restricted that they are excluded" (p. 158).[6] Without some demonstration that examples of this type are unlikely to arise in real cases (and none is given), the general applicability of the theory is called into question. What is more, vagueness is introduced by the requirement that situations be delineated and excluded in which *large* gains above the minimum would be sacrificed and/or the worst potential outcomes are not unacceptable alternatives to the one chosen under the difference principle.[7]

As noted above, the difference principle ignores information concerning the alternative payoffs to all citizens except the worst off under each strategy. Yet in defending the difference principle by his second and third arguments, Rawls is in the curious and somewhat contradictory position of using information about the relative payoffs to different citizens as a justification for adopting a decision rule which then ignores this very same information.

It would seem that either general information about the payoffs to all citizens is available or it is not. If it is, then Rawls' defense of the difference principle on the grounds that it requires less information is of no consequence (pp. 320–21). If this information is unavailable, then there is no way to separate those classes of situations in which the principle is applicable from those when it is not, and one must simply trust to fate to

6. Ironically, just two pages later, Rawls criticizes the utilitarians for resorting to exactly the same device for eliminating troublesome cases, and defends his own approach on the basis of its more general applicability (p. 160).

7. See, also on this point, David Lyons, "Rawls Versus Utilitarianism," *Journal of Philosophy* 69 (Oct. 5, 1972), 535–45.

provide a set of states of the world that will sustain the application of the principle.

With respect to the third justification for the application of the difference principle in the original position, Rawls argues that ". . . the third feature holds if we can assume that other conceptions of justice may lead to institutions that the parties would find intolerable" (p. 156). Rawls uses the example of slavery. The example does not demonstrate his point, however, as Lyons has shown.[8] Rawls' own theory will allow slavery to exist when the level of economic development is insufficient to support the special conception of justice, if slavery would be to everyone's advantage. And, there is no reason to expect that utilitarianism would not also reject slavery under the more favorable economic conditions of moderate scarcity that are necessary to ensure that the difference principle rejects slavery. A utilitarian could also eliminate the troublesome case of slavery by simply resorting to Rawls' device for eliminating theoretically difficult cases (e.g., the $1/n$ situation described above), namely exclude such outcomes from the choice set.

Thus, in our view Rawls does not offer adequate justification for his statement that ". . . the original position has been defined so that it is a situation in which the maximin rule applies" (p. 155). This is probably not correct as discussed above, and it is neither a good nor a workable definition of the original position as we will discuss in Sections II and V.

II. The Utilitarian Contract

All of the above criticisms of Rawls' defense of the difference principle can be eliminated by assuming that individuals in the original position maximize their expected utilities. In developing this utilitarian contract model, we shall make a number of the same assumptions about individuals Rawls makes. They are rational, egoistic and without envy. No special assumptions about benevolence are imposed. To begin with, we shall assume that each individual has all the information of a *general* nature that exists at the time he is to become a party to the contract. That is, in the original position when the social contract is made, he knows the state of natural, political, social and economic development of the society. He knows the tastes of all citizens for primary goods, and their attitudes toward risk. He does not have information about specific individuals, however. In particular, he does not know what his own income would be, under the various possible moral and political institutions he might choose, his own tastes for primary goods, his own attitude toward risk. We shall relax the assumption about the amount of general informa-

8. "Rawls Versus Utilitarianism," 539–43.

tion available in the original position, when the two theories are compared.

Fairness is introduced in much the same way Rawls employs it. Ignorant of his own position and preferences, each individual acts as if he had an equal chance of being any citizen in the society. He adopts their tastes, assumes their economic and social position, and assigns a utility index to being each individual. He does this for each possible state of the world (social contract). He then chooses that state of world which maximizes his expected utility, assuming he has an equal probability of being any citizen.[9]

Let us illustrate. Suppose there are two individuals and three possible states of the world (social contracts), yielding utility levels for the two individuals as in Table 1.

Table 1.

	S_1	S_2	S_3
I_1	100	60	40
I_2	0	30	40
W	50	45	40

An individual who assumed he had an equal probability of being either I_1 or I_2 would evaluate his expected utility or welfare under the three states as in row W. He would thus select row S_1 as the social contract promising the highest expected utility. This is the outcome from applying the Harsanyi approach.[10]

One may object, as does Amartya Sen, "that in social choices we are interested not only in the mathematical expectation of welfare with impersonality, but also with the exact distribution of that welfare over the individuals."[11] To claim that S_1 is preferred is to assume that the decision-maker in the original position takes an essentially risk neutral position on being I_1 or I_2. Clearly a risk averter might prefer S_2 or S_3.

This is a legitimate criticism of the Harsanyi approach, which represents what Rawls refers to as the "average principle." The response to this criticism need not be recourse to the maximin rule. Instead, it seems more in the democratic spirit of the contractarian approach for the various states to be compared using the citizens' own risk functions.

If each individual in the original position made these evaluations using

9. John C. Harsanyi makes the explicit assumption that the individual preference functions satisfy the von Neumann-Morgestern cardinal utility postulates. He then proves, under some additional weak assumptions, that this decision rule constitutes a social welfare function. See his "Cardinal Welfare, Individualistic Ethics, and Interpersonal Comparisons of Utility," *Journal of Political Economy* 63 (August, 1955), 309–21.

10. *Ibid.*   11. *Op. cit.*, p. 143.

his *current* risk preferences, one might get as many different choices as there were risk attitudes.[12] Thus, a full correspondence of opinion in the original position could break down due to individuals' adopting different attitudes with respect to risk. It is more in keeping with Rawls' depiction of the original position to assume that each citizen's current risk attitude is shielded from him by the veil of ignorance, but that he knows the risk attitudes of future citizens. A rational individual in the original position might reasonably maximize his expected utility by assuming he had an equal probability of having the risk attitude of any future citizen.

To illustrate this, assume that one of our future citizens is known to be risk averse; the other is risk neutral. Evaluating the three possible states using the risk neutral preferences, we get the simple utilitarian outcomes presented as row U in Table 2. Someone with "normal" risk aversion might evaluate the three states as row N. The expected welfare under the assumption the citizen has an equal probability of being each is row W^1. S_1 again promises a higher expected welfare, although its superiority has been reduced.

Table 2.

	S_1	S_2	S_3
U	50	45	40
N	35	40	40
W^1	42.5	42	40

One might again object, à la Sen, that a simple averaging of the risk neutral and risk averse preference functions weights the outcome too heavily in favor of the risk neutral solution. Just as someone who was risk averse might not be indifferent between being certain of experiencing 50 utility units and an even chance of being I_1 or I_2 under S_1, he might also not be indifferent between a certain 42.5 utils and even probabilities at being U and N.

This criticism may seem persuasive to some, although to us it is much less persuasive than when applied the first time. For the selection of S_1 on the basis of the outcomes of Table 2 does rest on an equal (impartial) weighting of all risk attitudes. Nevertheless, if it is felt that this single averaging gives too heavy a weight to the simple utilitarian choice, the averaging process can be repeated. The various social states can be evaluated using the future risk functions under the assumption one has an

12. This is the major criticism of the Harsanyi model raised in Prasanta K. Pattanaik, "Risk, Impersonality, and the Social Welfare Function," *Journal of Political Economy* 76 (November, 1968), 1152–69.

equal probability of being U or N. The utilitarian outcome under this averaging is presented as row U^1, the normal risk averse solution as N^1, in Table 3. Now, with the heavier weighting of the risk averse preference obtained via the second averaging, the equal probability calculation of expected utilities yields S_2 as the preferred social contract. The averaging could continue, but it is now clear that the elements in each column are converging to separate values, and that the convergent solution for the S_2 column will be greater than for either of the two other columns.

Table 3.

	S_1	S_2	S_3
U^1	42.5	42.5	40
N^1	40	42	40
W^2	41.25	42.25	40

Thus, a unanimous agreement on a social contract incorporating the risk attitudes of the citizens can be reached, if agreement on the weights to be attached to each risk preference, or the number of replications of the averaging experiment, can be obtained. That repeated averaging increases the weights attached to the more risk averse preferences, can be most vividly seen by assuming that one future citizen is maximin. Tables 4 and 5 present calculations similar to those in Tables 2 and 3, on the assumption there are three risk preferences involved: the two previously considered plus an extreme risk averter of the maximin or difference principle type (rows D and D^1). After only two iterations it is clear that S_3 will be the preferred state. What is more, the values of W for the 3 columns are

Table 4.

	S_1	S_2	S_3
U	50	45	40
N	35	40	40
D	0	30	40
W_0^1	28.33	41.67	40

Table 5.

	S_1	S_2	S_3
U^1	28.33	41.67	40
N^1	22.67	36.33	40
D^1	0	30.00	40
W_D^2	17.00	36.00	40

converging on 0, 30, and 40, respectively, the maximin values. This is because the maximiner only considers the minimum values, while the other two preferences give some weight to all values. Repeated averaging of the 3 preference functions must give heavier weight to the maximin outcome in the final outcome.

Thus, Rawls' maximin solution would emerge under the utilitarian contract only if two conditions were met: at least one future citizen has maximin preferences, and full (sole) weight is given to these preferences through repeated averaging.

Let us recapitulate. A menu of possible approaches to the averaging of individual utilities is possible in forming a utilitarian contract. On the one extreme, one can simply average the utilities giving equal weight to each. This simple utilitarian solution is equivalent to ignoring any risk aversion attitudes in the formulation of the contract, and giving full weight to the risk neutral outcome. The risk attitudes of future citizens can be incorporated by evaluating all future states of the world under each risk attitude and averaging the indexes. If the averaging is done only once, and the state with the highest index selected, the decision process is equivalent to giving equal weight to each risk attitude. Repeated averaging will give increasing weight to the more risk averse preferences.

Rawls objects to the assumption of expected utility maximization, presumably in both the simple and extended forms, on several grounds. At one point he argues that it is desirable to avoid "complicated theoretical arguments in arriving at a public conception of justice" and that "In comparison with reasoning for the two principles, the grounds for the utility criterion trespass upon this constraint" (pp. 160–161). This does not seem to be a relevant objection to expected utility maximization, since the theoretical justifications for his principles are hardly uncomplicated. Indeed, the conceptual experiment of expected utility maximization with a single averaging of risk attitudes may seem to many no more difficult than that proposed by Rawls for the original position.

Basically, however, Rawls objects to the average utility principle by arguing that individuals are extremely risk averse where knowledge of probabilities is poor and decisions are made for one's descendants. "The essential thing is not to allow the principles chosen to depend on special attitudes toward risk" (p. 172). Even if one shares Rawls' view that this is an essential property of the social contract, it is not clear that the utilitarian contract comes off any worse than the Rawlsian contract on this ground. The utilitarian contract *does* depend on the envisaged risk preferences of all future citizens, but is perfectly general in allowing those risk preferences to take any form imaginable and allowing any set of weights all can agree on. The Rawlsian contract is freed from all "special" attitudes toward risk only because it forces all participants to adopt a decision strategy of maximum risk aversion.[13]

Under the utilitarian contract, each person in the original position has the same general information about tastes and positions, and is ignorant of his own characteristics. Therefore, all should make the same evaluations of the possible states of the world, and unanimous agreement on a social contract be obtained. This approach is utilitarian in requiring the calculation of utilities for each individual under all possible institutions. It is contractarian (in the restricted sense of homogeneous individuals and equal ethical weights for everyone) in requiring that unanimous agreement by all individuals be reached by weighing impartially the payoffs to each citizen under alternative social arrangements. The incorporation of information about risk preferences into the decision process through averaging will ensure that the simple utilitarian outcome of highest arithmetic average of utilities is not to be produced.

III. The Rawlsian and Utilitarian Contracts
Compared: The Problem of Intergenerational Equity

When discussing justice between generations, Rawls is confronted with a dilemma. Straightforward application of the difference principle would require that a society undertake no net saving or dissaving, since any positive saving is likely to increase the welfare of the worst off in the next generation at the expense of the worst off in this generation. And dissaving would produce the reverse. Thus, a just society will undertake no net saving, experience no growth, and remain at a low level of economic development, if it applies the difference principle consistently.

Rawls is unhappy with this implication of his theory; he attempts to get around it by introducing the assumption that each generation recognizes a familial tie with the next and engages in positive net saving out of a pa-

---

13. Further, Rawls argues that "The principle of utility presumably requires some to forego greater life prospects for the sake of others" (p. 180) without appearing to recognize that this same qualification applies to his principles.

Rawls also seems to confuse *ex ante* and *ex post* interpretations of the average principle at several points. (See his discussion on Edgeworth on p. 170.) He tends to attack the *ex post* application where the relevant question is the *ex ante* application. For example, he argues that "Any further advantages that might be won by the principle of utility, or whatever, are highly problematical, whereas the hardships if things turn out badly are intolerable" (p. 175). Here, he does not seem to recognize the distinction between before the fact and after the fact equality or that even should things turn out badly, extreme risk aversion may not be justified in the original position. For further discussion of the concepts of *ex ante* and *ex post* equality see M. V. Pauly and T. D. Willett, "Two Concepts of Equity and Their Implications for Public Policy," *Social Science Quarterly*, June 1972 [Reading 19, above]; and D. C. Mueller, R. D. Tollison, and T. D. Willett, "On Equalizing the Distribution of Political Income," *Journal of Political Economy* 82 (March/April, 1974), 414–22.

ternal affection for its offspring generation, while retaining the assumption that an individual in the original position can conceptualize being a member of any generation (pp. 284–93). His argument seems forced. Why does he only posit parental affection for offspring? Why is there not an equal affection of the children for their parents? Someone in the original position would then envisage being both parent and child, and choose a zero saving rate again. More fundamentally, this assumption divorces the savings rate decision from the two principles of justice and makes it depend on the natural affection of one generation for the next.[14] Whatever the behavioral validity of this postulate, it essentially removes the important intergenerational equity question from the theory of justice.

In contrast, intergenerational equity can be easily treated in the model of expected utility maximization without necessitating a zero saving outcome. An individual in the original position would assume he had an equal probability of being a member of any generation and choose that set of savings rates that maximized his expected utility, again after making allowance for risk preferences. Extreme risk aversion of the maximin type would result in zero saving, but other possibilities are allowed.

Let us illustrate by considering the simple case with only two generations. The consumption options for the two generations can be depicted by the consumption possibility frontier CC (Figure 1). Each point on CC represents a level of present consumption C_t and the resulting level of future C_{t+1}. The negative slope of CC implies that the future consumption will increase if present consumption is reduced, i.e., via saving and investment. The curve is drawn concave to the origin to indicate diminishing returns to investment. If the society merely maintains its present net capital stock and undertakes zero net saving, we assume its consumption is 100 in both generations, point D.[15] Point D will be selected under the difference principle. D is preferred to all points to the left of or below dd, since they involve lower consumption in at least one period. No other points are attainable, so that D becomes the optimum allocation. Note that all points on or above dd are preferred to D, and that the difference principle creates a lexicographic ordering of all points in the diagram. A risk neutral individual is indifferent between any combination of consumption levels summing to the same total. His indifference curves are

14. A number of economists have justified government intervention to promote higher saving on these grounds. See, e.g., Amartya K. Sen, "On Optimising the Rate of Saving," *Economic Journal* 71 (September, 1961), 479–96; and "Isolation, Assurance and the Social Discount Rate," *Quarterly Journal of Economics* 81 (February, 1967), 122–24. See also, Stephen A. Marglin, "The Social Rate of Discount and the Optimal Rate of Investment," *Quarterly Journal of Economics* 77 (February, 1963), 95–111.

15. We ignore, as does Rawls, the question of the origin of the capital stock, and make a present time of entry assumption (pp. 140, 292).

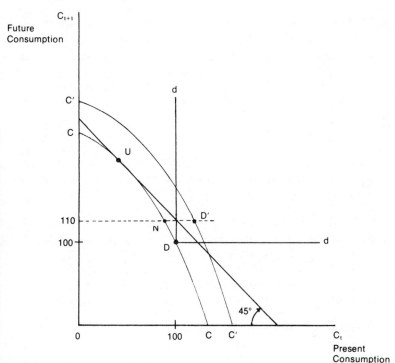

Figure 1.

straight lines making 45° angles with the axis, and he chooses point U where the slope of the consumption possibility frontier equals -1.0. At this point the marginal return on capital investment is zero. We have designated this point U to suggest that it is the decision a naive utilitarian makes. Assuming the marginal return on investment is positive at the starting point D, U is to the left of D, and positive saving occurs if the constitutional decision makers are risk neutral.

Between the cases of risk neutrality (U) and maximum risk aversion (D) there is a wide range of choices an individual with "normal" risk aversion can make. Some positive saving occurs under the more normal cases. The amount depends on *both* the extent of risk aversion in the individual and the shape of the consumption possibility frontier. Note that as long as the consumption possibility frontier is concave to the origin, i.e., there are diminishing returns to investment, a society never chooses to dissave, since the return from a unit of saving always exceeds the return on a unit of dissaving.

Suppose the society chooses N. The saving and investment implied by this choice shifts the consumption possibility outward to say $C'C'$, and the new initial point D' comes at a higher level of consumption. Again the risk trade-off between present and future consumption can be made and the process repeated. If there are diminishing returns to investment over time, the absolute value of the slope of the CC schedule declines as the society moves to successive D's, and D, N, and U converge. Two possibilities exist. D, U, and N may all come together at the same point in time and the society enters a steady state with zero marginal return on investment and zero saving. Alternatively, U and D may merge before N is reached and the zero-saving, zero-growth steady state occurs with a positive marginal return on investment. In this case, the society's risk avoidance preferences are strong enough to lead it to stop saving at the sacrifice of some consumption for future generations.[16]

This model could thus end up at the same place Rawls does, in a steady state with zero saving. Once there, the difference principle applies and each successive generation is no better off than its predecessor (pp. 288–93). The treatment of the choice of saving rates in moving to this steady state seems more satisfactorily contained within this conception of a theory of just social choices than it is in Rawls' conception, however.

IV. Further Comparison: The Evolution of a Just Society

At a number of points, Rawls suggests that the development of a just society is an evolutionary process requiring a rising level of economic activity, at least up to some point. This is most clearly stated in the following passage.

The supposition is that if the persons in the original position assume that their basic liberties can be effectively exercised, they will not exchange a lesser liberty for an improvement in their economic well-being, at least not once a certain level of wealth has been attained. It is only when social conditions (i.e., the level of economic development) do not allow the effective establishment of these rights that one can acknowledge their restriction. The denial of equal liberty can be accepted only if it is necessary to enhance the quality of civilization so that in due course the equal freedoms can be enjoyed by all. The lexical ordering of the two principles is the long-run tendency of the general conception of justice consistently pursued under reasonably favorable conditions. Eventually there comes a

16. It is also possible that the citizens may be more risk averse at very low and very high levels of income, as suggested below. For example, the indifference curves become more convex further out from the origin. This does not affect the saving decisions at earlier periods, however, even if an equiprobabilistic averaging of the risk preferences of all generations is undertaken. What is important is the shape of each generation's time preference map, *in the region where the choice is made.*

time in the history of a well-ordered society beyond which the special form of the two principles takes over and holds from then on.[17]

Although in this passage Rawls suggests a gradual transition from the general to the special conception, with the first principle getting increasing priority over the second, there is nothing in his theory that describes or accounts for this transition. The theory presented here can justify this transition in straight economic terms if liberty is essentially a luxury good. As a society's wealth increases, one can easily imagine it placing higher and higher priority on liberty over economic gain, and in some limiting case, adopting a lexicographic ordering of the principles governing liberty and distribution. Until such a point was reached, a rational society, like a rational individual, may be willing to make some trade-offs between liberty and wealth.

In much the same way, the utilitarian contract gives a plausible explanation of the circumstances under which the more egalitarian distribution of income, implied in the difference principle, will emerge. Casual observation suggests that people are both individually and collectively less willing to take (at least major) risks at subsistence income levels and at relatively high income levels. In the former situation the reason that an egalitarian income distribution may emerge as a consequence of high risk aversion is simply that a decision criterion like maximin may be sensible where the rejected alternatives have outcomes that one can hardly accept (Rawls' third justification for the difference principle), i.e., if one falls below subsistence, he dies. Thus, an egalitarian distribution of income along the lines of the difference principle may be quite a rational constitutional choice for subsistence income societies.[18]

An intermediate stage of constitutional choice with respect to the income distribution can be envisaged where a society adopts a utilitarian principle of distribution by maximizing the average economic well-being of the population. However, this same society may gradually return to the egalitarian income distribution implied by the difference principle as a part of its constitutional process, though for different reasons than in the subsistence case.

This sequence would involve the adoption of more and more redistributive measures as the society's standard of living rose, until it eventually had the egalitarian structure implied by the difference principle. (In terms of the gambling example presented in Section I, the *relative* amount of

17. Page 542. See, also, p. 503.
18. An excellent example of this sort of behavior in low-income societies is the egalitarian and diversified distribution of land by serfs in Anglo-Saxon England. Edward Mitchell explains this process as a response to agricultural risks in "Serfdom in Anglo-Saxon England: An Economic Analysis," mimeographed, 1972.

his income an individual would be willing to pay to play the game would decline toward zero as his income rose.) Returning to Rawls' three justifications of the difference principle, one can see that the second justification is plausible in an affluent society. The gains to the more wealthy may be sufficiently small in utility terms that they can be ignored and only the position of the worst off taken into account. In effect security becomes a luxury good in the affluent society. Similarly, once a society reaches a high enough standard of living, no further risks need be taken to improve the standard of living of future generations and saving may fall to zero.

Placed in this context, Rawls' difference principle might apply at several stages in a society's development. At these times, the institutions chosen by the utilitarian contract might resemble those implied by Rawls' theory. Under the behavioral assumptions assumed here, for example, the two theories converge at both low and high levels of income. Under this interpretation, the main advantage of the utilitarian contract approach is its greater generality and its capability of yielding normative conclusions in all constitutional choice situations.

V. Information and Morality

As stressed previously, Rawls' purpose in defining the original position is to ensure that the "desired solution" is obtained (p. 141). Specifically, he wishes to derive a set of "first principles . . . capable of serving as a public charter of a well-ordered society in perpetuity" (p. 131; also see pp. 137, 139), a set that will not be "biased by arbitrary contingencies" (p. 141). And he deems it "essential . . . not to allow the principles chosen to depend on special attitudes toward risk" (p. 172).

There are a number of alternative specifications of the degree of information and the mental experiment in the original position which also have attractive properties.

If the arguments presented in this paper are valid, the assumptions Rawls makes about the information available in the original position are not sufficient to sustain the main components of his theory: the two principles of justice and their lexicographic ordering. If this point is accepted, one next raises the question of the remaining relative advantages of different assumptions about the information available in the original position. Contrary to what it might seem, requiring that people *not* have information in the original position imposes a more stringent constraint on a contractarian model than allowing them to have full information about the future. Each individual starts with a large body of knowledge about himself and his society. He knows his own tastes, age, race, religion, sex, current income and wealth, likely future income and wealth and so on.

The major obstacle to his becoming a party to a social contract is the requirement that he shed this information and make decisions *as if* he were ignorant of his race, income, etc. The more information that must be shed, the more difficult the mental experiment the individual must conduct, and the less likely compliance with the theory is. The utilitarian contract is superior, in this regard, in that it places the minimum demands upon the individual that are needed to produce impartiality and unanimity in the original position. The individual may possess all information of a *general* nature that is available, only information specifically related to himself and his future position is denied to him.

It should be emphasized that the assumptions discussed at the start of the paper, that each individual have *full* information about the tastes, incomes, and other characteristics of the population are not required to justify employing the utilitarian contract. They merely serve to clarify the type of mental experiment made by an individual under this alternative theory. One could assume instead that only very aggregate information about the state of economic development is available: average income per capita, the distribution of income. This might still allow the calculations of probabilities of having a given level of income and the application of the model. Thus, if 5 percent of the population earned less than $2000, under a certain set of institutions, one would assume that his chances of earning less than $2000 were five in a hundred under these institutions.

Tastes could be handled similarly. Although one could not know the exact tastes of everyone, one might know that some people are conservative, some moderates, and some radicals; some hedonists and others stoics, etc. One might also be able to form some subjective probability estimates about the likelihood of being each, and use these to evaluate the different social states.

The question of whether one should use utility indexes or indexes of primary goods can be handled similarly. It is obvious that the amount of satisfaction people get from a loaf of bread differs from person to person. If one had a method for obtaining the actual utilities of individuals for each bundle of goods and comparing them, this would obviously be superior to simply comparing the bundles. One does not have this information, however, so in practice one would have to work with more objective proxies for utility levels like the actual bundles of goods or their dollar equivalents. In applying the model, one could easily substitute indexes of primary goods for utility indexes in the calculations (see Rawls, pp. 90–95).[19]

19. Michael Teitelman objects to Rawls' use of the concept of primary goods on the grounds that the definition of what is primary and not primary is dependent on cultural factors and thus cannot be made in an original position in which one is ignorant of all culture

It must be stressed that if insufficient information is available to make even very subjective probability estimates, one can still apply the general approach suggested by expected utility maximization. All possible states can be evaluated and the best one chosen by using a decision rule for evaluating uncertain outcomes, that is a composite of the decision rules of all citizens. This may not be the maximin rule. As noted above, the absence of information on probabilities is not sufficient to justify maximin. The essential virtue of the utilitarian contract is still preserved: all possible social states can be evaluated and compared, and the optimum chosen. No states need be ruled out by assumption. The more information of a general nature that is available at the original position, the more closely the set of institutions selected is likely to conform with the preferences of *all* of the people. But the decision rule can be applied with less than perfect information.

Although most versions of the utilitarian contract require that individuals suppress the minimum amount of knowledge necessary to achieve impartiality and unanimity, many may still feel that it requires that people engage in a conceptual experiment beyond their capacity. One simply may not be able to pretend he is in another's shoes. This problem plagues all models that demand the mental experiment of empathy or equal ethical weights for everyone. It implies that even where people try to perform the experiment, there are no mechanisms to ensure unanimity. Even a group of conscientious Kantians may disagree over conceptions of the general good.

There are various examples of how a complete correspondence of views regarding ethical weights may not be possible. We discussed Pattanaik's case of disagreement over risk attitudes above and demonstrated how repeated averaging of individual risk functions could lead to unanimous agreement. Repeated averaging to obtain unanimity has been suggested before by both Vickrey and Mueller.[20] As also shown above, however, repeated averaging in the presence of only one maximin risk averter will result in this individual's choice's emerging as the social choice, regardless of the preferences of all others.[21] This possibility of

---

specific knowledge. This criticism is not applicable to our model, in that we would have each individual evaluate each social contract and constitution using the utility functions he expects would exist under each culture. "The Limits of Individualism," *The Journal of Philosophy* 69 (October 5, 1972), 545–556.

20. See W. Vickrey, "Utility, Strategy, and Social Decision Rules," *Quarterly Journal of Economics* 74 (November 1960), 507–35, and Dennis C. Mueller, "Constitutional Democracy and Social Welfare," *Quarterly Journal of Economics* 87 (February 1973).

21. We ignore the possibility of a maximaxer existing and pulling the process in another direction.

one individual's preferences' dominating the outcome raises a serious question about the appropriateness of the repeated averaging technique. The rationale for the first round of averaging is straightforward. This represents the extension of the mental experiment from each individual to all other members, each putting themselves in every other individual's shoes. The behavioral interpretation of further rounds of averaging is less clear, however. And it is doubtful that the members of the group would regard as just or fair a decision rule which allowed the attitudes of one individual to so dominate the outcome.[22] Thus, a problem of getting unanimous agreement on a set of weights to be attached to each individual's risk preferences may still remain under the utilitarian contract.

Another obvious example would be a disagreement among constitutional decisionmakers over the set of ethical weights for future generations. Direct application of the utilitarian procedure would apply equal weights to each generation. Rawls, however, would apply a higher weight to the next generation out of parental affection. Someone else, unable to ignore entirely the knowledge that he is of the present generation, might apply a higher weight to it. Blacks and whites may disagree on the weights to be attached to the future consumption of these racial groups and so on. The basic point is that full equivalence of views may not be possible due to individual differences in abilities to engage in the mental experiment necessary to reach unanimity.[23]

Once the difficulty in reaching unanimity in the original position is recognized, practical methods for minimizing differences and achieving a homogeneity of views become important. The major requirement is to establish institutional structures in which the decisionmakers are not responsible for deciding issues that have a significant short run impact upon themselves. Many institutional devices for producing impartiality can be contemplated. Delegates to a constitutional convention might be drawn from the old (as many Indian societies do), from another community, or at random from the population.[24] Some decisions might be made on the stipulation that they not take place for another 25 years, say. Others might be entrusted to an impartial set of procedures, perhaps, carried out by a computer. If unanimity were still impossible, more drastic steps might be envisaged. Thus, the decision set might be divided into subsets in which unanimity was possible, and subsets where it was not possible.

22. Vickrey, *op. cit.*, recognizes this problem in averaging to avoid the case where there are as many social welfare functions as there are individuals.

23. See J. M. Buchanan and G. Tullock, *The Calculus of Consent*, Michigan, 1962, for similar arguments.

24. See our "Representative Democracy by Random Selection," *Public Choice*, Spring 1972 [Reading 26, below], for further discussion of this point.

Social contracts and constitutions could exist for the one subset, but not for the other.[25]

As social scientists, it is precisely these processes that concern us. In developing the utilitarian contract, therefore, we have employed that set of behavioral assumptions about individuals in the original position that come closest to reality, and yet preserve the central characteristics of the Rawlsian contract: impartiality and unanimity. In doing so we have minimized the problem of compliance, although at the cost of espousing a social contract, a constitution and other collective choice institutions that would be more closely tied to the *general* information on tastes, risk preferences, economic and social development, and so on, that exist at each point in time.

In contrast, Rawls, the moral philosopher, is interested in deriving a set of ethical principles that are clear, simple, and hold in perpetuity. His two principles of justice are precisely of this nature. In attempting to justify these principles, he places severe restrictions on the conditions defining the original position. And, by thus widening the gap between "ought" and "can," he increases the likelihood of noncompliance, and risks moving his theory into the group of ineffectual moral and political philosophies. This seems a pity since one of the truly important attributes of the justice through fairness approach is its potential for influencing the actual process of social and political institutional development.[26]

25. An example of a practical procedure would be to determine a proposed degree of progressivity in the income tax by simply taking the average of individual's disinterested preferences on a one man-one vote basis and then presenting to the polity this outcome for a yes-no vote. Presumably, where individuals' most desired outcomes did not differ significantly from the tax structure so determined, they would vote in favor of the proposal at this stage. Where some individuals differed so strongly from the proposal as to prefer to vote against it, then exit and the establishment of an alternative polity should be seriously considered.

Following this idea further, the loosest contractarian procedure would be to determine tentatively the outcomes of all major questions on a majority rule basis for yes-no questions and a one man-one vote weighted average process where the questions were in continuous terms. (An example of the distinction between yes-no questions and questions in continuous terms would be whether to have an income tax and if yes, what degree of progressivity should be adopted.) The whole package would then be presented to the polity on a non-amendable basis for a yes-no vote. Where a substantial majority agreed to the constitutional package and the cost of exit for others to form a new polity or join others would not be excessive, then a strong case for adoption of the constitution could be made, we believe, on utilitarian-contractarian grounds. On the other hand, where exit was impossible or extremely costly, greater care would have to be taken concerning the use of this procedure for constitutional decision-making.

26. James M. Buchanan argues along similar lines on his review of Rawls' book in *Public Choice* (Fall 1972).

VI. Conclusion

Let us close by emphasizing that the Rawlsian and utilitarian contracts have far more in accord than in contraposition. In their reliance on justice through fairness and impartiality, their contractarian approach, the role of ignorance of specific individual characteristics in the original position, the basic assumptions of egoism, rationality and nonbenevolence, etc., the two approaches are essentially identical. We regard the utilitarian contract as a bridge between the pure or naive utilitarian theories as embodied in the average utility principle, and the contractarian theories of Rawls, Rousseau and Kant.[27] It is utilitarian in that it builds on utility indexes (although they are not essential) and seeks a maximum choice over all individuals, although not a simple average. Yet, it is contractarian in making this optimal choice by unanimous consent of all parties on the original position. Thus while employing utility indexes, it satisfies the major requirement of the contractarian approach by ensuring that no man's interest may be ignored by society's general arrangements—only that is permitted which rational men pursuing their self-interest would freely accept.[28]

27. Within this triumvirate Rawls is closer to the utilitarians than he would probably admit. See, Lyons, "Rawls Versus Utilitarianism."

28. Michael Lessnoff, "John Rawls' Theory of Justice," *Political Studies* 19 (March 1971), 63–80. By Lessnoff's definition, our theory is contractarian, not utilitarian.

Part IV: Economists on Governmental and Political Failure

This section moves the discussion into areas traditionally reserved for political scientists. The papers introduce the reader to models of public choice and demonstrate their use in understanding problems of voter-consumer information, decision rules, and bureaucratic behavior. One of the main points they make is that governmental institutions are not cost-less correctors of private market failures. In fact, the failure of government in many areas is every bit as important a social problem today as the failure of private market processes. The unromantic but real choice is between two mechanisms that are both imperfect.

The first subsection examines deviations from the ideal in governmental behavior. James Buchanan's paper discusses the bridge between the behavior of persons in markets and the behavior of persons in the political process. Buchanan argues that the same people act in both processes and that they act from similar motivations. He suggests that unless self-interest behavior in the political process is analyzed as such, the economist is restricted in what he can contribute to the analysis of policy issues. In the second paper William Niskanen uses economic theory to develop a simple model of bureaucracy in order to analyze the nature of the economic activity carried out by bureaus. The main feature of bureaucracy, Niskanen stresses, is that a bureau does not sell its output at a per unit rate; rather it obtains lump-sum grants in exchange for all-or-none budget requests. Viewing the bureau in this manner and using the conventional economic theory of monopoly, Niskanen obtains the implication that bureaus' rates of output are higher than is socially optimal. In the third paper Roland McKean points out that many economists have curiously different attitudes toward the private and public portions of the economy. It is generally assumed that in the private economy individuals are utility-maximizers, but many analysts have assumed that in the public sector individuals are public-interest maximizers. McKean examines some implications of utility-maximizing individual action in the public sector. He stresses that there may be a process operating in governmental decision-making very similar to the externalities associated with private markets. In other words, when public officials make decisions, they do not always evaluate the total costs of their actions.

One important reason that political competition is not sufficient to force political actors to maximize voter interests is the difficulty and cost encountered by the electorate in getting information on the wide spectrum of government behavior. It is time-consuming and difficult enough to follow the major issues of the day. It is much harder to be informed and to try to do something about the broad spectrum of governmental decisions that may be based on bureaucratic or special interests. These deviations from the ideal in governmental behavior have led some economists to advance schemes to improve the democratic process. The second subsection thus consists of four papers examining problems of informed voting. In the first paper James C. Miller III proposes a method of increasing voter participation by means of computer technology that is likely to be available soon. In answer, Martin Shubik in the second paper suggests that such instant referenda via computer may not be wise, because of the wide disparity in the information possessed by voters. In the third paper Dennis Mueller, Robert Tollison, and Thomas Willett extend Shubik's argument to discuss how polling and representation can be combined to yield a system that is superior (on the grounds of information costs) both to the present geographically based national legislature and to Miller's referenda system. They propose the novel, though not new, idea of at-large representation via random selection of legislators. In the fourth paper Robert Tollison and Thomas Willett examine the literature on the importance of economic variables on the decision to vote and present some economic explanations of that decision. In particular, they stress the incentive effect of information. The decision to vote has for some time been the subject of detailed theoretical and empirical work by economists and political scientists. Most of these scholars have been interested in developing explanations of why people vote when in a statistical sense their vote is insignificant. Tollison and Willett survey this controversy, stressing that consumption-type motives (such as citizenship) must be invoked to explain absolute and relative voter turnouts.

Subsection C consists of two papers examining the possibility of systematic biases in the size of the government budget. In the first the editors review the literature on budget size in a democracy, literature that is concerned with possible bias in democratic processes which could skew the budget away from some notion of correct size. This literature touches on questions of social balance, dependence effects, collective decision rules, and bureaucratic behavior. The paper examines it with special attention to what benchmark for "correct" budget size each author employs in his discussion. We then extend the analysis to consider the effects of risk avoidance and political advertising specifically on the size of the defense budget. In the second paper Kenneth Greene assumes that public expenditures can be treated as analogous to insurance-type purchases and argues that voter attitudes toward risk can have important effects on the rate of growth in the public sector. In particular he stresses that attitudes toward risk will vary with income level. This yields the empirical implication that the public sector should grow at different rates over time. Using historical expenditure data for Great Britain and private life insurance data for the United States, Greene shows that his hypothesis is not inconsistent with past events.

Subsection D consists of a paper by Dennis Mueller, Robert Tollison, and Thomas Willett, in which they examine structural problems in the representation of minority interests under one-man, one-vote majority rule. To obviate these problems, they suggest a form of at-large, proportional representation. Polities, they propose, would be defined on the basis that individual voters have equal total utility gains from the issues decided within a polity—a condition called the equal-stake requirement.

A. DEVIATION FROM THE IDEAL IN GOVERNMENTAL BEHAVIOR

21. Toward Analysis of Closed Behavioral Systems

JAMES M. BUCHANAN

This book contains several applications of the "theory of public choice." This theory represents an attempt to close up the analysis of social interaction systems. In this respect it may be compared and contrasted with the familiar "open" system analyzed in traditional economic theory. The latter is a highly developed theory of market interaction. Beyond the limits of market behavior, however, analysis is left "open."

Reprinted from *Theory of Public Choice,* edited by J. M. Buchanan and R. D. Tollison (Ann Arbor: The University of Michigan Press, 1972), pp. 11–23, by permission of publisher and authors. Copyright © by The University of Michigan 1972.

The "public choices" that define the constraints within which market behavior is allowed to take place are assumed to be made externally or exogenously, presumably by others than those who participate in market transactions and whose behavior is subjected to the theory's examination. The limitation of analysis to open behavioral systems can be helpful if the objective itself is comparably restricted to that of making predictions about a few variables. If the behavioral elements that are neglected remain genuinely external, little can be gained by closing the system analytically. As applied to orthodox economic theory, this would suggest that the formation of "public choice" may be left out of account, provided that the objective of the theory is limited to making positive predictions about market structure and nothing more. Such a limitation would, of course, greatly restrict the usefulness that economic theory might have in policy discussion. Political economy or welfare economics could not represent a natural extension of the positive theory in this context.

The observed behavior of economists does not confrom to such a consistent and narrowly restricted role for their discipline. Many economists have examined the complexities of market structure on the assumption that economic motivation is pervasive. Utilizing such results, they have isolated and identified market failure. Much of modern welfare economics owes its origin to Pigou, whose primary contribution involved an emphasis on the possible divergence between private and social marginal product (cost). Almost without pause, Pigou and the economists who have followed him assumed that the behaving individuals in market process are motivated exclusively by private values, defined economically, and that social effects of their actions are neglected. This procedure represents a consistent extension of the behavioral assumption that is implicit in standard theory. Criticism becomes justified only when the "failures" of market process identified in this way are presumed to be correctable by political or governmental regulation and control. This last step represents an arbitrary and nonscientific closure of the behavioral system and, as such, cannot be legitimate. The critically important bridge between the behavior of persons who act in the marketplace and the behavior of persons who act in political process must be analyzed. The "theory of public choice" can be interpreted as the construction of such a bridge. The approach requires only the simple assumption that the same individuals act in both relationships. Political decisions are not handed down from on high by omniscient beings who cannot err. Individuals behave in market interactions, in political-governmental interactions, in cooperative-nongovernmental interactions, and in other arrangements. Closure of the behavioral system, as I am using the term, means only that analysis must be extended to the actions of persons in their several separate capacities.

I. The Elitist Model: An Open Behavioral System

Economists who have talked about "market failure" under the assumption that persons behave as automatons in market interaction have blithely, indeed almost blissfully, seemed willing to turn things over to the corrective devices of the politician-bureaucrat. What is the reason for this? Have the welfare economists assumed that persons are so much influenced by their institutional-environmental setting as to make ordinary men "socially conscious" when they take on political or bureaucratic roles? Some of the socialist romantics may have reflected this attitude, but this is not characteristic of those who have participated actively in sophisticated policy discussion. The practicing (and preaching) welfare economist does not really consider crossing the bridge. He does not think of the man who behaves in the marketplace, and whose behavior he examines, as the same person who either does or should make collective or public decisions for the whole community. This explains my usage of the term "open system." The implicit assumption has been that someone else, someone other than the participants in the marketplace, lays down the rules for collective order.

This limited and essentially open behavioral model can be made logically consistent and self-contained. The classical Italian scholars in public finance, such men as De Viti de Marco, Puviani, Einaudi, and Fasiani,[1] deserve credit for recognizing the necessity of defining specifically their assumed models of political order. Several of these scholars, and notably De Viti de Marco and Fasiani, developed parallel structures of analysis. On the one hand, fiscal phenomena were examined in a model where the producers-suppliers of collective-governmental "goods" are simultaneously consumers-demanders. This closure of the behavioral system is equivalent to that which "the theory of public choice," as presented in this book, embodies. Merely to define this interaction system (which was called "democratic," "cooperative," or "individualistic" by different writers) forces analysis of behavior of persons in separate capacities. On the other hand, and in sharp contrast, fiscal phenomena were examined in a model where collective-governmental decisions, effective for the all-inclusive community, are made by an elite or ruling group (members of a winning majority coalition, a party hierarchy, an aristocracy, an "establishment," a ruling central committee, a dictator). This model concentrates attention on the behavioral reactions of persons in the larger community, reactions to the set of collective decisions that are imposed

1. For a general discussion of the contributions of these scholars, along with appropriate bibliographical references, see the essay, "The Italian Tradition in Fiscal Theory," in my *Fiscal Theory and Political Economy* (Chapel Hill, 1960).

externally upon them. To make this model complete, however, the behavior of the members of the elite in choosing the decision set must be analyzed. Different persons act in different roles. As I have suggested, this is a consistent model and it contains implications that can be tested.

The criticism that may be lodged against those who have worked in the tradition of modern welfare economics is not that they have employed this ruling class or elitist model of analysis. Quite the contrary; had they done so, or had they expressed a willingness to do so, their work would have exhibited an internal coherence that has been largely absent. This lack of coherence warrants the legitimate criticism that the "theory of public choice" implies, whether directly or indirectly. The social theorist remains and should remain free to select his own model, and this selection should be informed by those aspects of reality which the theorist expects to explain more adequately. What the theorist should not be allowed to do is to work uncritically without being forced to look at the internal behavioral structure of his model. If the individual actors in the economic process are assumed to be divorced from the decision-making structure that defines the constraints on their behavior, the openness of the system must be acknowledged. A "science" that is limited to an analysis of reaction patterns can, of course, be constructed. This may be of value to those who do participate in rule-making. It is unacceptable, however, for the practitioner of this "reaction science" to infer "failure" or "inefficiency" if the latter are measured against criteria that are themselves derived from the valuation of the individuals who are reacting, and then to imply that such "failure" either will be, can be, or should be removed by some change in the behavior of others, namely those who participate in the establishment of the constraints. Before this can be done, a plausible "theory" of the behavior of the members of the ruling elite must be developed. Until midcentury, such a theory was almost wholly neglected by social scientists, with the Italian public-finance scholars again providing a notable exception. Some of the elements of such a theory are now emerging, and important contributions have been made by some of the same scholars who have worked in the theory of public choice.[2] The development of an acceptable theory of bureaucratic behavior can be interpreted as bridging the gap through an explicit recognition of dual decision structures.

II. Public Choice and Private Choice

The "theory of public choice" rests instead on a single decision structure. It involves the explicit introduction of a "democratic" model, one

2. I refer to such works as: Anthony Downs, *Inside Bureaucracy* (Boston, 1967); Gordon Tullock, *The Politics of Bureaucracy* (Washington, D.C., 1965).

in which the rulers are also the ruled. The theory examines the behavior of persons as they participate variously in the formation of public or collective choices, by which is meant choices from among mutually exclusive alternative constraints which, once selected, must apply to all members of the community. In acting or behaving as a "public choice" participant, the individual is presumed to be aware that he is, in part, selecting results which affect others than himself. He is making decisions for a public, of which he forms a part.

This characteristic feature of "public choice" distinguishes it sharply from "private choice." We may typify the latter by individual behavior in an idealized market setting: If a person acts, say, as a buyer or seller in a fully competitive market, he has no sensation that his own behavior modifies the environment of other persons. He acts as if he generates changes in his "private" economy only. Despite the analyst's recognition that each economic act influences, even if infinitesimally, the conditions confronted by all market participants, the participant himself is not cognizant of this.

It is precisely in the domain of welfare economics that this idealized behavior which I have called "private choice" becomes impossible. When a person is able to modify the economic environment of others through his own behavior, and when he can recognize this, the welfare economist refers to "externality." This is formally equivalent to the divergence between marginal private and marginal social cost or product, mentioned earlier. It is clear that when personal behavior generates externality, whether this be positive or negative, it must take on characteristics of "public choice," even if the actor does not explicitly acknowledge his role as a decision-maker for the relevant community of persons (small or large) that are affected. In one sense, individual behavior in an externality relationship may be interpreted as a sort of halfway house between the idealized "private choice" typified by buying and selling in competitive markets and the idealized "public choice" typified by voting in purely democratic referenda. It is not surprising, therefore, that several of the contributors of essays in this book have approached their subject matter through the technical analysis of externalities. By contrast, it remains surprising that Pigovian welfare economists, in general, have failed to sense the internal contradiction between their models of economic interaction where external costs and benefits become criteria for market failure and their models of political behavior where such externalities are presumed to be corrected.

There is, of course, a difference in the institutional-environmental setting for personal behavior in the market and in the political process. The individual whose private economic behavior pollutes the air and imposes external costs on others in his community (a classic example of an external diseconomy) may be partially unaware of the effects of his actions on others. Even if he is aware of these effects, he may treat as "his own property" the atmosphere elements (air) that others claim in common, implicitly or explicitly. By comparison, consider the individual who votes in a political referendum and who, say, supports the imposition of taxes on all persons in a well-defined political community. He is exerting an external diseconomy on others, and he may be fully aware that he is affecting their potential economic positions. But the voter claims no "property right" in the selection of the tax system, as such. His behavior may be tempered by his understanding that, in subsequent referenda on taxes and on other contraints, he will find himself in losing rather than winning political coalitions. On some such grounds as this, a plausible case can be made out that "political pollution" is subject to somewhat more intensive internal behavioral constraints than "economic pollution." The implications of such an argument should, however, be kept in mind. Once the welfare economist accepts such a defense of his orthodoxy, he is already partially in the "public choice" camp. He is, willy-nilly, being forced to close up his behavioral system.

At the current stage of development in social and behavioral science, this would represent significant progress. Whether or not and to what extent men behave differently under varied institutional-environmental constraints deserves much more inquiry and investigation. Some research along these lines will be carried out in due course. But the bridge has been crossed once it is so much as acknowledged that the same men are involved in the several decision processes.

III. The Economic Model of Behavior

This section introduces both the main strength and the main limitation of the "theory of public choice," as developed and applied in the papers in this book and by scholars elsewhere. This theory has been developed almost exclusively by scholars who are professional economists. As Gordon Tullock discusses in his essay in this book, the theory of public choice might be taken to reflect economic imperialism, interpreted as efforts by economists to expand the boundaries of their own discipline so as to make it applicable to more and more aspects of human behavior. As they have done so, it should have been expected that the explanatory potential of the strictly economic model of behavior would be gradually eroded, as indeed most of its users will readily acknowledge. The model has been demonstrated to retain surprising strength, however, even when applied to behavior that might initially have seemed to be almost wholly noneconomic. Methodologically, the economic model remains singular in its ability to generate conceptually refutable hypotheses regardless of its particular application.

The economic model of behavior is based on the motivational postulate of individual utility maximization. This postulate, in itself, remains empirically empty until further restrictions are imposed on the definition of utility or, technically, on the utility function. Once this step is taken, once the "goods" that the individual (in some average or representative sense) values are identified, the way is open for the derivation of hypotheses that can be tested against observations. The economic model is almost entirely predictive in content rather than prescriptive. The actors who behave "economically" choose "more rather than less," with more and less being measured in units of goods that are independently identified and defined. This becomes a prediction about behavior in the real world that the economist carries with him as a working professional scientist. As such, the economist neither condemns nor condones the behavior of those whose behavior he examines. He has no business to lay down norms of behavior for the consumer, producer, voter, or for anyone else. In its pure sense, economic theory is devoid of valuation at this normative level.

Failure to understand the descriptive and predicitive content of economic theory along with a proclivity to interpret all social "science" in prescriptive terms has caused many critics to deplore the "dismal science" and to rail against the "crass materialism" that economic behavior allegedly represents. The appropriate response of the economist to such criticism should be (but perhaps too rarely has been) that he is wholly unconcerned, as a professional scientist, about the ethically relevant characteristics of the behavior that he examines. To the extent that men behave as his model predicts, the economist can explain uniformities in social order. To the extent that men behave differently, his predictions are falsified. It is as simple as that.

The criticisms of the economic model of behavior, and of the science that embodies this model, have been long-continuing and pervasive even when the model has been limited in application only to the behavior of persons in well-defined market processes. These criticisms need not concern us here. But it should be apparent that when attempts are made to stretch the central predictive model beyond these confines, when the economic approach is extended to "public choice," the criticisms stemming from nonpredictive and nonscientific sources should be intensified. For precisely to the extent that the model loses some of its predictive content, its use to the nonscientist seems to become more and more suspect in some prescriptively relevant sense. A single example illustrates this point. The nonscientist may accept the use of an economic model of behavior, and he may acknowledge its explanatory power in relation to the price-making and price-taking by buyers and sellers of groceries. He may not condemn the economist out of hand for advancing the prediction that buyers will purchase more beans when they are cheapened relative to potatoes. By contrast, the same nonscientist may object, and strenuously, if the economist expands his horizons and uses essentially the same behavioral model to predict that the bureaucrat will increase his awards of public contracts to the prospect that sweetens the personal package of emoluments allowable within the legal constraints. Here the bureaucrat is, like the buyer at the corner grocery store, predicted to demand more of that "good" that is relatively cheapened in price. Because of the predictive-prescriptive confusion, however, the economist becomes suspect; he is interpreted as replacing the "is" by the "ought" in circumstances where prevailing moral principles make strict economic behavior partially or wholly unacceptable.

IV. Noneconomic Models of Behavior

Because of the predictive-prescriptive confusion, however, along with its subsequent creation of reluctance in noneconomist social scientists to undertake rigorous positive examination of behavior patterns, the extension of orthodox economic models to nonmarket behavior seems to fill an awesome gap in social analysis. Precisely because other approaches than the economic have been prescriptive, the latter appears initially to be more important in yielding predictive hypotheses about nonmarket behavior than it would be were alternative models also used in a positive or predictive manner. This latter would require that the noneconomic models be transformed. The traditional prescriptive norms *for* personal behavior would have to be converted into predicitive hypotheses *about* personal behavior. The "ought" would have to be replaced by the "is." If this transformation can be effected, noneconomic models can be extended to many aspects of behavior, including an invasion of the domain traditionally commanded by the economists. If the theory of public choice and related work represents "economic imperialism," the way is surely open for the noneconomists to turn the tables and extend behavioral models of their own into the realm of market interactions. All social scientists should applaud the emergence of competing means of closing up the analyses of behavioral systems. And, even in the strictly defined market process, there are surely important unexplained residues that may be examined against alternative behavioral hypotheses.

Consider first, and briefly, the dominant ethical system in the history of the West, Christianity. This system has been almost exclusively discussed and elaborated as a set of prescriptive norms for personal behavior, a set of "shoulds," "commandments," "precepts." Nonetheless, it is possible to convert this ethical system into hypotheses about behavior. We may do so by beginning with individual utility functions as methodologically helpful starting points even if they remain empirically empty. In its starkest form, Christianity is represented by an individual utility function in which "goods" attributed to others are valued equally with "goods" attributed to the person whose function is being defined. Furthermore, there can be no discrimination among the large set of "others" in the pure predictive model of Christianity. For predictions to be made, "goods" must be identified, but, once this is done, hypotheses may be derived and subjected to observation. Do individuals in some average or representative sense behave as the Christian model predicts? Casual empiricism alone suggests that the central hypothesis has at least some explanatory potential. We do observe individuals giving up "goods" to others, including the set of "others" where the individual units remain unidentified to the donor and wholly outside meaningfully drawn boundaries of personal relationship (funds are freely given for the feeding of starving children in Biafra). Research should be extended and carried forward to determine the explanatory limits of this strict Christian hypothesis. In this respect and at this point, the efforts of Kenneth Boulding should be especially noted. Almost alone among social scientists, and once again from a professional background in economics, Boulding has drawn attention to the explanatory potential of what he called the "integrative" system of interaction, which is essentially his version of what I have called here the Christian hypothesis. Other scholars, many of whom have also worked in theory of public choice, have joined Boulding in developing an "economics of charity." Such men as William Vickrey, Gordon Tullock, Earl Thompson, David B. Johnson, and Thomas Ireland have made contributions in this obvious attempt to include all forms of human behavior in a framework of positive analysis.[3]

Conversion of the prescriptive norm of Christianity into a predictive hypothesis in its pure or pristine form immediately suggests an intermediate approach, one in which the utility function attributes positive values to the "goods" of others, but where the "others' are personally iden-

3. See Kenneth Boulding, "Notes on a Theory of Philanthropy," *Philanthropy and Public Policy,* ed. by Frank G. Dickinson (New York, 1962); William Vickrey, "One Economist's View of Philanthropy," *Philanthropy and Public Policy, op cit.;* Gordon Tullock, "Information Without Profit," *Papers on Non-Market Decision-Making,* Vol. II (Charlottesville, Virginia, 1967); Thomas Ireland, "Charity Budgeting" (Unpublished Ph.D. Dissertation, Alderman Library, University of Virginia, 1968); David B. Johnson, "The Fundamental Economics of the Charity Market" (Unpublished Ph.D. Dissertation, Alderman Library, University of Virginia, 1968); Earl Thompson, "Do Competitive Markets Misallocate Charity," *Public Choice,* IV (1968), 67–74.

tified, either as individuals or as members of groups embodying certain descriptive characteristics. This approach yields a whole set of possible behavioral hypotheses, the working out and testing of which may be summarized in such various rubrics as "the economics of the family," "the economics of marriage," "the economics of clubs," "the economics of ethnic groups," and so forth. In each case, the word "economics" suggests only that the positive analyses in each case remain largely in the hands of professionally trained economists. But my point of emphasis here is only that work in each of these areas reflects an attempt to accomplish what I have called here the closing of the whole behavioral system.

V. The Kantian Generalization Principle Treated as an Explanatory Hypothesis

A more interesting approach, and one that seems hardly to have been explored at all, lies in converting the prescriptive norm of Kantian ethics into a predictive hypothesis about individual behavior. Like the more restricted but comparable Christian hypothesis, this could be treated as a complete model which may have more or less explanatory potential under different behavioral environments. Prescriptively, the Kantian principle instructs a person to consider as a duty that form of behavior that will, when generalized to the whole community of persons, generate results that are desired in some noninstrumental sense. Predictively, the Kantian hypothesis states that when behavior is recognized to affect others, these effects will be taken into account and behavior adjusted as appropriate. The interests of others than the actor are included, however, not out of "love" as in the Christian ethic, but out of a form of enlightened self-interest which is based on a generalized recognition of the reciprocity of social interaction. Translated into utility-function terms, the "goods" that are positively valued by the individual are those attributed to or assigned to himself and not to others. The utilities of others, generally or specifically, do not enter the utility function in any directly interdependent fashion. The interdependence that seems to be inferred from the results arises because the "goods" that the individual values are more inclusive and less instrumental than those upon which the orthodox economic models have concentrated attention.

Clearly, something akin to the Kantian hypothesis describes many aspects of human behavior. Large areas of social life are, and must be, organized essentially on anarchistic principles. Individual property rights are not well-defined, yet "pollution" is kept within reasonably tolerable limits by self-imposed constraints on behavior which can only reflect adherence to something like a generalization principle. And, indeed, this hypothesis offers some prospect for methodological reconciliation between the economist's analysis of market behavior and the noneconomist's analysis of nonmarket behavior. It may be plausibly argued that the Kantian hypothesis would yield predictions about market behavior that are identical to those produced by the more restrictive models of economic theory. The individual buyer or seller in a fully competitive market does not influence the position of others than himself. Hence, he may behave in strict accordance with Kantian precepts when he acts as the automaton of economic theory.

The two hypotheses may diverge only when externalities characterize the economic interaction process. If the Kantian hypothesis should be dominant, there may be no need for policy makers to express concern about environmental or atmospheric pollution or erosion arising from personal behavior, and there might be no inefficient congestion of available publicly used facilities. Similarly, there should be little concern about the narrow and possibly self-seeking behavior of political representatives and bureaucrats. If the Kantian hypothesis about individual behavior should be generally corroborated, individuals who participate in "public choice" would be acting in the genuine "public interest," as defined by the widespread adherence to the generalization principle.[4]

It should be apparent that what is needed is considerably more research to ascertain the explanatory power of competing behavioral hypotheses, any one or any combination of which will allow a closure of the social interaction system. One result of such research will surely be that the relative applicability of the competing hypotheses will vary from one institutional-environmental setting to another. And indeed a central part of the research may be the identification of those institutional characteristics that seem to exert an influence on personal behavior. In a paper that is not included in this volume,[5] I examined the possible influence of the sheer size of the interacting group on the individual's willingness to behave in accordance with the Kantian precepts. Charles Goetz has responded to my challenge, and he has demonstrated that, under certain conditions that involve the joint sharing of a collectively provided "good," the directional influence of numbers may be more than offset by the change in payoff differentials consequent on changing sizes of the group.[6] There are

4. Individuals may, of course, disagree as to what the "public interest" is, and conflicts may arise even when each and every person behaves in accordance with Kantian precepts. Resolution of such conflicts raises interesting problems, but the source of conflicts here would be quite different from the more familiar private interest-public interest dichotomy.

5. "Ethical Rules, Expected Values, and Large Numbers," *Ethics*, LXXVI (October 1965), 1–13.

6. Charles J. Goetz, "Group-Size and the Voluntary Provision of Public Goods," Working Paper 24 (Blacksburg, Virginia, November 1968).

other apparent, and less "economic," characteristics of interaction settings that may be examined for their influence on personal behavior patterns. The influence of the family, the tribe, the church, the local community, the political party, the civic club, the team, . . . all of these and more can be important and can affect overall social stability. Effective research seems only in its very early stages.

VI. We Cannot Have It Both Ways

In conclusion, I should emphasize the relevance of seeking closure of the behavioral systems in our analyses by returning to the comparison and contrast between the position taken by the post-Pigovian welfare economists and that taken by those who have contributed to the "theory of public choice," as represented variously in this book. Neither group should be allowed to operate in an open system of analysis. As I have stressed earlier, the post-Pigovian should not be allowed to generate excitement and ultimately to modify social policy by his alleged discoveries of "market failures" without, and at the same time, acknowledging the comparable "failures" of his proposed political-governmental correctives. The discovery of market failures is normally based on the usage of a narrowly constrained utility function which describes individual market behavior in terms of narrow self-interest. If, in fact, individuals behave in such a manner in the marketplace, the inference should be that they will also act similarly in other and nonmarket behavioral settings. The burden of proof must rest on the discoverer of market failure as he demonstrates that the behavioral shift into a nonmarket setting involves a dramatic widening of personal horizons.

The same restrictions should be imposed on those of us who have tried to extend the economists' model into nonmarket spheres of behavior. We should not be allowed to discover "political failures" because we have succeeded in isolating the self-seeking behavior of politicians and bureaucrats and, at the same time, be unconcerned about the "market failures" that show up because of externalities. Both the post-Pigovian welfare economists and the public choice economists should be required to work within broadly consistent analytical models. Both groups work essentially with an economic model; neither group should be allowed to slip into its own version of some Kantian-like hypothesis when and if this suits ideological prejudices.

The post-Pigovian may rescue himself from contradiction by either one of two routes. He may, as indeed several eminent welfare economists have done, join the ranks of the public-choice theorists and look critically at "government failures" alongside market failures. The result will be the emergence of some ideologically neutral grounds upon which both the public-choice theorists and the reformed Pigovians can evaluate alternative institutional arrangements on what must be a case-by-case comparative analysis.

The second escape from contradiction lies in the explicit extension of some variant of the Kantian hypothesis to market as well as to nonmarket behavior. The social scientist who sees bureaucracy as something other than the self-seeking of individuals within their own career hierarchy can also begin to look on market behavior and on the workings of markets differently. And indeed there are indications that some analysts are taking this route; witness the increasing attention that has been given to the so-called "social responsibility" of business.

The "theory of public choice" is only one step in the direction of an internally consistent social science. It should be interpreted as such by its proponents as well as by its critics. Its explanatory power varies greatly from application to application, but the number and the variety of these that are contained in this book alone should be sufficient to suggest both the generality of the theory and the promise of continued work.

22. The Peculiar Economics of Bureaucracy

WILLIAM A. NISKANEN

I. Introduction

Economics does not now provide a theory of the maximizing bureaucrat. The currently dominant approach to public administration is to provide the organizational structure, information system, and analysis to bureaucrats who, for whatever reason, want to be efficient. This approach, however, does not develop, or explicitly recognize as relevant, the conditions for which the personal objectives of the bureaucrat are consistent with the efficiency of the bureaucracy.

At present, with a large and increasing proportion of economic activity being conducted in bureaus, economists have made no substantial contribution to answering the following questions: What are the distinguishing characteristics of bureaucracies? What are the critical elements of a theory of bureaucracy? Specifically, what do bureaucrats maximize and under what external conditions? What are the consequences of maximizing behavior under these conditions? For example, what is the equi-

Reprinted from *American Economic Review*, May 1968, pp. 293–305, by permission of the publisher and author.

librium output and budget of a bureau for given demand and cost conditions? What are the effects of changes in demand and cost conditions? What are the welfare consequences of bureaucratic organization of economic activity? What changes in organization and the structure of rewards would improve the efficiency of a bureaucracy? This paper presents a simple model of the maximizing bureaucrat and, based on this model, a set of tentative qualitative answers to these questions.

II. The Model

The model outlined in this section is based on the following two critical characteristics of bureaus: (1) Bureaucrats maximize the total budget of their bureau, given demand and cost conditions, subject to the constraint that the budget must be equal to or greater than the minimum total costs at the equilibrium output. (2) Bureaus exchange a specific output (or combination of outputs) for a specific budget. For this paper, thus, bureaus are defined by these two characteristics.

Among the several variables that may enter the bureaucrat's utility function are the following: salary, perquisites of the office, public reputation, power, patronage, ease of managing the bureau, and ease of making changes. All of these variables, I contend, are a positive monotonic function of the total budget of the bureau.[1] Budget maximization should be an adequate proxy even for those bureaucrats with a relatively low pecuniary motivation and a relatively high motivation for making changes in the public interest. It is an interesting observation that the most distinguished public servants of recent years have substantially increased the budgets of the bureaus for which they are responsible.

The second characteristic—bureaus exchange their output for a total budget rather than at a per unit rate—is generally recognized, but the implications of this characteristic for the behavior of a bureau are not. This characteristic gives the bureau the same type of "market" power as a monopoly that presents the market with an all-or-nothing choice.[2] A bureau, thus, can appropriate all of the consumer surplus. As is shown later, however, this characteristic leads to significantly different output, budget, and welfare conditions for a bureau than for a monopoly.[3]

The equilibrium conditions for a bureau, as defined by these two characteristics, are developed below by considering a bureau faced by linear

1. This paper develops only the static model of a bureau and does not explore the time dimension of budget maximization.

2. I am indebted to Gordon Tullock for this powerful insight.

3. This characteristic applies strictly to a "pure" bureau, such as the Department of Defense. Many economic institutions such as the Post Office, most colleges and universities, and most hospitals sell part of their output at a per unit rate and a substantial proportion of their output for a budget.

demand and cost conditions. First, consider a bureau that buys factors in a competitive market and for which

$$V = a - bQ$$

and

$$C = c + 2dQ,[4]$$

where

$V \equiv$ marginal value to consumers
$C \equiv$ minimum marginal cost to bureau

and

$Q \equiv$ output of bureau.

For these conditions, then,

$$B = aQ - \frac{b}{2}Q^2$$

and

$$TC = cQ + dQ^2,$$

where

$B \equiv$ total budget of bureau

and

$TC \equiv$ minimum total cost to bureau.

The equilibrium level of Q, for these conditions, is determined as follows: Maximization of B leads to an upper level of $Q = a/b$. The constraint that B must be equal to or greater than TC, under some conditions, leads to a lower level of $Q = 2(a - c)/b + 2d$. These two levels of Q are equal where $a = 2bc/b - 2d$. For a bureau that buys factors in a competitive market, the equilibrium level of Q, thus, is where

$$Q \begin{cases} = \dfrac{2(a-c)}{b+2d} & \text{for } a < \dfrac{2bc}{b-2d}. \\[2em] = \dfrac{a}{b} & \text{for } a \geq \dfrac{2bc}{b-2d}. \end{cases}$$

4. The marginal cost function for a bureau that is not a discriminating monopsonist includes the factor surplus. The average cost function to this bureau and the corresponding marginal cost functions for a monopoly or bureau which is a discriminating monopsonist would be $C = c + dQ$.

Figure 1 illustrates these equilibrium levels of output for representative demand and cost conditions.

For the lower demand condition represented by V_1, the equilibrium output of a bureau will be in the budget-constrained region where the area of the polygon ea_1hi is equal to the area of the rectangle $efgi$. At the equilibrium level of output, there is no "fat" in this bureau; the total budget just covers the minimum total costs, and no cost-effectiveness analysis will reveal any wasted resources. The output of this bureau, however, is higher than the Pareto-optimal level. The equilibrium level of output is in a region where the minimum achievable marginal costs ig are substantially higher than the marginal value to consumers ih, offsetting all of the consumer surplus that would be generated by efficient operation at lower budget levels. If minimum marginal costs increase with output as a consequence of increasing per-unit factor costs (rather than diminishing productivity), this bureau will generate a substantial factor surplus equal to the triangle cfg—larger than would be generated at the lower, Pareto-op-

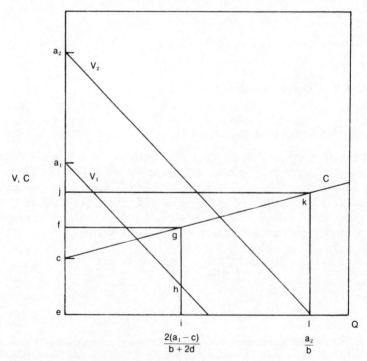

Figure 1. Equilibrium Output of Bureau.

timal output. Legislatures predominantly representing factor interests understandably prefer the provision of public services through bureaus.

For the higher demand conditions represented by V_2, the equilibrium output of a bureau will be in the demand-constrained region where the marginal value of output is zero. In this case the total budget will be equal to the triangle ea_2l and will be larger than the minimum total costs equal to the rectangle $ejkl$. At the equilibrium level of output, there is "fat" in this bureau. A careful analysis would indicate that the same output could be achieved at a lower budget, but the analyst should expect no cooperation from the bureau since it has no incentive to either know or reveal its minimum cost function. In this region, the equilibrium level of output is dependent only on demand conditions. The output of this bureau is also higher than the Pareto-optimal level, operating at an output level where the minimum marginal costs are equal to lk and the marginal value to consumers is zero, again offsetting all of the consumer surplus. The factor surplus generated by this bureau, of course, is also substantially larger than would be generated by a lower, Pareto-optimal output level.

III. Comparison of Organizational Forms

A better understanding of the consequences of bureaucratic organization of economic activity can be gained by comparison with the consequences of other forms of economic organization facing the same demand and cost conditions. Table 1 presents the equilibrium levels of output and related variables for a private monopoly which buys factors on a competitive market, a private monopoly which discriminates among factor suppliers, a competitive industry, a bureau which buys factors on a competitive market, and a bureau that discriminates among factor suppliers. Each form of organization faces the same following demand and cost conditions:

$$V = 200 - 1.00 \, Q$$
$$C = 75 + .25 \, Q.\,[5]$$

The traditional concern about private monopolies is that they produce too little output. Operating in an output region where marginal value is greater than marginal cost, they do not generate as much surplus value as would a competitive industry. For the demand and cost conditions shown in Table 1, a private monopoly would generate a sum of profit plus

5. This is the average cost function to a monopoly or bureau that is not a discriminating monopolist, the marginal cost function to a discriminating monopsonist, and the supply function to a competitive industry.

Table 1. Equilibrium conditions for alternative forms of economic organization facing same demand and cost conditions

Product market	Monopoly		Competitive	Bureau	
Factor market	Competitive	Monopsony	Competitive	Competitive	Monopsony
Measures					
Output	50	55.6	100	166.7	200
Revenue:					
Total	7,500	8,024.7	10,000	19,444.4	20,000
Average	150	144.4	100	116.7	100.0
Marginal	100	88.9	100	33.3	0
Costs:					
Total	4,375	4,552.5	10,000	19,444.4	20,000
Average	87.5	81.9	100	116.7	100.0
Marginal	100.0	88.9	100	158.3	125.0
Profits	3,125	3,472.2	0	0	0
Consumer surplus	1,250	1,543.3	5,000	0	0
Factor surplus	312.5	0	1,250	3,472.2	0

consumer and factor surplus around 75 percent that of a competitive industry.

For these demand and cost conditions, a bureau that buys factors on a competitive market will have an equilibrium output around two-thirds more than the competitive industry. This bureau will generate no profits or consumer surplus but will generate a factor surplus around 55 percent of the total surplus from a competitive industry. For these conditions, a bureau that discriminates among factor suppliers will have an equilibrium output twice that of a competitive industry and will generate no profits or surplus value.

A comparison of the supply and cost conditions is also helpful. A monopoly has no supply function; it will set an output such that marginal revenue equals marginal cost, with the output sold at a uniform price. A bureau also has no supply function; it will exchange increments of output at the demand price for each increment to an output level such that the budget equals the minimum achievable costs or the marginal value of the increment is zero. In a sense, a bureau also has no separate marginal cost function. The incremental resource withdrawal for a budget-maximizing bureau will be equal to the demand value, as the difference between this value and the minimum incremental cost will be financed from the consumer surplus appropriated at lower output levels. Only if a bureau is efficient at lower output levels, for whatever reason, would the incremental resource withdrawal be equal to the minimum incremental cost. One implication of this condition is that an analyst may not be able to identify a demand-constrained bureau's minimum cost function from budget and output behavior. All this may yield is the bureau's estimate of its demand function; in the static case, all bureaus will appear to have declining marginal costs and in a sense they do. An estimate of a demand-constrained bureau's minimum marginal cost function must be constructed from detailed estimates of the production function and factor costs—creating an extraordinary demand for analysis.

For different reasons, in summary, both private monopolies and bureaus operate in output regions that are inherently nonoptimal. The substitution of a bureau for a monopoly to provide some product or service, however, solves no problems; this substitution will reduce the aggregate surplus value and serve only the interests of the owners of specific factors.

IV. Effects of Changes in Demand and Cost Conditions

The model outlined in Section II may also be used to estimate a bureau's response to changes in demand and cost conditions.

Demand Shifts. Figure 2 illustrates the changes in a bureau's equilibrium output and budget, for given cost conditions, in response to shifts in demand.

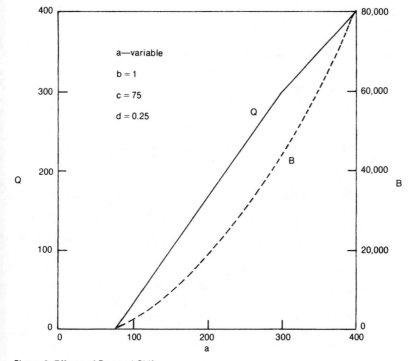

Figure 2. Effects of Demand Shift.

In the budget-constrained output region, the output of a bureau will grow by more than the amount of a demand shift, even when faced by increasing marginal costs. A bureau producing an output at constant marginal costs will grow at twice the rate of a competitive industry under the same conditions. In this region, the budget per unit output will increase only by the amount of the increase in the minimum unit costs.

In the demand-constrained output region, the output of a bureau will grow by the same amount as the demand shift, regardless of the slope of the minimum marginal cost function. The slower rate of growth of a bureau in this region is still higher than the rate of growth of a competitive industry facing increasing marginal costs. In this region, the budget per unit output increases rapidly, by an amount proportionate to the demand shift, regardless of the slope of the minimum marginal cost function.

A bureau, like a private monopoly, will often find it rewarding to try to shift its demand function. The incremental budget that would result from a demand shift will be particularly high in the demand-constrained output region. One would expect, therefore, that bureaucrats would spend a significant part of their time on various promotional activities, supported by the owners of specific factors.

Changes in the Demand Slope. Figure 3 illustrates the changes in a bureau's equilibrium output and budget, for given cost conditions, in response to changes in the slope of the demand function. The indicated changes in the intercept and slope are such that the output of a competitive industry, given the same cost conditions, would be constant at a level of 100 for each combination.

In the budget-constrained output region, the equilibrium output of a bureau will increase with increasing (negative) demand slopes; in the demand-constrained region, output will decline with increasing demand slopes. A bureau faced by a nearly horizontal demand function will produce an output at a budget per unit output only slightly higher than that of a competitive industry, but the total budget and the budget per unit output will increase monotonically with higher demand slopes. This suggests that a bureau may find it rewarding to try to increase the slope of the demand function for its output by promotional activities citing public "need" or military "requirement" to be fulfilled regardless of cost. A more important suggestion is that a bureau operating in a highly competitive output market would be relatively efficient. However, the present environment of bureaucracy—with severe constraints on the creation of new bureaus or new outputs by existing bureaus, and the passion of reformers to consolidate bureaus with similar output—seems diabolically designed

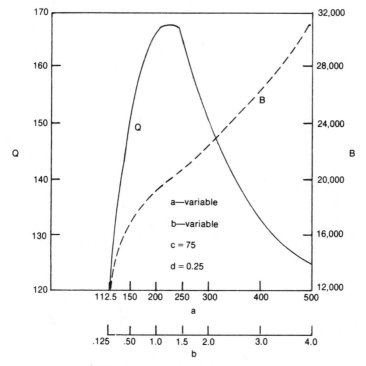

Figure 3. Effects of Changes in the Demand Slope.

to reduce the competition among bureaus and increase the inefficiency (and, not incidentally, the budget) of the bureaucracy.

Cost Shifts. Figure 4 illustrates the changes in a bureau's equilibrium output and budget, for given demand conditions, in response to shifts in the minimum marginal cost function.

In the budget-constrained output region, a downward shift of the minimum marginal cost function will increase the equilibrium output of a bureau at a rapid rate. A bureau producing an output at constant minimum marginal cost will grow at twice the rate of a competitive industry for the same downward cost shift. The bureau's budget will grow rapidly with the initial cost reductions and then very slowly as output approaches the demand-constrained output level. In the higher output region, further reductions in cost will not increase either the equilibrium output or budget.

These effects suggest that new bureaus or those facing exogenous

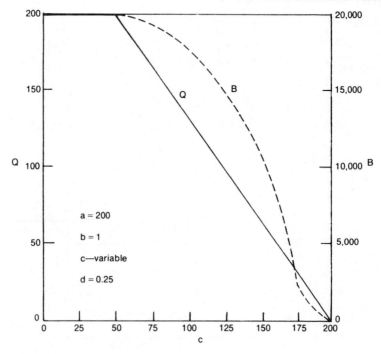

Figure 4. Effects of Cost Shifts.

increases in costs will be very cost conscious. Such bureaus will have an incentive to determine their minimum marginal cost function and to try to reduce the level of this function. Older bureaus or those facing a rapid increase in demand couldn't care less on either count. Tullock has been intrigued by the observation that bureaus both attempt to reduce costs and manifestly waste huge amounts of resources. This model suggests that, in equilibrium, a single-product bureau will be in one or the other of these conditions. A multiproduct bureau, such as Department of Defense, should be expected to attempt to reduce costs on the budget-constrained outputs and to assure that costs are sufficiently high to exhaust the obtainable budget on the demand-constrained outputs.

Changes in the Slope of the Minimum Unit Cost Function. Figure 5 illustrates the changes in a bureau's equilibrium output and budget, for given demand conditions, in response to changes in the slope of the minimum marginal cost function. The indicated changes in the intercept and slope are such that the output of a competitive industry, given the

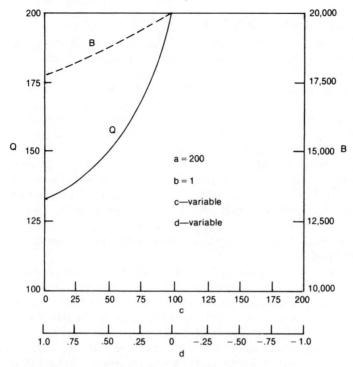

Figure 5. Effects of Changes in the Cost Slope.

same demand conditions, would be constant at a level of 100 for each combination.

In the budget constrained output region, the equilibrium output of a bureau that buys factors on a competitive market will increase with a reduction of the slope of the minimum unit cost function to a level, with constant unit costs, that is twice the output of a competitive industry. The bureau's budget will also increase with a reduction in the slope of this function, but relatively slowly. Both output and budget are invariant to changes in the slope of the cost function in the demand-constrained output region.

These effects suggest that bureaus may have an incentive to use production processes with a higher cost at low output levels and a lower cost at high output levels. In the static case, however, this incentive is not very strong and may be offset in part by pressure through the legislature from the owners of specific factors.

V. Critical Tests of this Model

This model suggests an image of a bureau with a level and rate of growth of output that is up to twice that of a competitive industry facing the same conditions. Demand by consumers may be the basis for establishing a bureau, but the interests of this group in preserving the bureau will diminish or disappear as the bureau creates no consumer surplus, except by negligence. A bureau, however, creates a substantially larger factor surplus than would a competitive industry, and the primary interests in continuing the bureau (or a war) are likely to originate from the bureau itself and the owners of specific factors. In the demand-constrained output region, a bureau's only concern about costs is to assure that they exhaust the obtainable budget. A bureau should be expected to engage in considerable promotion, in cooperation with the owners of specific factors, to augment the demand for its output, and to reduce—through persuasion, restrictions on entry, and consolidation—the elasticity of this demand.

These are serious charges. A set of critical tests of these assertions are difficult to pose. The best tests that I can conceive are to compare the output and costs of a bureau with those of a private firm with the same type of product. A comparison of the Social Security Administration and insurance companies, public and private hospitals, public and private statistics gathering organizations, or public and private police and garbage disposal services may be sufficient. Such tests, however, will be difficult as the existence of potential competition may present the bureau with a highly elastic demand, and some of the private firms producing a similar product have some of the characteristics of bureaus. A test of these assertions about a bureau that is the sole producer of a set of products, such as the Department of Defense, is even more difficult and probably more important. For such bureaus, an internal comparison at different points of time or, possibly, with bureaus producing a similar product in another political jurisdiction could be made.

VI. Further Implications for Analysis and Policy

Analytic Developments. The static model of a single-product bureau outlined in Section II should be extended in several dimensions. First, the consequences of the time-dimension of budget maximization should be developed. Louis DeAlessi's preliminary analysis suggests that a bureaucrat's concept of his property rights will lead to a preference for capital-intensive production processes. Second, the behavior of a multiproduct bureau that receives a single budget (or several budgets not specific to product type) should be explored. And third, the behavior of "mixed" bureaus, such as the Post Office, educational institutions, and public hospitals should be explored.

Policy Implications. This model of a bureau, if the suggested tests fail to disconfirm its assertions, has important implications for the organization for the production of the large and increasing proportion of our national output now produced by bureaus. What changes could be made to improve the efficiency of the production of these goods and services?

First, and probably most interesting, bureaucratic provision of these goods and services could be maintained, but each bureau would operate in a competitive environment and face a highly elastic demand function. The creation of new bureaus would be encouraged. Existing bureaus would be permitted and encouraged to produce products now provided by other bureaus. "Antitrust" restrictions would prevent collusive behavior to divide products or output among bureaus and to prevent the dominance of one bureau in a single product. The legislature would be willing to shift some part of the output of one agency to another, based on output and budget performance. The resulting bureaucracy would consist of many single and multiproduct bureaus without any obvious relation (in use) of the products offered by any single bureau. (As such, it would look a little like the corporate sector of our economy.)

Second, the incentives of bureaucrats could be changed to encourage them to minimize the budget for a given output or set of outputs. For example, the salaries of the top 5 percent of the personnel of a bureau could be a negative function of the budget of a bureau for a given set of outputs. This would still permit a political determination of the output level for the combination of bureaus providing the same product. Such a system would require more precise measurement of output than now, but would not require the monetary valuation of this output. Such a system may also attract better managers to the bureaucracy.

Third, the type of goods and services now provided by bureaus could be financed through government or foundations as is now the case, but the provision of these services would be contracted to private, profitseeking economic institutions. The bureaucracy, as such, would disappear, except for the review and contracting agencies. This system would also require better measures of output than now, but better measures are necessary for improved efficiency under any organizational form.

23. Divergences between Individual and Total Costs Within Government *

ROLAND N. McKEAN

It is a bit surprising to realize what different attitudes we have toward the private and public portions of the economy. This contrast is particularly marked with respect to divergences between individual and total costs or gains. By such divergences I mean differences between costs and rewards as perceived by decision-makers and total costs and rewards produced by their actions. These differences are often called external economies and diseconomies or, more briefly, spillover effects. They are impacts on others that are not taken into account by managers or individuals who take action.

Let me review our attitudes toward the two sectors in this respect. In the private sector we have assumed, first of all, that individuals are utility-maximizers. We have not claimed any precise knowledge of individuals' utility functions but have concluded that utility must be a function of many desired items, that there are trade-off or substitution possibilities among these items, and that, if one becomes more expensive relative to others, less of that item will be demanded. On this foundation, we have constructed most of economic theory, including many testable hypotheses.[1]

In this connection, we have believed that a producer recognizes costs he has to pay but is unlikely to recognize damages or resources used up for which he does not have to compensate anyone. He would have to sacrifice too many other things to make unnecessary compensations. For similar reasons we have assumed that a producer recognizes benefits for which customers compensate him but is unlikely to count other benefits that he does or could produce. Again it would be too costly in terms of other objectives. Indeed in a moderately competitive industry the sacrifice

Reprinted from *American Economic Review*, May 1964, pp. 243–249, by permission of publisher and author.

* I am greatly indebted to the Social Science Research Council for an award that made possible a larger study of governmental processes, from which the present paper stems.

1. The clearest discussion of these points that I know of is in an unpublished economics textbook by Armen A. Alchian. See also Armen A. Alchian and Reuben A. Kessel, "Competition, Monopoly, and the Pursuit of Money," in *Aspects of Labor Economics* (N.B.E.R., Princeton Univ. Press, 1962), pp. 157–83, and Gary S. Becker, *The Economics of Discrimination* (Univ. of Chicago Press, 1957).

entailed by a highly altruistic attitude would be bankruptcy. We have not meant, of course, that people always pursue self-interest narrowly defined. Rather we have meant that the higher the cost of pursuing one objective, the less of it one will try to achieve. Thus the more personal gain one sacrifices to be altruistic, the less altruism he will pursue. And the greater the divergence between individual and total costs and gains, the less likely one is to be guided by total costs and gains.

Second, with respect to the private sector, we have written and talked a great deal about ways to define property rights better or about other ways to intervene so as to induce people to take total costs and gains into account. In this writing and talking, a variety of issues has been explored. It has generally been accepted that it is not desirable for people to take pecuniary spillover effects into account. And some economists—especially Ronald Coase—have stressed that the cost of government intervention should itself be recognized—that divergences between individual and total costs in the private sector do not call for government intervention unless it would actually do more good than harm.[2] In any event, we have given quite a bit of attention to external economies and diseconomies in the private sector and what to do about them.

Third, it has not been uncommon to conclude that activities should be transferred to the public sector if serious divergences cannot be eliminated. As cities developed, for instance, it became obvious that private decisions had important spillover effects on other persons. Many concluded that the only thing to do was to have governments plan cities or, as cities grew older, plan their renewal. Flood control and education are also examples of activities that had significant external effects—divergences between individual and total costs and gains—and were placed to a considerable extent in the public sector. I am not suggesting that this was obviously a wrong solution—I am merely saying that we do often decide to turn to government in such instances. And even where lesser spillover effects occur, it is sometimes implied that, because the market system has "failed," the activity should be conducted by government.

In the public sector, however, our attitude has usually differed from the above. First, many of us, in our work, have tended to assume, unconsciously for the most part, that public officials are public-interest maximizers. In other words, we have assumed that government personnel pursue one type of gain and avoid one type of cost—those felt by the general public—and ignore other variables that would normally be in utility functions. To be sure, we have recognized the existence of outright graft

2. Ronald H. Coase, "The Problem of Social Cost," *J. of Law and Econ.*, Oct., 1960, pp. 1–44.

and corruption, attributing this to government personnel of another extreme variety—selfish-interest maximizers whose utility functions include a number of evil aims and little else. These evil men seem to be regarded as the exceptions that prove the general rule of public-interest maximizing. For some reason we have tended to neglect the intermediate possibilities: government officials who are ordinary utility-maximizers, with many items in their utility functions, with substitution possibilities existing among these items, and with negatively-sloped demand curves for each of these items. (Or, alternatively, government officials who are assumed for analytical purposes to have a smaller number of specific, though not wicked, aspirations.)

Second, given the above attitude, economists have naturally enough talked little about manipulating the costs of objectives sought by public officials so as to affect their behavior. We have talked little about rigging individual costs and rewards in government to make them more nearly consistent with total costs and rewards. Students of public administration and political science have searched for improvements in governmental organization, of course, implicitly seeking ways to bring individual criteria closer into line with higher-level criteria. Economists, however, have not given much attention to bargaining processes in government, the resulting cost-reward structures confronting officials, or ways to influence those cost-reward structures.[3]

Third, and again it is natural enough in view of the preceding remarks, we have rarely concluded that, because of gross divergences between individual and total costs or gains within government, certain activities should be shifted to the private sector. Again, I am not suggesting that

3. In recent years, though, there has been growing interest in economics as well as other social sciences in studying organizational behavior from vantage points of this sort. Some of the more directly relevant efforts are Armen Alchian's work on the implications for behavior of various kinds of property rights; E. C. Banfield, *Political Influence* (Free Press, 1961); James Buchanan and Gordon Tullock, *The Calculus of Consent* (Univ. of Michigan Press, 1962); R. A. Dahl and C. E. Lindblom, *Politics, Economics, and Welfare* (Harper & Brothers, 1953); Anthony Downs, *An Economic Theory of Democracy* (Harper & Brothers, 1957); George C. Homans, *Social Behavior: Its Elementary Forms* (Harcourt Brace, 1961); C. E. Lindblom, *Bargaining: The Hidden Hand in Government* (The RAND Corporation, RM-1434, 1955); Mancur Olson, Jr., "A General Theory of Public Goods" (Mar., 1963, unpublished manuscript); William Riker, *Theory of Political Coalitions* (Yale Univ. Press, 1962); Jerome Rothenberg's work in process on models of government behavior; Herbert A. Simon, *Administrative Behavior* (2d ed., Macmillan Co., 1961); J. G. March and H. A. Simon, *Organizations* (Wiley & Sons, 1958); and Gordon Tullock, "A General Theory of Politics" (unpublished manuscript). Also, this way of looking at organizational behavior, while often neglected, goes back a long way. For a review of the interest of one famous political economist in this subject, see Nathan Rosenberg, "Some Institutional Aspects of *The Wealth of Nations*," *J.P.E.*, Dec., 1960, pp. 557–70.

our policies have obviously been wrong. It simply strikes me as being a curious asymmetry in our thinking.

Or does each government official, in choosing his actions, weigh total gains to everyone against total costs to all? Is he unwilling to trade part of this objective for some degree of achievement along other lines? It may be true that public servants aim to promote the general interest more consistently than most other samples of the population. There is a selection process in the flow of personnel into any occupation, and those who choose public life may well be less selfish than most others. Nonetheless, it is unlikely that there is a sharp distinction between these two populations, especially since there are numerous transfers back and forth. Government officials too are surely utility-maximizers. They may attach less weight than others do to personal costs and gains and give greater consideration to the costs and benefits bestowed on strangers. But still, the greater the cost of achieving one aim, the less of it they will try to achieve; the greater the divergence between private and total costs, the less likely they are to reach decisions in the light of total costs. Moreover, to stay in office or to survive in the bureaucratic struggle, one cannot ceaselessly strive for the public interest. As in the competitive model, the cost is bankruptcy—this time career bankruptcy. The best one can hope for is that on balance he is "doing good" while compromising on many individual issues. A public official may not ask, "What can GNP do for me today?" but neither does he ask each morning, "What can I do for GNP?"

Even if civil servants and politicians do not constantly look at total costs and gains, however, are there serious divergences in government between private and total costs or gains? After all, there is a mechanism in any organization that forces each member to take into account many effects that might otherwise be externalities. This mechanism is the bargaining process, and it is crucial in making costs and gains felt by decision-makers in the public sector. It is similar in certain respects to the price mechanism, which is crucial in making costs and gains felt by decision-makers in the private sector. When a business firm takes action, it has to bargain with and compensate numerous persons who supply buildings, labor services, and other inputs. That is, if the firm's action uses up or damages property, the firm has to buy the consent of the owners. Wherever the firm's action has beneficial effects, the management tries to charge the beneficiaries. The greater the extent to which all these compensations are made, the less the extent to which the firm's costs and gains will diverge from total costs and gains. In government, similarly, if one official's action will use up someone's property or damage their interests, the official will probably find a cost associated with the action. He may endure embarrassing or expensive enmities, or suffer costly retaliations. One way or another he will have to bargain and pay a price, the size of which will depend on bargaining strengths and circumstances. If an official's action benefits a colleague or group, he will be able to bargain, tacitly if not explicitly, for some kind of *quid pro quo*. Thus the bargaining process can work in the direction of making individual costs and gains more nearly reflect total costs and gains.

In this grossly imperfect competition, however, the process does not work with much precision. Individual consumers have no incentive to put much effort into bargaining, for example, while advocates of tariffs, silver subsidies, or price-support programs have big stakes and develop powerful bargaining strengths. The process may lead to desirable things part of the time, for logrolling may help minorities protect their rights or achieve good things for which they are willing to pay a high price. In secret ballots, which could prevent any trading, majorities might well make laws to suppress individual rights for various minority groups. Perhaps many uneconomic or inequitable policies are simply part of the cost of protecting individual rights in a majority-rule society. But the main point is clear: this "price mechanism" in government performs most imperfectly. Often groups that in the aggregate are affected greatly, can bargain only weakly, and the "price-tags" that become attached to various actions are far from the "right" mark. Thus costs and gains as felt by officials can indeed diverge, and perhaps seriously, from total costs and gains.

It is fairly easy to think of examples. Consider the lease of rights to drill for oil in the deep waters offshore from Los Angeles. The City Council awarded such a lease several years ago. From the standpoints of at least a majority of the Council, the gains from this action outweighed the costs. When Mayor Yorty was elected, however, he felt differently. In fact he had the City Planning Commission zone most of these deep waters "for residential use only" to prevent any drilling; and then apparently considered awarding offshore leases for other ocean areas. In such situations it is hard to believe that everyone is looking at costs and rewards from the same overall viewpoint. It reminds me of the typesetter's Freudian slip when a New York paper stated in a different situation: "This will not hurt the mayor, some feel, in that he can say he was always on the side of the angles."

More seriously, though, in connection with almost any government decision, it is instructive to try putting yourself in various officials' places—Senator A, Governor B, Secretary of Department X, Chief of Branch Y—and imagining the gains and costs of alternative actions as you would perceive them. The magnitudes cannot be measured, but judgment suggests that serious divergences are pervasive, that checks and balances are crucial in preventing the outcomes from being disastrous, and that it may be possible to devise better bargaining arrangements yielding significantly improved cost-reward structures.

Perhaps the most important divergences between individual and total costs stem from the fact that government officials are spending other people's money., Almost no participant in the budget-formulation process is guided by a cost structure that is in line with total costs. The deck appears to be stacked in favor of gradual budget growth. First, there are groups of firms and individuals who find it worth while to press for favors. (One of the failures of marginal productivity theory is to consider the marginal productivity of effort devoted to obtaining favors from government.) Second, government personnel find these and other expansions attractive. For example, if the head of a bureau or department gets an increased budget, he reaps significant rewards: he can do a better job, or satisfy pressure groups, have greater influence, increase his chances for advancement, and so on. The costs include mainly effort devoted to appeasing rival department heads (usually by making his strategy consistent with the growth of other departments too), and efforts devoted to getting congressional support. If anything akin to the real resource cost enters into the calculations, it must do so by way of constraints from above.

When we turn to control by top levels of the executive branch, however, we find that here, too, spending other people's money pays. A government can win support by spending in strategic places and spreading the cost thinly over a large group of taxpayers. Tacit coalitions arise, and the restraint once exercised by Treasury Control in Great Britain and by the Bureau of the Budget here is gradually eroded.[4] But what about the top legislative body? Do members of Congress feel the real resource costs and transmit to government a corresponding constraint? No, as long as they do not go wild, they too can get more points by judicious spending than by voting against tax increases. Imagine that you are a senator, and compare the points you would score if, apparently singlehanded, you promoted a home state river project with the points you would rack up if you, along with several hundred other representatives and senators, reduced each voter's tax bill by $10.

4. See W. Drees, Jr., *On the Level of Government Expenditure in the Netherlands after the War* (H. E. Stenfert Kroese, N.V., Leiden, 1955), pp. 61–71; Alan T. Peacock and Jack Wiseman, *Growth of Public Expenditure in the United Kingdom* (Report of the N.B.E.R., Princeton Univ. Press, 1961); and Alan T. Peacock, "Economic Analysis and Government Expenditure Control," in Alan T. Peacock and D. J. Robertson (eds.), *Public Expenditure Appraisal and Control* (Oliver & Boyd, Edinburgh, 1963).

So much for this fragment of cost-reward structures within government. What about the taxpayer? Doesn't he feel the real resource costs and bargain for restraint? Let us look at the costs and rewards, from his standpoint, of pressing for tax reduction or opposing a tax increase. The gains from success in such an endeavor might amount to $100, but the probability of an individual influencing the outcome is infinitesimal. The expected gains from an individual's effort to oppose a tax increase, therefore, are virtually zero. In these circumstances, how much effort will he devote to bargaining?

Thus it may be that no one feels a cost that adequately reflects the real cost of budget increases. It is hardly surprising, therefore, to find that you as taxpayers are helping to put up a million dollars to rebuild the town of Wink, Texas, and half a million dollars to build a stadium in Bridgeport, Connecticut. Some people regard the latter example as being symbolic because Bridgeport was the original home of P. T. Barnum. But even if you believe such federal subsidies are wrong, no one is necessarily being a sucker, and no one is necessarily behaving in a reprehensible fashion. Gradual expansion of central government is probably where utility-maximization leads with the divergences between individual and total costs that exist under present institutional arrangements.

What can and should be done to reduce such divergences? Many devices may be worth considering: e.g., having numerous congressmen-at-large, elected by the whole nation; agreeing, because of our long-run interests, to have paid oppositions; or agreeing to have a "taxpayers' union," with closed shop and check-off system. Perhaps most of all at this point, though, we need to acquire a better understanding of the costs and rewards that organizational personnel find attached to alternative choices. In our familiar competitive model with its cost-reward structures, utility-maximization leads to fairly good outcomes. When you put governmental units (or an international community of governments!) into the model, however, where does utility-maximization lead? And where would it lead under modified arrangements affecting the various divergences between individual and total costs and gains?

B. PROBLEMS OF INFORMED VOTING

24. A Program for Direct and Proxy Voting in the Legislative Process *

JAMES C. MILLER III

People often speak of "participatory democracy" and other direct voting schemes in the context of local affairs,[1] but on a national as well as a state level we nearly always make legislative decisions through elected representatives. Why do we resort to representative democracy over public referendum? We may identify at least three interrelated reasons.[2] In the first place, space and time limitations rule out all but the smallest meetings. For instance, as New England town meetings become large, they grow into unruly mobs, inefficient in making public decisions. A second reason is that few people feel they have the expertise to make intelligent decisions on a wide variety of public issues. Few people, for example, are military experts, capable of deciding upon the necessity of a proposed anti-ballistic missile system; neither are most people trained in political economy. Because of this lack of expertise, people elect representatives whom they feel are competent to judge such matters and who will vote as they would if only they possessed such knowledge. A third reason for representation over direct voting is that it takes time to research and to decide upon public issues. Time is a scarce resource, and just to vote on all public issues would take much of an average person's time. (Indeed, we find that a major problem in securing large voter turnout is the opportunity cost of making the trip to the polls.)

Keeping in mind these reasons for representative democracy, let us consider a program for making compatible the better features of direct voting with the practical necessity of some representation.

Reprinted from *Public Choice,* Fall 1969, pp. 107–113, by permission of the publisher and author.

* The author wishes to acknowledge helpful comments from James M. Buchanan, Roger Sherman, Gordon Tullock, and Thomas D. Willett on an earlier version of this piece. Responsibility for errors and opinions remains, of course, with the author.

1. For an analysis of a particular circumstance, see Madelyn L. Kafoglis, "Participatory Democracy in the Community Action Program," *Public Choice,* Vol. V (Fall 1968), pp. 73–85.

2. For a comprehensive analysis of the problems of collective decision-making, see James M. Buchanan and Gordon Tullock, *The Calculus of Consent* (Ann Arbor: University of Michigan Press, 1962), esp. Part II.

I. The Proposal [3]

Through the researches of many, too numerous to mention here, problems of aggregating individual voter preferences are better understood, making (in theory, at least) public decision-making more efficient. And although the costs of collective decision-making remain high, we must face up to the fact that communication costs have been falling and it is now possible for a large number of people to express their opinions simultaneously.[4] Especially, one marvels at the advancing technology of electronic computers, indicating devices, and recording equipment. Some, in fact, have predicted that within 20 or 30 years every home will have a console tied into a computer upon which the children do their homework, the housewife will make out her grocery list, and the husband will pay the family's bills. Such a computer console also could be used to record political decisions, giving each voter an opportunity to cast his ballot on every issue and have it recorded through the machine. Safeguards, of course, would have to be installed so that no one could record decisions on the machine except its owner. For instance, a special metal key, a coded combination, or even a thumbprint might be required to operate the machine. Thus, the first feature of the proposal is a recording console for each voter upon which he may directly register his decisions on public issues.

Our Constitution calls for a bicameral legislature, and representatives in one body reflect constituencies of nearly equal population whereas in the other, expressing more or less in some measure the geographical and political autonomy of the several states, they reflect constituencies of unequal size. Votes in the two bodies are tallied in terms of the number of *representatives* favoring or objecting to the proposals. Actually, there is no reason why such votes could not be tallied in terms of the total number of *voters represented*. If direct voting (such as described above) were allowed, then final votes in Congress could be tallied with each and every voter's ballot decision being anonymously registered. Voting weights would remain the same as they are today. Whether voting is direct or by representation, my vote would be registered in the House tally among the other millions of votes, while in the Senate my "vote" would be counted as something less than a full vote, since Georgia has a voting population

3. Although the product of independent research, the proposal outlined here could be called an advance on the scheme suggested by Gordon Tullock in *Toward a Mathematics of Politics* (Ann Arbor: University of Michigan Press, 1967), Chapter X.

4. For example, in many localities television stations announce a controversial topic early in the evening; viewers then telephone in their positive or negative "votes" on the issue, and the results are announced at a later hour.

slightly greater than the national average. Thus, the second feature of the proposal is a provision for direct registering of voter decisions.

Another characteristic of our legislative system is that the elected representative votes on behalf of all people, in his district at all times, regardless of his degree of competence in the various matters of national concern. But this need not be the case: instead of electing representatives periodically for a tenure of two years or more, why not allow citizens to vote directly *or delegate proxy to someone else* for as long as they like (which is, of course, analogous to stockholder voting schemes in large corporations). Actually, there would be a wide range of alternatives available. The most concerned voter would vote on every issue at his personal console. Another may delegate proxy to someone he feels would vote as he would if only he had the time and knowledge to participate directly. Most voters, however, would utilize some combination of these extremes, voting on major issues personally and delegating proxy to someone else for the minor decisions. Thus, the third feature of the proposal is a provision for proxy as well as direct voting.

If voting is to be both direct and by proxy, what form will the actual debating and action-taking body (i.e., Congress) take? There still could be a House and a Senate, but representatives would not be chosen as they are now. At any point in time, there would be individuals—professional proxy voters or "politicians"—who have delegated to them from the entire voting population a number of proxy votes.[5] Ranking representatives each day according to the size of their constituency and choosing arbitrary cut-off members of, say, 400 for the House and 100 for the Senate, those 400 representatives having the most proxy votes for the House would sit in the House, and those 100 having the most Senate proxy votes would sit in the Senate. Of course, all proxy holders would cast votes, but only those with extremely large constituencies actually would sit in Congress and debate the issues. Thus, the fourth and final feature of the proposal is a provision for the maintenance of the congressional body via the proxy vote mechanism.

II. Merits of the Proposal

It has been pointed out that there are several reasons for having some representation in democratic decision processes, and there are, at once, a number of various institutional arrangements that come to mind, ranging from the town meeting to the election of a single representative to act as virtual dictator for a specified period of time. Our present system repre-

---

5. These professionals could receive remuneration, either through direct government payment (in some proportion to the number of proxy votes they held) or through fees paid by the individual voters.

sents a middle ground, but it is important to note that this middle ground is *the* system for everyone and it lacks flexibility. Let us consider a few features of the present system and contrast these with the proposed program. Under our present legislative system:

1. Representatives are elected on an all-or-nothing basis and represent or vote on behalf of their entire constituency whether supported by 100 percent of the voters or merely by 51 percent.

2. Representatives are chosen for a period of at least two years and continue to vote on behalf of their constituency—except for rare instances—even though at times their support might fall well below 51 percent.

3. Representatives vote on every single issue, regardless of the nature of the problem and their lack of competence or expertise.

4. Representatives stand for specific geographical areas of the country and must be indigenous to them.

One hears the cry, "one man, one vote" often these days and the point is usually raised with regard to the disenfranchisement of certain minority groups. However, in one important respect our present system would not be one-man-one-vote even under universal voter franchise. If a Democratic representative is elected from a certain district in Georgia, then theoretically he votes for and on behalf of those in his district. But in actuality, he mostly votes on behalf of those people who elected him. Suppose he is elected by a margin of 60-40. If I am a member of that dissenting 40 percent, then my judgment is registered little if at all. When the representative votes on a major issue, he does not cast 60 percent of his vote one way and 40 percent the other, but he casts it all affirmative or all negative (or, of course, he abstains from voting entirely). Where the membership of Congress is fairly evenly divided along political and ideological lines, it is possible that neither the House majority nor the Senate majority will reflect the composite judgment of the majority of the voting populace due to random elements or gerrymandering.

Under the proposal each voter's wishes at least would be registered in the final tally. Obviously, if my vote in the final tally is a minority one, then my personal wishes have little effect, just as if I had voted for a defeated candidate. But what is important is that my vote is reflected in the most direct way possible—the final tally—and not through the two-step process of representation.

Suppose for a moment that voting is not direct, but through proxy only. As a simple example, suppose that my district elects a Democrat, 60-40, and the adjacent district elects a Republican, 60-40. In essence, it may be argued that the two districts are fairly represented: the minority in one district is represented in the final tally by the majority winner in the other. But this is not quite the case. The majority winner in each district is answerable only to the majority voters in that district which elected him; he is in no way answerable to voters in the adjacent district. But under the proposed scheme, the 60 percent in one district could cast their proxies for a particular representative along with the 40 percent from the adjacent district (in addition to any number of other voters) and thus each voter would have a representative answerable to him, and each representative would be answerable to the whole of his constituency.

Under our present bicameral legislature, representatives in the House are chosen for a period of two years, while in the Senate they serve a term of six years. Only in very rare instances—a recall or Congressional refusal to deem the elected official qualified for office—is a people's representative forced out of office. But obviously there are many instances where a representative loses the support of his constituency and (if we are to be true to the ideal of representation) is not casting the appropriate votes and should be replaced by someone who will.[6]

Under the proposal, the representative would be subject to instant recall by each and every voter. If a representative did not maintain the approval of those whose proxy votes he held, he would have them withdrawn and would find himself no longer a representative (unless, of course, he picked up proxy votes somewhere else). Such recall would be on a day-to-day or even an hour-to-hour basis. In a way, such a scheme probably would allow greater freedom for a representative to practice statesmanship and vote his conscience. Under the present system a representative must conform his general actions to the wishes of his (regional) supporters in order to be reelected. But under the proposal, if a representative's ideas on policy issues changed and he conscientiously decided to reverse his stand, he could remain a representative by gathering proxy support from others holding the same general position.

Presently, representatives in the House and Senate vote on a wide variety of proposals, ranging from anti-ballistic missiles to subsidies for the

---

6. Some will argue that in such a case the representative should not be replaced, for it is only when he loses the support of his voters—acting on conscience—that he truly exercises "statesmanship." But it is begging the issue to point out *ex post* one who took the "right" (or perhaps lucky) action rather than follow the will of his constituency. Besides, it is quite likely that if the constituency trusts the representative's judgment it will remain with him even in the face of short-run dissatisfaction. On this, also see the next paragraph.

fine arts. A voter, if he is to choose intelligently on issues, must be an expert in each field. Likewise, a representative should be an expert, or at least competent, in each field. Just having the testimony of experts usually is not sufficient evidence upon which to make an intelligent decision. It is also necessary to weigh and perhaps determine the validity of the arguments these experts present. But it is not possible to be an expert on all matters; not since John Stuart Mill and Benjamin Franklin have there been individuals reasonably expert on all matters within the domain of public decision-making. Under the proposed legislative scheme, voters need not be experts in each field; neither should representatives. The way is open for the individual voter to give his proxy to a military expert whom he trusts to cast a vote as he would if only he had the required military expertise. At another time, the voter might delegate his proxy to an economist to decide upon issues affecting employment and inflation. The advantages of this provision are obvious. The committee system in use today is an effort to reach some sort of expertise on particular matters, but contrast quasi-experts on Senate and House committees hearing evidence on the National Aeronautics and Space Administration with a congress of seasoned specialists, chosen by the electorate, discussing the direction and possibilities for further experimentation. Not that the electorate would choose only spokesmen for the agencies being heard (as is the constant danger with ''expert'' testimony today), but hopefully they would select moderate, reasonable men to pass on the desirability of proposed ventures and changes in the law.[7]

Members of Congress currently represent specific geographical areas (districts or States) and must be indigenous to them. However, few political observers would argue that there is a uniform distribution of political talent across the country. Under the proposed scheme, there is no reason why a person living in one state might not give his proxy to someone indigenous to another state. Besides the distribution of competency, some areas of the country seem to generate an abundance of individuals of one ideological persuasion, while in other areas leaders tend to maintain a different slant on the issues. With the proposed scheme, each voter would, in his own conscience, choose as proxy (if indeed he chose a proxy) that individual from over all the nation that best reflected his own point of view.

Politics, it is often said, is the art of compromise. It might be argued that under the proposed program compromises would be impossible to conclude, for as soon as a proxy-representative voted in a compromise he

7. Obvious possibilities would exist for the formation of private-enterprise political ''parties.'' Such establishments would maintain a staff of experts and would base voting decisions on their recommendations.

would have his proxy-vote power withdrawn. But this is not necessarily true. A representative who compromises on issues of lesser importance to his supporters in order to gain advantage in areas of greater importance will retain his support, for those who give him their proxy will realize, through open communication if need be, that the final settlement is preferable to an all-or-nothing decision. In short, possibilities would remain for compromise and cooperative voting.

III. A Specific Limitation

The major weakness of the proposal is the lack of a specifically-formulated administrative structure for generating the public bills and bringing them in an orderly fashion to a vote. In other words, nothing has been offered to replace the bulk of the work now done by Congressional committees. Actually, some of this work would be unnecessary under the proposed scheme; for instance, lengthy hearings would be of less value since those voting on issues naturally would be, in the eyes of the voters, experts in the field. But some arrangement must be worked out for providing the bills and compiling the voting agenda. The agenda, especially, should receive much thought, for the voters must be made aware, via television monitor or other device, of the times the various bills will be called up for consideration so that they may plan their voting activities. This is not to say, of course, that no institutional solution exists; merely none is specified here.[8]

IV. Conclusion

This paper has argued that changing technology has increased opportunities for voter participation in the legislative process and has presented a proposal which takes some advantage of such possibilities. The objective has not been so much to criticize our present legislative voting arrangement, but to suggest for the future an alternative that might prove superior.

The New Left balks at the "establishment," and conservatives look with dismay upon the "liberal clique." Direct participation largely would solve these problems, by-passing intermediaries and allowing direct voter or voter-proxy approval of all legislation. If we accept the principal that, with constitutional guarantees, qualified individuals should determine as democratically and as directly as possible the decisions that affect their personal and corporate welfare, then the future holds opportunities for greater efficiency in collective action.

8. Another objection to the proposal often raised in private conversation is that it may prove to be an extremely unstable institution because of the instant recall feature. The question is whether elected representatives are more constant in their attitudes toward issues than

25. On *Homo Politicus* and the Instant Referendum

MARTIN SHUBIK

On Models and Political Man

It is the purpose of this note to suggest a crude categorization of the types of "political man" in our society and to suggest some of the implication of this categorization for the future of the instant referendum. In a recent issue of *Public Choice,* James C. Miller [1] wrote in somewhat optimistic terms about the possibilities of the new technology. I believe that some sort of computerized participation by large numbers of the public in opinion formation and direct policy making is in the cards in the next ten to twenty years. It may be that we will be able to turn this new technology to the improvement and defense of democratic institutions. I hope so. However, it is by no means evident that this will be the result.

Model building in political science is a hazardous art. Bare-bones, elegant simplicity is often appealing but inadequate. Models of man with considerable institutional detail tell a better story, but frequently as detail is piled in they become a mere story of a special case from which little if anything can be deduced.

Anthony Downs in his stimulating work, *An Economic Theory of Democracy,* [2] sketched a series of very enticing models of voting and other political processes. These models, while not mathematical in structure, were parsimonious in description and were presented in a form that makes further formalization a desirable and natural step. In contradistinction with this work, the further work of Downs on bureaucracy as well as the approaches of Cyert and March, Crecine and others to bureaucracy have gone in the direction of the construction of models of considerable detail. The behavioral approach, while having much to recommend it, ap-

---

are voters in general. To me the answer is not obvious, but there is some presumption in favor of instability. Since those responsible for actions are likely to be more moderate, this is to argue that representatives would be more stable than voters; yet under the proposal, the individual voter would have direct responsibility that he does not now have.

Reprinted from *Public Choice,* Fall 1970, pp. 79–84, by permission of the publisher and author.

1. J. C. Miller III. "A Program for Direct and Proxy Voting in the Legislative Process," *Public Choice* 7 (Fall 1969), 107–113.

2. New York: Harper & Row, 1957.

pears to be directed towards answering different questions someone might wish to answer with a more sparse analytical model.

In the behavioral sciences in general, it is a safe axiom that the correct model is very much a function of the question to be answered. A theory of bureaucracy needs to be developed undoubtedly. However, a theory of bureaucracy should not be confused with economic theory or with political theory. There are many political and economic questions which may be answered without having to become too deeply enmeshed with bureaucratic structure or detailed institutional information.

In particular, it appears to me that a fruitful way to modify political theory and economic theory is to go to a half-way house by keeping simple models, yet introducing in a parsimonious manner a restricted set of new variables and parameters to reflect some of the richness of the environment without immediately being swamped in the details of the process. The introduction of four or five types of political man might be a first step in this direction.

Robert Dahl,[3] in his perceptive study of the functionings of democracy from New Haven, categorized the political activity of the electorate into several different classes ranging from those actively seeking office to those who were basically not interested in the political process. Following this type of analysis, it appears to me that we can start to examine some of the possible implications of computerized voting.

In particular, I would like to suggest a categorization of five types of political behavior. In terms of the theory of games, two of the categories can be described as active "players" with strategic power; the third is a player with very little strategic power; and the fourth and fifth may be regarded as primarily behavioral mechanisms.

Class 1: The first category consists of the politically active, those who run for public office, and, if they are elected, the office becomes their major occupation during that period.

Class 2: Individuals whose livelihood and day-to-day existence depend in a direct and visible way on the political process. This includes high echelon governmental bureaucrats as well as many of the party functionaries and those actively engaged in running the patronage system. Included also are active lobbyists.

Class 3: In many societies there is a group of individuals who through education or indoctrination "take their politics seriously" even though they do not have a direct stake in the political process. There are those who both read and think about political problems. They can be character-

3. *Who Governs?* New Haven: Yale University Press, 1961.

ized as being moderately well informed and possessing a value system and a position concerning a fair number of political questions. They are to some extent analogous with the intelligent buyer in economic theorizing. Such individual has well-formed preferences and is rather well informed about his choices. However, he has rather limited short-run power over the market and is more or less constrained to acting as an intelligent price-taker.

Class 4: The fourth and fifth categories are those individuals who do not explicitly view themselves as conscious, active, calculating players in the game of politics. The first, and in the United States undoubtedly the largest of these two final categories, consists of those who view themselves as part of the political process and may frequently vote; however, their vote may depend more upon habit, custom, hearsay, ethnic or religious affiliations, and a host of other sociological variables rather than on the active application of time and effort in a manner which we might categorize as conscious problem-solving.

Class 5: This category consists of those individuals who implicitly or subconsciously do not regard themselves as part of the political process. They have accepted the role of "Indian" or Chinese or Jewish trader, or officially or unofficially disenfranchised minority group and do not participate in the political game as insiders.

This sketch of categories is intended neither to be totally complete nor necessarily utterly independent. For example, there are those among minority groups who consciously feel that they are disenfranchised, and do not wish to play in the political game, by those controlling "the house." Yet, nevertheless, they are actively concerned with overthrowing the current political system.

Even with these crude categories, however, we may start to explore some of the implications for an enriched political theory. The strategic models of the political process should contain the first two categories as the powerful players, the third category as strategically relatively powerless in the short run but with considerable potential in the long run, and the fourth and fifth categories are important inasmuch as their behavior can be influenced and possibly predicted by the other three.

It should not be assumed that the fourth and fifth categories bear any pejorative connotations. Reading the *New York Times* or keeping tabs on what the Secretary of State is doing is a time-consuming occupation. It is not difficult to make out a case in favor of being extremely politically inactive except in times of perceived utter emergency.

What does the distribution of the population into these categories look like? Making a pure guess, I suggest that in the United States Category 1 contains somewhat less than 0.1% of the population; Category 2 contains around 0.5% of the population; Category 3 might contain between 2% to 4% (where by population we mean the voting population); Category 4 around 80% and Category 5 around 15%. In a country such as Sweden, I suspect that the first two categories are approximately the same; the third category might be as high as between 3% to 8%, and the fourth category accounts for the remainder, with the fifth category virtually empty. In a country such as Peru, we might expect the fifth category to account for virtually the whole of the Indian population.

A key to the understanding of the political processes in the modern democratic world appears to be the understanding of the fourth and fifth classes of voters noted. Voter profiles are notoriously hard to obtain and even more difficult to interpret. Perhaps one of the things that has preserved a reasonable degree of democracy in many of our democratic states has been our lack of success in finding out what makes the Class 4 voter "tick." Fortunately, or unfortunately, it is possible that the behavioral sciences are improving to the extent that in the course of the next ten years there will be some moderately accurate answers to that question. Even without the answers, a change in communication technology may easily have a profound and conceivably dangerous effect on the functioning of the political system if the categorization of the political actors is anywhere near correct.

Information, Instant Referenda and the Democratic Process

It is my belief that the third voter class is critical to the functioning of a democratic system. Its power comes in its direct ability to influence the behavior of the fourth voter category and thereby influence those who control the political machinery. It has a certain amount of influence in the short run where the short run may be defined as a period of a few months. The major influence is in the long run where the long run refers to a period involving several years or more. The third voter type has virtually no influence whatsoever in processes which can be accomplished in a few weeks or less. In particular, the informed politically active and responsible voter can have virtually no influence on the behavior of his neighbors if such ultimates of misinterpretation of the democratic system as the instant referendum become possible. The time lags in the political process are precisely the critical periods needed to enable other influences to modify the instantaneous response of an unpremeditating voter. The power of the thoughtful voter comes in his ability to utilize the time lags in the political system to modify simplistic reactions to complex problems.

Communications technology will soon achieve a level of excellence when it will become possible to more or less wipe out the time lags in voter processes in referenda and in survey procedures. In doing so, the power of the consciously active voter may be attenuated to no more than his vote. This will result in an even greater concentration of power in the less than 1/2% of the voting population in the first two classes.

It would be false to present the new technology as only a force for evil. In particular, the population as a whole and the third class of voters in particular stand to gain considerably from availability of data banks on political issues. A natural and valuable contribution of computer technology would be to have files set up in timesharing systems on major issues with a multi-partisan committee in control, so that all sides have the opportunity to stock the files with their versions of "the facts." Further TV coverage could also be constructive.

Some Questions, Answers, and a Suggestion

Political problems are in general complicated. Adequate solutions to political problems are also usually complicated. Elegant and simple answers are more characteristic of quiz programs than they are of political life.

A general development of political theorizing which takes into account uncertainty, information costs and nonrational behavior is urgently needed to provide the basis for answering the many questions that will be posed to us by a huge population and advanced communications technology society.

Question: Is the instantaneous referendum economically and technologically eventually feasible? If it is, will this be desirable?

Answer: Given the growth of timesharing systems in the next ten to twenty years, it should be economically feasible to have the voting population cast their ballots via a timesharing system on virtually any subject at very little cost within a few days. The odds that it will be used are large. Without the appropriate controls this procedure could, in my estimation, prove disastrous to the democratic process.

A Suggestion: One possible form of control would be to have legislation which requires that any referendum be put to the public twice with a time lag of not less than six weeks between the two pollings. The time for debate and questioning and for influence of the independent voter on his fellow voters and on the political system in general must be preserved if the democratic system is to be preserved.

Technologists and hairdressers value neatness and elegance in and of themselves. Both of these qualities are desirable when they can be had.

Politics, however, in general, is neither neat nor elegant. Political man is not a neat, utilitarian abstraction. However, at the same time he is, also, not only a welter of special cases. The pressures of modern technology and of population are going to force the development of an operational political science as well as a rethinking through of the concepts of the democratic process if such a process is to survive.

Communications technology and population growth are forcing upon us the need to consider changes in our voting processes. Geographical contiguity of an electorate is no longer as important as it was. Simplicity of procedures, while still desirable, is no longer necessary. However, when we are confronted with added technological possibilities we must become more conscious of the gap between our theories and the realities of political behavior. I do not wish to suggest that Miller or others who foresee the great new possibilities of computerized voting are wrong. I wish to stress, however that the growth of the technology has raised far more problems than it has solved. In particular, we cannot estimate the results of change without first asking ourselves what does *Homo Politicus* look like.

26. Representative Democracy via Random Selection *

DENNIS C. MUELLER, ROBERT D. TOLLISON, and THOMAS D. WILLETT

It has been generally accepted in political science literature that no matter the advantages of full participatory (town meeting) democracy, for a large polity, such as almost any country, this form of government is not feasible. Hence, on purely technical grounds the closest that a country like the United States could come to a pure democracy would be representative government of some form. In a recent article in this journal [12], James C. Miller, III, pointed out that given present rates of technological advance, it may not be long before this technical constraint will not be binding for rich countries such as the United States, at least in the

Reprinted from *Public Choice,* Spring 1972, pp. 57–68, by permission of the publisher and authors.

* Useful comments were made on an earlier version of this paper by Professors James M. Buchanan, Edward Burton, C. M. Lindsay, J. C. Miller, III, Roger Sherman, and Gordon Tullock. Responsibility for any errors remains with the authors.

sense of conducting national referenda.[1] Miller proposes to employ referenda along with "proxy politicians," whose function is to represent blocs of voters on issues and to be subject to instant recall by them, as an alternative to present forms of representation. The goal of such a reform is to give primary control over democratic process to the voters.

In a subsequent paper [23] Martin Shubik questioned the desirability of Miller's proposal on the grounds that there is a wide disparity in the information possessed by various types of voters. Shubik's argument turns on a fear of getting "uninformed" choices in national referenda from a wide cross-section of voters and is closely related to the classic problems of obtaining adequate debate before voting or collecting opinions in a poll.[2] Shubik raised the correct issue because, if anything, the average complexity of public issues has increased over the same period that the technical capacity to conduct large referenda has been developed. The time costs of having the general public cast votes based on reasonable levels of information is still high, if not higher than in earlier periods. Thus, one could argue that the case for delegating authority to "experts" has increased. In this paper we extend the thrust of Shubik's argument to discuss how one can combine the advantages of collecting decentralized information through polling with the efficiency of representation and suggest a system of representation that we feel would yield a better mix of efficiency and information than either the present, geographic-based national legislature or Miller's referenda system.

I.

Proposals for holding a national town meeting via computer technology to obtain actual choices under some voting rule or to obtain advisory opinions on certain issues are open to objection on several grounds. To the pure elitist some people may be wiser, more intelligent, more moral, and so on. Hence, these persons "should" lead. However, even to one who wants to follow a form of democratic procedure, there will remain certain specialized or technical knowledge required for representation, and some members of the society may be more experienced in the "ways of government" (e.g., parliamentary procedure), perhaps due to professional necessity as in the case of the lawyer. Finally, and importantly, it is tremendously costly for everyone to become generally informed and to listen to the argument of experts, and where there is a need for quick legislative action, this problem would be compounded. Advanced tech-

1. For the mention of a similar proposal, see [20, p. 84] and the reference cited there. Also, for a general discussion of public policy toward emerging communications technology, see [17].

2. See, for example, the discussion in [4].

nology helps reduce these problems by lowering the money cost and increasing the speed and ease with which information could be received by the polity and their votes registered. But short of major advances in the efficiency with which individuals can absorb information, the value of the time the polity would have to expend in becoming reasonably well informed on political issues would remain staggering.[3] In essence, the principle of the division of labor implies that some degree of representation will generally be efficient, and all the reasons for representation that we have discussed here are variants of this principle.[4]

The reason that this elementary view of representation is important in the case of national referenda is because of the information possessed by the various individual voters. Political representatives who specialize in political activity will probably have more and a different mix of information on public issues than their constituents. One might argue in this case that the representative ought to educate his constituents, or distribute the different information that he has to them. Nonetheless, a difference in the information possessed by the representative and by his constituents seems inevitable in a system of political specialization.[5] Thus, if the populace is sampled, choices based on a different quality of information than if representatives decide will be obtained. Which method is better? This depends, among other things, on the amount and mix of information that one feels it necessary for decisionmakers to have and how representatives are chosen, and such decisions would be among the more important ones made in a constitutional period. Clearly, however, the possibility for different political outcomes is possible as between some form of representation and the national town meeting due to differences in the information possessed by the decisionmakers in each case.

Much of the interest in a national referendum procedure stems from dissatisfaction with the present form of national representation. One of

3. Of course, in calculating the cost of becoming informed, one should exclude the time spent talking politics and the like, which individuals expend directly for its enjoyment value. On the money or economic value of time see [1] and [22], and the references cited in these papers.

4. The sense in which we speak of efficiency here is that it is very costly for voters to become informed, and the gains over present forms of representation from having a political system where the responsibility for making informed decisions rests with the voters are probably nil. Also, the gains in terms of more accurate reflection of the underlying array of preferences of the polity are probably very slight.

5. Miller seeks to avoid this problem, as previously noted, by having socalled proxy politicians. This is an interesting proposal, but in addition to relying on the voters to become informed on issues as Shubik points out, Miller fails to clarify fully how his system would operate. What would happen to lobbyists? What would happen to party structure? What would be the role of bureaus? What would be the reaction of the media under such a system? It might well turn out in realistic circumstances that these proxy politicians are not such "proxies" after all.

the major problems with the present form of national representation, which is compounded by the monopolistic seniority system in the Congress, is its geographic base.[6] Tying representation to location gives rise to the much discussed incentives to logroll for the home district, forcing the polity into negative-sum games. Purely national issues presumably have no representatives except the President and Vice-President who are the only nationally elected officials in the present system, and even in this case there is considerable implicit logrolling via campaign platforms that serves to vitiate the President's ability to take a purely national stance on many issues. A related problem is that possibly intense minorities, which are not geographically concentrated, may not be represented at all where representation is based on geography and legislators are constrained to cast one vote per issue. Not is there any check that voters are reasonably informed in their voting choice, and there is considerable evidence that they frequently are not.[7] This results (at least in part) from the time costs of becoming informed through debate or otherwise in a specialized and complex world, and as stressed by Downs [7] and others, this may be quite rational. This defect in political procedure will persist so long as at some stage choices about representatives or policies are taken *directly* to the people. So a proposal, for example, to elect a national house of representatives from an at-large list of candidates would suffer from the same problem. Another problem with the present representative forms is that in a large number setting the individual voters may feel powerless to affect outcomes and may rationally decide to abstain on these grounds.[8] Finally,

6. For a more extensive proposal to deal with the following problems, see [15].

7. One of the more interesting examples of this—as an alternative to such perennial findings as that a sizable portion of citizens polled respond that the Bill of Rights may be considered subversive (when it is quoted to them without citation), or that "From each according to his ability, to each according to his needs" is a Biblical quotation—is the poll taken by one of the major television networks immediately preceding the 1968 New Hampshire Presidential primary which discovered that a majority of the voters polled did not know that Eugene McCarthy was a "dove" candidate. For a survey stressing that U.S. voters are typically not well informed on public issues, see [8]. For a discussion of the degree of public information and ignorance about fiscal variables, see [5, Chapter 13] and the references cited there.

8. Perhaps pure forms of democracy may be defended on the grounds that voters learn over time. This may be the case, but where you have rational abstention, democratic outcomes are controlled by less than the whole collectivity. Who actually controls in these circumstances is a function of the costs of voting and the individual's perceived stake in the outcomes. One way to handle the problem of non-voting would be to have poll payments instead of poll taxes. To the extent that the failure to vote is a reflection of a divergence between the private and social gains from democratic participation, this proposal would be appropriate to apply. Such a policy would not, however, guarantee informed voting, but only voting. To obtain informed voting some sort of information test would have to be applied. However, the issue of how to evaluate what constitutes informed voting or what requirements ought to exist for voting is complex, and the courts have been moving away from ex-

the present political process in the U.S. yields much power to the Executive and Administrative branches on expediency grounds.

II.

If we accept that some form of national representation is efficient, the remaining task is to decide on the best practical form of such representation. We would like to propose for consideration the selecting of a national legislature *at random* from the voting populace. Dahl [6, pp. 249–253] recently suggested a similar procedure, although only to give advisory votes, and the idea has historical origins in Athenian democracy [See 18, pp. 172–173] and in the work of Rousseau [21, Book IV, Chapter III].[9] Such a procedure would be a significant improvement over the existing political system in several ways. The incentive for pork barrel activities in order to secure votes would no longer be present since random selection would be independent of geographic base, and for the same reason minorities would be represented in correct proportion to their numbers in the society. Representation by random selection would also return political power to individual voters and give better articulation of voter preferences in the legislative process without sacrificing the efficiencies of representation. The legislature would not be composed of median position representatives as under two-party, geographic representation. Voter absention or uninformed voting would not be problems under this proposal, and perhaps voter alienation would be less in this case also.[10] If viewed as a replacement for the current forms of national

plicit requirements, such as literacy tests, for the right to vote. Nonetheless, even assuming that voters learn over time and also fully participate in democratic process, there may be frictions in realistic democracies so that lags in voters' learning functions may be very costly. Of course, many advocates of democracy as the best workable political system feel that this is not a major problem, because learning behavior over time will at least stimulate the polity to throw out of office over time those with whom they strongly disagree.

9. See also [3] for a proposed use of random sampling to estimate the demand for public goods; [15] for a discussion of the role of random selection in establishing and operating a system of proportional representation; and [25] for a proposal to use sample electorates to vote in various elections (e.g., the Presidential election). The latter, unpublished proposal of Ward is different from ours in that he does not extend his random selection proposal to a form of representative government, but only to choose groups of voters. Thus, although his system would probably be an improvement over existing methods of selecting representatives, we would argue that it would be hampered by many of the same problems of the existing system, such as high information costs to the sample electorates, that can only be minimized by combining random selection with a form of representative government.

10. We should note that it is true that randomly chosen individuals who are not concerned with re-election to office will have no direct incentive themselves to become informed. Even though absenteeism from legislative functions could be controlled, daydreaming could not be. Thus, there would be a problem similar to that of the absence of direct incentives for judges to devote much effort to reaching informed decisions which has recently been analyzed by Tullock [24] (university professors with tenure provide a somewhat simi-

representation, the random selection system removes direct sanctioning power through the ballot from the voter and replaces this control mechanism with a more subtle method of articulating voter preferences on national issues. We would argue that although the final outcome is not clearcut, such a change in representative procedure could be understood by voters as the formal embodiment of democratic equality in an *ex ante* rather than *ex post* sense.[11] One could also argue that the mass media aspect of political campaigning would be less of a problem under the random selection system, although this is not certain since the outcome depends on how this system of representation is meshed with existing political institutions (e.g., the Presidency). Finally, and importantly, it should be stressed that random selection of representatives avoids all of the traditional problems in voting theory of intransitivities in voting outcomes and the like in establishing a system of proportional representation [See 2, Chapter 11]. The application of voting theory is confined in this case to the operations of the random legislature once selected, and this feature of representation by lot is an important justification for establishing and operating proportional representation in this way.[12]

III.

The operational details of how such a body would be selected and how it would function are important considerations. Who would be eligible for the legislature? We would argue that everyone in the voting populace would be eligible except those barred by constitutionally agreed upon restrictions. Including as many people as possible in the selection pool would effectively guarantee the representation of the whole cross-section of voter preferences. Thus, there would be few deferments from electoral eligibility for the randomized legislature. When one is born, he automatically goes into the electoral pool. Practically speaking, however, the polity may wish to bar some groups of individuals constitutionally. Ex-

---

lar example). We feel, however, that in case of important, highly publicized decisions, social pressures such as desires to be respected and the like will generally provide rather strong personal incentives for informed choice. Thus, we would expect that with our randomly selected legislature, this would not be a major problem. This consideration could be one argument for public rather than secret balloting, however, and also for making terms fairly limited in duration so that the legislator's reputation might have some influence on his later career (similarly the prospects for advancement to higher courts may be an important incentive for lower court judges to make knowledgeable decisions).

    11. For the distinction between *ex ante* and *ex post* equity, see [19].

    12. In a related vein Niskanen [16, Chapter 20] recently suggested that review committees in the legislature be subject to random assignment and periodic reassignment. Under majority rule in the legislature this procedure would yield (with some sampling error) an approximation to the median committee member's demand for the outputs supplied by the bureau under review.

amples might be children, the mentally ill, criminals, civil servants, and individuals who receive government subsidies. The latter two categories raise the prospect of policing the random legislature to insure against the threat of the selected representative passing laws or raising subsidy rates for his particular pressure group. One might argue that the random legislature would have higher costs of policing against bribe taking and the like, since legislators do not have to run for re-election. However, the present system of electing representatives has similar problems, especially when pressure groups are geographically concentrated. The pool of eligible individuals for the random legislature might have to be restricted to achieve genuine representative behavior, but such restrictions, which set up basically a system of weighted voting would have to be balanced against the loss of sampling accuracy.[13]

How large would the legislature be and what sampling procedure would be followed? The size of the representative group would depend on how large a sample would be required to insure that on average over a series of electoral periods, a good depiction of the cross-section of voter preferences is obtained. In essence, more accurate measurement would have to be traded off against the additional costs of a larger legislature. Dahl argues that 500 or 600 at most is the number of people who could participate effectively in a random legislature [6, p. 152]. This may or may not be the case depending on the amount of sampling error one is willing to tolerate vis-à-vis the costs of a larger legislature and depending on how one meshes the random body with the existing legislative process. Given that there is no prior knowledge about the population proportion being sampled for (50-50), a sample size of 500 would yield a chance of 95 percent that the value being estimated lies within a range equal to the reported percentages, plus or minus an error of 4.9 percent. Doubling the sample size to 1000 would yield a 95 percent chance with a 3.6 percent error. So it is probably true that very accurate samples of the voting populace would have to be large. However, this does not mean that a large random legislature is not feasible or cannot be effective. To judge the feasibility of this method of representation one would have to compare its costs with the costs of the present system of elections and operation and with costs of high information voting. In terms of the effectiveness of such a representative body, it could be meshed with the existing political process by making it a purely advisory body, or as will be

13. For example, take the case of individuals who receive a government subsidy. Pursued literally, this would not only exclude welfare recipients, but also homeowners, holders of stock in oil and mineral companies, veterans, and so forth. Furthermore, it would be hard to argue that individuals should be excluded on the grounds of educational qualifications given current attitudes which do not allow literacy tests.

discussed below, one house of a bicameral legislature could be designated primarily to respond (i.e., vote on) rather than initiate legislation. In these cases large size would not necessarily be a constraint on its effectiveness. Finally, for less important issues, smaller subsets of the large random body could be used for decision making, allowing many less important issues to be handled at the same time.

The proposed sampling procedure would be random sampling with replacement. The latter condition is not strictly required with a large pool of voters from which to sample; so operationally one might argue that legislators could serve only one term, although this would cause the problem of perpetual "rookie" legislators. Although we propose random selection from the required pool of voters, one might be concerned about the selection of x percentage of a certain race or income level. In this case stratified sampling could be implemented and the legislature would be proportionally random by strata. Indeed, if such variables as tastes and income are highly correlated, then stratified sampling would lower the required total sample size. However, there would be a new set of problems associated with determining how many strata there should be and in what terms the strata are defined, and we would not want to employ stratified geographic sampling for previously mentioned reasons. Also, the problem of policing the legislature against pressure group legislation would be more difficult under stratified sampling.

Probably the strongest argument for some form of stratified sampling is that under a continuous system of unrestricted random sampling, the probability will approach 100 percent over time that for some draw of the legislature a set of representatives which reflect only a small portion of the underlying population will dominate the legislature (the American Nazi party, for instance) with the possibility of extremely adverse consequences as a result. Strong constitutional provisions and the use of a second house of Congress (see Section IV) could also be used to limit the effects that an unrepresentative, intolerant legislature might have while in office, and we would argue that the frequency of occurrence of such situations under our proposals is likely to be considerably less than what we have historically observed under alternative forms of government.

A problem related to the selection of the randomized legislature is how to compensate the selected legislators. One might argue that the opportunity costs of selected individuals ought to be paid and therefore a system of discriminatory wages would be required. In such a system an individual would be no more or no less better off for being selected.[14] However, while attractive on efficiency grounds (and in one sense of equity), this

14. In part this is a question of how much society should invest in government, and it is an implication of recent work on vote trading that a well-working government may embody

procedure is probably not feasible because of all the problems of estimating and discounting the appropriate opportunity costs and also of maintaining a well-working legislature with differential rates of pay. An obvious second-best solution would be to take existing Congressional pay scales as approximate to the "proper" common wage for national legislators and pay this wage and any extraordinary costs to those selected. The problem in this case consists of whether or not you require people to be in the selection pool. On the grounds of obtaining the proper sampling characteristics, there would probably have to be a requirement to be in the pool. However, this creates problems of compensation when, for example, an individual with a $100,000 opportunity cost is selected.[15] This problem is precisely analogous to the economics of conscription for military or jury duty where non-economic objectives such as racial balance may require violating strict opportunity cost dictates in recruiting or conscripting for such tasks.[16] In the case of the randomized legislature we would argue that an initial wage commensurate with existing Congressional pay scales would vitiate the major problems of requiring people to be in the selection pool. For those individuals with low opportunity costs who are selected, we would propose that they simply be allowed to earn the fortuitous rents caused by paying the uniform, high base wage. Also, if one were worried about random legislators voting themselves pay raises due to their lame duck status, Congressional pay scales could be set constitutionally and adjusted for productivity growth or increases in the cost of living. As another possibility, pay increases could be made for the subsequent session of legislators. So long as there were not a large proportion of staggered terms (see the discussion in the next paragraph), this procedure would help ensure against lame duck pay raises.

In terms of the functioning of the legislature, what would be the most desirable term of office? One cannot say for sure, but the fundamental reason for changing office under this system would be to detect changes in the distribution of voter preferences across the spectrum of national issues. In practice one would have to establish the trade-off between start-up costs (perpetual rookie legislators) and career dislocation costs (which would probably rise exponentially in relation to time in office) and the desire to collect accurate decentralized information while maintaining the

---

great potential gains from trade for democratic citizens. Hence, investments in democratic process may have big payoffs. See [14].

15. It might be possible to allow individuals with high opportunity costs to buy substitutes in this case. There would be a sacrifice of randomness here, but the rich may be "over-represented" in democracy in the first place.

16. To be fully analogous to the costs imposed by the military draft, any costs associated with the disruption of one's civilian career would also have to be estimated and discounted at the appropriate rate of time preference. See [13] and [26].

appropriate incentives for representative behavior. Possibilities would range from short, non-staggered terms to career appointments upon selection with staggered terms.

How would this legislature mesh with the existing forms of national government? Several of the following alternatives for the new legislature might be explored:

a) An additional national legislature to the present two,
b) An additional national legislature replacing one of the present two,
c) An exclusive national legislature replacing the present two,
d) An exclusive national legislature with another nationally elected body,
e) A mandatory national legislature to be used if requested by the present two legislatures or the President, and
f) An advisory national legislature to be used if requested by the present two legislatures or the President or to be required to give advisory votes on selected issues.

Perhaps the more feasible alternative, at least on a short-run experimental basis, is the last. In this case, the central problem is whether the votes of the randomized legislature would be binding (and if so, in what form, i.e., what voting rule would be required to pass a law?). If the votes of such a body were binding in some form, then the political system could be characterized as government by randomized jurors. In this form the randomized legislature could be viewed as a more formal embodiment of its current functional equivalents—the Presidential commission, the White House conference, and the like. The Presidential commission, for example, is a method under present institutional arrangements to gather a range of informed public opinion on a given issue (of course, this is not the only function which commissions sometimes perform). Also, the advisory random body would officially sanction and improve (due to fuller information) public opinion polls. If the voters of the randomly selected body were to be only advisory, a smaller body could be maintained, and in a sense the polity would seek the counsel of a smaller number of randomly selected qualified persons on certain issues.[17]

17. Another interesting issue is whether the votes of the random body would be open or secret. The present national legislature has to have open voting so that constituents know how their representatives vote. This is not necessarily the case with the random body, particularly if one does not allow re-election of legislators. Thus, the issue of open or secret voting in the random body would revolve partially around the kind of voting response bias that the collectivity desired since *both* open and secret balloting would have inherent response bias. Of course, under either open or closed voting, care would have to be taken to insulate the legislators from lobbying pressures and to see that they cast informed votes.

Our basic point is that the use of randomly selected bodies is a powerful method for reconciling the specialization advantages of representation with a fuller representation of voter preferences and to show that one can get a better representation of voter preferences than exists under the present system without going to a pure referenda system. Also, one avoids traditional voting theory problems of aggregating voter preferences by selecting representatives (though not in the operations of the random legislature) in this method. While the operational details under any given embodiment of our proposal present problems and we have surely missed many important points that would have to be considered in meshing the random body with the rest of the process of government, these are no more insurmountable than those of organizing our present national legislatures, and we would urge experimentation along the lines of our proposal. Following Dahl [5], we could argue that such experimentation is essential if democracy is to be given an opportunity to work and democratic power is to be returned to the people.

IV.

A final point is that political entrepreneurship would probably suffer under an exclusive random system. In some respects, such as the problems of mass media and the technology of modern politics (dollar democracy), this would be desirable. However, to maintain the production of innovative policies and to produce what one might term "political X-efficiency," we might add to the random system a sort of executive committee or senate, to be elected nationally from an at-large list of candidates. For example, twenty seats for this group could be established, and political entrepreneurs could campaign for seats. This group in a sense would represent the formal continuation of the present Senate in much smaller size and would serve to lessen the problem of Executive discretion in the present system. This senate could be elected by the general public or by the larger random body. The advantage of having the senators elected by the general public would be to maintain a sense of voter participation in the system whereas the advantage of having them elected by the random body would be the attainment of virtually the same electoral outcomes for less costs of political entrepreneuring. There would be problems with defining which decisions this group would control and which decisions the President would control, but the principle on which such a division of issues would be undertaken would basically be how quickly a decision needed to be taken by the Executive Branch. Also, if

---

Closed voting might help in the former regard if it increased the uncertainty in vote buying, whereas open voting would help the latter cause since the impact of one's decision can affect his future career.

one desired a very large random body for sampling accuracy reasons, then this smaller body could originate legislation. In this way the larger random group could function effectively, despite its size, with its primary function being to vote on proposals originated and debated by the smaller, elected senate.[18]

The persevering reader may be convinced by now that we are writing a piece of science fiction rather than analyzing a serious proposal to reform democratic decision making.[19] We argue, however, that the time is long since past when this country should have a commissioned body to look analytically at its electoral procedures. In such a setting proposals like ours and Miller's and the work of others in this vein can be discussed seriously on their practical and theoretical merits.

References

1. Becker, Gary. "A Theory of the Allocation of Time," *Econ. Jour.* 75 (Sept. 1965), 493–517.
2. Black, Duncan. *The Theory of Committees and Elections.* New York: Cambridge University Press, 1958.
3. Bohm, P. "An Approach to the Problem of Estimating the Demand for Public Goods," *Swedish Jour. Econ.* (Mar. 1971), 55–66.
4. Bowen, H. R. "The Interpretation of Voting in the Allocation of Economic Resources," *Quar. Jour. Econ.* 58 (Nov. 1943), 27–49.
5. Buchanan, J. M. *Public Finance in Democratic Process.* Chapel Hill: University of North Carolina Press, 1967.
6. Dahl, Robert. *After the Revolution.* New Haven: Yale University Press, 1970.
7. Downs, Anthony. *An Economic Theory of Democracy.* New York: Harper and Row, 1957.
8. Dye, T. R. and Zeigler, L. H. *The Irony of Democracy.* Belmont, California: Wadsworth, 1970.
9. Heinlein, Robert. *The Moon is a Harsh Mistress.* New York: Putnam, 1966.
10. Livingstone, Dennis. "Science Fiction Models of Future World Order Systems," *International Organization* 25 (Spring 1971), 254–270.
11. Mill. J. S. *Considerations on Representative Government.* London: Parker, Son and Bourn, 1861.

18. Mill advocated an executive council or small group of experts to write and initiate legislation in his system of proportional representation. Presumably, this group in Mill's system would be the functional equivalent of the modern committee staff. This is related, but somewhat different, from our proposal where the initiating body is elected. For Mill's discussion, see [11, Chapter V].

19. He is somewhat justified in this regard as Robert Heinlein discusses a random selection proposal in [9]. However, as we indicated earlier, there are also precedents for this type of consideration in the practice of Athens, the work of Rousseau, and more recently, the work of Robert Dahl. Indeed, in popular commentary William F. Buckley's frequently repeated statement that "he would rather be governed by the first thousand names in the New York telephone directory than the faculty at Harvard" also comes to mind. We might also note that more than one work of science fiction has made worthwhile contributions to political science. See, for instance, the discussions in [10] and [20, pp. 5–7].

12. Miller, J. C., III. "A Program for Direct and Proxy Voting in the Legislative Process," *Public Choice* 7 (Fall 1969), 107–112 [Reading 24, above].

13. —— and Tollison, R. D. "The Implicit Tax on Reluctant Military Recruits," *Social Science Quarterly* 51 (Mar. 1971), 924–931.

14. Mueller, Dennis, Philpotts, G. C., and Vanek, Jaroslav. "The Social Gains from Exchanging Votes: A Simulation Approach," *Public Choice* (forthcoming).

15. ——, Tollison, R. D., and Willett, T. D. "A Normative Theory of Representative Democracy," Cornell University, mimeo., 1971.

16. Niskanen, W. A. *Bureaucracy and Representative Government.* Chicago: Aldine-Atherton, 1971.

17. Owen, B. M. "Public Policy and Emerging Technology in the Media," *Public Policy* 18 (Summer 1970), 539–552.

18. Parkinson, C. N. *The Evolution of Political Thought.* New York: Viking Press, 1958.

19. Pauly, M. V. and Willett, T. D. "Two Concepts of Equity," *Social Science Quarterly* (June 1972), 8–19 [Reading 19, above].

20. Price, D. K. *The Scientific Estate.* New York: Oxford University Press, 1965.

21. Rousseau, Jean-Jacques. *The Social Contract.* Amsterdam: M. M. Rey, 1762.

22. Sherman, Roger and Willett, T. D. "The Standardized Work Week and the Allocation of Time," *Kyklos* 25 (Fasc. 1, 1972), 65–82.

23. Shubik, M. "On Homo Politicus and the Instant Referendum," *Public Choice* 9 (Fall 1970), 79–84 [Reading 25, above].

24. Tullock, Gordon. "Public Decisions as Public Goods," *Jour. of Pol. Econ.* 79 (July/Aug. 1971), 913–918.

25. Ward, B. "Toward More Democratic Elections?," unpublished manuscript, July 1969.

26. Willett, T. D. "Another Cost of Conscription," *West. Econ. Jour.* 6 (Dec. 1968), 425–426.

27. Some Simple Economics of Voting and Not Voting *

ROBERT D. TOLLISON and THOMAS D. WILLETT

In the literature on the economic approach to politics there has been considerable attention given to the development of models to explain observed voting behavior, e.g., see Downs [5], Fraser [6], Frey [7, 8],

Reprinted without appendix from *Public Choice,* Fall 1973, pp. 59–71, by permission of the publisher.

* Without implicating them, we would like to thank Ryan Amacher, Dennis Mueller, Roger Sherman, and Gordon Tullock for helpful comments on an earlier draft of this paper.

Riker and Ordeshook [18], Russell [19], Stigler [22], and Tullock [24]. A major reason for the interest in this topic is that there appears to be no generally acceptable explanation of the importance of the role of economic variables in the decision to vote. One of the problems in this literature is the intermingling of two questions about voting and the consequent failure to distinguish what hypothesis about voting behavior is being specified. In one case the issue is raised as to why individuals vote, especially in large polities, or what factors explain the absolute turnout of voters in a given election. In another case the related, but distinct, empirical issue of why do greater proportions of high income than low income individuals vote is raised. There also has been controversy over what role variables that are not strictly economic in nature (sometimes termed "sociological") play in economic models of the voting decision. Further, the effect of information on the incentive to vote has, to our knowledge, not been fully clarified in the economic theory of democracy.

Our purpose in this paper is to offer a critical review of the current state of the literature and to explore further the questions mentioned above. In Section I economic models to explain the absolute turnout of voters in a given election are discussed. The role of "sociological" variables as a source of benefits from voting is stressed in explaining absolute voter turnouts. In Section II economic explanations of the relative turnouts of rich and poor voters in a given election are considered. Sociological variables are again important determinants of relative voter turnouts. The effects of information on the incentive to vote are also considered in Section II, especially with respect to how it might affect the relative turnouts of rich and poor voters. In Section III a brief analysis of non-voting in a democracy and ways to internalize this sort of externality using the economist's standard approach of taxes and subsidies are presented.

I. Absolute Voter Turnouts

There are at least two important predictive hypotheses about voting behavior which an economic model of the voting decision should address. First, can the model explain the absolute level of voter turnout? Second, can the model explain the relative turnouts of rich and poor voters?

Consider what we term a narrow economic model of the voting decision, i.e., one which not only makes use of the logical or economic approach to the voter's decision calculus, but also limits the arguments considered to economic variables. In such a model the potential voter balances the direct cost of voting (C) against the expected benefits (PB) which accrue only to the individual in the sense that he computes the expected value that his vote will be decisive in the election of his preferred candidate.[1] One would rationally vote only when expected benefits exceeded costs. Since in most reasonably sized polities the expected benefits from casting a vote would be quite low for rich and poor voters alike, we doubt that even if very accurate and correct measures indicated reasonably small opportunity costs to voting the narrow economic model would be able to explain to an important quantitative extent either the relative turnouts of rich and poor voters or the absolute turnout in a given election. In fact, very few individuals should vote at all in these circumstances, except in elections where the number of voters in quite small.

For example, consider the predictive ability of this model to forecast the absolute level of turnout in a Presidential election where 60 million votes are cast. Even assuming a trivial level of opportunity costs for all voters, and a reasonably small proportion of "swing" voters—for example, $1 and 10 million respectively—the voter's odds of making a difference in the outcome are approximately 1 in 10 million (i.e., $P = 10^7$), and the value of the possible range of election outcomes to the individual (B) would have to exceed $10 million for it to be rational to vote within the context of narrow economic factors.[2] This is, of course, an inconceivable outcome for almost any voter. Normally, there would be few voters for whom the value of an election (in the sense of the amount of compensation required for indifference between the election of the most and the least preferred candidates) would be more than a few thousand dollars.[3] In the frequent case of tweedle dum-tweedle dee candidates the value for most voters would of course be considerably lower. On narrow economic grounds, then, few people would rationally go to the polls to vote even where the number of voters in the election were only a few thousand and a close election was expected.[4]

It seems doubtful, therefore, that the narrow economic model of the

1. Downs [5, Ch. 14] develops this type of model of the short-run voting decision, and Frey [8] essentially amends this model (ignoring the benefit side) with a point about possible efficiencies in voting for higher income voters. We discuss the models of Downs and Frey in greater detail below.

2. For a more detailed discussion of how P should be calculated, see Riker and Ordeshook [18].

3. Another way to measure the income effect in this case would be the amount (which may not be the same as that mentioned in the text) that the voter is willing to pay to avoid the least preferred candidate.

4. We suspect that this conclusion holds even when additional plausible reasons for voting in a narrow economic model are admitted. For example, there may be risk avoidance effects where voters participate in the sense of paying an insurance premium against the small probability of a large loss if the least preferred candidate is elected. One would therefore vote to keep the Fascists from gaining electoral power, even though the chances that they will be able to do so are small.

voting decision can explain the absolute level of turnout in a given election or the relative turnouts of rich and poor voters where opportunity costs, even of a trivial size, vary directly with income. Indeed, it is hard to explain why anyone votes at all in elections with large numbers of voters if one sticks strictly to this model of the voting decision.

Rather, as has been argued by Riker and Ordeshook [18], to explain the relatively high voter turnouts which occur, one must consider the set of direct benefits from the act of voting which are perceived by many voters and which are independent of the outcome of the election. These "sociological" benefits include such factors as the satisfying of a felt obligation or duty and response to social pressures to vote. Thus, the benefit-cost ratio for voting becomes $(PB + D)/C$, where D summarizes the effect of sociological benefits. While some economists, for example, Downs [5] and Frey [8], have evidenced a distaste for the consideration of such variables in a model of the rational calculus of voting (in the case of Downs because of the potentially tautological nature of the resulting model), Riker and Ordeshook have illustrated how this model can be used to confront empirical evidence in a non-tautological manner.[5] Thus, logical or economic models of voting can productively include non-economic arguments in the citizen's decision calculus. Where social conditioning has affected individuals' response patterns in a significant manner, for instance, by instilling in individuals a sense of duty to vote, then to be useful, explanatory models must take this into account, even if this comes at the costs of the disciplinary pureness of the resultant model. We see no inherent contradiction in taking into account sociological variables within the context of an economic approach to political questions. The ability to do so greatly increases the power of the economic approach.[6]

5. Specifically, using estimates of P, B, and D, for a sample of voters and employing survey research methods, they were able to construct a test of the consistency of the model in explaining the relative turnouts of groups classified by different values of the independent variables. The results supported the underlying model at a highly significant level. See also Riker and Ordeshook's [18, n. 7, pp. 26–27] commentary on Downs' discussion of the meaning of rationality in this context.

6. In a recent paper Stigler [22] develops a model of political competition which emphasizes a possible self-interest (investment) motive for voting. He argues that it may be premature to introduce arguments about the utility of voting for its own sake (consumption) and that the investment motive is more likely to have fruitful empirical application than the consumption motive. Apart from the issue of the empirical support for Stigler's model, voting is a case where empirical testing of hypotheses about the consumption motive is not difficult due to the availability of data (a feature not readily possessed by Stigler's investment motive) and where non-tautological tests for the explanatory power of the consumption motive can be conducted in fruitful ways, as Riker and Ordeshook demonstrate.

II. Relative Voter Turnouts and the Effect of Information on the Incentive to Vote

Whether higher or lower income individuals have greater net incentives to vote and participate in other political activity is an important question both because of intrinsic interest in its own right and because, as was recently emphasized by Frey [8], of its possible implications for the empirical testability of economic models of political behavior. The value of time spent in voting will generally be greater for higher than for lower income citizens. Hence, simple economic theory would suggest, *ceteris paribus,* less voting by higher income individuals because of the higher cost to them. There is considerable empirical evidence, however, that a greater percentage of higher income individuals vote than do lower income individuals, e.g., see Milbrath [14]. Has the economic approach to politics led to an important testable hypothesis which has proven to be false?

Frey attempted to reconcile observed voting patterns with a broader economic explanation of voting behavior. In this model the higher opportunity costs of voting of higher income voters can be offset by the efficiency with which they may be able to participate in political activities such as voting. For example, higher income voters may be able to work (e.g., think about an investment project) on the way to and from the polls. Frey's discussion attempts to rescue the economic approach from the false predictive hypothesis that higher income individuals should vote less, although it must be acknowledged that on this question the approach secures the protection of the impossibility of falsification because it concludes that either result can occur.[7]

Downs [5] argued earlier that higher income voters should vote *more* even though their opportunity costs are higher because they have a greater "advantage" in bearing the higher costs (an ability-to-pay criterion). Frey argues that Downs' analysis is incorrect and that the simple economic model would predict less voting by higher income voters because of the higher price of voting which they face, i.e., the higher opportunity costs of their time. Frey then attempts to rescue the explanatory power of the economic approach by introducing a factor stressing the efficiency with which higher income voters can participate in politics.

Neither Downs nor Frey gives a fully correct analysis of the implications of the simple economic approach. Downs considered only the income effect on voting behavior and ignored a substitution effect where

7. Frey [8, p. 103] discusses how the "economic hypothesis" might be interpreted in an *ex ante* sense and thereby falsified. For example, in his argument one would have to find high income groups with low productivity in voting.

higher income voters face a higher relative price for voting, while Frey considered the nature of the substitution effect and ignored the income effect. In a complete model of voting both effects are, of course, relevant, and one cannot derive an unambiguous conclusion from purely qualitative assumptions in the simple economic approach, even in the absence of Frey's refinement. While Frey's argument concerning the cost of voting is undoubtedly correct in qualitative terms, it is doubtful that his increased efficiency factor is sufficiently powerful to offset the higher value of time of higher income individuals so that the effective cost of voting is really lower on average for higher income individuals.[8] Thus, the conflict between income and substitution effects probably remains for most individuals.

Again, sociological factors can provide the major explanation for voting behavior by income level. There is evidence [14] to the effect that there is a strong positive association between income and individuals feeling a sense of duty to vote. Hence, even though C may be higher for higher income individuals, so on average is D, and no qualitative conclusion can be derived on the relationship of D/C to income, e.g., see [18].

It is also possible that PB could vary systematically with income. For instance, Downs argues that the cost of information tends to be lower for better educated, higher income voters and that they consequently are likely to perceive better the differences in candidates and tend to place a higher value on the difference between possible outcomes. Thus, higher income voters may tend to participate more heavily for these reasons. This need not be the case, however. If one takes Downs, for example, to argue that starting from a situation of no information, the general introduction of information about the difference in two parties will increase the incentive to vote, then no doubt he is correct. In this case party positions would be clarified over the no-information state, and in effect, Downs would be arguing that the mean positions of the two parties move apart with the introduction of information, introducing a differential in the positions of the parties and creating a great incentive to vote.

However, consider the probability density functions of the outcomes

8. As a footnote to the discussion of the relation of income to voting behavior, it should be noted that with a workweek constraint, which may be important for production workers, income may not properly gauge the full opportunity cost of voting. For example, some workers may work longer hours than they would if they could individually adjust their workweek and may have a higher opportunity cost of time outside of work as a result. While such an effect is plausible and may help reconcile somewhat a narrow economic model of voting behavior stressing opportunity costs with observed voting patterns, we do not regard such effects as being strong enough to enable a narrow economic model to predict the relative turnouts of rich and poor voters. See the discussion by Sherman and Willett [21].

from parties $\bar{x}_1$ and $\bar{x}_2$, if elected. With respect to the effects of information on the individual estimates of the means of the x_1 and x_2 functions, ($\bar{x}_1$ and $\bar{x}_2$), it is not clear that changes would always be in the direction of increasing $[\bar{x}_1-\bar{x}_2]$. Frequently, party propaganda may attempt to exaggerate the difference between candidates. In this case, the initial exposure to campaign literature may increase a voter's estimate of $[\bar{x}_1-\bar{x}_2]$, but, additionally, more objective information may tend to reduce it again. Hence, at any particular point on an individual's information vector, the addition of more information could either increase or decrease $[\bar{x}_1-\bar{x}_2]$. We cannot conclude, as did Downs [5, p. 273], that an increase in information will necessarily increase B.

Furthermore, the level of information may also have an important effect on the individual's subjective estimate of P. As has been suggested by Riker and Ordeshook [18], public commercials aimed at inducing people to vote frequently give the impression that the likelihood of an individual's vote making a difference is much greater than it "objectively" is. There is some evidence, e.g., Dennis [4], that suggests that higher income voters also tend to be more informed about the likelihood of their votes making a difference. People may, of course, be rationally uninformed about this. If one introduced this type of information effect, the model would more strongly predict that, *ceteris paribus,* higher income individuals would vote *less,* since they would be expected to be more likely to understand the probabilistic futility of voting under more circumstances, i.e., their estimates of P would be lower.[9] Of the two types of information effects, we would expect the effect on P to have generally a greater impact on the incentive to vote than the effect on B.

Another effect of changes in the general level of information may be not to change the means of the x_1 and x_2 density functions, but rather to narrow their dispersions, as is illustrated in Figure 1. This will reduce the area of intersection between the two density functions thereby reducing the probability that the voter will make a "mistake" by supporting *ex ante* a party whose policies *ex post* turn out to be less preferred (x_p denotes the voter's preferred position in Figure 1). On this score, the incentive to vote is increased. However, the reduction in dispersion also reduces the degree of the possible difference in the outcome from the two parties. On this score, the incentive to vote is reduced. The net resultant of these two conflicting pulls could go in either direction, depending on the individual's utility function with respect to the actual outcomes. For example if the rate of change in voter utility is a constant over the relevant range, then B will be a function only of the means, $\bar{x}_1$ and $\bar{x}_2$.

9. This effect is probably primarily a function of education rather than income, but since education and income are highly correlated, it does show up for higher income voters.

We present further theoretical discussion of the effect of information on the incentive to vote in the appendix to the original paper, in which several additional classes of information effects are considered. In general we find that there is no theoretical reason to expect information to affect the incentive to vote in a systematic way. Downs overstates the case when he assumes that uncertainty definitely reduces the returns from voting [5, p. 273]. In the absence of additional empirical research on the problem, the most reasonable general conclusion would seem to be that information has no systematic effect on the incentive to vote.

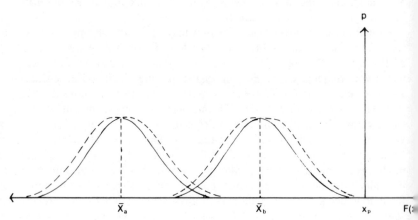

Figure 1.

An interesting implication of the analysis is related to another reason why poor voters may participate less heavily in politics. There may be alienation effects in a system of electoral competition that cause some voters in the extremes to refuse to participate on the grounds, for example, that where parties cluster in the middle of the issue space, they are not "represented" in the political competition. In several recent papers, Hinich, Ordeshook, and Ledyard [10, 11, 12] develop this concept. For example, they assume an alienation effect such that "π [the utility a citizen derives from voting] diminishes as the loss a citizen associates with his preferred candidate increases." [12, p. 75]

In terms of Figure 1 this situation could be depicted by a leftward shift (away from the voter's most preferred position, x_p) of one set of the distributions of party outcomes, with the difference in the mean positions remaining constant and no change in the dispersions of the distributions. Thus, the party differential remains the same, and there are no information effects on the dispersions of the two distributions of party outcomes.

Under these conditions for Hinich and Ordeshook's assumption to be valid, it is necessary that over the relevant range of total utility associated with the shift in the distributions, $u''(x) > 0$, i.e., the voter must be a risk seeker. As the alienation assumptions seem plausible but general risk seeking by potential voters does not, it would appear that the typical voter's utility function may be the Friedman-Savage-Markowitz [9, 13] type which has been used to explain the possible coexistence of both gambling and insurance buying by rational individuals.[10]

Another implication of the analysis of the effect of information on the incentive to vote is that, if one is interested in turning out the vote, more information about candidates should have no systematic effects in this regard.[11] A strategy of providing more information about candidates to increase voter turnouts would work only in the case of supplying additional information about candidates where no information (or very little) previously existed, and this condition is not likely to be widespread in most real world polities.[12] Thus, in terms of a predictive hypothesis from the analysis of information effects on voting, one might argue that the growth of information about candidates via the growth of media coverage of political events has not had a significant differential impact on voting turnouts over earlier periods, such as the nineteenth century when media coverage was much less extensive. Furthermore, if one is interested in turning out the vote, consideration should be given to the imposition of poll taxes or subsidies, which we discuss in the next section.

While no systematic conclusions can be drawn on the effect of information on the incentive to vote on the basis of qualitative theory alone, sociological variables would appear to play a large role in explaining the patterns of voting with respect to income. We turn now to a brief consideration of the other side of the coin of the economics of voting: the economics of non-voting.

III. Non-Voting

One of the reasons that economists interested in public choice have written about voting is that externalities (positive *and* negative) for the

10. For an empirical study which finds results consistent with the Friedman-Savage-Markowitz utility function, see Weitzman [25].

11. For a related analysis, see Shepsle [20].

12. The information effects considered here are those with respect to information about candidates. As noted above, information stressing one's duty to vote or attempting to give voters the impression that their votes actually "count" more heavily than an objective assessment would lead one to believe may have systematic effects on the incentive to vote. Likewise, if people's interest in political affairs is kindled, this could carry over to their feeling a greater duty to vote, even though this might not be consistent with narrowly self-interested behavior.

polity flow from the existence of the vote.[13] In the case of non-voting, should such behavior become widespread, say as a result of reading among the polity of the work of Downs [5] and Tullock [24], the possibility of a serious negative externality from non-voting arises. If only a few vote, outcomes may not be very representative of the preferences of the general community causing dissention among the polity. Furthermore, when voter turnout is small, the general legitimacy of the political system may be called into question, especially if the outcomes determined by the few who vote diverged widely from the general consensus. In the extreme these effects could lead to a collapse of the political system.

Downs [5] fully recognized the problem posed by non-voting and stresses the prisoner's dilemma that this recognition poses to the democratic voter. Although participation may be required for the long-run viability of democracy, a rational calculus in the short-run may indicate non-voting as optimal. Downs suggests the way out of this dilemma may be to rely on some form of long-run cooperative behavior where voters recognize their stake in the preservation of the system and in fact suggests that such behavior may be rational. This, however, seems unlikely.

Recognition of everyone's having a stake in the system can explain how everyone might rationally agree to impose on themselves binding rules requiring voting. In the absence of such enforceable rules, however, "cooperative behavior" will not generally be rational in the large-number setting. To the extent that some voters do, at least to some extent, take into account the effects of their voting on the preservation of the system, then there would appear to be a presumption that on this count higher income individuals would have greater incentives to vote than lower income individuals. This would be true if higher income individuals placed on average higher values on the preservation of the system. However, this factor is likely to be offset in narrow economic calculations by the greater tendency among higher income individuals to make reasonable es-

13. Gordon Tullock [23] makes the important point that although the vote creates an externality, the externality is positive for some people and negative for others. In the same paper he also argues that under plausible conditions a tax on voting sufficient to cover the entire cost of the voting process can be a Pareto optimal move. The type of negative externality from non-voting that we discuss in this section is not strictly equivalent to the externalities from the vote that Tullock analyzes. He basically emphasizes externalities that are related to the voter's direct self-interest in voting or abstaining, e.g., how is one's political power affected by extending the suffrage or how are outcomes on a particular issue changed if compulsory voting is introduced? The negative externality from non-voting which we discuss is really an extreme case where non-voting threatens the viability of the political system and greater participation may be desired by all voters, pretty much independent of the type of considerations raised by Tullock, as a way to preserve or stabilize the existing political and social system.

timates of the probabilities that their vote will make any difference as to whether the total vote is sufficient to ward off negative externalities.

The voting problem is similar in structure in the pollution problem. It is rational in the narrow economic sense for individuals to vote for antipollution laws, where they would not "voluntarily" stop polluting themselves. In small-number, repeated play prisoner's dilemma games, there is a tendency to arrive at a cooperative solution, but this outcome is much less likely in the large number case which is more germane to voter behavior.[14] The sociological sense of duty would seem a much stronger explanation than the psychological one of cooperative, long-run, prisoner's dilemma behavior in the large-number case.

If voting is widely considered as a duty and a sufficient amount of political participation is forthcoming as a result, then the negative externality from non-voting that we have been discussing may be inframarginal. For example, in the U.S. 65 percent turnouts for major elections may be enough to qualify the "stability of the system" problems caused by non-voting as inframarginal.

However, there may be cases where this negative externality from non-voting is Pareto-relevant. Recalling that we concluded in the last section that additional information about candidates under normal circumstances should not lead to a presumption of more voting, one may wish to impose an appropriate tax (or subsidy) on non-voting to internalize the relevant part of this negative spillover from such behavior. In terms of applying the economist's solution in this case, there would be no conceptual difference in a policy of applying a tax or subsidy to non-voting in terms of the opportunity cost imposed on the individual voter. However, political feasibility might suggest a tax on non-voting as the desirable policy, given the widespread feeling noted previously that voting is a duty. Indeed, most observed policies toward voting behavior have been of the form of fines on non-voting (e.g., Australia).[15]

14. Officer and Willett [17] develop a model of the stability of the international monetary system in which the participants' recognition of their stake in the stability of the system parallels Downs' discussion of the voters' stake in the preservation of the political system. Tullock [23] discusses this problem in the context of a case where compulsory voting may be the optimal policy. Also, the literature on public goods theory on free riding behavior in large and small groups is directly relevant to the type of problem discussed here. See, e.g., Buchanan [3, Chapter 5, and the references cited there].

15. Operationally, one would have to question whether there is any elasticity in voter response to such a policy. On this question a little casual empiricism suggests that the answer is clearly yes. For instance, in Australia where there is a vote tax and in Italy where non-voting is recorded in one's police record (which appears to be viewed as a reasonably strong nonpecuniary incentive), voting rates are typically in the range of over 90 percent, as compared with U.S. voting rates in national elections in the range of 65–70 percent.

Of course, whether relying on long-run cooperative behavior or a poll tax, it may be the case that simply an increased proportion of active voters may not be linked to a lessening of, say, general dissatisfaction with political outcomes. Much of the literature on alienation suggests that this could be possible, e.g., see Andrews and Karlins [1]. Also, one may not just want voting *per se*, but informed voting. In these cases, consideration should be given to alternative ways to organize and run the polity to lessen dissatisfaction with political outcomes and obtain informed voting, e.g., see Mueller, Tollison, and Willett [15, 16].

References

1. Andrews, L. M. and Karlins, M. *Requiem for Democracy?* New York: Holt, Rinehart and Winston, 1971.
2. Buchanan, J. M. "Politics, Policy, and the Pigovian Margins." *Economica,* 29 (1962), 17–28.
3. ———. *Demand and Supply of Public Goods.* Chicago: Rand McNally, 1968.
4. Dennis, J. "Support for the Institution of Elections by the Public." *American Political Science Review,* 64 (1970), 819–35.
5. Downs, Anthony. *An Economic Theory of Democracy.* New York: Harper and Row, 1957.
6. Fraser, J. "Why Do High Income People Participate More in Politics? The Wrong Answer." *Public Choice,* 13 (Fall, 1972), 115–18.
7. Frey, B. "Political Participation and Income Level: Reply." *Public Choice,* 13 (Fall, 1972), 119–22.
8. ———. "Why Do High Income People Participate More in Politics?" *Public Choice,* 11 (Fall, 1971), 101–05.
9. Friedman, M., and Savage, L. "The Utility Analysis of Choices Involving Risk. *Journal of Political Economy,* 56 (1948), 279–304.
10. Hinich, M., Ledyard, J., and Ordeshook, P. "Nonvoting and the Existence of Equilibrium Under Majority Rule." *Journal of Economic Theory,* (April, 1972), 144–53.
11. Hinich, M., and Ordeshook, P. "Plurality Maximization Versus Vote Maximization." *American Political Science Review,* 64 (1970), 772–91.
12. Hinich, M., and Ordeshook, P. "Social Welfare and Electoral Competition in Democratic Societies." *Public Choice,* 11 (Fall, 1971), 73–88.
13. Markowitz, H. "The Utility of Wealth." *Journal of Public Economy,* 59 (1952).
14. Milbrath, L. W. *Political Participation.* Chicago: Rand McNally, 1965.
15. Mueller, D. C., Tollison, R. D., and Willett, T. D. "Solving the Intensity Problem in Representative Democracy." Reading 30, below.
16. ———. "Representative Democracy Via Random Selection." *Public Choice,* 12 (Spring, 1972), 57–68 [Reading 26, above].
17. Officer, L. H. and Willett, T. D. "The Interaction of Adjustment and Gold Conversion Policies in a Reserve Currency System." *Western Economic Journal,* 8 (March, 1970), 47–60.

18. Riker, W. H. and Ordeshook, P. C. "A Theory of the Calculus of Voting." *American Political Science Review*, 62 (1968), 25–42.
19. Russell, K. "Political Participation and Income Level: An Alternative Explanation." *Public Choice*, 13 (Fall, 1972), 113–14.
20. Shepsle, K. A. "The Strategy of Ambiguity: Uncertainty and Electoral Competition." *American Political Science Review*, 66 (1972), 555–68.
21. Sherman, R. and Willett, T. D. "The Standardized Work Week and the Allocation of Time." *Kyklos*, 25 (Fasc. 1, 1972), 65–82.
22. Stigler, G. J. "Economic Competition and Political Competition." *Public Choice*, 13 (Fall, 1972), 91–106.
23. Tullock, G. "Optimal Poll Taxes." Unpublished manuscript, Aug. 1972.
24. ———. *Toward a Mathematics of Politics*. Ann Arbor: University of Michigan Press, 1968.
25. Weitzman, M. L. "Material Balances under Uncertainty." *Quarterly Journal of Economics*, May 1971.

C. ARE THERE SYSTEMATIC BIASES IN GOVERNMENT BUDGET SIZE?

28. Risk Avoidance and Political Advertising: Neglected Issues in the Literature on Budget Size in a Democracy

RYAN C. AMACHER, ROBERT D. TOLLISON, and THOMAS D. WILLETT

The literature concerned with budget size in a democracy is extensive and diverse. A wide spectrum of opinion exists as to whether—and why—budgets are too small or too large. Most of this discussion pertains to the overall size of the government budget vis-à-vis the private sector. It is possible, however, to examine systematic forces at work in the U.S. political and economic system that may bias the size of the government budget in a direction away from what the average voter-consumer desires. In this paper we examine these potential biases as they relate to a significant portion of the U.S. federal budget, namely the defense budget. It is argued that differential advertising, lobbying, and possible dependence effects among different activities in the public sector may induce biases that are in themselves more important than any resulting imbalance in

aggregate public versus private spending. A number of budgetary and bureaucratic factors are discussed that influence the provision of such
"risky" public goods as defense and give reason to suspect that the
defense budget is "too large." Our analysis results in a counterargument
to Downs' point that the budget in a democracy tends to be "too small"
for outputs with benefits that are uncertain and ill perceived by voters. A
number of questions that may prove fruitful for future empirical research
are considered. It should be noted that while most of the discussion is
devoted to the defense budget, it may be applicable to other segments of
the federal budget and even to state budgets.

In Section I we review the literature on budget size in a democracy.
Section II discusses the defense budget as an example, giving primary attention to the question whether there are structural reasons why defense
officials may *want* to expand their budgets more than their counterparts in
other bureaus. Section III investigates whether there are institutional
mechanisms in the budgetary process that enable defense officials to convert their desires into effective demands for larger budgets. Section IV
considers some of the empirical issues raised by this analysis, and Section
V offers some concluding remarks about the relationship between risk,
advertising, and the size of the budget.

I. Background: The Literature on Budget Size in a Democracy

There is no lack of opinion that the public sector in the United States is
either too large or too small, and there may be even a few people who
would argue that the public-private mix is the correct one. In this first
section we review the literature in order to categorize the political-
economic forces that might influence budget size. Any categorization is,
in some senses, arbitrary. This is particularly the case with regard to the
literature on the size of the budget in a democracy because of the difficulty in tracking down explicit statements of the benchmarks used by
many of the authors. In one sense all the literature is the same in that it
takes the democratic process as we know it and the market system as we
know it and searches for any biases that might influence the size of the
budget. It is, therefore, necessary to look for subtle differences in the
benchmarks employed. Some of the literature (à la Galbraith) concentrates on the private market as the influencing agent with the state playing
a passive role. Other literature examines competition for resources within
the state sector. In order to analyze these subtle differences, we find it
useful to categorize the literature with respect to the type of benchmark
an author employs for gauging "correct" budget size. This criterion leads
to the grouping of papers and books in four categories: (1) those works on
social balance by Galbraith, Hayek, and others that argue from an essen-

tially empirical conception of the appropriate budget size (i.e., observed budget size is either "too small" or "too large" according to one's particular view of the strength and pervasity of dependence effects—defined below—among public and private goods). The antecedents of these writings are the empirical propositions contained in Wagner's Law of ever increasing government size and the more recent discussions of displacement and scale effects in the growth of the relative size of government, especially during war; (2) those works by Downs, Buchanan, Tullock, and others which argue primarily in terms of a collective decision benchmark (e.g., in the case of Downs, the budgetary outcome where voters and parties have perfect information about the costs and benefits of government action); (3) those by Niskanen, McKean, and others which emphasize the behavior of bureaus in supplying public goods vis-à-vis comparable competitive supply of the same goods via markets; (4) those by Greene and others that treat government expenditures as a form of insurance and examine the influence of risk on budget size.

Social Balance

The question of balance between private and public sectors finds its modern analytical origin in Alfred Marshall's recognition that external economies will prohibit competitive firms from reaching the optimal level of output. Building on Marshallian foundations, A. C. Pigou prescribed government intervention to bring about social balance in the presence of external economies and diseconomies.[1] Modern extensions and refinements in welfare economics have emphasized the problems in the original Pigovian prescription of government intervention as the appropriate corrective device. Perhaps the most important theoretical development is Coase's paper on social cost, and certainly the most important practical emendation of Pigou is the observation that governments intervene in private processes in a less than perfect (costless) way.[2]

But while recent developments in welfare economics do bear on the issue of budget size in democracy, and this area has much to contribute in deriving the appropriate normative presumptions about budget size, a review of this literature would lead us too far afield from the more limited and more distinct question of what systematic forces are at work in democratic politics to affect the size of the government budget.[3] Hence, we will begin instead with probably the most widely known discussion of the

1. Recent contextual evidence indicates, however, that Marshall was skeptical of various aspects of Pigou's extensions in this area. See Bharadwaj (1972).

2. See Coase (1960). J. M. Buchanan has expounded the latter point forcefully throughout his writings; in particular, see Buchanan (1962).

3. This literature has recently been reviewed thoroughly by Mishan (1971).

appropriate size of the public sector in the United States, that offered by Galbraith in *The Affluent Society*.[4]

Galbraith argues that there is a systematic imbalance between the private and public sectors because of heavy advertising in the private sector and because of dependence effects associated with private economic activity such that new suppliers tend to generate their own demand.[5] Both these points, especially the latter, rest on the view that man's wants are not independent of the production processes which satisfy them, and harken back to a Veblenian view of the economic process. Thus, the dependence effect in a market economy with private advertising presumably leads to an overabundance of private goods and too few goods provided by government. Galbraith therefore argues that additional public goods are required in order to create dependent demands for more public goods and services and a better balanced economy.

These arguments rest on easily challengeable empirical assumptions. As Hayek has pointed out, some important publicly supplied goods are also subject to dependence effects, education being his classic example, while not all private goods generate such an effect.[6] It is also clear that lobbying and public relations by government agencies and their suppliers, and free press coverge of proposed government projects, are at present *functional equivalents* of private advertising activity.[7] Along these same lines, Harry Johnson has argued that general benefit public activities, such as defense, tend to be overextended in democratic budgets because they can be advertised as being in the public interest.[8] In addition, it is clear that in many cases private goods and public goods are complements, e.g., cars and roads. In this case private advertising will affect the demand for both public and private goods. Thus, there are many arguable exceptions within Galbraith's analytical framework, and the question of imbalance becomes an empirical one, on which, as yet, little systematic research has been done.

Of course, there has been a great deal of empirical work on the growth

4. Galbraith (1958).
5. Dependence effects refers to Galbraith's contention that the demands for some goods are created because the demand for them is not innate. Galbraith also argued that the real value (i.e., corrected for price increases) of government expenditures was more susceptible to inflation than private expenditures. A major difficulty with this argument is that it assumes the rate of inflation is given exogenously, while, in fact, inflation is frequently itself caused by an expansion of government expenditures not financed by additional taxation (e.g., the inflation in the United States following the large and rapid expenditures associated with the Vietnam War). Thus, this portion of Galbraith's analysis is more appropriate when applied to state and local government expenditures, rather than those at the national level.
6. Hayek (1961).
7. See Demsetz (1970a), for a discussion emphasizing this general point.
8. Johnson (1968).

of the public sector, some of which is associated with largely *ad hoc* rationalizations about why governments tend inevitably to grow. These contributions should be noted here, since in some respects they are similar to the more recent discussions of social balance. Perhaps the best known such rationalization (assertion?) is Wagner's Law of increasing government activity.[9] As Greene stresses, however, Wagner's Law embodies an organic conception of the state, that is, the state is inevitably subject to growth because it *ought* to grow and not because it is *predicted* to grow.[10] Still other examples of empirical propositions about the rate of growth of the public sector are the displacement and scale effects discussed by Peacock or Wiseman.[11] In effect, the public sector grows in discrete steps as a function of wartime growth of expenditures and taxes and never returns to prewar levels since (a) taxpayers recognize that a higher level of taxation is sustainable and (b) bureaucracies learn to perform certain functions during the war period and do not voluntarily relinquish them later.

In general the discussion of social balance has spawned propositions covering the entire range of empirical possibilities. At this point it would appear fruitful to narrow this range by careful testing of consistant theoretical formulations of the various hypotheses about dependence effects.

Collective Decision-Making Models

Anthony Downs has obtained a conclusion similar to Galbraith's—namely, that the government budget in two-party democracy tends systematically to be too small.[12] Extending the logic of his earlier published model of democratic political behavior,[13] he argues that democratic budgets are not expanded enough in certain directions when vote-maximizing parties compete for the support of utility-maximizing voters. The "correct" budget by Downs' benchmark is the budget which would emerge if political parties and voters had perfect information. This criterion is clearly ethical in character (as Downs stresses), requiring the value judgment that democracy works well under such conditions. Following this guide, he argues that many benefits of government action will not be produced in a complex and interdependent democracy where parties must appeal to voters lacking perfect information. Some governmental benefits

9. See Wagner (1890), Buchanan (1960), pp. 48–50, and Bird (1971) for discussions of Wagner's Law.

10. Greene (1973).

11. Peacock and Wiseman (1961) employed empirical data about the growth of the public sector in the U.K. For a recent argument in this same tradition with supporting data to the effect that provincial-state-local governments have been growing faster than central governments, see Davies (1970).

12. Downs (1960).   13. Downs (1957).

are remote and uncertain in nature, for example, the potential benefits of foreign aid expenditures in preventing a future war or those from safety and food and drug regulation. Voters are simply (and rationally) not aware of the potential returns from governmental activity in such areas and would not recognize such benefits *even if* political parties invested in an advertising program to make them known. On the other side of the fiscal account Downs argues that under realistic circumstances taxes, even indirect ones, are more accurately capitalized than the remote benefits.[14] This keener perception of taxes also inherently limits the process of minority or producer interest legislation (i.e., negative-sum games) which otherwise would overextend the democratic budget in terms of resource use. So, on net, the imperfectly capitalized benefits carry the day, and the budget size in a democracy tends to be too small. As society becomes more complex and interdependent, this tendency will become more pronounced.[15]

James M. Buchanan and Gordon Tullock have mounted arguments generally counter to those of Downs and Galbraith. They arrive at their position by employing a methodology similar to, though not identical with, Downs'.[16] Tullock argues that majority voting tends to result in overinvestment in specific benefits projects (e.g., rivers and harbors) at

14. It is possible that different tax institutions can affect the size of the budget due to different degrees of fiscal illusion associated with different financing measures. Buchanan has written extensively along these lines. See especially Buchanan (1964) and (1967), chapter 11. For another similar analysis, see Johnson and Pauly (1969).

15. Wheeler reports the results of some limited tests (based on educational data for the state of Maine) of models of underproduction of public outputs. See Wheeler (1967). Among the models that he purports to test are Downs' model of budget size and an argument by Margolis that the more fractionalized the governmental structure in an urban area, the smaller will be the local government budget. See Margolis (1961). Margolis bases his argument on the view that the closer government is to the voters, the more likely the individual voter is to discern his stakes in public action (i.e., being informed is less costly) and public expenditures are more restrained as a result. Thus, larger governmental units would tend to make informed voter choices more difficult and thereby expand these governmental units vis-à-vis smaller jurisdictions or lower-level units. Wheeler points out that this is a counterargument to Downs because less information for voters leads to larger, not smaller, budget sizes. Also, it is possible that voters are more conscious of the taxes employed by the smaller governmental units, and governments at this level do not expand as much as those at higher levels for this reason. Unfortunately, Wheeler reports inconclusive results from his tests.

16. Buchanan, (1961); Tullock (1959); Buchanan and Tullock (1962), especially chapters 10, 11, 12 and 14. The primary difference in methodology between Downs and Buchanan and Tullock is that Downs employed vote-maximizing parties *and* utility-maximizing voters as his units of analysis while Buchanan and Tullock adopt a purely individualistic methodology which stresses individual utility maximization as the basis for deriving implications regarding political institutions. For further discussion of the differences in these two approaches, see Buchanan and Tullock (1962), especially chapters 1–4, and Downs (1957), chapter 1.

the expense of general benefit items such as defense.[17] He adopts as benchmark a median voter's choice based on his perceived personal costs from collective action, a benchmark that includes no form of strategic or anti-social voter behavior, and is similar to Downs' in that it is an ethical criterion. If people deviate from this behavioral norm and form coalitions to exploit minorities for general benefits through discriminatory taxation, the government budget will be too large by the resource cost of such activity. In game-theoretic terms, negative-sum games are being played under simple majority rule, and resource wastage in such games equals the amount by which the value of the game to all participants (majority and minority) exceeds the value of the game to the winning coalition. If majority rule is viewed as the lowest acceptable collective decision rule, then resource wastage can proceed to the point where public investment is only slightly more than one-half as efficient as private investment. Buchanan and Tullock point out that whether the budget is pushed too far in terms of specific or in terms of general benefits, relative to the controlling median voter, depends on the fiscal taxation norm that applies in reality.[18] Assuming that the general taxation norm, albeit heavily eroded by pressure group exemptions, "fits" real-world democratic fiscal institutions, the implication is that general benefit items suffer at the expense of specific benefit items. Under these conditions the absolute budget size will be too large by the amount of the negative-sum games that such coalitions play. This outcome of resource wastage is strongly implied by Buchanan and Tullock and has been made explicit in a later paper by J. R. Davis and C. W. Meyer. Applying the game-theoretic approach to the issue of budget size, Davis and Meyer define the "correct" budget in a democracy as the summed dollar value of all positive-sum coalition games (zero-sum games are just pure transfers).[19] Thus, to the extent that democratic coalitions tend to play negative-sum games, the budget in a democracy will be "too large" by the amount of resources involved in these games.

Of course, the fact that negative-sum games can be played in political trading implies that such games are not played in a strictly voluntary setting. If participation were voluntary, one would not observe negative-sum games, since the affected minority could always refuse to particpate and thus avoid, for example, discriminatory taxation. Buchanan and Tullock explicitly discuss this point and argue convincingly that politics is not a voluntary process, but rather a coercive one where, under less than a unanimity decision rule, stable negative-sum games can be played.[20]

Indeed, the distinction between negative-sum and positive-sum games

17. Tullock (1959).   18. Buchanan and Tullock (1962), chapter 11.
19. Davis and Meyer (1969).   20. Buchanan and Tullock (1962), chapter 11.

is crucial to deciphering the confusion in the literature about what is good and bad about logrolling or vote-trading. Mueller, Tollison, and Willett discuss this point, focusing on structural characteristics in the system of representation that can lead to the negative-sum attributes of logrolling.[21] For example, negative-sum results can proceed from the fact that, given geographic representation, any representative is confronted with high payoffs from representing local interests in the national legislature by trying to logroll off the general tax system, and with virtually zero payoffs from campaigning on a platform of national efficiency. This asymmetry in payoff to the geographically based legislator is partly attributable to the greater information voters have about localized and specific public sector benefits, as compared with their knowledge about more remote general benefits.[22] Given also a seniority system in the legislature which gives monopoly power on important committees (e.g., in terms of which issues are put on committee agendas) to those districts that send back the same representative over a long period of time, the problem of overrepresention of local interests in the national legislature is compounded because legislative survival and the attainment of monopoly power within the legislature become functions of representing local interests.

What is bad, then, about this form of logrolling at the national level is not that it serves as a means for revealing relative intensities of preferences on national issues—indeed this is essential if one is to avoid imposing the will of passive majorities upon intense minorities (i.e., intensity problems)—but that in its most blatant forms it is used to reveal relative intensities of preference on essentially local issues that never should come before the national legislature.[23] When restricted to positive-sum games, logrolling can be beneficial in revealing voter preferences on issues. The confusion as to whether logrolling applies to positive- or negative-sum games can help to explain the disagreements among many observers over its possible benefits.[24]

Collective decision models, based on differing methodological approaches to the analysis of political behavior (in the case of Downs, a "realistic" approach emphasizing vote maximization by political parties and utility maximization by voters, and in the case of Buchanan and

21. Mueller, Tollison, and Willett (1974a).

22. Such geographically influenced negative-sum games are usually typical of "pork barrel programs," e.g., making Tulsa, Oklahoma, a seaport. Tullock (1970) stresses the difference in local voter information.

23. Mueller, Tollison, and Willett (1974a) present a "solution" to the intensity problem, emphasizing point voting and at-large proportional representation.

24. For examples of pro-logrolling arguments, see Buchanan and Tullock (1962), Coleman (1966) and (1970), Dahl (1971), Bentley (1938). See Lowi (1969) and McConnell (1966) for anti-logrolling positions.

Tullock, a thoroughgoing exposition based on methodological individualism),[25] also lead to diverse conclusions about budget size. Again, as in the last section, it is appropriate to emphasize the need for an empirical resolution of these conflicts, but we should also note that the theory of public choice provides a theoretical basis on which to build empirical tests. This is a marked improvement over the more widely known *ad hoc* discussion of social balance considered in the preceding section.

Models of Bureaucratic Behavior

An alternative approach to the issue of budget size in a democracy is that of developing positive models of bureau behavior. Interest in this aspect of public choice behavior is relatively recent and was pioneered by Downs and Tullock.[26]

Perhaps the most rigorous and intellectually appealing treatment of bureau behavior is contained in the recent work of W. A. Niskanen.[27] He develops a tentative model of bureau supply where the budget-maximizing monopoly bureau is predicted a priori to be "too large" becaue of the inherent all-or-none monopoly power embodied in the exchange of bureau output for a total budget, rather than for a per unit rate. In other words, one of the primary conclusions of his analysis is that under some conditions bureaus produce too much vis-à-vis the level of output that a comparable competitive industry would produce. Indeed, in a special case Niskanen obtains the fascinating result (Chapter 7) that whereas a competitive industry produces an optimal amount and a comparable monopoly one-half the optimal output, a comparable budget-maximizing bureau produces exactly *twice* the optimal output! Thus to Niskanen the output of the comparable competitive industry is the benchmark for the optimum budget size for a bureau, and his analysis indicates that budget size in democracy will generally be too large insofar as it is affected by the maximizing behavior of bureaus.

In a recent review of Niskanen's book, Thompson argues that Niskanen's implication of a too large budget is the result of his assumption that the bureau is in a superior bargaining position vis-à-vis its trustee, e.g. a congressional committee, with the result that the bureau can freely choose its output and obtain all-or-nothing prices for it.[28] Thompson points out that the situation is actually one of bilateral monopoly, and the solution of outputs and prices will be determined by the relative bargaining positions of the two parties. He stresses that the trustees are in a

25. Downs (1967) and Buchanan and Tullock (1962).
26. Downs (1967) and Tullock (1965).
27. See Niskanen (1968) and (1971), Enke (1968), and Stockfish (1972).
28. Thompson (1973).

stronger position and can in fact replace the bureaucrat if he refuses to produce their output at their price. He also suggests that the size of the budget in this context depends on how successful the bureaucrat is at misrepresenting actual expected costs and outputs so that the trustees select the output the bureaucrat wants to produce. In fact, given the logic of Niskanen's model and the condition that the bureau's customer is a monopsonist, it may be that the bureau underproduces rather than overproduces.[29]

In another review of Niskanen's book, Tullock takes exception to Niskanen's explanation that the budget grows over time because government services are superior goods.[30] Tullock argues that the budget expands because civil servants have an incentive to vote for those congressmen who are interested in expanding bureaus. Once the bureau is enlarged, it changes the ratio of civil servants to general citizens in such a way that one would expect further increases in the bureau's budget as the electorate becomes increasingly employed in the public sector. Tullock concludes by pointing out that though his alternative proposition as to why bureaus tend to expand is speculative, Niskanen's book serves a useful function in setting the stage for empirical testing.

Several other papers have drawn inferences about budget size from potential bureaucratic and political behavior. McKean argues the general point that there may be a divergence for government actors between individuals' perceived cost and the total costs of individual actions. Such divergences, stressed as social costs or negative externalities in the private sector, can turn out to be quite costly in the public sector as well, and the lack of institutional constraints on them can lead, following the traditional Pigovian logic, to a supraoptimal public sector.[31] On the other hand, more recent papers by Thomas Borcherding and Robert Bish and Patrick O'Donoghue stress the possibility of *underconsumption* of public goods due to the potential of bureaus to purchase factors monopsonistically to produce public outputs.[32] This is certainly a distinct practical

29. We would argue that in a "closed" model the link between geographic representation, majority rule, and vote-trading is the key in resolving the issue of over- or underproduction by bureaus. In this context the trustee and bureaucrat may both be motivated to influence the budget in the same direction, with the implication being overproduction. Niskanen's model addresses this issue when he discusses the demand conditions that could characterize the selection of the trustees of the bureau. See Niskanen (1971).

30. Tullock (1972).

31. See McKean (1964), (1965), and (1968), chapter 2. Recently, McKean has expressed a quite different view, arguing instead that government constraints such as the volunteer army will not have significant effects on efficiency because of a lack of appropriability. See McKean (1972), and Amacher and Tollison, (forthcoming).

32. See Bish and O'Donoghue (1970), and Borcherding (1971). Borcherding seems to withdraw his earlier analysis in Borcherding (1972). Olson (1965) recognized such a possi-

possiblity because of the monopsony situation that arises when consumers cooperate to demand public outputs under conditions of increasing costs.

In contradistinction to this discussion of how government bureaus behave in producing public outputs, it is useful to recognize that not all public goods are supplied by government. Parodoxically, many of the best examples of goods that fit the Samuelson definition of publicness (e.g., a melody) are supplied through normal market channels.[33] In contrast to Samuelson's original conclusion that public goods would be undersupplied in a market system, Thompson has argued that pure public goods, characterized by full divisibility over units of production and yet complete indivisibility among consumers, can be produced by competitive private markets.[34] In fact, he argues, a system of rational price discrimination will be used in the pricing of such goods so that each consumer will be charged his marginal valuation, and since average valuation exceeds marginal valuation, these kinds of public goods will be *oversupplied*.[35] In this case we therefore end up with a counter-Galbrathian conclusion that private markets will oversupply a certain subset of public goods.[36]

Even if we neglect the large quantity of additional contributions, especially those in the area of welfare economics, which could be related in one way or another to the question of budget size in a democracy, it is clear from the number of arguments reviewed in this section that qualita-

---

bility in the development of a public goods interpretation of group behavior. Olson discusses the social imbalance hypothesis in terms of the tendency of large groups of voters to attain suboptimal supplies (i.e., the government budget is too small) of public goods because of free-riding behavior.

33. See Samuelson (1954) and (1955).

34. Thompson (1968).

35. Thompson's analysis was controversial and spawned a discussion over what level of output would be produced. See Owen (1969), Rodgers (1969), Ganguly (1969), and the reply by Thompson (1969).

36. The economic theory of the private provision of public goods has also been applied to the issue of whether the standard public goods model can be interpreted as fully analogous to the Marshallian model of joint supply. Demsetz argues, in defense of the earlier arguments by Buchanan, that the two models are fully analogous, i.e. that a competitive equilibrium is consistent with differential prices among consumers of the public goods. See Buchanan (1961), Samuelson (1969), and Demsetz (1970b). However, in a recent paper Ekelund and Hulett (1973) argue convincingly that Demsetz's analogy hinges on a peculiar definition of competition, where producers do not compete (in the case of television tapes) across all viewing hours. They argue that the appropriate test of whether joint supply (competition) or price discrimination (monopoly) describes the case of the private provision of public goods is what happens under open price competition. They show that under open price competition monopoly emerges and the differential prices that go hand in hand with monopoly are the result of price discrimination and not any competitive, joint-supply properties of the model. Indeed, Head (1973) states (p. 5) that the correct analogy "would be the joint supply of various descriptively different products, the demand for which is monopsonistic."

tive economics alone cannot offer an answer. There are clearly several important conflicting tendencies. Empirical research to attempt to approximate the quantitative importance of the various factors discussed is essential if one hopes to find an answer to the question of whether government budgets tend to be systematically too large or too small according to commonly accepted criteria of desirable size. Indeed, the answer may well vary from one country to another.[37]

Risk Uncertainty, and Social Balance

Investigations into the possible existence of relationships between attitudes toward risk and the size of the budget have only recently begun. For example, Due has argued (in a passing reference) that since the benefits from public expenditures are uncertain, in the sense that the voter is unsure of the incidence of the expenditure, while privately provided goods are more certain in this respect, there will be a bias against outputs produced by the public sector.[38]

In a recently published paper, Greene has addressed the issue of risk and budget size in a more thorough and substantive manner. He stresses that many budget expenditures can be characterized as insurance-type activities and argues that the size of the budget may be responsive to the electorate's attitudes toward risk.[39] Interpreting the Friedman-Savage risk hypothesis in absolute rather than relative terms, Greene contends that expenditures on insurance-type public programs will be responsive to the absolute level of income in a country. Thus, at a low absolute level of income the electorate will be risk-averse and the public sector will be relatively large as a consequence. As a country advances into an absolute "middle-income" range, there will be a decline in public, insurance-type expenditures because the populace will become relatively less risk-averse. As a country's income increases to a high absolute level (the affluent society), insurance-type government programs will in relative terms increase again as the voters become relatively more risk-averse, since they now have greater wealth endowments to protect.[40] Greene tests his hy-

---

37. For example, it is an implication of some of the existing theory of alliances that defense spending for alliance purposes tends to be lower in the smaller member countries of the alliance. International interaction can thus have important effects on democratic budget sizes and the effect of this interaction is directly related to the relative size of the democracy. Thus, for instance, a conclusion that the defense budget in the United States tends to be too large might not carry over to a smaller country. For this discussion, see Olson and Zeckhauser (1966).

38. Due (1969).   39. Greene (1973).

40. For a related discussion in a different context, see Rawls (1971) and Mueller, Tollison, and Willett (1974b).

pothesis against data about the growth of the public sector in Great Britain and finds preliminary support for it. It represents a clear exception, at least in the middle-income range, to Wagner's Law of ever increasing government activity.

Summary

This literature review serves as a point of departure for our inquiry into risk avoidance and political advertising and their effects on the size of the budget. The following analysis begins from the position of Greene, who has analyzed the effect of risk and uncertainty on the size of the budget through the attitudes of the electorate, and interestingly, comes full circle to reconsider Downs' work, but stressing bureau behavior, a factor which Downs specifically excluded from his discussion. In this sense our analysis might be viewed as an extension of Downs' basic work, though it contradicts his major conclusion when applied to budget activities such as defense.

II. Risk and Uncertainty: A Neglected Issue in the Size of the Defense Budget

In this section we adopt a methodological position that takes the budget size preferred by the informed median voter as a benchmark and then investigate how bureaucratic behavior under conditions of risk and uncertainty can drive budgetary levels above that. As we have seen, this is the most typical assumption made in the literature on budget size in a democracy.

Traditional Structural Factors

The traditional view of bureaucratic behavior offers various explanations of why a bureau chief will generally want to expand his own bureau's activities beyond what the average voter-consumer or his legislative representative would approve. The bureau manager, in defense or elsewhere, may be better informed on the prospective benefits from government activity. Alternatively, he may be motivated simply by normal desires for promotion and larger budgets. As another possibility, the recruitment practices of each agency may naturally attract individuals who believe in the value of the bureau's product, be it defense, the SST, or conservation, and believe in it with a zeal which goes beyond the preferences of the informed median voter. Thus, defense managers may be personally more hawkish and less attuned to domestic problems than the average voter, may wish to allocate more funds to defense, and less to private and other public spending. There are, in fact, some observers who argue that this does tend to occur.[41]

A traditional factor unique to the military bureaucracy is the early retirement of military officers, relative to civilian officials. This may create a conflict of interest in that some military personnel can look forward to private employment with defense contractors at high renumeration after retirement. If the important officers of the military bureaucracy are able, or forced, to retire in their fifties, this means that crucial decisions on bureaucratic structure and function are being made by people still intent on capitalizing for their own future. Increasing the size of the Air Force is additionally attractive to Colonel X if he expects to spend some active years yet working for the company that produces the airplanes.

Risk and Uncertainty: A Conceptual Experiment

At least one other structural factor exists to suggest that defense managers tend to seek more budgetary expansion than their opposite numbers on the non-defense side. Bureaucrats are assumed to be always concerned with preserving their reputations. A visible "disaster" for the nation arising from one's bureaucratic domain is typically a personal disaster for the bureaucrat who is held responsible. The possibility of a major disaster may thus lead "responsible" officials to want to buy insurance (perhaps more insurance than the representative voter would find appropriate) in the form of larger budgets for their bureaus. But some parts of government do not deal with outputs which are subject to the strong possibility of disastrous outcomes. What, for example, can go wrong in the Census Bureau that would compare with a major foreign policy failure?

Consider the following conceptual experiment. Hold constant personality factors in the sense that the informed average voter-consumer is made a defense manager without a change in his tastes for alternative uses of defense resources. Assume also that his level of information does not change (he was already fully informed on defense problems) and that the individual's preference for risk does not change in the transition. Under these conditions (assuming he would be charged his pro rata share of the tax costs), would the individual choose the same level of defense as before as optimal for himself?

Any individual decision-maker's demand for national defense will be a function of decision-making under risk and uncertainty, since the alloca-

41. For example, in his survey of defense managers, Richard J. Barnet observes, "for a generation we have put in charge of the national security bureaucracy men who by virtue of career, training, and interests, have little sensitivity to public problems in domestic society." Barnet (1971), p. 21.

tion of additional domestic resources to defense should reduce, but cannot fully eliminate, risks of a major policy failure. A best estimate of the production possibilities schedule relating defense expenditure and probability that defense will be successful may be imagined.[42] Differences in levels of effectively demanded defense by defense managers, given the perceived transformation curve, will depend upon their views of and information about the benefits of preserving peace (or avoiding the costs of destruction), the desirability of the anticipated alternative uses of the resources involved, preferences toward risk, and the host of other factors conveniently summarized as "tastes." Given these factors, a decision-maker's indifference curves can be traced out between expenditures on national defense (again, assuming the individual pays the pro rata tax price of these expenditures) and the risk that defense will be inadequate. A simple analytical model of bureaucratic decision-making, where preferred equilibrium budget size depends on the individual decision-maker's perceived production possibilities schedule and indifference curves, can thus be represented.

The determinants of the indifference curves are now held constant, and the question posed is whether the average voter-consumer as defense manager will prefer the same size defense budget. Under these conditions it seems likely that the individual as a defense manager will behave in a more risk-averse manner because he perceives more personal costs of failure than he would face as an ordinary citizen. This effect exists because of the great degree to which the responsibility for defense is personified in the defense manager. In terms of operational behavior he will want to buy more insurance in the form of a higher defense budget (and higher pro rata tax payments). Likewise, a given individual may wish to buy more national defense as a member of the Armed Services Committee than he would as an ordinary member of Congress, and perhaps more as a member of Congress than he would as an ordinary citizen. So the systematic evaluation of the costs of policy failure in defense is predicted to vary directly with the individual's position in the decision-making hierarchy and to lead to insurance purchasing in the form of larger budgets as that position rises.[43]

42. This assumes, of course, that counterproductive programs—i.e., those that would stimulate a foreign response that would more than nullify the effects of the initial expenditure—are not adopted. Considerations involved in trying to make adversaries use up resources in this manner are ignored in this paper.

43. A similar point would apply in a private context to the analytical discussions of the separation of ownership and control in the modern corporation. Thus, conceptually at least, it is possible that stockholders may desire a "more risky" set of investments than management undertakes.

A Dependence Effect: Where We Are is not Independent
of How We Got There

There can also be a discrepancy between the defense manager's perception of efficient defense policies and the perception of the informed median voter, even where both have the same information about the relative costs and benefits of defense expenditures. In graphical analysis a dependence effect would be reflected in the shape of the production possibilities curve (between defense budgets and risks that defense will not be adequate) perceived by defense managers.[44] Quantitatively, an excessive defense budget (relative to that preferred by the median voter) may thus result from judgments made under uncertainty by defense decision-makers about their perceived set of efficient defense policies. For example, this effect could be reflected in defense managers lobbying not only for larger budgets (stocks), but also for faster rates (flows) of acquisition of new weapons systems. Some of the debate over ABM centered on whether or not that policy was on the defense spending/risk of policy failure production frontier. Much of the debate surrounding the SST was over the fate of Seattle—a clear dependence effect in budgetary discussions. Indeed, perhaps the clearest example of a dependence effect in defense decision-making is the arms race, where current choices on weapons acquisition are not independent of the path (i.e., past weapons systems) by which the United States arrived at its current stock of weapons systems. Huntington provides some evidence on the origin of possible dependence effects in the attitudes of defense managers: "By recruiting the National Security Manager from those who have been successful as conservators and managers in the booming domestic economy, we have built into the system a powerful bias in favor of a dynamic status quo—i.e., preservation of America's preeminent economic and military position as the continually increasing and projecting American power abroad." [45]

Summary

The traditional reasons why defense managers may be biased toward budgets that are "too large" have been reviewed, and we have introduced the additional concept of risk as it influences defense managers to ask for larger budgets as a form of insurance against a policy failure. However, there is a difference in what defense managers *want* and what they are *able* to obtain in the budgetary process. In the following section,

44. Galbraith (1958) discusses dependence effects associated with private economic activity such that new suppliers tend to generate their own demand.
45. Huntington (1961), p. 267.

the relationship between the inherent risk associated with defense expenditures and the *ability* of the Department of Defense to secure larger budgets is discussed.

III. Effectiveness of Defense Lobbying

In terms of traditional analysis, success in the budgetary process has been linked to having powerful advocates in the appropriate committees of Congress, and also powerful clientele groups lobbying in favor of budget extensions.[46] Defense activity has had the good fortune to have both. Note is also often taken of the "dynamic leadership" supplied by defense managers and by the congressional committee leaders supporting defense. Yet if the biases identified in the previous section have any reality, none of this "good fortune" and "dynamic leadership" should be surprising or unpredictable.[47] Indeed, as far as the various factors which yield an insurance-purchasing bias in defense decisions go, the powerful committee chairmen in Congress are virtually in the same position as upper-level defense managers within the executive branch.[48]

Differential Efficiency in Defense Advertising

An important determinant of the ability of defense managers to win budgets larger than those of "civilian-sector" and state and local bureaus

46. For a recent survey of literature on the budgetary process, see Sharkansky (1969). An excellent discussion of the defense budgetary process and the defense economy is Enthoven and Rowen (1961).

47. Of course, Presidential leadership in budgetary procedures is also important. A primary example of this in modern times is the so-called "Remainder Method" of determining defense spending used by President Truman and at some points by President Eisenhower. In this essentially balanced budget procedure, governmental revenues were estimated (or possible expenditures within the existing debt limit), domestic and foreign aid expenditures were deducted from this figure, and the remainder was allocated to defense. For a discussion, see Huntington (1961), p. 221. In fact, however, the services have frequently, in recent times, responded to spending vetoes or limits set by the secretary of defense or the President by taking their case directly to "friendly" congressmen. See Yarmolinsky (1971), p. 42.

48. In this sense, merely shifting more decision power over defense activity to Congress would probably not yield a defense budget more reflective of average voter preferences. One might argue, however, that congressional reforms that would result in involving a wider group of congressmen in actual decision-making about defense policies could help in this regard, especially in terms of offsetting the risk effect noted earlier. The behavioral psychology argument to support this argument is contained in the literature surrounding the risky-shift hypothesis. This literature stresses that in some cases groups are willing to tolerate more risk than individuals, although the reason for this is not clear (e.g., group leaders may be more tolerant of risk or groups may be able to spread risk more effectively or some combination of the two). For a survey of the literature on this subject, see Mandler, Massen, Kogan, and Wallack (1967), esp. pp. 111–266.

or to bias resource allocation decisions between defense and private sectors lies in defense advertising, lobbying, and their functional equivalents. The term "advertising" is employed here in a highly aggregated
sense. The functional equivalents of private sector advertising in the
Defense Department (defense expenditures for public demonstrations of
military effectiveness, other military public and press relations, lobbying
for budget approvals, and so forth) are all included in the definition of
defense advertising. The broad functional equivalence of these expenditures resides in the fact that they are similarly motivated, and this is the
sense in which the aggregate activity of defense advertising, or the selling
of defense spending, is introduced.[49]

Since some portion of a bureau's budget goes to lobbying for next
year's budget, one might expect economies or diseconomies of scale to
show up in comparing the effectiveness of the persuasive advertising or
lobbying of two public bureaus which differ in budget size. There are
various ways in this context that the Defense Department may be able to
bias budgetary outcomes both within the public sector and in relation to
the private sector.

To begin with, all public bureaus have one source of special effectiveness in advertising compared with the private sector: their ability to
concentrate the bulk of their efforts on a small group of decision-makers
in the Congress. Indeed, the structure of representative government generally enables public bureaus to obtain great efficiency from lobbying expenditures by selecting a relatively small number of effective decision-
makers. Private sector advertising, on the other hand, must influence
large numbers of decision-makers (consumers) to be effective.

A source of potential differential efficiency of defense advertising vis-
à-vis other public bureaus may be seen in the analogy of the private industry problem of the inter-firm versus inter-industry effects of advertising. The cigarette industry provides a convenient example of an oligopoly, where decentralized and uncoordinated advertising efforts tend to
reduce industry profits in a cancelling effect. A large portion of each
firm's advertising increases its costs without expanding the total demand
for cigarettes. The implication of this argument, usually discussed with
reference to the prisoner's dilemma, is that industry collusion would lead
to lower levels of advertising expenditures and both lower prices and
higher profits. Antitrust statutes make it impossible for firms in the private sector to do this openly. However, such collusion may exist in the
public sector whenever a large bureau such as Defense is able to coordi-

49. It will become clear as the discussion proceeds that useful analytical and empirical
work can be done by disaggregating the concept of defense advertising and looking at its
components.

nate the otherwise competitive advertising efforts of its component parts.

The Defense structure, of course, has also shown significant internal competition and lack of coordination, e.g., between the Air Force and Naval Air Force, between the Army and Marine Corps, and so on. What is important empirically in this context is whether the advertising by the various defense bureaus is competitive or complementary, and how these relationships compare with those between categories of non-defense spending. In other words, does the expansion of one defense bureau tend to result in the expansion or contraction of other defense bureaus and do similar or different relationships hold between non-defense bureaus? More generally, there exists for the public sector the problem of identifying "industries" in terms of demand relationships (cross-elasticities) among bureaus and in terms of which public outputs tend to be substitutes and which tend to be complements. Empirical work to classify public outputs in these terms where an industry concept is used would be helpful in discovering the degree of any differential efficiency that exists in public sector advertising.[50]

Some Procedural Aspects of Defense Advertising

When compared with domestic governmental activities, the defense establishment also has a couple of possible procedural advantages in selling itself to Congress. A small number of important legislators can make all the difference to the approval of a spending program (e.g., in terms of having items placed on a committee agenda), and a bureau can have a strategy that matches the spatial allocation of its expenditures with that of its important relations in Congress. If enough bureau spending can be channeled into the districts of these particular representatives, their support may be secured.[51] Defense expenditures may lend themselves more readily than others to being spatially allocated in this way. Defense

50. Such an attempt would involve the extension of B. Russett's work on the opportunity costs of defense to compute the relationships among other categories of public and private outputs. See Russett (1969) and (1970), chapter 5. This point is discussed further in section IV. Niskanen has an analytical discussion of the effect of changes in demand and cost conditions on bureau behavior. See Niskanen (1971), chapter 8.

51. Evidence on congressional voting behavior and military activity (especially the location of military employment) is presented in Russett (1970), especially chapter 3. For example, ". . . Department of Defense expenditures for military installations go to support and reinforce, if not to promote, a set of hawkish and strongly anti-communist postures in American political life. This support may be inadvertent, but it does exist. In turn, the Pentagon is supported, and its expenditures promoted by those voters and political leaders" (pp. 75 and 77). This issue is discussed, in the context of whether Defense Department or defense contractor lobbying is more important, at the end of the next subsection. The discussion is, of course, related to the possibility of geographically based legislators engaging in negative-sum political trades. For a discussion of this point, see Mueller, Tollison, and Willett (1974a).

spending may, for example, be able to generate more home district employment than HEW spending on cancer research.

There may also be links between military secrecy and the effectiveness of defense advertising. The procedure of selective declassification of information on increased Soviet threats just before votes on defense spending indicates such a link. In this manner the Defense Department's monopoly on certain information (quite aside from its interpretation of such information) can be used effectively in advertising the credibility of its budgetary requests.

Risk, Uncertainty, and Defense Advertising

As was argued above, bureaucrats may want to overinsure in the case of defense spending. However, can bureaucrats seeking their insurance premiums through the budgetary-political process induce the public to go along? In other words, where the voter-consumer must make a decision with respect to a form of insurance purchase against, for example, the small probability of a nuclear conflict, are his preferences particularly susceptible to advertising by bureaus for more spending?

On the one hand it may be argued that when faced with decision-making where there is a small probability of a large loss, the consumer-voter treats the relevant probabilities as zero. The traditional argument for the provision of social insurance is typically made in a similar form, where, for some reason, be it individual myopia or free-riding behavior, individuals tend to underinsure for retirement, against illness, and so on. But it should be stressed that in terms of our argument this view translates into a bias in the expression of decentralized, average voter preference. If bias toward underinsurance among voters exists, then risk-averse bureaus (if successful in the budgetary process) would tend to counterbalance the bias and push supplies of these public outputs toward optimal levels (or perhaps past optimal levels, depending on the relative strength of the two biases). In the following discussion we shall continue to refer to the benchmark of informed median voter outcomes while granting that it is possible that in some cases biases may be desirable on the basis of more comprehensive criteria.

On the other hand, it may be argued that the consumer-voter is very susceptible to advertising under the functionally equivalent conditions of the act of purchasing insurance. Bain has argued that it is in areas where consumers lack information that advertising is more effective, and defense purchases would seem to fall into this category.[52] Indeed, Fellner's

---

52. See Bain (1956), chapter 4. It should be noted, however, that his argument has to do with the establishment of separate and distinct brand identities by the firms in a competitive oligopoly. He does not discuss aggregate industry purchases in any simplified way.

work on the subjective skewing of probabilities suggests systematic limitations on the ability of decision-makers to make effective judgments about extremely important, but extremely improbable, events.[53]

Because decisions on the defense budget are subject to particularly high levels of risk and uncertainty, and generally fall into the category of the latter argument both in terms of outcomes and in terms of expected costs, systematic differences in administrative and median voter preferences in regard to national defense expenditures may thus be resolved in favor of the administrator's preferences.[54] Politically, it seems that arguments for the purchase of more insurance are almost always considered morally superior to arguments that one's insurance premiums are already excessive; even when one decides that it is wise to purchase less insurance, or forego purchasing more, a faint hint of impropriety remains. The intense discussion of the "missile gap" in the 1960 Presidential campaign is an excellent example of this point.

Thus consumer-voter decisions with respect to risky "insurance" activities may be particularly susceptible to the effects of advertising. In addition, decisions about activities with highly uncertain costs or returns may also be particularly susceptible to advertising influencing the individual's perception of the set of efficient policies which he faces (i.e., his production possibilities schedule). It is very hard to make a solid estimate of the probability of attack, and in such a situation the Defense Department may be able to influence strongly the individual's perception of the riskiness of a particular strategy, especially when the agency has near-monopoly power over the dissemination of pertinent information.[55]

Similarly, uncertainty on the costs of new weapons systems has allowed the military leeway to sell programs on the basis of prospective costs well below those eventually incurred. The greater the uncertainty over the eventual costs and benefits of a program, the greater should be an agency's ability to undertake advertising activity which will raise the "purchasers' " perception of the benefits and lower the perceived costs.

53. See Fellner (1965), especially chapter 6. The paradoxes proposed by Allais designed to refute the Von Neuman-Morgenstern utility-maximizing hypothesis were of a similar form. On this, see Samuelson (1966)., pp. 127–136.

54. Some forms of civilian activity (e.g., the prevention of epidemics), may fall into the same category, as we will give our medical advisers larger appropriations if they warn us urgently enough about smallpox.

55. The discussion of advertising and uncertain defense outcome is related to Galbraith's discussion of the use of fear in lobbying for defense spending. "There is the use of fear. This, of course, is most important. Anything which relates to war, and especially to nuclear conflict, touches a deeply sensitive public nerve. This is easily played on. The technique is to say, in effect, 'Give us what we ask, do as we propose, or you will be in mortal danger of nuclear annihilation.' " U.S. Congress (1969), p. 4. The use of "worst case analysis" (a minimax strategy) by defense officials is another example of the same kind of behavior.

If it is correct that the purchase of insurance is particularly susceptible to the effects of "advertising," then defense administrators who wish to purchase more defense insurance than the average voter can launch political advertising with great impact on the quantity finally demanded or accepted. Similarly, advertising by defense suppliers affects the amount of defense insurance that the public and defense decision-makers wish to buy, although there is some reason to believe that lobbying by defense contractors is the less important phenomenon. As Charles Schultze has observed:

The uniformed Armed Services and large defense contractors clearly exist. Of necessity, and in fact quite rightly, they have views about and interests in military budget decisions. Yet I do not believe that the "problem" of military budgets is primarily attributable to the so-called military-industrial "complex." If defense contractors were all as disinterested in enlarging sales as local transit magnates, if retired military officers all went into selling soap and TV sets instead of missiles, if the Washington offices of defense contractors all were moved to the west coast, if all this happened and nothing else, then I do not believe the military budget would be sharply lower than it now is. Primarily we have large military budgets because the American people, in the cold-war environment of the 1950's and 1960's, have pretty much been willing to buy anything carrying the label "Needed for National Security." The political climate has, until recently, been such that, on fundamental matters, it was exceedingly difficult to challenge military judgments, and still avoid the stigma of playing fast and loose with the national security.[56]

Additionally, Russett's finding that employment (e.g., bases) rather than contracts is an important explanatory variable in congressional voting on defense appropriations tends to support the view that lobbying by the military is more important than that by defense contractors.[57]

When one considers also the potential magnitude of defense insurance purchases as a proportion of the total budget, one realizes that there may be very significant distortion in the public sector due to the effects of defense advertising. Indeed, the distortion may not be confined to the federal level. To the extent that insurance-type activities are proportionately more prevalent at the federal than at the state or local government level, activity undertaken at the lower levels may be "too small" relative to total government activity.

IV. Tentative Empirical Examples

Some tentative evidence to support the argument that the expansion of public activities has the characteristic of an insurance purchase is given in R. F. Fenno's data on House Committee appropriations as a percentage

56. U.S. Congress (1969), p. 54.   57. Russett (1970), pp. 79–86.

of requests.[58] Many of the agencies that tended to fare best over a sixteen-year period in these terms could be characterized as insurance-type activities, including the FBI, FDA, and the Bureau of Narcotics. Empirical study of the budgetary process designed to discover the links between type of output and success in budgetary procedures would be extremely useful in generalizing the basis for the hypothesis on risky public outputs.

Another example of the hypothesis of overexpansion of risky, insurance-type government activities may be found in the economics literature on optimum levels of international reserves. Central bank and Treasury desires to hold high and growing levels of international reserves for defense of their currencies provide a very close analogue to Defense Department desires for high levels of military expenditure. One could note parallels with respect to secrecy and low levels of public or general congressional information, a strong lobby outside of government (the banking and financial community), and a high level of risk aversion among agency authorities recruited heavily from the banking and financial community.[59] In addition, the two public activities share a basic similarity as insurance-type activities. Fritz Machlup, in his investigation of the reserve-holding behavior of various countries, concluded that the demand for reserves could best be explained in terms of what levels and rates of growth made financial authorities happy.[60] H. Robert Heller found that countries' holdings of international reserves were generally much higher than his calculations of optimal reserve levels in terms of insurance against the risk of running out of reserves or having to meet a balance of payments deficit by internal deflation.[61] Both these analyses suggest that the dominance of financial authorities in the decision-making process leads to overinvestment in international reserves, as compared with an outcome based on informed median voter preferences.

Also an interesting aspect of the problem of public "industry" definition and differential efficiency in public sector advertising is the popular discussion of "national priorities." In effect this discussion may be a method used by non-defense bureaus of aggregating the guns-versus-butter dilemma so as to exploit any complementary advertising effects for domestic programs and to offset potential differential efficiency in coordinated and perhaps complementary defense advertising.[62]

Another method that may give some insight into demand relationships among defense spending, other public activities, and private spending, is Russett's work on the opportunity costs of defense spending. An appro-

---

58. Fenno (1966).   59. For the United States, see Canterbery (1968).
60. Machlup (1965).   61. Heller (1965).
62. For examples of this type of discussion, see Schultze, Hamilton, and Schick (1970), and Benson and Wolman (1971).

priate extension of this work would be to perform the same exercise for other public outputs and thus obtain the "cross-partials" to give approximations on the relationships among all major categories of public and private sector outputs.[63]

These empirical links are sketchy at best. Our discussion of advertising activity by public agencies raises a host of empirical questions that cannot be settled in this paper, but their resolution is especially important since the existing literature contains several competing hypotheses about budget size. The problems to be confronted can be mentioned. Are there empirical economies of scale in defense advertising? If so, how are they achieved?[64] Is advertising more effective where the public output is the purchase of an uncertain outcome? What are advertising-sales ratios for public agencies and how do they compare to private industry advertising-sales ratios?[65] Research along these lines would be very useful in developing an understanding of the intricacies of public policy formation and might indeed even raise problems that have not been addressed in the economics literature on industrial organization. For example, do large private firms that produce risky outputs tend to have higher advertising-sales ratios?

As was suggested earlier, a starting point for work in this area might be

63. Russett (1969) (1970). In extending Russett's measurements to other public outputs, what one wants to measure is the cross-elasticity of demand among the various categories of public and private outputs. Thus, for relationships among substitutes, this cross-elasticity measure would be negative, and for complements the relation would be positive. However, as between two outputs, regressions should be run *both* ways since one would get different results and, a priori, there is no reason to expect that the relationship runs strictly in one direction. Such estimates would ideally provide information on questions such as, if the Air Force is allocated X more budget dollars, what will happen to the budgets of the Army, Navy, HEW agencies, and so forth? In estimating cross-elasticities, care should be taken to hold constant as many factors influencing budget size as possible. In this regard, earlier empirical studies of the budgetary process which identified important independent variables in the determination of an agency's budget could be useful in estimating cross-elasticities. An important study of this type is Davis, Dempster, and Wildavsky (1968).

64. For efforts to determine empirically if there are economies of scale in private advertising, see Telser (1962), Simon (1965), and Peles (1971).

65. If one takes the recent estimate (by CBS News) of a Defense Department public relations budget of $200 million (recognizing that, as a real cost estimate, this figure would be biased heavily downward) and computes an advertising-sales ratio based on a defense budget of $70 billion, the result is approximately .003. This estimate compares very favorably with most private industry advertising-sales ratios and suggests that Galbraith may be correct about the comparatively heavier advertising in the private sector. However, the question whether there are economies of scale in defense advertising is especially interesting given the low computed advertising-sales ratio and the large absolute level of expenditures for such purposes. It should be noted, however, that the Pentagon admitted in 1969 to a public information force of 2800, with salary and operating costs of $27.9 million. The Pentagon also maintains a legislative liaison office with a budget of $3.3 million (1967). For these figures, see Yarmolinsky (1971), pp. 197 and 42, respectively.

to disaggregate the concept of defense and public agency persuasive activity in order to establish a taxonomy of such behavior. In the process it would perhaps be possible to collect reliable data series on the expenditures for advertising functions by public bureaus. Once such foundations had been established, an attempt could be made to integrate advertising behavior and attitudes toward risk with the existing economic and behavioral theories of bureaucratic activity. This is only a suggestive scheme. There are obviously difficult theoretical and empirical issues to be confronted. Nonetheless, important and useful work should be possible along these lines.

V. Conclusion

Downs argues in his seminal article on budget size that a two-party democracy will not produce enough of public outputs with highly uncertain or vaguely perceived returns. This paper, concentrating on the size of the defense budget, has argued the contrary case. The view presented here is that advertising exists in the public sector and that where agencies are both informing and persuading, Downs' argument that budgets for uncertain benefits are too small is open to question. Rather than viewing advertising as a well-defined form of public sector behavior, we have examined it in terms of functional equivalents such as a free press, lobbying, and so forth. Crucial to any empirical argument on this point would be the untangling of the propaganda and information content of current public sector advertising, a judgmental problem on which one would not expect unanimous agreement. Within the logic of the behavioral model we presented, pressure groups may play an important role in advertising the benefits of a public output and will possibly have an important impact on voter preferences where voters are purchasing an uncertain outcome. Defense suppliers are, of course, an excellent example of such a pressure group. Furthermore, if one introduces a Congress with monopolistic elements such as a strong committee system ruled by seniority, patronage and the activity of suppliers can interact in a less than perfectly competitive manner. This is especially the case with the defense budget. Here, the localized nature of defense spending, the small number of important decision-makers on defense expenditures, and the possibility of Defense Department public relations activity having an important impact under these conditions could be emphasized.[66]

66. The problem of introducing more realistic circumstances is perhaps best considered in terms of developing an analogue in models of public sector behavior to the concepts of imperfect competition and monopoly power in the private sector. The existing literature on pressure groups does not consider such problems in terms of analogues to imperfectly competitive private markets, even though it is clear that on many counts the activity of defense

It should also be noted with respect to the general problem of public-private imbalance that even if low advertising-output ratios are observed for public activities, one cannot conclude that comparatively heavier advertising by the private sector makes the public budget too small. This is again because of the possible existence of economies of scale in public sector advertising vis-à-vis private advertising activity.

Finally, it should be stressed that our discussion has raised many empirical questions that remain unsettled. It is hoped, however, that it offers a suggestive scheme for further empirical investigation.

References

Amacher, R. C., and R. D. Tollison. "A Note On Property Rights Within Government, and Devices to Increase Governmental Efficiency." *Public Finance Quarterly,* forthcoming.

Bain, J. *Barriers to New Competition.* Cambridge: Harvard University Press, 1956.

Barnet, Richard J. "The National Security Managers and the National Interest." *Politics and Society,* February 1971.

Benson, Robert, and H. Wolman, eds. *Counterbudget: A Blueprint for Changing National Priorities, 1971–76.* The National Urban Coalition, 1971.

Bentley, A. *The Process of Government.* Bloomington, Ind.: Principia Press, 1938.

Bharadwaj, K. "Marshall on Pigou's Wealth and Welfare." *Economica,* February 1972.

Bird, H. R. "Wagner's Law of Expanding State Activity." *Public Finance* 26, 1971.

Bish, R., and P. O'Donoghue. "A Neglected Issue in Public-Goods Theory: The Monopsony Problem." *Journal of Political Economy,* November–December 1970.

Borcherding, T. "A Neglected Cost of the Voluntary Military." *American Economic Review,* March 1971.

———. "Bureaucracy and the Welfare Consequences of Conscription and Voluntarism." (The Western Agora) *Western Economic Journal,* September 1972.

Buchanan, J. M. *The Public Finances.* Homewood, Ill.: Richard D. Irwin, 1960.

———. "Simple Majority Voting, Game Theory, and Resource Use." *Canadian Journal of Economics and Political Science,* August 1961.

———. "Politics, Policy, and Pigovian Margins." *Economica,* February 1962. Reprinted in J. M. Buchanan and R. D. Tollison, eds., *Theory of Public Choice.* Ann Arbor: University of Michigan Press, 1972.

———. "Fiscal Institutions and Efficiency in Collective Outlay." *American Economic Review,* May 1964.

———. *Public Finance in the Democratic Process.* Chapel Hill: University of North Carolina Press, 1967.

pressure groups can best be explained by such models. For an interesting discussion of such analogues, see Curry and Wade (1968), especially chapter 4.

——. *The Demand and Supply of Public Goods*. Chicago: Rand McNally, 1968.

——, and M. Kafoglis. "A Note on Public Goods Supply." *American Economic Review,* June 1963.

——, and G. Tullock. *The Calculus of Consent*. Ann Arbor: University of Michigan Press, 1962.

Canterbery, E. Ray. *Economics on a New Frontier*. Belmont, Cal.: Wadsworth, 1968.

Coase, R. "The Problem of Social Cost." *Journal of Law and Economics,* October 1960.

Coleman, J. "The Possibility of a Social Welfare Function." *American Economic Review,* December 1966.

——. "Political Money." *American Political Science Review,* December 1970.

Curry, R. L., and L. L. Wade. *A Theory of Political Exchange*. Englewood Cliffs, N.J.: Prentice-Hall, 1968.

Dahl, R. *After the Revolution*. New Haven: Yale University Press, 1971.

Davies, D. "The Concentration Process and the Growing Importance of Noncentral Governments in Federal States." *Public Policy,* Fall 1970.

Davis, J. R., and C. W. Meyer. "Budget Size in Democracy." *Southern Economic Journal,* July 1969.

Davis, O., M. Dempster, and A. Wildavsky. "A Theory of the Budgetary Process.' *American Political Science Review,* September 1966.

——, and A. Whinston. "Externality, Welfare and the Theory of Games." *Journal of Political Economy,* June 1962.

Demsetz, H. "Discussion." *American Economic Review,* May 1970.

——. "The Private Production of Public Goods." *Journal of Law and Economics,* October 1970b.

Downs, A. *An Economic Theory of Democracy*. New York: Harper and Row, 1957.

——. "Why the Government Budget is Too Small in a Democracy." *World Politics,* July 1960.

——. *Inside Bureaucracy*. Boston: Little, Brown, 1967.

Due, J. *Government Finance: Economics of the Public Sector*. Homewood, Ill.: Richard D. Irwin, 1969.

Ekelund, R., and J. Hulett. "Joint Study, the Taussig-Pigou Controversy, and the Competitive Provision of Public Goods." *Journal of Law and Economics,* October 1973.

Enke, S. "Comment." *American Economic Review,* May 1968.

Enthoven, A., and H. Rowen. "Defense Planning and Organization," in J. M. Buchanan, ed., *Public Finance: Needs, Sources, and Utilization*. Princeton: Princeton University Press, 1961.

Fellner, W. *Probability and Profit*. Homewood, Ill.: Richard D. Irwin, 1965.

Fenno, R. F. *The Power of the Purse*. New York: Little, Brown, 1966.

Galbraith, J. K. *The Affluent Society*. Boston: Houghton Mifflin, 1958.

Ganguly, S. "The Perfectly Competitive Production of Collective Goods: Comment." *Review of Economics and Statistics,* November 1969.

Greene, Kenneth. "Attitudes Toward Risk and the Relative Size of the Public Sector." *Public Finance Quarterly,* April 1973 [Reading 29, below].

Hayek, F. A. "The *Non Sequitur* of the Dependence Effect." *Southern Economic Journal*, April 1961.

Head, J. "Public Goods: the Polar Case." In R. Bird and J. Head, eds., *Modern Fiscal Issues*. Toronto: University of Toronto Press, 1973.

Heller, H. Robert. "Optimal International Reserves." *Economic Journal*, June 1965.

Huntington, S. *The Common Defense*. New York: Columbia University Press, 1961.

Johnson, D., and M. Pauly. "Excess Burden and the Voluntary Theory of Public Finance." *Economica*, August 1969.

Johnson, H. G. "An Economic Approach to Social Questions." *Economica*, February 1968.

Lowi, T. *The End of Liberalism*. New York: W. W. Norton, 1969.

Machlup, Fritz. *The Need for International Reserves*. Princeton: Princeton University International Finance Section, 1965.

Mandler, G., P. Massen, N. Kogan, and M. A. Wallack. *New Directions in Psychology III*. New York: Holt, Rinehart, and Winston, 1967.

Margolis, J. "Metropolitan Finance Problems: Territories, Functions, and Growth," in J. M. Buchanan, ed., *Public Finances: Needs, Sources, and Utilization*. Princeton: Princeton University Press, 1961.

McConnell, G. *Private Power and American Democracy*. New York: Alfred A. Knopf, 1966.

McKean, R. M. "Divergences Between Individual and Total Cost Within Government." *American Economic Review*, May 1964 [Reading 23, above].

———. "The Unseen Hand in Government." *American Economic Review*, June 1965.

———. *Public Spending*. New York: McGraw-Hill, 1968.

———. "Property Rights Within Government, and Devices to Increase Governmental Efficiency." *Southern Economic Journal*, October 1972.

Misham, E. J. "The Postwar Literature on Externalities: An Interpretative Essay." *Journal of Economic Literature*, March 1971.

Mueller, D., R. Tollison, and T. Willett. "Solving the Intensity Problem in Representative Democracy." Mimeo., 1974a [Reading 30, below].

———, Robert Tollison, and Thomas Willett. "The Utilitarian Contract: A Generalization of Rawls' Theory of Justice." *Theory and Decision*, 1974b [Reading 20, above].

Niskanen, W. A. "Nonmarket Decision Making: The Peculiar Economics of Bureaucracy." *American Economic Review*, May 1968.

———. *Bureaucracy and Representative Government*. Chicago: Aldine, 1971.

Olson, M. *The Logic of Collective Action*. Cambridge: Harvard University Press, 1965.

———, and R. Zeckhauser. "An Economic Theory of Alliances." *Review of Economics and Statistics*, August 1966.

Owen, B. M. "The Perfectly Competitive Production of Collective Goods: Comment." *Review of Economics and Statistics*, November 1969.

Peacock, A. T., and J. Wiseman. *The Growth of Public Expenditure in the United Kingdom*. New York: National Bureau of Economic Research, 1961.

Peles, Y. "Economies of Scale in Advertising Beer and Cigarettes." *Journal of Business,* August 1971.

Rawls, J. *A Theory of Justice.* Cambridge: Harvard University Press, 1971.

Rodgers, J. "The Perfectly Competitive Production of Collective Goods: Comment." *Review of Economics and Statistics,* November 1969.

Russett, B. *What Price Vigilance?* New Haven: Yale University Press, 1970.

———. "Who Pays for Defense?" *American Political Science Review,* June 1969.

Samuelson, P. A. "The Pure Theory of Public Expenditure." *Review of Economics and Statistics.* November 1954.

———. "Diagrammatic Exposition of a Theory of Public Expenditure." *Review of Economics and Statistics,* November 1955.

———. "Utility Preference and Probability." In J. E. Stiglitz, ed., *The Collected Scientific Papers of Paul Samuelson.* Cambridge: M.I.T. Press, 1966.

———. "Contrast between Welfare Conditions for Joint Supply and Public Goods." *Review of Economics and Statistics,* February 1969.

Schultze, C., E. K. Hamilton, and R. Schick. *Setting National Priorities: The 1971 Budget.* Washington: Brookings Institution, 1970.

Sharkansky, I. *The Politics of Taxing and Spending.* New York: Bobbs-Merrill, 1969.

Simon, J. L. "Are There Economies of Scale in Advertising?" *Journal of Advertising Research,* 1965.

Stockfish, J. *The Political Economy of Bureaucracy.* New York: General Learning Press, 1972.

Telser, L. "Advertising and Cigarettes." *Journal of Political Economy,* October 1962.

Thompson, E. "The Perfectly Competitive Production of Collective Goods." *Review of Economics and Statistics,* February 1968.

———. "The Perfectly Competitive Production of Public Goods: Reply." *Review of Economics and Statistics,* November 1969.

———. "Review of *Bureaucracy and Representative Government* by W. A. Niskanen." *Journal of Economic Literature,* September 1973.

Tullock, G. "Problems of Majority Voting." *Journal of Political Economy,* December 1959.

———. *The Politics of Bureaucracy.* Washington: Public Affairs Press, 1965.

———. "A Simple Algebraic Logrolling Model" *American Economic Review,* June 1970.

———. "Review of *Bureaucracy and Representative Government* by William Niskanen." *Public Choice,* Spring 1972.

U.S. Congress. *The Military Budget and National Economic Priorities.* Hearings before the Subcommittee of the Joint Economic Committee. Washington: U.S. Government Printing Office, 1969.

Wagner, A. *Finanzwissenschaft.* Leipzig, 1890.

Wheeler, H. J. "Alternative Voting Rules and Local Expenditure: The Town-Meeting v.s. City" *Papers on Non-Market Decision Making,* II, 1967.

Yarmolinsky, A. *The Military Establishment.* New York: Harper and Row, 1971.

29. Attitudes toward Risk and the Relative Size of the Public Sector *

KENNETH V. GREENE

While much recent research in economic theory has been devoted to the problems of choice under uncertainty, little has considered the effect of uncertainty in the benefit streams of collectively provided goods and services on the choice mechanism of the individual taxpayer-consumer.[1] In discussing the differences in the qualities of collectively provided goods and services, as compared to their privately provided counterparts. John Due (1969) has maintained that the former involve a greater "degree of uncertainty" for the consumer-taxpayer. This is true, he contends, both on the benefit and on the tax side of the ledger. He concludes that a "bias"[2] exists against collectively provided goods and services; that because of uncertainty the taxpayer-consumer will prefer privately provided goods.

Due offers this observation only in passing, while discussing the "peculiar" characteristics of public goods and services. When his argument is subjected to critical scrutiny, interesting questions arise. Are the benefit streams of publicly provided goods or services inherently more or less uncertain than those of private goods and services? If so, would this mean that there would always be a "bias" for or against public goods' provision? If not, can the preferences of certain income classes be identified and changes in a society's income distribution be used to predict the relative size of the public sector through time?

This paper attempts to cast at least some light on these questions. The initial section examines the nature of benefit and cost streams to the individual taxpayer-voter. There follows a discussion of the relevance of the Friedman-Savage (1948) hypothesis to the preferences of different in-

Reprinted from *Public Finance Quarterly,* Vol. 1, No. 2 (April 1973) pp. 205–218 by permission of the Publisher, Sage Publications, Inc.

* The author wishes to thank Daniel Newlon, James Buchanan, and an anonymous reviewer for comments which improved this paper.

1. This is not to deny that much has been written on uncertainty and the proper criterion for government investment decisions. See, for instance, Arrow and Lind (1970) as a recent example. Moreover, Zeckhauser (1969) has contributed an excellent summary piece on uncertainty as a justification for governmental action.

2. A strong taste for or against something arrived at on rational grounds is usually not identified as a bias by economists. Such an identification would be the economist's own value judgment—hence, our quotation marks.

come groups for public services. Next, this hypothesis is allied to the changing structure of absolute income distributions to derive implications for the relative size of the public sector. Historical data for one market-oriented democratic society, Great Britain, are presented. While in and of itself, such data prove little, they illustrate that the hypothesis is not necessarily inconsistent with past events.

The Nature of Public Goods and Services

While a subtle distinction is often made between risk and uncertainty,[3] here the precise demarcation line will be ignored. Professor Due's statement to the effect that the benefits from public goods and services are uncertain is interpreted to mean that the consumer-taxpayer-voter contemplating a purchase can attach only a subjective probability to each of a number of distinct benefit levels possible after the purchase.[4]

Do benefit streams from collectively provided goods involve more uncertainty than those from private goods? The answer is moot. Many private goods have fairly certain benefit streams. The enjoyment derivable from a box of cornflakes or a bag of pretzels varies very little for the same individual within a reasonable period of time. Conversely, the benefits from many public services are quite uncertain. The returns from an additional $1 million spent on local libraries are but conjectural for the individual taxpayer-voter.

On the other hand, although categorization is difficult, an examination of Table 1 may imply that the bulk of governmental services may well fall into the category of insurance-type services.

These services are designed to minimize possible fluctuation in real-income streams and provide such insurance in areas where the market finds it extremely difficult, if not impossible, to do so. At the federal level, national defense and the interest on the debt incurred for national defense are the most obvious examples. They are a means by which the populace agrees to pool its resources to prevent large and severe losses of economic, nationalistic, and moral capital. Again, at least in terms of realpolitik, expenditures on international affairs may be similarly conceived. Most health and welfare expenditures lend themselves to a parallel interpretation. Health expenditures are designed to minimize economic losses and even welfare expenditures may be designed to ensure the citi-

3. The classic example is Frank H. Knight's (1921) distinction.
4. It must be admitted that this interpretation may be unfair to Professor Due. Although he is not clear, he may be referring to uncertainty in the Knightian sense. In that case, however, there is no definite line of reasoning which would lead to the conclusion that uncertainty creates a "bias." Ignorance of the benefits of a good need not prejudice one against it. There may be some truth to the maxim that "the grass is always greener on the other side of the fence."

Table 1. Categories of federal, state, and local direct government and social insurance trust fund expenditures in the United States (fiscal 1969)

Function	Amount (in millions)	% of total	% of total excluding 1 and 2
1. National defense and international relations	$ 84,253	26.2	—
2. Interest on federal debt	14,037	4.4	—
3. Space research and technology	3,691	1.2	1.7
4. Health and hospitals	13,588	4.2	6.1
5. Public welfare	17,517	5.5	7.9
6. Social insurance administration	1,790	.5	.8
7. Natural resources	11,649	3.6	5.2
8. Social insurance trust fund expenditures	48,521	15.1	21.8
9. Police protection	4,903	1.5	2.2
10. Fire protection	2,024	.6	.9
11. Education	55,771	17.4	25.0
12. Other	63,624	19.8	28.5
Total	$321,368	100.0	100.0

Source: U.S. Bureau of the Census (1971: 23).

zen a certain floor level of real income. Expenditures on natural resources ensure against floods, drought, and against the possibility that our heirs will be left penniless as far as their natural environment is concerned. Space research and veterans' benefits may be connected with ensuring national defense on the one hand and as a pure insurance scheme on the other.

At the state-local level, fire and police services are obviously risk-averting activities. So are most health and welfare expenditures. The most important expenditure category on the state-local level, education, is usually justified on the grounds of interpersonal spillovers of educational benefits and as a means of assuring a more egalitarian society. Insofar as it fulfills the latter purpose, it too can be thought of as a social insurance scheme. Such expenditures assure the voter that even if his own or others' heirs do not have sufficient economic resources, they will not be condemned to a cycle of indefinite poverty created by their lack of education. The same motive drives an individual to take out a private life insurance policy.[5]

It appears that the vast bulk of government expenditures may be considered insurance against the risks of various possible but unforeseen events. Approximately eighty percent of total direct and insurance trust

5. There is considerable economic literature which interprets redistributive governmental programs as a form of social insurance (see, for instance, Buchanan, 1967, and Newlon, 1970).

fund expenditures, and seventy percent of total nondefense, nonfederal debt service spending may be classified in the insurance category. In fact, this, in essence, has been the criticism of those who decry the rise of the welfare state. They argue that mankind is trading risk, progress, and growth for the sweet serenity provided by the "great insurer"—the state.

But there is another side to the argument that the "purchase" of public services involves more uncertainty. One may argue that the individual taxpayer, when considering public expenditure and revenue measures, is highly uncertain of his own tax price. His own behavior, which will influence his total tax bill, is in the future. Moreover, his own tax will be influenced by the uncertain actions of other taxpayers. The prices of private goods and services, or so the argument goes, are fixed and certain.

Such reasoning is a bit misleading. It forces one to compare the price of buying a bag of pretzels with the taxes to be paid over one's lifetime if the federal government decides to subsidize the development of an interplanetary transportation system. A proper comparison involves choices with consequences which reverberate over equally long time spans. If such comparisons are made, it is by no means obvious that the price of private goods is necessarily more certain. For instance, if I decide to buy a house, the real cost of the mortgage payments is neither more nor less certain than the property taxes I will pay over the next thirty years to finance a community college. I possess only a subjective probability distribution of both real interest rates and real property taxes. Nor is it only the possibility of price instability that creates the uncertainty for my housing costs, the true costs of the mortgage are my alternative investment returns, and these depend as much on the actions of a whole host of economic agents as do my tax payments.

Even if the prices of public services were inherently less certain, tax institutions tend to be rather stable, and tax structure decisions tend to be separated from expenditure decisions. The implication is that when individuals decide whether or not they approve of a government expenditure program, they rarely are confronted with any idea of the method of its financing. One can discuss, therefore, the preferences of individuals for or against public goods provision without dragging in the tax side of the fiscal account.

The Friedman-Savage Hypothesis and the Demand for Public Services

Whether an individual has a "bias" for or against certainty depends on the shape of his marginal utility of income curve. If it is assumed that the marginal utility of income is constantly declining, the consumer-voter tries to maximize his expected utility, and the joys of gambling are nonexistent, then he will prefer a certain outcome to a series of uncertain outcomes with the same expected payoff. If the marginal utility of income is increasing, the exact opposite will be true. Presuming that most public goods are of the insurance type, then there will be a "bias" toward publicly provided services in the one case, and a bias against them in the other.

The shape of the utility-of-income curve hypothesized by Friedman and Savage (1948), has some interesting implications for preferences for and against public goods of the insurance type. Their hypothesis sometimes has been interpreted to mean that those individuals relatively high or low in the income distribution have declining marginal utilities of income, while those in the middle-income class place increasing marginal utilities on successive increments in income. On this interpretation, the implication is that the lower- and upper-income classes, ceteris paribus, would be favorably disposed to the bulk of public expenditures which are of the insurance type. The middle-income class would be inclined to oppose such expenditures; to prefer that the money be used in the private sector for the purchase of goods and services with the same expected payoffs, but with some potential variability in their payoffs.

Of course, this factor will be only one of many determining an individual's taste for public spending programs. Surely, in any one expenditure decision, it will be the individual's own contemplated benefits and tax burdens which will weigh most heavily in his mind. But here the purpose is to abstract from any of the distributional considerations and focus in solely on the effects of uncertainty on the demands for public services by different income groups.

If the Friedman-Savage hypothesis is applicable here, then presuming a purely democratic decision-making rule, the distribution of income is a relevant parameter in determining the size of the public sector. For instance, a symmetric distribution of the three classes would tend to lead to the conclusion that a majority would favor many insurance-type public services. As a result, the public sector might be large. But what is more important is that, if the relative income distribution shows a certain pattern of change in the case of economic growth, a pattern of change in the relative size of the government sector may be predicted.

The Friedman-Savage hypothesis, however, has been subjected to some rather devastating criticisms. Markowitz (1952) notes that it implies behavior not observed in reality. In the first place, it predicts that neither those in the upper nor those in the lower reaches of the income distribution will ever accept fair bets. Neither group would ever enjoy a night of poker with the boys.[6] Moreover, insurance salesmen would rarely call on middle-class clients—there would be none! Hirschleifer (1966) points out an even more damaging implication of the Friedman-Savage hypothesis. If it were true, the middle-income class would be quite unstable. Its members would tend either to sink into the lower classes or to become nouveau riche.[7] Such a U-shaped income distribution has not been witnessed. The thesis is therefore contradicted by reality.

It is the contention here, however, that the Friedman-Savage hypothesis has been misconstrued. Properly interpreted, it may have essential validity, does not contradict observable behavior, and may have implications for the relative size of the public sector in a democracy through time. The solution lies in distinguishing relative from absolute income.

To a large extent, it may be an individual's absolute income level which determines his attitude toward risk. Those who receive only a small level of real income will be risk averters, at least with respect to bets of a significant size, precisely because they will be particularly adverse to literally playing with their lives. Those who receive an income considerably in excess of that necessary for "the good life" will be prone to risk that portion of their income over and above subsistence for a chance at such a life. Those who already have the real income necessary for all necessities and the bulk of amenities will be interested in preserving the latter and will be risk-averse. Although the concept of absolute income is by no means unambiguous, it is difficult to deny that it does influence behavior. This is a substantial difference between those who are in the middle of the relative income distribution in the United States and those in the same position in Zambia. It seems reasonable to presume that it might affect the attitude toward risk.[8]

On this interpretation, it is no wonder that we observe the bulk of the population in a country like the United States buying insurance. Absolutely speaking, most are rich and hence are risk averters. Still it is not surprising that parimutuel and off-track betting flourish. No one denies that there are joys of gambling and that they probably have a positive income elasticity.

Nevertheless, the Friedman-Savage hypothesis interpreted in absolute-income terms does have an implication for the growth of the public sector

6. Actually, this is putting things a bit too strongly. The "joys of gambling" could always be introduced as a deus ex machina but the purpose of the Friedman-Savage hypothesis is to explain behavior in risky situations without such a ploy.

7. It is interesting to note that Friedman and Savage (1948: 303) recognized this. In fact, they predicted the instability of the middle classes.

8. It must be admitted that the reader certainly comes away from the Friedman-Savage piece assuming that they are discussing relative income positions. This leaves them open to the charges made by their critics.

of an economy during its stages of development. If, for instance, in the early stages of economic growth, the vast bulk of the population is poor in absolute terms, with but a few in the middle- and upper-income classes, there will be a "bias" for public provision, since most public services are designed to avert risk. If a democratic decision-making rule exists and if legislators act according to the wishes of their constituents, then a rather large proportion of GNP will tend to be devoted to the public sector.

If the economy possesses the sources of growth, the absolute income distribution will tend to change. The majority of the lower classes will be transferred into the middle-income class, where they will receive at least some amenities in addition to their share of necessities. This middle class, however, will possess increasing marginal utilities of income and will be risk-prone. They will be "biased" against the insurance-type services of the public sector. If the preferences of the majority are reflected, a laissez faire attitude toward government will evolve. In fact, neither public nor private insurance schemes will be particularly attractive.

Because of the fact that most investments have substantial positive payoffs, however, the absolute income distributions will continue to rise. The majority of the population will become absolutely rich. Having "made it," they will become risk-averse. The "bias" toward insurance and the public sector will appear again, and the "welfare state" will begin to develop.[9]

The paucity of very long-term data on total public expenditures does not permit us to test this hypothesis explicitly. Moreover, practically, it might prove impossible to test even with the best of data or expenditures and GNP levels. The hypothesis does not deny that other things, most importantly the distribution of the benefits and tax burdens by income class, do influence the preferences of different income groups for public goods. Attempts to measure these interclass benefits and burdens through history

9. An interesting addendum may be added to these predictions if we conceive of the tax structure being determined by the controlling coalition and if this coalition passes tax structures which are extremely favorable to this coalition. In the initial and terminal stages of development, the poor and rich would then favor public expenditures even more so, and this would tend to strengthen the predictions. In the middle stage, if the controlling middle-income group passes tax structures favorable to itself, our prediction will be muted.

Of course, if the tax structure is considered set at the "constitutional stage" of decision-making and remains invariant, the predictions are left unmodified.

On the other hand, a progressive tax structure could be interpreted as a form of insurance and, therefore, more likely to be adopted in the first and last stages. Thus, the prediction of a relatively large public sector in the first stage would be reinforced. The prediction of a relatively large public sector in the last stage would be muted, but, perhaps, not greatly, because, if there are relatively many rich people, a progressive tax structure could still mean a low percentage of any given tax bill paid by the "rich" individual.

would be extremely difficult. The best that can be done is to draw on the work of Peacock and Wiseman (1961) and Veverka (1963) for the United Kingdom. This is the only country for which data, on GNP and total government expenditures: central state and local are available for more than a century. Compiled U.S. data, for instance, do not provide total state and local expenditures before 1880.

The data in Table 2 do tend to conform at least roughly to the predictions derived from the hypothesis presented here. The tendency is more striking when we look at total government expenditures as a percentage of GNP. Given the Napoleonic Wars, however, this may be misleading. But, for what statistics we do have, it is also present for non-defense-debt expenditures as a percentage of GNP. In general, if we placed time on the horizontal axis and expenditures as a proportion of GNP on the vertical, the observations would be more or less U-shaped.

Table 2. Government expenditures as a proportion of GNP in Great Britain

Year	Total expenditures in current prices as a % of GNP in current prices	Total expenditures, less defense, interest on the debt and other war-related expenditures as a % of GNP in current prices
1790	12	4.3
1800	22	—
1810	23	—
1820	17	—
1830	15	—
1840	11	3.7
1850	11	—
1860	11	—
1870	9	—
1880	10	—
1890	8	4.8
1900	14	6.5
1910	12	8.0
1920	26	10.6
1932	29	18.3
1938	30	16.4
1951	40	25.9
1961	38	26.4

Source: Veverka (1963: 114, 119).
Note: Figures before 1890 are Veverka's estimates. Those after 1890 are those of Peacock and Wiseman. Although in this article, Veverka promised a book containing data for intermediate years, it has not been forthcoming; hence, the blanks for most years before 1890. Note also the last column estimates for 1900, 1920, 1938 are not in Veverka's article and have been calculated directly from Peacock and Wiseman (1961: Table 2, and Table 3, 55).

The rest of the published studies which provide long-run estimates of both government expenditures and gross national product (for example, Andic and Veverka, 1964; Musgrave and Culbertson, 1953) at best stretch back only into the 1890s and therefore prove rather useless for testing the hypothesis put forward. Cross-section studies of different countries in the same relative stages of development may be thought capable of giving us some evidence. As Musgrave (1968) reports, there is no significant correlation between income and the proportion of gross national product spent by the government for either underdeveloped (below $300 per capita in the mid-1950s) or developed (above $600 per capita) countries. A significant positive relationship was found within the intermediate group of developing countries.

The relevance of the results of these studies for our hypothesis is unclear. What is considered subsistence income and what is considered enough income to sustain some amenities will differ among countries. A country classified in the intermediate category of these cross-section studies may psychologically consider itself to have most of the good things of life. Moreover, if there were not these intercountry differences, there would still exist the ambiguity involved in choosing the correct breakoff points between "underdeveloped," "developing," and "developed" countries. The hypothesis is suitably tested only by looking at particular countries over long periods of time, including their period of development.[10]

One further piece of evidence lending some credibility to the thesis should be noted. It implies that, during the stage of development, private insurance schemes should also be unpopular.

Financial markets were not well enough developed for the life insurance industry to become very significant in the United States until the 1850s. But one can infer from Table 3, the relative decline of the industry from a peak in 1871 which was not reached again until 1892. Once again, however, one cannot contend that these figures prove the thesis. Other conditions, including some financial upheavals, occurred during the period.

In summary, the attitude toward risk on the part of different income classes may be a factor which qualifies Wagner's Law. The hypothesis developed in this paper may meet the same objections as Wagner's own hypothesis. There are many qualifying circumstances. Certainly no all-embracing explanation of the pattern of growth of the public sector has been established. But, as Richard Bird (1971: 24) writes in a recent article concerning Wagner's Law, "Yet which is more important in the final analysis, the sweeping statement, wrong in many details but pointing to new horizons or the careful, rigorous tidying up and testing of

10. Note this is quite a different hypothesis than our own, because Wagner's hypothesis is based on an organic conception of the state. There is no role for individual preference and choices; the state's role expands because it ought to. Moreover, note that Wagner implies a continuing increase in the relative share of the public sector, rather than a cyclical pattern.

Table 3. Life insurance in force in the United States as a percentage of Gross National Product

Year	%	Year	%
1850	3.76	1881	14.25
1855	2.72	1884	18.19
1860	4.51	1887	20.46
1865	8.99	1890	25.41
1870	27.27	1891	27.41
1871	27.58	1892	30.52
1872	24.39	1895	37.39
1875	22.80	1898	38.04
1878	18.94	1901	39.68

Source: Gross National Product estimates taken from Berry (1968: 32). Life Insurance estimates from Institute of Life Insurance (1970: 16–17).

previously formulated hypotheses? I am inclined to opt for the former annoying as it may often be.''

References

Andic, S. and J. Veverka (1964) "The growth of government expenditures in Germany since the unification." *Finanzarchiv* 23: 169–278.

Arrow, K. J. and R. C. Lind (1970) "Uncertainty and the evaluation of public investment decisions." *Amer. Economic Rev.* 60: 364–378.

Berry, T. S. (1968) *Estimated Annual Variations in Gross National Product, 1789–1909.* Richmond: Univ. of Virginia Press.

Bird, R. (1971) "Wagner's law of expanding state activity." *Public Finance* 26: 1–26.

Buchanan, J. M. (1967) *Public Finance in Democratic Process.* Chapel Hill: Univ. of North Carolina.

Crowley, R. W. (1971) "Long swings in the role of government: an analysis of wars and government expenditures in Western Europe since the eleventh century." *Public Finance* 26: 27–43.

Due, J. (1969) *Government Finance: Economics of the Public Sector.* Homewood, Ill.: Richard D. Irwin.

Friedman, M. and L. Savage (1948) "The utility analysis of choices involving risk." *J. of Pol. Economy* 56: 279–304.

Hirschleifer, J. (1966) "Investment decisions under uncertainty: applications of the state preference approach." *Q. J. of Economics* 80: 252–277.

Institute of Life Insurance (1970) *The Historical Statistics of Life Insurance.* New York.

Knight, F. H. (1921) *Risk, Uncertainty and Profit.* New York: Kelley.

Markowitz, H. (1952) "The utility of wealth." *J. of Pol. Economy* 50: 151–158.

Musgrave, R. M. (1968) *Fiscal Systems.* New Haven, Conn.: Yale Univ. Press.

—— and J. M. Culbertson (1953) "The growth of public expenditures in the United States 1890–1948." *National Tax J.* 6: 97–115.

Newlon, D. H. (1970) "Redistribution as insurance or investment." Ph.D. dissertation. University of Virginia.

Peacock, A. T. and J. Wiseman (1961) *The Growth of Public Expenditures in the United Kingdom*. Princeton: Princeton Univ. Press.

U.S. Bureau of the Census (1971) Governmental Finances in 1969–70. Washington, D.C.: Government Printing Office.

Veverka, J. (1963) "The growth of public expenditure in the United Kingdom since 1790." *"Scottish J. of Pol. Economy* 10: 111–127.

Wagner, A. (1890) *Finanzwissenschaft*. Leipzig.

Zeckhauser, R. (1969) "Uncertainty and the need for collective action," in *The Analysis and Evaluation of Public Expenditures, the PPB System*. Washington, D.C.: U.S. Congress Joint Economic Committee.

D. RATIONALIZING OUR POLITICAL DECISION-MAKING

30. Solving the Intensity Problem in Representative Democracy

DENNIS C. MUELLER, ROBERT D. TOLLISON, and THOMAS D. WILLETT

The problem of the representation of minority interests under one man–one vote majority rule has never been satisfactorily resolved in democratic theory or in its application. The typical statement of the problem depicts the victory of a lethargic majority over an intense minority, to the detriment of either one's sense of equity and efficiency or, in the extreme, of the viability of the political process itself.

In this paper we present mechanisms for both direct and representative democracy that take into account the relative intensities of each voter's preference over issues.[1] In essence, we address the challenge posed by

From *Economics of Public Choice,* edited by Robert D. Leiter (Boston: Twayne, forthcoming). Used by permission of the editor.

1. Our proposal may not resolve the type of problem where, for example, an intense majority faces an intense minority on an issue (e.g., racism). This sort of issue is not strictly an intensity problem, but rather a problem perhaps best characterized as a "crisis of the state," where resort to a constitutional setting is generally regarded as necessary and one constitutional option is the division of the state. As noted, such issues should be resolved at the constitutional stage where, ideally, citizens take a longer-run, more disinterested view of outcomes. The references cited in n. 3 recognize the need of recourse to constitutional procedures in such cases. We discuss constitutional decision making in section III and n. 11 below. In addition to the type of intensity problem described in the text, there is also the possibility that even in a well-working democratic model such as the one presented in this paper, there can be long-run *persistent* majorities and minorities. Thus, even where relative intensities on issues can be taken into account (*ex ante*) in setting up a democratic system,

Robert Dahl: "Is it possible to construct a system for arriving at decisions that is compatible with the idea of political equality and at the same time protects the rights of minorities?"[2]

The answer to this question can be found in neither of the two leading theories of American democracy, the Madisonian and Populist theories, as Dahl and others have shown.[3] The Populist theory, with its emphasis on the normative significance of one man—one vote majority rule, essentially ignores the problem, or implicitly assumes it away. Madisonian theory has as its greatest virtue the preservation of minority interests through the various "checks and balances" created in the constitution by the separation of the government into three branches, the separation of the legislature into two branches, and the decentralization of government into a federalist system. The strengthened position of the minority under Madisonian democracy reduces the "tyranny of the majority" problem at the cost of creating a "tyranny of the minority," in which any lethargic minority can block the preferences of an intense majority. Although the American system is a blend of Populist and Madisonian democracy, few seem convinced that this blend has adequately resolved the dilemma between the two tyrannies of majority and minority control. Nor do we believe that the more modern theories of interest-group democracy and implicit mechanisms of bargaining between majorities and minorities provide a satisfactory answer.[4]

The solution to the intensity problem presented here combines elements of all of these theories. It is Populist in that it requires that each voter have an *equal stake* (to be defined below) in the set of outcomes to be decided by any polity of which he is a member, and that he have an equal number of votes over the set of issues of the polity. It is Madisonian in requiring that the tasks of government be broken into separate branches, with particular emphasis placed on the judicial branch's control over the legislative through the delineation of political boundaries and issue sets. It emphasizes as well a federalist arrangement of government authority.

Our theory incorporates elements of the modern public choice theories

there can still be permanent winners and losers over time (*ex post*). We discuss this type of intensity problem in more detail in section III (n. 21) and in a separate paper entitled, "On Equalizing the Distribution of Political Income," *Journal of Political Economy,* 82 (March–April 1974).

2. Robert A. Dahl, *A Preface to Democratic Theory,* (Chicago: University of Chicago Press, 1956), p. 90.

3. *Ibid.* See, also, Wilmoore Kendall and George W. Carey, "The 'Intensity' Problem and Democratic Theory," *American Political Science Review,* 62 (March 1968), pp. 4–24; and V. Ostrom, *The Political Theory of a Compound Republic,* Center for the Study of Public Choice, 1971.

4. For a discussion of implicit mechanisms, see Kendall and Carey, *op. cit.,* pp. 16–19, and some of the literature on logrolling cited in n. 15.

in that it starts from a set of assumed voter preferences over issues, and allows voters to satisfy these preferences by voting. In this sense we are presenting a generalization of the intensity problem which emphasizes a solution to the problem of voting for public goods that is analogous (subject to the constraint of majority rule on non-constitutional decisions) to the manner in which the market solves intensity problems for private goods. The model can also be adapted to allow for logrolling and bargaining.

This, of course, is not the only criteria for judging the desirability of government institutions. While in passing we do derive some of the effects which a more responsive voting mechanism might have on other attributes of desirable government institutions, we are not attempting to present a blueprint for the most desirable form of democratic institutions based on a careful weighing of all relevant criteria. We are attacking a much more limited question: how to design public choice mechanisms to "solve" the intensity problem and accurately reflect in voting outcomes the underlying preferences of the electorate. This is an intriguing intellectual question in its own right and is not without practical implications. But while we feel that our "solution" to the intensity problem has important implications for the design of "good" democratic institutions, we wish to make very clear that we are not proposing to offer a solution for all of the problems of democratic government.

In section I we propose a direct democracy solution to the intensity problem that emphasizes giving voters a stock of votes to allocate over issues decided by a given polity. This process traces out relative utilities among issues for a voter and is called point voting.[5] Also in section I, we discuss the requirement for the optimality of point voting in resolving the intensity problem, the equal-stake requirement.

In section II we extend the advantages of point voting and the equal-stake requirement in representing the underlying structure of preferences to a form of representative government. We propose a system of at-large proportional representation for polities defined on the equal-stake condition either with a legislator's vote stock proportioned to the number of

5. To our knowledge the point-voting scheme was first proposed by Richard Musgrave in *The Theory of Public Finance* (New York: McGraw-Hill, 1959), pp. 130–131. J. Coleman discusses the concept of point voting, but cites no precedent discussion and never analyzes the concept. See his "Political Money," *American Political Science Review*, 64 (December 1970), pp. 1074–1087. Kendall and Carey, *op. cit.*, p. 19, mention point voting, but never with respect to resolving the intensity problem. Also, Zeckhauser has discussed some problems in the use of lotteries as an alternative way to handle varying intensities of voters' preference. See R. Zeckhauser, "Majority Rule with Lotteries on Alternatives," *Quarterly Journal of Economics*, 83 (November 1968), pp. 696–703.

votes he received in an election or with random selection of legislators, each of whom receives one vote per issue.

In section III we consider the kinds of constitutional decisions that are required in our model and some mechanisms for making them.

Sections IV and V contrast our model with the present system, discussing primarily the advantages of at-large versus geographic representation in section IV and the possible effects of our model of proportional representation on party structure and stability of political parties in section V.

Section VI presents a summary of the results of the paper.

I. Resolving the Intensity Problem in Direct Democracy

In his review of the intensity problem Robert Dahl concludes by blankly stating that no solution exists.[6] In another well-known paper on the intensity problem Kendall and Carey stress that in a Madisonian form of democracy the intensity problem can be contained by deliberations between goodnatured majorities and intense minorities, but that Populistic democracy simply cannot solve the problem.[7] However, they also discuss problems caused in the Madisonian model by minorities taking advantage of majorities in the deliberative body by bluffing about the intensity of their feeling on issues, and their analysis of this problem stresses mechanisms to raise the cost of bluffing to minorities and the partial nature of resolutions of the problem along these lines. In this analysis they mention clearly the concept of point voting and vote trading (p. 19), but never with respect to resolving the intensity problem. Indeed, they fail to grasp that in either Madisonian *or* Populistic models of democratic decision making, point voting can resolve the intensity problem fully in an ideal sense and to an approximation in an operational sense. In the remainder of this section we apply point voting to resolve the intensity problem in direct democracy, and in section II the solution is extended to a form of representative democracy.

As an example of the type of intensity problem that we consider, take one of the simplest of all democratic processes: a local referendum to increase the property tax by a stated amount and use the funds to build a new school. This situation can easily lend itself to an intensity problem. For example, a majority of the voters may not have children and may be slightly opposed to the measure because of the (let us say) small tax

6. Dahl, *op. cit.,* p. 119.

7. Kendall and Carey, *op. cit.* For example, they state that "Put otherwise: it remains true, as a matter of history, that the intensity problem has arisen as a special problem in the theory of populistic democracy; but it has not, on our showing here, arisen there properly, because populistic democracy has no hooks for grappling with it" (p. 11).

increase that accompanies it. The parents of school age children may be intensely for the tax-school package, however, because of the poor condition of the existing school. Thus, the parents would lose to a relatively indifferent majority in the defeat of the school issue. Conversely, one could envisage a situation in which the parents are in the majority, the proposed tax increase is substantial, the present school is in good condition, and the nonparents are "tyrannized" by the passage of the tax-school referendum. In either case the lesson is clear—for one man–one vote majority rule on separate issues to have normative authority, each voter must have an equal expected utility gain or loss from the outcome of any given issue. If this condition is not met, then voting, where each voter has one vote per issue, will not accurately reflect underlying voter preferences.

Kendall and Carey tend to characterize this type of electoral situation as a conflict between majority rule and political equality, emphasizing that its resolution may involve getting rid of majority rule *or* destroying political equality.[8] The solution to the intensity problem advanced here maintains majority rule for direct or legislative decision making on nonconstitutional issues, but broadens the definition of political equality under which majority rule prevails. As will be discussed with respect to the equal-stake requirement, the all-or-none trade-off between majority rule and political equality does not exist when political equality is defined over the whole set of issues to be decided by a polity rather than in terms of one vote per issue.

To clarify the example further, consider the distribution of potential welfare or utility gains for a single voter over a set of n issues in Figure 1. The height of the curve is an index of the potential gain to the voter from a favorable outcome on that issue, where a favorable outcome may represent either the passage of a desired bill or defeat of an undesired bill. In order for there *not* to be a potential tyranny of the majority problem under majority rule, each voter must have the identical utility distribution as in Figure 1 (i.e., it is not enough for the integral to be the same; the utility distribution of voters must be identically distributed) with the only differences coming in whether they favor passage or defeat of an issue. For example, all voters must experience a y gain in utility from the outcome on issue x, although some voters receive the gain only if it passes and others only if it loses.

Suppose, however, that all the issues to be decided by a polity are formulated so that they can be decided by a yes or no vote. Each issue involving an expenditure is presented with a self-financing tax so that all voters know precisely the cost to them of the passage of a particular

8. *Ibid.*, pp. 5–7.

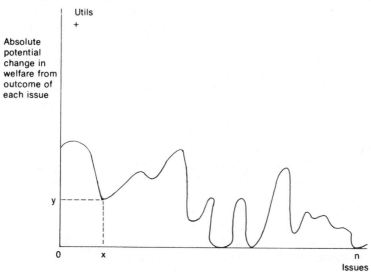

Figure 1.

issue. Taking these costs into account, each voter determines his net benefits from the passage or defeat of every issue. These net benefits constitute the vertical distances given in Figure 1.

Now, instead of having one vote on each issue, suppose the voter is given a thousand votes and is asked to allocate these in proportion to his utility index over the n issues. Thus, if issue j provides 7 times as much benefit as issue k, the voter allocates 7 times as many votes to it. In voting he returns a form indicating how his thousand votes are to be assigned to each of the n issues and whether he casts them for or against each issue (he votes against all issues promising negative benefits). Ideally, each voter's allocation of votes will trace out a distribution exactly proportioned to the utility distribution in Figure 1. The issues are decided by aggregating the vote distributions over all voters, and passing all issues that receive more yeses than noes.[9]

This type of "point-voting system" will give accurate information about the *relative* intensities of each voter's preferences over the n issues and thus removes the necessity of assuming that each voter has exactly the same relative utilities over the same n issues (i.e., that all voters have the same utility curve in Figure 1 except for signs). Operationally, the concept of point voting itself is not difficult to understand. This is partic-

9. See n. 5.

ularly true for market economies where voters are faced with the same sort of allocation decisions in their market behavior. In the direct democracy variant, the amount of sophistication required to allocate points over issues seems less demanding than the typical family's weekly budget decisions or the computations inherent in filling out a tax form.

Further, the use of point voting to resolve the intensity problem does not rely on implicit and indirect bargaining mechanisms between majorities and intense minorities to approximate, however inaccurately, the revelation of relative utilities in a political process. Point voting reveals relative intensities directly and in a theoretical sense both *solves* and *measures* the intensity problem straightforwardly.[10] In terms of the objective of reflecting the underlying array of voter preferences in public choice outcomes, point voting–direct democracy reveals individuals' marginal rates of substitution among issues analogously to the manner in which marginal rates of substitution among private goods are revealed in markets as consumers allocate their budgets. In effect point voting is the first step here in setting up a public choice process that operates similarly to markets.

There is, however, an important condition which must be met for point voting to be completely optimal in an ideal sense. The social welfare W will be maximized by aggregating the votes cast by each citizen over the n issues *if and only if every voter has an equal total expected utility gain* from the outcome of the voting process over the *set* of n issues. This too is a strong condition. It is clearly unrealistic if the set of n issues consists of *all* the collective choices affecting a voter. An urban resident's welfare is more heavily dependent upon the outcomes of all political choices he can influence than is the farmer's. Many public services have a localized geographic effect, e.g., police and fire protection, education (particularly at the lower levels), recreation facilities, and health services. It is less unrealistic to assume, therefore, that the total set of issues affecting an individual can be broken down into subsets on a geographic basis, so that within each geographically determined polity all voters have an equal potential utility gain from the outcome of the decisions of that polity. That is, boundaries should be drawn for each neighborhood, city, regional, and national government such that all voters in any political jurisdiction have an equal expected utility gain over the subset of issues decided by that polity. Voters in each polity would be given an equal number of votes to be allocated among the issues decided by that polity.

One way of approaching the problem of drawing boundaries and allo-

---

10. Dahl, *op. cit.,* chapter 4, is especially concerned with the problem of measuring differing intensities of preference as an issue. The point-voting system does this directly in the sense of revealed preference.

cating issues is to assume that these decisions are made at an earlier, constitutional stage in the democratic process. If one makes the further assumption that citizens at the constitutional stage are ignorant of their future tastes and positions, then the allocation of issues and boundaries so that voters have equal expected stakes becomes a necessary condition for maximizing social welfare at the constitutional stage. Under uniform ignorance about future preferences and positions, *unanimous agreement* could be reached at the constitutional stage, and the equal-stake criterion, voting rules, redistributive measures, certain allocative measures such as contained in the Bill of Rights, etc., embodied in the constitution could be regarded as the main elements of the social contract. With the equal-ignorance condition satisfied, our approach to constitutional decision-making may be consistent with the Paretian criterion since we could advance our proposed form of democratic decision-making as presumed Pareto-optimal at a constituional convention and see if unanimous consensus could be found to support our model.[11]

Thus, the designation of political boundaries for each level of government and the allocation of issues among the various governments become key conditions in the creation of a voting system that accurately reflects

11. For a further discussion linking the voting rules and boundaries of parliamentary democracy to the constitutional decision, see D. Mueller, "Fiscal Federalism in a Constitutional Democracy, *Public Policy,* 19 (Fall 1971), pp. 567–593; and "Constitutional Democracy and Social Welfare," *Quarterly Journal of Economics* 87 (February 1973). In practice, of course, one would not get the ideal solution even if the appropriate measurements for boundaries could be made because such factors as transactions costs would have to be traded off against the gains from setting up exactly optimum governments. In operation, say in the United States, most of the changes in governmental boundaries would probably be at the metropolitan and regional levels. See Gordon Tullock, "Federalism: Problems of Scale," *Public Choice,* 6 (Spring 1969), pp. 19–29 [Reading 14, above], for an example of the discussion of transaction costs. Mueller points out that a certain amount of "good citizenship" by voters is required if point voting is to reveal individuals' marginal rates of substitution among issues. In a large number setting, such behavior is plausible. In a small number setting, for example, a small representative legislature, all voting systems are subject to strategic voting, and it is an open question whether point voting is better or worse in this regard than, for example, are one man–one vote systems. We will return to this problem in the next section.

We also note that in the discussions of the intensity problem the prospect of non-voting also raises the general problem of the representativeness of collective decisions under majority rule, and there may be cases where a polity would wish to enforce participation via a poll tax or subsidy as a way to internalize any publicness involved with attaining the full expression of underlying voter preferences. Then, the intensity problem could be solved by point voting, and representation of underlying preferences would be "full." Also, the empirical form of the potential bias due to non-voting is that voting and political participation tend to vary positively with income. For discussions of the economic theory of voting and non-voting behavior, see R. D. Tollison and T. D. Willett, "The Simple Economics of Voting and Not Voting," *Public Choice* 15 (Fall 1973) [Reading 27, above], and the references cited there.

relative intensities of preference among all groups in the polity. While we recognize that these conditions as a practical manner cannot be exactly met, we think that operational equivalents of these conditions (see n. 20), combined with the other mechanisms of the model, would be an improvement over other possible voting systems.

Previous theories that have failed to recognize these conditions have often encountered serious conceptual difficulties. The well-known Arrow Impossibility, where cycling can take place under majority rule, can be attributed to the fact that *all* citizens are allowed to participate in the making of *all* decisions, regardless of their interests in the outcomes of the process. Indeed, since point voting and vote trading are devices for combining *cardinal* utilities, intransitivities and cycling cannot occur as in the Arrow Impossibility where with *ordinal* rankings there is no single alternative uniformly considered as the best, the worse, etc. Thus, cycling cannot occur because intransitivities are eliminated by introducing cardinality and because all issues are more or less decided at the same time. In effect by basing the optimality of the point-voting system on the characteristic of voters deciding all issues simultaneously at either the parliamentary or constitutional stage of the model, the Arrow Impossibility is bypassed by violating his postulate of the independence of irrelevant alternatives.[12]

This part of the theory is quite consistent with traditional American political thought. The defense of minority rights through guarantees of local political authority was one of the major issues in the drafting of the Constitution.[13] The condition that every voter have an equal stake in the outcomes over the set of issues affecting him also seems fully consistent with America's Populist democratic traditions. Again, however, its importance has not been fully recognized in the literature and its violation in the large is probably a major cause of frustration with the democratic process. When issues are decided with vote trading or logrolling, the out-

12. For Arrow's discussion, see his *Social Choice and Individual Values* (New York: John Wiley, 1951). Also see E. J. Mishan's criticism of Arrow with regard to allowing all voters a stake in all decisions in "A Survey of Welfare Economics: 1939–1959," *Economic Journal*, 70 (June 1970), pp. 197–265. For the full discussion of how point voting avoids the Arrow Impossibility, see Mueller, "Constitutional Democracy and Social Welfare," *op. cit.*

13. See *Federalist Papers*, Nos. 45, 46. Note, however, Madison's arguments for preserving minority rights by transferring authority from the local to the national level in Papers 10 and 51. Also, we should note that following Dahl, *op. cit.*, we employ a "Populistic democracy" model in this section, where elections are thought of as expressions of voter preferences for public policies. In Section III where we discuss constitutional decisions, the implicit model of democracy will be closer to "Madisonian democracy," where elections are viewed as the selection of "good" decision makers. On this distinction see Kendall and Carey, *op. cit.*, 20–24.

comes on *all* issues are interdependent and sensitive to the selection of issues. The addition of issues to the choice set (e.g., that would hurt some groups and leave the others unaffected) can lower the realized utility gains of the former even if they are eventually defeated because the potentially injured voters must trade away votes on the potentially harmful issues to ensure their defeat, and thereby lower their power to affect other decisions that might benefit them. The selection of issues is also important under point voting. The addition of an issue to the set alters the vote-point allocations and has a potential impact on all outcomes. Care must be taken when selecting the issues to be voted upon to ensure that all voters stand to experience roughly equal utility gains from the outcomes of the decision process.[14]

A number of papers have explored the possibilities of getting voters to reveal the relative intensities of their preferences by trading votes.[15] Mueller, Philpotts and Vanek have shown in a polar version of this model, in which voters literally do trade votes (or fractions thereof) in vote markets, that the outcomes from vote trading closely approximate those one would obtain under point voting.[16] Although it is a long leap from this kind of vote trading to the implicit trading that takes place via logrolling in actual assemblies, at least one observer has been willing to argue that logrolling tends to approximate the results one would get with actual trading.[17] Thus, the results we seek might tend to be approximated

14. The normatively disturbing interpersonal utility comparison problem inherent in the equal-stake condition may be removed by assuming boundaries are drawn and issues allocated at the constitutional stage by voters who assume they have an equal probability of assuming the position and tastes of other voters in future generations. The determination of the fiscal federalism questions so as to satisfy the equal-stake condition then becomes a necessary condition for maximizing the expected utility of the voter at the constitutional stage (which we will discuss in Section III). Also, see Mueller, "Fiscal Federalism in a Constitutional Democracy," for a discussion of this problem, and E. Haeferle, "A Utility Theory of Representative Government," *American Economic Review*, 61 (July 1971), pp. 350–367, for a discussion of the importance of how issues are formulated and how the legislative agenda is drawn up to democratic decision making.

15. See, for example, J. M. Buchanan and G. Tullock, *The Calculus of Consent* (Ann Arbor: University of Michigan Press, 1962); J. Coleman, "The Possibility of a Social Welfare Function," *American Economic Review*, 56 (December 1966), pp. 1105–1122, and "Political Money," *op. cit.*; Mueller, "The Possibility of a Social Welfare Function: Comment," *American Economic Review*, 57 (December 1967), pp. 1304–1311; and Parks, "The Possibility of a Social Welfare Function: Comment," *American Economic Review*, 57 (December 1967), pp. 1300–1304.

16. D. Mueller, G. Philpotts, and J. Vanek, "The Social Gains from Exchanging Voters: A Simulation Approach," *Public Choice*, 13 (Fall 1972), pp. 55–80. See, also, Robert Wilson, "An Axiomatic Model of Logrolling," *American Economic Review*, 59 (June 1969), pp. 331–341.

17. Coleman, "The Possibility of a Social Welfare Function," *op. cit.* See also "Comments" by Mueller and Parks and "Reply" by Coleman in *American Economic Review*, 57 (December 1967), pp. 1300–1317.

via some form of vote trading without having to resort to point voting *if the equal-stake criterion were satisfied and proportional representation were adopted* (we discuss the latter condition in the next section).

Most criticisms of the actual results of logrolling can be traced directly to the violation of the equal-stake criterion. The ill effects of pork-barrel legislation come about because those with very small stakes in the total set of issues to be decided can trade away votes on all but the relatively few issues they consider important and thus ensure their victory to the likely detriment of the community at large. The tendency for these asymmetries to exist, and for local issues to gravitate to higher levels of government is enhanced by the geographic selection of representatives. We will consider the effects of geographic representation on the propensity of legislators to play negative-sum games in more detail in section IV.

II. Extending the Solution to Representative Democracy

If point voting were employed at each level of government, and legislative decisions at each level were made via direct democracy, then the utility distributions of each voter as depicted in Figure 1 would be employed directly in the legislative process. All of the available information about the relative intensities of voter preferences on issues would be utilized in legislative decision making by a point voting–direct democracy.

Direct democrary is often impractical, however.[18] Historically, town meetings were reasonably efficient in a small numbers setting. As society grew and the number of voters became large, direct assembly and debate became difficult, and the deliberative step in the legislative process was not viable in a direct form of democracy. Today, as issues become more complex, the amount of information needed to vote intelligently increases and it becomes inefficient to have each voter gather all the necessary information himself. Thus, representative government is superior to direct democracy, chiefly because of the greater informational efficiency inherent in it. The standard institutions of representative bodies such as committees, staffs, hearings, and the like are all embodiments of this point.

18. Note, however, the suggestion of James C. Miller III, to take advantage of advances in communications technology and institute a national referendum. We reject the national referendum as a device for returning to direct democracy on the grounds that representation properly economizes information gathering and the making of informed choices. See James C. Miller III, "A Program for Direct and Proxy Voting in the Legislative Process," *Public Choice,* 7 (Fall 1969), pp. 107–113 [Reading 24, above], and Martin Shubik, "On Homo Politicus and the Instant Referendum," *Public Choice,* 9 (Fall 1970), pp. 79–84 [Reading 25]. For a fuller discussion of the issues raised by Miller and Shubik, see our "Representative Democracy via Random Selection," *Public Choice,* 12 (Spring 1972), pp. 59–68 [Reading 26].

We seek a method for choosing representatives that will preserve the advantages of point voting in revealing the relative intensities of individual preferences and still incorporate the informational efficiency of representative government. This can be accomplished if each voter selects a legislator who will *represent* his general preferences on the issues, given the greater information the latter will typically have. Each voter must thus choose a representative who promises to take positions on the issues in rough correspondence to the voter's preference map. If the voters in a polity can be broken down into a number of subgroups each of which is composed of voters of homogeneous tastes (identical preference maps), then each voter can have his tastes accurately represented in the legislature if a representative is chosen from his subgroup. Suppose, for example, that the m voters in a city can be divided into s subsets of v_1, v_2, . . . v_s voters respectively, where the members of any subset have identical preferences. Then, ideally, a perfectly representative body could be established by selecting s representatives, one each from the s subsets of voters. If point voting were employed in the legislature, each representative could accurately depict the relative intensities of his constituents on the issues. In order to make the aggregation of points an accurate reflection of the aggregate gains and losses from deciding each issue, the total numbers of vote-points representatives received would have to be proportioned to the number of votes they represented. Thus, the representatives could start with numbers of points proportional to v_1, v_2, . . . v_s.

If voter preferences are such that voters in any polity can be grouped into a number of subsets of voters with homogeneous tastes that is sufficiently small to allow the creation of an assembly with a single representative from each subset, then the informational efficiency of point voting can be extended to a representative form of government. The representatives to the legislative branches at each level of government would have to be selected from a list of at-large candidates presented to all the voters in the several polities. The x seats in each legislature would be filled by the x candidates receiving the most votes, and each candidate would receive a number of vote-points proportioned to the number of seats in the assembly. Voting in the legislature would take place following the same point-voting scheme described in section I. The points cast by a representative would give the relative intensities of his constituents weighted by their number.[19]

19. One problem with some of the experiments with at-large proportional representation (e.g., as practiced in New York City in the 1930's) is that representatives were not given votes in the legislature in proportion to the numbers of supporters they had. Thus, minority party representatives had equal strength with major party representatives, producing the potential for a "tyranny of the minority." We should also note that an early champion of a

   Additional flexibility can be added to the selection of representatives to
the various levels of government by using a form of point voting to select
representatives. That is, instead of giving each voter one vote to cast for a
representative at each level of government, voters could be given *m* votes
to allocate to the representatives over all levels of government. In this
way, voters could express their relative intensities of preference *within*
each level of government by voting for those candidates who had platforms most closely resembling their own, and *across* levels of government by allocating their points for selecting representatives in proportion
to their relative intensities of preference on the different levels. The latter
allocation would give more political power to those representatives
elected at the levels of government about which the voter felt more
strongly. A modified form of the equal-stake criterion would now be
required in which each voter in a *local* polity received the same number
of points to be allocated to representatives to *all* polities of which he was
a member. Since urban dwellers will typically receive greater benefits
from the political process than rural dwellers (they are affected by more
social interdependence and market failures), urban dwellers will have to
receive more total points, although within any urban area (or within a
neighborhood of an urban area if that is the lowest political unit) all
voters would receive the same number of votes.[20] This modification to
the electoral process would require more information on the part of those
constructing the initial boundaries, since not only would boundaries giving equal stakes be required, but also decisions as to the *relative* intensities of total utility gains among voters in different areas would have to be
made. On the other hand it is less restrictive in its constraints on voter
preferences, since it only requires that voters in the same local community receive an equal utility gain over the set of *all* issues affecting them.
The optimality of election of representatives by one man–one vote assumes equal utility gains for voters in the same local area over *each* set of
issues affecting them.

   A system for proportionally *electing* legislators to each level of government would make greater demand on the abilities of voters to gather and
evaluate information about candidates. If, for example, the national assembly had 100 seats, the voter might have to evaluate 150 candidates

---

proportional voting system based on the Hare system and without point voting was John
Stuart Mill. See Mill, *Considerations on Representative Government* (London: Parkinson
and Bourn, 1861).

   20. One way to approximate the correct difference in initial vote stocks would be to take
existing differences in government budgets between urban and rural areas as evidence of the
correct dispersion in vote stocks. This procedure would allow *equally weighted* voters a
chance to decide which equal-stake issues they felt more strongly about (e.g., national
versus local).

(including the primary election) in deciding which one would best represent his views. Similar evaluations would have to be made when he selected his representatives to the state (regional), metropolitan, and neighborhood legislatures. If information were supplied to voters in the same way as it is today, the task of evaluating candidates might be impossible.

Fortunately, under proportional representation candidates will have incentives to provide more accurate information to voters. Under a two-party system where only one candidate emerges as a winner, candidates have an incentive to take positions close to the median voter's position and to cloud their stands on controversial (polar) issues. Under proportional representation, candidates compete for a much larger number of seats and need to secure a much smaller number of votes to be elected. Their incentives are, therefore, to differentiate their positions from those of other candidates and convince voters that their platforms most closely correspond to the voters' own preferences.

A simple way to supply voters with information about candidates would be to publish a manual that listed each incumbent candidate and his allocations of vote points in the preceding congresses. Challengers could list the way they would allocate their vote points once in office as opposed to the incumbent's proposed allocation. More radical innovations in the use of the media to supply voters with information about candidates could also be considered.

There would remain, however, after these improvements in information flow, a trade-off between the number of candidates and decision making costs faced by the representative individual voter as Figure 2 illustrates.

The decision costs function in this case would increase at an increasing rate as more candidates imposed greater complexity on the choice facing the voter. Thus, the trade-off between having a large legislature to reflect voters' tastes more accurately and decision making costs for voters would be present in any democratic system where voter participation is required. Selecting a point on this trade-off curve would determine a voter's trade-off between the amount of choice he desires in selecting a representative and the cost of making this choice. One suspects that in a complex society with a highly educated and wealthy population the optimal trade-off point is somewhere to the right of the two-party point, and it probably shifts rightward over time as the society develops.

It is possible, nevertheless, that the number of seats needed to reflect adequately the spectrum of individual preferences might be so large, that a proportionally elected assembly fully representative of the range of individual preferences would be infeasible. In this case, one might want to

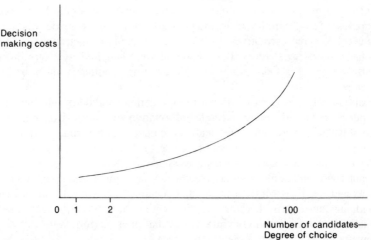

Figure 2.

abandon a democratic voting process for choosing representatives in favor of a random selection process. The same conceptual outcome as proportional representation with point votes allocated accordingly can be achieved by selecting *at random* legislators for the governments in the rational federalism.[21] In all cases the size of the legislature could be fixed at a large enough number so that random selection (with only highly qual-

21. Rousseau proposed a similar system for choosing an executive in an "ideal" democracy. See *The Social Contract* (Amsterdam: M. M. Rey, 1762), Book IV, Chapter III, "Concerning Elections." See also Dahl, *After the Revolution* (New Haven: Yale, 1970), pp. 149–153. Democracy by lot also was practiced in Athens. See C. N. Parkinson, *The Evolution of Political Thought* (Boston: Houghton Mifflin, 1958), pp. 173–175. On the origins of representation by lot, see Fustel de Coulanges, *The Ancient City,* 1864. He writes:

It is surprising that modern historians represent the drawing of lots as an invention of the Athenian democracy. It was, on the contrary, in full rigor under the rule of the aristocracy (Plutarch, *Pericles,* 9), and appears to have been as old as the archonship itself. Nor is it a democratic procedure: we know, indeed, that even in the time of Lysias and of Demosthenes, the names of all the citizens were not put in the urn (Lysias, *Orat., de Invalido,* c. 13; *in Andocidem,* c. 4): for a still stronger reason was this true when the Eupatrids only, or the Pentakosiomedimni could be archons. Passages of Plato show clearly what idea the ancients had of the drawing of lots; the thought which caused it to be employed for magistrate-priests like the archons, or for senators charged with holy duties like the prytanes, was a religious idea, and not a notion of equality. It is worthy of remark, that when the democracy gained the upper hand, it reserved the selection by lot for the choice of archons, to whom it left no real power, and gave it up in the choice of strategi, who then had the true authority. So that there was drawing of lots of magistracies which dated from the aristocratic age, and election for those that dated from the age of democracy (p. 183, fn. 13).

For a more complete discussion of the random selection proposal, see our "Representative Democracy via Random Selection," *op. cit.*

ified exemptions from the sample) would yield an accurate picture of the distribution of voter preference. For example, if 10 percent of the voting populace were radical leftwingers, then on average over time 10 percent of the random legislature would be radical leftwingers. Clusters of representatives would form around the various points in the distribution of voter preferences in the random body, and one man–one vote (i.e., an equal allocation of vote points) in the random body would yield the proper proportional weights to the various intensities of voter preference. The selected representatives could then still allocate their stock of one vote per issue in any way they chose, i.e., point voting. In such fashion the random selection system would yield the *same conceptual* result as proportional representation with vote points allocated accordingly.

Representation by random selection would return political power to individual voters and give better articulation of voter preferences in the legislative process without sacrificing the efficiencies of representation. If viewed as a replacement for the current forms of national representation, the random selection system removes direct sanctioning power through the ballot from the voter and replaces this control mechanism with a more subtle method of articulating voter preferences on national issues. We would argue that although the final outcome is not clearcut, such a change in representative procedure could be understood by voters as the formal embodiment of democratic equality in an *ex ante* rather than *ex post* sense.[22] Finally, and importantly, it should be stressed that random selection of representatives avoids all of the traditional problems in voting theory of intransitivities in voting outcomes in establishing a system of proportional representation.[23] The application of voting theory is con-

22. See Pauly and Willett, "Two Concepts of Equity," *Social Science Quarterly,* June 1972, pp. 8–19 [Reading 19, above], for the general discussion of the concepts of *ex ante* and *ex post* equity. Also, as we noted before, where voting is costly and non-voting is a problem, election returns, even under point voting, may be unrepresentative. With these conditions it is an open question as to whether direct election of a proportional legislature or random selection gives a better articulation of underlying preferences. One alternative discussed previously would be to have public investment to lower the costs of voting via computer technology, requiring voting, or rewarding or penalizing voting through poll payments or poll taxes. Indeed, to the extent that the failure to vote is a reflection of a divergence between the private and social gains from democratic participation, the latter proposal would be appropriate to apply. The advantage of random selection in this regard is that it offers a lower cost method of obtaining a reasonable approximation of preferences. On the general problem of voting and non-voting see Tollison and Willett, *op. cit.* Further, this problem is in part a question of how much society should invest in a government. And it is an implication of recent work on vote trading that a well-working government may embody great potential gains from trade for democratic citizens, and hence, investments in reforming democratic process may have big payoffs. See Mueller, Philpotts, and Vanek, *op. cit.*

23. On this problem, which is endemic to democratic systems where voters directly elect legislators and which would also apply to our proposal for electing a proportionally repre-

fined in this case to the operation of the random legislature, once selected, and this feature of random representation is an important justification for establishing and operating proportional representation in this
way.

In summary, both a *proportionally elected* assembly that employed
point voting and a *randomly selected* assembly would provide an accurate
depiction of the preferences of the population if they were large enough
relative to the spectrum of preferences of the voters. In the former each
subset of preferences would be represented by a single representative who
would have a total number of vote-points to allocate over issues in proportion to the number of voters he represented. Under the random selection process each representative would have the same number of vote-
points, and the different numbers of voters in each preference subset
would be revealed through the random selection process. The choice between these two systems must rest basically on (1) the advantages of having all voters *participate* in democracy by *electing* a representative versus
having an *equal chance* to be selected as a representative, and (2) the
range of preferences of voters and the costs of making decisions among
candidates. It should be noted, however, that both proposals have inherent in them an increase in the amount of information about issues that the
average citizen possesses. Under the proportional election system *all*
voters would be expected to incur greater decision costs in selecting representatives. Under the random selection process those citizens chosen to
be representatives would have to acquire information about issues at least
during their term of office.

---

sentative body from an at-large list of candidates, see D. Black, *The Theory of Committees
and Elections* (New York: Cambridge, 1958), chapter 11. Many of the operational details
and the costs and benefits of the random procedure are discussed more fully in our "Representative Democracy via Random Selection." We should clarify one problem with the random procedure—namely, how large it would have to be to reflect accurately the distribution
of voter preference—especially since Dahl argues (*After the Revolution*, p. 152) that 500 or
600 at most is the number of people who could participate effectively in a random legislature. This may or may not be the case depending on the amount of sampling error one is
willing to tolerate vis-à-vis the costs of a larger legislature and depending on how one
meshes the random body with the existing legislative process. Given that there is no prior
knowledge about the population proportion being sampled for (50–50), a sample size of 500
would yield a chance of 95 percent that the value being estimated lies within a range equal
to the reported percentages, plus or minus an error of 4.9 percent. Doubling the sample size
to 1000 would yield a 95 percent chance with a 3.6 percent error. So it is probably true that
very accurate samples of the voting populace would have to be large. However, this does
not mean that a large random legislature is not feasible or cannot be effective. For example,
such a representative body could be meshed with the existing political process by making it
a purely advisory body, or one house of a bicameral legislature could be designated primarily to respond to (i.e., vote on) rather than initiate legislation. For such a body, large
size would not necessarily be a constraint on its effectiveness.

Although there is no need for a bicameral legislature if conditions are appropriate for either of the above two representative schemes, one might want to adopt a bicameral system to capture the best features of both, especially if these conditions are not met. Random selection could be used to select a large proportionally representative body, and proportional voting to elect a much smaller body. The smaller body would be responsible for initiating, debating, and amending legislation, and the large body would serve as a fully representative cross section of the population with veto power over the elected assembly. The smaller assembly could also serve as the home ground for political entrepreneurs.

Finally, we should stress that, on the assumption of homogeneous tastes among blocs of voters and the satisfaction of the equal-stake requirement for the various politics implied in our model, the solution of the intensity problem is carried over to a representative setting. The underlying array of preferences is reflected in voting outcomes in a proportionally representative legislature, and issues are decided at the correct level of government by optimal jurisdictions based on the satisfaction of the equal-stake requirement. The latter conditions of agenda setting and drawing the boundaries of governments raise the important problems of constitutional decision making which we consider in the next section.

III. Constitutional Decisions

The selection of issues and delineation of boundaries for each level of government is such an important component of our theory that some discussion of the method by which these decisions would be made is necessary.

One must quickly reject any existing legislative bodies for this task, at least under current voting rules. Representatives are now selected geographically, and one would expect that any decisions made by an existing legislature would tend to preserve present asymmetries in political power among different areas and the tendency to kick local issues up to the national level. The U.S. Constitution's strong emphasis on preserving the power of certain geographic areas can be traced directly to the selection of delegates to the Constitutional Convention on a geographic basis. More recently, the Bretton Woods agreement on the international monetary system set up after World War II is a good example of such short-sighted behavior by rule makers with the positions of major powers being strongly influenced by their expectations as to whether they would have balance of payments surpluses or deficits over the early post-war years.[24] Indeed, since the whole idea of the equal-stake assumption is to

24. See L. H. Officer and T. D. Willett, *The International Monetary System* (Englewood Cliffs, N.J.: Prentice-Hall, 1967), and the references cited there.

straighten out geographic biases currently prevailing, it is hard to see how we could get any part of the existing political system to make correct constitutional choices unless the choices were not to take effect until a time so distant, say three generations hence, that they would be irrelevant to the current reform of democratic decision making. And it would be extremely hard, if not impossible, for any existing political body to resist overcentralizing geographic issues.

One way out of this dilemma would be to hold a constitutional convention, but select delegates by proportional representation with the point-voting method or via random selection. These procedures would lessen the geographic incentives toward overcentralization and would at least yield a constitutional reform based on the full range of voter preferences. For example, selecting the delegates at random and allowing the decisions to take effect only after an elapsed period of time might vitiate many of the problems here. In a sense one is trying to solve the intensity problem in a constitutional setting and also to obtain a constitutional state of mind of uniform ignorance about one's future position in the society (see n. 8).

The partisanship inherent in the geographic selection of representatives is reinforced by the requirement that representatives run for re-election. This kind of partisanship may be desirable with regard to the day-to-day decisions of a legislature since it provides the citizen a means of ensuring that his views are in fact being represented in the democratic process. It is not suitable, however, for obtaining the kind of disinterestedness called for in establishing the equal-stake requirement. The typical way in which the Constitution seeks to ensure impartiality in decision making by an officer is to preclude his concern with selection or reappointment. Thus, judges on the highest courts are appointed for life, governors on the Federal Reserve Board and commissioners in the regulatory agencies are appointed for fixed, nonrenewable terms, and jurors are selected randomly and for fixed time periods. In a similar manner, impartiality could be obtained in settling jurisdictional issues in a federal system and constructing a new form of representative body. A constitutional convention could be called, and either of the two methods of selecting representatives described above could be used; i.e., representatives could be randomly drawn or voted on from an at-large list of candidates. What is essential is that they do not have to run for re-election on the basis of the *justice* they exhibit in drawing the federation's local and regional boundaries and allocating issues.

Two primary tasks of the convention would be to draw political boundaries to approximate the equal-stake criterion and to allocate issues to the appropriate level of federalism. In effect the setting of the equal-stake requirement and the allocating of issues to the appropriate level set the income distribution requirement of the model, and the model at this point would be analogous to setting an equitable income distribution and letting the market work, though again with majority rule arbitrating legislative decisions.

In addition, an important function of the convention would be to decide in effect whether an issue is constitutional in an *ex ante* sense. This is the manner in which issues (intense minority–intense majority) that can potentially break down the system and traditional items in the Bill of Rights could be handled, if they are foreseen at the time of the convention. In the latter case all-or-none rules could be set up at the convention outlawing or sanctioning certain rights. If such issues are not foreseen, then the convention would be faced with the task of setting up constitutional procedures to take effect in the future to resolve such issues.

This task of setting up future constitutional machinery should be broadly construed. For example, Braybrooke has an interesting test to allow individuals to be in a winning *or* losing coalition only 90 percent of the time that would qualify in our terms as a constitutional device. In effect this would be a system of progressive taxation of political income that could be imposed by a constitutional convention to lessen the problems of persistent majorities over future political periods, i.e., the long-run form of the intensity problem.[25]

Two possibilities exist for arbitrating future jurisdictional disputes. The constitutional convention could be reconvened periodically to take up the redrawing of boundaries and allocation of issues in light of changing population densities and environmental factors. In this way the convention would function as a sort of jury for deciding federalism issues. Alterna-

25. See Braybrooke, *Three Tests for Democracy: Personal Rights, Human Welfare and Collective Preference* (New York: Random House, 1968). In effect our model to this point, in setting up the equal-stake requirement, allocating issues to the correct level of government, and giving voters in any polity an equal stock of votes, has established the traditional form of *ex ante,* or before-the-fact, type of political equality, although going beyond the usual one man–one vote form of this type of equality. As noted earlier, however, it is still possible that even with the above conditions of our model satisfied, there can be *persistent* majorities and minorities over time. In such a case one may wish to consider the imposition of a vote-tax at the constitutional stage which would take away votes from abnormally high winners and subsidize abnormally high losers in such a way as to force everyone in the polity to win on average roughly the same amount of the time. The vote-tax system would thus solve the long-run form of the intensity problem where a majority persistently wins on the issues in a given polity and establish political equality in an *ex post* sense. This sort of vote-tax system would be very analogous to handicapping systems in sports (e.g., golf). For a thorough discussion of the concepts of *ex ante* and *ex post* equality and of the resolution of long-run "tyranny of the majority" problems, see Pauly and Willett, "Two Concepts of Equity," *op cit.,* and Mueller, Tollison and Willett, "On Equalizing the Distribution of Political Income," *op. cit.*

tively, the equal-stake criterion could be broadly written into federal and state constitutions, and the courts could be relied upon to draw the boundaries in an equitable manner. Clearly, the recurring constitutional convention approach is time-consuming and costly and perhaps not flexible enough to apply in the modern world. The judicial approach meets these objections, but poses problems of how one selects the judges in a way that is totally free of interest-group bias. In essence, efficiency considerations probably imply movement toward more judicial democracy so long as the judges are selected in a way to reflect accurately the distribution of voter preference.[26] An effective way to combine the judicial approach to redrawing boundaries and allocating issues with our electoral proposals would be to maintain a small random jury of judges to make such decisions over time.

Such a procedure could be set up to function independently of other governmental institutions in the spirit of Madisonian checks and balances. Thus, the important constitutional tasks of drawing political boundaries and setting legislative agendas would fall to an independent judicial body. This constitutional body, if selected in such a way as to offset any short-run geographic bias in decision making, would serve to check tendencies for the legislative branch to overcentralize issues (discussed in the next section).

IV. Problems of Geographic Representation

Our model has four central characteristics: (1) point voting to reveal relative intensities of preference over a set of issues; (2) a federation of governments such that every citizen in a given polity has an equal expected welfare gain from the set of outcomes in that polity; (3) an active judiciary or constitution drafting process for redrawing political boundaries and screening issue sets to ensure that the equal-stake criterion is satisfied in each polity; and (4) at-large proportional representation through either proportionally elected or randomly selected legislative bodies.

A primary difference in the model presented here and the present American political system is that of at-large versus geographic representation. We will thus contrast some of the problems caused by geographic representation under the present system with the at-large representation system implied in the foregoing model in this section.

Under geographic representation the main characteristic a representative's constituents have in common is that they reside in the same area. Any bill he can get through the legislature that benefits all of the members of his district should win him votes. In effect a geographi-

26. This is consistent with the drift of Theodore Lowi's argument in *The End of Liberalism* (New York: Norton, 1969).

cally–based system confronts the legislator with high payoffs from representing local interests in the national legislature by trying to logroll off,
for example, the general tax system and with virtually zero payoffs to
campaign on a platform, for example, of national efficiency. This asymmetry in payoff to the geographically based legislator is partly attributable
to the greater information voters have about localized and specific public
sector benefits compared with more remote general benefits.[27] Coupled
with a seniority system in the legislature which gives monopoly power on
important committees (e.g., in terms of which issues are put on committee agendas) to those districts that send back the same representative over
a long period of time, the problem of representing local interests in the
national legislature is compounded because legislative survival and the attainment of monopoly power within the legislature become functions of
representing local interests.

One of the most important concerns individuals in a community have
in common is their interest in the vitality of the community's economic
base. In many instances a majority of the members of a polity may directly or indirectly receive their income from a single firm or industry.
Company towns, geographically concentrated industries like steel, autos,
textiles, lumber, defense, and regionally concentrated agricultural industries are all examples of this. When economic activity is thus concentrated, it is possible for representatives to win political support by serving as
spokesmen for the economic interests in their home districts. Tariffs, industry and company oriented tax concessions and subsidies, local public
works projects, and defense contracts are all examples of issues that often
are decided, in part, on the basis of their economic impact on certain
regions.

Such attempts to redistribute income toward certain regions through the
legislative process frequently result in negative-sum games. Examples of
this kind of negative-sum game legislation in the form of tariffs, Department of the Interior pork-barrel public works legislation, Christmas tree
tax "reform" bills, and so forth, are plentiful in legislative history.[28]

27. Tullock stresses this difference in information possessed by the local voter in "A
Simple Algebraic Logrolling Model," *American Economic Review,* 60 (June 1970), pp.
419–426.
28. A classic example of this is the tariff protecting a geographically concentrated industry. Since a tariff typically benefits only a small minority and hurts everyone through higher
prices, no single tariff can typically pass (unless part of a general logroll where, for example, a defense base is traded for a tariff) in the legislature. The Christmas tree package of
tariff legislation generated by Congress in 1970 in response to the President's support for
tariff protection for one industry only (textiles) is an example of this point. Fortunately,
none of the versions of the Christmas tree bill reached the floor of the House, and no trade
legislation was raised during the session. A bill containing tariffs favoring a large number of
geographically concentrated industries might pass, however. Such a bill would produce ran-

What is bad about this form of logrolling, at say the national level, is not that it acts as a means for revealing relative intensities of preferences on national issues—indeed this is essential if one is to avoid the imposition of the will of passive majorities over intense minorities—but that in its most blatant forms it is used to reveal relative intensities of preference on essentially local issues that never should come before the national legislature. When restricted to positive-sum games, logrolling can become a beneficial means for revealing voter preferences on issues. This confusion as to whether logrolling applies to positive- or negative-sum games can help to explain the disagreements among many observers over the benefits from logrolling.[29]

Our model would reduce the likelihood that legislatures would engage in negative-sum games in two ways. First, at-large representation eliminates the direct link between a representative and local interests. Although he can still adopt platforms based on local issues, the legislative candidate would have an incentive to broaden his appeal to a larger constituency in order to increase the number of votes he receives. Candidates who stressed economy in government, free trade, consumer protection and similar positive-sum game issues would be able to increase their political strength under proportional representation by appealing directly to a national constitutency (for example, by proposing the potential tax reductions inherent in such platforms).

The control over the issue selection process by the judicial branch provides the second check on the legislative branch's engaging in negative-sum games. Bills that favored special economic or geographic interests would not be allowed on the agenda because of the likelihood that they would violate the equal-stake criterion. They would be channeled, along with intense majority–intense minority issues, into the constitutional amendment process. Although this may sound novel, it is quite consistent with the spirit of the Constitution. The right to engage in commerce is guaranteed by the Constitution, but it is immasculated by tariffs, quotas, state and privately enforced monopolies, etc. Given a choice between a free trade–free competition bill and a Christmas tree tariff–monopoly–

dom and probably small changes in the distribution of income, and most likely leave society worse off on balance, by distorting world prices and relinquishing some of the gains from trade. Thus, the bill would be a negative-sum game in that some industries might increase their real incomes at the expense of others and on average real incomes in the nation would go down.

29. For examples of pro-logrolling arguments see Buchanan and Tullock, *The Calculus of Consent;* Coleman, "The Possibility of a Social Welfare Function," and "Political Money"; the various works of Robert Dahl; Arthur Bentley, *The Process of Government* (Bloomington, Ind.: Principia Press, 1938) (first published 1908); and Madison's *Federalist Papers.* See Lowi, *The End of Liberalism,* and G. McConnell, *Private Power and American Democracy* (New York: Knopf, 1966), for anti-logrolling positions.

monopsony bill, a constitutional convention bound by a unanimity rule should select the former. Similarly, it was deemed necessary to pass a constitutional amendment to enable the government to tax personal income. Yet, the defining of income and selection of tax rates was left up to legislative logrolling, thereby eliminating the equity implicit in the constitutional sanction for the tax. The way, the only conceivable way, to achieve horizontal and vertical equity in the definition of income and tax rates, is to decide these issues by some form of judicial process. A constitutional convention charged with the responsibility of establishing an equitable income tax might come up with such a tax, if its members could adopt a sufficient degree of detachment so that they weighted the tax's likely impact on all citizens, and if they did not have to run for re-election by appealing for the votes of a certain subset of the citizens. Once established, all changes in tariff, monopoly, and income tax policy would be made by the same constitutional process under unanimous consent, thereby ensuring the positive-sum nature of any changes.[30]

When this process for selecting issues is contrasted with the present system in which small committees of the legislature determine the issue set, the composition of the committees is relatively stable over time, the legislators are selected geographically and often favor special local and economic interests, and the seniority system allows certain regions and localities to have more power within the committees than others, one gets a far different picture of the likelihood of negative-sum game playing in the legislature.

V. Stability and Parties

Another primary difference between the model and the present American political system is that the performance of the latter is strongly determined by the outcomes achieved under a two-party system of government, while the model presented here emphasizes a multi-party system. The issue of stability has been raised with respect to multi-party systems in at least two senses. First, in the literature on the economic theory of democracy the stability of party positions along an ideological spectrum has been questioned (see n. 31). Second, on pragmatic and empirical grounds the "stability of the government" under a multi-party system is often questioned. We discuss both these issues in this section, although primary attention is given to the first.

It is well known that under a two-party system candidates tend to take median positions. Assume, for example, preferences on issues can be

---

30. Again, it is interesting to note how John Stuart Mill recongized the importance of establishing a separate body (in his case a commission to select the issues upon which the legislature must act), *op. cit.*, pp. 235 ff.

depicted as lying along a spectrum running from radical left to reactionary right as in Figure 3. If one party's candidate adopts the median position, *M*, he guarantees himself at least a tie in the election. If the second party's candidate adopts any other position, e.g., *R*, he will get less than 50 percent of the votes if each citizen votes for the candidate closest to him. Thus, the best strategy for the second party candidate is to adopt the same position as the other candidate, *M*, and hope that by random error on the part of voters, he emerges a winner.

Note what happens if a third party candidate enters the race, however. If he adopts *R*, while the other two are at *M*, he gets all votes to the right of *R* and half of those between *M* and *R*, and beats both of the other candidates. This should induce one of the other two candidates to move from *M* to, say, *L* isolating the candidate at *M* with a small fraction of the vote. The candidate at *M* will then have an incentive to move outside of the *L–R* segment, thereby trapping one of the other candidates and so on. Starting from a position in which all candidates are at the center, at least one candidate in a multi-party (more than 2) system will have an incentive to move away from the center.

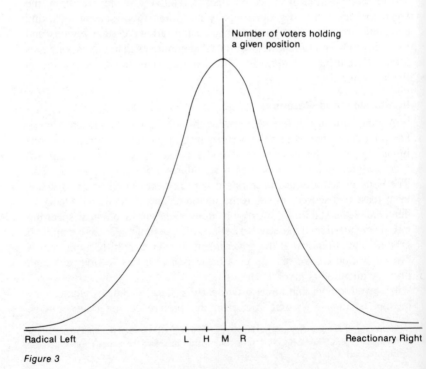

Number of voters holding
a given position

Radical Left   L H M R   Reactionary Right

Figure 3

In the extreme, one can envisage this spreading out to continue until the total range is covered and each candidate receives an identical fraction of the vote. In a 100-man legislature, each candidate would locate at the center of a percentile, and receive 1 percent of the vote. Starting from this distribution of positions, however, candidates will have an incentive to move back toward the center. With the peak in the center, a candidate can increase his percentage of the vote by moving slightly toward the center. This can be seen in Figure 3 by noting that with candidates at L, M, and R, the two outside candidates can increase their votes by moving toward M.

Thus, in general, the positioning of the candidates along an ideological spectrum in a multi-party system is unstable.[31] Depending upon the starting point, there may be incentives to move toward the center or away from it, and movements in both directions could be occurring at the same time. (The situation is analogous to the instability that occurs in the Edgeworth duopoly model. Starting from the joint profit maximizing price each duopolist has an incentive to cut prices; starting from competitive price, each duopolist has an incentive to raise prices.)

There are a number of reasons for believing that a considerable (although perhaps not complete) spreading out of candidates along the left-right spectrum would occur under the multi-party (multi-candidate) system discussed here, however. In the primary in which, say 150 to 200 candidates are entered, and only the 100 highest vote getters are on the final slate, many candidates will probably adopt positions along the two tails of the distribution. In the primary a candidate can guarantee a position on the final slate with 1 percent of the vote. Thus, adopting a position relatively far removed from the other candidates, unless it is way out on the tail, can get one elected. New candidates, in particular, will want to differentiate their positions clearly from the incumbents.

Let us assume that the candidates do apportion themselves along the political spectrum, so that following the primary each of the 100 winning candidates is in the middle of a percentile of voters. Each now faces the strategy choices of moving toward the center or staying put (see Table 1). If he stays and all other candidates stay, he is assured of 1 percent of the vote. If he moves in the direction of the median immediately beside the adjacent candidate, and all other candidates stay, he increases his share of the vote to somewhere between one and one and a half percent. If all other candidates adopt a similar strategy, and the process is followed to

31. For a discussion of the convergence toward the center and instability in a multi-party system, see Melvin J. Hinich and Peter C. Ordeshook, "Plurality Maximization vs. Vote Maximization: A Spatial Analysis with Variable Participation," *American Political Science Review*, 64 (September 1970), pp. 785–788.

completion, all arrive at M with expected shares of the vote all equal to 1 percent with voters randomly choosing among the candidates.

The case in which all other candidates move and one stays in place is a little more complicated. Suppose L is the candidate who stays in place. All candidates to his right move to M, and L gets the percentage of the vote represented by the area under the curve between L and H, a point halfway between L and M. All candidates to the left of him move to his immediate left. The expected percentage of votes for one of these candidates is now slightly greater than 1 percent. Any one of them can increase his percentage of the vote by jumping L and taking the furthest position to the left of M in the bunch at the center. If all other candidates on the left do this, L is left alone to the left of M and gets all votes to the left of H.

Table 1.

Candidate L	All other candidates stay	All other candidates move beside the next candidate toward the center
Stays	$S = 1\%$	$S = \int_{-\infty}^{H} f(X)dX$
Moves next to the candidate to his immediate right	$1\% < S < 1.5\%$	$E(S) = 1\%$

$S =$ candidate L's share of the vote
$f(X) =$ frequency distribution

If we assume candidates prefer the certain 1 percent they achieve if all candidates stay to the risky 1 percent they can expect if they all plunge into the center, the stay strategy is preferred under the maximum criterion. Although the instability of the outcomes when all or almost all are moving places a high variance around the payoffs in the second column, the rather high payoff from staying in place in the polar example should dominate and make staying the preferred strategy under most decision rules. Only if a high probability is placed on other candidates staying will moving toward the center produce a slight expected gain.

The attractiveness of moving is still further reduced once possible voter reactions are introduced. A risk-averting voter may prefer a candidate who steadily maintains a position somewhat near his own, to one who is currently at the voter's position, but is constantly moving. To the extent that voters favor candidates who adopt (or appear to adopt) attitudes out of conviction rather than as strategies for winning votes, shifting positions is further discouraged.[32] Finally, the already difficult task of acquainting voters with one's platform, when there is a long list of candidates, will be made even more difficult if the candidate is constantly changing his position.

Thus, under the proposed form of proportional representation the candidates would tend to spread out along the full spectrum of preferences and remain in their positions under plausible conditions, in contrast to the two-party outcome. Each voter could select a candidate close to his own position; each voter would be assured that the candidate he voted for in the final election would be in the legislature to represent him. And with a randomly selected legislature, at least some of the chosen members would probably be close to any individual voter's position.

When only one winner is selected from each district, parties that are thinly spread across a country will not win seats in an election. Since it is hard for parties out of office to remain visible, the ins and outs characteristic of geographic representation reduces the number of parties over time to those with sufficient geographic concentration to win some seats in assemblies. On the other hand, any party with some national following, no matter how it is dispersed geographically, can elect some representatives to the national assembly under at-large proportional representation or random selection, and thereby maintain its visibility, creditability, and existence.[33]

Under a proportionally representative system the importance of political parties would probably decline. The two-party system would most certainly be replaced by a multi-party structure, and even within parties it would be the individual platforms of the candidates that would determine the number of votes they got. Party designations might aid voters in concentrating on those subsets of candidates that are most likely to approximate their views, but the same kind of information could be provided by subdividing the voter's manual by ideological position (liberal-conservative, hawk-dove, segregationist-integrationist).

One of the chief pragmatic virtues claimed for the two-party system is stability.[34] This stability stems from the tendency of two-party democracy

32. Hinich and Ordeshook, *ibid.,* find that there can be as many as 3 conversion points for a unimodel distribution, if voters abstain from voting (due, for example, to alienation effects) as candidates move from their positions. See also A. Downs, *An Economic Theory of Democracy* (New York: Harper and Row, 1957), pp. 103–112.

33. Downs, *op. cit.,* pp. 122–127. Downs' book touches on a number of the issues raised in this paper about two-party and multi-party systems. See also Gordon Tullock, *Toward a Mathematics of Politics* (Ann Arbor: University of Michigan Press, 1967), chapter 10.

34. S. M. Lipset, *Political Man* (Garden City, N.Y.: Doubleday, 1960).

to satisfy the middle voters by producing median outcomes and comes at the expense of frustrating the voters on both tails of the political spectrum. In times of profound ideological disagreement, when the middle ground gives way to an enlarging of the numbers of voters at the two extremes, the frustration produced by two-party democracy may produce political instability, however, and even the demise of the two-party system. The political history of the United States is replete with examples of third and fourth parties forming out of the frustration of a lack of voice under the two-party system.[35] At-large proportional representation or random selection would institutionalize the multi-party framework and provide all minority groups of moderate size a legitimate voice in the political process.

With respect to the second type of stability problem raised by a multi-party system ("stability of the government"), it should be noted that proportional representation need not result in the political instability that characterizes some multi-party parliamentary governments. The chief executive could still be elected for a fixed term of office with impeachment a difficult and rare occurrence. Stability could thus be preserved in the executive branch.[36]

VI. Summary and Conclusion

The preferences of minorities can be reflected under majority rule by giving each voter an equal number of vote-points which he can allocate over all issues in proportion to his relative intensity of preference. The information needed to make decisions in a modern, urban society precludes the gathering of information on voter preferences by direct democracy. Still, the advantages of direct democracy–point voting in reflecting voter preferences can be preserved by selecting representatives to each legislature in proportion to the number of voters in each polity having similar preferences. As an added advantage, the selection of legislators on an at-large basis would reduce the link between concentrated economic power and political power that geographic representation aids in producing. Fur-

---

35. See in particular Lipset's discussion of the election of 1860 when there were four viable parties with presidential candidates, *ibid.*, chapter 11.

36. For an empirical survey of the effect of parliamentary party structure on the stability of governments (196 cases), see M. Taylor and V. M. Herman, "Party Systems and Government Stability," *American Political Science Review*, 65 (March 1971), pp. 28–37. This study finds that there is a strong relationship between stability of government and fragmentation of the parliamentary party system and of the government parties. No relation is found between fragmentation of opposition parties and stability. Also, the ideological disparity of parties did not seem to explain stability any better than a fragmentation stressing the number and size of parties. Interestingly, the proportion of seats held by "anti-system" parties did seem to be linked to stability.

ther, under plausible conditions of voter and party behavior, the multi-party system implied in our model would be stable.

The optimality of proportional representation with point voting rests heavily upon a requirement that political boundaries be drawn and issues allocated among polities so that each voter in a polity has an equal potential utility gain from that polity's decision. This equal-stake criterion is quite consistent with the Populist spirit of American democracy, but again places several requirements on the way fiscal federalism decisions are resolved. Indeed, the impartiality required in the equal-stake condition could only be achieved by a judicial or quasi-judicial body, like the courts or a constitutional convention. Thus the political system which we discuss would place increased demands on the judicial process, as well as on the legislative process, and the citizens themselves. But, such shifts in power will obviously be necessary under any attempt to strengthen democracy by returning power to the people.

Part V: Economics and Economists in the Policy Process

The final section of the volume turns once again to a direct examination of the role of economics and economists in the policy process, concentrating especially on the proper role of the economist giving policy advice. The questions addressed concern the relative merits of advice given within the system and outside advice, and what balance of professionalism and politics enables advisers to be most effective.

The first paper, by Arthur Okun, discusses the economist and presidential leadership, arguing that economists should be involved in policy formation and considering how they can be effective in that area. After describing the workings of the present system of economic advice in the Executive Office, Okun suggests that the economics profession needs something like a Supreme Court to represent it in areas of professional concern. In other words, he makes a distinction between inside and outside economic advice.

In the second paper George Shultz (former Secretary of the Treasury and Labor, and Special Economic Assistant to the President) argues that the economist giving policy advice must be aware of the institutional structures underlying the government's decision-making process. Policy makers operate in a complex institutional setting, and Shultz urges economists to realize that one cannot attain perfection in government policy. The role of the economist, he believes, should be to argue for economic solutions to social problems and in particular to stress the relationship between economic behavior and individual liberty.

In the third paper Henry Wallich (member of the Board of Governors, Federal Reserve System) describes the formation of the West German equivalent of the U.S. Council of Economic Advisers, the *Sachverstaendigenrat,* and compares the two bodies. The major distinction between them is that the German council operates independently of the government and passes purely professional judgments on matters of social pol-

icy, in contrast with the U.S. Council (CEA) where political considerations also enter into the framing of policy.

Charles Schultze, in the fourth paper, discusses criticisms that have
been made of one institutional management device that has been implemented to improve the provision of public policy—namely the planning,
programming, and budgeting system (PPB). He considers criticisms of
PPB by examining a theory of political decision-making that has evolved
in the political science literature. Essentially his paper serves to compare
elements of the political science approach with the economic approach.

The last two papers again deal with the Council of Economic Advisers.
Gordon Tullock argues that the CEA is inappropriately structured and
should be radically redesigned in order to improve the likelihood that the
government will act in an economically informed way. In effect he
suggests an outside council of experts to render opinions on matters of
economic policy. Robert Tollison and Thomas Willett, commenting on
Tullock's paper, argue that his proposal should be considered as an addition to, rather than a substitute for, the present CEA—in other words,
that both inside and outside advice on economic policy serve a useful purpose.

31. The Economist and
Presidential Leadership

ARTHUR M. OKUN

The economists in our universities and research institutions toil in the
field of values as well as that of fact and theory. When they come to
Washington, they cannot leave their ideologies behind. Indeed, they
should not. Political economists necessarily move in the realm of social
values, and that is the way they become most useful, especially as advisers to the President. Presidential leadership consists of selecting priorities, making commitments, identifying the aims of the nation, and then
working to fulfill them. To exercise this leadership effectively, the President needs the advice of people with diverse professional training.

Nobody comes out of graduate school with a Ph.D. in priority setting
or applied political ideology. And yet these are major tasks in the executive's policy making. Some group of people is going to do this job and it

Reprinted from Arthur M. Okun, *The Political Economy of Propersity* (New York: Norton, 1970), pp. 23–30, by permission of the Brookings Institution. Copyright © 1970 by the
Brookings Institution, Washington, D.C.

should include economists. Unless there is evidence that deep thinking about social problems can be done best by those whose minds are uncluttered by formal training in the social sciences, the economist should not yield this territory entirely to those with no professional background. As Gardner Ackley argued:

. . . Those in authority get plenty of advice from others who show no great delicacy in distinguishing technical questions within their competence from questions of values. The President hears from other members of his Administration, from businessmen, from labor leaders, from journalists—yes, from economists. If his economic adviser refrains from advice on the gut questions of policy, the President should and will get another one.[1]

To be effective, the adviser must operate with sensitivity and understanding of the President's values and aims. He must know the President's tastes, just as a good wife has to know how her husband takes his coffee. Thus after Kennedy pledged to "start this country moving again,"[2] his economists convinced him that a 4 percent interim target for unemployment was an appropriate translation of that goal.[3] Once that commitment was made, it had broad and pervasive implications for subsequent policy decisions. When President Johnson set forth the vision of the Great Society, his economists shaped the strategies in the war against poverty to fit. They showed how prosperity could contribute to the fulfillment of a great society. They stressed the fundamental compatibility—indeed, complementarity—of material goods and spiritual goals when some of the President's staff urged him to downplay economic considerations in order to emphasize human values. Because President Johnson wished to avoid a Robin Hood or class-struggle theme in social aid to the disadvantaged, it was important to develop programs and justifications that emphasized the long-term benefits to the entire nation from investment in human resources. When President Nixon counseled the nation to lower its voice, his economists followed, in their pronouncements, with a stress on moderation and gradualism. President Nixon's preference for the middle of the road must influence many of the staff efforts to develop program initiatives.

Efforts to flesh out the framework of the President's leadership are of

1. Gardner Ackley, "The Contribution of Economists to Policy Formation," *Journal of Finance*, Vol. 21 (May 1966), p. 176.

2. *Freedom of Communications*, Pt. 1: *The Speeches, Remarks, Press Conferences, and Statements of Senator John F. Kennedy, August 1 through November 7, 1960*, Final Report of the Senate Committee on Commerce, Prepared by its Subcommittee of the Subcommittee on Communications, S. Rept. 994, 87 Cong. 1 sess. (1961), p. 542.

3. See "The President's News Conference of March 15, 1961," in *Public Papers of the Presidents of the United States: John F. Kennedy, 1961* (1962), p. 187.

particular importance within the Executive Office of the President. Many of the top officials of other agencies in the executive branch are assigned the role of advocates within the administration. For example, the Secretary of Labor is expected to be a spokesman for manpower programs. An imaginative and energetic secretary ought to be able to generate a volume of high priority manpower programs whose costs would far exceed the amount of resources and legislative energy that can be reasonably allocated to his department. Kermit Gordon, former Director of the Bureau of the Budget, recited the warning of the bureau's very first director, General Charles G. Dawes: "Cabinet members are vice presidents in charge of spending, and as such they are the natural enemies of the President." [4] In point of fact, the members of the Cabinet serve the President by making the strongest possible case for their efforts and their programs. They also serve him by developing a special liaison with private interest groups. This pluralistic system within the administration functions very well. But it does confront the President with some hard choices, which he cannot hope to make all on his own. He needs some staff and some advisers who are not assigned a role of advocacy. Here he is bound to look to the executive office agencies, including the White House staff, the Bureau of the Budget, and the Council of Economic Advisers, to exercise a check on the pluralistic structure of the administration.

To assure this check, our presidents have selected members of the Council of Economic Advisers who were not affiliated with particular interest groups. CEA members have generally moved into public office from a university or nonprofit research institution. To be sure, most of our leading academic economists have taken fees from private groups for consulting or speech making. Moreover, an academic or public service background is no guarantee of objectivity and impartiality, nor does private activity foreclose them. The nation has been served with distinction by economists in public service who previously practiced their profession on behalf of banks, business firms, trade associations, and labor unions. But it is added insurance when the economists sitting closest to the President have a background of concern for the public interest. [5]

The effectiveness of officials in the Executive Office depends entirely on their relationship with the President. They have no programs to run and no responsibilities or powers that they can exercise on their own. The only statutory claim that the Council of Economic Advisers has on the

4. Kermit Gordon, "Reflections on Spending," in John D. Montgomery and Arthur Smithies (eds.), *Public Policy*, Vol. 15 (Harvard University, Graduate School of Public Administration, 1966), p. 15 (Brookings Reprint 125).

5. For a contrasting view, see William H. Chartener, "The Business Economist in Government," *Business Economics*, Vol. 4 (January 1969), p. 10.

President's eye or ear is the writing of the Economic Report. If the President's attention to the CEA were limited to that once-a-year effort, the Council would be a most uninteresting and ineffective agency. It becomes interesting and effective to the extent that it wins his confidence.

But this confidence must flow two ways. No adviser can expect to have his advice taken all or even most of the time. If he feels in disharmony with the general position and posture of the administration, he ought to leave his job. But if he considers his job worthwhile and is to do it effectively, he must accept certain standards of loyalty. He must agree to confine battling to internal councils and cannot publicly oppose administration decisions once they are made. At most he can hope that, with the President's blessing, he may occasionally launch trial balloons and thus move in the vanguard of administration policy. Loyalty may even dictate that he prepare briefs for others to use with legitimate arguments in favor of positions with which he does not agree. He can and should maintain personal integrity by refusing to say publicly anything that he does not believe even though he cannot say publicly everything he does believe.

Given these constraints, members of the Council of Economic Advisers are clearly recognized as the President's men. If they speak publicly, they will be identified as spokesmen for administration positions. A Council chairman can respond to this dilemma, as Edwin Nourse and Arthur Burns did, by speaking very rarely for the public record. As Nourse strongly expressed his view:

For the President to permit or encourage intervention of Council members in any manner in the legislative process or in the public promotion of measures or policies is to make them politically expendable and to destroy the unique usefulness of the Council as an institution designed for scientific service to the executive branch.[6]

Most of the other six Council chairmen have not subscribed to this view. They have advocated and explained publicly many administration economic policies and proposals. When the President's case was their case and when the issues could be illuminated by economic education of the citizenry, they have spoken out—as partisans, but as partisans with expertise and professional integrity.

In such cases, both the speaker and the listeners know that the discussion is pursued within, and not above, the political fray. The mere fact that the Council agrees with the President can never be news and can never enhance an administration position. No CEA member has ever claimed to be the spokesman for a purely professional view. Woodrow

6. Edwin G. Nourse, *Economics in the Public Service: Administrative Aspects of the Employment Act* (Harcourt, Brace, 1953), p. 500.

Wilson once said with obvious facetiousness, "The trouble with the Republican party is that it has not had a new idea for thirty years. I am not speaking as a politician; I am speaking as an historian." [7] Neither presidents nor their advisers can hope ever to convince their audiences that their pronouncements on partisan issues are professional and nonpolitical.

In short, when the President's economists decide to go on public record, they cannot serve two masters. They cannot speak both for the President and for the profession. And they cannot speak for the profession publicly and still maintain confidence and rapport internally with the President. The choice should be clear. It is far more important for society and for the profession to have economists who maintain rapport with the President and thus can have greatest influence on the inside.

A Voice for Consensus

Yet this is not an entirely satisfactory conclusion. One wishes for a more effective way of influencing public and congressional opinion in the areas of professional consensus. There is a role to be played by a Supreme Court of the profession, although a less important one than that actually fulfilled by the Council and the Bureau in recent years.

This is not necessarily an either-or choice. One can conceive of another and separate institution outside the administration consisting of economic experts ready to speak up on policy matters involving technical results or widespread professional agreement. Somebody would have to select a group of "outside" economic experts, clearly bipartisan in composition. They could not be self-selected not should they be named by the President. Perhaps the minority and majority leadership of the Congress could best handle this assignment; they might wish to consult with officers of the American Economic Association for suggestions. Perhaps the majority and minority might each choose six economic experts. This group of twelve could perform the specific and limited function of defining the scope of bipartisan professional agreement. They would make recommendations only when the group was nearly unanimous—perhaps ten signatures out of the twelve might be required on any report. One would expect to hear from the group only rarely on specific pieces of legislation, but it might set forth important principles and positions on both macro- and microeconomic policies. Such a group would probably have supported appropriately restrictive fiscal and monetary actions in 1966–68. It might have done considerable good, and it could hardly have done much harm.

7. Albert Shaw (ed.), *President Wilson's State Papers and Addresses* (New York: Review of Reviews Co., 1917), p. 81.

Some risks attend the initiation of any institution in the policy process, no matter how modest its conception and objectives. If too much were expected from the advisory group in terms of either influence or specific recommendations, it could be condemned to failure. If its silence on certain issues would be viewed as incriminating, it might add further to the suspicion that economists are hopelessly divided. If this group would seem to introduce a technocratic element in policy issues or to present a picture of a medieval tribunal of wise men ruling on the theology of social issues, its creation would not serve the nation.

I am confident that it would not endanger the place of the maverick in the profession; he would still find a receptive audience. Nor would it be likely to interfere with the functions of existing institutions; indeed, it would help to clarify the fact that the Council of Economic Advisers simply cannot and should never be expected to fulfill the nonpolitical, purely professional function. In the last analysis, such a group would be beneficial only if it influenced our legislators, directly or indirectly. If they would take such a group seriously and find its judgments helpful, its creation could be a way of resolving a dilemma of the political and nonpolitical role of the economist in public policy.

Whether or not new institutions are created, there will be a continuing challenge to narrow the gap between the judgment of the profession and the law of the land. It must be demonstrated that there *is* a professional view on many matters. The day ought to come when informed noneconomists are no longer surprised that the negative income tax can be strongly advocated by "new economists" like James Tobin and Joseph Pechman and also by Milton Friedman.

To convey the professional view effectively requires the talents of a missionary, an outstanding pedagogue, and a super-salesman; it also takes skillful and sympathetic understanding of opposition views and, especially, of noneconomic considerations in policy choices. These requirements and skills differ from those most vital to successful academic research. The areas of professional consensus are rarely on the frontier of economic inquiry. They are typically built on the foundation of theoretical and empirical results that have been established and accepted by the profession long ago.

The political economist's task can be aided by some types of academic research that can nail down, dramatize, and quantify his message. But the academic researcher will rarely regard these as the most challenging scientific problems. Meanwhile, the political economist will find that much of the exploration on the frontiers of economic knowledge is irrelevant to his task of providing ammunition for the battles waged in a political arena. And so political economy has to be a separate and distinct activity of the profession. It is not science, but it is a source of potential benefit to the nation. And it will remain alive and well in Washington, whichever party occupies the White House.

32. Reflections on Political Economy

GEORGE P. SHULTZ

There is a lot of politics in economics these days, although this is hardly surprising when political survival so often seems tied to government action. As economists, we are hardly to blame for this state of affairs. But, having bolted from the seminar room to the policy scene, we can, it seems to me, be more effective in our contributions if we think of ourselves as engaged in—to use the words of an earlier day—political economy. This is more than a call for a greater overlay of common sense, uncharacteristic humility, and renewed attention to the analysis of policy issues; it is a call for an extension of institutional analysis beyond the firm and the union so that we might better understand—and thereby affect—economic decision-making by government.

Present Institutional Arrangements

Economic policy issues seldom present themselves to the policymaker in disembodied terms. If they did, economic policy could be handled by statisticians and computer experts—no doubt for the lasting benefit of all. Rather, those issues are served up to the policymaker by a variety of political and economic forces outside his direct control. In addition, the time horizon for resolving a policy issue is usually short: an economist's "lag" may be a politician's catastrophe.

Proposals for policy actions typically are put forward by a party in interest. I leave aside proposals advanced in letters to *The New York Times* and academic articles, as well as other proposals that, whatever their intrinsic merits, are likely to sink directly to the bottom of the Washington political seas. Those that stay afloat long enough to have a chance of surviving must have the strong support of at least one party in interest.

The first interest group is the one the term usually suggests—a group in the economy that will benefit directly from the legislative or administrative action proposed. It has long been apparent to many companies,

Reprinted from *Challenge*, March–April 1974 pp. 6–11, by permission of the publisher and author.

unions, professional bodies, associations, and the like that they can achieve profits or other advantages as easily by government actions as by their own efforts in the marketplace. Sometimes they seek subsidies, sometimes tax relief, sometimes protection from competition. Should we economists be surprised that they seek the gold at the end of the government rainbow? We should indeed expect them to use government until at the margin the costs exceed the benefits received.

The second interest group is the executive branch, department, or bureau that represents the first interest group. It may seem odd to refer to an executive department as an interest group, but the fact is that the interests of a particular department are quite often remarkably allied with those of its "clients" in the society. Here I speak of no conspiracy or even any lack of civic virtue on the part of cabinet secretaries and their faithful civil servants. Such clientele representation is expected in Washington. Advocacy government is part of our unwritten constitution. Everyone expects the Department of Agriculture to represent the farmers, the Department of Interior to represent the western reclamation interest, and even the Department of State to represent the impact on foreigners in the interagency forums where executive branch decisions are hammered out. Even if such advocacy relationships were not so universally expected, a cabinet secretary would find it difficult to avoid representing his clients at the White House court. Many quickly become captured by the permanent bureaucracy that does not doubt the desirability of client representation, and others find that the way to gain public support and to avoid brickbats is to support their clients' interests.

Members of the bureaucracy have limits placed on their income, of course; and predictably they seek their satisfaction in other ways. Parkinson has said most of what there is to say on this subject, and the tendency toward bureaucratic edema is familiar to all diagnosticians of governmental ailments. The waste and inefficiency would be tolerable if it were not for the systematic bias toward expansion of the role of government. Cabinet secretaries and other departmental political appointees, whatever their initial good intentions, all too often slip into the role of "hired guns" for their departments in interagency struggles.

To understand fully the role of the departments, it is important to grasp the nature of the third interest group—the legislative committees in the Congress. Congressmen represent the interests of their constituents, and this is as it should be. Farm-state legislators tend to vote for farm programs whether or not those programs contribute to efficiency in the allocation of resources. Economists may remonstrate, but they seldom have had to meet a precinct captain.

What is less widely appreciated is the extent to which self-selection results in agricultural committees' being dominated by farm-state legislators, interior committees by Westerners and so forth. Only one of the thirteen members of the Senate Interior Committee is from east of the Mississippi. The consequences are predictable.

Congress and the executive branch are joined in bureaucratic wedlock by the fact that for nearly every congressional committee, there exists an executive department or bureau in the same substantive area. The department's attention to the wishes of the committee members is assured by the increasingly pervasive requirement that the spending programs of the department be authorized once each year in addition to the constitutional requirement of appropriation of funds. Recently, the practice has taken the form of trying to require the annual authorization not merely of spending programs but also of employee salaries and expenses—that is, the annual authorization of the existence of the department itself.

This state of affairs gives a committee chairman great strength. It also has a more subtle effect. If the legislator is to achieve success in his calling and concomitant rewards in prestige and national attention, then his legislative efforts must be focused on topics within his committee's competence. Here we see a little-perceived, but persistent, force pushing for a larger government role. If the committee's jurisdiction is health, then it can be predicted with high probability that the members, and particularly the chairman, will favor expanded government health programs. The same goes for national defense, agriculture, and so on down the line of government programs.

What has kept this process in check is not so much the self-restraint of the members of the substantive committees: more important is the inevitable shortage of resources for doing everything at once. The organizational embodiments of this resource constraint are the appropriations committees which trim the ambitions of the substantive committees down to size in the annual appropriations cycle. But even the appropriations committees cannot exercise their traditional discipline over the process. Their jurisdiction over the resource allocation function has been steadily eroded through the growth of various backdoor spending practices. And, of course, they too can and do become part of the interest-group alliances.

Nevertheless, the budget process is a great check on private ambitions over public funds and one of the most effective checks to bureaucratic expansionism. More importantly, it provides to the public resource allocation process the necessary overall spending constraint that the price system imposes on private resource decisions.

Today, budget discipline is breaking down in three ways. The first is the growth in the Congress of backdoor spending techniques which exclude the appropriations committees from the resource allocation process and thereby assure that Congress never looks at the budget as a whole. Examples of these backdoor practices include the crop support payments of the Commodity Credit Corporation and grants to airports from the Federal Aviation Administration. The second way in which budget discipline is eroding is through the tendency over the years of both Presidents and Congresses to take favored programs off the budget and thereby to avoid making overall resource allocation decisions. The Federal National Mortgage Association, the Export-Import Bank, and the Rural Electrification Administration are all funded off the budget. Today, over a third of the debt obligations of the federal government reflect off-budget credit and guarantee programs. The third pernicious influence on budget discipline is now just arising. It stems from the desire of congressional committees to free favored programs from any executive-branch allocation decision by permitting various executive agencies to submit their proposed budgets directly to the Congress and thereby end-run the annual presidential budget proposal to the Congress. Funding for the Consumer Protection Agency is an example of this end-run technique. Moreover, recent law prohibits the executive branch from making any reduction in the budget of the Consumer Protection Agency. While each of these techniques of circumventing the budget may be expedient to particular interests at particular times, they threaten a breakdown of the system, a breakdown that will be harmful to all. At minimum they facilitate the use of government for private gain.

Fortunately, presidential and congressional perception of the budget problem has grown. It has been recently and forcefully expressed in the form of a joint committee on this subject, and proposals for new institutional arrangements are well advanced. They deserve all the support they can get. To succeed they will need sustained effort both for enactment and for use in the intended manner.

Thus far we have considered how outside economic interests, executive departments and substantive legislative committees—each acting out of self-interest and without any element of conspiracy—tend to form alliances to serve their common interests. This process extends beyond narrowly economic issues to the social and even the national security and foreign policy arenas. What economist should be surprised? Is it not now standard theory that utility maximization extends to organizations as well as individuals and to matters other than simple pecuniary gain? Economists should be able to appreciate and extend concepts of self-interest in a complex political environment in which the quality of democratic representation as well as efficiency is at stake.

The approach that I have described can help to illuminate many features of the national scene. The outside interest groups need not be limited to the behemoths of industry operating the military-industrial complex but can as easily be the hospital and school administrators, the organized social workers, and others with a vested interest in doing things in the same old way. It was mildly instructive, for example, to observe the opposition of social workers to the family assistance plan under which federal dollars would have been channeled directly to the poor to permit each poor family to decide for itself how best to spend its allotment. We should not be surprised that many social workers supported the retention of the existing system, under which a large portion of those dollars go to social workers, a middle-income group, in return for supervising the allocation of in-kind benefits and the expenditure of funds by the poor.

Good or Bad

The system I have described has both strengths and shortcomings. Aside from democratic considerations concerning the right of groups to be heard in the hall of government, the advocacy element may be cited as a positive factor. Although it is possible to make decisions in a hermetically sealed, systems-analysis environment, abstract economic analysis too often ignores vital factors that are likely to be brought to the policymaker's attention through the advocacy process.

Let me cite controversial areas in which economists have been prominent in public debate yet in which the limitations on our professional judgment seem to me apparent. The first is in energy. Proceeding from the simple thesis that oil could be extracted more cheaply abroad, economists have in the past usually argued on grounds of welfare and efficiency for relatively free importation. Counterarguments based on a quite different and noneconomic thesis of national independence were viewed with suspicion at best. Yet today the case for independence in energy supply can be seen not just as the pleading of a "special interest" but as a valid national goal. Economists will and should have a lot to say about how we can reach that goal—but it was and is simply wrong to discount the validity and importance of this goal.

The approach of economics toward oil imports is, of course, on application of the powerful and persuasive case for freer trade generally. Yet, in pursuing that goal, how do we weigh the diffused and generalized gains from trade against the very real pains and costs of the dislocations that shifting trading patterns cause in particular congressional districts that elect particular Congressmen?

We need a process to reconcile these objectives—for example, to accompany reduced trade barriers with new "safeguard" provisions and to recognize the national interest in an assured energy supply. The process of reconciling these goals should not be seen as a distortion of the purity of our economics, but rather as a valid national requirement working through political institutions.

On the negative side of the advocacy process, there is, in my view, one major disadvantage: the system creates almost irresistible incentives for the expansion of the government without careful attention to the costs or implications of such a process. All of the advocates in the system seek to better their positions; and in nearly every case, whether they be outside economic interests, executive departments, or congressional committees, bettering their positions means expanding government action.

Now some of you may favor a larger role for government. Perhaps this is only a question of values. My conviction that we must do our best to hold the line against the encroachment of government on private institutions has been greatly strengthened by my experience over the last five years. In any case, assuming that the question of the proper size of government is amenable to rational debate, I see no grounds for concluding that the process I have described would lead to an optimum size of government or the assumption of functions for which government has a clear comparative advantage. This judgment may help to explain why economists are unlikely to be elected president of any organization other than the American Economic Association, but it also raises issues to which economists should be especially sensitive.

What does it all mean for the Policymaker?

How does the policymaker deal with the advocacy system that I have described? First of all, he must be realistic about the environment in which he must function. Some cynics have said that success in Washington can be equated with survival, and it is certainly true that one cannot ignore political and bureaucratic factors to the point where he is excluded from the decision-making process. But that is merely a negative condition of access to decisions. There is a more positive way to approach the question. When I first came to Washington I used to think that there were two kinds of people: substantive folks, like you and me, who analyze problems and propose optimal solutions; and the politicians who do their thing, for good or for ill, with the proposals we make. I never had a sillier idea. One cannot make, much less implement, effective policies without taking political and bureaucratic factors into account and, on occasion, turning them to advantage.

I have a reasonably well-known failing for thinking of the government process in sailing terms. A theory—a compass—is needed as a basic guide for the helmsman. For me, economic reasoning and, particularly, notions of efficiency provide such a guide. However, the application of an economist's principles must accommodate both notions of equity and a sense of political feasibility. If efficiency is the cutting edge of economics, then equity—or fairness—is the *sine qua non* of politics, even though the concept may be used to support claims that arise from self-interest. In a governmental process, efficiency and equity often conflict—or appear to conflict—so that the economic policymaker must often temper intellectual purity with equitable considerations that are defined in political terms. In familiar language, efficiency is not a free good.

Economic theory thus provides both a notion of where we want to sail and a compass for knowing where we are on the relatively uncharted governmental seas. With the changing political winds—winds that sometimes seem to change 180 degrees within a few weeks in Washington—one who sets sail directly toward his distant goal will never get there. The skill lies in tacking. The successful policymaker is one who can turn the opposing wind to advantage as he moves in the direction shown on his compass.

What does it all mean for the Professional Economist?

If you accept my description as a reasonably accurate report from a professional economist who has made a short, albeit intensive, exploration of the distant land of policymaking, then you may fairly ask what contribution the professional economist can make to such an undisciplined process.

I believe the economist has a primary responsibility to stick to his knitting: to point out and point up both the conclusions derived from strict application of economic logic and the relative power of the economic forces involved. Just as there are many cases in which noneconomic considerations (such as the importance of a capacity for independence in energy) dominate, there are others in which market forces hold sway (such as those preventing successful government support of exchange rates that are seriously out of balance). Such a strategy preserves what is best in economics—its vigor, its perspective, its capacity for satisfying one's desire for logic and symmetry in thought, its ability to destroy the myths that plague popular discussion of economic issues, and its power as a teaching vehicle. Such a strategy provides the policymaker with the map and compass he needs to sail the seas of Washington.

Aside from strict application of professional economics in policymaking, there is lots of room for a more systematic study of the constraints and the institutional environment within which government policies influencing the economic system are determined. This is the domain of political economy, and the time has come for a return to this nineteenth-century subject. I am aware that much work has already been done, but so far as I know it has not yet reached the point of usefulness that, for example, standard price theory has long had.

Last, it seems to me that economists have a special role to play in explaining, if not dramatizing, the relationship between economic behavior and the exercise of individual liberty. By this I do not mean to assert doctrinaire support of the Chicago school or any other school. It is true, however, that where a man works, the wage he commands for his labor, how he spends or invests his money, and what prices he charges for his products are integral to the personal freedoms that define his everyday life. Both Marx and Smith recognized these facts and projected alternative paths to the good society.

As a subject of considerable technical virtuosity, modern economics often obscures this relationship between personal freedom and economic behavior in a tangle of assumptions and computations. For the ordinary citizen inconvenienced by a strike, the controversy over free collective bargaining usually seems an exercise of distant relevance. When economic issues do intrude on the public's consciousness—as in the current energy crisis—they are often cast in terms of avarice or undeniable needs. Thus, in my judgment economists have a particular responsibility to relate policy decisions to the maintenance of freedom, so that when the combination of special interest groups, bureaucratic pressures, and congressional appetites calls for still one more increment of government intervention, we can calculate the costs in these terms. Thus, economists may have an impact on policy that extends beyond the most current crisis and reflects the best traditions of the discipline.

33. The American Council of Economic Advisers and the German *Sachverstaendigenrat:* A Study in the Economics of Advice *

HENRY C. WALLICH

At the time when the Council of Economic Advisers (CEA) was moving toward the peak of its success and influence, with the approaching tax cut of 1964, the government of West Germany, after long deliberations, decided to establish a body similar to the CEA in name and appearance but very different in substance. The *Sachverstaendigenrat fuer die Begutachtung der Gesamtwirtschaftlichen Entwicklung* (SR hereafter), a "Council of Experts for the Evaluation of Aggregative Economic Developments" came into being on August 14, 1963. The history of the SR thus is much shorter than that of the CEA. The initial policies and procedures of the SR nevertheless have been sufficiently well defined and original to make a comparison fruitful.

The CEA has long been a reliable spokesman for successive administrations. The SR has been, with rare exceptions, a vigorous critic of the government in power. Among the many economic advisory bodies that today are in operation, it probably has gone farthest in the direction of opposing the hand that appointed it. This choice of strategy in giving economic advice reflects partly the nature of the legislation and partly the interpretation that the SR has given to it. The purpose of such legislation, whether the Employment Act or any other, must be to elicit an advisory strategy conducive to advice that is both good and effective. In this sense, comparison of the relative performance of the CEA and the SR is also a test of the relative merits of the respective legislations.

In contrast to the CEA, which is an inside adviser, the SR is an outside adviser. Its five members are economic experts and predominantly profes-

Reprinted, in abridged form, from the *Quarterly Journal of Economics*, August 1968, pp. 349–379, by permission of the publisher and author.

* I am greatly indebted to my colleague William Fellner for constructive suggestions, to William Dodson for his substantial contribution to the discussion, pp. 370–73, and to Herbert Giersch and Horst Schulmann for a critical reading and numerous corrections of the manuscript.

sors. Unlike the CEA members, however, who serve full time at the President's pleasure, the SR members serve less than full time for periods of five years. They communicate with the government principally through published annual reports, to which the government must respond in kind. The SR is not allowed to make explicit policy recommendations but must analyze prospective developments under alternative assumptions. In practice, of course, it is virtually impossible to do so without making implicit recommendations, and the SR has taken full advantage of this form of expression. All this differs greatly from the corresponding provisions of the Employment Act of 1946.

A strong similarity is exhibited by the historical roots of the two councils. Both go back to serious concern about the economic outlook. In the postwar United States, unemployment was the prevailing fear. Unemployment also happened to be the dominant trauma in the economic experience of the United States. In post 1960 Germany, inflation was the chief concern. Inflation, rather than unemployment, probably also represents the most traumatic economic experience of the German people.

In the United States early discussion of the Employment Act had briefly dwelt on the possibility of creating the CEA as an independent agency. The original Full Employment Bill of 1945 had made no mention of the CEA. The proposed "National Budget," i.e., the national economic plan, was to be prepared in the Executive Office of the President. Conservative influences succeeded in making the anonymous authors visible, and changed the "National Budget" to the "Economic Report." They also subjected the advisers to Senate confirmation. But they failed in their efforts to place them in an independent agency or to make their communications to the President available to the Congress. These two provisions, if enacted, would have produced something very like the SR at least in legal format.

Given the existence of an Executive Office, its use as the place to anchor the advisers was consonant with U.S. government organization. An independent agency, not in close touch with the President, would have had to rely for its effectiveness in good part upon the respect that Congress and the public might feel for the views of a body of professors, in the United States not a very strong base of power. Such pronouncements as this agency might make, moreover, always subject to public view, would not have differed greatly from similar pronouncements by private academic, business, and labor groups, which already were being made in large numbers.

In Germany all this was different. In a parliamentary system with Cabinet responsibility, it is not easy to find a good spot for an advisory group to the government, although the former British system of an adviser to the government with a Cabinet Secretariat is one way of doing it.

The type of economic analysis undertaken in the United States by the CEA, moreover, in Germany is practiced quite fully by the Grundsatzabteilung (Principles Division) of the powerful Economics Ministry. There is still alive in Germany, on the other hand, a modicum of respect for the scientific authority of professional pronouncements, even in the area of economics. Objective economic truth exists and can be discovered by experts if these remain untainted by politics or interest group allegiance. There is a relative paucity of economic analysis from other sources. Much of what exists is deservedly suspect. An independent group fits these specifications.

Objectivity or Maximization?

Such, broadly, were the circumstances helping to shape the U.S. and German legislations that were destined to elicit such widely differing advisory behavior in the two countries. To judge by the law, the German legislator had in in mind something like Max Weber's purely objective scientist, free of value judgments (*wertfrei*) as the ideal member of the SR. Max Weber said that science and value judgments are incompatible. Abstention from value judgments clearly is the implicit prescription for an independent agency that is to analyze economic policy under alternative assumptions without making recommendations.

The legislative history of the SR does not quite bear out this presumption concerning the legislator's state of mind. The creation of the SR had been promoted by Professor Erhard in his earlier capacity as Minister of Economics. Erhard, engaged in a constant effort to restrain inflation by suasion, and encountering diminishing returns, hardly would have supported such plans had he not expected help from the SR. Chancellor Adenauer, apparently clearly foreseeing that a group of independent professors would cause mostly trouble, at first blocked the proposal. When later the SR came into being under somewhat different circumstances, it was with the apparent presumption on the part of Erhard, then the prospective Chancellor, that it would take a strong stand against union pressure. Erhard viewed the unions' high wage demands as chiefly responsible for inflation. These auspices seem to imply, on the part of some of the sponsors, a bias against labor not readily reconcilable with perfect objectivity.

The general impression that freedom from value judgments is expected of the SR nevertheless remains. It is noteworthy, therefore, that Dr. Edwin Nourse, the first chairman of the CEA, appeared to have had something similar in mind. That seems to be the obvious interpretation of his frequent insistence, in *Economics in the Public Service* that CEA advice should be professional and objective.[1]

Two methods seem to offer themselves to the scientist ill-advisedly turned adviser who wants to be truly objective. He may leave on his client's desk memoranda outlining a large variety of policies and withdraw discreetly, allowing the client to make up his own mind. Alternatively, he may accept a set of values from another source, be it his client, or the law, and proceed from there.

Nourse, as the Economic Reports during his chairmanship show, did not follow the first route. Neither did he adopt the values of his client, as the disappointing nature of his relations with President Truman demonstrates. Nor could a consistent objective function have been derived from the Employment Act, a confused piece of compromise legislation demanding an impossible maximization of three goals at once, expressed in noneconomic language and subject to constraints that do not even parse unambiguously.

One must conclude, therefore, that Nourse believed economists to be capable not only of professionalism, which none would dispute, but also of objectivity, which many would regard as too high a compliment. Economics deals with choice, and choices are determined by values. Economic advice therefore inevitably seems to reflect some ordering of preferences. The degrees to which particular economic advisers depart from perfect objectivity may naturally differ. First, the adviser may give advice, based on the best ordering of preferences of which he can convince himself, but refrain from strongly pressing this advice upon his client. Nourse, perhaps not altogether voluntarily, seems in effect to have operated in this style. Second, he can press strongly in private his economic advice upon his client. This may reflect the methods of Dr. Burns and Dr. Saulnier. Third, he may become a public advocate of his advice, which then naturally cannot conflict with the views of his client. This was the *modus operandi* of Walter Heller. Finally, he may in public utterance give his economics an avowedly political slant, as Leon Keyserling did.

The first and second chairman of the CEA between them therefore seem to have explored the extremes of the advisory strategies available. Subsequent chairmen have operated well within these extremes, because the style of the first was less than fully effective, while that of the second attracted criticism. None of the feasible strategies is free of value judgments.

Not so the German SR. One of its most articulate spokesmen. Professor Herbert Giersch of Saarbruecken, firmly states, and at least some of

1. Edwin G. Nourse, *Economics in the Public Service* (New York: Harcourt, Brace, 1953).

the other members concur, that their advice is broadly free of value judgments. The values, and their ordering, is given by the law. All the SR
does, conceptually, is to solve the decision equations for the values of the
instruments required to reach the prescribed targets.

Two pieces of evidence support this remarkable claim. The SR, a
group of five economists, under no pressure from operating duties or
from a client, has nevertheless continuously maintained unanimity in its
published reports. The law specifically authorizes expression of minority
views.

Second, the law itself was unanimously approved by the legislature,
with the support of all political parties. The inference is that the legislators apparently believed they had successfully curbed any temptation for
the advisers to take targets into their own hands.

On the other hand, it needs to be pointed out that the SR's belief that
its hands are tied turns out to be extraordinarily convenient as an instrument for maintaining unanimity. Unanimity, meanwhile, is needed to
maintain popular belief in the scientific accuracy of SR pronouncements,
a need not eased by the circumstance that the law requires the SR to make
forecasts.

Analytical Approaches

To enter into a detailed comparison of the substantive analysis and policy recommendations of the two groups of advisers would exhaust the
reader without beginning to exhaust the subject. Only a few general comments can be attempted.

The CEA's "Economic Report" and the SR's "Jahresgutachten" are
not very dissimilar in format and coverage. Both deal exhaustively with
the past and rather gingerly with the future. The projections of the
"Jahresgutachten" are more detailed than those of its American contemporary but also better hedged. The SR's product is generally at a higher
level of technical difficulty and at times academic abstractness. Its generally critical attitude protects it, on the other hand, from the election
speech flavor that the inside-adviser role tends to inject into the "review
of the year" chapter of the CEA's Economic Report. One of the SR's
volumes even takes the unsuspecting peruser through a condensed course
in elementary statistics. The SR is also more venturesome in its macroeconomic hypotheses than is its opposite number. The latter, on the other
hand, while claiming less, usually has a more solid econometric base.

The SR offers a well-developed cyclical hypothesis for the German
economy. With rare exceptions, cyclical expansions are exogenous. In so
open an economy as the German this is prima facie plausible. The export

boom, via an accelerator process, and with a lag, expands the investment goods sector. Prices and wages begin to rise faster, again with lags. The upper turning point is brought on by stochastic events—such as a downturn abroad or central bank credit restrictions. The schema would lend itself to testing by a detailed model and simulation. No major efforts in that direction have been made by the SR, however, which indeed lacks the staff for such a venture.

The SR bases a good part of its stabilization policy upon this analysis. Because the lags are long, short term measures are viewed as of little value. Nor is action necessarily appropriate against the macro variables that are most obviously out of balance at any given moment. Their condition may have its roots in earlier developments. If these were not counteracted in time, it may be useless to attact the consequences.

This analysis is applied particularly to inflation. The SR bypasses the issue of cost push and demand pull inflation on the grounds that it is a chicken and egg problem. Demand pull inflation and high profits induce subsequent high wages increases. It would be technically wrong as well as socially unjust to pin the blame for inflation on labor. The main source of inflation, the SR believes, as of cyclical disturbances, is exogenous.

Inflation is imported into Germany by several routes which the SR, however, regards as basically coincident. Rising prices in undisciplined trade partner countries are one of them. Another and very interesting one is the above average growth of productivity in the export industries. Because their prices are largely determined abroad, these do not fall when costs fall. Hence export industries can pay high wage increases that then spill over into domestic industries with lower productivity gains. Their prices then must rise.

This analysis lets off the hook the two most often cited perpetrators of the German inflation: the labor unions and the United States. Exoneration of the unions undoubtedly was a great shock to the Ehard government. Exoneration of the United States follows logically from the assertion that it is not the balance-of-payments surplus per se, much of it indeed due to the American deficit, but the rising level of foreign prices that pushes up the German price level. A look at the very modest role that payments surpluses have played in the great German monetary expansion, both at the commercial and the central bank level, indeed gives the United States a fairly clean bill of health.

To halt the inflation of the 1960's that eventually was terminated by drastic credit tightness and a subsequent recession, the SR proposed and to some extent initiated a "concerted action." This is the German version of the guideposts, with appropriate variations on the American theme.

Emphasis is placed on wage restraint, since key industry prices are largely determined externally. The German wage guideposts differ from those of the CEA in one important particular. They are not intended to reduce wage increases below their equilibrium level, given demand and supply conditions in the factor markets and specified price expectations. The guideposts only seek to establish a lower level of price expectations than labor and management would otherwise have in mind in their wage and price setting. This, the SR believes, will reduce the rate of wage increases and hence the rate of inflation. In subsequent wage rounds, price expectations are to be further reduced by common agreement, until price stability is reached.

The SR does not mention that wage increases based on the assumption of a specified price increase will be consistent with that price increase in only one special case: when the prevailing level of unemployment is consistent with wage increases equal to productivity gains. The rate of unemployment, in other words, must be the equilibrium rate. At a lower unemployment rate, nominal wage increases will exceed productivity gains by more than the anticipated price increase. The realized price increase will then exceed the anticipated unless profit margins can be reduced. The Phillips curve will shift upwards, inflation will accelerate. Except in the rare case when unemployment is at or above its equilibrium rate, the only permanently effective form of incomes policy is one that pushes the Phillips curve to the left, thereby lowering the equilibrium rate. That is the principle implicit in the guideposts propagated by the CEA. Unless the Phillips curve is shifted, incomes policy indeed does not act as an instrument of policy.

The most dramatic and least practical proposal put forward by the SR, and that most forcefully rejected by the government, has been the variable exchange rate. The SR views it as part of its integrated, all or nothing, approach. Full employment, stable prices, rapid growth and payments equilibrium cannot simultaneously be attained by a small open economy in an inflationary world. Ergo it is the exchange rate that has to give, with the DMark appreciating. In the United States the same argument has been made on behalf of a downward floating dollar—not, of course, by the CEA. To avoid repeating the unacceptable, the SR has varied its porposal in the direction of a "crawling peg." How the notoriously high German interest rate structure is to be brought down sufficiently to keep an appreciating DMark from attracting foreign capital, how the existing government is credibly to commit future governments so that international traders and investors can rely on the peg to keep crawling is not spelled out. An alternative is offered in the shape of absolute commitments to everlastingly fixed exchange rates with vigorous and implausible international policy coordination to match. But the heart of the SR or at least of its analysis, clearly has been on the side of exchange rate variability in one form or another.

Where the heart of the CEA has been in the matter of exchange rates during the long payments agony of the United States has not been revealed to outsiders. Its voice certainly has been firmly in the right spot, but it may have been only its master's voice. This possibility of a discrepancy between an adviser's view and his utterance on a matter of such substance leads to some concluding observations about the differences between the two councils.

When the U.S. Congress instructed the CEA to "evaluate Government programs" it may have wanted the CEA to do what governments notoriously avoid: to compare fundamental alternatives. It has been convincingly argued by Charles E. Lindblom that governments do not make the universal comparisons of all possible alternatives that economic theory demands of them.[2] Instead, they move incrementally, feeling their way, and more often away from an evil than toward a goal. The CEA is perhaps the only agency in the American government that is sufficiently unbureaucratic, imaginative, and free from agency self-interests to proceed differently.

With some notable exceptions, the CEA's close attachment to the President has kept it from doing so. As a result, the CEA has limited itself to doing better what without it would have been done less well by others: to formulate a normal government program. All governments evolve an economic policy, by design or default, even if it is no more than the name they give to their mistakes. The CEA has helped to improve, but not basically to change.

The SR has attempted a greater design. It has tried to do, however unsuccessfully, what governments ordinarily do not do—to move by more than incremental steps. Does it, despite initial disappointments, point a lesson for the United States?

Given the ex officio critical role that for the most part the SR has assumed toward the German government, it is hard to believe that another government in its right mind would again establish a similar institution. Nevertheless, among the early proposals featuring in the Employment Act debate, as pointed out above, there was one for a group independent of the President. That might have been the beginning of an American SR.

A prosperous career for such a group is not easy to envisage. A Presi-

2. David Braybrooke and Charles E. Lindblom, *A Strategy of Decision* (New York: The Free Press of Glencoe, 1963), pp. 61–143.

dent would have little use for a group of advisers not chosen by him, imbued possibly by the philosophy of the opposition party. They might criticize, and some would listen, but who would react?

An alternative possibility might be a more thorough review of the CEA's output, especially of the Economic Report. That function, to have any impact, would have to be performed by the Congress, as it is at present by the Joint Economic Committee (JEC). It could indeed be argued that the German SR bears more resemblance to the JEC than to the CEA. But the Congress, like the JEC, is a group of politicians. Its majority is likely to be of the President's party. If these men disagree with his policies, it is probably because they want, not something else, but more of the same. There will be, most of the time, a majority and a minority report. Being political, neither will change many minds.

The miscarriages of economic policy in 1966 and 1967 make it tempting to suggest quite a different expedient. It must by now have been demonstrated to the satisfaction of even the most optimistic that the Congress is unlikely to yield discretionary power for anticyclical tax changes to the President, and cannot be relied upon to make needed changes quickly under its own procedures. The less optimistic meanwhile have begun to wonder whether the President could be relied upon to use these powers even if the Congress did delegate them. The logic of the situation points to a solution as inescapable as it is hopeless: turn these powers over to an independent body. Whether this group were a reconstituted CEA with term appointments, or the Federal Reserve, or still another group makes no vital difference. One can assume with great probability that any independent body would do a better job than the politicians, and with absolute certainty that it would never get the power.

Ruling out this device as utopian (some would say undemocratic), there remains only the slow and painful process of improving our policy-making and policy reviewing within existing channels. Many improvements in American public life have come from presidential or congressional leadership. But it is perhaps asking too much that this leadership should also provide better and stronger criticism of its own activities. The chances are that, if better and stronger criticism is to be had, it must come from public opinion. The last few years have shown that the public is capable of learning economics. Some ancient errors and prejudices have been unlearned. The events of 1966–67 do not demonstrate very convincingly that we have not just substituted one set of misconceptions for another. But if we can trust the dictum that every nation gets the kind of government it deserves, Americans certainly can get better government policymaking if they take enough interest to demand it.

34. Muddling Through: An Alternative View of the Decision Process

CHARLES L. SCHULTZE

The planning, programming, and budgeting system as it is applied in civilian agencies of the federal government differs substantially from earlier improvements in the budgetary process insofar as it impinges, at virtually every level of detail, directly on the political process. PPB attempts to influence the choice of both ends and means with a problem-solving approach—that is, it emphasizes analytical criteria of effectiveness and efficiency rather than political criteria of consensus; it deliberately seeks to force examination of a wider range of alternatives than those typically dealt with in the political process; it stresses long-run planning rather than "muddling through."

In the political science and public administration literature of the past decade, there has developed a sophisticated and realistic theory of the political decision-making process which implicitly, and in a few cases explicitly, seems to raise very fundamental criticisms of PPB. It is primarily associated with Charles E. Lindblom, who has developed it in a series of books and articles over the past ten years or more.[1] An outline of this theory and a comparison of its approach to decision making with that incorporated in PPB will provide a useful basis for subsequent examination of how PPB can realistically fit into and support the political process by which decisions are reached.

The fate of anyone who develops a well-articulated theory is to watch helplessly as others shamelessly oversimplify its subtle shadings in an attempt to summarize and compress. Here, the contrast between Lindblom's approach and PPB will deliberately be sharpened in order to stress the important points which need to be made. Consequently, I cannot

Reprinted from Charles L. Schultze, *The Politics and Economics of Public Spending,* (Washington: The Brookings Institution, 1968), pp. 35–53, by permission of publisher and author. Copyright © 1968 by the Brookings Institution, Washington D.C.

1. Charles E. Lindblom, "The Science of 'Muddling Through,' " *Public Administration Review,* Vol. XIX, No. 2 (Spring 1959), pp. 79–88; "Decision-Making in Taxation and Expenditures," in National Bureau of Economic Research, *Public Finances: Needs, Sources, and Utilization* (Princeton University Press for NBER, 1961); David Braybrooke and Charles Lindblom, *A Strategy of Decision: Policy Evaluation as a Social Process* (Macmillan, 1963); and Charles Lindblom, *The Intelligence of Democracy* (Macmillan, 1965).

guarantee that Mr. Lindblom and his associates would be willing to claim parentage for what is described. However, I think my outline captures the spirit of their approach.

The Lindblom theory of the decision process implicitly attacks the PPB approach on the following grounds.

First, PPB is unrealistic. The actual decision-making process is not suited to the problem-solving approach. Therefore, PPB will wreck itself upon the rocks of reality.

Second, not only is PPB incompatible with the realities of politics, it would not represent a desirable decision system even if it were politically acceptable. In a free political society, the problem-solving approach does not usually arrive at "good" decisions. It attempts, at too many points, to substitute efficiency criteria for the more meaningful criterion of achieving consensus through adjustment of conflicting values. And by its emphasis on the explicit statement of ends and objectives PPB can intensify unproductive ideological debate.

Third, the analytic approach associated with PPB—in particular its attempt to specify and measure ends, to separate means from ends, and to examine a wide range of alternatives—is unattainable and undesirable when applied to social and institutional problems.

Before elaborating on the Lindblom approach it is important to note two points. First, Lindblom's writings preceded the installation of PPB in the civilian agencies of the federal government. At no point does he explicitly mention PPB. Second, and more important, Lindblom's primary concern was to establish the limits of the comprehensive problem-solving approach as a means of arriving at decisions that deal with complex and highly political matters. I will examine the *apparent* conflict between PPB on the one hand and the political bargaining process on the other within the framework of Lindblom's analysis. As a result of this approach, the contrast between Lindblom's emphasis on the limitations of analysis and my emphasis on pushing out those limits appears sharper than it really is. But just as I would not deny that there are limits to the application of PPB, so Lindblom would not deny that there is a role for PPB and that the limits he describes can be pushed out.[2] Indeed, the aim of this book is not to sharpen the differences between the political bargaining approach and the analytical approach to decision making, but rather to find a partial synthesis between the two, at least in the sense of defining the appropriate role of each. The relatively sharp contrast between the two decision techniques drawn (or perhaps "overdrawn") in this chapter is a necessary first step toward this goal.

2. Lindblom explicitly makes this point in a letter to me, July 5, 1968.

Ends and Means

Central to the Lindblom approach is its emphasis on the difficulty of specifying the ends or objectives of public programs and the impossibility of separating ends from means.

We can start with the obvious proposition that various social ends or values are in conflict with each other. I am not speaking of opportunity costs in the allocation of resources—with a limited budget the cost of having more of one good in accepting less of another. There is a deeper conflict of values associated with most choices.[3] The more ambitious our goals in terms of full employment, the more we must sacrifice goals of price stability and balance-of-payments equilibrium. Programs that seek to raise farm prices and incomes conflict with the objective of lower consumer prices. The goal of reducing traffic accidents conflicts with the desire for rapid transportation and widespread car ownership. The goal of efficient urban transportation often conflicts with aesthetic values and values associated with displacing low-income residents. Altruistic values are an important part of the policitcal process, and professional cynics are unrealistic in denying their existence. Nevertheless, altruistic values conflict among themselves as well as with self-interest values.

Not only do our social ends or values conflict, but being quite subtle and complex, they are exceedingly difficult to specify. We simply cannot determine in the abstract our ends or values and the intensity with which we hold them. *We discover our objectives and the intensity that we assign to them only in the process of considering particular programs or policies.* We articulate "ends" as we evaluate "means."

Consider the examples of conflicting values cited above. No one can specify in advance the weight he attaches to traffic safety versus rapid transportation except when considering a specific traffic safety program and evaluating its particular impact on the transportation system. We all subscribe to both the goals of ending poverty and of preserving work incentives. But we do not have an abstract social welfare function that predetermines our tradeoffs between these two goals and that can be applied toward making a choice in any given situation. Yet we can make a decision about a particular piece of social welfare legislation that sets certain specific income limits on welfare payments and exempts a specified portion of earned income from that limit. We all are interested in reducing the crime rate, and also in preserving individual rights, but we

3. This proposition does not apply when the existing situation constitutes an "inferior" solution—that is, when some change can be made that allows us to have more of one value without a sacrifice of others. Whether "most" choices involve conflicts of values depends on whether in "most" situations we are living with inferior solutions.

can handle problems of the tradeoff between the two only when considering a concrete program which effects both these goals.

In brief, our values or goals become meaningful only when the means to achieve them are examined. The reason for this is twofold: First, since our values and the weights attached to them are extremely subtle and complex, no attempt to articulate them in advance will encompass all their shadings and intensities. But we can handle the subset of those shadings and intensities that are raised by a particular policy issue. Second, any given course of action usually involves many different values. In the case of the unemployment-inflation tradeoff, we might conceivably specify in advance the tradeoff function that reflects our value system. But any particular fiscal policy will involve other values besides these two. We may be especially concerned, at a particular moment, about the impact of unemployment on summer riots, or on depressed economic areas. We may not like the income distribution consequences of a given tax measure designed to achieve a desired unemployment-inflation mix, or the consequences of an expenditure cut on federal social programs. But the tradeoff we might have chosen, considering only the objectives of unemployment and inflation, may not be acceptable when the particular policy actions affect many other values. And these various values cannot, usually, be measured in terms that allow one to be directly compared with others—that is, weights cannot be assigned to them. Conceptually this kind of problem can be handled in terms of a multidimensional social welfare function. In practice, however, there are so many "dimensions" to most public programs that there is no possibility of determining, in the abstract, multidimensional tradeoff functions among different, usually noncommensurable, values.

The detailed legislative specifications and appropriation structures for most social programs stem from the fact that the particular provisions of a public program usually impinge upon a number of political values. What may appear to the analyst as a technical means to affect one generally accepted objective usually has subsidiary implications for many other objectives about which there is much less agreement. The obvious analogy is with consumer preference theory. Our preference function is revealed to us only by the act of making a particular choice among goods, and then only in the region of the function immediately surrounding the choice point.

Not only do we indicate our objectives through the consideration of particular means to achieve them, but we actually discover new objectives at the same time. For example, imagine a world in which there were no Polaris missiles, or similar systems, but one in which multiple independently targeted reentry vehicles (MIRVs) of large yield and great accuracy were a reality. It would then be impossible to provide a strategic force that could survive an enemy's first strike; every attempt to do so, for example, by adding numbers of hardened missiles, could be offset, at a fraction of the cost, by the enemy adding MIRVs to his force. In such a world I doubt whether the current strategic deterrence objective of "assured destruction capacity" [4] could have been conceived. The existence of large bodies of oil-yielding shale and the necessity to develop a policy for their exploitation has generated policy studies that may well lead to the formulation of objectives concerning U.S. energy policy which might otherwise never have been articulated. Senator Richard B. Russell opposed the Defense Department's request for authorization of the fast deployment logistics ships (FDLs), not on grounds of cost or effectiveness, but because—according to him—they would provide an excessively easy means of intervening militarily in limited wars. Here is a significant objective—the limitation of our military fast response capability—which, I am convinced, was not part of Senator Russell's social welfare function. It evolved, in all probability, during consideration of the specifics of a particular program.

Our ends or values are also hierarchical in nature. Most objectives are valued because they help achieve some higher values, which become more difficult to articulate the further up the scale we go. Ends are simply means to higher ends. Price stability is an objective of public policy because, among other reasons, it affects the distribution of income and the efficiency of forward business planning. We use the grant-in-aid approach in most new social programs partly because it tends to preserve the powers of state and local governments in a federal system. We value this system because it is decentralized, which we value in turn for the sake of political freedom and diversity.

The dual fact that we discover our values while considering the means to achieve them and that values are hierarchical in nature results in a continual change and evolution of our objectives. Experience constantly teaches us that some of our values have less of a connection than we thought with the achievement of higher values. Federal aid to elementary and secondary education was vigorously opposed by many conservatives on grounds that it would lead to a federalized school system. A few years after passage of the Elementary and Secondary Education Act of 1965, this element of opposition has virtually disappeared. The presumed connection between the subordinate goal of financial independence for local school systems and the higher goal of policy independence has been

4. Assured destruction capacity, as an objective for U.S. strategic retaliatory forces, requires that those forces always be sufficient to absorb an enemy's first strike and survive with sufficient capability to inflict irreparable damage on the enemy.

shown by experience not to be as strong as originally thought. Moreover, the constant change in the availability of new instruments of social policy, and the growth of income with which to finance their application, leads to a steady shift and expansion of our social values. The means and resources generate the values and the objectives.

In short, ends are closely intertwined with means, are subtle, complex, constantly being discovered, and are usually in conflict with one another. Moreover, the most obvious fact of political life is that individuals and groups differ widely from each other in the values they hold and the intensity with which they hold those values. If the articulation of a multidimensional set of objectives is difficult for a single individual or group, it is infinitely more difficult for the body politic. Value conflicts arise from the immediate self-interest of various groups—depletion allowances, the location of public works projects, farm and maritime subsidies—and from conflicts over more general values, which stem from long-term self-interest—the power of federal versus the state and local governments, the overall level of federal expenditures and revenues. Other conflicts arise because different groups have quite different visions, in an altruistic sense, of the "good society."

In the Lindblom view values and means are so closely intertwined, policy decisions affect so many different values, and there is such a wide network of conflicts over values that decisions about public programs, even at a relatively low level of detail, are saturated with value choices. Technically, maximizing a known social welfare function subject to a given set of production functions and resource constraints does not fit political reality.

The Consequences of Policy Decisions

In addition to the difficulty of establishing ends apart from means, the Lindblom school lays great stress on the inherent difficulties in predicting the consequences of any particular programmatic means on the wide range of ends or values that exist. In different terminology, the difficulties associated with specifying a social welfare function are compounded by the difficulty in establishing production functions. The more important the policy measure under consideration, the more difficult the problem of predicting its consequences.

In 1962 President John F. Kennedy proposed removing from the Interstate Commerce Commission authority to establish minimum rates on certain classes of freight carried by railroads. The principal immediate effect of this "minimum rate bill" would have been to increase competition between the railroads, on the one hand, and trucks and barge lines, on the other. The administration expected, and received, opposition from the trucking and barge lines. But the death-blow to the bill more probably came from opposition from local interests and port authorities scattered through the country. The existing location of many industries is heavily dependent on the structure of freight rates. Any change in those freight rates could produce changes in comparative advantages in ways that are hard to predict for thousands of communities and industries. It proved to be impossible to determine, in advance, what the impact of the bill would be on industrial location. But uncertainty and the threat of unknown consequences played a major role in killing the bill.

Who could have forecast the diverse impact on local political structures of the language in the original antipoverty bill relating to the "participation of the poor" in the decision structure of community action agencies? Who can now predict the consequences of the new model cities program on social structures, political power, integration, and all the other relevant values in the many urban areas involved? The 41,000 mile interstate highway program, inaugurated in the mid-1950s, has had consequences for almost every aspect of American life—speedier intercity transportation being only one of the effects. The comparative advantage of industrial locations on the outer fringes of urban areas has been sharply increased; the tax structure of metropolitan areas has been significantly affected; the recreation habits of the population have been altered, and the demand for national parks dramatically increased. The chain of consequences was so wide as to defy prediction at the time the program was launched—and indeed its ramifications defy ex post analysis. G. L. S. Shackle, in his 1966 presidential address to the Royal Economic Society aptly stated the problem:

"Is the nature of things, the so-called human predicament, such that we face an endless examination in arithmetic, each hour presenting its sum, and the subsequent hours or years marking our answer right or wrong? If so, policy-making is problem solving, there is an algebra of business which only needs to be supplied with a sufficiency of information to guarantee success. Or is the logic of things such that no such sufficiency of information can ever exist? Is policy-making, by necessity, an originative art? Art is the manipulation of constraints. . . . Art is not arbitrary, unconstrained caprice. But the required knowledge may be knowledge of what *can* be done rather than what *must* be done." [5]

Uncertainty about the performance of hardware systems can be substantially reduced with additional information, and the consequences of uncertainty in terms of the assigned task of the system can be systematically examined by techniques such as sensitivity analysis. However, it

5. G. L. S. Shackle, "Policy, Poetry and Success," *Economic Journal,* Vol. LXXVI, No. 304 (December 1966), pp. 755–56 (italics supplied).

is much more difficult to reduce uncertainty over the effects of federal programs on social and institutional behavior. And the consequences of uncertainty for decision making are similarly more difficult to unravel. Difficult as it is to predict the output of a major missile system in terms of assured destruction capacity, it is substantially easier to analyze than, say, the impact of the model cities program on the social and institutional structure of the ghetto. Of course, the ultimate objective of a strategic missile system is its affect on the behavior of Soviet and Chinese decision makers, and this is no easier to predict than the consequences of a model cities program. In terms of *ultimate* objectives or values, that observation is correct. Insofar as missile systems and space programs have, as objectives, an influence on men's minds, their ultimate output is as hard to predict as that of any social program. But the difference between the analysis of hardware systems and social programs is that the *proximate* consequences of the social programs are substantially less susceptible to prediction than are those of hardware programs. This inherent limitation of the human mind to analyze the full sweep of the social and institutional consequences of major programs is a key element in the Lindblom approach.

Another aspect of the decision process, heavily stressed by Aaron Wildavsky,[6] relates to the political costs of political decisions. There are political opportunity costs to any decision, just as real as the economic opportunity costs. Because values conflict among different groups and among themselves, securing the agreement necessary to pursue one line of action most often reduces the opportunity to pursue other lines of action. This is a different kind of opportunity cost. Securing the support of one particular bloc in Congress for passage of, say, an education bill, may require commitments out of a limited pool of appointment patronage, or that hostages may be given the bloc in terms of support for or opposition to other measures. An education bill may, for example, be associated with a series of public works projects. Another cost incurred in passing one bill may be the alienation of support for other bills. A civil rights bill may ''cost'' a housing bill. To take another hypothetical example, an administration might have the votes to override opposition and sharply increase the repayment formula on irrigation projects—requiring irrigators to pay back a higher proportion of project costs. But irrigation appears absolutely vital to a particular group of congressmen. Overriding their ''veto'' on irrigation policy may well insure their opposition to other decisions on which they might have been neutral or mildly favorable.

6. Aaron Wildavsky, ''The Political Economy of Efficiency: Cost-Benefit Analysis, Systems Analysis, and Program Budgeting,'' *Public Administration Review*, Vol. XXVI, No. 4 (December 1966), pp. 292–310.

These considerations not only enter the relations between the executive and the Congress, but also affect the internal decision process within the executive, which also represents a coalition of divergent interests.

More generally, because most programs have consequences for a wide range of values about which there are sharply divided views, it is impossible for any political leader to consider a single program decision in isolation. The effect of any one decision on a whole system of decisions must be taken into account. Beyond the more immediate opportunity costs of decisions—the cost of one decision in terms of others—there are opportunity costs for the decision process as a whole. To secure the enactment of a positive program of actions, a consensus or coalition must be put together which bridges a wide divergence of values. That consensus or coalition is usually elastic, but not infinitely so. Decisions that put a radical strain on the consensus may take their toll not only on individual future decisions but on the whole process. The consensus may be destroyed, the coalition fragmented, the process disrupted. These costs dictate a set of efficiency criteria for political decisions equally as real and valid as the resource costs which lead to the efficiency criteria of systematic analysis.[7]

The Science of Muddling Through

All the foregoing considerations indicate a particular type of decision process that seems, at first glance, quite different from the rational problem-solving approach associated with PPB. This decision process is presented by Lindblom and others both as a description of reality and as a prescription for "good" decisions.

Minimizing Debate about Values

The first rule of the successful political process is, "Don't force a specification of goals or ends." Debate over objectives should be minimized partly because ends and means are inseparable. More important, the necessary agreement on particular policies can often be secured among individuals or groups who hold quite divergent ends.

The Elementary and Secondary Education Act of 1965 broke new ground in terms of federal aid to education. It was enacted precisely

7. The analogy between political opportunity costs and economic opportunity costs can be pushed still further. An economic system is judged not only for efficiency in the static sense—that is, allocating resources efficiently toward satisfying the economic demands of its members, given the existing set of production functions—but also for efficiency in the dynamic sense—that is, expanding the level of output by discovering and using new production functions. Similarly, an effective political leader not only maximizes what he can achieve from the existing constellation of political forces, but also finds means of changing that constellation of forces to make possible a wider range of potential achievements.

because it was constructed to attract the support of three groups, each with quite different ends in view. Some saw it as the beginning of a large program of federal aid to public education. The parochial school interests saw it as the first step in providing, albeit indirectly, financial assistance for parochial school children. The third group saw it as an antipoverty measure, since the distribution formula for Title I of the bill—containing the largest part of the funds—is based on the number of poor children in each school district. Two other crosscutting values were taken care of in the bill: Title I provided formula grants to school districts over which the federal government had little control. Title III, on the other hand, provided individual federal project grants for specific innovative programs.[8] If there had been any attempt to secure advance agreement on a set of long-run objectives, important elements of support for the bill would have been lost, and its defeat assured.

Another example is the wheat price-support program enacted in 1964. The earlier proposed program was built around mandatory federal controls over wheat acreage, aimed at reducing supply and maintaining income. The controls would have applied to all wheat farmers. But to become effective the law required a favorable vote from wheat farmers, in a referendum, on the establishment of acreage controls. The referendum resulted in a negative vote. The consequent lack of any wheat program would have led to a drastic fall in wheat prices and incomes. The new program, developed in response to this situation, provided for direct federal payments to farmers who agreed "voluntarily" to reduce their wheat acreage. This program secured the support of two quite distinct groups. One group sought a subsidy program acceptable to farmers that would avoid a sharp fall in wheat prices during an election year. The other group saw in the direct payment scheme the possibility, at some future time, of placing a limit on the subsidies paid to high-income farmers. (Under the older programs, it was technically impossible to tailor the benefits to the income of the farmer.) The two groups had diametrically opposite objectives. Yet both were able to agree on the same program— precisely because ultimate goals and objectives were not forced into the debate.

Income distribution is another example. Ideally, the nation should agree on a "desired" distribution of income, and adjust tax rates and program subsidies on the basis of that decision. But clearly the attempt would be disastrous. No agreement could be reached on a global specification. But we can and do agree on specific pieces of legislation that have fairly predictable consequences for income distribution.

8. Subsequently, in the "Green" amendments of 1967, the federal government's selection among project applicants was sharply reduced in favor of state boards of education.

In the political world depicted by Lindblom, specification of objectives is not only intellectually difficult but pragmatically objectionable. Ideological dispute accomplishes nothing substantial but it blocks pragmatic agreement among diverse interests on specific measures. A decision technique that emphasizes the precise and careful statement of objectives can, under this view of political reality, prove positively harmful.

Incrementalism

The second feature of a desirable decision process, in the theory we are examining, is its incremental nature. Because political decision costs tend to mount the more the decisions conflict with the values held by important groups, and because our ability to foresee the full social consequences of any program change is so limited, movement toward objectives should proceed by small steps.

Radical actions take us beyond the realm of reasonable foresight. We make progress by sequential steps, correcting and adjusting for unforeseen consequences as we go. The whole route is not planned in advance. This form of planning by small increments has been called "Lewis and Clark" planning as opposed to "Cook's tour" planning.[9] Both goals and steps toward the goals should be modest. In most cases we can neither specify nor get agreement upon more radical goals—goals that require large departures from present experience. Moreover, since the consequences of social programs are so complex and far reaching, it is difficult to predict whether any major departure from current policies will move us toward a particular goal and virtually impossible to foresee the consequences of our actions on other values or goals. According to this theory, inertia of government bureaus, which so limits the flexibility and freedom of action of cabinet secretaries and Presidents, reflects not merely bureaucratic caution but the built-in wisdom of making progress by small steps.

Political incrementalism has its analogue in analytic incrementalism. It does not pay, in analyzing a federal program or any proposed course of political action, to scan a wide range of fundamentally differing alternatives. Analysis should be confined to a relatively small number of alternatives, differing not too drastically from current policies or programs. While evaluating alternatives, only a few of the major and more immediate consequences of proposed actions should be examined. Attempts to predict the full range of consequences of actions mislead policy makers by giving the appearance of more certainty than can possibly be had.

9. James R. Schlesinger, "Organizational Structures and Planning," in Roland N. McKean (ed.), *Issues in Defense Economics* (Columbia University Press for National Bureau of Economic Research, 1967).

Incrementalism urges modest goals for analysis and policy. For longer-term planning it substitutes policy making by sequential trial and error.

The Advocacy Process

Another major element in the Lindblom approach is the great emphasis placed on the advocacy process as a means of reaching decisions. The individual analyst or analytic staff cannot possibly trace the consequences of policy decisions for the wide range of values that are important to various groups in society. But if the decision process is so structured that advocates of every significantly affected interest have a voice in policy making, then self-interest will insure that each advocate traces out, and vigorously presents, the consequences of any action for the value or values he represents.

In actual practice the political process is structured to give wide scope to this advocacy process. It is impossible to make a policy proposal in Washington without stirring up an incredible array of interest groups, each joining in the debate and uncovering real or alleged relationships between the proposed policy and its own interests—relationships that the policy proponents may never have dreamed existed. There are thousands of individuals whose full-time occupation is the careful examination of proposed legislation or executive actions, seeking to discover implications for the interests of the groups they represent.

The committee system of the Congress and the executive branch are both structured to promote this advocacy process. Few policies are decided on without the participation of many federal agencies in addition to the one that has primary responsibility. The decision process within the executive branch is geared to maximize rather than minimize policy debate among agencies.

Of equal importance is the pervasive web of relationships between the executive and the Congress. There are long-standing channels between federal bureaus and congressional subcommittees, along which information and influence pass as cabinet secretaries come and go. The decision process is fragmented and widely distributed, with many centers of advocacy brought to bear on almost every significant decision.

Decisions are reached, therefore, through an advocacy or bargaining process in a highly pluralistic decentralized system. In this way a mutual adjustment of widely differing values is achieved, not by ideological agreement on specified ends but by pragmatic agreement on particular means. Progress in this system (presumably toward the "good," the "true," and the "beautiful") is made by trial and error, through successive approximations, with both ends and means being continually modified by increments.

This approach is pragmatic and meliorative rather than radical and idealistic. It follows the spirit of the common law rather than the Napoleonic code, emphasizing muddling through rather than long-term planning. It stresses process rather than substantive criteria. A "good" decision is one which gains consensus rather than one which meets outside criteria of efficiency or effectiveness. The political decision process has evolved in this direction because it is a successful means of coping, in a reasonably free society, with the reconciliation of divergent interests and values and the inherent limitations of the human mind to predict the consequences of social policies.

This outline of the decision process is, in many respects, a reasonably accurate description of the existing state of affairs. Many of its normative prescriptions are attractive. At the same time it appears, at least on first glance, to be in sharp contrast with the outlook and methodology underlying the planning, programming, and budgeting system. Let me now turn to an examination of the role of PPB in the context of this decision model.

35. A Modest Proposal

GORDON TULLOCK

Any government is compelled to make many decisions which have economic effects. Further, for a great many of these decisions, economists can provide valuable guidance. Economists cannot tell the government what it should or should not do, but in many cases the economist can accurately predict the consequences of some particular action and point out that these consequences are (or are not) in accord with the desires of the government. In other areas, although the economist cannot make a highly accurate prediction, he can at least offer a better estimate as to the likely effect of the given policy measure than can the noneconomist. Lastly, the economist may be able to suggest areas where a change in policy would lead to an output which most people would regard as an improvement over the status quo.

Since economists are not now and are not likely *ever* to become a majority of the population, the method by which economic knowledge is used to improve the output of public policies can hardly be direct majority voting. Democracy requires the economist, in a sense, "as a consul-

Reprinted from the *Journal of Money, Credit, and Banking,* Vol. 3 (May 1971), pp. 263–70. Copyright © 1971 by the Ohio State University Press. All Rights Reserved.

tant.'' Currently, our government obtains its economic "advice" mainly from the Council of Economic Advisers. It is the thesis of this note that this council has been inappropriately designed and that it should be radically revised with the idea of improving the likelihood that our government will act in an economically informed way. It should be said, in passing, that the inadequate design of the present Council of Economic Advisers is a consequence of its historic origin. The Council was not set up primarily to offer general economic advice to the government, but to solve a particular problem—unemployment. It was indeed established by the Employment Act of 1946. It has not, of course, solved the problem of unemployment because the problem is a good deal more difficult than it was thought to be by the sponsors of the Act. It has instead developed into an agency which, in part, advises the president as to policies he should adopt, and, in part, engages in public relations activities supporting whatever policies the president *has* adopted.[1]

In practice, then, the Council of Economic Advisers has tended to be a partisan institution, which is more likely to come to the attention of the average citizen (and, for that matter, of Congress) when it is engaged in controversy than when it is offering economic advice which is relatively uncontroversial among economists. The result has been a general reduction in respect, both for the Council and for economics as a policy tool. The Council, instead of demonstrating publicly that economics is a science which gives fairly definite answers to many problems, engages in controversies in fields in which there is wide disagreement. Under the circumstances, economic advice is apt to be accepted only when it happens to be in accord with the presuppositions of a political leader or citizen. Thus, it is probable that economic knowledge is much under-utilized in forming policy.

It might be thought from what I have said above that simply abolishing the Council of Economic Advisers is a suitable remedy for the situation. It is true that, if the Council of Economic Advisers did not exist, the government would still have access to economic advice. Individual economists could, as they do now, express opinions on policy issues. Any government agency, including the Office of the President and the Congress, could hire economists for the specific purpose of advising them. Thus, without any special institutional structure, the government could obtain a good deal of economic advice. It seems to me, however, that the amount of advice which would be obtained would remain suboptimal, and the situation which now pertains in which the common man and politician have economics brought to their attention only in those cases in which econo-

1. For some reason, the Council under Republican administrations has been much less active in the second sphere than it has been under Democratic administrations.

mists disagree and, hence, tend to think that there is little upon which they *do* agree, would also continue. Not only would the amount of economic advice received by the government be suboptimal, the government would give it less respect than it deserves.

A third defect of having no formal economic advisory institution for the government would be one which the Council of Economic Advisers has done little to overcome. In this respect, our present situation is only marginally different from what it would be if the Council did not exist. Under present circumstances, there is very little payoff to economists for applying their science to practical policy questions. In general, it is easier to build a reputation by writing a number of articles on the arcane technicalities of economic science than by a careful application of economics to some area of government policy. Indeed, outside the field of macroeconomics, it is quite hard to get such articles even published. A radical change is needed in the payoff structure so that economists are motivated to offer economic advice.[2]

What, then, do I recommend? I have two proposals: one for a drastic change in the Council of Economic Advisers, which is almost unique among modern calls for reform in that it will not involve any significant increase in the cost of the organization, and a second suggestion for establishing another institution, perhaps under government sponsorship and perhaps under foundation control.

As for the first proposal, somewhat paradoxically I propose to increase the respect in which the Council of Economic Advisers is held and reduce its partisan nature by making it more overtly partisan. Currently it purports to be an advisory council which gives "correct" advice to the government, but in practice it represents the party in power and its public activities are largely in support of the existing policy. If, instead, the Council consisted of a number of economists who were slected to represent different points of view and if their duties were simply to make public statements about desirable economic policy (not necessarily as a unit), then on those occasions when they did agree (and this would occur more often than the layman might think), their advice would carry much greater weight than it does now.

When they did disagree, the policymaking organs of our government would have presented to them several economically literate points of view on problems which are genuinely controversial among economists. Thus, the ultimate decision would be better than if they receive only one opin-

---

2. Although this [article] is appearing in a journal devoted to monetary policy, the need for economic advice is by no means confined to this area. Indeed, it is probable that the amount of economic policy advice received by the government today in the monetary field is larger and its general quality higher than in any other area.

ion. Further, the fact that this advice would be given publicly would mean that the economists would be subject to pressure not to say things which would look foolish five years in the future. The politicians could hardly maintain that they had not been warned if they chose to disregard the advice.

Obviously, if both major parties are represented, the Council will have to be larger than three.[3] Without any strong belief that it is the right number, let me suggest seven as an appropriate size.[4] In order to make certain that they are genuinely representative of the two parties, we must avoid the traditional procedure for getting "nonpartisan" officials in government. Under this traditional procedure, if the President and Senate are of one party, the people that they select to represent the other pary always turn out to be among the least partisan of men.

As a possible selection process, suppose that the American Economic Association provides to the government a list of twenty-five or thirty prominent Democratic economists and twenty-five or thirty prominent Republican economists. With these lists to guide them, let us suppose that the Republican leadership of the House and the Senate select (and fire) three, the Democratic leadership of the House and the Senate three, and the president one. This would guarantee a board of seven which would contain genuine representatives of both parties.

I would suggest that instead of hiring the seven economists full-time, they would be hired half-time and be permitted to remain in residence at their universities, visiting Washington only periodically. With present-day air travel, a weekly meeting would be no great inconvenience, even to a man who lived in Seattle.[5]

By hiring the members of the Council half-time instead of full-time, we could get our seven members for only a trifle more than the present three. Further, it seems to me likely that we would be able to get a higher average quality. It is a peculiar but fairly obvious characteristic of the Council of Economic Advisers that it has not, on the whole, attracted many of the real leaders of the economic profession. Substantially any economist can name four or five people who have served on the Council in the last twenty years who are indeed drawn from the first rank of the profession. This, however, is a small fraction of the total number of

3. Perhaps it would be desirable to include other groupings, such as Southerners, Negroes, etc.

4. Not only is this number offered somewhat tentatively, all of the details of the program I am offering are subject to revision. I would be delighted with suggestions for changes in details.

5. There would, of course, be no basic reason why the meetings of the Council would have to be held in Washington in any event. Chicago might be more convenient for many routine meetings.

members. With part-time appointments, it seems likely that it would be possible to obtain a higher quality membership.

In addition to pay and prestige, we could offer an additional incentive to attract economists to membership on the Council. At the moment, the Council maintains a small bureaucracy engaged in economic research under its direction. This small bureaucracy could be decentralized. Each member of the new, larger Council could be given the right to hire one or two economists to engage in full-time research under his supervision, or a larger number of economists doing part-time research. Similarly, he would be given suitable clerical assistance. Thus, the individual economist could not only spend half his own time on government activity, but he could direct a sizable quantity of economic research into problems which he thought were of immediate importance.

Note that this would not replace *all* the work done by the present Council bureaucracy. In addition to directed research on specific problems, the Council staff currently produces certain statistical series which are not produced elsewhere in the government. If these series are thought worthwhile, they can of course be continued. There is no obvious reason, however, why this should cause any great problem for this program. The necessary personnel for producing these statistics could be attached to the president's office or the Department of Commerce or some other government agency. Needless to say, the Council of Economic Advisers would probably have considerable weight in deciding what statistical series should be collected. Indeed, one of its functions would be to advise the government on statistical problems.

Individual members of the Council should be permitted—indeed, encouraged—to make public statements on any matter of economic policy which strikes their fancy. They would, however, realize that their statements would carry more weight if backed by the full Council than if produced as an individual statement. The Council should hold regular meetings at which it discusses problems of economic policy and issues statements about economic policy as a Council. These statements would not, of course, have to be unanimous any more than decisions of the appellate courts have to be unanimous.

One of the functions which this Council would serve—and which our present arrangements do not—is to distinguish for the layman between those problems on which there is general consensus among economists and those on which there is a legitimate difference of opinion. Surely economic advice in the first category is far more reliable than in the second. If the Council regularly issued statements which had attached to them minority opinions or, perhaps in some cases, in which there was no majority, it would be fairly easy for the layman to distinguish those policies which were generally agreed upon by economists from those which were not. I am myself convinced that the result of this exercise would be that a great many noneconomists would find that economists have a surprising amount of agreement on a surprising range of questions.

One problem that might arise would be a tendency of economists on the Council to make their disagreements very conspicuous by writing more about them than about their agreements. This danger, I think, could be avoided largely by depending on the good sense of the Council members. They are more likely to be influential in those areas where they happen to be agreed. Thus, if they wish to maximize their influence in the government, they should give a good deal of prominence to those matters upon which they *do* agree and not spend all of their time wrangling about those upon which they disagree.

It is likely that bringing out into the open issues upon which prominent economists are in disagreement would tend to stimulate research in desirable directions. We can, however, go further. There is no reason why the Council could not make recommendations for research in various areas which it thought important. It seems to me that these recommendations would be regarded as quite significant by the National Science Foundation, the Ford Foundation, Congress, and various other agencies which are in a position to fund economic research. Thus the Council could play a role in directing economic research into areas which are of policy importance. The present Council, of course, plays some role in this direction, but it seems to me that far more could be done.

If these recommendations were implemented, when the Council agreed it would not only have the confidence of the president, but also the confidence of his opposition because the opposition have appointed part of it. When the Democratic appointees disagreed with the Republican appointees, I presume the shrewd politicians who man the elective part of our federal government would correctly deduce that this was a matter of partisan politics and that economics had not a great deal to say on the issue. When they all agreed, however, I believe that the politicians would realize that they were facing not a statement made by supporters of one party, but a genuine professional opinion.

Further, the individual members of this revised Council probably would be very reluctant either to make statements that they believed to be untrue or to remain silent while other members of the Council made such statements. At the moment, there is relatively little discredit reflected upon an economist who, during his period as a member of the Council of Economic Advisers, refrains from criticizing vigorously certain presidential policies of which he disapproves. He is thought of as presidential appointee and that is not his duty. The new Council would not have this characteristic. An appointee by, let us say, a Democratic president who remained silent or supported the president while his Republican co-members of the Council were criticizing the president for some piece of economic illiteracy might well find that his reputation as an economist suffered. Under these circumstances, he would be motivated to join in the chorus and, as a Democrat, would add a gret deal of weight to the advice tendered to the government by the economists.

Although to reorganize the Council of Economic Advisers in the way I have specified so far would be a great help in obtaining a government whose activity is more in accord with economic knowledge than we have now, this is not enough. We need to enlist a much larger part of the economic profession in the search for better government policy. Examination of almost any part of the functioning of our government—whether it be procurement, the Post Office, the CAB, or even some such apparently noneconomic areas as law enforcement—will indicate that improvements could be made by application of economics.

In part this need would be met by the Council and its ability to stimulate special research projects in various areas. Still, it would be better if we had an even wider participation from the economic profession. There is today one field, usually called macroeconomics, in which economists regularly provide economic knowledge for government policy. Not only is there a specialized journal (*Journal of Money, Credit, and Banking*), but articles in this field appear regularly in other journals as well. There are large numbers of economists specializing in the field and economists who are not so specialized are normally *au courant* on developments. Our objective should be to develop a similar situation in other fields where government policy could be benefited by application of economics. Economics draws its real justifications from the possibility of improving the functioning of our society. Much of modern economics has retreated from this task into the intricacies of pure theory. It is time that we turned more attention to the real problems of government policy.

In order to achieve this goal, it is necessary to establish fairly strong incentives to economists to do work in the policy area. As I mentioned before, today the payoff to economists for investigating minutiae of theory are, generally speaking, much higher than for applying elementary economics to important problems. Socially the payoff is reversed. The social gain from a minor theoretical advance is probably much smaller than that which can be obtained from the application of elementary economics in many areas where it is now ignored.

In order to attract economists into this area, we must provide incentives. Most economists today live in universities that follow a publish-or-perish system. This system is much criticized and it certainly is not a suitable way to obtain good teaching; but as a way of promoting research, it has great advantages. The university, in essence, pays its personnel in terms of their scientific achievements, while it leaves the actual judgment of the value of those scientific achievements to the editors and readers of the various specialized journals.[6]

The system works, however, only if the editors of the journals and the colleagues of the scientists in any given profession have tastes which are in accord with social needs. It would appear to me that this criterion is, in part, not true in today's economics. The articles that *do* pay off are not those which we most need. Indeed, there are only two journals which specialize in the application of economics to political problems outside the field of macroeconomics. One, the *Journal of Law and Economics,* is distinguished but read by a rather narrow circle. The other, *Public Policy,* has so far had little impact. What we can say about both of these journals, however, is that, at the moment, the payoff from publishing an article in either of them is much less than the payoff from publishing an article in the *American Economic Review,* the *Journal of Political Economy,* or the *Quarterly Journal of Economics.* Thus the existence of these two journals, although it certainly stimulates research in practical government problems, is not enough. Further, any attempt to pull the profession into an area in which it is not currently much interested faces an automatic threshold problem. The new field is one which *ex definition* does not have prestige. Further, a new journal will not have prestige. Under the circumstances, it will be difficult for it to attract really first-rate people to write their best articles in the area. This will be particularly true if we are attempting to get articles in areas in which people are not already doing research. The rewards for publishing an article in an obscure journal are quite modest, and if publishing an article in that obscure journal requires a change of research and/or a learning of new research skills, it is unlikely that very many people will undertake the experiment.

To economists, a solution immediately suggests itself. Why not pay? The only reason we do not offer large honoraria for publishing in scientific journals is that, in general, the rewards provided by the publish-or-perish system are adequate. In an area where that is not so, cash payments would seem to be desirable and these payments should be large enough to attract first-rate people into the area. I would suggest honoraria of $1,000 per article. This would not only lead a number of people voluntarily to take up work in applying economics to such areas as military procurement, the ICC, local government, taxation, etc., but would also make it possible to commission articles from very prominent economists.

6. See Gordon Tullock, *The Organization of Inquiry* (Durham, N.C.: Duke University Press, 1966), pp. 36–39.

Further, with honoraria of this size being paid for articles, the prestige of the journal would almost instantaneously be established and the publish-or-perish rule would begin rating it—if not as high as the *American Economic Review*—nevertheless, very highly.

Thus, I suggest the foundation of, at first, a single new journal. Eventually, we would hope that many specialized journals in many fields, modeled perhaps after the *Journal of Money, Credit, and Banking,* would develop—but, for a beginning, one journal. This journal would have to be heavily financed if it were to be able to pay very large honoraria for individual articles. Further, it seems to me it would be desirable to arrange a good deal of editorial help in the journal's office in order to make the articles readable by people who have not had Ph.D.'s in economics. In many applied areas, this would be perfectly possible. Certainly, it would greatly increase the impact of the journal. Lastly, the journal should be so organized as to stimulate a continuing discussion. It might, for example, have two editors selected because they have different points of view. Each could be responsible for half of the articles published.

With time, as we developed a large group of economists who are interested in applying their knowledge to practical governmental problems, we could create further specialized journals, thus developing specific sub-communities of economists interested in special areas of government policy. Alternatively, it might not be necessary to take any such steps at all. Once articles in this field develop prestige and leading economists begin writing them, it is likely that the existing economic journals would increase the number of such articles which they publish. In any event, we need a channel which will both attract economists into applied research on policy problems and provide them with the facilities for learned discussion, which is, after all, the basis of scientific progress.

It may be seen that, of my two proposals, the first is superficially much more drastic. Further, it clearly would have more immediate effect. The second, which appears to be a relatively modest proposal for establishing one more journal, would probably have relatively little immediate effect, but in the long run might have a very great effect. In any event, it does seem that, whether you like my proposals or not, the present situation is clearly not optimal and we should try to improve it.

36. A Defense of the CEA as an Instrument for Giving Economic Policy Advice

ROBERT D. TOLLISON and THOMAS D. WILLETT

We should like to offer some brief commentary on Gordon Tullock's proposal for reform of the Council of Economic Advisers in the United States.[1] We find attractive Tullock's suggestion of the formation of a bipartisan council of economic experts to represent to the public and the government areas of consensus among professional economists. In fact in at least two countries, Canada and Germany, councils of experts such as Tullock suggests already exist.[2] A similar proposal was recently made by Arthur Okun,[3] and as Okun noted, this idea was discussed during the hearings on the Employment Act of 1946 which established the present Council of Economic Advisers.

Where we differ with Tullock is over whether some such body should replace the present council. We agree with Okun (p. 28) that this need not be an either-or question. We strongly share Tullock's desire to see economic analysis play a greater role in the formulation of public policy and believe that this would be obtained better by having both a group of part-time "outside" economic experts to act as some sort of "Supreme Court of the profession" (Okun's terminology) and an "inside" council

Reprinted from the *Journal of Money, Credit and Banking,* Vol. 7 (February 1975). Copyright © 1975 by the Ohio State University Press.

1. Gordon Tullock, "A Modest Proposal," *Journal of Money, Credit, and Banking,* 3 (May 1971), 263–70.

2. For a recent discussion of the German Council, see Henry C. Wallich, "The American Council of Economics Advisers and the German Sachverstaendigencrat: A Study in the Economics of Advice," *Quarterly Journal of Economics* (August, 1968), 349–79.

3. Arthur Okun, *The Political Economy of Prosperity* (Washington: The Brookings Institution, 1970), pp. 17–30. For a skeptical view of Okun's proposal see Martin Bronfenbrenner, "The Kennedy-Johnson CEA," *Public Policy,* (Fall, 1970), 743–44. Bronfenbrenner is concerned that there is not yet enough concensus among economists to make such a scheme for economic advice viable. Should this be the case, one could argue that it would be preferable for groups of experts be called on to do evaluations of selected policy issues. An example of the use of a professional organization in this way is the recent report of the Operations Research Society on the quality of arguments (pro and con) on the ABM issue. (See the *New York Times,* Friday, October 1, 1971, p. 23) and the many groups of technical experts (e.g., the National Research Council) that give scientific advice to the government. On the latter, see M. L. Perl, "The Scientific Advisory System: Some Observations," *Science* (September 24, 1971), 1211–15.

which participates fully in policy formulation and debate within the government. (Yes, Gordon, better things do cost more!) The two roles are really quite separate and both are worthwhile. Tullock is concerned that the policy advocacy of the Council of Economic Advisers has led to "a general reduction in respect, both for the council and for economics as a policy tool." While we would question whether the net effect is in the direction Tullock suggests, he is certainly correct that the council often does represent political rather than professional consensus in its policy pronouncements. And despite the correctness of Okun's statement that "No CEA member has ever claimed to be the spokesman for a purely professional view," the fact that there is only one CEA-type body at present must lead to confusion in the minds of the public.[4] The creation of a second body which would be designed to reflect more accurately professional consensus would help reduce this problem.

Such a council of experts would not provide a close substitute for most of the present functions of the CEA, however. Public pronouncements of the CEA, both partisan political advocacy and relatively "neutral" economic analysis and education, provide only a minor portion of its activity (and its importance). Of much greater importance on the formation and implementation of economic policy in the United States is the quiet, internal role that the members and senior staff of the council play within government.

Tullock is no doubt correct that a part-time outside council of economic experts could maintain on average a more distinguished group of professional economists than has the CEA. But such part-time advisers just cannot fully substitute for ongoing economic analysis within the government.[5] There are of course a number of distinguished economists in permanent government employment or in temporary positions such as political appointees (e.g., George Shultz) or visiting professors at various

4. It was not clear when the council was set up whether it would be more of an "inside" or an "outside" body, and under its first chairman, Edwin Nourse, it followed more of an outside role. Since then, however, the "inside" role of the council has become firmly established. On the development of the CEA see E. Ray Canterbery, *Economics on a New Frontier* (Belmont, California: Wadsworth, 1968), chaps. 10 and 11; Edward S. Flash, Jr., *Economic Advice and Presidential Leadership* (New York: Columbia University Press, 1965); Gardner Ackley, "The Contribution of Economists to Policy Formation," *Journal of Finance* (May, 1966); and Walter Heller, *New Dimensions on Political Economy* (Cambridge: Harvard University Press, 1965); and L. D. Taylor, "The 1970 Annual Report of the Council of Economic Advisers," *Public Policy* (Summer, 1970).

5. For a recent discussion of why outside consultants or experts cannot fully substitute for professional economists within government stressing the function of economic intelligence, see Sir Alex Cairncross, "Economists in Government," *Lloyds Bank Review* (January, 1970). On the intelligence functions of the CEA, see H. Wilensky, *Organizational Intelligence* (New York: Basic Books, 1967), 94–109.

government agencies (e.g., with the Board of Governors of the Federal Reserve System, but we think that there can be little question that the existence of the council has had a substantial impact toward raising the average level of economic analysis within the U.S. government. This is due not just to the level of competenence of the economists who serve as members and senior staff economists at the council, but also to the fact that the rapid turnover of members and staff (the staff is usually on leave from universities or research institutes and serve one or two years; members average somewhat longer) provides a constant flow of new insights into the early stages of policy formation and tends to minimize incentives to play bureaucratic games when giving economic advice. A council member's future is not likely to be substantially influenced by the internal policy advice he gives. This may not always be the case with career government employees. The key to bureaucratic advancement is often in coming out with conclusions that one's superiors find agreeable, rather than with the analysis that is most correct.[6]

Thus while sharing Tullock's concern over the public role of the CEA, we feel that its generally high reputation within the profession allows the government to attract a revolving source of internal economic advice which it would otherwise find extremely difficult to obtain. Thus, we would suggest that Tullock's proposal should be considered as an addition to, rather than a substitute for, the present Council of Economic Advisers.

An additional advantage of keeping the present type of council is that the flow of academic economists through the council tends to raise the average level of policy interest in the profession. We strongly agree with Tullock on the desirability of increasing the professional incentives to apply economics to political problems, but feel that Tullock, besides overlooking this above consideration, also failed to mention a number of important incentives that already exist. One which we feel has generated a substantial amount of excellent analysis is the opportunity to testify before congressional committees, especially the JEC.[7] Incentives are also generated by organizations such as the CED, Brookings, Rand, and the

6. In passing, we should like to take exception to Tullock's characterization of the council staff as "a small bureaucracy engaged in economic research under its [the council's] direction." The professional staff of the council has been purposely kept small (around 15) despite the wide range of activities in which the council engages so that each professional economist on the staff works directly with a council member, in effect serving as his deputy. This both facilitates close communication within the CEA, and greatly increases the influence that analysis by staff economists has within the government bureaucracies.

7. For a recent discussion of the high value of the testimony before the JEC and of papers prepared for, and published by, the JEC, see N. Beckman, "Congressional Information Processes for National Policy," *The Annals of the American Academy of Political and Social Science* (March, 1971), 46.

American Enterprise Institute. Likewise, the resurgence of interests in political economy by both economists and political scientists (inspired to an important degree by Tullock's contributions to this area) may enhance the academic prestige of such activity.

Indeed, the issue of developing greater professional research in the area of public policy is largely separable from the question of how the system of economic policy advice ought to be set up. The former problem concerns how the economics profession operates its system of scientific research and communication and how to encourage additional research in the specific area of public policy applications, and of course, both of these aspects of the problem of scientific communication have important indirect feedbacks to the policy formation process. As he notes, Tullock has addressed the problem of scientific communication in *The Organization of Inquiry,* and we would argue that suggestions such as Tullock's to subsidize articles by economists in the area of public policy research and a recent proposal to pay journal referees merit serious consideration as a part of a general study of how professional disciplines communicate and what the properties of a good system of professional communication are.[8] The fact that different disciplines have different publication procedures and that the natural science disciplines exhibit a considerably shorter lag between completion of research and publication due largely to different editorial and refereeing procedures suggests that the present system used by economics may not be the best.[9] Thus, the consideration of how to obtain more research by economists on public policy may involve subsidies, but it also to some extent may be a function of the general organization of communication in the economics profession and the more or less haphazard development of specialty journals under the present system. Study and reform of the way we communicate as economists would certainly be desirable and would also probably have desirable feedback effects on the formation of economic policy.

8. See H. Mohring, "A Remission from Baumol's Disease: Ways to Publish More Articles—Comment," *Southern Economic Journal* (July, 1970), 106–7, for the proposal to pay journal referees.

9. See, for example, H. Zuckerman and R. Merton, "Patterns of Evaluation in Science: Institutionalism, Structure, and Functions of the Referee System," *Minerva* (January, 1971). Also, see R. Amacher, R. Tollison, and T. Willett, "Alternative Screening Devices for the Dissemination of Economic Research," Texas A. & M. University, mimeo., 1975.

Index of Names

WOLFGRAM LIBRARY

Library of Congress Cataloging in Publication Data
(For library cataloging purposes only)

Main entry under title:

The Economic approach to public policy.

Includes bibliographical references and index.

1. United States—Economic policy—Addresses, essays, lectures. 2. United States
—Social policy—Addresses, essays, lectures. 3. Policy sciences—Addresses, essays,
lectures. I. Amacher, Ryan C. II. Tollison, Robert D. III. Willett, Thomas D.
HC105.7.E27   338.973   75-38425
ISBN 0-8014-0914-4
ISBN 0-8014-9860-0 pbk.